SAMS

EPIC GAMES

MASTERING UNREAL® TECHNOLOGY

VOLUME I:

Introduction to Level Design with Unreal® Engine 3

Jason Busby, Zak Parrish, Jeff Wilson

Sams Publishing, 800 East 96th St., Indianapoli

POWERED BY

UNREAL TECHNOLOGY

Mastering Unreal® Technology, Volume I

Copyright © 2010 by Epic Games, Inc.

ISBN-13: 978-0-672-32991-3

ISBN-10: 0-672-32991-3

Library of Congress Cataloging-in-Publication Data:

Busby, Jason.

Mastering Unreal technology / Jason Busby, Zak Parrish, Jeff Wilson.

p. cm.

ISBN 978-0-672-32991-3

1. Computer games—Programming. 2. Entertainment computing. 3. UnrealScript (Computer program language) I. Parrish, Zak. II. Wilson, Jeff. III. Title.

QA76.76.C672B8685 2009

794.8'1526—dc22

2009003414

Printed in the United States of America

First Printing July 2009

Trademarks

Warning and Disclaimer

Bulk Sales

Sams Publishing offers excellent discounts on this book when ordered in quantity for bulk purchases or special sales. For more information, please contact

U.S. Corporate and Government Sales
1-800-382-3419
corpsales@pearsontechgroup.com

For sales outside of the U.S., please contact

International Sales
international@pearson.com

Editor-in-Chief
Karen Gettman

Executive Editor
Neil Rowe

Development Editor
Mark Renfrow

Managing Editor
Kristy Hart

Project Editor
Anne Goebel

Copy Editor
Water Crest Publishing, Inc.

Indexer
Erika Millen

Proofreader
Dan Knott

Publishing Coordinator
Cindy Teeters

Multimedia Developer
Dan Scherf

Cover and Interior Designer
Gary Adair

Compositor
Nonie Ratcliff

Contents at a Glance

Table of Contents

About the Authors

Jason "Buzz" Busby is the president and chief executive officer of 3D Buzz, Inc., a company dedicated to teaching the world the arts and skills behind today's hottest technical industries, including 3D animation, programming, and game development. Through his website, www.3dbuzz.com, Buzz distributes his signature Video Training Modules (VTMs), which contain hours of training content that is professional, informative, and entertaining. His site also boasts one of the most robust, friendly, and helpful online communities in the world of 3D animation.

Zak Parrish is 3D Buzz Inc.'s chief of operations. For the past six years, he has worked with Jason Busby and 3D Buzz, Inc., to help provide top-quality education to students across the world. His work can be seen on many of the 3D Buzz VTMs, as well as in the Unreal Tournament 2004 and Unreal Tournament 3: Limited Collector's Edition training video series. He is also an aspiring student of graphic design and is in the process of wrapping up his Bachelor of Fine Arts degree at Austin Peay State University.

Jeff Wilson is a student at the University of Advancing Technology, where he is pursuing a degree in game design. He has been studying the Unreal Engine for four years, while creating various modifications for Unreal Tournament 2003 and Unreal Tournament 2004. During his period of self study, Jeff developed a thorough understanding of the internal workings of the Unreal Engine, allowing him to create several unique gaming applications using his programming skills and 3D artistry. He has since become a professional consultant working for 3D Buzz, Inc., aiding in the development of many training videos over Unreal Technology.

Dedications

Jason:

None of my endeavors would succeed without the concern, compassion, and unquestioning support of my beautiful wife Angela, my two daughters Heather and Meagan, and my loving mother, Belinda. To these wonderful women, I most lovingly dedicate this book.

Zak:

I dedicate this book to my parents, Don and Carolyn; to my younger brothers, Micah and Daniel; to my elder brother Josh, his lovely wife Lesley, and my soon-to-be niece; and to Emily Ruth Averitt, who always seems to be ready with a patient ear, a warm smile, and that perfect cup of tea.

Jeff:

I dedicate this book to my parents, Tom and Wanda. They have put up with more from me than two people should have to and supported me all along the way; to my brother Michael and his family; and to my grandparents, Albert and Virginia, who more than anyone showed me what it means to be a good person and made me who I am today.

Acknowledgments

Jason: I would like to thank my family and my mom for putting up with me throughout this project and providing the love and support that allowed me to get the job done. I'd like to thank Zak for dealing with me through all my ups and downs and using his incredible writing talent to help make this book run as smoothly as possible. I also want to thank Jeff for his professionalism, his seemingly endless knowledge of the Unreal universe, and his indomitable will in seeing this project through to its completion.

Zak: I would like to thank Jason for seeing potential in me and helping me see it in myself. Without his vision and insight, I could never have learned or achieved so much. Thanks certainly go to Jeff for helping all of this make sense when it seemed that nothing else out there possibly could.

Jeff: I would like to thank Jason first and foremost for taking a chance on me and for allowing Zak to talk him into writing this book in the first place. I can't really imagine where I would be right now if he hadn't. I would also like to thank my parents for instilling in me the work ethic and determination I have needed to make it this far in life. I never made things easy on them, but they were always there for me and encouraged me when I needed it the most.

All Authors: We would all like to extend a most hearty thanks to those who helped make this book a reality from behind the scenes. First, thanks go to Logan Frank, who can always be counted on for technical assistance, no matter how complex the problem. We'd also like to thank Terry Wilson, for his countless hours of testing and screen capturing. Thanks also go out to Lee Jae Chi, for his amazing drawing skill and help with illustrations.

We would also like to thank Mike Capps and Mark Rein for making this book a reality, as well as Tim Sweeney for designing the Unreal Engine and starting this gaming phenomenon. Special thanks to the people at Epic who also reviewed this book: Jim Brown, Andrew Bains, Scott Dossett, Wyeth Johnson, Chris Mielke, Greg Mitchell, Mikey Spano, Ken Spencer, Jordan Walker, and Alan Willard. Finally, we would like to give a very large thanks to the Unreal community, which has been a massive source of support and inspiration in all our Unreal projects.

We Want to Hear from You!

As the reader of this book, *you* are our most important critic and commentator. We value your opinion and want to know what we're doing right, what we could do better, what areas you'd like to see us publish in, and any other words of wisdom you're willing to pass our way.

You can email or write me directly to let me know what you did or didn't like about this book—as well as what we can do to make our books stronger.

Please note that I cannot help you with technical problems related to the topic of this book, and that due to the high volume of mail I receive, I might not be able to reply to every message.

When you write, please be sure to include this book's title and authors, as well as your name and phone or email address. I will carefully review your comments and share them with the authors and editors who worked on the book.

Email: feedback@samspublishing.com

Mail: Neil Rowe
            Executive Editor
            Sams Publishing
            800 East 96th Street
            Indianapolis, IN 46240 USA

Reader Services

Visit our website and register this book at informit.com/register for convenient access to any updates, downloads, or errata that might be available for this book.

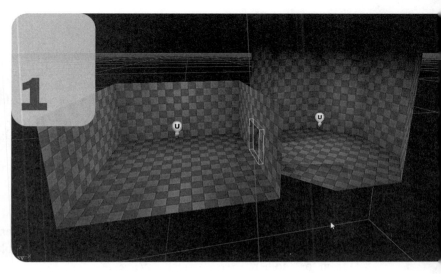

Chapter 1

Introduction to Unreal Technology

OK, life's as it should be: *You're playing a game.* Xbox 360, PS3, PC, whatever. Stop, think. What's throwing that character up there on the screen? What's making that explosion look, sound, act like that? What's moving you from one room, one world, one level to the next? What's controlling how that game reacts to you? What's bossing around all your fancy hardware, making it jump through hoops? What makes it all so *real?*

A *game engine*, that's what. And if you're playing something really hot—like, say, Gears of War 2 or BioShock—that engine is Unreal Engine 3.

1

You, yes, *you* can make Unreal Engine 3 jump through hoops in your games, your levels. You just have to know how. That'll take a little work—but, hey, you've already started. In this chapter, we give you a quick nano-history of the Unreal Engine, then a copter's eye view of its components and how they fit together to do stuff that's—hey, we apologize, but it's a fact—absolutely *unreal*.

History of Unreal

Neither Rome nor the Unreal Engine was built in a day. Took the centurions and senators centuries to get Rome running right. Took the good folks at Epic Games barely a decade to create the Unreal Engine and transform it into the world's most incredible game engine. How'd Epic get from there to here? Here's a quick timeline...

June 1998: Unreal

Remember Unreal (see **FIGURE 1.1**)? Hey, you're dating yourself. It hit the big time way back in the summer of 1998. (Along with Monica Lewinsky, Mark McGwire, dotcoms, 'N Sync...) But, hey, compared to all that stuff, Unreal was unforgettable. Engrossing story, incredible graphics, lush environments—including some of the best 3D outdoor landscapes ever seen in gaming. And that's just the *single-player* game; Unreal also gave you the chance to take on artificially intelligent "bots": players controlled by the computer.

That's the stuff most gamers saw—but, just underneath the surface, something even more remarkable was happening: the birth of the Unreal Engine. Epic Games wasn't just creating a game: It was creating a modular set of programs and tools for building and customizing practically any game.

The Unreal Engine gave Epic Games—and other companies who licensed it—a gigantic head start. Suddenly, there was no need to re-create everything from scratch. You could combine the Unreal Engine with your own content, tweaking its behavior however you wanted. The result: You could get from idea to state-of-the-art game a whole lot faster. And once you'd delivered your game, you could port it to other kinds of hardware faster, because the Unreal Engine managed many of the differences between gaming platforms for you.

But there was even more. The Unreal Engine also paved the way for mod makers. Its UnrealScript made it easier than ever to take *existing* games to a whole new level. (*Literally.*)

FIGURE 1.1 The original Unreal was a landmark in 3D gaming.

November 1999: Unreal Tournament

Unreal was great, Unreal Tournament was positively mindblowing. First intended as an expansion pack for the first Unreal game (and fully compatible with Unreal's maps), Unreal Tournament supercharged Unreal's multiplayer features (see **FIGURE 1.2**). Transforming the concept of "death match" into a series of spectator sports, Unreal Tournament wowed players

1

with incredible online play, plus some of the most advanced bot artificial intelligence (AI) that gamers had ever seen. They could see Unreal Tournament in a lot more places, too; in addition to PC and Mac, it was also ported to PlayStation 2, as well as the late, somewhat lamented Sega Dreamcast console.

FIGURE 1.2   Unreal Tournament was eventually ported to several different platforms.

March–July 2001: The Unreal Developer Network

By 2001, thousands of game developers and modders were hard at work with the Unreal Engine. In response, Epic Games launched The Unreal Developer Network—commonly called "UDN"—a central location where the users of the Unreal Engine, from licensees to mod makers, could find up-to-date documentation and tutorials for making the most of Unreal Engine (see **FIGURE 1.3**). To this day, the site —udn.epicgames.com—remains the most respected online source for knowledge about Unreal Engine development.

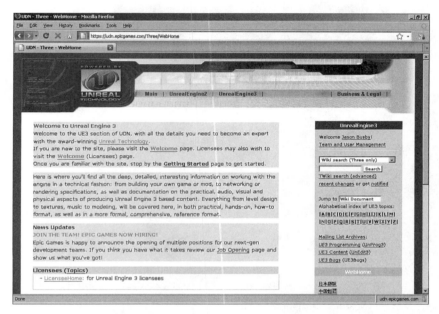

FIGURE 1.3   UDN is still the largest single source of Unreal Technology information.

September 2002: Unreal Championship and Unreal Tournament 2003

Unreal Championship brought the Unreal franchise to Microsoft's Xbox game console; hot on its heels came Unreal Tournament 2003 for the PC (see **FIGURE 1.4**). Both games focused heavily on multiplayer gameplay, and Unreal Championship was one of the first games to take advantage of the broadband multiplayer capabilities built into Microsoft's Xbox Live! (see **FIGURE 1.5**).

These games were driven by Unreal Engine 2, which ushered in a whole new era of flexibility and power for game development and mod making. Game developers found a powerful new particle system for creating everything from fire to fog, and handy static mesh tools for adding richer detail with cheaper hardware. They found the Karma physics engine, which brought new realism to everything from collisions to explosions. Then there was Matinee, an integrated system for

1

creating in-game *cutscenes*—brief, noninteractive movies that advance a game's plot or provide important background. You learn more about these Unreal Engine tools and features later in this chapter and throughout the book.

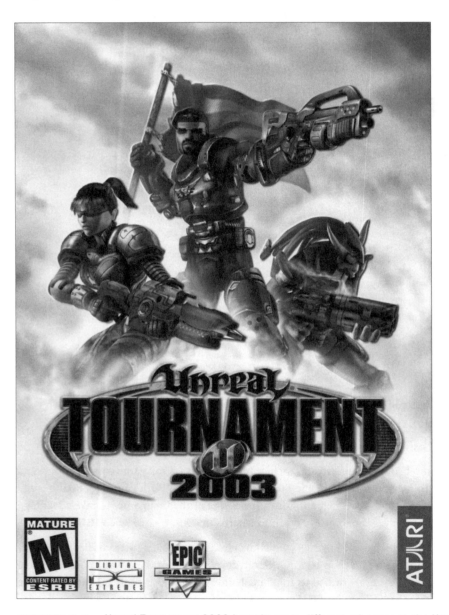

FIGURE 1.4   Unreal Tournament 2003 brought many different advances to the Unreal franchise.

FIGURE 1.5   Unreal Championship was an Unreal Tournament-style game created strictly for consoles.

February 2003: Unreal II

In February 2003, Unreal II: The Awakening launched, revitalizing single-player gaming on the PC. Unreal II returned to the storyline of the first Unreal game, pitting the individual player

1

against the merciless forces of the Skaarj (see **FIGURE 1.6**). The game also included extensive interaction with computer-controlled non-player characters (NPCs). Unreal II's lush environments pushed the underlying engine to new levels, and the game's animations were also supplemented by Legend Entertainment's powerful Golem animation system.

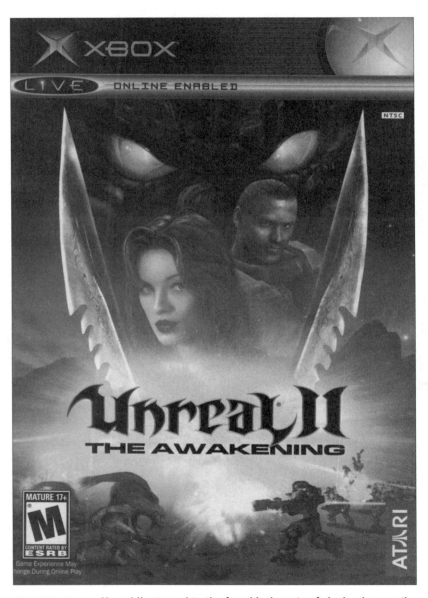

FIGURE 1.6   Unreal II returned to the franchise's roots of single-player action.

March 2004: Unreal Tournament 2004

With the advent of Onslaught, Unreal Tournament 2004 brought even further leaps in online multiplayer gaming. This new gaming mode put players in a vast battlefield populated with capturable control points, outposts, weapons, and vehicles—making all-out warfare possible on a tremendous scale (see **FIGURE 1.7**). Some Unreal Tournament 2004 levels even took place in outer space, forcing players to infiltrate a space station with space fighters before landing to take over the station on foot.

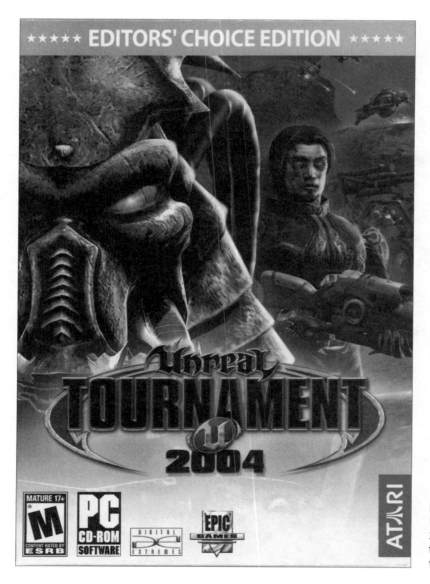

FIGURE 1.7
Unreal Tournament 2004 introduced tremendous battle-fields and vehicles.

1

April 2005: Unreal Championship 2: The Liandri Conflict

This second installment of the Unreal Championship franchise was created exclusively for the first-generation Xbox game console, using Unreal Engine 2.5, a special version of the Unreal Engine built specifically for Xbox (see **FIGURE 1.8**). Unreal Championship 2 offered enhanced graphics and solid multiplayer gameplay, either through system linking or via Xbox Live!. It also added melee combat, presented through a new third-person camera that gave players a whole new view of the hardcore gaming action.

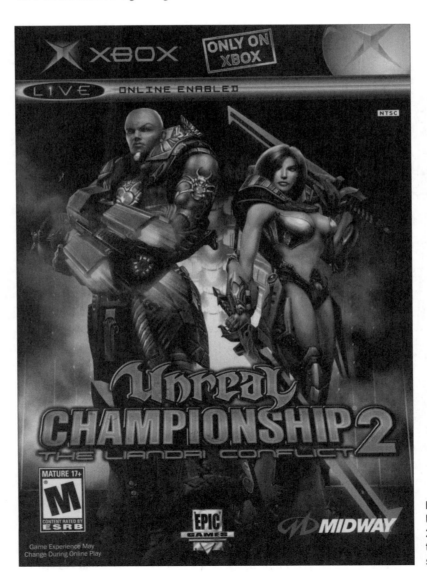

FIGURE 1.8
Unreal Championship 2 was exclusive to the original Xbox system.

November 2006: Gears of War

With all these versions of Unreal in the marketplace, Epic Games was working on an entirely new family of games—and an entirely new version of the Unreal Engine to drive them. That engine, Unreal Engine 3, is the subject of this book—and if you're here, you've almost certainly played some of the stunning games that run on it.

Epic Games' own Gears of War was the first game to demonstrate the full capabilities of Unreal Engine 3. Featuring a unique third-person camera style, rich and extremely detailed environments, frighteningly realistic enemies, and some of the most visceral combat ever portrayed in gaming, Gears of War became an instant hit—and some of the bestselling intellectual property in history (see **FIGURE 1.9**). And Gears of War 2 (see **FIGURE 1.10**), which released exactly 2 years later, has proven to be even more successful.

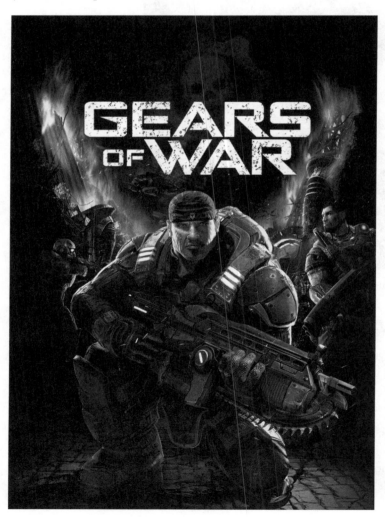

FIGURE 1.9   Gears of War was one of Xbox 360's most anticipated titles.

1

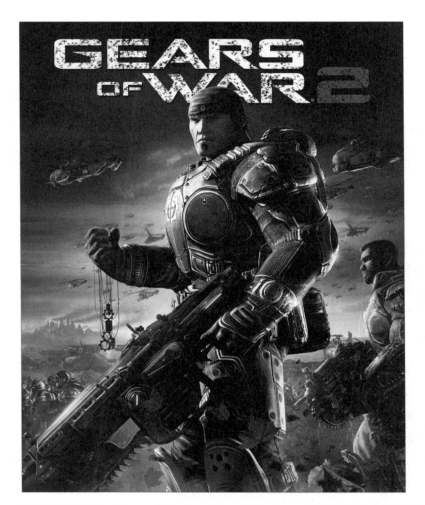

FIGURE 1.10   Gears of War 2 continued to advance the technology behind the Unreal Engine.

November 2007: Unreal Tournament 3

And finally we get to the game that you use to follow the tutorials found in this book, Unreal Tournament 3. This game brought the power of Unreal Engine 3 to the fast-paced multiplayer world of the Unreal Tournament universe (see **FIGURE 1.11**). Never before had the vast battlefields of the tournament been portrayed with such visceral realism and detail.

The intense realism in both Gears of War games and in Unreal Tournament 3 was made possible, in large part, by innovations in the Unreal game engine. These improvements shake virtually every last bit of performance out of today's advanced hardware: DirectX 9/10 PCs, the Xbox 360, and the PlayStation 3, with its near-supercomputer power.

FIGURE 1.11   Unreal Tournament 3 allows the Unreal mod community access to the power of Unreal Engine 3.

One example (well, three): Both lighting and materials have been completely revamped, and courtesy of Ageia (now part of NVIDIA), there's an entirely new physics engine. You might find one other feature even more exciting: the new Kismet visual scripting system. Kismet replaces huge amounts of old-fashioned computer programming with simple gameplay flowcharting that practically anyone can do—most assuredly, including you.

But we're getting ahead of ourselves. Let's take that copter-level view of Unreal Engine 3 you were promised...

Overview of the Unreal Engine

What *is* the Unreal Engine, exactly? In short, it's a system that organizes your "assets"—your characters, artwork, props, weapons, music, sound effects, voiceovers, etc.—into a visually stunning interactive environment.

But not just "any" visually stunning environment: one that behaves just the way you want it to—as a *game*, in other words!(see **FIGURE 1.12**).

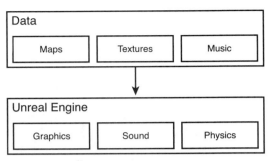

FIGURE 1.12 The flow of data through the Unreal Engine

Unreal Engine Components

The Unreal Engine contains several components. Each can work independently, but they're kept humming along in harmony by a central "core engine." Since everything's neatly modularized, licensees of the Unreal Engine's technology can easily customize or replace any individual component without drastically changing the core engine (and raising costs or delaying delivery—two of the industry's worst no-nos). This section introduces you to each Unreal Engine component, and shows how they work together to deliver an Unreal gaming experience.

The Graphics Engine

The graphics engine controls what you see while you're playing a game; it produces the jaw-dropping visuals that appear as you blast your way to victory. Without it, you'd just see a tremendous list of ever-changing property values, such as the player's location, health, any weapons they are carrying, ammo, what animation is currently playing, and so on. Fat lot of fun *that* would be. Thankfully, the graphics engine translates this information into the lush environments you see during gameplay (see **FIGURE 1.13**).

The graphics engine is responsible for "behind-the-scenes" calculations few players ever think about. For example, it determines which objects display in front of others, and which objects should "occlude" (hide) others from view.

In Unreal Engine 3, when you occlude "rear" objects from view, they don't render at all. That frees up processing cycles for something more useful. Previously, developers had to perform these intricate manual level optimizations themselves. Now, Unreal Engine 3 handles that for you—just one way it's been optimized to improve performance and save you time.

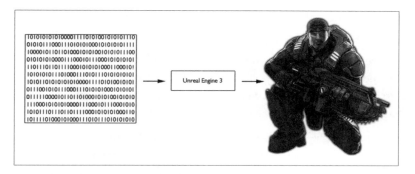

FIGURE 1.13   The graphics engine is responsible for turning vast lists of properties into interactive imagery on the screen.

Certain aspects of level optimization *are* still in place, and work with the rendering engine to help control what the player can and can't see. Unreal Engine 3 supports Level Streaming, which allows different sublevels to be loaded or unloaded from memory during gameplay. With Level

Streaming, when a player enters one section of a level, the area he's exiting can be dumped from memory and no longer rendered by the graphics engine. This means you can present the player with truly vast environments without ever exposing them to a loading screen or a break from the action. For more about Level Streaming, see Chapter 12, "Level Streaming."

> **NOTE**
>
> You'll hear that term—rendering—a lot in this book. What does it mean? It's just the way a computer graphics program generates an image from the information it's been handed: information about things like geometry, viewpoint, texture, lighting, and shadows.

The Unreal graphics engine also renders the various shaders and materials that are applied to all your objects. (For now, all you need to know about shaders is that they give you a *lot* more flexibility in controlling how your graphics render.)

As we've mentioned, one important part of rendering is *lighting*. Unreal Engine 3 boasts an extremely robust lighting system. That allows for dynamic lighting and shadowing, soft shadowing effects, and, well, more realism. You learn a lot more about this in Chapter 7, "Introduction to Lighting."

The Sound Engine

It's been said that 90 percent of what you perceive is in what you hear. Indeed, even the most visually entertaining films and games lose their punch with the sound turned off. Many players take the nuances of game sound for granted, not realizing the tremendous sound layering that takes place in today's games: the active sounds of the player running through sand, the shattering of glass, the report of gunfire, the ambient noises such as running water or wind and rain... even the

1

dynamic, fully orchestrated soundtracks that change as the action changes. There's a lot to sound in games these days.

The sound engine makes these effects possible in your game. It takes all the sound effects you've recorded and imported, queues them based on certain events in the game (such as playing an explosion sound when a grenade is thrown), and re-creates them as closely as possible, using the sound hardware built into the computer or gaming console.

Unreal Engine 3's sound engine is surprisingly easy to use. You import your sound effects or music, and use them to construct SoundCues—lists of instructions that control how sounds are played. For example, SoundCues might control whether a sound loops, whether its pitch or modulation should be tweaked, or whether it should be combined with other sound bites.

The Physics Engine

You live in the universe. You see how objects react when they bounce off each other. At a deep, instinctual level, knowledge of the laws of physics is built right into you. But that knowledge isn't built right into your PC or game console. If you want realistic collisions and explosions in your game, those have to be programmed. Trust us. You *don't* want to have to do that on your own. With Unreal Engine 3, you don't have to; your in-game physics are handled through NVIDIA's state-of-the-art PhysX physics engine.

PhysX supports a whole laundry list of physical simulations, including rigid bodies, constrained bodies, dynamic skeletal meshes (think "ragdolls"), and even cloth. Each of these can be interactive in the game and can be manipulated by the player, either directly or through scripted sequences. The physics system can also work with the sound engine to produce dynamic sound—say, whenever a physics-driven object strikes the ground (see **FIGURE 1.14**).

The Input Manager

Without inputs from a player, you don't have a game; you just have a piece of game engine-driven animation, or "machinima." As a gamer, you know where these inputs come from: button presses, mouse movements, applications of pressure to analog controls—nowadays, maybe even vocal commands. Whatever its source, each input must be recognized, and then converted into a command that tells your game how to react. In Unreal Engine 3, that's the job of the Input Manager.

Each time a player produces an input, the Input Manager sets a series of properties that control what should happen in the game. For example, when a player presses the "Jump" button, the Input Manager sends a signal to the core engine, which causes it to play a jump animation, send the relevant information to the graphics engine to render that action on the screen, and queue a jump sound effect from the sound engine. All that happens *very* quickly; so fast, players almost never notice the delay between their input and the game's reaction.

FIGURE 1.14   Using the physics engine, characters can turn into ragdolls.

One great thing about Unreal Engine 3's Input Manager is that it's extremely flexible. You can adjust easily when you're moving between different gaming platforms or input devices.

Network Infrastructure

As Epic Games developed its Unreal Tournament series, it learned more about fast, efficient multiplayer gaming than just about anyone else – and those lessons are built into Unreal Engine 3's highly optimized network infrastructure.

During a multiplayer game, each player's computer is in constant communication with another computer that acts as a server. This server computer can also run a "client" application, which means another player can actually join in and play from the server computer. When a computer is running strictly as a server (with no client), it's called a "dedicated server." Dedicated servers are generally preferred for online gaming, as the server can use all its resources for serving, not playing.

The key to efficient network gaming is to limit the data that's sent across the network to only the most important aspects of gameplay, such as each player's position and interactions with his immediate environment. By sending only the most relevant details, you can have very fast gameplay even on slower connections. The Unreal Engine has been designed to do just that.

1

The UnrealScript Interpreter

UnrealScript is one of the most revolutionary aspects of the Unreal Engine. It's a scripting language that allows programmers or users to adjust virtually anything the Engine is doing, without touching the actual game source code. UnrealScript may be the #1 reason why so many people are out there creating mods and new levels for games that run on the Unreal Engine.

If you've done much programming, you may find UnrealScript familiar. In many respects, it's a lot like the popular languages Java and C++. But, as a scripting language, it's intended to be relatively easy—in fact, its creator, Tim Sweeney, said that where he had to make tradeoffs, he chose simplicity over execution speed.

The UnrealScript Interpreter is the component of the engine responsible for transforming the UnrealScripts you create into code that the engine can process (see **FIGURE 1.15**).

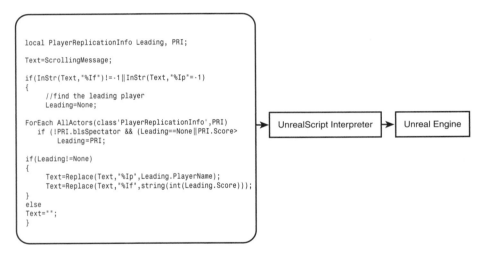

```
local PlayerReplicationInfo Leading, PRI;

Text=ScrollingMessage;

if(InStr(Text,"%If")!=-1||InStr(Text,"%Ip"=-1)
{
    //find the leading player
    Leading=None;

ForEach AllActors(class'PlayerReplicationInfo',PRI)
    if (!PRI.blsSpectator && (Leading==None||PRI.Score>
        Leading=PRI;

if(Leading!=None)
{
    Text=Replace(Text,"%Ip",Leading.PlayerName);
    Text=Replace(Text,"%If",string(int(Leading.Score)));
}
else
Text="";
}
```

UnrealScript Interpreter → Unreal Engine

FIGURE 1.15   The UnrealScript Interpreter

(Note that this book won't focus on UnrealScripting. It's primarily intended to cover artist-level game asset creation.)

Overview of Component Interaction

Now that you know the basic components of the Unreal Engine, here's how they work together to deliver an actual gaming experience.

Most games are driven by a *game loop*: a part of the game's programming code that constantly repeats itself, checking for any input from the player and updating all aspects of the game accordingly (see **FIGURE 1.16**). Within this loop, the game engine repeatedly performs many individual checks to see what's changed in the gaming environment. For instance, *has a player moved? Fired his weapon? Taken damage? Have his enemies moved?*

The game loop generally also keeps track of "generic" tasks. For example, it queues the graphics engine to redraw the screen, tells the sound engine to play any sounds that have come up, and sends data across the network. Typical game loops are designed "linearly," which means that each cycle of the loop runs through its series of checks in the exact same order every time, and give each check equal priority. But, as you'll see in a moment, the Unreal Engine's game loop is a bit smarter than that.

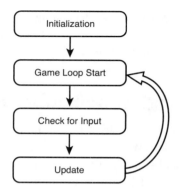

FIGURE 1.16   This diagram illustrates a basic game loop.

The Unreal Engine uses an *event-driven* game loop. This means the engine contains a list of events that the various components of the engine needs to address. These events are created from many different sources, such as player inputs, data from the physics system, or communication between components. Everything is passed through the system via this event list (see **FIGURE 1.17**).

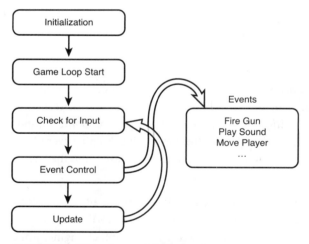

FIGURE 1.17   An event-based system

In Unreal Engine 3, each event is given a specific priority. Rather than updating every single aspect of the game during every game cycle in an order that's "written in stone," events are processed based on their importance. For example, you fire a weapon. The game loop recognizes this, then reacts by sending multiple new events into the queue, such as instructions to launch a projectile and play a sound. Obviously, the projectile's launch is more important, as it directly

1

affects gameplay depending on whether it strikes an enemy or some other object that must react to it. Therefore, the Unreal Engine gives the projectile launch a higher priority than the "noncritical" gunfire sound.

Engine Components at Work

Let's take a closer look at how these components work together during gameplay (see **FIGURE 1.18**). When you start an Unreal Engine-based game, each engine component is *initialized*. (This is like starting your sports car: It's idling, waiting for your input, shifting into gear, flooring the gas pedal, turning the steering wheel, or whatever else you have in mind.) Initialization takes place during the loading time between launching the game and seeing the opening title screen.

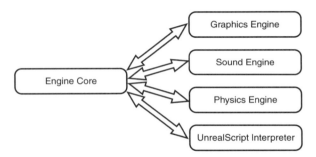

FIGURE 1.18   Unreal Engine component interaction

Now the engine components start communicating with one another. At startup, the core engine initializes the graphics engine, the sound engine, the physics engine, and the UnrealScript Interpreter. The core engine also begins sending commands to each component. Some components, such as the physics engine, begin sending data back to the core engine, keeping everything in sync. Once all components are initialized, the game's user interface is displayed, and the engine waits for the player's input.

To start the playable part of the game, the core engine loads a level that contains all assets needed for gameplay: textures, materials, sounds, meshes, animations, scripts, and so forth. Each asset is routed to the proper engine component. Materials are processed by the graphics engine, while rigid body objects are calculated by the physics engine. The event queue now "comes to life" and is quickly populated with events the core engine needs to manage as it delivers the gaming experience.

To summarize:

1. Game initialization:
    a. The core engine initializes each engine component.
    b. Components begin sending data back to the core engine for synchronization.
    c. Game is ready for user input.
2. Game launch (choosing and starting a level):
    a. A map is loaded, containing all game assets and their corresponding properties.
    b. Each asset's information is routed to its respective engine component.
3. Gameplay (excessive use of flak cannons, shock rifles, and weapons):
    a. Each engine component sends information to the core engine, which is sorted as a series of prioritized events in the event queue.
    b. The Unreal Engine's game loop runs constantly, evaluating each event by priority and performing the highest-priority tasks first.

Creating Your Own Worlds with the Unreal Engine

You now have a rudimentary grasp of the engine, its components, and how they work together to present an actual game. Now, let's start looking at what *you*, the game designer, need to create in order to actually *use* the engine in your own games.

(And, by the way, not just games. The worlds you create are entirely up to you. The Unreal Engine can be used for virtually any visualization project. Imagine attending a bid meeting for a large-scale construction job, and showing your potential client a fully interactive 3D walkthrough they can control, powered by the jaw-dropping visuals of Unreal Engine 3. *Ka-ching*—sale made!)

Game Assets

Virtually all data that the Unreal Engine uses is stored in *packages*: collections of the assets needed for your game or project. Packages are often separated by the kind of assets they contain. You might, for example, have a package called ComputerMeshes that held only the static meshes needed to construct a game scene. However, you might also include the textures for those meshes in the same package.

In the end, just think of a package as a container used to load assets into the game. Except for maps (which in a sense are their own packages), all game assets are contained within packages. You learn more about each kind of asset as you move through this book.

Maps

Maps, also called *levels* and sometimes called *scenes*, are where you create environments in the Unreal Engine (see **FIGURE 1.19**).

Technically, a *map* is simply a collection of various game assets that are shown to the player, with many of these assets pulled from the packages you've created. Artistically, the map is where you set the stage for your game or visualization experience. It's where you construct the overall shape of your environment, and use your assets to decorate it and bring it to life.

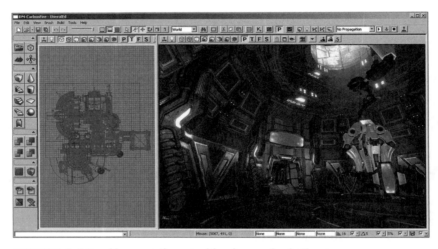

FIGURE 1.19   Maps are the actual levels you play in the game.

For convenience, each map contains its own package, where you can store assets that are only used in the game level the map displays. Most assets, however, are stored in separate packages, where they're accessible to any level that needs them.

> **NOTE**
>
> The culling behavior described below is only true when using level packages. This is one of the reasons why, in most cases, you are better off using an entirely separate package, rather than relying on level packages.

If you place an asset in a map's package, but don't actually use it the level, it is culled from the map's level package next time the level is saved. For example, imagine that you add the texture of a brick wall to your level's package, but you never actually display a brick wall. Unreal Engine 3 realizes it doesn't need to waste precious memory on that brick wall texture, and dumps it from the package.

Textures and Materials

As you probably realize by now, both textures and materials are stored in packages. Textures are simply 2D images used to create materials in your levels and on other game assets (see

FIGURE 1.20). We dedicate a whole chapter to materials and textures; for now, just know that every visible surface you create has a material applied to it, and most materials contain at least one texture. Think of a texture as part of a material: the 2D image that supplies color and other important information. Think of a material as an instruction for how light plays on your object's surface. In Unreal Engine 3, each surface must have a material applied, and the material contains textures and other rendering instructions. (There's a lot more to it, but that'll hold you for now.)

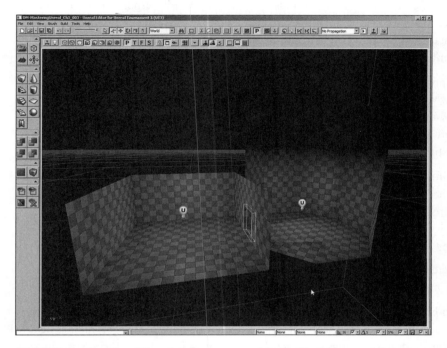

FIGURE 1.20　Two different textures: one painted in Photoshop and the other acquired with a camera

Some textures, such as normal maps, present an illusion that the surface has much more physical detail than your hardware can actually render. Through the use of normal maps, models that are only comprised of a few thousand polygons can look like they were constructed from *millions* of polys!

You create textures using 2D graphics software that isn't part of the Unreal Engine—for example, Photoshop, ZBrush, or Painter. You can also use images you've captured with digital cameras or scanners.

Once you have created your textures, you use them to create materials within the Unreal Editor. A single material can use multiple textures (though using too many can waste precious system resources). These materials can be applied to any surface in your maps. More on this in Chapter 6, "Introduction to Materials."

Sounds

Like textures, sounds must be created outside of Unreal Engine 3. You can use an external software application, or get your sounds from audio file compilations, such as sound effect CDs or royalty free sound files available online. Sounds are usually played in response to events during gameplay, such as the opening of a door, the starting of a lift, or the firing of a weapon. Ambient sounds—for instance, running water, chirping crickets, or running machinery—might also run throughout an entire scene.

Once you've imported your sounds, Unreal Engine 3's SoundCue Editor gives you tremendous flexibility in how you use them. You can mix multiple sound effects into a single sound, play certain sounds randomly, and even adjust the volume, speed, and modulation of individual effects. Using the SoundCue Editor, you can transform even the simplest audio into a complex and powerfully realistic symphony of effects.

Using Kismet, Unreal Engine 3's embedded visual scripting system, you can also create complex music systems that play certain songs and effects in response to specific events, such as when a player's health drops below a certain level, or when the player accelerates to high speed.

Static Meshes

We've already referred to static meshes a couple of times, in passing. As you work with Unreal Engine games, you use them constantly. So, what exactly *are* they?

Let's step back a bit. In 3D graphics, objects are built from *polygon meshes*—collections of vertices, edges and faces that define the shape of objects. Different kinds of polygon meshes behave differently. You can do different things with each, but some work faster than others. Static meshes render really fast, and you can use them to create very complex shapes, which makes them great for gaming. They can't be used for everything, however. (Among their limitations, you can't animate their vertices.) But most modern Unreal Engine 3 game environments are so completely covered in static meshes that you can't even see their underlying geometries.

Static meshes are designed to be *instanced* (reproduced) multiple times completely within your video card. They require essentially no work from your PC's or game console's main processor. This means they can be drawn extremely fast, even when you're using thousands of them. Don't get carried away, though. You still get the best performance if you reuse meshes wherever possible instead of creating new ones. Only the first instance of a static mesh uses a significant portion of memory. For all other copies, only positional, rotational, and scale information is stored in your video card's memory and the other rendering bits don't need to be copied again. It goes without saying that the more efficiently you use memory, the better your game performs.

Sometimes, of course, you'll have good reasons to create new meshes. Just remember, with everything in game creation (and life), you need to know the tradeoffs. Using the Unreal Editor's Primitive Stats browser, you can sort all of a level's assets by memory usage (see **FIGURE 1.21**). Notice that your level is playing a tad slow? Find your biggest memory hogs. If static meshes are at the top of the list, maybe you want to throttle back on how many you're using, or how complex they are. (We talk more about the Primitive Stats browser in Chapter 11, "Level Optimization.")

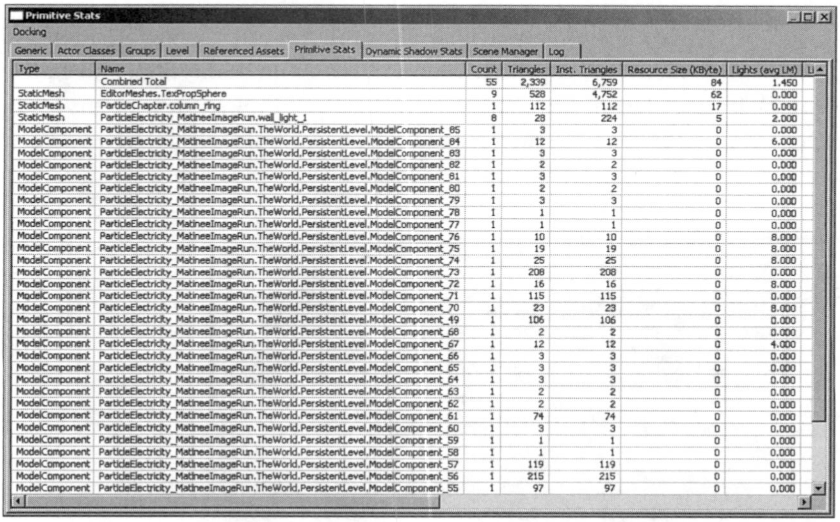

Type	Name	Count	Triangles	Inst. Triangles	Resource Size (KByte)	Lights (avg LM)
	Combined Total	55	2,339	6,759	84	1.450
StaticMesh	EditorMeshes.TexPropSphere	9	528	4,752	62	0.000
StaticMesh	ParticleChapter.column_ring	1	112	112	17	0.000
StaticMesh	ParticleElectricity_MatineeImageRun.wall_light_1	8	28	224	5	2.000
ModelComponent	ParticleElectricity_MatineeImageRun.TheWorld.PersistentLevel.ModelComponent_85	1	3	3	0	0.000
ModelComponent	ParticleElectricity_MatineeImageRun.TheWorld.PersistentLevel.ModelComponent_84	1	12	12	0	6.000
ModelComponent	ParticleElectricity_MatineeImageRun.TheWorld.PersistentLevel.ModelComponent_83	1	3	3	0	0.000
ModelComponent	ParticleElectricity_MatineeImageRun.TheWorld.PersistentLevel.ModelComponent_82	1	2	2	0	0.000
ModelComponent	ParticleElectricity_MatineeImageRun.TheWorld.PersistentLevel.ModelComponent_81	1	3	3	0	0.000
ModelComponent	ParticleElectricity_MatineeImageRun.TheWorld.PersistentLevel.ModelComponent_80	1	2	2	0	0.000
ModelComponent	ParticleElectricity_MatineeImageRun.TheWorld.PersistentLevel.ModelComponent_79	1	3	3	0	0.000
ModelComponent	ParticleElectricity_MatineeImageRun.TheWorld.PersistentLevel.ModelComponent_78	1	1	1	0	0.000
ModelComponent	ParticleElectricity_MatineeImageRun.TheWorld.PersistentLevel.ModelComponent_77	1	1	1	0	0.000
ModelComponent	ParticleElectricity_MatineeImageRun.TheWorld.PersistentLevel.ModelComponent_76	1	10	10	0	8.000
ModelComponent	ParticleElectricity_MatineeImageRun.TheWorld.PersistentLevel.ModelComponent_75	1	19	19	0	8.000
ModelComponent	ParticleElectricity_MatineeImageRun.TheWorld.PersistentLevel.ModelComponent_74	1	25	25	0	8.000
ModelComponent	ParticleElectricity_MatineeImageRun.TheWorld.PersistentLevel.ModelComponent_73	1	208	208	0	8.000
ModelComponent	ParticleElectricity_MatineeImageRun.TheWorld.PersistentLevel.ModelComponent_72	1	16	16	0	8.000
ModelComponent	ParticleElectricity_MatineeImageRun.TheWorld.PersistentLevel.ModelComponent_71	1	115	115	0	8.000
ModelComponent	ParticleElectricity_MatineeImageRun.TheWorld.PersistentLevel.ModelComponent_70	1	23	29	0	8.000
ModelComponent	ParticleElectricity_MatineeImageRun.TheWorld.PersistentLevel.ModelComponent_49	1	106	106	0	0.000
ModelComponent	ParticleElectricity_MatineeImageRun.TheWorld.PersistentLevel.ModelComponent_68	1	2	2	0	0.000
ModelComponent	ParticleElectricity_MatineeImageRun.TheWorld.PersistentLevel.ModelComponent_67	1	12	12	0	4.000
ModelComponent	ParticleElectricity_MatineeImageRun.TheWorld.PersistentLevel.ModelComponent_66	1	3	3	0	0.000
ModelComponent	ParticleElectricity_MatineeImageRun.TheWorld.PersistentLevel.ModelComponent_65	1	3	3	0	0.000
ModelComponent	ParticleElectricity_MatineeImageRun.TheWorld.PersistentLevel.ModelComponent_64	1	3	3	0	0.000
ModelComponent	ParticleElectricity_MatineeImageRun.TheWorld.PersistentLevel.ModelComponent_63	1	2	2	0	0.000
ModelComponent	ParticleElectricity_MatineeImageRun.TheWorld.PersistentLevel.ModelComponent_62	1	2	2	0	0.000
ModelComponent	ParticleElectricity_MatineeImageRun.TheWorld.PersistentLevel.ModelComponent_61	1	74	74	0	0.000
ModelComponent	ParticleElectricity_MatineeImageRun.TheWorld.PersistentLevel.ModelComponent_60	1	3	3	0	0.000
ModelComponent	ParticleElectricity_MatineeImageRun.TheWorld.PersistentLevel.ModelComponent_59	1	1	1	0	0.000
ModelComponent	ParticleElectricity_MatineeImageRun.TheWorld.PersistentLevel.ModelComponent_58	1	1	1	0	0.000
ModelComponent	ParticleElectricity_MatineeImageRun.TheWorld.PersistentLevel.ModelComponent_57	1	119	119	0	0.000
ModelComponent	ParticleElectricity_MatineeImageRun.TheWorld.PersistentLevel.ModelComponent_56	1	215	215	0	0.000
ModelComponent	ParticleElectricity_MatineeImageRun.TheWorld.PersistentLevel.ModelComponent_55	1	97	97	0	0.000

FIGURE 1.21   The Primitive Stats browser can help you see if you are using too many static meshes in your level.

Animations and Skeletal Meshes

Game characters typically aren't static meshes. They're *skeletal meshes*: meshes that deform based on a digital skeleton. You create them and add their skeletons through a process called "rigging." That's another task that happens outside the Unreal Engine, typically in 3D applications such as 3ds Max or Maya. Once a skeletal mesh is rigged, it can be animated to make it look like it's running, jumping, shooting, doing pelvic thrusts, or whatever else your wild imagination conjures up.

Meshes and their corresponding animations are, unsurprisingly, stored in packages. Animations are stored as a separate type of asset that you can assign to any character with a similar skeletal structure. This simplifies animation, and frees up precious game resources by reducing the number of animation sequences that must be loaded into memory.

1

The Tools of the Trade

Now that you have a general idea of the types of game assets you'll build, let's talk tools. As you've seen, many assets must be created in external software applications. In this section, we mention a few of the most popular, but you can certainly use others. We start, however, with an immensely powerful tool that *is* part of the Unreal Engine, and one that every Unreal level and game developer needs: the Unreal Editor itself.

Unreal Editor (UnrealEd)

The Unreal Editor (a.k.a., UnrealEd) is the central application you use to create maps, populate them with meshes, create your materials, construct sound effects from audio files, and much more (see **FIGURE 1.22**). It's also the only program used to open and browse the contents of an Unreal package. It's *not* a content creator. It *is* an outstanding tool for transforming raw content into breathtaking games.

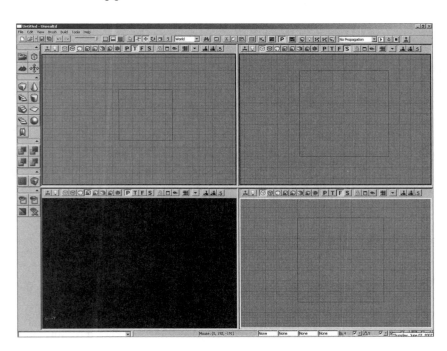

FIGURE 1.22   The Unreal Editor user interface

3D Applications

Because Unreal Engine 3 is a 3D gaming engine, you need 3D assets—whether they're characters or the static meshes you pour all over your Unreal environments. Plenty of 3D applications can create content for Unreal Engine 3, but the two most popular are Autodesk's 3ds Max and Maya (see **FIGURE 1.23**). You can find out more about them at www.autodesk.com, which sometimes—not always—makes trial or training copies available for download.

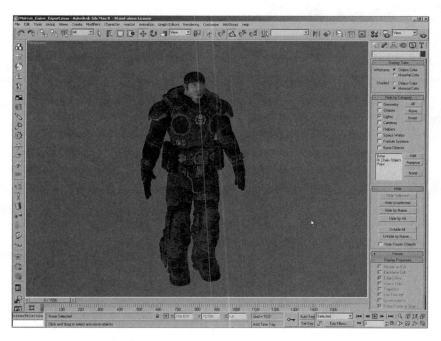

FIGURE 1.23 The 3ds Max user interface

Texturing Programs

To create textures for your game's materials, you need graphics editing software such as Adobe Photoshop or Corel Painter (see **FIGURE 1.24**). Each of these contains huge palettes of tools for working with photographic references as textures, or for painting your own.

There are other applications as well, including some that enable you to paint directly on the surface of your models. For instance, there's Pixologic's ZBrush. This nifty package doesn't just enable you to create textures; it allows you to model multimillion polygon meshes for producing super-realistic normal maps for your meshes. (Don't understand all that just yet? You will soon. But for now, trust us: that's *impressive*.)

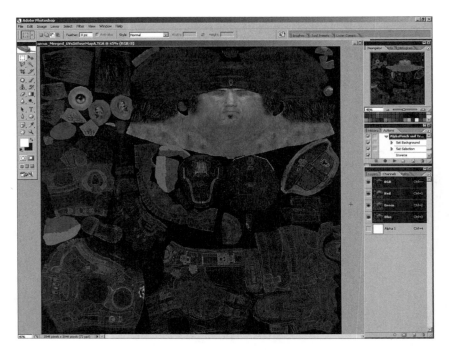

FIGURE 1.24   Textures can be edited inside Photoshop.

Collada

With all the 3D applications out there, each with its own fave formats, it would be cool to standardize a single format for sending information into Unreal Engine 3. Then, users of any application could freely create and swap Unreal game assets without switching to different software. Unreal Engine 3 supports the Collada file format, which has plug-in versions for virtually every major 3D application on the market (see **FIGURE 1.25**). For more information about Collada, and to download its latest plug-ins, visit collada.org.

Sound Programs

For audio, Unreal Editor's SoundCue Editor uses WAV files. Yup, theoretically you *could* use Windows' ancient Sound Recorder application to create those. And you *could* rely on the SoundCue Editor itself to adjust modulation and volume. But we suspect you'll want an audio environment that's a little more comprehensive. Two good options are

Sony's Sound Forge and Adobe Audition (see **FIGURE 1.26**).

Whatever program you choose, make sure it lets you edit waveforms to remove any slight pauses at the end of your effects. That's essential for easy blending between different effects.

FIGURE 1.25   Collada offers a unified file format for 3D assets.

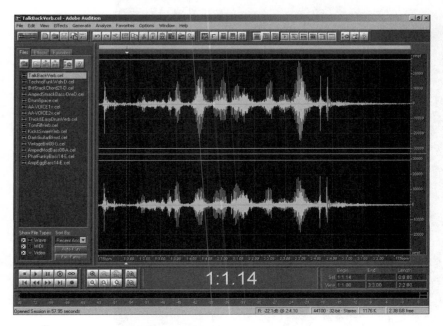

FIGURE 1.26   Adobe Audition

Training Sources

This book gives you an incredible amount of information on creating and using game assets. But, let's face it: Some of these third-party applications are pretty technical. Many aspiring game artists will want some sort of training to help them along the way.

There are plenty of online and offline locations for 3D application and texturing training. Your humble authors would like to recommend their own site, 3DBuzz.com. Come visit: We have hundreds of hours of free training videos available for download, as well as professional level training videos that help us pay the rent (see **FIGURE 1.27**).

FIGURE 1.27   3DBuzz.com, the original home for free 3D training

A quick commercial (just one, we promise): 3D Buzz has been in the online 3D training business for over five years now. We work very closely with Epic Games; in fact, we produced the 60+ hours of training videos released with the Unreal Tournament 2004 DVD Special Edition as well as a series of training videos included with the Special Edition PC release of Unreal Tournament 3. So, yeah, *we know this stuff.*

Chapter 2

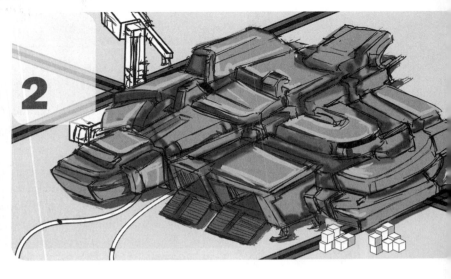

Overview of Game Development

So, what's the game development process like? Where does it start? When (if ever!) does it end? What'll happen on the way? How do you overcome the obstacles that practically every game development team runs up against, whether they're working on a simple mod or a whole new game? We can't cover everything that happens in every development cycle, but this chapter hits the highlights. We also offer up some hard-won guidelines, ideas, and (dare we say it) solutions for working together better and getting done sooner.

The Importance of Iteration

Game development is a huge process. It's long, it's involved, and it definitely isn't easy. It's a job for a team. Nowadays, no one person can create the next great first-person shooter by themselves—at least not in one lifetime!

Nope, you need lots of folks—people with many different ideas and skill sets. And realize upfront that the game you imagine won't be the same as the final result. Your ideas will change. Certain elements may not pan out, or may not be as cool as you'd hoped. Or you may simply not have enough time or funding to produce everything you want. It's an organic process. Your game will be created, reworked, re-envisioned, and then created again based on the feedback you get.

This process is known as *iteration*, and if you do it right, your game won't just start great: It'll get better as you move through production. Iteration keeps your development cycle from stagnating by allowing all team members to get their say. Your game grows almost like an organic creature: assimilating new and worthwhile ideas while shedding those that don't lend themselves to the experience you want to deliver.

Here's how iteration should work. You come up with an idea. You refine it. You develop a game (or a gaming element) based on it. Your group critiques it. Did it work? Could it be better? How? New ideas emerge. New implementations are added. And you review those. Rinse and repeat, throughout the development cycle. The changes are major at first, and gradually become smaller as the game moves toward completion. But don't expect the iterative process to end quickly. In a good, energetic production environment, some things can change right up to the last minute.

(What does all this tell you about the team you're going to need? They'd better be flexible. Eager to work with new ideas. Ready to listen to each other and willing to respect the opinions of their peers! Otherwise…well, let's just say, otherwise, it won't be fun.)

In this chapter, we put iteration to work. We walk you through some of the key elements of a successful game development cycle, showing how iteration helps drive a game from original idea into something you can actually ship to real players. Even if you're not building a full-scale AAA game title—even if you're just working on a mod—this chapter will give you a huge headstart. You'll learn how to tackle your project effectively, and how to keep it moving forward, no matter what.

Start with the Idea

Every game starts with an idea. It could be the idea of a certain style of gameplay. It could be the concept of a new gaming element—such as letting a player control several characters at once. Or the idea could arise simply from a story. However, in a best-case scenario, your ideas should take you beyond the norm. Simply re-creating an existing idea is a sure way to create an instantly forgettable game.

No, not every game must be original through and through. (If you set that standard for yourself, you may never get started!) You don't always have to reinvent the wheel: Sometimes, it's helpful for players to recognize "conventions" that help them get started playing your game. But if you've been playing games for a few years, you already know how derivative some games are. If all you're going to do is rehash an existing game, why bother creating it or buying it?

Start with the kind of game you want to make, and then work on ways to make it stand out. Want to make a third-person shooter? What could you add that separates it from, say, Gears of War?

How do you come up with great ideas for games that are compelling, and just plain fun? Simple: Play games. If you're reading this book, you're probably already a gamer. You've got games you love and games you hate. You've played games that leave you breathless. You've played other games with one awful moment where you eject it, put it on the shelf, and leave it to rot. Cliff Bleszinski, Lead Designer for Gears of War, calls these "shelf moments." You're trying to avoid shelf moments at all costs, of course. But remember, you can't please everybody!

As you design, think about your gaming experiences. What games have you absolutely loved? Why were they so great? Why did other games fail? Take notes. Write down ideas. Even write down features and ideas you'd like to borrow from. Many newcomers shun the idea of using ideas deriving from other games. It's OK if you combine those ideas with your own inspiration. Change what you've seen. Give it a twist. Re-create it in your own image. And above all, don't get too attached to any idea: Be ready to discover that it might not work. Sometimes the best thing an idea can do is lead you to an even better one!

Next, develop your idea. At this stage, many people become excited and are itching to share their idea with their team members or friends. This is not necessarily a problem; however, it may be too soon. If things are still "sketchy" or vague and you're not sure you can express your idea clearly, you might end up misrepresenting it to your team. They might lose interest before you even get started. What your Mom told you about first impressions is the truth! Get your idea fully fleshed out (or as close to it as possible) before you try to present it. If you want to get some input or feedback, that's fine, but don't present the full idea until it's ready to be seen.

You might start developing an idea by writing out a story. Or you might draft some concept art (or commission someone else to do it if you don't draw). Or you might even prepare a very rough mockup of the game itself. This mockup could exist entirely on paper if it needed to—whatever it takes to help you understand what it is you're trying to achieve and what it'll take to get there.

Often, this stage of development may involve creating a "treatment" for your game in the form of a story. As games keep pushing toward cinematic-quality experiences, the need for a good story to drive the player through the game becomes ever more important. To give you a feel for what treatments look like, the next section shows you a mock treatment for a game we call *Outworlder: Surviving the Fringe*.

Story Treatment

The story: The war had taken perhaps everything that Earth really had left. We started off, like we usually do, fighting each other. Brutally. One side of the planet was completely obliterated in a nuclear firestorm, and it wasn't the side everyone expected it to be either (see **FIGURE 2.1**).

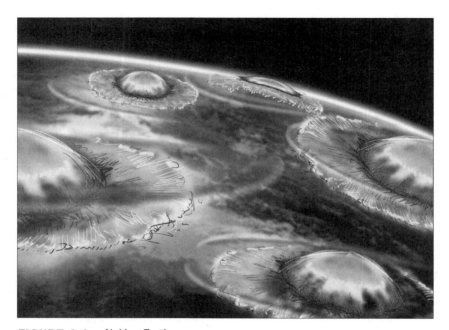

FIGURE 2.1   Nuking Earth

The rest of the planet would have been lost due to fallout if the Turgen Shield hadn't been activated, effectively sealing off one side of Earth from the other (see **FIGURE 2.2**). Unfortunately, the multiple warhead detonations had already affected the planet's rotation, and the result was apocalypse. All ocean life died first, and the rest of the planet started to follow.

Over the next ten years, the remnants of the population came together and worked hard to fast track a planet abandonment operation. A few planets had been located on the fringes of Earth's monitoring range that, while being extremely hostile environments, could support human life. Some 50 years after the end of the war, most of Earth's population had loaded into massive capital starships (see **FIGURE 2.3**) powered by a new type of engine created for long-distance space travel. Those who remained had only a few decades until the Turgen Shield's systems would fail, and the Earth would be taken by glowing fires and radioactive gasses.

FIGURE 2.2   The Turgen Shield

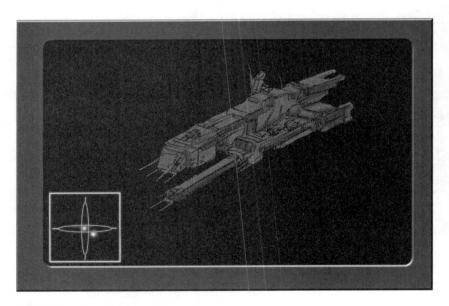

FIGURE 2.3   Settlers frigate

About 100 years into mankind's excursion into space, we came into contact with our first non-human lifeform: the Geshar (see **FIGURE 2.4**).

2

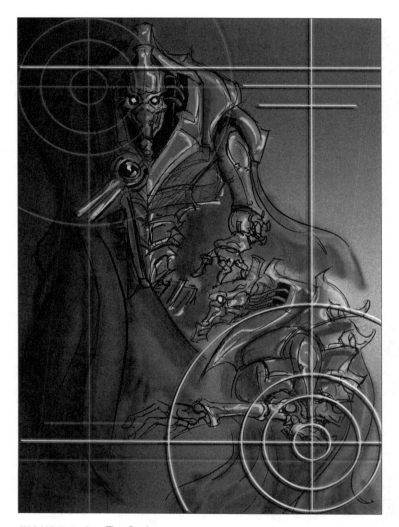

FIGURE 2.4   The Geshar

Their civilization was much older than ours, older by several millennia. They had been so close all this time, hidden by a cloaking technology they used to shroud their entire planet. And they knew us. They'd been watching us. They knew our language and how to communicate. They knew how to kill us. We were the thing they feared most. They said we were a planet-killing contagion, not worthy to traverse the cosmos.

The Geshar wiped out many colonies, captured others, and often transported captured vessels back to Earth, where they would initiate a forced landing on the surface—a death sentence they declared was the only ending fit for an Earthling. We fought them for decades (see **FIGURE 2.5**).

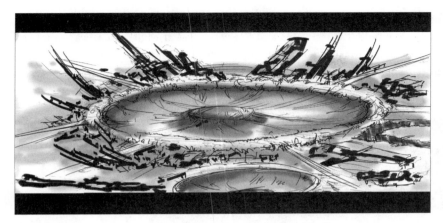

FIGURE 2.5 The aftermath of the Geshar attack on colonies

They were technologically superior, but they weren't invincible. They weren't prepared to handle our "primitive" methods of combat. At close range, no human battalion can take down a small army of Geshar infantrymen. However, their armor isn't all that tough, and they are actually weaker than humans when it comes to dealing with injuries. One good shot to the torso will drop a Geshar; it seems their brains are scattered throughout their bodies. It makes them very efficient thinkers, but also very easy to snipe.

But all that was a while ago. The three planets that Earth has colonized haven't had much trouble from the Geshar in many years. And, as humans tend to do, we're already starting to forget how much of a threat they can be.

Not that any of this bothers me. I'm what some of you might call a pirate. I steal spaceships for a living. I sell off their cargoes, break the pieces down, and sell those. Then I move on, looking for something else. I try not to kill anyone. There are plenty of killers out there who will simply decompress a ship with one good hull detonation. I don't like having blood on my hands if I can avoid it (see **FIGURE 2.6**).

So, that's how I ended up here. I caught a tip that a new weapon tech was being transported via the Night Feather freighter (see **FIGURE 2.7**). I had no idea what the tech was, or what it was for—just that there was a several million credit reward for

FIGURE 2.6 The main character

anyone who brought it in. The ship wasn't even heavily guarded. Apparently, no one on board knew what they had in the hold. I work alone, and I'm very good at what I do. It was simple to get the ship while it was in repair dock. The two guards they left on board were pretty easy to remove with a pair of twin Tirellian prostitutes I brought with me. Their dancing would distract anyone.

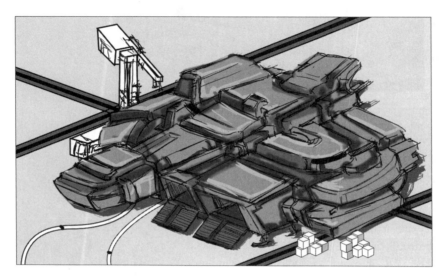

FIGURE 2.7   The Night Feather concept

I hadn't gone far when the Imperial Militia frigate appeared behind me, ordering me to shut down my engines immediately and prepare for boarding. I *knew* this had been too easy. So I did what any good pirate would do, up against much greater firepower. I ran like hell. I set the jump-drive for the fringe of Gesharian space; I didn't think they'd follow. I was wrong. I was racing toward one of the Gesharian homestead planets, hoping they would break off the chase as I got nearer and nearer to orbit. The Geshar are relatively tolerant of transport ships, but a warship could start another interstellar conflict.

Just then, a deafening impact roared through the ship, followed by alarm claxons. The ship had been hit by a missile! Plummeting toward the Geshar planet, no engines, no guidance systems, I was a meteor in the making. At the last instant before complete decompression, I activated a stasis field in my section of the ship. Hopefully it will last until the crash is over (see **FIGURE 2.8**).

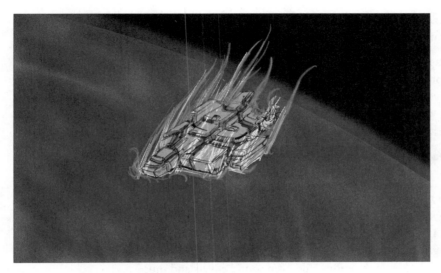

FIGURE 2.8 Night Feather entering atmo

With a solid story in place, you can start discussing gameplay with your team. Which direction will it take? How will it fit with the story? How will it make your scenario more believable to the player and more enjoyable?

For instance, you might decide that the player will start out aboard Night Feather looking for the cargo. This could force the player to immerse himself in the story more deeply, as he would experience the crash for himself. You might also decide that the player is heavily injured on impact, or poorly armed when he exits the ship. This storyline and game title also suggest that the player will be working hard to stay alive on this alien, enemy world. Perhaps the gameplay dynamic will include tasks such as keeping the player character fed and full of energy. All these issues need to be ironed out before game development can move forward.

However, keep the iterative process in mind at all times. Within your team's limits, you could try out several ideas to discover which work, which don't, and which can be augmented. Even ideas that don't make it into the actual project might spawn other ideas that will be valuable.

Considerations for Production Scheduling

Every project needs a production schedule, and every schedule is different. Even if you're just working on a mod in your free time, a schedule gives you motivation to move your project forward. Of course, if someone's paying you to deliver a game, creating a realistic schedule (and following it) is even more important. In this section, we identify some issues to keep in mind when you work on your schedule—including crucial considerations associated with creating the highly detailed assets you're going to need.

Time can easily be the key factor in whether major areas of gameplay or storyline in your game actually get explored. Sometimes you simply don't have enough time to do everything you want. The key: Do everything you can do, without getting so caught up in details that you wind up shooting the rest of your production in the foot.

Making games using Unreal Engine 3 is an art-intensive process. When you use Unreal Engine 3, the engine is already "done": You're heavily focused on creating the objects that will be displayed within it.

You can sum up the attraction most players feel to Unreal Engine 3 in a single word: *visuals*. Games created with Unreal Engine 3 provide heart-stopping realism with lightning-fast gameplay, if you take the time to take advantage of the engine's true power. Hyper-realistic multi-million polygon game characters aren't created overnight; neither are the other assets you need, including models, textures, animations, and even sound effects and music.

Creating high-resolution geometry for your visual assets takes time. Getting your geometry properly textured does, too. In the case of characters, getting everything properly rigged and animated takes a lot of time. Nowadays, most games deal with thousands of different assets: That's why many game development companies outsource much of the asset creation labor. It takes more time to get assets done in modern games, and you need plenty of people to work on them.

Creating your assets isn't the whole story, either: You need time to try them out in the game, to make sure you've captured the right look and feel, and that they fit into the overall flow of production.

The great thing is that you can apply the iterative process here as well. Even the model for a character or item can start with concept art, which can be discussed and refined until the team (or some portion of it) approves it for modeling. Then, the model can be created and critiqued in much the same way. You don't want to go too overboard (or you'll never get anything done), but the key is to make the most of your team environment and work this process into your schedule. It won't be lightning fast, but it won't take forever either!

We don't want to totally ignore the nonvisual side of the Unreal Engine. The engine is constructed so licensees can easily change virtually any aspect of it, and even nonlicensees can make dramatic changes by writing UnrealScripts. Your idea and the way you've acquired access to Unreal Engine 3 (either by licensing it, or by modding a game using it) drives how much time you must invest in the programming end of development. In general, you'll to want to complete as much of your original coding early in the process as possible, so you'll have time to fine-tune and perfect it.

You'll want to talk to the team members who handle each aspect of production and get an idea of how long they expect their responsibilities to take. Tight time constraints are OK—in fact, they're inevitable—but people must have enough time to get the work done. By feeling out their experience level and the speed at which they can realistically complete their assigned tasks, you can create a far more realistic schedule—one that comes close to fitting everyone's needs. And you can prepare for the unexpected, too. Setbacks will occur, and you will have to adjust parts of your schedule to stay on track with your overall goals.

Communication

Iteration demands great communication among all members of the team. Remember, people are repeatedly reviewing game elements and deciding what they like and don't like—over and over again. Communication problems are one of the leading causes of production setbacks. In particular, ambiguity kills: You need to be crystal clear about everything.

Have Regular Meetings

The best way for people to communicate clearly is to bring them together in one room. Meet often. Depending on your team and how closely they work together, you might meet every morning, though once a week will sometimes have to do. The goals of your meeting? To discuss everyone's progress on their assignments, give suggestions and critiques to one another, make decisions on ideas that need refinement or reconsideration, and come up with a plan of attack based on all these considerations.

But there's another purpose to meetings: to promote a creative environment where new ideas can be heard much more quickly. In some meetings, you might not want to adjourn until you've heard and agreed on at least a few new ideas. When everyone's talking about ideas that "would be cool" or "might make something better," iteration happens faster and games get better.

Make Yourself Heard

Meetings do no good if you just sit there and nod the whole time. Say what you're thinking about the topic at hand. Don't understand where an idea is headed? Say so! Think you've come up with a way to make another idea better? Speak up! You offer nothing to the team if you can't speak your mind about their ideas, or bring them some of your own.

Respect Your Teammates

Your teammates are here for a reason. They're on your team because you trust them to know what they're talking about, and you value their opinion. (Right? If not, you're doing something wrong!)

Never shut down opinions out of hand. Listen to what people have to say, even if they disagree with you or your idea. Even if your idea gets shot down, or their take on your idea doesn't get applied, merely having the discussion can help you fix problems in the future—or help identify other issues that would have been left hidden until it was too late to deal with them.

Artists Versus Programmers: Round One, Fight!

Artists and programmers tend to speak two different languages. If you're an artist, you might throw out the occasional idea that makes every programmer in the room get suddenly very queasy. Some ideas are easy to implement. Others might be extremely difficult, or even impossible because they might require changes that you can't perform. (For example, if you're not an Unreal Engine licensee, you can't access the source code needed to make certain changes.) More often, programmers simply may not have enough production time left to do what artists are suggesting or vice versa.

The key is to make sure artists and programmers are talking to one another. Keep those lines of communication flowing. It's not the artist's job to know what is and isn't possible through code, just as it's not the programmer's job to make the models look realistic. At the same time, artists and programmers must work closely together to come up with adequate compromises for incorporating new ideas into the game. You may not fully understand what your colleagues are doing, but don't be afraid to talk it out!

Pick Your Battles

Not all your ideas will make it into the game. Some won't work. Your team will hate some of them. Some will need refinement (sometimes tweaks, sometimes big changes.) That's just the way it is. When a team member doesn't agree with you on a point, don't fight for it too hard if you don't have to. Some battles aren't worth fighting.

Some, however, are. You might feel passionately about some ideas, even when no one else shares your vision. If you end up in a situation like this, you may need to be ready to defend your idea against an onslaught of opposition. That's where your communication skills and your ability to convey your ideas are truly put to the test. You've got to make your colleagues see why your idea is so important.

Sometimes, persistence is key. Other times, pulling back saves face and helps production move along more smoothly. You may need to concede a battle so that you can get the upper hand in the war later on. More to the point, you might have to let your idea be pushed to the background for a time. You can sometimes bring it up in subsequent meetings, or present it from different angles until you find just the right one that sways your colleagues. Whatever the result, respect your teammates; if an idea just won't work and your other teammates are adamant about dropping it, know when to let it go.

Stay Creative

One of the hardest things to do in a team environment is to keep things from stagnating. If you are the lead designer of a project, it's your job to keep the ideas flowing. Be outlandish. Come up with crazy ideas if you have to. It's better to shoot down fifty ideas on the way to finding five great ones than to struggle to come up with three good ideas and fail miserably.

Again, remember: even ideas which don't get accepted can spawn ideas that do. For example, you might toss out the idea that it would be really cool if you could throw ammunition magazines into fire and have them explode and kill surrounding enemies. However, your other teammates might not like it (or your programmers may tell you that it can't be done on your schedule). But, just bringing up that idea might make someone suggest another option: setting guns to self-destruct and then throwing them at the enemy. You'd be out a gun, but you've effectively created a powerful grenade. That idea could be wildly successful, and no one would have thought of it if you hadn't been thinking outside the box in the first place.

Testing and Feedback

Testing is one of the most critical parts of your development cycle. In larger productions, it's often outsourced. If you're keeping it in house, you and your team will play through the game—or perhaps specific parts—and then reconvene in a meeting to discuss what everyone finds. This is just another part of the iterative process. Realize that at the outset, there won't be much to play. It takes some time to come up with a playable shell, and team members have to recognize that certain areas contain only "rough visualizations" of effects or assets to come.

This type of testing is commonly called *alpha testing*. In the stage, you're not ready to bring in the public. Chances are, they would not understand the visualization aspects or the incomplete components and might get the wrong idea about the project. This type of testing leads to many meetings where the team discusses what is working and what is not and makes suggestions; then everyone will separate and incorporate those changes, preparing for the next meeting. Yes, iteration again. Each time you meet, the game has changed.

At some point, your game will be nearly finished. Maybe you're just running out of time (and cutting out features that aren't working or can't be refined in time). Maybe you're getting close to the game you originally envisioned. At this point, you're ready to consider *beta testing*.

There are several ways to beta test. You could hire a staff to handle it. Or, you could allow members of the public to apply for permission to beta test. This is considered *closed* beta testing, because you can choose who can test your game, while keeping it off-limits to everyone else. For example, you might not want to let anyone test your game unless they have a computer that's fast enough to fairly assess its performance.

Or, in *open* beta testing, you can release a playable version of the game to the general public. This is usually the final type of testing before the game finishes its production cycle. Those who download and test your game or project will (in a best-case scenario) supply you with feedback as to what is and isn't working on their end. This is different from the feedback you'd expect to get during alpha testing, however. In alpha testing, you're getting feedback on things that don't necessarily correspond to whether the game is functioning properly. You're often changing things that

2

members of your team didn't like or just didn't add as much to the game as you would have hoped. Beta testing isn't about what the testers "like" or "don't like." It's about finding and rooting out problems and malfunctions.

So, how long do you test? Well, remember that game development, like many other ventures, could theoretically go on forever. That's why the production schedule is so important. Testing continues as long as it can without offsetting the production schedule too much.

Ending Production

At some point, your production cycle must cease. You may feel like you still have work left to do, or that there were things that you wanted to see in the game that never made it in. This is very common and shouldn't concern you too much. But what happens when the production is over? In a larger production, the release "goes gold": The final software is sent to a publisher who duplicates discs and case labels, and packages the game for retail sale.

If you're on a smaller production cycle, such as one for a mod, you're ready to prepare your mod for download and start telling people about it. Smaller productions rely heavily on word-of-mouth advertising, although you may have budgeted enough for some low-cost banner ads, or found a website that's willing to help you generate hype. Either way, it's time for people to find out how awesome your efforts really are, and to get people playing it and talking about it.

However, even after your game or mod or other project has gone out the door, your job's not necessarily done. You might be responsible for handling bug fixes and patches. Alpha and beta testing never pick up every problem, and some problems just won't get picked up that way—for example, game balance issues that only become obvious when large numbers of people are playing. You may need to handle these with a software patch. Unlike 15 years ago, even console games receive minor fixes from time to time, as modern consoles increasingly rely on interaction via the Internet.

Still, though, even with all this to do, the end of your production is a time to celebrate, and some heavy congratulations are definitely in order. The next step? Take a short break. Then, plan the next project, and get cracking!

Chapter 3

Up and Running: A Hands-On Level Creation Primer

If your weird, disturbing imagination can conjure it up, it's a pretty good bet that Unreal Engine can make it happen. The power of this engine can seem overwhelming—specially when you're first starting out. It's your job to narrow the Unreal Engine's field of infinite possibility: to sculpt it into the gaming experience of your dreams. It's like being handed the keys to an F-22 fighter jet: Where do you start? You ultimately need to develop skills in many different areas. To give you a feel for the real experience of working with Unreal Engine, we designed this chapter to get your hands dirty with as many aspects of the Unreal Editor as possible. Worry not. We hold your hand every step of the way. It'll be simple. Easy. Fun. We promise…

Starting Your First Level

This chapter does not contain in-depth explanations over each action you perform, but rather provides a quick run-and-gun crash course on the Unreal Editor, enabling you to acquaint yourself with many of the actions you'll be performing throughout this book. This chapter can also help those who have previous experience in earlier versions of Unreal Editor with finding the changes that have been made as of the release of Unreal Engine 3.0.

It is highly recommended that you follow this chapter from beginning to end, rather than simply selecting a tutorial in the middle. Remember that this is a primer chapter intended to give you a brief tour of Unreal Editor and demonstrate as many of the concepts found throughout this book as easily as possible.

> **NOTE**
>
> The tutorials in this chapter assume that the reader can generally identify the primary areas of the Unreal Editor user interface. For an in-depth look at the Unreal Editor user interface, please turn to Appendix A, "The Unreal Editor User's Guide."

TUTORIAL 3.1: Creating Your First Room

1. Launch Unreal Editor. You can do this by launching the Unreal Tournament 3 Editor application found within the Windows Start menu. If you don't see this option, you may need to create your own shortcut to access the Editor, which you can do by appending the flag "editor" to the end of your executable's Target property. If you're unsure, simply follow these steps within Windows (see **FIGURE 3.1**):

   a. Navigate to the installation folder where you have installed Unreal Tournament 3, and locate the game's launch executable. In many cases, this will be something like the following:

      C:\Program Files\Unreal Tournament 3\Binaries\UT3.exe

   b. Right-mouse drag a copy of your executable icon to a blank space in your installation folder (or to the desktop, if you prefer) and choose Create Shortcuts Here from the Context menu.

   c. Right-click on your new shortcut, and choose Properties from the Context menu.

   d. On the Target line in the Properties window, add a space to the end of the line (after the quotes), and then add "editor."

2. The Generic browser might open once Unreal Editor launches. If so, close it for now by clicking the Close button in the upper-right corner and then choose File > New from Unreal Editor's main menubar (see **FIGURE 3.2**).

> **NOTE**
>
> Your final target should look something like this:
>
>   "C:\Program Files\Unreal Tournament 3\Binaries\UT3.exe" editor
>
> Double-clicking this new shortcut launches Unreal Editor.

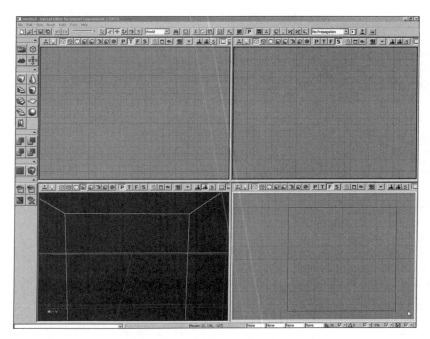

FIGURE 3.1   This is the Unreal Editor user interface.

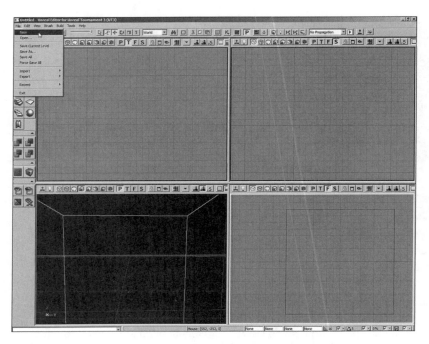

FIGURE 3.2   Here are the New options from the main menubar.

3

3. The New Level dialog appears, from which you can choose to create an additive or subtractive world (see **FIGURE 3.3**). Choose Subtractive, and click OK. You may be asked if you would like to save any changes, in which case you should click No.

This creates a world of solid volume (as if we were inside the center of a mountain) from which we can carve out our level.

4. On the left side of the screen (in the Toolbox), you see the Cube button 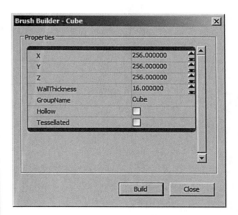. Right-click on it. A window containing various dimensional properties appears in the center of your screen (see **FIGURE 3.4**).

5. Enter the value 1024 for the X and Y properties (length and width), and a value of 512 for Z (height). Refer to **FIGURE 3.5** if you need help.

> **NOTE**
>
> For this introductory level, we use subtractive space as a matter of simplicity. In most cases, you will want to use additive levels in order to speed up lighting pre-calculations.

FIGURE 3.3   This is the New Level dialog.

> **NOTE**
>
> You can assume that any properties we do not explicitly tell you to set can be left at their default values!

FIGURE 3.4   This is the Brush Builder— Cube Properties window.

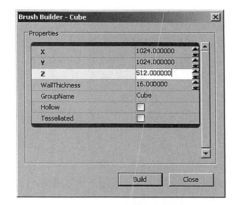

FIGURE 3.5   Enter the values into the Cube Properties window as shown.

Click the Build button, and then the Close button when finished. The Red Builder Brush has now changed its size to match your specifications. However, don't become alarmed if you notice the Brush disappear from some viewports altogether. You may need to navigate the camera around in those viewports before the Red Builder Brush becomes visible!

Use the following controls to navigate the camera in your viewports and see your level:

In the Perspective Viewport (typically the lower-left quadrant):

Left Mouse Button—Drag to move the camera forward and back and to rotate left and right.

Right Mouse Button—Drag to rotate the camera similarly to how you would turn your head.

Left and Right Mouse Buttons (simultaneously)—Drag to slide the camera up, down, left, or right without turning.

In the Orthographic (Top, Side, Front) Viewports (typically upper-left, upper-right, and lower-right quadrants):

Left Mouse Button—Drag to move the camera up, down, left, or right.

Right Mouse Button—Drag to move the camera up, down, left, or right, just like holding down the left mouse button.

Left and Right Mouse Buttons (simultaneously)—Drag to zoom the camera toward or away from the level.

6. From the Toolbox (again, on the left side of the screen), choose the CSG: Subtract button ▉. This creates a subtractive brush using the shape and position of the Red Builder Brush. The purpose of this subtractive brush is to "carve" a room out of our world of solid mass. However, because we currently have no lighting in the level, you will not be able to see anything.

7. From the toolbar at the top of the Perspective viewport, click the Unlit button ◯. This displays your level without calculating any lights. Because there are no lights in our level, this is an easy way to view or work so far! Feel free to navigate around the Perspective viewport to have a look at your room (see **FIGURE 3.6**).

8. Save your progress thus far by choosing File > Save Current Level from the main menubar. Name your level with the name DM-Ch3_001.ut3.

> **NOTE**
>
> Be sure to practice these navigation skills! We assume their use throughout the remainder of this book!

> **NOTE**
>
> Adding the prefix "DM-" to the beginning of our map name means that when we later play-test the map, it will load up as an Unreal Tournament Deathmatch map. This enables the player to spawn with a gun, health, and controls just as he would if playing the game. Without this prefix, the level tests in Editor Mode, in which there are no weapons and only basic controls.

> **TIP**
>
> To alleviate errors, make sure that you never put a space in the filename for a map, and that you give each map a completely unique name! Also, make sure that your filename is never longer than 30 characters!

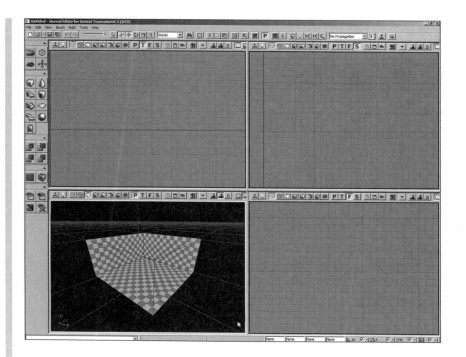

FIGURE 3.6   The current progress of our first room.

END TUTORIAL 3.1

Congratulations! You've just created your first room in an Unreal level! Currently, however, it's not going to be much to look at. In **TUTORIAL 3.2**, we add on to our existing room and start to turn it into a more interesting level!

Now that you know how to carve a room out of your level, you can easily add more rooms by following a similar workflow. However, in order to attach those rooms and keep your level's geometry clean and efficient, you're going to have to pay attention to the exact positioning of each room, and make sure that each of your brushes are aligned precisely.

Currently, our level is pretty bland. In **TUTORIAL 3.2**, we continue the process of laying out the key areas by adding on another room.

TUTORIAL 3.2: Adding a Second Room to Your Level

1. Continue from **TUTORIAL 3.1**, or open the DM-MasteringUnreal_Ch3_001.ut3 map included in the files for this chapter.

2. In the Toolbox, right-click on the Cylinder button ▣. In the Cylinder Properties window, enter 1024 for Z, and leave the other properties at their default values, as shown in

FIGURE 3.7. Click Build and Close when finished. This changes the Red Builder Brush into a tall hexagon.

3. Before we create the subtractive brush for our hexagonal room, we should position the Red Builder Brush appropriately. To do this, we rely on the Translation Widget 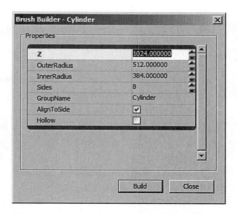, which can be found in the Unreal Editor main toolbar. You may recognize the widget as being very similar to the translation manipulator found in many 3D applications, such as 3ds Max and Maya.

Select the Red Builder Brush by left-clicking on it in any viewport. You should now notice that not only does the brush highlight to a bright red, but also that the Translation Widget is visible inside of it (see **FIGURE 3.8**).

FIGURE 3.7 Use these settings for Cylinder brush creation.

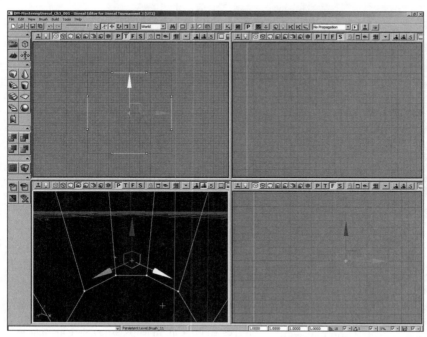

FIGURE 3.8 This is the Translation Widget seen in a Lit Perspective viewport.

4. In order to make sure that all movements in the Editor are precise, we
need to verify our Drag Grid settings,
which control how many units your
objects snap (or instantaneously jump)
as you move them. The settings for
the Drag Grid can be found near the
lower-right corner of the Console bar at

> **NOTE**
>
> Make sure you have selected not only the Translation
> Widget, but also the Show/Use the Widget icon,
> located just to the left. Without this button activated,
> you are not able to see the widget.

the bottom of the interface. Verify that the checkbox is checked, and that the
Drag Grid is set to 16. If you need to change the Drag Grid settings, simply click on the
small black arrowed button next to the Drag Grid setting, and choose 16 from the menu
(see **FIGURE 3.9**).

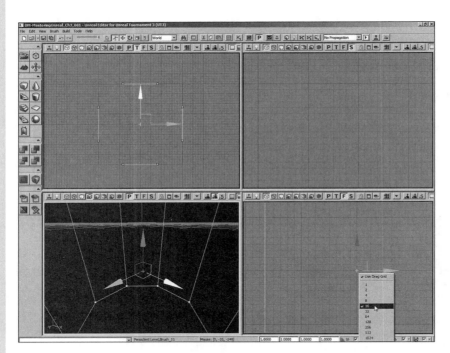

FIGURE 3.9   Here is the Drag Grid settings menu.

5. For this step, make sure that you are
focusing on the top viewport (upper-left
quadrant). Zoom out so that you can
see all the Red Builder Brush. Verify
that the brush is selected and that you
can see the Translation Widget. Click
and drag on the red arrow (X-axis) of

> **NOTE**
>
> In general, it is a good idea to always leave the Drag
> Grid on. This enables you to precisely snap your
> brushes end-to-end, which is extremely important in
> maintaining clean BSP geometry in your level. For
> more information on BSP, please see Chapter 4, "A
> Universe of Brushes: World Geometry In-Depth."

the Widget, moving the Red Builder Brush upward until its bottommost wall is two grid spaces from the top of the cube.

Because your Drag Grid settings are at 16, a gap of two grid spaces is equal to a space of 32 units (16×2) between the cube and the hexagon (see **FIGURE 3.10**). This will be important in a moment.

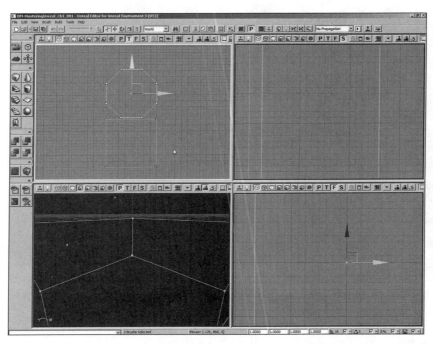

FIGURE 3.10   The cube and hexagonal cylinder properly positioned in the top viewport

6. Next, look at the side view (upper-right quadrant). You will notice that the bottom of the cylindrical brush is lower than the bottom of the cube brush. This needs to be fixed or you will have a wildly uneven floor in your level, resulting in an open pit when the player enters the cylindrical room!

> **TIP**
>
> If you are unsure as to exactly how many units are between the cube and the hexagon, you can drag along the grid using the middle mouse button to see a measurement tool!

While still looking at the side viewport, use the blue arrow handle of the Translation Widget to move the cylindrical Red Builder Brush up in the Z-axis so that its base is flush with the bottom of the cube-shaped room.

7. Once you have verified that the hexagon shape has been positioned such that the distance between the walls of the hexagon and the cube are exactly 32 units, and that the floors of each room are level to one another, click the CSG: Subtract button 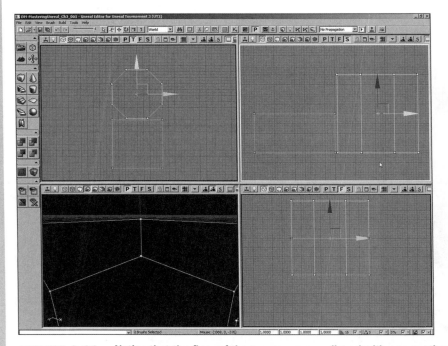 to carve out your second room (see **FIGURE 3.11**).

FIGURE 3.11   Notice that the floor of the two rooms are aligned with one another.

8. From the top viewport, use the Translation Widget to move the Red Builder Brush out of the way so that you can more easily view the rooms in your Perspective viewport. Notice how there is currently no way for a player to pass from one room to the other (see **FIGURE 3.12**).

9. From the File menu of the main menubar, choose Save Current Level to save your progress.

> **NOTE**
>
> Be aware that lighting has been added into the level for **FIGURE 3.12** to help the reader visualize the level's layout! The results on your computer will likely look very flat while being viewed in Unlit mode.

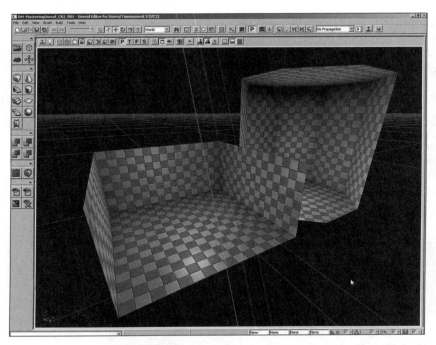

FIGURE 3.12 Here you can see our two current rooms. However, if you look closely, you'll see that they are not currently connected.

END TUTORIAL 3.2

Now we have two separate rooms in our level, but at this time we have no way to go from one room to the other. In **TUTORIAL 3.3**, we solve this problem by creating an adjoining doorway between the two rooms. At this stage, we have two rooms but no way to traverse between them! In **TUTORIAL 3.3**, we add the doorway that connects the two chambers into a single level.

At this stage, we have two rooms but no way to traverse between them! In **TUTORIAL 3.3**, we add the doorway that connects the two chambers into a single level.

TUTORIAL 3.3: Connecting Your Rooms

1. Continue from **TUTORIAL 3.2**, or open the DM-MasteringUnreal_Ch3_003.ut3 map included with the files for this chapter. We are now going to create the doorway that connects the two rooms together.

2. Right-click on the Cube button 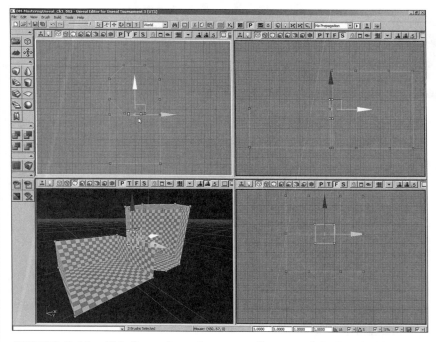 and input the following values into the properties; then click Build and Close:

   X: 32

   Y: 256

   Z: 256

> **TIP**
>
> You can use the down arrow key to move between input fields in the Builder Brush Properties window.

3. In the top viewport, use the Translation Widget to position the Red Builder Brush so that it fits exactly in between the cube and the hexagonal cylinder and the cube rooms. Verify that the Red Builder Brush is centered so that its edges touch each of the two rooms, and that it is horizontally aligned (again, in the top view) to fit precisely between the cube brush's sides, as shown in **FIGURE 3.13**.

FIGURE 3.13　This figure shows the proper alignment of the Red Builder Brush for the creation of the doorway, as seen from the top viewport.

4. Now that the Red Builder Brush is aligned in the top view, you need to align it in either the front or side view. If you don't, the bottom of your doorway will be several feet in the air! In the front viewport (lower-right quadrant), use the Translation Widget to move the Red Builder Brush so that its base is flush with the bottom of the two rooms.

5. Once you have confirmed the position of the Red Builder Brush, click the CSG: Subtract button to carve out a doorway between the two rooms. You can verify this doorway in your Perspective viewport, although you may need to navigate the camera inside one of the rooms in order to see it (see **FIGURE 3.14**).

> **NOTE**
>
> Be aware that lighting has been added into the level for **FIGURE 3.14** to help the reader visualize the level's layout! The results on your computer will likely look very flat while being viewed in Unlit mode.

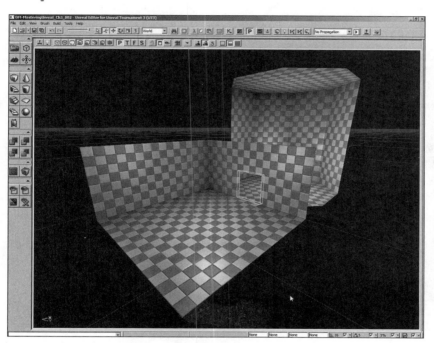

FIGURE 3.14   Here is the doorway connecting the two rooms, as seen in the Perspective view!

6. Be sure to go to File > Save Current Level from the main menubar to save your changes!

END TUTORIAL 3.3

For our current purposes, this is as complex as we need to make this level. However, if we were to try to play the level right now, we'd find that we couldn't see anything! This is because there is currently no lighting in this level whatsoever. In **TUTORIAL 3.4**, we fix this problem by adding lights to our level.

Without some sort of lighting in place, your level appears to be a strictly black screen, only illuminating for brief flashes when weapons are fired. In **TUTORIAL 3.4**, we add some lights into our level so that our player can see!

3

TUTORIAL 3.4: Illuminating the Level

1. Continue from **TUTORIAL 3.3**, or open the DM-MasteringUnreal_Ch3_003.ut3 map included with the files for this chapter.

2. There are many ways to create a light. In this case, we're going to use a simple shortcut. In the top viewport, hold the L key and then left-click in the center of the cube-shaped room. This adds a light to the center of that room (see **FIGURE 3.15**).

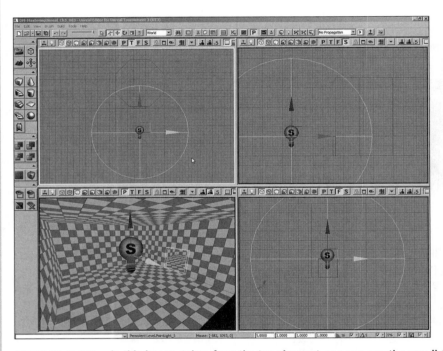

FIGURE 3.15   In this image, taken from the top viewport, you can see the new light icon (scaled up for visibility).

3. Currently, you cannot see the result of your light. In the Perspective viewport toolbar, click the Lit button 🔲 so that you can see what your light looks like (see **FIGURE 3.16**).

4. With the light selected, press the F4 key. This opens the light's Properties window. This window is divided into several expandable categories. First, click on the Light category. Underneath you see the LightComponent subcategory. Clicking on this subcategory expands a large list of properties that affect the look and behavior of the light (see **FIGURE 3.17**).

> **NOTE**
>
> If the window does not appear when you press the F4 key, it is possible that you have changed focus away from one of the viewports by perhaps clicking on another window or control. Try reselecting the light in any viewport and immediately pressing F4. Alternatively, you can double-click an object to open its properties directly.

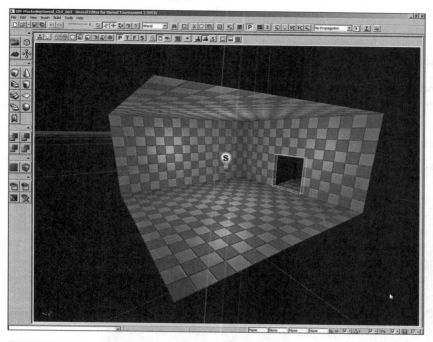

FIGURE 3.16   You can now see the result of our lighting.

5. Within the list of settings found under the LightComponent subcategory, set the following properties (technical explanations of what these properties do are approached later in Chapter 7, "Introduction to Lighting"):

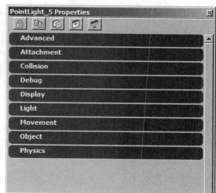

> **Brightness**—Set to 0.25.
>
> **CastDynamicShadows**—Check this box.
>
> **LightingChannels**—Expand this subcategory by clicking on the black arrow to the left of its name, and check the Dynamic box.
>
> **LightShadowMode**—Use the dropdown to set this to LightShadow_Modulate.

Close the Properties window once you have finished setting these properties.

FIGURE 3.17   This is the light's Properties window.

6. We now need a duplicate of this light so that we can illuminate the cylindrical room. With the light still selected, hold the Alt key and from the top view, use the Translation Widget to move the light up in the X axis to the center of the cylindrical room. By holding down the Alt key while you move, you will notice that the selected object is duplicated.

7. With the newly duplicated light selected, press the F4 key to open its Properties window. If necessary, re-expand the Light Category, and then the LightComponent subcategory. Set the following:

> **Radius:** 768

This increases the area of effect for the light in the cylindrical room (see **FIGURE 3.18**).

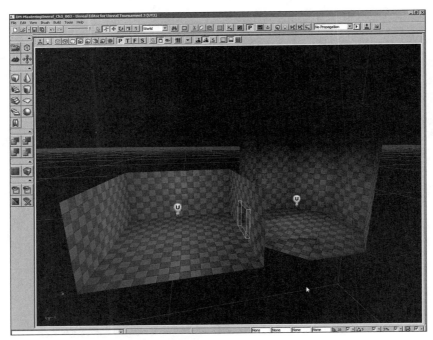

FIGURE 3.18   As you can see in this image from the Perspective viewport, both of our rooms are now lit.

8. Be sure to go to File > Save Current Level from the main menubar to save your changes!

END TUTORIAL 3.4

Your room is now lit! At this point, it would be easy to test it out and see what it's like to walk around inside it. In **TUTORIAL 3.5**, that's just what we're going to do!

Of course, building your level is a lot of fun, but at some point you need to jump in and see how it plays! In **TUTORIAL 3.5**, we show you how you can test your levels within Unreal Editor.

TUTORIAL 3.5: Testing Out the Level

1. Continue from **TUTORIAL 3.4**, or open the DM-MasteringUnreal_Ch3_004.ut3 map included with the files for this chapter.

2. Before we actually enter our level, we need to build it. Building is one of the most important things you do while editing an Unreal level. It allows Unreal Editor to compile your geometry, lights, and other items into a playable environment. In general, you will want to rebuild anything you've changed before you test a level.

    For our purposes, simply click on the Build All button  (available in the main toolbar), which builds everything all at once. Because we have created a subtractive level, this build process may take several moments. Just remember that until you rebuild, you might not be looking at an accurate representation of your level (see **FIGURE 3.19**)!

    FIGURE 3.19   The Building Map dialog shows the progress of your current build operation.

3. Upon completion of the Build process, you will likely see the Map Check window appear, alerting you that some of your brushes have null reference materials. This is currently of no concern to us, as it is simply alerting us that we need to apply some genuine materials to the walls, floor, and ceiling at some point. For now, you may ignore this warning (see **FIGURE 3.20**).

    Close the window by clicking the Close button.

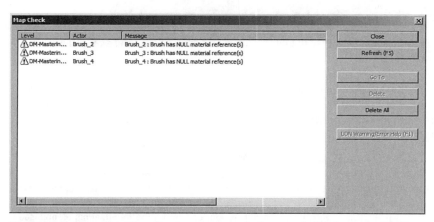

FIGURE 3.20   The Map Check appears each time you build the map, alerting you to any warnings or errors in your map.

4. Once everything is built, it's time to try out your level. There are two ways to go about this. One requires that you place a PlayerStart actor at the point where you want your player to enter the level. The second requires that you simply right-click somewhere in your level (preferably on the floor) and tell Unreal Editor that you'd like to play the level from there. For this first test, we use the second method.

Right-click on the floor of the cube room, and choose Play From Here from the Context menu. The In Editor Game window appears, and you can run around your level as if you were playing it in a game (see **FIGURE 3.21**). When finished, press Esc to return to the Editor.

FIGURE 3.21   In this figure of the Play In Editor window, you can see the level as if you were playing it in Unreal Tournament 3!

5. Now we're going to test the level using a PlayerStart actor. This is important if you know you want your player to enter the level at a specific location. Begin by right-clicking on some part of the floor of your level. From the Context menu that appears, choose Add Actor > Add PlayerStart.

You can use the Translation Widget to position the PlayerStart wherever you like. Notice the small arrow that points out of the PlayerStart icon? This enables you to control what orientation

> **NOTE**
>
> After you right-click on the floor, you can hold Ctrl as you left-click on the Play From Here option. This enables you to test the map as a spectator, which means your camera will be free-floating, as opposed to being attached to a character.

the player has upon entering the level. For now, leave the orientation at its default value (see **FIGURE 3.22**).

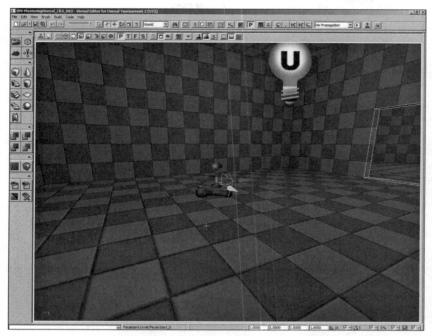

FIGURE 3.22 This view in the Perspective viewport shows that the PlayerStart actor is now placed in the level.

6. You can now test the level by going to the Build menu on the main menubar, and choosing Play Level. Had you tried this without first adding a PlayerStart actor, you would have received an error message.

   When you are finished testing your level, press Esc to return to the Editor.

7. Save your level progress!

END TUTORIAL 3.5

We now have our level's geometry constructed, and some lights in place so that we can navigate it. However, all we currently see is the default material, which is not very pleasing to the eye. In the next few tutorials, we're going to add some materials to the walls, floor, and ceiling of our level to really start to change the environment.

Our basic level is built and lit. We now need to control the types of surfaces from which it has been built. In **TUTORIAL 3.6**, we explore this process by adding materials to the world geometry.

TUTORIAL 3.6: Adding Materials to World Geometry

1. Continue from **TUTORIAL 3.5**, or open the DM-MasteringUnreal_Ch3_005.ut3 map included with the files for this chapter.

2. Before we can add materials to our level, we need to open up the package that currently holds all the materials and meshes that we use in the creation of this level. To begin, open the Generic browser by choosing View > Browser Windows > Generic from the main menubar (see **FIGURE 3.23**).

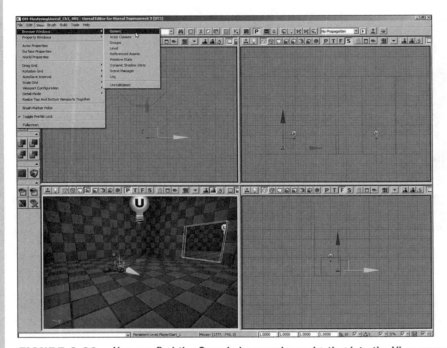

FIGURE 3.23   You can find the Generic browser by navigating into the View menu.

3. From within the Generic browser, choose File > Open from the menubar (see **FIGURE 3.24**). Navigate to the Chapter_3_LevelAssets.upk package file that is included with the files for this chapter. If you have not yet copied this file, it is included on your book's DVD inside the packages folder for this chapter.

4. In the Perspective viewport, navigate the camera so that it is inside the square-shaped room. Then, using the left mouse button, click on one of the walls of that room. Notice that the wall turns blue. This tells you that that surface is selected.

   While holding the Ctrl key, click on all the walls and the ceiling of the cube-shaped room to select them, along with all the surfaces within the doorway except for the floor (see **FIGURE 3.25**).

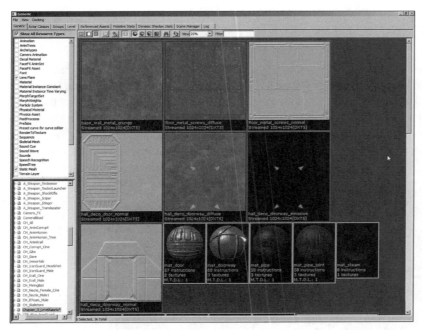

FIGURE 3.24 The Generic browser now shows the contents of our level package.

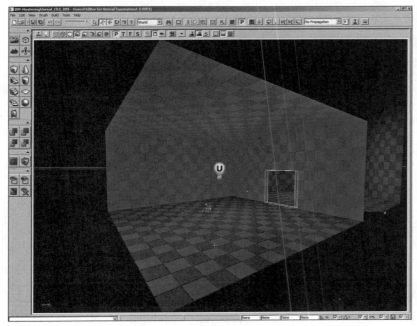

FIGURE 3.25 The walls of the cube room are currently selected.

5. Back in the Generic browser, click on the mat_wall_plates material. Materials can be recognized in the Generic browser as green boxes containing a textured sphere. This sphere is a preview of what the material looks like.

Clicking on the mat_wall_plates material while the walls are selected apply the material to all the selected surfaces. If you now deselect all the surfaces in your Perspective viewport by simply clicking on one of the currently selected walls, you can see the result of the applied material (see **FIGURE 3.26**).

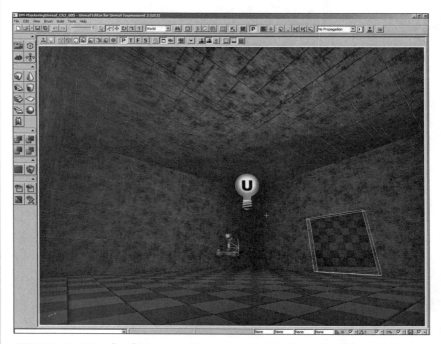

FIGURE 3.26   Our first material is now applied to the walls of the cube room.

6. Select the floor of the cube-shaped room, and from the Generic browser, click on the mat_wall_screws to apply it to the floor.

Also apply this material to the floor of the doorway.

7. Navigate the Perspective view camera into the cylindrically-shaped room, and select all the walls, as well as the ceiling. As a shortcut, you can select only one of the walls, and then press Shift-B to select all the surfaces that correspond to that brush. Then, simply hold Ctrl and click on the floor to deselect it, leaving only the walls and ceiling selected.

Once your surfaces are selected, go to the Generic browser and click the mat_stone_ mossy material to apply it.

8. Using the skills you've gained so far, apply the mat_stone_dark material to the floor of the cylindrical room (see **FIGURE 3.27**).

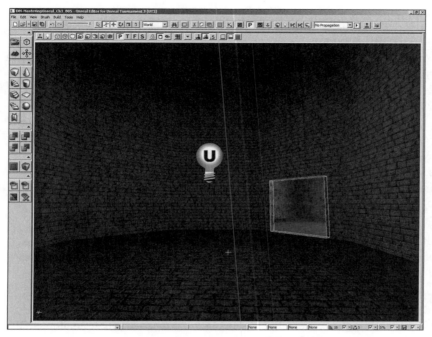

FIGURE 3.27   Here is the cylindrical room with all of its materials applied.

9. Feel free to test your level, but be sure to save your progress when you are finished!

END TUTORIAL 3.6

Our level is really starting to shape up! The walls are in place, the lights are working, and we've got some "paint" on the walls. However, things still look fairly bland overall. We need some objects to place in our level to give it some more character. In **TUTORIAL 3.7**, we start populating our level with static meshes, which are models that are constructed from exterior 3D applications, such as 3ds Max or Maya. For our purposes, the meshes are already created. For technical information regarding static meshes, please turn to Chapter 5, "Static Meshes."

Although we've spent time adding our world geometry, most of the levels you see in Unreal Tournament 3 are almost completely covered in static meshes. In **TUTORIAL 3.7**, we keep things simple by only adding a few, but don't be afraid to experiment and really start decorating your environment!

TUTORIAL 3.7: Placing Static Meshes in the Level

1. Continue from **TUTORIAL 3.6**, or open the DM-MasteringUnreal_Ch3_006.ut3 map included with the files for this chapter.

> **NOTE**
>
> If you are opening an existing file, you might notice that the package is in the package list in the Generic browser, but that it appears grayed out. If this is the case, simply right-click on the Chapter_3_LevelAssets package and choose Fully Load from the Context menu!

2. To begin, launch the Generic browser by choosing View > Browser Windows > Generic. If necessary, make sure that you have loaded the Chapter_3_LevelAssets.upk package file that is included on your book's DVD inside the packages folder for this chapter.

3. In the Resource Types list in the upper-left corner of the Generic browser, check the box for Static. This excludes all assets that are not static.

> **NOTE**
>
> You might need to click in the main window of the browser to refresh your view, because sometimes using the Resource Types list causes all assets to disappear temporarily.

We now place one of these meshes in our scene. Click on the sm_pipe_straight mesh in the browser. In order to place the mesh in your level, it must be selected in the browser (see **FIGURE 3.28**).

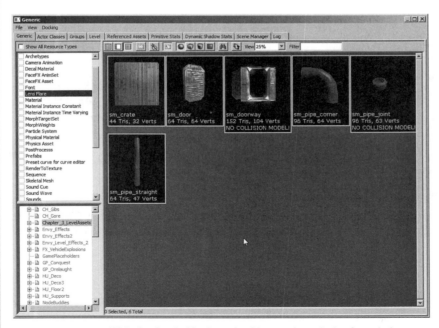

FIGURE 3.28   With the Static Meshes checkbox activated, the Generic browser only displays the static meshes included in the selected package.

4. In the Perspective viewport, navigate the camera into the large square-shaped room. Right-click on the floor near one of the walls and choose the following from the Context menu that appears: Add Actor > Add StaticMesh: StaticMesh Chapter_3_LevelAssets.sm_pipe_straight.

It does not really matter which wall you place the pipe near, although you may later have to adjust the rotation of some objects to make them face the center of the room!

This places the selected static mesh at the point where you clicked the right mouse button. Make sure the mesh is about 32 units (two grid spaces) away from the wall in the top viewport; move the mesh with the Translation Widget if necessary (see **FIGURE 3.29**).

> **NOTE**
>
> The Add StaticMesh option from within the Context menu changes based on which static mesh you currently have selected in the Generic browser.

FIGURE 3.29   Our first static mesh is now placed, which should appear as a vertical pipe protruding from the floor.

5. Next, select the sm_pipe_joint mesh in the Generic browser. To place it, navigate your Perspective camera so that you can see the top of the straight pipe mesh you just added. Right-click on the top surface at the end of that mesh as if you were selecting a cap at the top of the pipe. Choose Add Actor > Add StaticMesh: StaticMesh

Chapter_3_LevelAssets.sm_pipe_joint from the Context menu. This places the small joint mesh at the very top of the pipe.

If necessary, move the joint mesh in the top viewport (upper-left quadrant) to make certain that it aligns to the pipe mesh. You might also need to verify in the side or front viewports that the joint mesh is placed vertically right at the end of the pipe (see **FIGURE 3.30**).

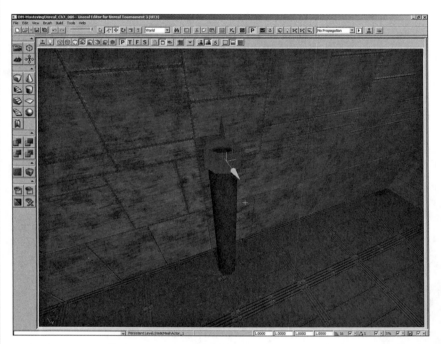

FIGURE 3.30   Here you can see the joint mesh correctly placed on top of the vertical pipe mesh.

6. Choose the sm_pipe_corner static mesh in the Generic browser, right-click on the top of the static mesh you just added, and choose Add Actor > Add StaticMesh: StaticMesh Chapter_3_ LevelAssets.sm_pipe_corner from the Context menu to add the static mesh to the map.

The mesh should appear right on top of the joint mesh, although you may need to rotate it so that it points away from the wall. To do this, choose the Rotation Widget 🔄 located in the toolbar. Then, simply drag the blue rotation axis (Z-axis) to spin the mesh around until it points into the room.

> **NOTE**
>
> You can select all three of the meshes by holding Ctrl, and then rotate them all as a single unit if you like.

> **TIP**
>
> You can cycle among the Translation, Rotation, and Scale widgets by tapping the spacebar!

7. If you were to click the Build All button 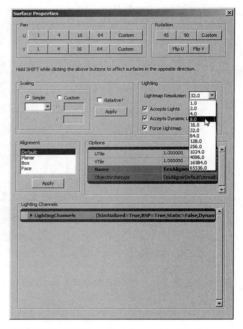 right now, you would notice that your pipe mesh does not appear to have a shadow. This is because shadows are calculated on a surface-by-surface basis, and the shadow resolution for the wall surface behind the mesh is not sharp enough. Basically, the shadow is diffusing so much that we can no longer make it out. We now fix this by first clicking on the wall behind the mesh so that it highlights in blue, and then press the F5 button, which opens the Surface Properties dialog (see **FIGURE 3.31**).

8. Within the Surface Properties dialog, go to the Lighting group, and from the Lightmap Resolution dropdown, choose a value of 8.0. This sharpens up the shadows behind the pipe mesh so that they are visible. When finished, click the Build All button to see the result (see **FIGURE 3.32**). Note that you may incur a longer build time due to the higher resolution shadows!

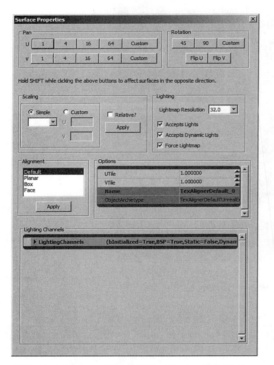

FIGURE 3.31   The Surface Properties dialog appears when you pres the F5 key.

FIGURE 3.32   Here you can see the Lightmap Resolution dropdown expanded.

Close the Surface Properties window.

The Lightmap Resolution property may seem counterintuitive, as the lower you place the number, the sharper the shadows get. Think of the number as the number of Unreal units used to calculate a single point of shadow. Thus, lower values tighten up the shadows (see **FIGURE 3.33**). At the same time, having smaller shadow points requires more points to be placed to create a contiguous shadow. This means that lower Lightmap Resolution settings require more processing

> **NOTE**
>
> If you'd like a fun challenge, add multiple copies of the meshes to populate your room with a series of connected pipes!

power and could slow down your level. Be careful about doing this to too many surfaces!

9. You can test your level at this time. Be sure to save your work when you are finished!

FIGURE 3.33   Notice that the shadow behind the pipe is now visible.

END TUTORIAL 3.7

We have placed our first static meshes into the level, but we could still go much further. In an actual level, you typically place many static meshes throughout your environment. The general idea is that the base layout and proportion of your level is created with world geometry, whereas the actual rich detail and populated objects are all created with static. Naturally, you can end up with hundreds (if not thousands) of static meshes in your level. However, due to the nature of how static meshes are calculated, multiple instances of the same mesh require only slightly more processing power than just a single instance, and most of that calculation is handled by the video card. This means that you can place many copies of a mesh throughout a level without creating significant overhead on your computer.

We still have a few more meshes to go. In **TUTORIAL 3.8**, we place the remaining static meshes in the level, including a door that eventually opens as we approach it.

Currently, the passageway between our two rooms is a simple square-shaped hole. In **TUTORIAL 3.8**, we place a static mesh doorframe around this opening to give a more pleasant look to the doorway.

TUTORIAL 3.8: Adding the Doorway Mesh

1. Continue from **TUTORIAL 3.7**, or open the DM-MasteringUnreal_Ch3_007.ut3 map included with the files for this chapter. We are now going to add the doorway mesh that surrounds the door separating our rooms.

2. Open the Generic browser, expand the CH_03_LevelAsset package, and choose the Meshes group. Click on the sm_doorway static mesh.

3. In the Perspective viewport, right-click on the floor in the middle of the doorway between the two rooms. From the Context menu, choose Add Actor > Add StaticMesh: StaticMesh Chapter_3_LevelAssets.sm_doorway. This places the doorway mesh in your doorway, although it likely requires alignment. Using the Translation Widget, along with the front viewport, move your doorway mesh so that it fits perfectly into the doorway. Be sure to verify alignment in your Perspective viewport (see **FIGURE 3.34**).

4. Click the Build All button [icon] to make sure that your level exhibits appropriate lighting and shadows.

5. Save and test your map.

> **NOTE**
>
> If you are opening an existing file, you might notice that the package is in the package list in the Generic browser, but that it appears grayed out. If this is the case, simply right-click on the Chapter_3_LevelAssets package and choose Fully Load from the Context menu!

> **NOTE**
>
> If you have created your room in a different direction such that it moves side-to-side rather than up and down when viewed in the top viewport, you may need to use the Rotation Widget to rotate the doorway mesh 90 degrees so that it fits appropriately into your doorway!

> **NOTE**
>
> We have not yet placed the actual door that opens and closes in our doorway. Do not be tempted to skip ahead by placing this as a static mesh! This object will be created later using a different actor type that allows for animation!

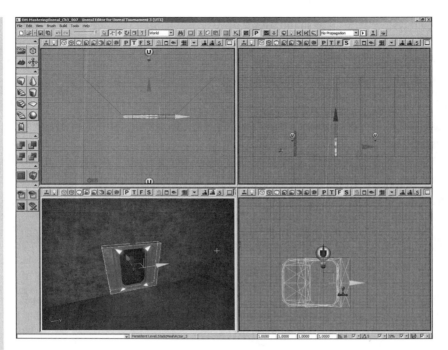

FIGURE 3.34   The doorway mesh correctly placed in the level

END TUTORIAL 3.8

We have now placed all of our static meshes into this simple level. Next, we add some simple accent lighting to our doorway so that the glowing areas appear to be emitting light. Currently, they are simply using a material emissive effect to get the orange glow, but no light is being emitted into the level. If we want them to emit light, we must "fake" the effect by strategically placing accent lights.

Lights do more in your levels than just show your players where they are going. They also serve to add more life to your levels! In **TUTORIAL 3.9**, we add some low-radius colored lights around the door to help make the glow effect around the doorway appear more realistic.

TUTORIAL 3.9: Placing Accent Lighting Around the Doorway Mesh

1. Continue from **TUTORIAL 3.8**, or open the DM-MasteringUnreal_Ch3_008.ut3 map included with the files for this chapter.

2. In the Perspective viewport, navigate the camera so that you are close to the doorway mesh. Next, while holding the L key, left-click on the illuminated orange wedge-shape on the upper-left corner doorway mesh. This creates a new light right on the surface of that shape (see **FIGURE 3.35**).

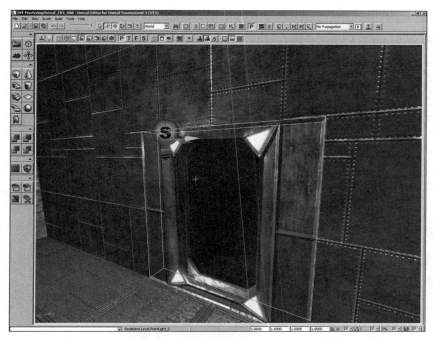

FIGURE 3.35   Your first accent light is in place.

3. Using the Translation Widget, move the light a few units away from the doorway mesh. Precision is not really a factor, so just pull it away so that the icon is not sitting right on the surface, but not so far away that the lighting effect is ruined—about 12 units should suffice.

> **TIP**
>
> You can watch the Console Bar (bottom center of the interface) for an indication of how far you are moving an object with the Translation Widget!

4. With the light selected, press F4 to open the Properties window. Expand the Light tab and the LightComponent category, and then set the following properties:

> **Brightness**—0.25
>
> **CastDynamicShadows**—Check this box.
>
> **LightColor**—Expand this property with the small black triangle and enter the following values:
>
> > **B:** 91
> >
> > **G:** 198
> >
> > **R:** 255

LightingChannels—Expand and check the Dynamic box.

LightShadowMode—LightShadow_Modulate

Radius: 96

5. Holding Alt, use the Translation Widget to move a copy of the light across the doorway to the opposite side, thus creating a duplicate right in front of the opposite illuminated wedge. Release Alt when finished.

6. Hold Ctrl and select both of your new lights together, and then, while holding Alt, drag them down to simultaneously create two more duplicates in front of the bottom wedges. This should create a copy in front of all four orange wedges on one side of the door (see **FIGURE 3.36**).

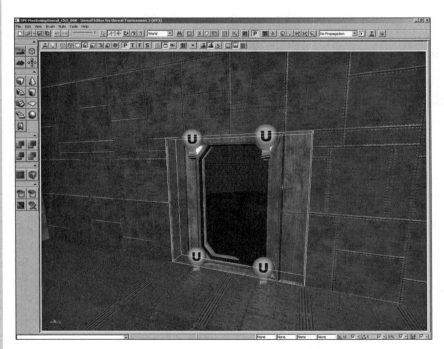

FIGURE 3.36   You can now see all four copies of the light.

7. Now, hold Ctrl again and select the two upper lights, so that you have all four lights selected. Then, holding Alt one more time, use the top viewport to move the lights through the doorway and create four copies of the lights on the opposite side of the doorway.

8. Click the Build All button to recalculate your lighting for the new lights. Then test and save your map.

END TUTORIAL 3.9

Accent lighting is an important aspect of lifelike levels. Material emission, which provides the glowing bloom effect, is a powerful tool that looks great when used in the appropriate areas of a level. However, the addition of lights to create actual illumination can push the look of your level closer to the edge of reality. Over the next few tutorials, we are going to supplement our existing level by adding special effects to the level in the form of particle-based steam!

Particles are points in space that can be used to create a variety of effects from steam to smoke to fire to dust and even debris! A particle setup in Unreal can be very simple, or can grow to become quite complex. Although this book does not explore in-depth the creation of complex particle systems in Unreal, we still wanted to show you how easy particle effects were to create and place into existing levels, so that you can start making your own basic effects. For this initial primer, we're going to keep things very simple by making a steam effect.

It is time to start taking your first steps into Unreal Editor's robust special effects system. In **TUTORIAL 3.10**, we create a basic emitter that we will eventually use to pump steam into the room!

TUTORIAL 3.10: Creating Your First Particle Emitter

1. Continue from **TUTORIAL 3.9**, or open the DM-MasteringUnreal_Ch3_009.ut3 map included with the files for this chapter. It's time to spice up our level with some particle effects!

2. Open the Generic browser, and check the Show All Reference Types checkbox above the Reference Types list in the upper-left corner of the browser.

3. Right-click on a blank area of the preview window. This opens an object creation Context menu, from which you choose New ParticleSystem (see **FIGURE 3.37**). The New Object dialog appears.

4. In the New Object dialog, verify that Chapter_3_LevelAssets is visible for the Package name; then enter the following:

       Group: Particles

       Name: part_steam

   Click OK when finished (see **FIGURE 3.38**).

> **NOTE**
>
> If you just opened the level, you might receive a warning telling you that you must fully load the package before proceeding. If this happens, click Yes.

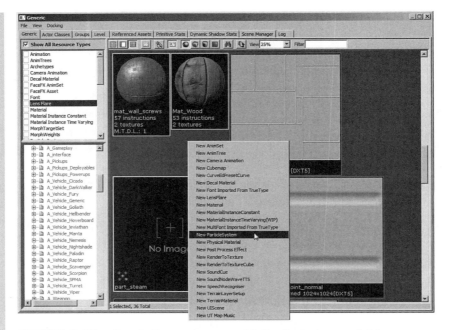

FIGURE 3.37 Here is the preview area with the Context menu visible.

The UnrealCascade Particle System Editor (just Cascade for short) now appears with your new particle system already loaded in and ready to edit (see **FIGURE 3.39**). For a more in-depth look at the interface of the Cascade, please see Appendix A.

5. Right-click in the Emitter List (the large black area in the upper-right quadrant of the Cascade Editor) and choose New ParticleSpriteEmitter from the Context menu that appears. A new particle emitter node appears. This is the object that actually fires particles into our level, and is the object we must edit to create our effect (see **FIGURE 3.40**).

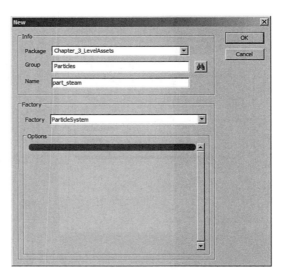

FIGURE 3.38 The New Object dialog with the appropriate fields filled in.

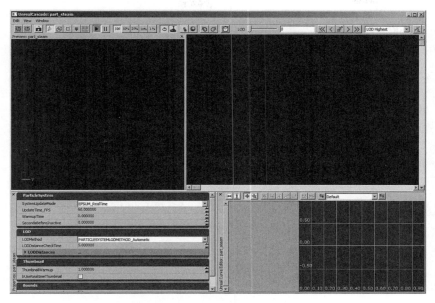

FIGURE 3.39   The Cascade Particle Editor interface

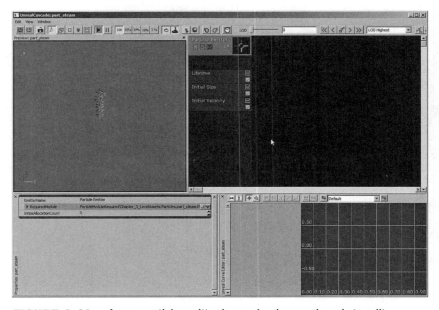

FIGURE 3.40   A new particle emitter is now in place and ready to edit.

6. Select on the Particle Emitter node at the top of the Emitter List by clicking on it. It turns orange to indicate its selection, and you will notice its properties appear in the properties area at the lower-left quadrant of the Cascade Editor. We begin by adding a material to the emitter. Follow these simple steps:

> **NOTE**
>
> In some cases, your particles seem to disappear after this final step. If this happens, simply close Cascade and then reopen it by double-clicking on the part_steam particle system in the Generic browser.

    a. In the properties area of the Cascade window, expand the Required Module property, and then click on the Material property.

    b. Next, click on the Show Generic Browser button [⊞] to bring up the Generic browser.

    c. Select the Chapter_3_LevelAssets package, and select the mat_steam material.

    d. Close the Generic browser.

    e. Back in the Cascade Editor, click the Use Current Selection in Browser button [◀] to apply the material to your particles (see **FIGURE 3.41**).

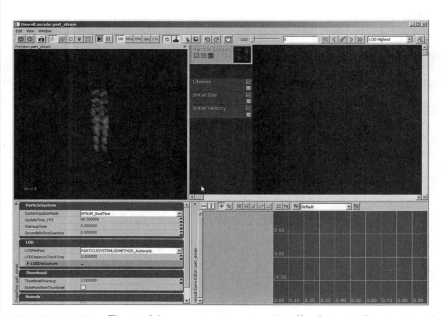

FIGURE 3.41   The particles now appear as small puffs of steam! The preview window has had its background changed to black in this image.

7. We're going to need to set a variety of properties on the emitter to get the behavior that we're looking for. For the sake of simplicity, we begin by adjusting values that are included with the particle emitter, and later we add on modules of new properties.

In the properties area, expand the RequiredModule category, and do the following:

a. Expand the SpawnRate, and then the Distribution subcategories. Set Constant to 25. This causes the emitter to emit 25 particles per second.

b. Set InterpolationMethod to PSUVIM_Linear_Blend. We do this because the texture for the steam is comprised of several different images, and this causes the particles to blend in between the different images in order.

c. Set both the SubImages_Horizontal and SubImages_Vertical properties to 2. This is because the multiple images of the steam texture are laid out in a 2×2 grid (see **FIGURE 3.42**).

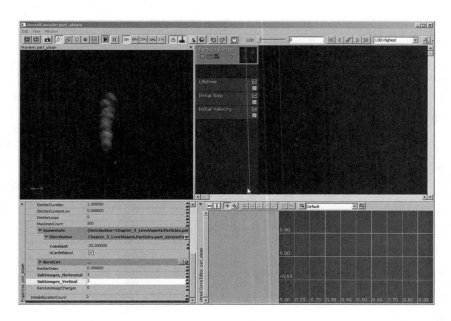

FIGURE 3.42   You'll notice that the steam has changed slightly, no longer appearing as dual streams of vapor.

8. Save your progress so far by choosing Edit > Save Package from within Cascade. There is currently no need to test the map, as nothing has yet changed.

END TUTORIAL 3.10

We have now created our emitter, but there are several properties that we need to set in order to get our desired effect. However, there are so many properties available to a particle system, you must add only the properties you want to use to your emitter. If all potential properties for an emitter were in place, the list of properties would be unmanageable! In Unreal, groups of properties that perform specific functions on particle systems are called *modules*. Some of these modules are already in place on a default particle system, whereas others need to be added. In **TUTORIAL 3.11**, we set up the modules that came by default with our emitter, and later we add new modules.

The emitter itself is only a small part of the process to produce our special effect. In **TUTORIAL 3.11**, we start to place the key modules that control the behavior of the particles in our level.

TUTORIAL 3.11: Establishing Base Emitter Modules

1. Continue from **TUTORIAL 3.10**, or open the DM-MasteringUnreal_Ch3_010.ut3 map included with the files for this chapter. If you cannot currently see the Cascade Particle Editor, simply do the following:

    a. Open the Generic browser and select the Chapter_3_LevelAssets package.

    b. If the package appears grayed out, right-click on it and choose Fully Load from the Context menu.

    c. Click on the small plus sign next to the Chapter_3_LevelAssets package and select the Emitters group.

    d. Double-click on the part_steam_Tut_3-11 emitter.

2. We begin by setting the properties of our base modules that are already added to our particle system. In the Emitter List (again, in the upper-right quadrant), click on the Lifetime module, which turns orange when selected. The properties for this module appear in the properties area in the lower-left quadrant (see **FIGURE 3.43**). Set the following properties under the Distribution category:

    Min: 1.25

    Max: 2.0

    This causes each of the particles to live for a random range of time between 1.25 and 2.0 seconds.

3. Back in the Emitter List, select the Initial Size module, and set the following properties under the Distribution category (see **FIGURE 3.44**):

    Max X: 150.0

    Max Y: 150.0

    Max Z: 150.0

    Min X: 75.0

    Min Y: 75.0

    Min Z: 75.0

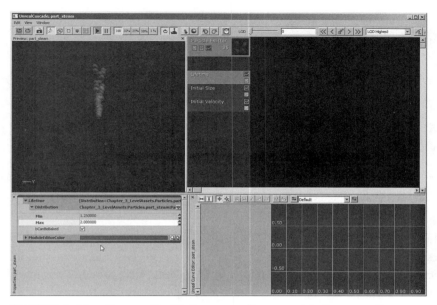

FIGURE 3.43   Here are the Lifetime properties as seen in the properties area.

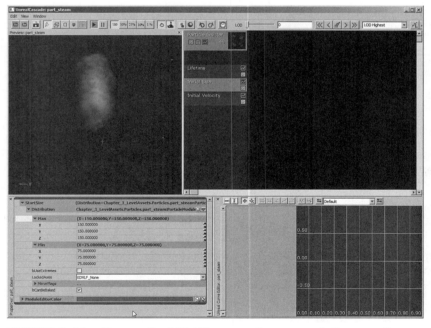

FIGURE 3.44   Here are the Initial Size properties as seen in the properties area.

4. Now select the Initial Velocity module, and set the following properties:

> **Max X:** 40.0
>
> **Max Y:** 40.0
>
> **Max Z:** 200.0
>
> **Min X:** -20.0
>
> **Min Y:** -20.0
>
> **Min Z:** 175.0

> **NOTE**
>
> You might need to zoom the camera back in the preview window to see your particle system at this point! You can do this by right-mouse dragging in the preview window.

5. Save your package by choosing Edit > Save Package from within Cascade.

END TUTORIAL 3.11

Our base modules are now set up, but for our effect to look the way we want it to, we need more than just the basic modules that came with our emitter. In **TUTORIAL 3.12**, we add a few modules to our particle system, as well as establish the associated properties with each one.

There are many different modules that can be added to your particle system. In **TUTORIAL 3.12**, we expand upon our existing setup by adding sub-image indexing, enabling each particle to show a series of different textures throughout its lifespan.

TUTORIAL 3.12: Implementing Additional Emitter Modules

1. Continue from **TUTORIAL 3.11**, or open the DM-MasteringUnreal_Ch3_011.ut3 map included with the files for this chapter. If you cannot currently see the Cascade Particle Editor, simply do the following:

    a. Open the Generic browser, and select the Chapter_3_LevelAssets package.

    b. If the package appears grayed out, right-click on it and choose Fully Load from the Context menu.

    c. Click on the small plus sign next to the Chapter_3_LevelAssets package and select the Emitters group.

    d. Double-click on the part_steam_Tut_3-12 emitter.

2. We now add our first module. In the Emitter List, right-click on the empty space below the Initial Velocity module. From the Context menu that appears, choose SubUV > SubImage Index. This adds a SubImage Index module to the list (see **FIGURE 3.45**).

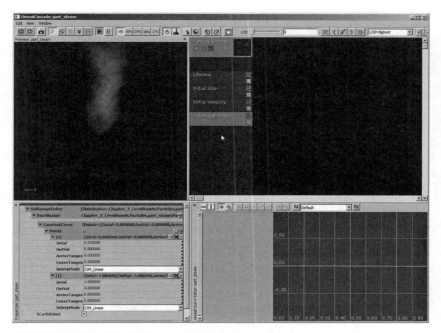

FIGURE 3.45   The SubImage Index has been added.

3. Make sure this new module is selected, and then, in the properties area, set the following properties:

   a. Click on the Distribution category. The blue-arrowed Create A New Object button ▼ (look closely, it's very small) appears on the far-right side of the properties area. Click it.

   From the Context menu that appears, choose DistributionFloatConstantCurve. This actually creates a curve that the particle system reads in order to control how the images of the particle blend from one to another. You control the shape of the curve by adding points to it, and by controlling the values at each of those points.

   b. Expand the new Constant Curve category; then click on the ellipsis (the "...") right next to Points. The Add New Item button ▣ appears on the far right. Click it two times. This adds two points, named [0] and [1], to your constant curve.

   c. Expand Point [1] and set the following:

   InVal: 1.0

   OutVal: 3.0

4. Back in the Emitter List, right-click on the empty space below the SubImage Index module. From the Context menu that appears, choose Size > Size By Life. This adds a new Size By Life module to your list (see **FIGURE 3.46**).

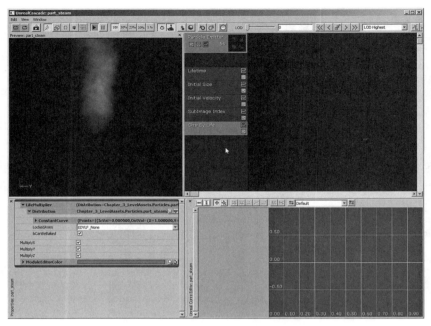

FIGURE 3.46   The emitter now contains a Size By Life module, seen here in the Emitter List.

5. Just as you did with the SubImage Index, click on the Distribution category, and then click on the Create A New Object button 🔽. Choose DistributionVectorConstantCurve from the Context menu.

As before, this creates an internal curve, now controlling how the particles flow from one size to the next over the course of their lifetimes. This time, the curve is much more complex with many more points.

Within the Distribution category, complete the following steps:

a. Expand the newly created ConstantCurve category.

b. Click on the ellipsis (the "...") next to the Points category. This again exposes the Add New Item button 🔳.

Click this button four times to add four new points to the curve.

c. Expand point [0]. Expand the OutVal category. Set the following:

> **OutVal:**
>
> **X:** 0.2
>
> **Y:** 0.2
>
> **Z:** 0.2

d. Expand point [1] and set the following:

> **InVal:** 0.6
>
> **OutVal:**
>
> > **X:** 1.5
> >
> > **Y:** 1.5
> >
> > **Z:** 1.5

> **NOTE**
>
> As you complete the first part of this step, you will notice that your particles seem to disappear in your preview window. Do not be alarmed—we fix this with the remaining steps.

e. Expand point [2] and set the following:

> **InVal:** 0.85
>
> **OutVal:**
>
> > **X:** 0.75
> >
> > **Y:** 0.75
> >
> > **Z:** 0.75

> **NOTE**
>
> As you complete this last step, you will notice your particle system start working again in your preview window.

f. Expand point [3] and set the following:

> **InVal:** 1.0

6. Save your package by choosing Edit > Save Package from the Cascade menubar (see **FIGURE 3.47**).

7. You can now close the Cascade window.

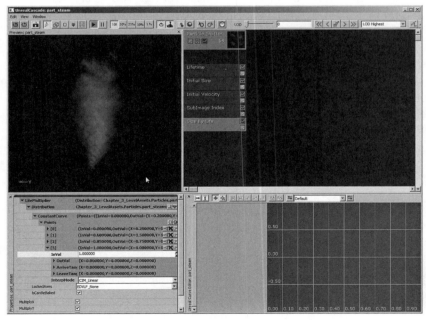

FIGURE 3.47
This is the steam particle system's final behavior, as seen in Cascade.

END TUTORIAL 3.12

3

At this point, you have created your particle emitter, although it is currently not placed in your level. This is the standard workflow for particle creation; you use the Cascade window to establish the type of effect you're looking for. When you are finished, you place the emitter in your level to actually add the effect into your level. In **TUTORIAL 3.13**, that is exactly what we're going to do.

Our design process for the effect is now complete and our emitter is ready for action! In **TUTORIAL 3.13**, we show how to place your particle system into the level through the use of the Emitter Actor.

TUTORIAL 3.13: Placing the Steam Emitter into the Level

1. Continue from **TUTORIAL 3.12**, or open the DM-MasteringUnreal_Ch3_012.ut3 map included with the files for this chapter.

2. From the Generic browser, open the Chapter_3_LevelAssets package and select the Emitters group. You should now see your part_steam emitter in the preview window. Be sure that it is selected.

> **NOTE**
>
> If you did not complete **TUTORIAL 3.12**, you can choose part_steam_complete instead!

3. In the Perspective viewport, right-click on the end of the pipe corner mesh that currently points into the room. From the Context menu that appears, choose Add Actor > Add Emitter: part_steam (or Add Emitter: part_steam_complete) to place the emitter into your level (see **FIGURE 3.48**).

4. At this time, you probably cannot see the result of your emitter in your viewport. You can fix this by clicking the Real Time button ![icon] located on the far-left side of the viewport's toolbar (see **FIGURE 3.49**).

> **NOTE**
>
> If the steam appears to be blue, it's simply because the emitter is currently selected. Click anywhere in the level to deselect the emitter.

5. Save and test your level. As a challenge, see if you can adjust the necessary values of the particle system so that the steam sprays outward from the pipe as it rises! Here's a hint: You can start with the Initial Velocity module!

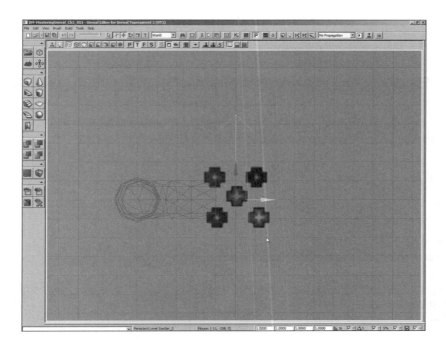

FIGURE 3.48
The emitter's icon appears as five dots grouped closely together.

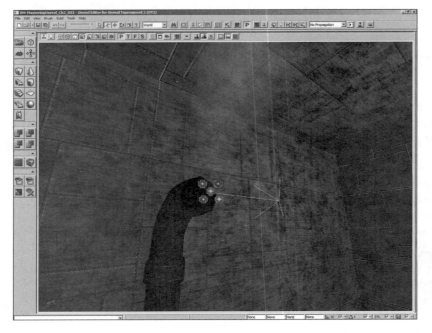

FIGURE 3.49
Our pipe mesh now appears to be emitting steam!

END TUTORIAL 3.13

We've certainly come a long way for such a basic level, but there are still more elements to add before we're finished. Our next step is to add a door that actually opens and closes into our doorway. This requires the use of Matinee (which, if you've used earlier versions of Unreal, you might remember from creating in-game cinematics and scripted sequences), as well as Kismet, the new visual event-scripting system in Unreal Engine 3.0.

By its nature, world geometry is static—it cannot move. To create a moving door, we need to add a special animated mesh, called an InterpActor, to the scene.

3

TUTORIAL 3.14: Adding an InterpActor and Trigger

1. Continue from **TUTORIAL 3.13**, or open the DM-MasteringUnreal_Ch3_013.ut3 map included with the files for this chapter.

2. Our first step in creating an object that moves through our level is to add the appropriate mesh. However, rather than add it in as a static mesh, which does not by its nature ever move in the level, we add it as an "interpolation actor," which can move through space using animation specified in the Matinee system.

   From the Generic browser, select the Chapter_3_LevelAssets. Then, check the Static Meshes option from the Resource Types list, which shows only the static meshes included with the package (see **FIGURE 3.50**).

   > **NOTE**
   >
   > If you are opening an existing file, you might notice that the package is in the package list in the Generic browser, but that it appears grayed out. If this is the case, simply right-click on the Chapter_3_LevelAssets package and choose Fully Load from the Context menu!

3. Choose the sm_door mesh, and then close the Generic browser for now. In the Perspective viewport, right-click on the floor in or near your doorway and choose Add Actor > Add InterpActor: StaticMesh Chapter_3_LevelAssets.sm_door from the Context menu. This adds the mesh into your map as an InterpActor rather than a static mesh.

   > **NOTE**
   >
   > You might need to click in the main window of the browser to refresh your view, because sometimes using the Resource Types list causes all assets to disappear temporarily.

4. Use your Translation Widget along with the top, front, and side viewports to make sure that the door mesh is aligned appropriately in the doorway as if the door was closed. If necessary, use the Rotation Widget to rotate the door 90 degrees (see **FIGURE 3.51**).

   > **NOTE**
   >
   > It is critical that you do *not* add this mesh into the level as a static mesh! Doing so precludes the door from being able to move in your level.

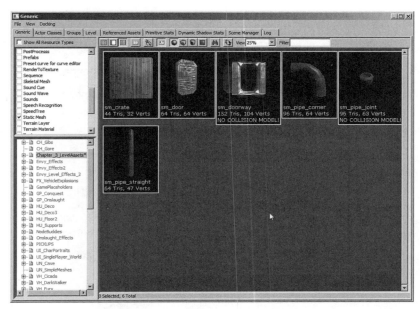

FIGURE 3.50   All the meshes in the Chapter_3_LevelAssets package are shown.

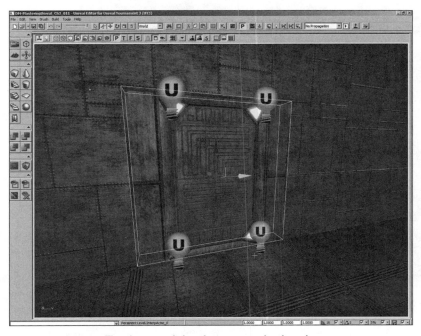

FIGURE 3.51   The door mesh has been properly placed.

5. There are a few settings that we need to place on the door in order for it to behave properly without any problems. With the door InterpActor selected in your viewport, press F4 to open the Properties window and do the following:

    a. Expand the DynamicSMActor tab; then expand the StaticMeshComponent category.

    Under the Lighting tab, set bCastDynamicShadow to false (unchecked). This prevents the door from casting a shadow that is visible through the wall while it is opening.

    b. Close the DynamicSMActor tab. Open the Collision tab.

    c. Set both the CollisionType property to COLLIDE_BlockAll. This keeps the player from being able to walk through the door while it's shut, as if the door was a hologram.

    d. Close the Properties window.

6. We must now add the "switch" that causes our door to open. In Unreal, such switches are known as triggers. Like lights, these are always available in the Add Actor Context menu.

    Right-click on the center of the door mesh and choose Add Actor > Add Trigger. This adds a new trigger into the level (see **FIGURE 3.52**).

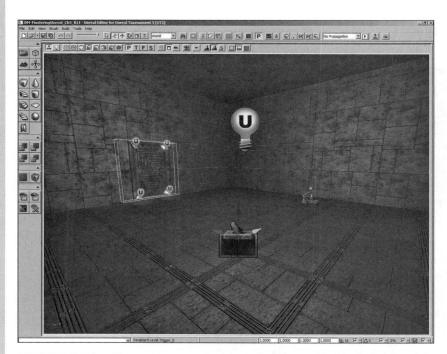

FIGURE 3.52   Here you can see the trigger has been added to the center of the room.

7. With the trigger selected, press F4 to open the trigger's Properties window. Expand the Trigger tab, and then the CylinderComponent category.

    Set both the CollisionHeight and CollisionRadius properties to 96.0.

8. With the trigger selected and visible in the top viewport, press the C key to display the collision geometry for the trigger. Then, use the Translation Widget along with the orthographic viewports to position the trigger into the very center of the door mesh. Make sure the collision geometry protrudes from both sides of the door (see **FIGURE 3.53**).

> **NOTE**
>
> The visibility of collisions is independent in each viewport. This means that if you press C to turn it on in one viewport, you will not see it in any other viewports in which you have not also pressed C to turn it on. You can turn it off by pressing C a second time.

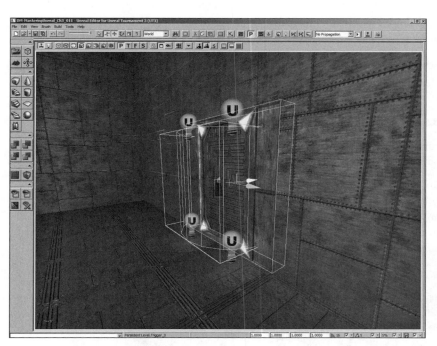

FIGURE 3.53   If the trigger has been placed properly, its collisions extend evenly from the center of the door.

9. Save your level.

END TUTORIAL 3.14

Our InterpActor and trigger are now placed in our level. However, before the door actually works, we need two more elements to make the effect come alive: a Kismet sequence and a Matinee sequence. Essentially, Kismet "listens" for input from the trigger (in this case, that a player has entered the collision radius). As soon as this happens, Kismet triggers the Matinee sequence and Matinee then tells the InterpActor how it needs to animate.

In **TUTORIAL 3.15**, you are introduced to Kismet as you create your first basic sequence, into which we later tie in the appropriate Matinee animation.

To put it simply, Kismet is a visual scripting system that enables you to create complex in-game events by simply connecting a series of nodes together into a network, rather than having to create any programming code. As your sequences get more involved, you will find yourself creating more and more complex networks of nodes.

The true beauty of Kismet is that it enables non-programmers (that is, artists and designers) to create complex in-game sequences that were previously only possible through code. Keep in mind that we could easily write an entire book just on how to create various sequences in Kismet. In **TUTORIAL 3.15**, however, we create one of the simplest possible sequences. For more information on using Kismet effectively, please read Chapter 9, "Introduction to Unreal Kismet."

It's time to add some functionality to our door. In **TUTORIAL 3.15**, we create the simple network that opens the door based on the player's proximity.

TUTORIAL 3.15: Creating Your First Kismet Sequence

1. Continue from **TUTORIAL 3.14**, or open the DM-MasteringUnreal_Ch3_014.ut3 map included with the files for this chapter.

2. Open the UnrealKismet (just Kismet for short) Editor by clicking the Open Kismet button K on the main toolbar at the top of the Unreal Editor interface. We create our Kismet sequence within this Editor (see **FIGURE 3.54**).

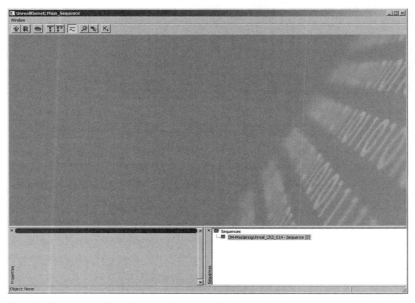

FIGURE 3.54   The Kismet Editor interface

3. Make sure that your trigger is selected in your level, and then right-click in the main work-space (the large area that dominates the upper portion of the Kismet window) and choose New Event Using Trigger_0 > Touch from the Context menu. This creates a new Touch sequence object that is automatically tied to Trigger_0 (see **FIGURE 3.55**).

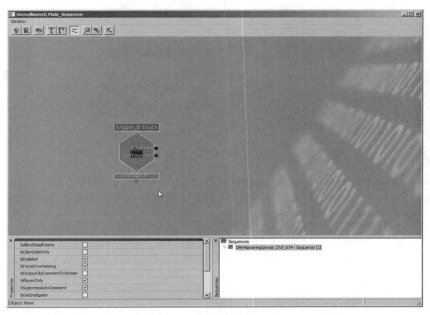

FIGURE 3.55   A new Touch sequence object has been created.

4. Navigate the Kismet workspace so that the Touch sequence object is on the left side of the window. Then right-click in a blank area to the right of the Touch sequence object and choose New Matinee from the Context menu that appears (see **FIGURE 3.56**).

Navigating the Kismet Editor:

Left Mouse Button—Drag to move the view up, down, left, or right.

Right Mouse Button—Drag to move the view up, down, left, or right, just like holding down the left mouse button.

Left and Right Mouse Buttons (simultaneously)—Drag to zoom the view closer or farther away from the network.

Ctrl + Left Mouse Button—This enables you to move around the selected sequence object (or node) in the view. This is helpful for rearranging a network of sequence objects for easier readability.

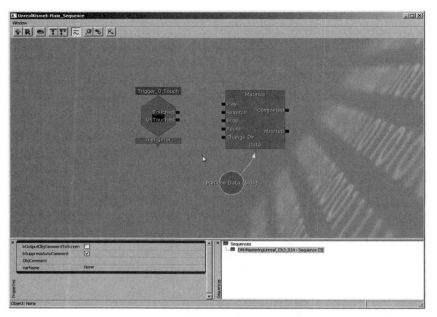

FIGURE 3.56   The Matinee sequence object is now visible next to the original Touch sequence object. Aligning them makes connections easier, as these connections tend to run left-to-right.

5. Move your mouse over the small handle next to the Touched output property on the Touch sequence object, and notice that it highlights yellow.

Next, drag with the left mouse button to connect a "wire" from the Touched output of the Touch sequence object to the Play input property of the Matinee sequence object. This means that the Matinee sequence "plays forward" when the trigger is touched. In essence, this sets up the system that allows the door to open once the player steps into the collision radius of the trigger.

6. Using the techniques provided in step 5, connect a wire from the UnTouched output property of the Touch sequence object to the Reverse input property of the Matinee sequence object. With this connection in place, your Matinee animation reverses (or play backwards) once a player is no longer touching the trigger. With this in place, the door can automatically close when the player steps away from it (see **FIGURE 3.57**).

However, we see no animation until we establish within Matinee exactly what type of motion takes place. Don't worry about that now, as we set it up in **TUTORIAL 3.16**.

7. Finally, select the Trigger_0 Touch sequence object, and in the properties area, set the MaxTriggerCount property to 0. This allows the trigger to be fired an infinite number of times, thereby allowing your door to close behind players and re-open as they approach it again.

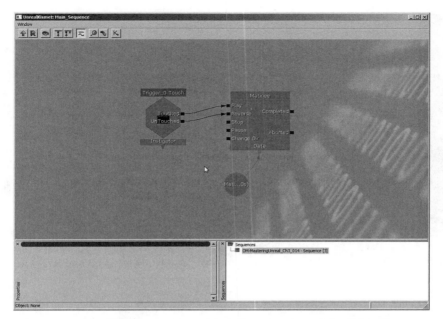

FIGURE 3.57   The two sequence objects have now been "wired" together.

8. Save your level's progress so far. Currently, there is no need to test the map, as no playable changes have been added.

END TUTORIAL 3.15

We have now established our InterpActor in the level, and through the use of Kismet have set up a sequence such that when a player touches the trigger, *something* happens. However, we have not yet established exactly what that something is. In **TUTORIAL 3.16**, we set up the InterpActor with Matinee so that when our Kismet sequence fires, the door moves.

Kismet alone cannot handle the animation we need to make our door open and close. For that, we need to incorporate the Matinee system into our Kismet sequence.

TUTORIAL 3.16: Setting Up the InterpActor with Matinee

1. Continue from **TUTORIAL 3.15**, or open the DM-MasteringUnreal_Ch3_015.ut3 map included with the files for this chapter. Open the Kismet Editor via the Kismet button in the Main Toolbar.

2. In the Kismet Editor, double-click the Matinee object. This opens the Matinee Editor, which is very similar to a non-linear video editing environment (see **FIGURE 3.58**).

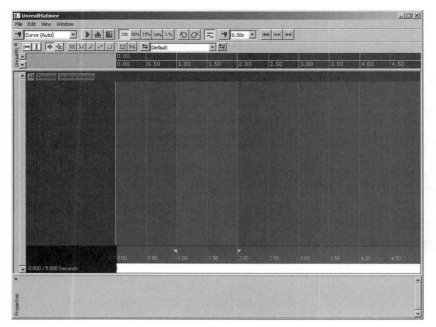

FIGURE 3.58 This is the Matinee interface.

3. Right-click in the Group List (the wide vertical dark-gray bar in the upper-left area of the Matinee window, located just below the All, Cameras, and Skeletal Meshes buttons). From the Context menu that appears, choose Add New Empty Group. You are prompted to enter a name for the group. Enter SteamRoomDoor (see **FIGURE 3.59**).

> **NOTE**
>
> Important! In one of the viewports, make certain that you have selected your InterpActor (identifiable by the purple wireframe). If your mover is **not** selected, the next step will not work properly!

4. Next, right-click on the SteamRoomDoor group and choose Add New Movement Track from the Context menu. This creates a new movement track for the group, as well as produces the first keyframe for the animation (see **FIGURE 3.60**).

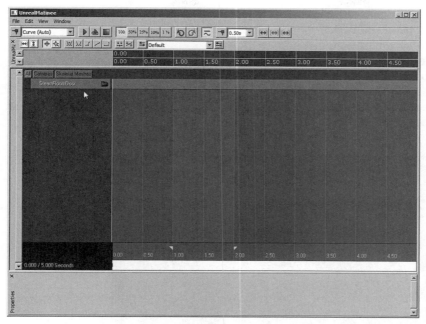

FIGURE 3.59   You can see the new group has appeared in the upper-left corner of the interface.

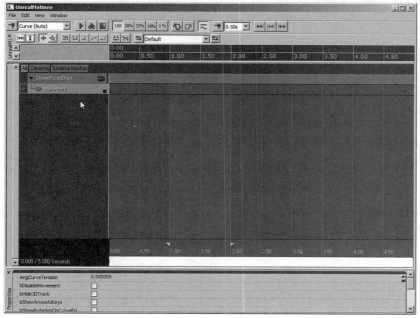

FIGURE 3.60   A new movement track has now been added to the group.

5. In the Matinee window, select the newly created movement track by clicking on it. Then, make sure that the time slider is currently set to 0.0 by dragging on the number-covered gray bar that runs across the bottom of the Matinee track area (see **FIGURE 3.61**).

NOTE

You may not see the time slider at first. Just click and drag anywhere along the numbered rules, and verify that the green text at the left changes to update with the time slider's new position. When finished, be sure to set the time slider back to 0.000/5.000.

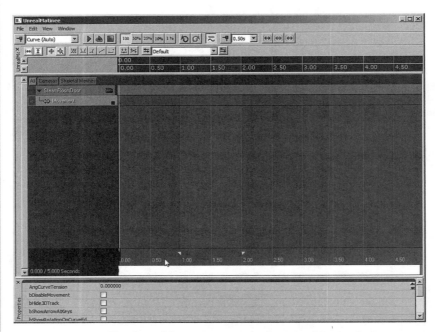

FIGURE 3.61   The time slider runs across the bottom of the track view.

6. Move the time slider to 1.0 (or as close to 1.0 as you can get it) and click the Add Key button. This places a second keyframe. However, we still do not have movement in our door, as this second keyframe has been recorded with the door in the same position. In effect, we've just animated the door sitting still for one second (see **FIGURE 3.62**).

7. Select the newly created second keyframe by clicking on the small orange triangle visible in the same line as the movement track at time index 1.0. Your Perspective viewport should have ADJUST KEY 1 in the lower left corner.

In the top viewport, move the door 128 units to the left (that's eight grid spaces if your Drag Grid is still set to 16). You have now recorded a new position for the second keyframe, thereby animating the door opening over the course of one second (see **FIGURE 3.63**).

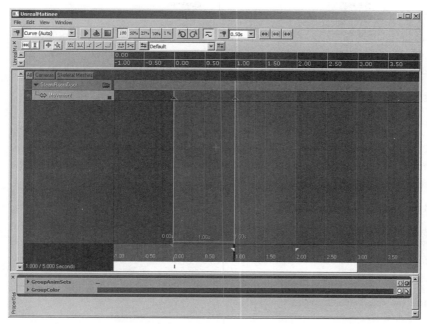

FIGURE 3.62 The two keyframes are visible as upwardly pointing triangles.

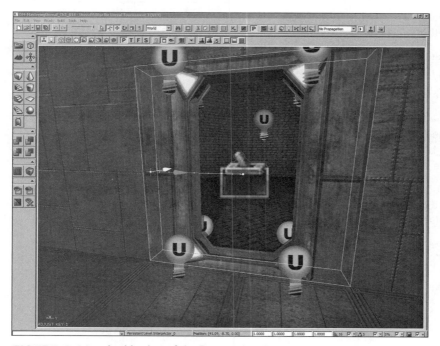

FIGURE 3.63 In this shot of the Perspective viewport, you can see the door has been moved to the open position. Notice the indication in the lower-left corner that we are adjusting Key 1.

8. Close the Matinee Editor and the Kismet Editor, if it's open.

9. Save your map and give it a try. Your door now opens and closes as you approach it or walk away. If you move too quickly, you'll notice that it also prevents you from entering until it has opened.

END TUTORIAL 3.16

Our door is now functioning properly in the level. To users who have experience with previous versions of Unreal, it may seem like it took quite a bit of setup just to make a simple door open, but this new system allows for much more versatility than earlier versions. Plus, once you get the workflow down, setup of InterpActors is a breeze.

In **TUTORIAL 3.17**, we're going to push our level a little further by adding in some dynamic objects that the player can interact with, knocking them over based on a simulation of real-world physics. This is a two-stage process. First, we set up our physics objects, and then we apply a physical material that controls how the object responds to outside forces.

In **TUTORIAL 3.17,** we add interactive physics objects into our level. These crates can be picked up, thrown, shot, and knocked over by your players!

TUTORIAL 3.17: Creating Physics Objects

1. Continue from **TUTORIAL 3.16**, or open the DM-MasteringUnreal_Ch3_016.ut3 map included with the files for this chapter.

2. In the Generic browser, select the Chapter_3_LevelAssets package. If the package is grayed out, right-click on it and choose Fully Load from the Context menu.

3. Select the sm_crate mesh in the Generic browser; then close the browser

4. Navigate the Perspective viewport into the cube-shaped room; then right-click at some point on the floor and choose Add Actor > Add RigidBody: StaticMesh Chapter_3_LevelAssets.sm_crate. This adds the crate mesh as a rigid body, which is a special type of actor that can react to physical forces (see **FIGURE 3.64**).

5. Position the box against the wall that includes the door, just to the left of the door itself (see **FIGURE 3.65**).

> **NOTE**
>
> You need to release the Alt key in between each duplication!

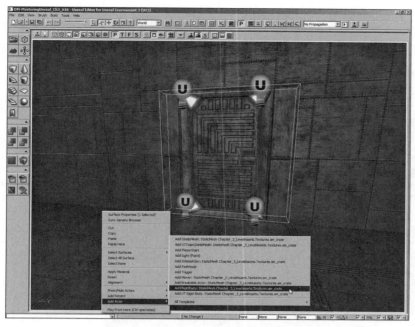

FIGURE 3.64 This is the Context menu selection for adding rigid bodies.

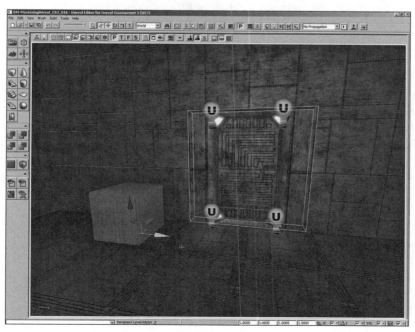

FIGURE 3.65 Here you can see the box positioned just to the left of the door.

6. Holding Alt, use the Translation Widget to move a clone of the mesh right next to the first. Repeat this process until you have four boxes lined up next to one another in front of the door, as shown in **FIGURE 3.66**.

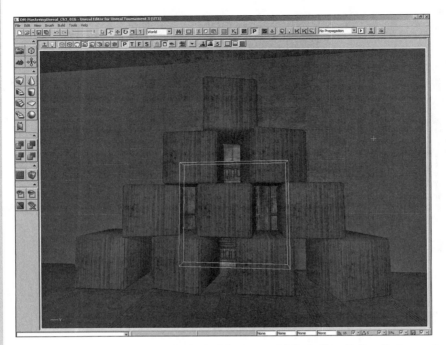

FIGURE 3.66   The boxes are stacked in a pyramid formation. Notice that some boxes have been rotated individually to give the stack a little more character.

7. Select the first three boxes and Alt-move them using the same technique to create a row of three boxes resting atop the first row. Repeat this process with the first two boxes of the second row, and then with a single box to create a pyramid of 10 boxes, as shown in **FIGURE 3.66**.

8. Save your level.

END TUTORIAL 3.17

Now that we have placed our physical objects, we need to control how they react when forces are applied to them, such as the force of a player colliding with or moving them. In **TUTORIAL 3.18**, we apply the physical material that actually controls this aspect of the rigid bodies.

Physics materials control the physical attributes of a physics object. In **TUTORIAL 3.18**, we construct a basic physics material and add it to our crates.

TUTORIAL 3.18: Creating and Applying a Physical Material

1. Continue from **TUTORIAL 3.17**, or open the DM-MasteringUnreal_Ch3_017.ut3 map included with the files for this chapter.

2. Open the Generic browser. Right-click in a blank area of the preview window, and choose New PhysicalMaterial from the Context menu. This opens the New Object dialog. Enter the following values (see **FIGURE 3.67**):

   > **Package:** Chapter_3_Level Assets
   >
   > **Group:** Physics
   >
   > **Name:** physMat_crate

3. This creates a new physical material and displays its current properties for editing. From within it, set the following values:

   > **Density:** 0.25
   >
   > **Friction:** 0.5

   Close the Physical Materials Properties window when done.

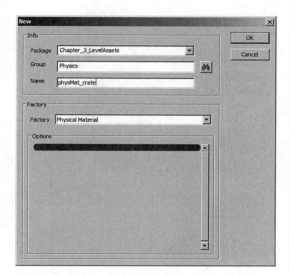

FIGURE 3.67   This is the New Object dialog with the appropriate settings in place.

4. Make sure you still have the physMat_crate material selected in the Generic browser; then select all 10 of the crates in the Perspective viewport. Press F4 to open their Properties window and do the following:

   a. Expand the DynamicSMActor tab. Then expand StaticMeshComponent.

   b. Go to the Physics section and click the word "None" next to the PhysMaterialOverride property. Click the Use Current Selection in Browser button 🔄 on the far-right side of the window to apply the physMat_crate material to all the crates (see **FIGURE 3.68**).

5. Rebuild lighting; then save and test your map.

6. The crates are in your way right now. Because we don't have a weapon handy that enables us to blow them out from in front of the door, we use a special console command to access the Physics Gun. This is a great way to test dynamic simulations in your level.

   While viewing the Play In Editor window, press the Tab key to access the console. Then, type **physicsgun** and press Enter.

FIGURE 3.68　You can now physically interact with the boxes in your level!

You can now pick up the crates by walking up to them and holding the right mouse button. If you quickly sweep the mouse and release mid-motion, you can throw the box across the room! Have fun!

In **TUTORIAL 3.20**, we take a look at how we can add weapons to make the box removal process much easier (and not require cheat codes).

END TUTORIAL 3.18

Now that we've got some physics objects in the level to play with, there's only one more effect that we're going to add before we consider this very simple level to be complete. We're going to put in some height fog to give the level a hazy feel.

A common visual effect in video games is the use of fog. Unreal provides a simple height-based fog system, which we demonstrate in **TUTORIAL 3.19**.

TUTORIAL 3.19: Adding Height Fog

1. Continue from **TUTORIAL 3.18**, or open the DM-MasteringUnreal_Ch3_018.ut3 map included with the files for this chapter.

2. From the main menubar, choose View > Browser Windows > Actor Classes. This brings up the Actor Classes browser, which gives you an organized list of all the actors available for your level (see **FIGURE 3.69**).

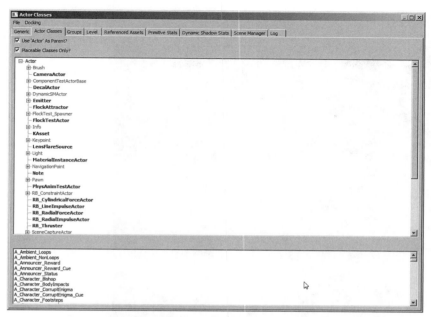

FIGURE 3.69   The Actor Classes browser interface

3. Within the Actor Classes browser, expand Info and select HeightFog.

4. Right-click on the floor of the cube-shaped room and choose Add HeightFog Here from the Context menu that appears. This places the height fog at the location you clicked.

5. Double-click the HeightFog actor icon to bring up its Properties window, and then do the following:

   a. Expand the HeightFog tab and then expand the Component category.

   b. Set the Density property to 0.0015 (see **FIGURE 3.70**).

6. Use the Translation Widget to move the HeightFog actor to the altitude at which you would like the fog to start. Moving it to the ceiling fills the entire room with fog. Alternatively, you could leave it close to the floor. Also, fee free to adjust the density to taste (see **FIGURE 3.71**).

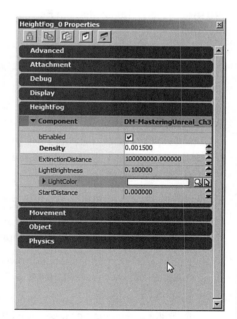

FIGURE 3.70   The HeightFog Properties window

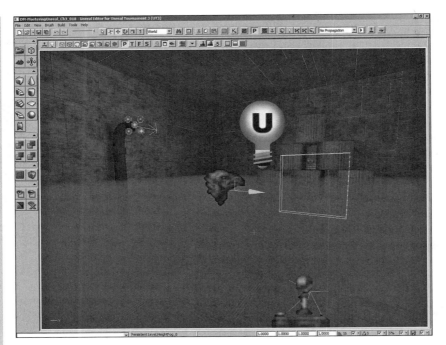

FIGURE 3.71   Notice that the HeightFog icon rests atop the actual fog. Moving it up increases the fog level.

7. Save and test your level.

END TUTORIAL 3.19

Something you need to pay close attention to in your levels is the placement of various pickups such as weapons, armor, and ammo. In **TUTORIAL 3.20**, we add a rocket launcher to help us knock those rigid body boxes out of the way.

TUTORIAL 3.20: Adding Weapons and Ammo Pickups

1. Continue from **TUTORIAL 3.19**, or open the DM-MasteringUnreal_Ch3_019.ut3 map included with the files for this chapter.

2. From the View menu, choose Browser Windows > Actor Classes. This brings up the Actor Classes browser (see **FIGURE 3.72**).

3. Weapon pickups are used by the AI system to help the AI-driven bots know where to get their guns. Because of this, weapons seem to be a little buried; in terms of their actual class, they derive from the base NavigationPoint. To find weapons, you need to expand (click the small plus sign next to) the following:

NavigationPoint

PickupFactory

UTPickupFactory

Select UTWeaponPickupFactory, and then close the Actor Classes browser (see **FIGURE 3.73**).

FIGURE 3.72   This is the Actor Classes browser.

FIGURE 3.73   Here you can see the UTWeaponPickupFactory selected.

4. On the floor of the level somewhere near the steam pipe, right-click and choose Add UTWeaponPickupFactory Here. This places the small weapon pickup base on the ground (see **FIGURE 3.74**).

5. Next, we need to specify which weapon we'll be using. We need something with some force to knock those crates out of the way, so we use the shock rifle.

   With the weapon base selected, press the F4 key to open up the Properties window. Locate and expand the UTWeaponPickupFactory category. Within, you see a dropdown for the WeaponPickupClass property.

   In the dropdown, select UTWeap_ShockRifle, and then close the Property window (see **FIGURE 3.75**).

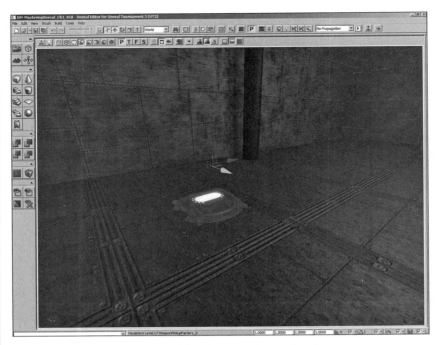

FIGURE 3.74   The weapon pickup base has been placed.

6. Next, let's add some ammo. Reopen the Actor Classes browser, and this time expand the following:

> **NavigationPoint**
>
> **PickupFactory**
>
> **UTPickupFactory**
>
> **UTItemPickupFactory**
>
> **UTAmmoPickupFactory**

Select UTAmmo_ShockRifle, and then close the Actor Classes browser (see **FIGURE 3.76**).

7. Right-click on either side of the weapon pickup base and choose Add UTAmmo_ShockRifle Here. This places the ammo item. You can use the Translation Widget to place it however you want, or move it with the Translation Widget while holding the Alt key to make duplicates as you like. In our case, we made one copy on either side of the pickup base (see **FIGURE 3.77**).

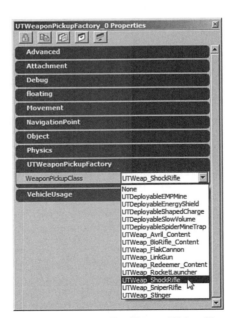

FIGURE 3.75   The WeaponPickupClass property enables you to choose which weapon the base generates.

FIGURE 3.76   Here you can see the UTAmmo_ShockRifle item selected in the browser.

FIGURE 3.77   We've now added some ammunition for the shock rifle.

8. The last thing we need to do is add the pickup light that illuminates the weapon base. From the main menu, choose Tools > Add Pickup Lights. This adds a small light above your pickup base (see **FIGURE 3.78**).

> **NOTE**
>
> If you fail to add a pickup light, you receive a warning after you build your lighting!

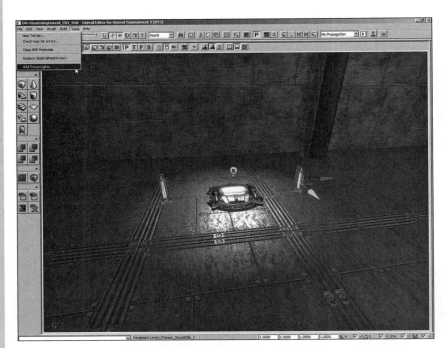

FIGURE 3.78   The Tools menu makes adding pickup lights very easy.

9. Click the Build All button to rebuild lighting. You'll notice that after you build, you have some floating lines in the air running between your PlayerStart and the new pickups. These are AI paths. We won't be getting into these in this book, but they are used to handle how the bot AI runs around your maps (see **FIGURE 3.79**).

10. Save your level and feel free to test your results by pressing the Play In Editor button. You can now pick up the shock rifle and knock the boxes out of the way (see **FIGURE 3.80**)!

Feel free to go back into the Editor and add other pickups as well. You *do* have to work pretty hard to get through the door; maybe it would be nice to put a powerup of some kind in the other room! Experiment with different pickups and see what you come up with!

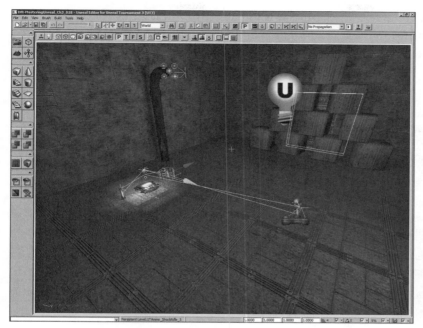

FIGURE 3.79
You can see AI paths connecting any object that derives from the NavigationPoint class.

FIGURE 3.80
Your level now contains a useable weapon!

END TUTORIAL 3.20

The final step in the process of level creation is to publish your level. This performs the final building and cooking for your level, allowing you to share the files with other Unreal players. In **TUTORIAL 3.21**, we demonstrate this simple process.

TUTORIAL 3.21: Publishing Your Level

1. Continue from **TUTORIAL 3.20**, or open the DM-MasteringUnreal_Ch3_fin.ut3 map included with the files for this chapter.

2. We're now going to publish our level so that it can be played within Unreal Tournament 3. However, before you do this, always make sure your map has been saved with the proper gametype prefix. Because we're building a deathmatch-style map, we've saved the level with the prefix "DM-." This causes the game to recognize our map as being intended for deathmatch (as well as Duel or Team Deathmatch)-style play. The available prefixes include the following:

   DM-: Deathmatch, Team Deathmatch, and Duel.

   CTF-: Capture the Flag.

   VCTF-: Vehicle Capture the Flag.

   WAR-: Warfare.

> **TIP**
>
> Remember the hyphen in the prefix!

   As soon as the level is open in the Editor, push the Publish button located on the far-right side of the toolbar.

3. A small window pops up, asking if we want to save packages. Because we've made no changes to our packages, we can click No (see **FIGURE 3.81**).

   This brings up a small commandlet that automatically cooks all your content and saves copies of everything (including your level) to the appropriate folders in your Unreal Tournament 3 installation folder. The upshot to all of this is that once the process is finished, you're ready to play the game in Unreal Tournament (see **FIGURE 3.82**)!

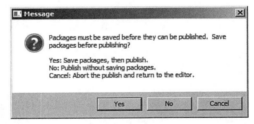

FIGURE 3.81   The Publish action starts by asking if you want to save your packages.

> **NOTE**
>
> This publishing process can be time consuming, even on smaller levels. On larger levels, it can take several minutes. Be sure to be patient!

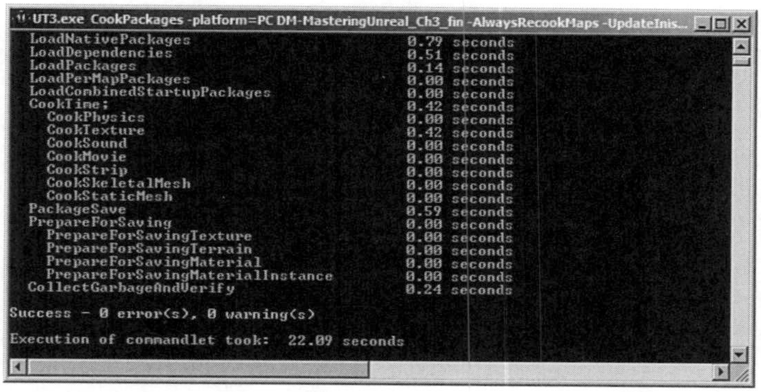

FIGURE 3.82   After a few moments, you should be good to go!

4. Once publishing is done, you can close Unreal Editor. Launch Unreal Tournament 3.

5. Once the game launches, log in and choose Instant Action, and then choose Deathmatch as your gametype. Within the list, find the level you just published (ours was named DM-MasteringUnreal_Ch3_Fin.ut3), and double-click it.

> **NOTE**
>
> If you don't see your map in the list, it's probably because there is no prefix for its gametype. See step 2 for details!

6. In the level options screen that appears, set the bot number to 0 for now, and click Start Game. This launches your map inside of Unreal Tournament 3. Have fun!

END TUTORIAL 3.21

Summary

This chapter has introduced you to many of the concepts that you will use over and over throughout your career as a game modder or developer. It would be a good idea for you to go back over what you've done and see if you can apply them without the book's guidance. Also, try experimenting with what you've learned and see if you can come up with your own levels and effects! Just playing around can yield tremendous knowledge, so don't be afraid to get your hands dirty!

Throughout the rest of this book, we expand upon and add to many of the concepts that you have seen here. However, keep in mind that all the skills that you have picked up from these tutorials will be vital, and hopefully will accelerate your progress through the remaining chapters of the book.

Chapter 4

A Universe of Brushes: World Geometry In-Depth

One tool is essential for creating the base layout and geometry for your levels: BSP brushes. These brushes can also be invaluable in "prototyping" your levels: quickly previewing what they'll look like and how they'll play, without creating all their individual assets. You took a quick glimpse of BSP brushes in Chapter 3, "Up and Running: A Hands-On Level Creation Primer." In this chapter, we drill down, showing you all you need to know to use BSP brushes in level creation.

Key Terms and Concepts: BSP and CSG

In discussing brushes, we've used the term BSP several times. It's about time we defined it! BSP stands for *Binary Space Partition*, which is a computer graphics technique for breaking up complicated polygons into smaller, simpler ones that can render more quickly. Among other things, BSP calculations instruct the game engine in the proper order for rendering each polygon. All most level designers really need to know is that Unreal Engine's brushes use BSP. (If you simply *have* to know more, last time we looked, there was a pretty solid explanation of BSP over at Wikipedia.)

While we're at it, let's get one more acronym out of the way: *Constructive Solid Geometry (CSG)*. That's just another term for *world geometry*—the geometry that's created from your BSP brushes. You first create BSP brushes to define the area and volume of a level. Then, Unreal Editor uses those brushes to create the level's CSG.

Brush Types

All BSP creation revolves around the construction and placement of *brushes*. By now, you've read the term "brush" several times, but may not be familiar with what it means. In Unreal Editor, a brush is simply a three-dimensional object used to designate a certain area of space. There are three different types of brush that you use most often during level creation: the Red Builder Brush, additive brushes, and subtractive brushes.

The Red Builder Brush

The Red Builder Brush is the most important brush in your level design process because it defines the shape from which all other brushes are created (see **FIGURE 4.1**). You can think of it as a template to create additive and subtractive brushes. It is displayed as a red wireframe object in your Unreal Editor viewport. It can have many different shapes based on the primitive object you have selected, which we cover later.

The Red Builder Brush is always present in your level, even when you first start Unreal Editor. Initially, it exists merely as a vertex, and remains so until you define a new shape for it. However, because the brush does not render in game and has no effect on gameplay, its position is irrelevant. If you need to hide the Red Builder Brush while working in Unreal Editor, you can simply enter Game Mode by pressing the G key.

Additive Brushes

Additive brushes enable you to add mass into your level. They are created from the Red Builder Brush by clicking the CSG: Add button in the Toolbox. Additive brushes appear in your viewports as blue wireframes. Additive brushes are created in the precise shape of the Red Builder Brush (see **FIGURE 4.2**).

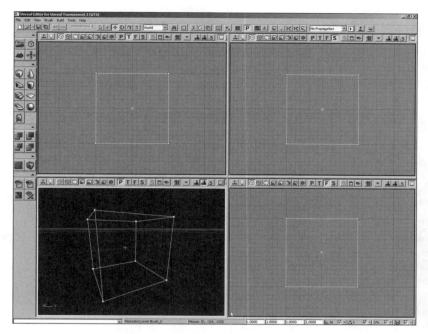

FIGURE 4.1
Here we can see the Red Builder Brush, which appears as a wireframe box, in all four viewports.

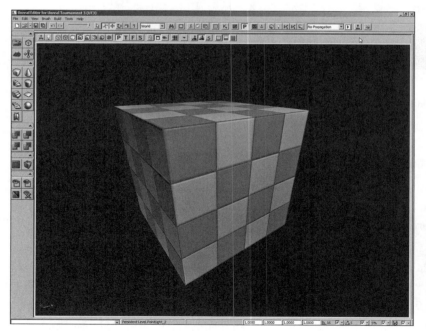

FIGURE 4.2   An additive brush adds solid mass into the level. Here an additive cube has been added into an empty additive level.

Subtractive Brushes

Subtractive brushes are used to remove mass from your level, similar to carving out the current shape of the Red Builder Brush. You can create them by clicking the CSG: Subtract button in the Toolbox. Subtractive brushes appear as yellow wireframes in your level (see **FIGURE 4.3**).

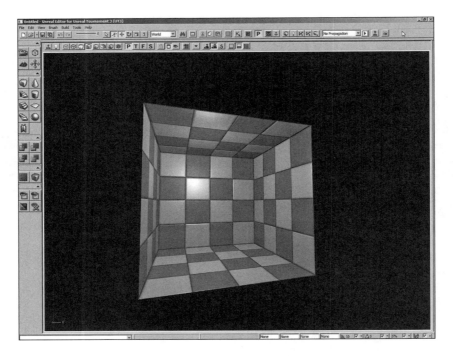

FIGURE 4.3   A subtractive brush created in a subtractive level

A Quick Word on Building

The most important thing to remember about BSP is that it is used to *create* your world geometry. A BSP brush itself is not world geometry. For Unreal Editor to make the conversion from BSP brushes to CSG world geometry, you must "Build" your level.

Building is as easy as clicking a single button. If you are only recalculating your world geometry, you can click the Build Geometry button located in the Toolbar. If you have applied lighting to your scene, you will instead use the Build All button, which recalculates your geometry, as well as the shadow maps resulting from any changes.

The key is to keep in mind that whenever you change *anything* about your BSP brushes, be it a simple edit, adding a new brush, or even moving an existing brush, you *must* build your geometry. Because this will in nearly every case require a change in shadows, you may as well just click the Build All button 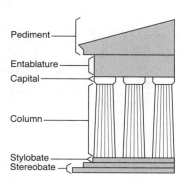.

In that regard, one of the more important aspects to remember about building is simply that it takes time. Small basic levels tend to build very quickly. However, you'll soon discover that as you start to create more intricate and vast levels with more complex lighting setups, building everything takes longer and longer. This is where having a fast processor (or two) can come in handy, but in most cases, you'll just have to be patient.

Cleaning BSP Materials

Sometimes when you're building your levels, you'll receive a warning after clicking the Build button in the Map Check window that you need to run the Clean BSP Materials command, as a certain number of BSP surfaces have "unnecessary material references." This is due to the result of having two brushes that have touching faces, and those faces have some sort of material that accepts lighting. As an example, consider two painted blocks that are pressed up against each other. The surfaces that are in contact cannot be seen, and so there is no reason for those surfaces to have paint on them.

Having those extra materials upon surfaces that are in contact with one another can give a performance hit during rebuilding, as the rendering engine still tries to calculate lights and shadows for those surfaces. A good practice would be to place a material on any such surfaces that did not receive lighting. This means the rendering engine could "skip" those surfaces and thereby give you a faster result during rebuild.

Fortunately, Unreal Editor does this for you. Simply select the Tools menu at the top of the main user interface, and click Clean BSP Materials. This tracks down any instances where two contacting BSP surfaces share a lit material and apply to those surfaces an invisible unlit material, saving a bit of precious time during your next rebuild.

As you progress through this chapter, we will use many of the topics covered thus far—as well as several others—through the creation of a very simple ancient Greek temple. We begin by creating the base of the temple, and move up through all the other elements as the chapter progresses.

Before you begin, you may want to use the simplified diagram in Figure 4.4 to review the elements of a Doric temple.

FIGURE 4.4   Simplified diagram of the elements of an ancient Greek temple

In **TUTORIAL 4.1**, we begin construction of our temple by placing a single stair—called the stylobate—upon which we place the rest of the building.

TUTORIAL 4.1: Constructing the Stereobate Step

1. Launch Unreal Editor and open the DM-Ch_4_BSP_Temple_Start.ut3 map. In the Generic browser, verify that the Chapter_4_BrushDemo.upk package is available. Both of these files are included on the DVD in the files for this chapter.

2. Set your Drag Grid value to 16 (see **FIGURE 4.5**).

> **NOTE**
>
> In practicality, the techniques shown throughout the tutorials in this chapter would be most effective for rapidly prototyping out a level as opposed to creating a finalized gaming environment. For the final game-play version of the level, most (if not all) of the geometry would be comprised of static meshes, as they are far more efficient in terms of required processing power. We cover the process here simply as a way to help familiarize you with the use of BSP brushes.

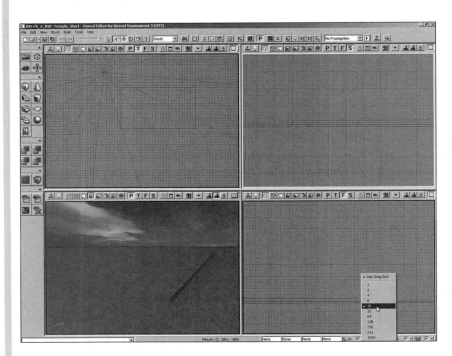

FIGURE 4.5   The Drag Grid can be set from the Status Bar at the bottom of the UI.

3. In the Generic browser, select the mat_concrete material located within the BrushDemo package, so that it will be applied to all new BSP brushes.

4. We're going to start with the stereobate step, which in layman's terms is simply a single stair that extends up from the base. Right-click the Cube builder button , and enter the following values (see **FIGURE 4.6**):

X: 1792   **Y:** 3328   **Z:** 32

Click Build and Close, and then select the Red Builder Brush.

5. In the Top viewport, use the Translation widget to move the Red Builder Brush so that it is centered on the concrete base in the X and Y axes. From the Top viewport, the Red Builder Brush should be inset by 128 units from the base X and Y directions.

6. In either the Side or Front viewport, move the Red Builder Brush so that its bottommost face is flush with the topmost face of the base. In simpler terms, rest the Red Builder Brush on top of the base.

7. Finally, click the CSG: Add button in the Toolbox to create an additive brush in the location of the Red Builder Brush (see **FIGURE 4.7**).

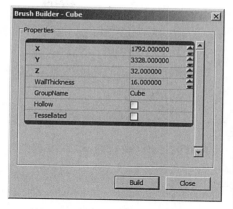

FIGURE 4.6   Your Cube Builder settings should appear like so.

TIP

In the orthographic viewports, you can move the Translation Widget to any corner of a brush by simply right-clicking on the corner! This can make precise movements that reference other points much easier!

FIGURE 4.7   The new additive brush forms a new step.

8. Click the Build All button ![icon]. After the build, you may receive a warning that you need to run Clean BSP Materials. Do this now by choosing Tools > Clean BSP Materials from the main menubar.

9. Save your level as DM-BSP_Temple_01.

END TUTORIAL 4.1

Working with Brushes

Now that you know the types of brushes that are available to you, it is important for you to understand a few points about brush workflow. Knowing these simple topics can speed up level design by helping you choose which brush you need, how you can position that brush, and some easy ways to avoid problems while working with brushes.

Additive and Subtractive Levels

Whether you primarily use additive or subtractive brushes in your level usually depends on the type of level you create. As of the release of Unreal Engine 3.0, users can create levels in an additive or subtractive manner, rather than being limited only to subtractive levels as they were in previous generations of the engine. The difference is quite simple; an additive level can be thought of as a massive area of open air, into which you *add* the geometry of a level. A subtractive level, on the other hand, is a massive area of solid mass, much like being inside a mountain. From this mass, you remove or carve out your environment.

It should be noted, however, that as of Unreal Engine 3 and current games such as Unreal Tournament 3, level designers should only be using additive levels. Subtractive levels should be avoided generally.

The Almighty Drag Grid

One of the most important things you'll need to remember about placing brushes is that when it comes to precision, a miss is as good as a mile. Gaps and overlapped brushes can lead to problems in your level, and should be

> **TIP**
>
> Should a brush that you're working with not be aligned to the current grid, simply select the brush and right-click on one of its corners in an orthographic view (such as the Top, Side, or Front views). This snaps that vertex to the nearest grid point!

avoided at all costs. For example, let's say you're trying to attach a subtractive corridor to a subtracted room, but you accidentally leave a tiny gap between the brushes. Once you build your geometry, you'll find that the small gap has resulted in a wall between the room and the corridor.

To avoid this situation, you can make use of the Drag Grid, which is activated by default in Unreal Editor. The Drag Grid forces your brushes to snap to a given grid value, designated in the Drag Grid settings. As a rule, do not turn off the Drag Grid while working with brushes, and be sure to adjust the snap value frequently to make large or small snaps more accommodating.

Moving with Pivots

Brush pivots provide center of movement for your brushes. When you're snapping to the grid, this pivot determines the point at which the brush snaps. The pivot is also used as a point of rotation. For example, say you have a cube-shaped brush with its pivot precisely at the center of the cube. If you rotate the brush, you would see the cube appear to spin in place. However, if you relocated the pivot to the corner of the brush, you would see the cube rotate about its corner. You can change the pivot of a BSP brush by right-clicking on one of its vertices, or by right-clicking anywhere on the screen and using the options under Pivot (see **FIGURE 4.8**).

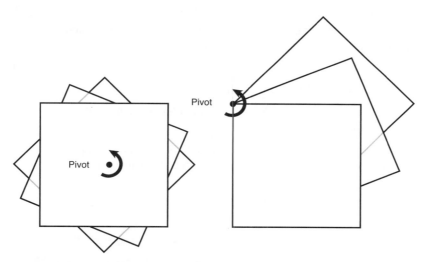

FIGURE 4.8   The effect of changing the pivot's location

Brush Order

Brush order is another important aspect to BSP creation. Say you've constructed a level of a multistory building out of BSP brushes, which is contained within a large cube-shaped subtraction. Perhaps you later decide that placing the building inside a cylindrical subtraction would make more sense, and so you delete the subtractive cube and replace it with a cylinder. However, when you build your geometry, you find that the entire building has disappeared! This happens because the brushes were created in the wrong order. Think about it: If the *last* operation you perform is a large subtraction, all of the additive brushes within that subtraction would be removed.

You can change the order in which each brush is calculated, thus fixing this problem. If you were to tell Unreal Editor to calculate the large cylindrical subtraction first, all the additive pieces within it would still be intact once the geometry was built. To change a brush's order, right-click on it and choose Order from the context menu that appears. Underneath, you find options for calculating the brush first or last, as well as swapping its order with another selected brush.

Building to the Proper Scale

Scale is important in level design, and is a key element in BSP brush creation. Choosing the proper scale can be tricky without a point of reference. In general, it's a good idea to make your designs relate to your playable character. For example, in Unreal Tournament 3, the player's character is roughly 96 Unreal units tall when standing, and around 64 units when crouched. This means all of your doorways need to be at least this tall to accommodate the player, and that all ceilings should be well above this value. Always keep scale in mind when designing your levels, and remember to keep your levels from feeling too constrained or too spacious.

Please continue from **TUTORIAL 4.1**, or open the DM-Ch_4_BSP_Temple_01.ut3 map included with the files for this chapter. In **TUTORIAL 4.2**, we move forward with the construction of our temple, adding the second tier of the foundation, known as the stylobate.

TUTORIAL 4.2: Adding the Stylobate to Our Temple

1. Make sure the mat_concrete material is selected from the Chapter_4_BrushDemo package in the Generic browser.

2. We now create the stylobate, which is the step that actually leads onto the floor of the temple. Right-click the Cube builder button 🔘, and enter the following values:

   X: 1536

   Y: 3072

   Z: 32

   Click Build and Close, then select the Red Builder Brush (see **FIGURE 4.9**).

3. In the Top viewport, use the Translation widget to move the Red Builder Brush so that it is centered on the stereobate step in the X and Y axes. The Red Builder Brush should inset 128 in all four directions from the stereobate step created previously.

4. In the Side or Front viewport, move the Red Builder Brush so that its bottommost face is resting on top of the stereobate step.

5. Finally, click the CSG: Add button 🔲 in the Toolbox to create an additive brush.

6. Click the Build All button 🔳. Run Clean BSP Materials from the Tools menu; then save your map's progress (see **FIGURE 4.10**).

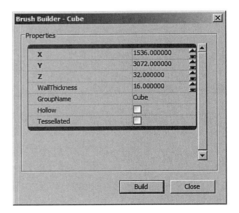

FIGURE 4.9   Your Brush Builder settings should appear like so.

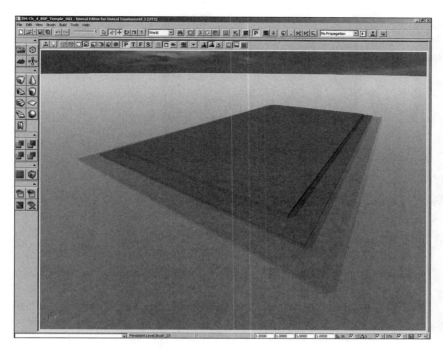

FIGURE 4.10   All the necessary steps for the temple are in place.

END TUTORIAL 4.2

Primitives

The brush primitives are a set of quick, pre-made brush factories that can be applied to the Red Builder Brush in order to add or subtract geometry of a given shape from your level. Each of these primitives comes with a set of parameters that make it easy to customize the resulting shape. Although most of the parameters for each primitive are self-explanatory, feel free to check out the Unreal Editor User's Manual in Appendix A, "The Unreal Editor User's Guide," for detailed explanations of each of the primitive's parameters.

Cube

The Cube is one of the most frequently used primitives in your level-building arsenal. Despite its name, it does not have to have sides of equal length. This primitive is a good starting point for most rooms. Using the available settings, this primitive can be hollow with an adjustable thickness for its walls (see **FIGURE 4.11**).

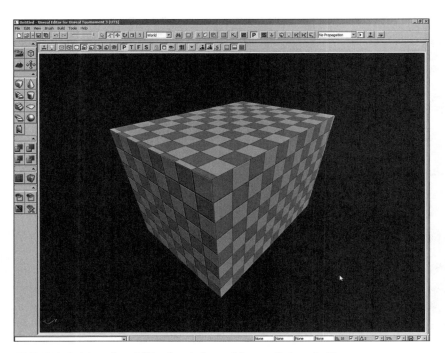

FIGURE 4.11   An additive brush formed from a Cube primitive

Cone

The Cone primitive is basically a cylinder with one end collapsed to a single point. It might be easier to think of it like a pyramid in which you can specify the number of sides around its base. Although not as frequently used as the Cube primitive, it can be handy in specific situations. Using the available settings, this primitive can be hollow with an adjustable thickness. The height of the inside cap of the hollowed primitive can be specified as well (see **FIGURE 4.12**).

Cylinder

The Cylinder primitive is most often used for creating cylindrically-shaped rooms. Although this primitive can be used for creating objects such as pillars, pipes, and so forth, you should note that in current versions of Unreal Editor, such objects are usually created in a 3D modeling application and imported as static meshes. Using the available settings, the Cylinder primitive can be hollow with an adjustable thickness. Unlike the Cube primitive, when hollow, the cylinder brush ends are open, giving it a tube-like appearance (see **FIGURE 4.13**).

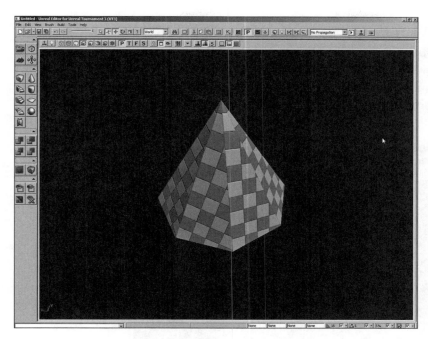

FIGURE 4.12   An additive brush formed from a Cone primitive

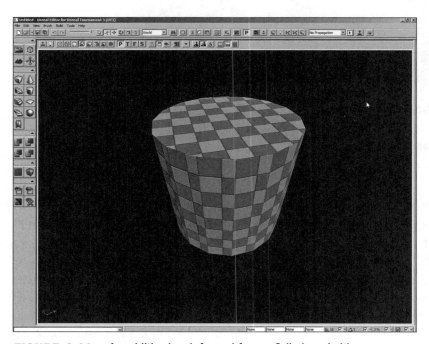

FIGURE 4.13   An additive brush formed from a Cylinder primitive

4

Sheet

The Sheet primitive is a simple four-sided plane. A Sheet has no collision, so players and other objects can pass through it. This can be used to create decorative trim, hide seams, create basic fluid surfaces, and produce a variety of other effects. It should be noted, however, that once placed in a level, a sheet brush is only visible from one side, unless the material on it is two-sided (see **FIGURE 4.14**).

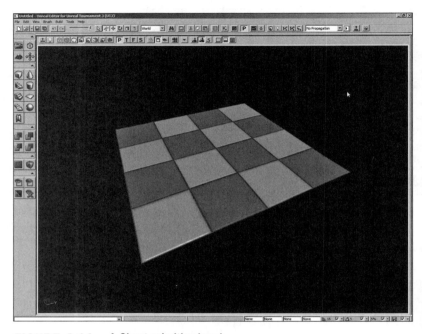

FIGURE 4.14   A Sheet primitive brush

Tetrahedron (Sphere)

The Tetrahedron primitive is the closest approximation to a sphere that can be achieved with a brush. It is basically a spherically-shaped brush composed of an adjustable number of triangles (see **FIGURE 4.15**). In nearly every case, it is better to use a static mesh instead of this brush, because the number of polygonal faces and erratic texture placement make the tetrahedron brush impractical.

Curved Staircase

The Curved Staircase primitive is a set of stairs that curve about a specified angle and extend solidly all the way up from the floor (see **FIGURE 4.16**). For this reason, this primitive should not be used to create a set of stairs that curves about an angle greater than 270 degrees, or they wrap over themselves. This primitive should generally be avoided in favor of using a custom-made static mesh, because its large number of BSP tessellations can result in a performance loss.

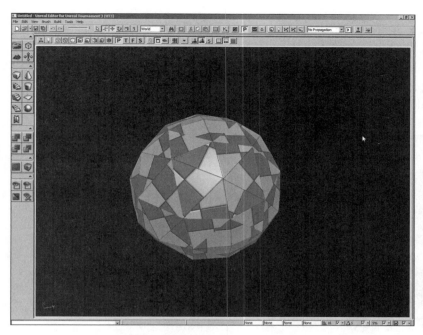

FIGURE 4.15   A Tetrahedron primitive

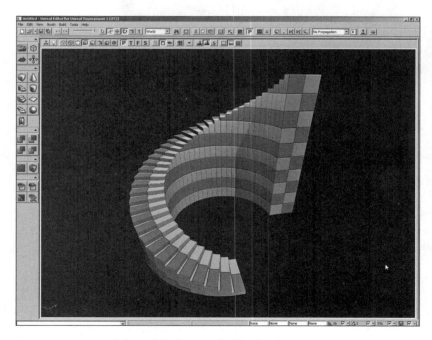

FIGURE 4.16   A Curved Staircase primitive brush

Linear Staircase

The Linear Staircase primitive is a straight set of stairs that reaches from all the way up from the floor (see **FIGURE 4.17**). This is a very straight-forward primitive to use, but like the Curved Staircase primitive, it also should be avoided in favor of a custom-made static mesh because of performance considerations.

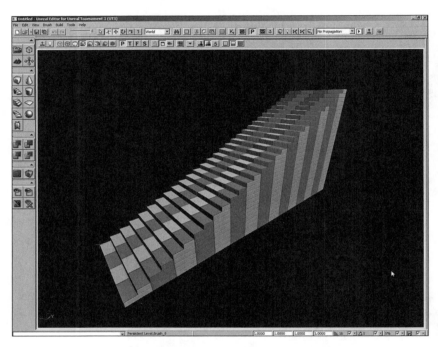

FIGURE 4.17 A Linear Staircase primitive brush

Spiral Staircase

The Spiral Staircase primitive is much like the Curved Staircase primitive in that it is a set of stairs that curves about a specified angle. The difference here is that the stairs do not reach up from the floor (see **FIGURE 4.18**). Instead, each section of the staircase is only as thick as each individual step, enabling you to create a staircase that wraps around many times without ever overlapping itself. As with the other Staircase primitives, this primitive should be avoided in favor of a custom-made static mesh.

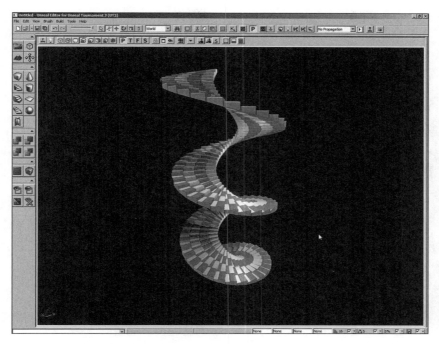

FIGURE 4.18   A Spiral Staircase primitive brush

Volumetric

The Volumetric primitive is actually just a specified number of vertical sheets rotated about the Z-axis to give the effect of having volume (see **FIGURE 4.19**). This can be used for creating effects such as fire, smoke, plasma, chains, or trees, where exact three-dimensional detail is not necessary or would become a hindrance to performance. In most cases, however, a similar effect could be created with a very simple particle system or static mesh. As such, Volumetric primitives seldom need to be used.

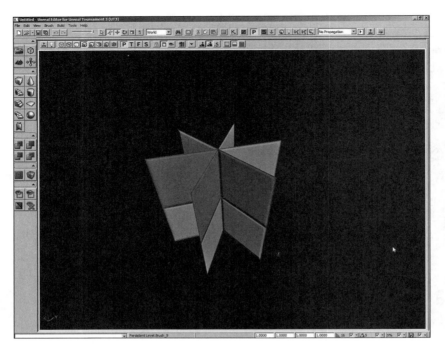

FIGURE 4.19   A Volumetric primitive brush is a series of rotated planes.

Boolean Operations

You can also create new shapes for the Red Builder Brush by using Boolean-style operations with other brushes in your level. This is accomplished using the Intersect and De-Intersect operations, both located in the Toolbox. However, please note that both of these operations can yield undesirable BSP cuts in your geometry, and are therefore seldom used in level design. Again, in most Unreal Engine 3 levels, you want the BSP to be as simple as possible, leaving more complex geometry for static meshes. However, there may come a time when knowing these operations can speed up your workflow!

Intersect Tool

The Intersect tool removes all areas of your Red Builder Brush that are *not* inside solid geometry. The following figures demonstrate how this tool works. Note the shape of the Red Builder Brush before and after intersection (see **FIGURE 4.20**).

Note that the Intersection operation has only changed the shape of the Red Builder Brush and nothing else. At this point, you are ready to create an additive or subtractive brush from the new shape.

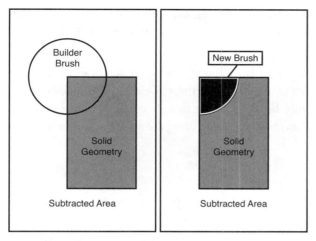

FIGURE 4.20   Before and after Intersecting

De-Intersect Tool

Think of the De-Intersect tool as the opposite of Intersect. It removes all parts of the Red Builder Brush that are *inside* another BSP brush. Check out **FIGURE 4.21** for details.

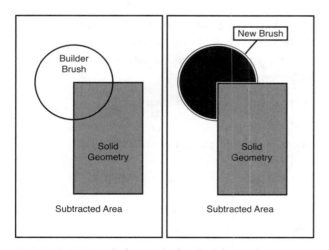

FIGURE 4.21   Before and after De-Intersecting

Brush Solidity

Brush solidity plays an important role in how your level's world geometry is created. If your brushes are too complex, you can end up with many divisions in your world geometry, which can harm performance. In general, it's best to remember that BSP brushes should be used for proto-typing your levels and to create the most basic general volume, not for any sort of decoration. Save your decoration for static meshes!

However, if there comes a time where you need a fairly complex brush or you need a brush that performs a specific task, you would do well to remember the three levels of brush solidity: Solid, Semi-Solid, and Non-Solid. Although Solid brushes are the default type of brush you use in Unreal Editor, Semi- and Non-Solid brushes must be created using the Add Special Brush button ▣ located in the Toolbox.

Solid

Solid brushes are by far the most common. In fact, every brush you have created so far has been a solid brush. Solid brushes have the following main properties:

- ▸ Solid brushes block players and projectiles in the game. This means you can't run through them or shoot through them.
- ▸ Solid brushes can be additive or subtractive.
- ▸ Solid brushes create BSP cuts in their surrounding world geometry.

Semi-Solid

Semi-Solid brushes can be places in a level without adding any extra BSP cuts to the surround-ing world geometry. This can be beneficial when using brushes to create things such as pillars and beams, but you should note that such objects are typically reserved for static meshes. The follow-ing is a list of key attributes for Semi-Solid brushes:

- ▸ Semi-Solid brushes block players and projectiles, just as Solid brushes do.
- ▸ Semi-Solids can *only* be additive, never subtractive.
- ▸ Semi-Solids don't leave BSP cuts in their surrounding world geometry.

Non-Solid

Non-Solid brushes behave similarly to a hologram. They have no collision capabilities and are therefore of fairly limited use. The following is a list of their properties:

- ▸ Non-Solid brushes do not block players or projectiles.
- ▸ Non-Solids can *only* be additive, never subtractive.
- ▸ Non-Solids do not leave BSP cuts in their surrounding geometry.

> **NOTE**
>
> In many cases, rather than use a non-solid brush, it would be better to simply use a static mesh that has no collision model!

Brush Manipulation

Although the brush primitives and the Intersect and De-Intersect commands do allow for tremendous variety in the shapes of your brushes, you eventually run into a situation where you simply need more creative power to create the shape you need. As of the release of Unreal Engine 3.0, Unreal Editor provides an entirely new method for brush manipulation, offering virtually as much flexibility as what is found in most 3D modeling applications, such as 3ds Max or Maya. However, before we discuss how you can adjust your geometry, let's take a moment and look at the structure of BSP brushes.

Brushes in Unreal are composed of polygons, which are shapes with many sides. When you are working in 3D, a *polygon* is a surface comprised of vertices, edges, and at least one face. Before you see how these three components can be used to edit your brushes, take a moment to review them in **FIGURE 4.22**:

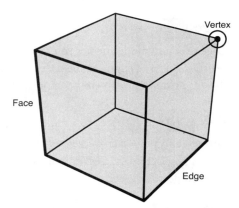

- ▸ A *vertex* is defined as a point in space. In terms of a polygonal object, it is a point where two or more edges meet. You can think of a vertex as a dot in a three-dimensional connect-the-dots game.

- ▸ An *edge* is a line between two vertices. For example, the lines between the corners of a polygonal cube are classified as edges.

- ▸ A *face* is a surface stretched between three or more edges. In the case of a cube, a face would be one entire side of the object.

FIGURE 4.22   A visual representation of the polygon components

Geometry Mode

Geometry Mode is new to Unreal Engine 3.0 and encapsulates the previous methods of manipulating brushes with a selection of new tools into one clean interface. To anyone who has used any of the popular 3D modeling applications available, Geometry Mode seems very familiar. Those of you who are new to 3D modeling need not worry because the tools are so well designed and easy to use that even complete newcomers will be creating and manipulating BSP geometry in ways that could only be imagined in previous versions of Unreal Editor.

Activating Geometry Mode is as simple as selecting a BSP brush and clicking the Geometry Mode button located near the top of the Toolbox. Once activated, the Geometry Tools window appears, giving you access to a great variety of manipulation methods for your brush. Best of all,

Geometry Mode can be used on any additive or subtractive brush, as well as on the Red Builder Brush!

> **NOTE**
>
> Multiple brushes can be selected and manipulated at the same time in Geometry Mode by holding Ctrl and clicking them with the Left Mouse Button.

Selection Modes

Vertex

Vertex selection mode likely becomes the mode you will use most often. It enables you to select, move, delete, and weld the vertices of the currently selected brushes. You can also create new vertices and make a perpendicular cut between two selected vertices. In Vertex selection mode, you also have the option of using soft selection.

Edge

Edge selection mode enables you to select, move, split, and turn the edges of the currently selected brushes. Turning edges can be useful if you have triangulated a polygon of a brush, but you want the edge running between the opposite vertices.

Poly

Poly selection mode enables you to select, move, extrude, triangulate, and flip the polygons of the currently selected brushes. With its many useful tools, Poly selection mode is the next most-often-used mode after Vertex.

Object

Object selection mode enables you to select, move, rotate, scale, and clip brushes. Clipping is a quick and easy way to make irregularly shaped brushes. Keep in mind that transformations made to a brush in Object selection mode are actually being applied to all the vertices of the selected brushes. The pivots of the brushes are not affected at all.

Please continue from **TUTORIAL 4.2**, or open the DM-Ch_4_BSP_Temple_02.ut3 map included with the files for this chapter. With the base of our temple completed, we now create the first of our series of columns in **TUTORIAL 4.3**.

TUTORIAL 4.3: Creating the First Column Shaft

1. Make sure that the mat_concrete material is selected from the Chapter_4_BrushDemo package in the Generic browser.

2. In the Toolbox, right-click the Cylinder builder button ▣ and enter the following values:

   Z: 1024

OuterRadius: 64

Sides: 8

Click Build and Close; then select the Red
Builder Brush when finished (see **FIGURE 4.23**).

Click the Geometry Mode button 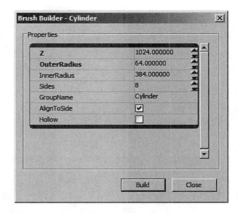.

3. In the Toolbox, the Geometry Tools dialog
   appears. In the Selection Mode section, click
   the Vertex button if it is not already
   pressed.

4. Make sure the Drag Grid is still set to 16 units.
   Select each vertex in the Top viewport one at a
   time; then right-click each one to snap them to
   the grid. You can't do all the vertices of the
   brush at once, but selecting each one individually also snaps those that are stacked directly
   beneath the selection (see **FIGURE 4.24**).

FIGURE 4.23   Your brush builder
window should appear like so.

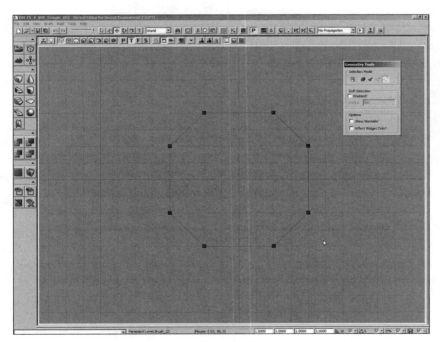

FIGURE 4.24   Once snapped, your vertices appears like so in the Top viewport.

5. Click the Camera Mode button in the Toolbox to exit Geometry Mode.

6. In the Top viewport, use the Translation widget to move the Red Builder Brush so that it fits into the lower-left corner of the innermost step, but with a 32-unit gap (that's two grid spaces if your Drag Grid is set to 16) on either side. Use **FIGURE 4.25** if you need help.

> **NOTE**
>
> You might notice as you re-enter camera mode that the wireframe of your brush seems to disappear. Do not be alarmed; this is simply a redraw issue of the viewport. If you deselect your brush, the wireframe returns!

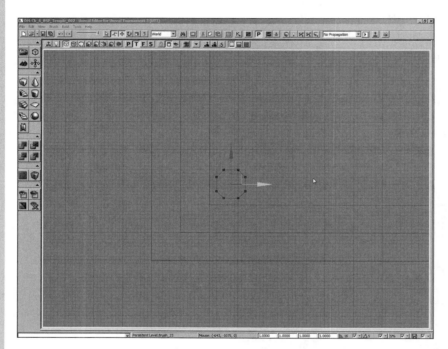

FIGURE 4.25   The column should fit into the lower-left corner of the stylobate step.

7. Using either the Side or Front viewport, move the Red Builder Brush so that the bottom-most face is resting on top of the stylobate step.

8. Finally, click the Add Special Brush button ▣ in the Toolbox to open the Add Special dialog. Select Semi-Solid in the Solidity section and click OK to create a Semi-Solid brush. Using a Semi-Solid brush enables us to have a shape that blocks the character without making any unnecessary BSP cuts (see **FIGURE 4.26**).

9. Rebuild your geometry and lighting with the Build All button ▣; then Clean BSP Materials. When finished, save your level.

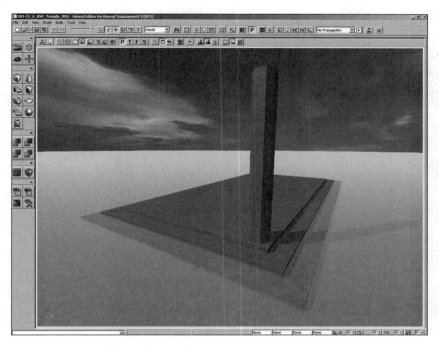

FIGURE 4.26   The column has now been added to the level.

END OF TUTORIAL 4.3

Toggle Modifier Window

Geometry Mode's Toggle Modifier Window shows or hides the Geometry Modifiers dialog (see **FIGURE 4.27**). This dialog provides access to a series of geometry modifications that enable you to create some truly unique BSP shapes!

Soft Selection

Soft selection uses a specified spherical radius from the selected vertex to determine all affected vertices' selection weights. The weight falls off from 1 at the selected vertex to 0 at the specified radius. All vertices at or beyond the radius are essentially unaffected. Any transformation is applied based on the weight of all affected vertices. The selected vertex receives the full transformation, whereas a vertex halfway along the radius from the

FIGURE 4.27   The Modifier Window holds many functions you can perform on your BSP geometry.

selected vertex receives only half the transformation, and a vertex at or beyond the radius does not receive any transformation at all (see **FIGURE 4.28**).

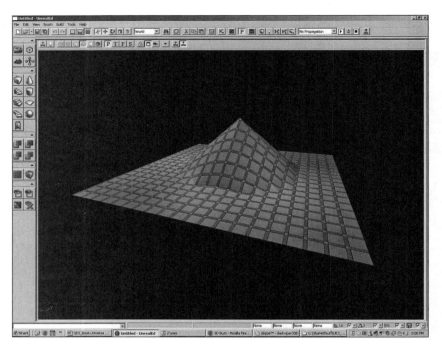

FIGURE 4.28   The vertices in the sheet were translated with soft selection enabled.

▶ **Enable**—Soft selection is only used if it is enabled. Otherwise, normal selection is used.

▶ **Radius**—Radius determines how far the soft selection reaches and, in turn, the quickness of the falloff.

Show Normals

Show normals display the normals of all the vertices, edges, or polygons (depending on the current selection mode) of the currently selected brush in all viewports (see **FIGURE 4.29**).

Affect Widget Only

The Affect Widget Only property enables you to adjust the point about which the transformations are calculated. With this option checked and the Translation widget active, you can move the widget without affecting any of the selected geometry. Turning off this property and switching to one of the other transformation modes enables you to perform transformations using the new location of the widget as the center of motion.

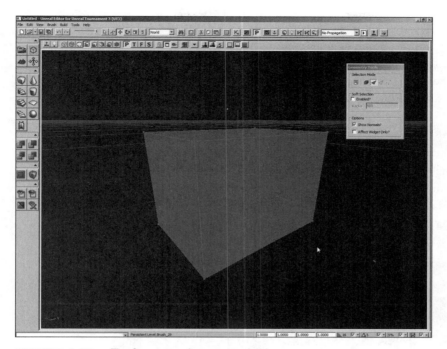

FIGURE 4.29   The face normals are now visible.

Geometry Modifiers

The Geometry Modifiers are the real guts of the new Geometry Mode. These are the actual functions that enable you to perform transformations and other manipulations on the BSP geometry in your level. There are two types of modifiers in Geometry Mode: Passive and Active. Passive modifiers require input from the user in order to be performed. These modifiers can be performed through the use of the mouse in the viewports, or they can have parameters that can be filled in for exact results. When using keyboard entry, the operation is performed when the user clicks Apply. The two types of modifiers are separated in the Geometry Modifiers dialog, with Passive being at the top and Active being at the bottom. Passive modifiers require some input from the user to have an effect, whereas Active modifiers are simple one-click buttons whose operations take effect immediately.

Passive Modifiers

The passive modifiers enable the user to perform various operations to the geometry through direct manipulation. Each of these passive modifiers is exclusive, meaning that activating any one of them allows the user only to perform the function related to the modifier. For instance, when the Edit modifier is active, you cannot extrude.

Edit

The Edit modifier is probably going to be your most often-used modifier. It allows basic transformations such as moving, rotating, or scaling to be carried out on the selected vertex, edge, or polygon (depending on the current selection mode). See **FIGURE 4.30**.

Extrude

The Extrude modifier is only available when in Poly selection mode, and is an extremely useful addition to Unreal Editor's brush manipulation tools. Extruding is a very easy way to create additional polygons on your brushes. In simple terms, the selected polygon or polygons are dragged out a certain distance and new polygons are created to fill in the gaps from the polygon's previous location (see **FIGURE 4.31**).

FIGURE 4.30 The Geometry Tools window is currently in Vertex Selection Mode.

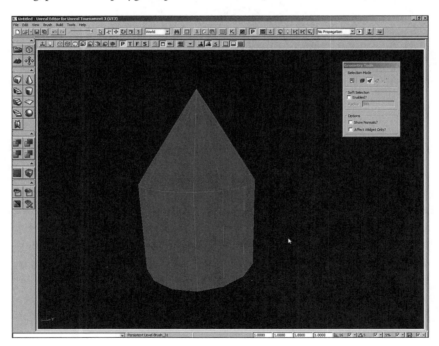

FIGURE 4.31   The bottom face of the cone has been extruded.

The Extrude modifier also has keyboard entry parameters that can be used to make exact extrusions. *Length* is the distance the selected polygon is moved, or more precisely, the distance of the extrusion. *Segments* refers

> **NOTE**
>
> Rather than create an extrusion numerically, you can create one intuitively by moving a polygon with the Translation Widget while the Extrude modifier is active.

4

to the number of extrusions that are performed when Apply is clicked. For instance, if values of 16 and 5 are entered for Length and Segments respectively, five new sections each with a length of 16 units are created when Apply is clicked.

Clip

The Clip modifier replaces the brush-clipping tools from previous versions of Unreal Editor. It is only available when in Object selection mode. Those of you familiar with previous versions of Unreal Editor will be happy to note that it works in very much the same manner as in the past. The user sets two or three clipping points by holding Ctrl and right-clicking in one of the orthogonal viewports. These points can then be selected and moved to define a plane in space that is used to clip, or slice, the selected brush (see **FIGURE 4.32**). If only two points are created, the clipping plane contains those two points and should be perpendicular to the orthogonal viewport used to create them. If three points are created, the rotation of the clipping plane is defined by the third point.

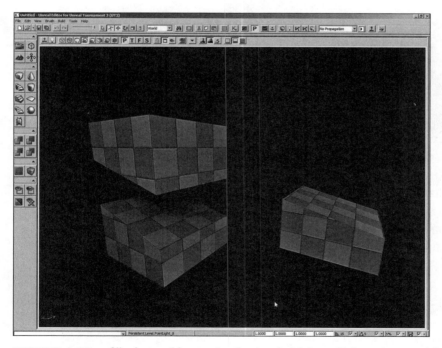

FIGURE 4.32   Clipping enables you to slice brushes into multiple parts or to delete a portion of a brush.

When the clipping plane is created, you will notice a small line running from it at a perpendicular angle (see **FIGURE 4.33**). This line designates the normal, or positive, side of the clipping plane. It is important to note which direction the normal is facing, as by its default nature, the clipping operation deletes the portion of the clipped brush that is on the same side as the normal. The clipping operation is performed on the currently selected brushes when the user clicks Apply.

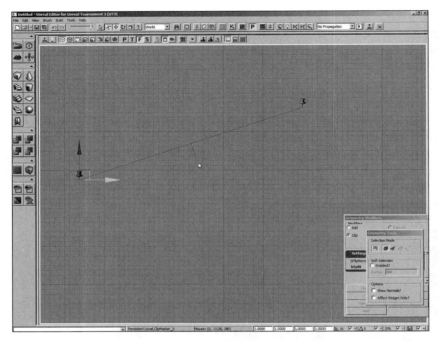

FIGURE 4.33   The small perpendicular line designates the clipping plane's normal.

The Clip modifier has parameters that control the results of the clipping operation. The bFlipNormal parameter determines which way the normal of the clipping plane is facing. This setting is very important, as the direction of the plane's normal controls which half of your brush will be removed during a standard clipping operation.

The bSlice parameter determines whether or not the clipping operation discards any part of the selected brushes during the clipping plane. If bSlice is checked, the current brush splits into two new brushes along the clipping

> **NOTE**
> When you activate bFlipNormal, you will not see the normal change to the other side!

plane, and both pieces are left intact. If bSlice is not checked, the portion of the brush that is on the normal side of the clipping plane will be deleted during the clipping operation, unless bFlipNormal is also checked, which will of course delete the opposite side.

Please continue from **TUTORIAL 4.3**, or open the DM-Ch_4_BSP_Temple_03.ut3 map included with the files for this chapter. We now have our first column in place. In **TUTORIAL 4.4**, we make use of Geometry mode to extrude out a capital.

TUTORIAL 4.4: Creating the Column Capital

1. Make sure that the mat_concrete material is selected from the Chapter_4_BrushDemo package in the Generic browser.

   We are done with the Red Builder Brush for now. Using the Translation widget, move the Red Builder Brush off to the side so it is out of the way.

2. Select the Semi-Solid column brush, and click the Geometry Mode button ⬡ in the Toolbox. Click the Poly button ◁ in the Selection Mode of the Geometry Tools dialog, and then click the Toggle Modifier Window button ▤ to show the Modifier window (see **FIGURE 4.34**).

3. In the Modifier window, select the radio button next to Extrude. In the Perspective viewport, select the top face of the semi-solid column.

4. Make sure your Drag Grid is set to 16.

FIGURE 4.34 Geometry Mode and the Modifier Window are now active.

5. Using the Translation widget, move (or extrude) the selected face 16 units (one grid space) upwards in the positive Z direction.

6. With the column's topmost face still selected, select the radio button next to Edit in the Geometry Modifiers window, and use the Scale Widget to scale the face up 135% uniformly (see **FIGURE 4.35**).

> **NOTE**
>
> It is absolutely *critical* that you switch back to Edit mode *before* attempting to scale in the next step! Scaling while in Extrude mode has been known to crash Unreal Editor!

7. With the top face still selected, go to the Geometry Modifiers window and reactivate Extrude mode. Set the Extrude length parameter to 16 (if it is not already) and click Apply. This creates the extrusion numerically rather than intuitively.

8. Switch back to Edit mode, and then scale the topmost face 65% larger using the Scale Widget.

9. Finally, make one last 16 unit extrusion to finish off the capital using whichever method (numerically or intuitively) that you prefer (see **FIGURE 4.36**).

10. Click the Build All button ⬚ and then save your level.

4

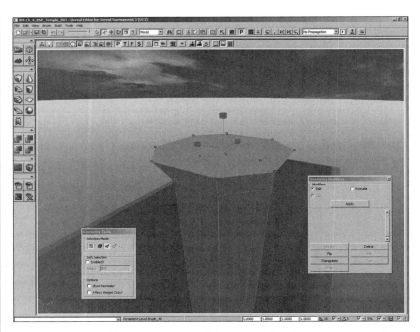

FIGURE 4.35   The topmost face of the column has been extruded and scaled.

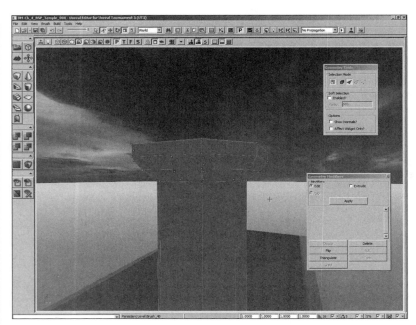

FIGURE 4.36   The capital should appear like so when finished.

END TUTORIAL 4.4

Please continue from **TUTORIAL 4.4**, or open the DM-Ch_4_BSP_Temple_04.ut3 map included with the files for this chapter.

TUTORIAL 4.5: Adding the Colonnades and the Entablature

1. Make sure that the mat_concrete material is selected from the Chapter_4_BrushDemo package in the Generic browser.

2. Set your Drag Grid to 32. In the Top viewport, select the column brush and, while holding down the Alt key, use the Translation widget to move it 320 units (10 grid spaces in total) to the right, in the positive Y direction. This creates a duplicate of the column (see **FIGURE 4.37**).

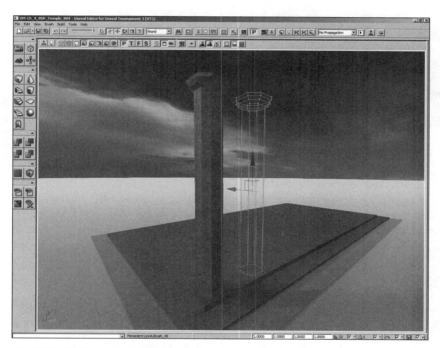

FIGURE 4.37   The initial column has now been duplicated.

3. Repeat Step 2 until you reach the other end of the stylobate creating one row of columns. Click the Build All button ![icon] when done (see **FIGURE 4.38**).

> **NOTE**
>
> The column appears as a wireframe until geometry is rebuilt!

4

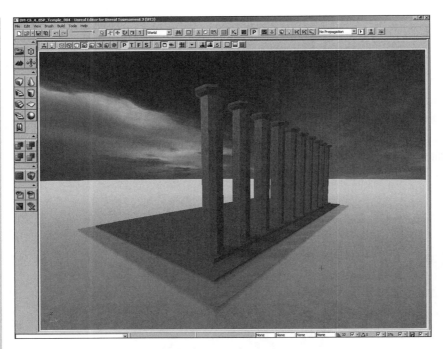

FIGURE 4.38   You now have a full row of columns.

4. In the Top viewport, hold down Ctrl and Alt and drag the left mouse button to make a mar-quee-selection around the entire row of columns you just created. Now, while holding down the Alt key, use the Translation widget to create duplicates of all the columns at once, moving them 1344 units in the positive X direction (see **FIGURE 4.39**).

   Click the Build All button when done.

5. In the Top viewport, select the columns in the upper-left and upper-right corners (remember to hold Ctrl to select multiple objects). While holding down the Alt key, use the Translation widget to create duplicates of the columns, moving them 320 units in the negative X direction (see **FIGURE 4.40**).

6. In the Top viewport, select the columns in the bottom-left and bottom-right corners and, while holding down the Alt key, use the Translation widget to create duplicates of the columns and move them 320 units upward in X.

FIGURE 4.39 Duplicate the entire row across the temple.

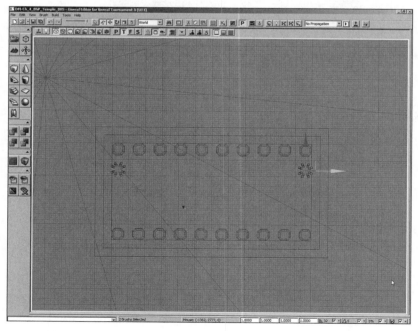

FIGURE 4.40 Make duplicates of the two upper-corner columns.

7. In the Top viewport, select the column you just created on the right and, while holding down the Alt key, use the Translation widget to create a duplicate of the column and move it 320 units in the upward in X (see **FIGURE 4.41**).

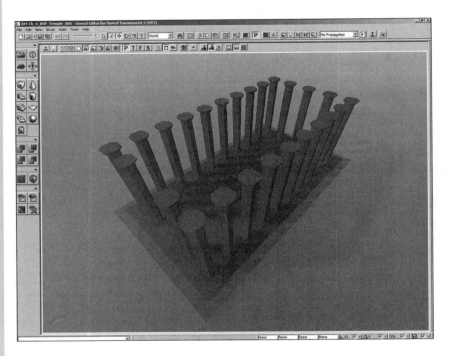

FIGURE 4.41   The final column is now in place.

8. Set your Drag Grid back to 16. In the Side viewport, select the stylobate brush (the top-most stair) and Alt-drag a duplicate that rests on top of all the columns. This creates the entablature (see **FIGURE 4.42**).

9. Click the Build All button , clean your BSP materials, and save your level.

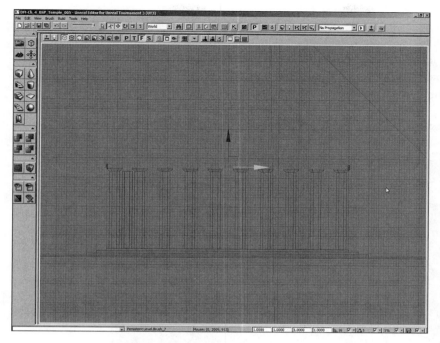

FIGURE 4.42   A duplicate of the stylobate forms the entablature.

END OF TUTORIAL 4.5

Active Modifiers

Active modifiers differ from passive modifiers in that they require the user to perform some sort of direct function before they can work properly. For instance, the Delete modifier requires that you select a piece of geometry to be removed before clicking the button. Each of these modifiers has their own specific selection protocol.

Create

The Create modifier can be a little confusing at first glance because it is only available in Vertex selection mode. For this reason, you might assume its function would be to create new vertices. This is not the case. The Create modifier is actually for creating new polygons from a selection of vertices. These vertices must be selected in a continuous loop, and the order in which these vertices are selected is extremely important because it determines which way the resulting polygon faces. If the vertices are selected in a clockwise loop, the new polygon faces toward you. If the vertices are selected in a counter-clockwise loop, the new polygon faces away from you. If you create the polygon facing the wrong direction, do not worry. There is another modifier we cover in a moment that helps you to correct that problem by flipping the polygon.

Delete

The Delete modifier is only available in Vertex and Poly selection modes and is extremely straightforward. It simply deletes the selected geometry. Keep in mind that any geometry that depends on the deleted geometry is affected by this operation. For instance, if a vertex is deleted, any polygons containing that vertex will be collapsed accordingly (see **FIGURE 4.43**).

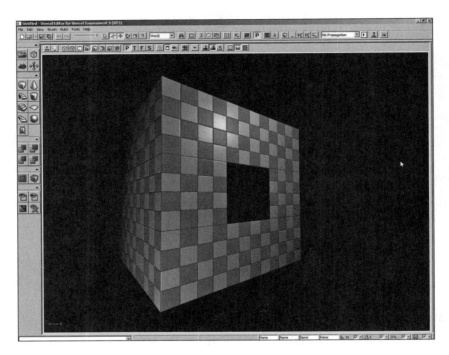

FIGURE 4.43   A polygon has been deleted from this cube.

Flip

The Flip modifier is only available in Poly selection mode, and enables you to change the direction that the selected polygons are facing. This is extremely important because, by default, Unreal only renders the positive side of a polygon, meaning that the back of a polygon appears completely transparent. As mentioned previously, this modifier can be helpful if you use the Create modifier to make a polygon that is facing the wrong direction.

In **FIGURE 4.44**, you can see an additive Cube brush that has had all of its sides flipped. It appears as it were a subtractive brush in a subtractive level, because the negative sides of the polygons—which are now facing outward—are not rendering. If you were to navigate the camera inside the box and look outward, it would look as if you were inside a room.

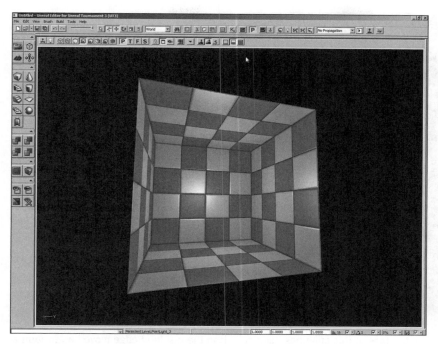

FIGURE 4.44   This box has had one of its sides flipped to face inward.

Split

The Split modifier is only available in Vertex and Edge selection modes and only works on components belonging to a single polygon at a time. If two edges are selected, the Split modifier splits the polygon along the midpoints of those edges. If more than two edges are selected, each of the edges will simply be split in half. If two adjacent vertices are selected, the polygon will be split along the midpoint of the edge connecting them. If two catty-cornered vertices are selected, the polygon will be split along the opposite diagonal. It is best to only select two vertices when using the Split modifier, as selecting more may yield unpredictable results (see **FIGURE 4.45**).

Triangulate

The Triangulate modifier splits the selected polygons into triangles. This is useful when you want more control over the final appearance of the brush and enables you to turn edges using the Turn modifier, which is explained next (see **FIGURE 4.46**).

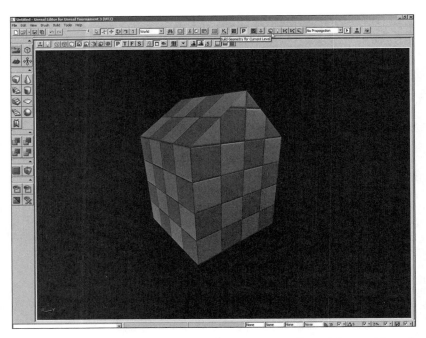

FIGURE 4.45   The top face of this cube has been split, and the resulting edge moved up to form a wedge.

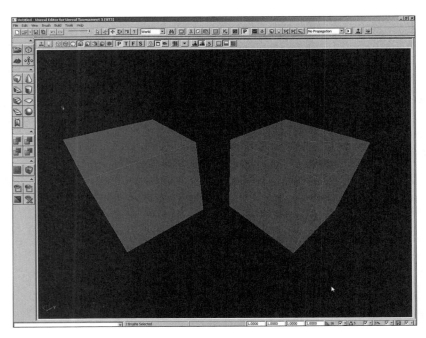

FIGURE 4.46   A cube before and after triangulation

Turn

The Turn modifier only works when the polygons on both sides of the selected edges are triangles. In essence, the Turn modifier causes the selected edges to run along the opposite diagonal of the four-sided polygon, consisting of the triangles on either side of the edge (see **FIGURE 4.47**).

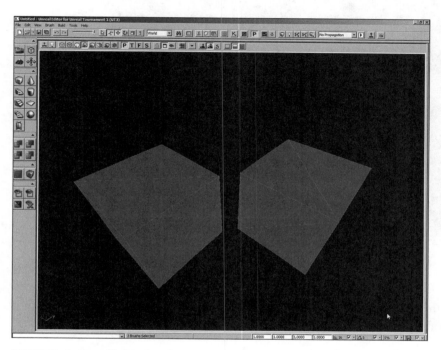

FIGURE 4.47 Notice the triangle edge on top of the cube on the right is turned in the opposite direction from the left.

Weld

The Weld modifier is used to weld, or merge, two or more vertices into one. The first selected vertex determines the location of the resulting single vertex. The operation can result in the deletion of polygons and holes in your brushes, which may need to be filled using the Create modifier (see **FIGURE 4.48**).

> **TIP**
>
> Dragging vertices on top of one another is another way of welding vertices, although both vertices must be placed in precisely the same location!

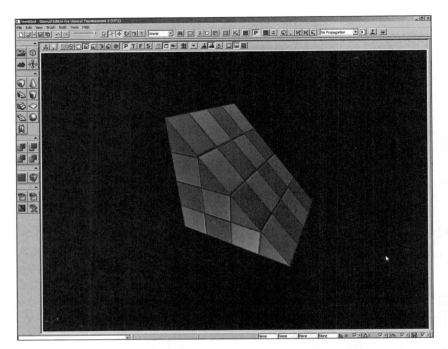

FIGURE 4.48   The vertices at the top of the cube were welded together, turning the shape into a wedge.

Please continue from **TUTORIAL 4.5**, or open the DM-Ch_4_BSP_Temple_05.ut3 map included with the files for this chapter.

TUTORIAL 4.6: Creating the Pediment

1. Make sure that the mat_concrete material is selected in the Generic browser.

2. In the Side or Front viewport, select the large rectangular brush resting atop the columns and use the Translation widget to Alt-drag a duplicate of the brush 32 units upward in Z, which places it directly on top of the original brush (see **FIGURE 4.49**).

3. Click the Geometry Mode button ⬡ in the Toolbox. Click the Edge button ▮ in the Selection Mode section of the Geometry Tools dialog. Then, click the Toggle Modifier Window button ▤ to show the Modifier window.

4. In the Perspective viewport, select the two top edges of the polygons facing in the positive and negative X directions. In the Geometry Modifiers window, click the Split button ▭ Split ▭. A new edge is created connecting the two selected edges at their midpoints. This new edge should be running lengthwise along the brush, as shown in **FIGURE 4.50**.

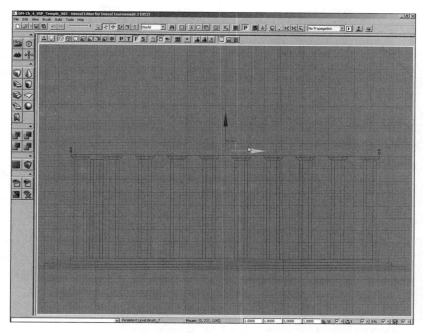

FIGURE 4.49   The new duplicate of the entablature rests atop the original.

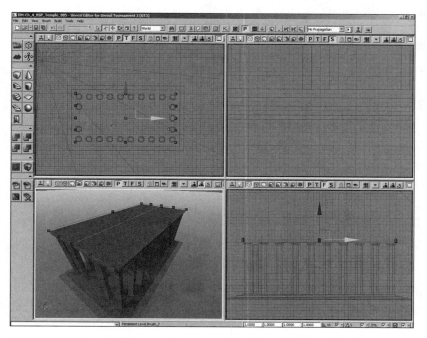

FIGURE 4.50   Splitting creates a new edge down the top of the cube.

5. Select the new edge and move it 416 units upward in the positive Z direction. Next, go ahead and click the Build All button ![icon] so that we can view our progress (see **FIGURE 4.51**).

FIGURE 4.51   The pediment has now been created.

6. Save your level.

END TUTORIAL 4.6

Please continue from **TUTORIAL 4.6**, or open the DM-Ch_4_BSP_Temple_06.ut3 map included with the files for this chapter. Our temple is essentially finished, but to help us add a little character to it, we're going to break some of its parts up and make it appear to be ruined. We do this using the Clip modifier in Geometry Mode in **TUTORIAL 4.7**.

TUTORIAL 4.7: Destroying the Temple with Clipping

1. Make sure that the mat_concrete material is selected in the Generic browser.

2. In the Top viewport, select the column in the lower left corner.

3. Click the Geometry Mode button ![icon] in the Toolbox. Click the Object button ![icon] in the Selection Mode section of the Geometry Tools dialog. Then, click the Toggle Modifier Window button ![icon] to show the Geometry Modifiers window and click the Clip radio button in the Modifiers section (see **FIGURE 4.52**).

4. In the Front viewport, hold the Ctrl key and right-click in the viewport anywhere to the left of the selected column. Then, while still holding Ctrl, right-click again on the right side of the selected column.

The clipping line now appears. Notice the small red line coming out perpendicularly. This is the clipping normal.

5. Each of the new clipping markers can be selected and moved, just like any other object in Unreal Editor. Do this now; select each of the clipping markers, and position them to create an interesting angle that we could use to slice the column.

6. Currently, your clipping plane is perpendicular to the Side viewport. If you needed a more complex angle, you would need a third clipping marker.

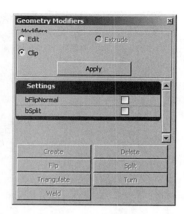

FIGURE 4.52 Your Modifier window should appear like so.

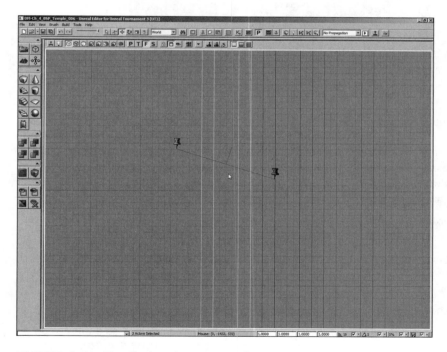

FIGURE 4.53 The clipping plane, as seen from the Front viewport

In the Top viewport, hold Ctrl and right-click somewhere away from your two clipping markers. This creates a third marker, defining a plane. You see this plane in the Perspective viewport as a triangle that connects the three clipping markers (see **FIGURE 4.54**).

4

FIGURE 4.54   Your new clipping plane appears like so in the Perspective viewport.

7. Although the plane appears to be a small triangle far away from the corner column we're trying to clip, it actually has infinite extents across your level. However, it might be difficult to gauge exactly where the clip takes place with such a vast distance between the plane and the object being clipped. Because of this, it might be easier to surround your object to be clipped with your three markers, so that the triangle wraps around your object. In this way, you'll have a clearer idea of where the clip takes place!

Do this now by using the Translation widget to position the markers around the corner column you selected earlier (see **FIGURE 4.55**).

8. Now that you have the markers positioned, it's time to chop through the column. In the Settings area of the Modifier window, check bSplit. This prevents part of the column from being deleted.

When finished, click Apply to create the split. The column is now in two separate pieces.

9. Use the Move and Rotate widgets to reposition the upper piece to look as if it broke off and fell away. Click the Build All button 🔧 when finished (see **FIGURE 4.56**).

10. Feel free to clip other parts of the geometry as well. See if you can make a destroyed temple! Rebuild and save your level when finished.

> **TIP**
>
> You can clip multiple objects with the same clipping plane simply by selecting those objects before clicking the Apply button!

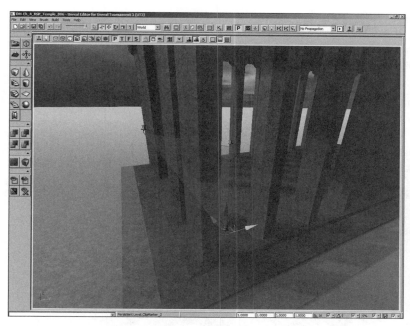

FIGURE 4.55   The clipping markers now surround the column.

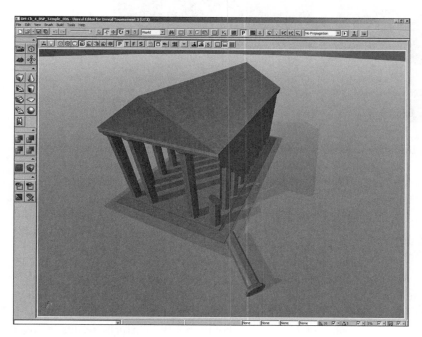

FIGURE 4.56   The upper portion of the column was moved to look broken.

END OF TUTORIAL 4.7

Working with Shadows

Up to this point, we have focused primarily on ways that you can create and edit BSP brushes in your level. Another important factor that contributes to the look of your levels is how shadows are cast on your BSP. Granted, most of your levels will likely have your BSP covered completely in static meshes, but it may be handy to know how shadows are mapped onto BSP and how you can change the clarity of your shadows (see **FIGURE 4.57**).

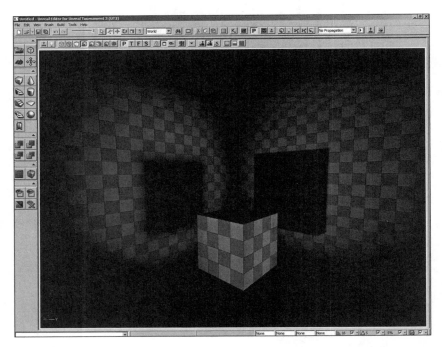

FIGURE 4.57   On the left, you see low-quality shadows, with high-quality shadows on the right.

Changing this is done very easily from within the Surface Properties window. Simply select a surface, and change its Lightmap Resolution to a lower property. Unlike setting the map resolution for static meshes (covered in Chapter 5, "Static Meshes"), a *lower* value results in a crisper shadow. This is because the number assigned to Lightmap Resolution pertains to the size of the pixels used to calculate the shadows.

Although this does mean that a smaller number tightens up your shadows, care must be taken because this also results in a larger calculation in your game, and the need for more memory usage. The smaller the pixels of your shadows, the more pixels are needed to make your shadows completely solid. Therefore, lowering the Lightmap Resolution setting actually results in *larger* lightmap textures with a sharper shadow result. The trick is to use this technique only when necessary, lest you notice a performance hit in your levels and increased building times. Also, keep in mind that in many modern levels, BSP may not often be visible, because they are often hidden behind static meshes. Setting your Lightmap Resolution to a very high setting (resulting in a lower-quality shadow map) may help speed up build times and save memory!

In the preceding tutorials, you created a simple ancient Greek temple. You might have noticed that the shadows appearing from the columns are not very clear. In **TUTORIAL 4.8**, we remedy this and take a look at the Surface Properties window's Lighting group.

Please continue from **TUTORIAL 4.7**, or open the DM-Ch_4_BSP_Temple_07.ut3 map included with the files for this chapter. In order for our lighting to appear realistic, we need greater control over the look of our shadows. In **TUTORIAL 4.8**, we adjust the shadow settings of our temple's floor to get nice cast shadows from the columns.

TUTORIAL 4.8: Controlling Shadows on BSP Surfaces

1. You notice that the columns are not casting clear shadows onto the floor of the temple. Select the surface of the temple's floor, and from the main menu, choose View > Surface Properties (see **FIGURE 4.58**).

2. In the lighting group, you see the Lightmap Resolution setting. By default, this is set to 32. Set it down to 2.0, and build your level (see **FIGURE 4.59**).

3. You'll notice that it takes longer to rebuild, and that the shadows on the floor of the temple are much clearer. Set the Lightmap Resolution value all the way up to 1024 and build to see the results (see **FIGURE 4.60**).

   What happens is that the shadows are now being calculated in pixels that are stretched to 1024 Unreal units in size. This means that fewer pixels are needed to cover the area, but that the shadows have far less definition as a result!

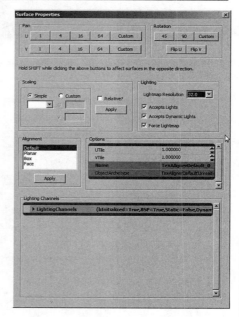

FIGURE 4.58 We focus on the Lighting group of the Surface Properties window.

4

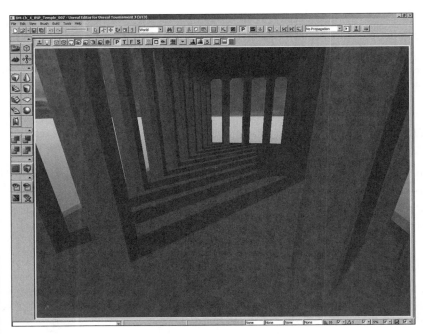

FIGURE 4.59   The temple floor now has very crisp shadows.

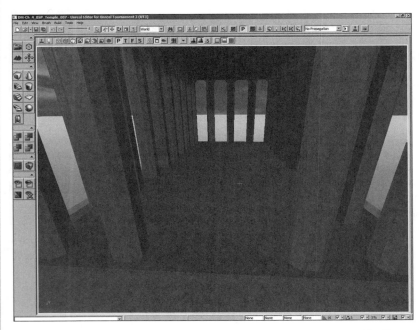

FIGURE 4.60   With a very high Lightmap Resolution, you see practically no shadows at all.

4. Finally, set your Lightmap Resolution to 4, click Build All 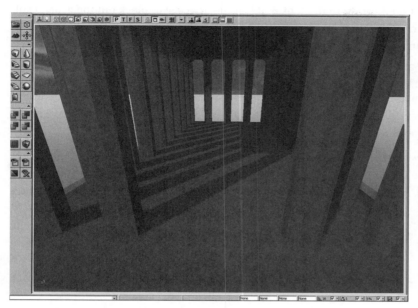, and save your level (see **FIGURE 4.61**).

FIGURE 4.61   A value of 4 gives you fairly crisp shadows.

END OF TUTORIAL 4.8

Summary

This chapter has introduced you to several concepts and techniques pertaining to the use of BSP brushes as you design your levels. Although good use of BSP is going to be important as you design your own environments, it is also important that you remember that in most modern Unreal Engine 3 games (such as Unreal Tournament 3 and Gears of War), the role of BSP has been significantly diminished from what it was in previous versions of the Unreal Engine. With the advancing technology of video cards and the tremendous increase in their on-board memory and processing power, well-built static meshes can serve as a far more efficient means to create most of the surfaces with which the players can interact.

However, this is not to say that you won't be using BSP brushes or the knowledge contained in this chapter. Indeed, you might find that you'll often be constructing BSP frameworks to proto-type out levels early on, before sitting down and working on static mesh layouts. Also, you can use

BSP brushes to create invisible collision surfaces (known as Blocking Volumes) that can be used as simple sources of collision around complex surfaces.

In most cases, you'll find it easiest to think of BSP brushes as a way to block out the general volume of your level, knowing that you will often completely cover up that BSP with static meshes later on. There is some debate, because of this, as to whether BSP is even necessary in additive levels. However, Epic—as an example—often used at least a BSP base on the ground to help with the calculation of dynamic collisions in levels for Gears of War, sort of like a catch-all if something goes awry. You'll also find BSP brushes in levels of Unreal Tournament 3 wherever a designer needed a very simple object that used only a basic material, and there was no need to trouble an artist to generate a model, UVs, a texture, and so on.

Our advice is simply to leave your BSP construction to the minimal arrangement of your level's general space and volume, and to let static meshes take care of anything that's not there just to define a certain area. However, don't be afraid to make use of simple BSP brushes here and there if you need them!

4

Chapter 5

Static Meshes

Play a game built with the Unreal Engine, and one thing jumps right out at you: the amazingly rich visual detail. Static meshes make that rich visual detail possible. You don't create these polygon models within Unreal Engine: You do that in exterior applications such as 3ds Max, Maya, and Photoshop. In this chapter, we show you exactly how static meshes work, how to create them, and how to import them into your levels.

The Importance of Static Meshes

Static meshes are drawn by the computer's graphics card, allowing them to be rendered much more quickly than BSP brushes (see **FIGURE 5.1**). Because they never change position, they can be cached to video memory. This means that multiple copies of a single static mesh can be placed throughout a level with very little overhead on your machine—how many copies depends on the amount of memory in your video card.

FIGURE 5.1   In this image, nearly every visible surface is a static mesh.

In many of the game levels produced by Epic, nearly every visible surface of a level is a static mesh. Remember when designing your levels that BSP surfaces tend to be flat and drab, whereas static meshes can easily add copious amounts of visual depth.

Static Mesh Workflow Overview

The creation of static meshes can take place in a number of ways. For our purposes, we're going to narrow it down into two primary workflows. Both of these workflows can be described in the flow chart shown in **FIGURE 5.2**.

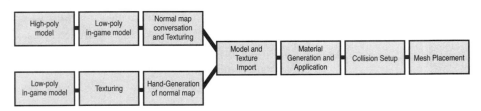

FIGURE 5.2   This flow chart describes two popular methods of static mesh design.

The first workflow involves the creation of static meshes in the form of a high-resolution, or high polygon, mesh, which is later used to produce a normal map. This technique enables the modeler to create tremendous detail at the physical level. Once this high-resolution mesh is completed, a lower-resolution model is created. This low-resolution mesh is what is actually displayed in-game, but using the normals generated from the high-res version.

The second workflow requires only a low-resolution mesh. Instead of modeling a high-rez mesh to create normals, a normal map is generated inside Photoshop from a grayscale bump map using a free plug-in from nVidia. Free plug-ins to convert height maps into normal maps also exist for PaintShop Pro and GIMP, and can be found quickly with an Internet search. If your static mesh is fairly simple, you may find that this method can save you considerable time over having to create high-resolution geometry for every single mesh in your level.

In both workflows, the next steps are similar. You create a layout of the UV texture coordinates for the object, and then use the layout to paint a series of textures in Photoshop. In some cases, these textures are pulled back into a 3D application where some form of lighting can actually be baked into the texture itself. This causes the texture to appear to be shadowing itself, such as when two plates of armor overlap. Also, if you are using the high-resolution mesh workflow, this is where you would generate the normal map, typically by using features in a 3D application, such as 3ds Max, Maya, or ZBrush.

From there, the mesh is imported into Unreal Editor, and a material is generated for the mesh using the textures that have been created. Once this is done, a collision hull is established for the object, allowing other actors to collide with the mesh. Sometimes, especially if an object is going to be unreachable by a player, a collision surface for your mesh is not needed.

Finally, your new static mesh is ready to be placed into your level. Over the next several tutorials, you are shown how to create a simple static mesh using 3ds Max and Photoshop. For purposes of simplicity, because this is not a 3ds Max training book, we use the low-resolution method, in which we would create our normal maps inside of a 2D image editor later.

Over the next several tutorials, we create a simple archway mesh in 3ds Max. To begin, we create a box, from which we model the final shape.

> **NOTE**
>
> To follow most of the tutorials in this chapter, you need to have 3ds Max installed on your machine. If you do not own 3ds Max, you may download a free 30-day trial version of it at www.autodesk.com! These tutorials use 3ds Max 2008, although just about any version since 3ds Max 7 or so should work fine. Also keep in mind that these tutorials assume a very basic knowledge of the 3ds Max user interface and navigation (see **FIGURE 5.3**).

> **TIP**
>
> If you are completely new to 3ds Max, it would be a very good idea to watch the Essential Skills Movies that are included with the installation of the free 30-day trial version of 3ds Max. A screen showing these movies appears the first time you launch 3ds Max.

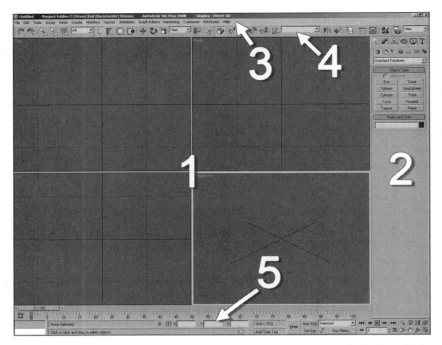

FIGURE 5.3   1) Viewports; 2) Command Panel; 3) Menu Bar; 4) Toolbar; 5) Coordinate Entry Area

TUTORIAL 5.1: 3ds Max: Modeling a Simple Static Mesh, Part I: Creating an Editable Poly

1. Launch 3ds Max.

2. From the Command Panel at the right of the screen, click the Box button (see **FIGURE 5.4**).

3. Expand the Keyboard Entry rollout, and input the following dimensions (see **FIGURE 5.5**):

   Length: 256

   Width: 16

   Height: 256

   Click the Create button when finished.

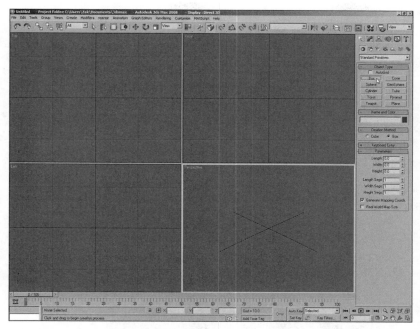

FIGURE 5.4   The Box button is located in the Create Panel of the main Command Panel.

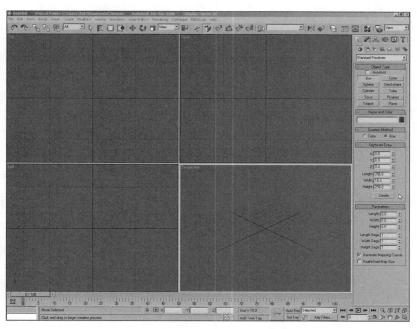

FIGURE 5.5   The Keyboard Entry area should appear like so when you are finished.

4. Right-click in any of the viewports to exit Box creation mode; then press the F4 key to display the box's wireframe on top of the surface (see **FIGURE 5.6**).

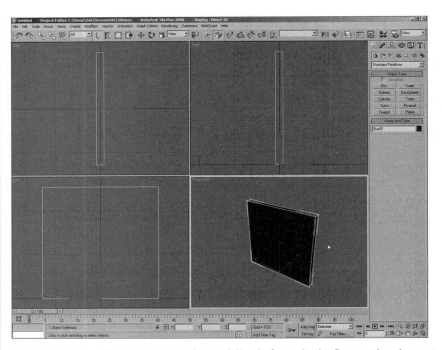

FIGURE 5.6   Here you can see the model's wireframe in the Perspective viewport.

5. With the box selected, right-click it, and from the lower-right portion of the Quad menu, choose Convert To > Convert to Editable Poly (see **FIGURE 5.7**).

6. In the Command Panel, change the name of Box_01 to ArchedDoorway (see **FIGURE 5.8**).

7. Save your scene as archedDoorway_1.max.

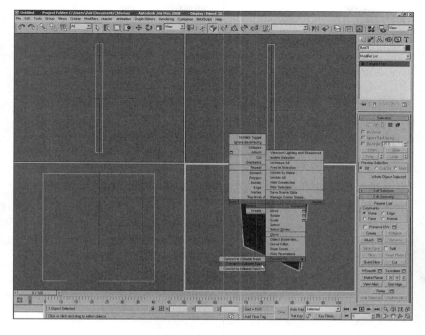

FIGURE 5.7
The Quad menu is available whenever you right-click within one of 3ds Max's viewports.

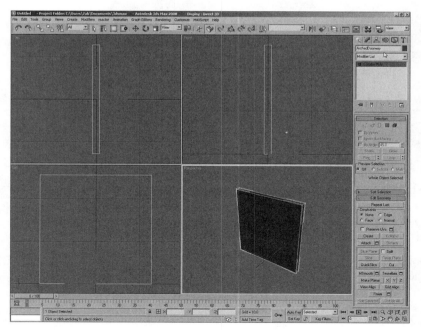

FIGURE 5.8
You will find the name field at the top of the Create Panel.

END TUTORIAL 5.1

Please continue from **TUTORIAL 5.1**, or launch 3ds Max and open the Chapter_05_ ArchedDoorway_01.max file included with the files for this chapter. Now that our box is created, we can start adding in the edges that form the shape of our archway.

TUTORIAL 5.2: 3ds Max: Modeling a Simple Static Mesh, Part II: Creating the Basic Shape

1. With the editable poly object (the box) selected, click on the Modify Panel, located within the Command Panel (see **FIGURE 5.9**). Expand the Editable Poly sub-object list in the Stack, and choose Polygons.

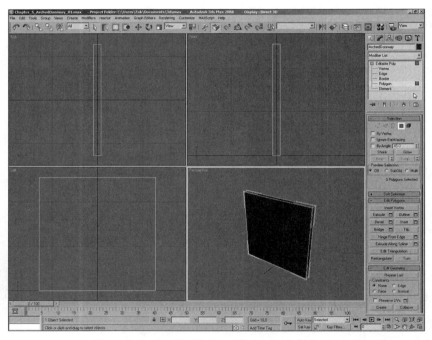

FIGURE 5.9   The tab for the Modify Panel is located at the top of the Command Panel.

2. Select the large polygonal faces on both sides of the box. It may help to marquee-select them from the Left viewport.

3. In the Edit Polygons rollout in the Command Panel, click the Settings button next to the Inset button. Set the Inset Amount to 32 and click OK (see **FIGURE 5.10**).

> **TIP**
>
> As a shortcut, you can press the 4 key while the object is selected!

FIGURE 5.10 Use an Inset value of 32 to create an inset copy of both of the faces.

4. Select the two large polygons that were just inset. Then, while holding the Ctrl key, also select the three polygons that wrap around the underside of the box shape. The easiest way to do this is to hold the Ctrl key while dragging a marquee in the Left viewport around all of the polygons that make up the center and bottom of the shape (see **FIGURE 5.11**).

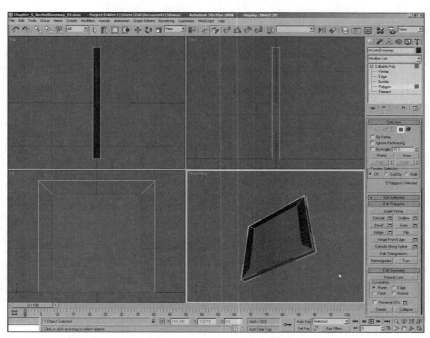

FIGURE 5.11 Your final selection should look similar to those. Note that the selection includes faces on both the front and the back.

Once all five polygons are selected, press the Delete key to remove them.

5. In the Stack, select Vertices (or press the 1 key). In the Left viewport, marquee-select the four vertices near the bottom of the shape, as shown (see **FIGURE 5.12**).

NOTE

Because the Left view has no depth, the four vertices appear as only two!

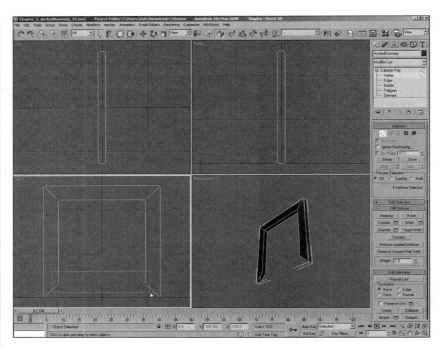

FIGURE 5.12   You need to select these vertices to adjust the shape of the frame.

6. Press W to select the Move tool. In the Coordinate Inputs at the bottom of the UI, you see that the Z value of these vertices is currently 32. Type in a value of 0 and press Enter. The vertices should fall to the grid (see **FIGURE 5.13**).

7. Press the 2 key to make Edges selectable. In the Left viewport, individually marquee-select each of the five edges surrounding the deleted polygons, as shown in **FIGURE 5.14**. Marquee-selecting causes you to select edges on the front and back of the object simultaneously, meaning that although it looks like only five edges from the Left viewport, you're actually selecting 10!

> **TIP**
>
> Rather than having to type a 0, you could simply right-click the spinner next to the coordinate value. The spinner is the small pair of arrows right next to the input field.

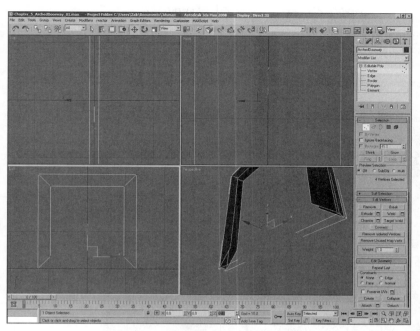

FIGURE 5.13 The coordinate fields are located just beneath the viewports and enable you to change the position, rotation, and scale of objects numerically.

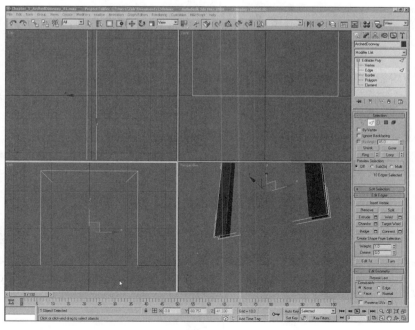

FIGURE 5.14 You need the following edges selected for the next step.

8. With the edges selected, click the Bridge button, located in the Edit Edges rollout of the Command Panel. This closes in the surface, creating an inverted U-shape. When finished, press the 6 key to exit Sub-Object mode (see **FIGURE 5.15**).

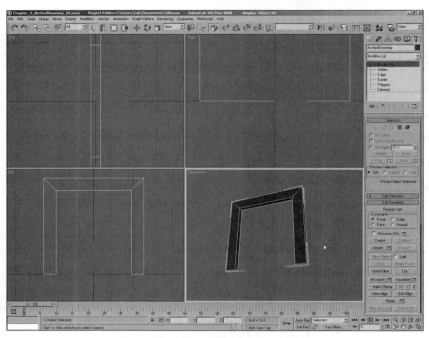

FIGURE 5.15   Your final object should look like this.

9. Save your scene as archDoorway_2.max.

END TUTORIAL 5.2

Please continue from **TUTORIAL 5.2**, or launch 3ds Max and open the Chapter_05_ArchedDoorway_02.max file included with the files for this chapter. In **TUTORIAL 5.3**, we wrap up the final shape of our model.

TUTORIAL 5.3: 3ds Max: Modeling a Simple Static Mesh, Part III: Finalizing Our Simple Model

1. With the object selected, press the 2 key to make Edges selectable; then select the two edges in the inner corners of the archway (see **FIGURE 5.16**). You need to hold Ctrl to select them both.

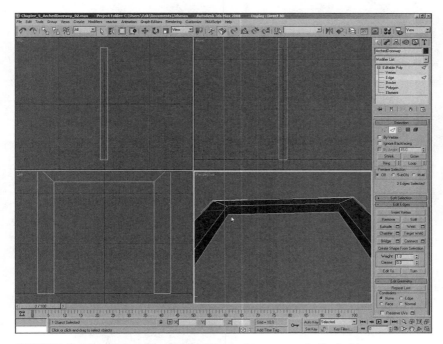

FIGURE 5.16   Select the edges of the inside corners, indicated here.

2. In the Edit Edges rollout, click the Settings button next to the chamfer. Set the amount to 48 and click OK (see **FIGURE 5.17**).

3. Press 1 to make Vertices selectable. In the Left viewport, marquee-select the vertices across the very top of the arch, and in the Edit Vertices rollout, click the Settings button next to Weld. Set the value to 0.1 (if necessary) and click OK (see **FIGURE 5.18**).

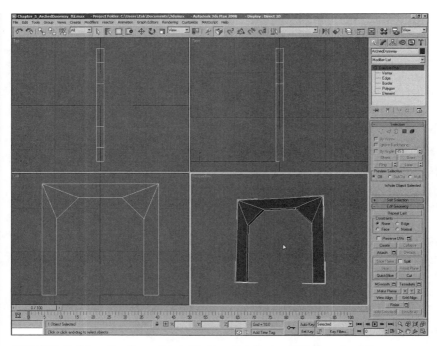

FIGURE 5.17   Use the settings for the chamfer to create bevels at the corners.

4. In the Edit Geometry rollout, click the Slice Plane button; this brings up the Slice Plane gizmo (see **FIGURE 5.19**).

5. Make a pair of slices using the following steps:

    a. Click the Reset Plane button located in the Command Panel.

    b. Activate the Move tool (W key), and in the Coordinate Entry area, set the Z value to 96.

FIGURE 5.18   Welding these vertices prevents shading issues later in Unreal.

    c. Click the Slice button located in the Command Panel.

    d. Back in the Coordinate Entry area, set the Z value to 72.

    e. Click the Slice button again to create a new slice.

    f. Click the Slice Plane button again to deactivate it (see **FIGURE 5.20**).

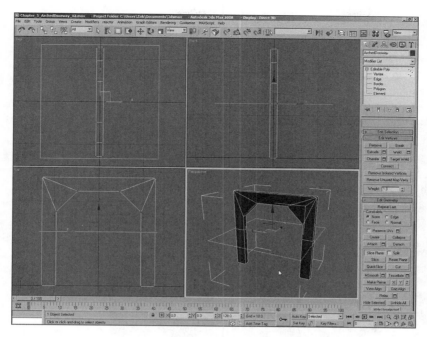

FIGURE 5.19   The Slice Plane gizmo appears as an outline of a plane in the viewport.

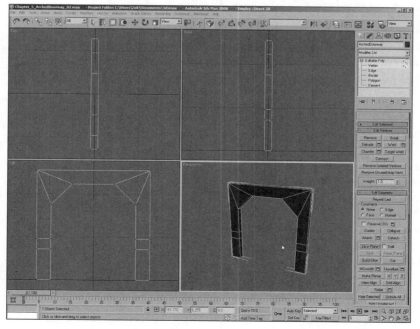

FIGURE 5.20   When finished, your arch's legs should have two new edges in them.

6. With the Move tool still activated, set your Transform Coordinate Center to Use Selection Center.

7. Press 4 to make Polygons selectable. Select the two faces on the bottom front of the arch shape, as shown in **FIGURE 5.21**. In the Coordinate Entry area, set their X value to 32. Repeat for the opposite side, setting the value to -32 instead.

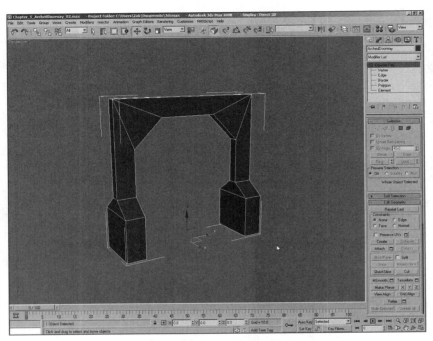

FIGURE 5.21   When finished, your new shape should appear like so.

8. Our last step is to adjust our surface normals so that the corners of our object are creased, and to avoid shading issues later. Press the 5 key to make Elements selectable, and click the model. This selects all the faces of the model.

In the Polygon: Smoothing Groups rollout, set the value next to Auto Smooth to 25, and then click the Auto Smooth button (see **FIGURE 5.22**). The result is that all of our model's edges are hard, or sharp, instead of soft, which helps prevent shading problems in Unreal.

> **NOTE**
>
> Depending on which side you select first, you may have to use the opposite of the preceding values.

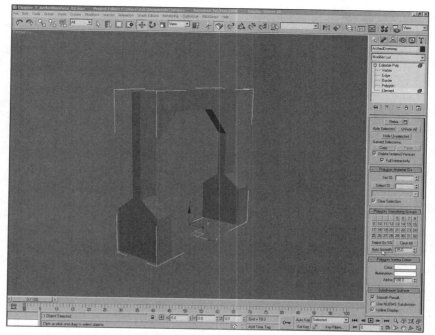

FIGURE 5.22   The Auto Smooth button enables you to adjust the smoothing groups of the model based on a particular angle.

9. Press 6 to exit Sub-Object mode. Save your scene as archedDoorway_3.max.

END TUTORIAL 5.3

UV Texture Coordinates

Once your object has been modeled, you need to create a series of textures for it. These textures eventually plug into the various material channels of the mesh's material.

Before you can create textures, however, you need to create a layout for the model's UV texture coordinates. Consider the idea of printing colors onto a world globe using your computer's printer. Naturally, a globe won't fit into your printer's paper feed. What you need to do is create a flattened version of the globe, and then place it across the surface of the sphere later. Laying out UV texture coordinates uses the same principle.

A model's UVs enable you to determine exactly how the texture is placed across the surface. In a sense, you break up your model into pieces, place those pieces into a flattened layout, and then use that layout to paint a texture. Fortunately, because a model's UVs are different from their actual 3D vertices, you do not have to make any changes to the model's actual 3D geometry to accomplish this.

In **TUTORIAL 5.4**, we create a simple UV layout for our model, which could later be used in a 2D image editor as a pattern to paint a texture. However, rather than going deep into the world of game texturing, a subject worthy of its own book series, we are simply going to show you how to create and render out your own UV layout, and then provide you with a completed texture on a finished version of the model.

Please continue from **TUTORIAL 5.3**, or launch 3ds Max and open the Chapter_05_ ArchedDoorway_03.max file included with the files for this chapter. Now that our archway has been modeled, we need to lay out its texture coordinates for painting in an image editing application, such as Adobe Photoshop.

TUTORIAL 5.4: 3ds Max: Creating a Simple UV Layout

1. Select the ArchedDoorway object. Make sure you are not in sub-object mode (nothing in the stack should be highlighted in yellow). In the Command Panel, select the Modify Panel, and click on the Modifier List, located just below the object's name.

   Press the U key once to select the UnwrapUVW modifier; then press Enter (see **FIGURE 5.23**).

2. Once the modifier is applied, click the Edit… button located in the Parameters rollout in the Command Panel. This brings up the Edit UVWs window (see **FIGURE 5.24**).

3. Rather than show you how to create a layout piece by piece, we're going to show you a simple method that enables you to create a basic layout automatically. This layout can then be used as a basis from which you can customize how you'd like each face to be placed.

> **NOTE**
>
> Although **TUTORIAL 5.4** does cover enough information for a beginner to create a simple UV layout, some knowledge of 3ds Max helps considerably!

> **NOTE**
>
> In 3ds Max, UV coordinates actually contain a third dimension, designated W. However, for our purposes, we do not need this third dimension, so we refer to texture coordinates simply as UVs.

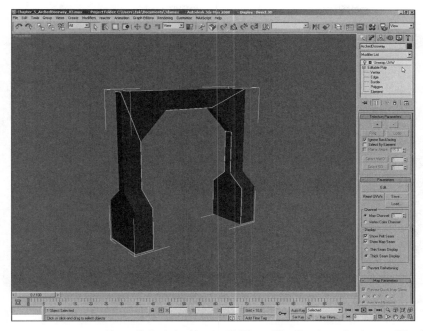

FIGURE 5.23   You will find the UnwrapUVW modifier far down in the modifier list.

In the Selection Mode area, located near the bottom of the Edit UVWs window, make sure the Faces button is pressed. Then, drag a marquee-selection box around all the faces in the window (they appear to be a tangled mess). Alternatively, you could press Ctrl-A (see **FIGURE 5.25**).

4. From the Edit UVWs toolbar, select Mapping > Flatten Mapping. This brings up the Flatten Mapping dialog (see **FIGURE 5.26**).

Set the Face Angle Threshold value to 60, and click OK.

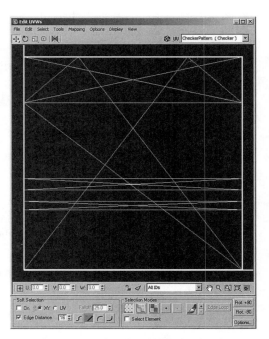

FIGURE 5.24   The Edit UVWs window is where you create your UV layouts for your models.

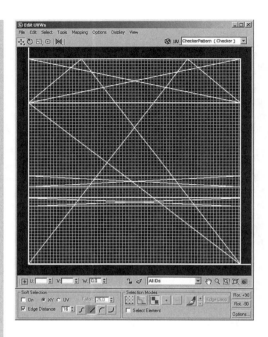

FIGURE 5.25   Once selected, the faces appear to be a massive overlapping jumble of polygons.

5. In the Selection Mode area, check the Select Element checkbox. This enables you to select an entire piece of the layout with a single click, rather than selecting a single face (see **FIGURE 5.27**).

Take a few moments to select various pieces in the Edit UVWs window, and see how they coincide with selections in the Perspective viewport. You can use this to help you see exactly what it is you have selected.

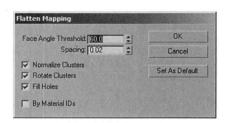

FIGURE 5.26   The Flatten Mapping operation creates a basic layout that we can then edit to suit our needs.

6. In the upper-right corner of the Edit UVWs window, you'll see some icons for Move, Rotate, and Scale. You can use these to position each one of the pieces however you like. To place them as we did to create our textures, follow these steps:

   a. Select the uppermost of the two archways in the Edit UVWs window. Select the Move tool and drag it on top of the first (see **FIGURE 5.28**).

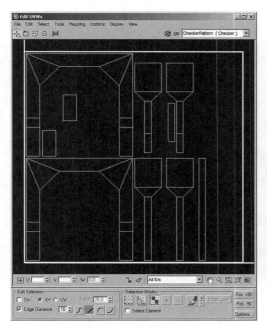

FIGURE 5.27 When finished, you should get a layout similar to this (grid hidden for clarity).

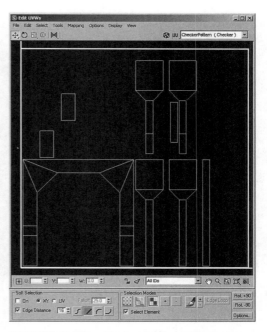

FIGURE 5.28 The two archway pieces have been stacked together, which places the same texture on both sides of the mesh.

b. Locate the two shapes that form the insides of the legs, and stack them on top of one another as precisely as possible (see **FIGURE 5.29**). Then, marquee-select both pieces selected and click the Rot +90 button twice to turn them right-side up.

c. When finished, with both pieces selected, place them both underneath the archway, as shown in **FIGURE 5.30**. Take care to leave a small gap between these pieces and the archway!

> **TIP**
>
> You can zoom the Edit UVWs window with the mouse wheel, or by holding Ctrl + Alt and left-dragging. Zoom in very close to verify that the two archways are placed exactly on top of one another. This means that whatever texture is painted on one side is automatically placed on the other!

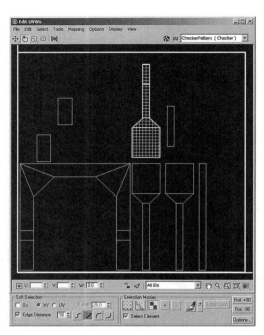

FIGURE 5.29   The inside faces of the leg have now been stacked together.

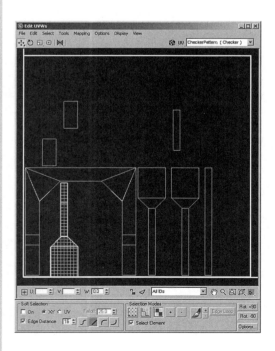

FIGURE 5.30   Place the pieces underneath the archway.

d. Locate the two shapes that form the outside of the legs and stack them in a similar manner, rotate them 180 degrees, and place them just to the right of the archway, as shown in **FIGURE 5.31**.

e. Find the two pieces that make up the bottom of the feet. Stack them as precisely as possible, and position them somewhere inside the arch (see **FIGURE 5.32**).

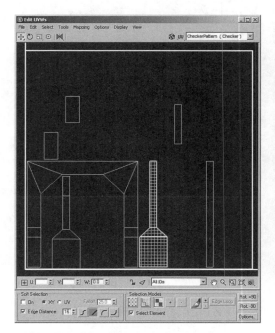

FIGURE 5.31   The stacked outer pieces should be placed right next to the archway.

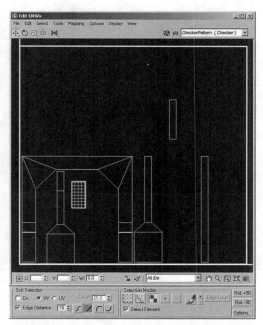

FIGURE 5.32   The bottom of the feet can be placed anywhere under the archway.

f. Locate the underside of the crossbeam, and place it inside the arch (see **FIGURE 5.33**).

g. Locate the top of the crossbeam, rotate it 90 degrees, and place it above the arch (see **FIGURE 5.34**).

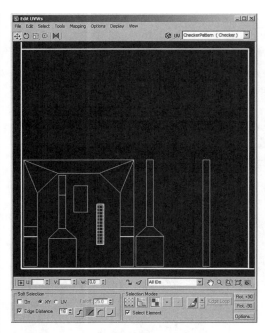

FIGURE 5.33 Place the underside of the crossbeam somewhere underneath the arch.

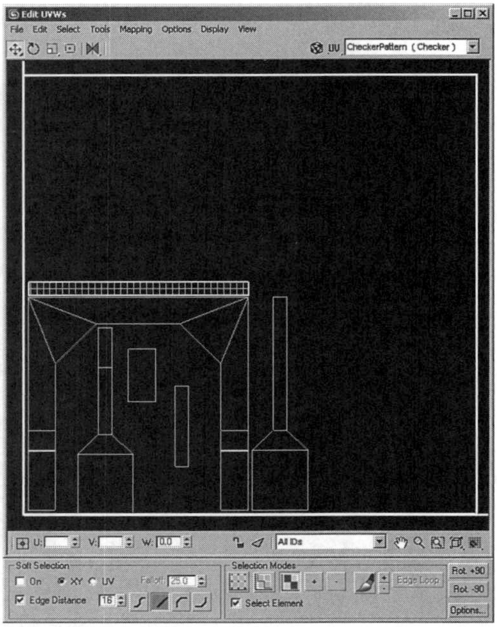

FIGURE 5.34 The top part of the crossbeam should go above the archway.

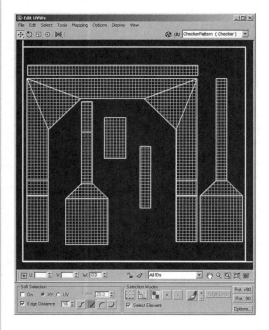

FIGURE 5.35 Make sure the final layout fits completely into the square!

h. Finally, select all your pieces and use the Scale tool to scale them up to fill as much of the texture space (the thick dark blue square) as possible. Your final layout should look something like **FIGURE 5.35**.

7. Close the Edit UVWs window and save your scene.

END TUTORIAL 5.4

Considerations When Creating UV Layouts

When laying out the UVs for an object, there are some things you should always keep in mind. Although this book is not intended to make you a professional texture artist, there are some simple guidelines that you can use to keep your layouts nice and efficient, as follows:

1. Make sure all of your pieces fit within the placement square, which means between the UV coordinates (0,0) and (1,1). Do not let them extend past the boundaries of the square!

2. Try to keep the polygon faces of your layout relative to one another in size.

3. Try to maintain the aspect ratio of a polygon when creating its layout; this helps you avoid texture stretching.

4. If you want to reuse parts of a texture in multiple areas, consider stacking the UVs for those different areas on top of one another.

5. Weld vertices of UV layouts when possible to help avoid seams.

6. Don't waste space in the layout! Large open areas result only in wasted texture memory!

7. Don't be afraid to label your layouts so that you know which faces coincide with each part of the model.

8. If you are creating layouts for another artist to use, make sure you communicate with that artist so that you are both clear on how they want to texture the surface.

9. There is no "right" or "wrong" way to create a layout. Create a layout that makes sense to you, or whoever is doing the texturing. As long as you're using as much of the texture space as possible and not distorting your layout too much, then you're doing well.

Please continue from **TUTORIAL 5.4**, or launch 3ds Max and open the Chapter_05_ArchedDoorway_04.max file included with the files for this chapter. Now that we have created our texture layout, we need to export it so that we can paint on it.

TUTORIAL 5.5: 3ds Max: Rendering UV Layouts for Use in Image Editing Software

1. Select the arched doorway model, and in the Modify Panel, locate the UnwrapUVW modifier within the stack. Select it, and then click the Edit... button to open the Edit UVWs window.

2. From the Tools menu of the Edit UVWs window, choose Render UVW Template (see **FIGURE 5.36**).

3. The most important setting in the Render UVs window is the resolution of your texture. For most static meshes, you do not need to go any higher than 2048×2048. However, do keep in mind that because your layout has been created in a square fashion, you always want your aspect ratio to be 1:1; as always with Unreal, make sure you choose a resolution that is a power of 2!

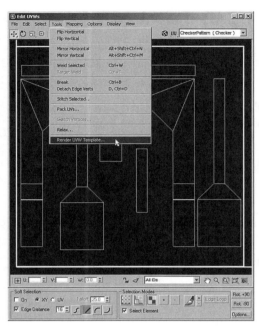

FIGURE 5.36   The RenderUVs window enables you to adjust settings for the type of layout you'd like to render.

4. For our purposes, set the value to 1024×1024, if it is not already.

5. Click the Render Template button (see **FIGURE 5.37**).

6. The Render window appears, from which you can save the template in any format that you like. Once the template is saved, you can open it up in the image-editing software of your choice and paint new texture for your model!

> **NOTE**
>
> If you see that your UV layout render looks incomplete, as if it is missing some edges, you can relax; this is perfectly normal, and is the result of the render being displayed at a ratio other than 1:1.

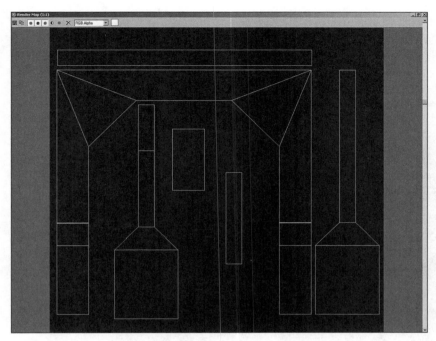

FIGURE 5.37 The new render shows the layout for your UVs.

END TUTORIAL 5.5

Creating Textures

Texturing a static mesh can often take longer than the actual modeling process. Remember that most of the rich detail you see in individual objects is created via materials in Unreal. Therefore, to power those materials, you need a series of detailed textures in place. Once you have created a UV layout, you are ready to take that layout into Photoshop (or any other 2D paint application) and create your texture, using the layout as a pattern.

You must keep in mind, however, the great number of possibilities that materials allow. Do you want some parts of the object to glow? Are some areas shinier than others? Does the texture animate in some way? You need to answer these questions and more before you can determine exactly what it is your material, and therefore your textures, need to accomplish. Hopefully, you already have a good idea of the final look before you even begin modeling. Even so, a good plan is to have some sketches or notes on hand during texture creation to help keep you on track.

In the case of the model we created earlier in this chapter, we want the final look to have a weathered metallic appearance, with some steel rivets holding it together and a couple of glowing edges for good measure. The archway should be fairly shiny in some areas, but not at all in others (see **FIGURE 5.38**).

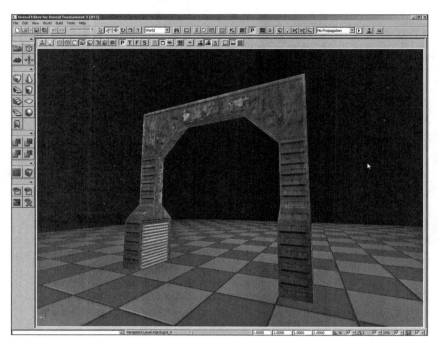

FIGURE 5.38   The final texture that we came up with has a weathered sci-fi look.

To accomplish all of these effects, we need multiple maps for our material—one that gives the overall color, another that handles what areas are emissive, one to affect shininess, and so on. Still, there may be other maps whose only job is to mask out an area of effect. In the end, you might find yourself creating many different textures to be applied to the same mesh, so knowledge of a good 2D texturing package is useful.

At the same time, this book is not going to try to compete against the vast quantities of great Photoshop resources out there. Instead, we're going to show you the textures we came up with, and provide them to you on the DVD so that you may peruse them yourself (see **FIGURE 5.39**).

Using these textures, along with the skills picked up in Chapter 6, "Introduction to Materials," we created a material for our archway. The material can be found in the ImportingStaticMeshes package located on the DVD in the files for this chapter.

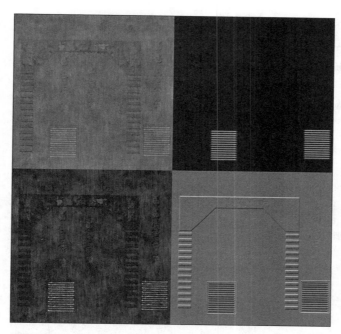

FIGURE 5.39   Clockwise from the upper left are the textures used for Diffuse, Emissive, Specular, and Normal.

Importing Static Meshes

Once your model and textures are complete, it's finally time to put everything together inside Unreal Editor. This requires the import of your static mesh and all your textures, the creation and application of your material, and the addition of a collision model, provided that one is needed. Here, we are going to focus on getting the model from 3ds Max into Unreal Editor.

The first step is to get the model out of 3ds Max in a format that can be read by Unreal Editor. There are a few formats that we could use, though for simplicity, we're going to use the ASCII Scene Export (ASE) format, which is included with 3ds Max.

Please continue from **TUTORIAL 5.5**, or launch 3ds Max and open the Chapter_05_ArchedDoorway_05.max file included with the files for this chapter. In **TUTORIAL 5.6**, we take our model from 3ds Max into Unreal Editor.

TUTORIAL 5.6: 3ds Max: Exporting a Mesh from 3ds Max Using the ASCII Scene Export (ASE) Format and Importing into Unreal Editor

1. We begin by finalizing our model. This simply entails collapsing the stack so that we do not lose the UV data we set up previously.

   Select the model, and in the Modify Panel, right-click on the UnwrapUVW modifier and choose Collapse All. You get a warning box, but you can disregard it by clicking Yes (see **FIGURE 5.40**).

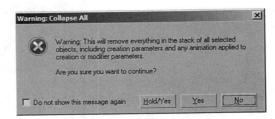

2. Select the mesh, and from the File menu, choose Export Selected. In the dialog that appears, set the file format to ASCII Scene Export (ASE) and set the name to ArchedDoorway. Make sure to save the file in a place where you can easily find it later!

   When you click OK, you see the ASCII Export window appear. Make sure the following are checked when creating static meshes (see **FIGURE 5.41**):

   Mesh Definition

   Materials

   Mesh Normals

   Mapping Coordinates

   Geometric

FIGURE 5.40 You always receive such a warning when collapsing an object's stack.

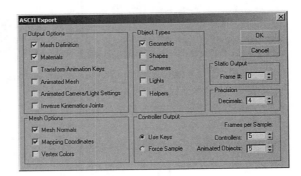

FIGURE 5.41 Check the boxes shown here to export your model.

For our purposes, no other check boxes need to be checked and no other settings need to be adjusted.

3. Save your scene and close 3ds Max.

   Now that the mesh has been properly exported from 3ds Max, we can bring it into Unreal Editor and continue our workflow. Because the ASE format has been natively supported by Unreal Editor since the beginning, importing a static mesh in this format is extremely simple.

4. Launch Unreal Editor and, if necessary, open the Generic browser.

5. From the Generic browser's File menu, choose Import. Navigate to the ASE file you saved for your ArchedDoorway and click OK. In the Import dialog that appears, set the following:

Package: MyStaticMesh

Group: Meshes

Name: sm_archedDoorway

You get a warning message indicating that your object has no material reference and that the default material will be applied. At this time, this is acceptable.

6. In the Generic browser, locate the new MyStaticMesh package and save it (see **FIGURE 5.42**).

> **NOTE**
>
> Keep in mind that the origin of the scene (coordinate location 0,0,0) is used as the pivot once our mesh is taken into Unreal. In this case, the pivot is located in the center at ground level, which is perfect for our purposes.

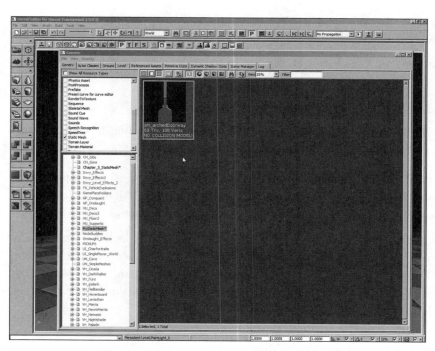

FIGURE 5.42 Your model now appears in the new package of the Generic browser.

END TUTORIAL 5.6

Using the Static Mesh Editor

The Static Mesh Editor is the primary tool for setting up a static mesh for use in your levels. With it, you can change a static mesh's global material, set up its collisions, and adjust its properties. Its interface is fairly simple, providing you with a preview of the mesh itself, as well as a few tools and list of properties (see **FIGURE 5.43**).

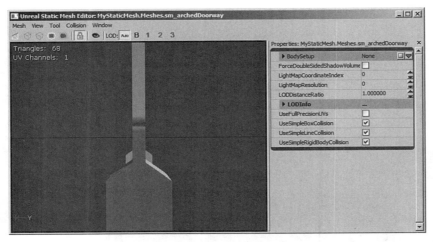

FIGURE 5.43   The Static Mesh Editor has a very simple user interface, allowing for quick changes in mesh settings.

The most important use of the Static Mesh Editor is to provide you with the final setup you need before your new static mesh is ready for placement in your level. In **TUTORIAL 5.7**, we take a look at how we can use it to adjust our preview snapshot and to get our new material applied.

Launch Unreal Editor and open the Chapter_05_StaticMesh.upk package included with the files for this chapter. For **TUTORIAL 5.7**, we are going to use the assets included with the book. You can use the skills learned in this tutorial and apply them to your own mesh later. Now that our static mesh is inside Unreal Editor, there are some settings we need to establish for it; we do so using the Static Mesh Editor.

TUTORIAL 5.7: Using the Static Mesh Editor

1. In the Generic browser, locate the sm_archedDoorway_01 static mesh, and double-click it. This opens the Static Mesh browser.

2. The first thing we need to do is set up our material. Placing a material on a static mesh within the Static Mesh Editor applies that material to every copy of the mesh that is

placed in your level. If you need to change the material on a specific mesh only, you need to change the properties for that individual mesh, which we explore later in **TUTORIAL 5.11**.

In the Static Mesh Editor, expand LOD > [0] > Elements >[0], and click on the Material property. Use the Generic browser to locate and select the mat_archedDoorway_plain material, and click the Use Selection in Browser button ⏏ to apply it (see **FIGURE 5.44**).

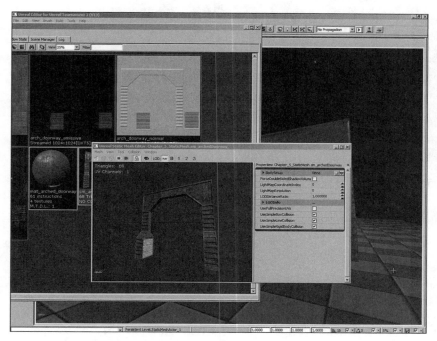

FIGURE 5.44 Once you place the material into the Material property, it appears on the mesh.

3. Now that the material is applied, the last thing we do is set up a new snapshot for the static mesh in the Generic browser. Drag the left and right mouse buttons to position the archway in the preview window in an interesting angle. When finished, click the Save Thumbnail Angle button ▣ (see **FIGURE 5.45**).

4. Save your package.

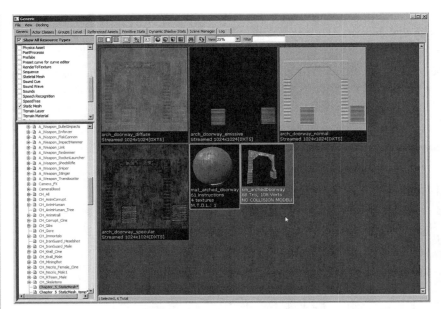

FIGURE 5.45   The new thumbnail appears on the object in the Generic browser.

END TUTORIAL 5.7

Collisions

Currently in the Generic browser, our mesh has a warning stating that there is no collision model. This means that currently, players and other actors can pass through it as if it had no physical substance. For some meshes, especially distantly placed decorations, this may be acceptable. However, in many cases, you will want some sort of collision to take place when actors come into contact with your mesh.

To create this collision, you need to establish a collision model for your object. A *collision model* is a simple polygonal mesh that is invisible to the player, and acts sort of like a "force field" to prevent actors from passing through the static mesh. In most cases, it surrounds the outside of the static mesh, although it will be very close to the surface. Fortunately, Unreal Editor makes the process of creating these collision objects extremely simple. However, it helps if you know a few things about the types of collisions you can create, so that you can choose the proper one for your model.

In the Static Mesh Editor, you will find the Collision menu, which contains a list of all the types of collision models that Unreal Editor can generate for your mesh. Most of these collision models contain a DOP value. DOP stands for *discrete oriented polytope* and refers to how many planes are used to create the collision object. For example, a 6-DOP collision object is created from six planes, creating a simple bounding box. 10-DOP objects are boxes in which all the edges along a particular axis (the Z-axis, for example) have been beveled. 18-DOP objects are boxes in which all the edges have been beveled, and 26-DOPs are cubes in which all edges and vertices have been beveled.

However, you will notice that all the DOP-based objects in the Collision menu are "simplified" collisions. This means that Unreal Editor uses an algorithm to eliminate extraneous vertices of your collision model, keeping it as simple as possible. Remember, the simpler your collision model, the faster its calculation will be!

Unreal Editor also provides access to a simplified spherical collision model and the Auto Convex Collision option, which enables you to create a collision model out of multiple parts. We discuss the use of this option in **TUTORIAL 5.8**.

Please continue from **TUTORIAL 5.7**, or launch Unreal Editor and open the Chapter_05_ StaticMesh.upk package included with the files for this chapter. In **TUTORIAL 5.8**, we demonstrate the process of creating collision surfaces within the Static Mesh Editor.

TUTORIAL 5.8: Creating Collisions

1. Double-click on the sm_archedDoorway_collision static mesh to open the Static Mesh Editor. Then, click the Show Collision button ⬛ in the Static Mesh Editor's toolbar. Currently no collision appears.

   In the Static Mesh Editor, click on the Collision menu and choose 6DOP simplified collision. You will notice a green box appear around the model, indicating its collision surface. This is the surface that a player or other actor collides with during gameplay (see **FIGURE 5.46**).

   If you don't see the collision mesh, make sure that the Show Collision button 🔲 is still activated.

2. The problem with a simple bounding box collision is that our player cannot walk though it. Even though the model is of an arch, its collision box means that it is calculated as if it were a solid wall. However, before we create a more suitable collision, click on the Collision menu again and choose 10DOP-Z simplified collision. Click Yes on the warning menu that appears.

   Notice that the bounding box model does not change. That is because the simplification algorithm detected that the extra planes of a 10-DOP object were not necessary, and collapsed down the vertices, forming another simple box.

3. Click on the Collision menu again, and this time, choose Auto Convex Collision. The Convex Decomposition window appears, enabling you to change three settings, which control how precise the new collision mesh will be. Remember to keep your collision meshes as simple as possible.

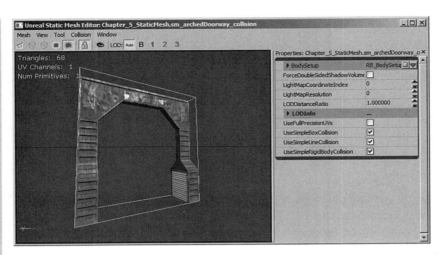

FIGURE 5.46   Once you apply a 6DOP collision, a bounding box appears around the model.

Use the sliders to set the following values:

Depth: 3

Max Hull Verts: 9

Allow Splits: 12

When finished, click Apply and then Close. Notice that the new collision model is made up of several different pieces, which are color-coded from one another. This type of collision surface is perfect for objects that contain open areas, like our archway (see **FIGURE 5.47**).

4. Close the Static Mesh Editor and save your package.

> **TIP**
>
> If you're new to the Auto Convex Collision system, the trick to getting the simplest collisions you can out of the Convex Decomposition window is to start with the sliders at their highest values and click Apply. Then, start sliding them each backward one notch at a time and clicking Apply after each one. As soon as you create a collision that is unacceptable (for instance, if the player can't walk through it anymore), go back up a notch. Do this with each slider in turn!

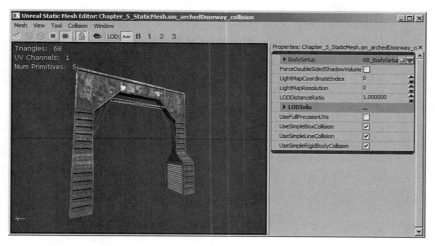

FIGURE 5.47 The new collision model enables the player to walk beneath the archway.

END TUTORIAL 5.8

Creating Custom Collisions

As your skills progress in static mesh creation, you will eventually come to a point where it is a benefit to create your own collision mesh, rather than relying on Unreal to create one for you. This process is fairly simple, although it does require that you know a few things about convexity.

All collision meshes *must* be convex. Simply, this means that a straight line drawn through the shape at any angle should only enter and exit the shape once. See the example in **FIGURE 5.48**.

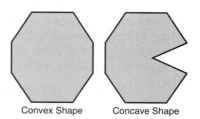

Convex Shape   Concave Shape

FIGURE 5.48 On the left, you can see a convex object; on the right, a concave object.

Collision models must also be named using a special convention. By using this convention, you allow Unreal Editor to automatically detect the presence of the collision model and apply it to your static mesh. The convention is simple: Merely append a special prefix onto the name. The list of prefixes and their uses is as follows:

- ▶ **UBX_:** If using an unedited box as a collision mesh.
- ▶ **USX_ :** If using an unedited sphere as a collision mesh.
- ▶ **UCX_ :** If using a customized convex shape as a collision mesh.

Creating your own custom collisions offers you a great deal of flexibility and power, but you must remember that the key is to keep your meshes as simple as possible. Too many vertices can result in extra processing required for calculating collisions. Fortunately, the archway mesh that we created earlier is so simple that we can use its actual shape to create a collision surface. However,

> **NOTE**
>
> The underscores in the prefixes are necessary in the naming convention. So, if you had created a collision model named "collideBox" out of an unedited box, its name would be UBX_collideBox. Also be aware that by "unedited," we mean that you have not moved or changed any of the vertices, edges, or polygons of the object!

as you may have realized, the archway itself is a concave shape. In **TUTORIAL 5.9**, we take a look at how we can split up the archway into a series of separate meshes that we can use to calculate collision.

Launch 3ds Max and open the Chapter_05_ArchedDoorway_06.max file included with the files for this chapter. In many cases, the best collision for a custom mesh is one created by hand with as few vertices as possible. In **TUTORIAL 5.9**, we demonstrate this process within 3ds Max.

5

TUTORIAL 5.9: 3ds Max: Creating Custom Collision Surfaces from an Existing Model, Part I

1. Select the archway object, and activate the Move tool with the W key. Then, holding Shift, drag a copy of the model away from the original in the Y-axis. In the Clone dialog that appears, make sure the Option group is set to Copy and the number of copies is set to 1; then click OK (see **FIGURE 5.49**).

> **NOTE**
>
> If you performed any custom modeling operations during the creation of the archway, you should open the file included on the DVD rather than using your own model! If you made any changes, these instructions may not work!

2. Select the original model, and right-click on it. From the upper-right quadrant of the Quad menu, choose Freeze Selection. The original model should turn gray, and is now unselectable.

3. Select the duplicated model and, in the Coordinate Entry Fields at the bottom of the UI, set the Y translate value to 0 (as a shortcut, simply right-click the spinner). This places the duplicate right on top of the original (see **FIGURE 5.50**).

4. With the new duplicate selected, press the 1 key to make Vertices selectable. Then, in the Command Panel, under the Edit Geometry rollout, click the Slice Plane button to bring up the Slice Plane gizmo.

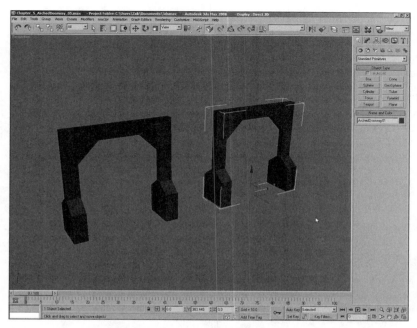

FIGURE 5.49 The object has now been cloned.

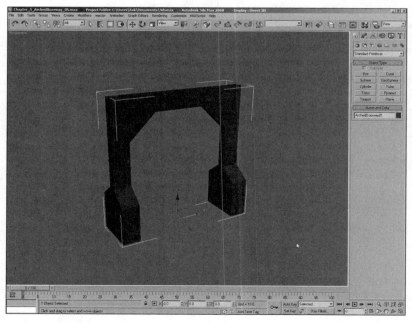

FIGURE 5.50 When both models are on top of one another, it looks like only one arch.

5. We are going to slice the object into several separate convex parts, and then divide those parts into different meshes. To do this, follow these simple steps:

    a. Next to the Slice Plane button in the Command Panel, check the Split checkbox. This causes the Slice Plane to act like a cutting laser, actually dividing the mesh.

    b. Make sure the Move tool is selected, and in the Coordinate Entry Fields, set Z to 96 and click Slice.

    c. Set the Z coordinate value to 176 and click Slice.

    d. Press the E key to activate the Rotate tool, and set the X coordinate value to 90.

    e. Press W to return to the Move tool. Set the Y coordinate to 48 and click Slice.

    f. Set the Y coordinate to -48 and click Slice.

    g. Click the Slice Plane button again to deactivate the Slice Plane (see **FIGURE 5.51**).

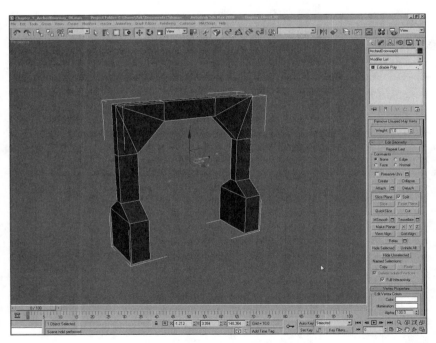

FIGURE 5.51   Your model does not appear to be different, but it is now divided into several pieces.

6. Save your work as Archway_collision.max.

END TUTORIAL 5.9

Please continue from **TUTORIAL 5.9** or launch 3ds Max and open the Chapter_05_ArchedDoorway_07.max file included with the files for this chapter. In **TUTORIAL 5.10**, we continue with the process of creating our own collision surface for our archway mesh.

TUTORIAL 5.10: 3ds Max: Creating Custom Collision Surfaces from an Existing Model, Part II

1. Your model is now separated into different parts, but we need to make each of those parts into its own individual object. Press the 5 key to make Elements selectable, and then click on the lower-left foot of the archway. In the Command Panel under the Edit Geometry rollout, click the Detach button.

   In the dialog that appears, set the name to UCX_leftFoot and click OK; then press 6 to exit Sub-Object Mode.

2. Repeat step 2 for each of the other elements, naming them as shown in **FIGURE 5.52**. On the last object, you do not need to Detach; simply change the name.

3. Your next step is to cap off any open ends from the Split procedure.

   a. Select one of the pieces, and press the 3 key to make Borders selectable.

   b. Marquee-select the entire piece. At least one edge should highlight (press F4 if you cannot see edges). This edge is a border, and it needs to be closed in before proceeding.

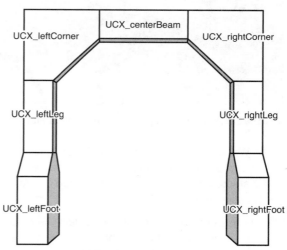

FIGURE 5.52 This diagram shows the naming convention for the pieces of the archway.

   c. In the Command Panel under the Edit Borders rollout, click Cap. There is no visible change, but the open ends are enclosed. In **FIGURE 5.53**, you can see the result with a piece that has been moved away from the object.

   d. Repeat this process with all the remaining pieces, capping off any open ends.

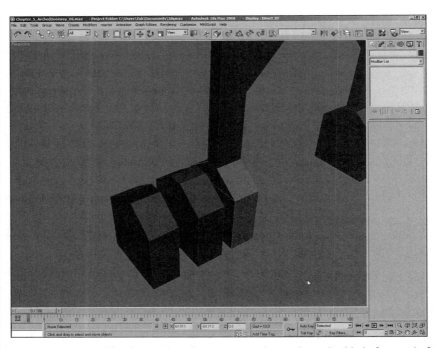

FIGURE 5.53   The Cap tool encloses open ends, as shown in this before and after.

4. We could move on with the collision objects as they are. However, for most professional-level game productions, what we have here is a bit overcomplicated. In the following steps, we remove the pieces we don't need and create a much more optimized group of collision meshes.

   a. In the Command Panel, select the Display tab. Scroll down the panel to the Hide Rollout and check the Hide Frozen Objects checkbox. This makes the frozen original arch disappear temporarily.

   b. Select the UCX_leftLeg, UCX_rightLeg, and UCX_centerBeam objects. Press Delete to remove them. You should only have the feet and legs remaining (see **FIGURE 5.54**).

   c. Select the UCX_leftFoot object and press 4 to make Polygons selectable.

   d. Select the small polygon at the top of the object and press W to invoke the Move Tool. In the Coordinate Entry Area, set the Z-Axis field to 176. Repeat steps c and d for the opposite foot.

   e. Exit Subobject Mode and select the UCX_leftCorner object. Press 4 to make Polygons selectable.

   f. Select the small vertical polygon that faces the opposite corner, and right-click the Y-Axis spinner to move the polygon to the middle of the shape. Repeat steps e and f for the opposite corner.

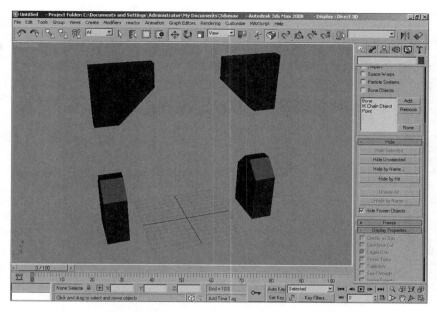

FIGURE 5.54   With the legs and center beam gone, you only have 4 shapes left.

    g. Uncheck the Hide Frozen Objects checkbox set earlier. As a reminder, it is located in the Command Panel under the Display Tab.

You should now only have 4 objects that form a simpler version of the arch (see **FIGURE 5.55**).

5. You may want to test your convexity before you export the model. To do this, click on the Utilities Pane in the Command Panel. This is on the tab on the far right. At the bottom of the Utilities Pane, you'll see the Reactor button. Click it, and at the bottom, you'll find the Utils rollout.

Within the Utils rollout, you find the Test Convexity button. You can select any object and click this button to automatically detect whether the object is convex or concave (see **FIGURE 5.56**).

Test all your objects now.

6. Right-click in a blank area of the viewport and choose Unfreeze All from the upper-right quadrant of the Quad menu.

> **NOTE**
>
> If one of your objects is reported as concave, it is probably because you still need to cap its ends!

7. Next, marquee-select all objects in the scene and export them to ASE format, as shown in **TUTORIAL 5.6**. You can use any name you like, as long as you can find the file in Unreal momentarily. Note that you will export them all simultaneously; do not export them one-at-a-time!

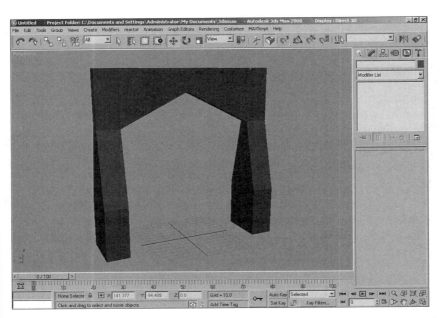

FIGURE 5.55   The new collision meshes form a much more optimized version of the original model.

8. Close 3ds Max and launch Unreal Editor. In Unreal Editor, open the Generic browser and choose Import. Locate the ASE file, and enter the following for the Import settings:

   Package: StaticMeshImport

   Group: Meshes

   Name: sm_archwayWithCollision

   If you look at the mesh in the Static Mesh Editor, you'll notice that it already has its collision mesh (see **FIGURE 5.57**)!

9. Save your package.

FIGURE 5.56   The Test Convexity button provides a quick way to tell if your object makes a good collision mesh.

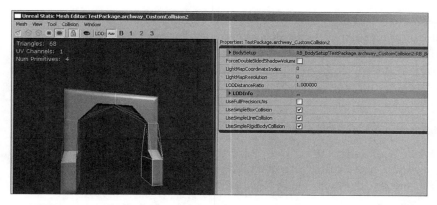

FIGURE 5.57   If you click the Show Collision button, you can see your custom collision mesh!

END TUTORIAL 5.10

Placing Static Meshes

At this point, your static mesh should be ready for placement in a level. Placing static meshes is easy; it's simply a matter of selecting a particular mesh from the Generic browser and placing it with a right-click. However, when placing your static meshes, keep a few things in mind, as follows:

1. You'll get the most benefit from static meshes by placing multiple copies of the same mesh throughout your level. This is because of the way the graphics card handles the information regarding each mesh. For instance, placing 1,000 copies of the same mesh in a level would have little relative overhead on the machine, whereas placing 1,000 different meshes would have much more overhead.

2. Keep in mind that static meshes should form most of the physical detail of your levels. Do not rely on BSP for more than just the general form and layout, as BSP is much slower in calculation.

3. Try not to place static meshes randomly throughout your level. Your level looks much more complete if you place your meshes with a purpose. Think of yourself as an interior designer whenever possible.

4. Rotating or rescaling a static mesh can give the mesh a completely new purpose. For example, a simple plumbing pipe can become a massive column with just a simple change in scale!

In **TUTORIAL 5.11**, we are finally going to place our new static mesh in a simple level, and have a look at how we can change around some of its properties. Launch Unreal Editor. Open the Chapter_05_BasicRoom_01.ut3 level and the Chapter_05_StaticMesh.upk package, both included on the DVD with the files for this chapter. We show how to place your new customized mesh into a level.

TUTORIAL 5.11: Placing and Adjusting Static Meshes in a Level

1. In the Generic browser, select the sm_archedDoorway_placement static mesh. In the Perspective viewport, right-click in the center of the large open space, and from the Context menu, choose Add Actor > Add StaticMesh:...sm_archedDoorway_placement.

   Use the Translation, Rotation, and Scale widgets to place the mesh in your level however you like (see **FIGURE 5.58**).

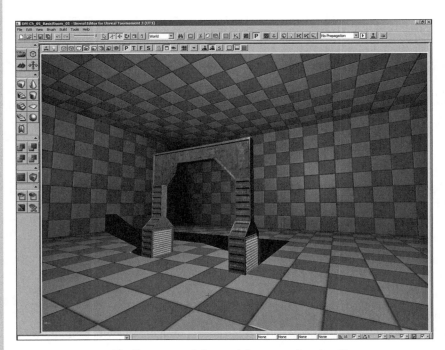

FIGURE 5.58   Finally, a copy of the model appears in a level!

2. While holding the Alt key, use the Translation Widget to move the mesh, which creates a duplicate. Feel free to make several different copies; see if you can come up with an interesting layout!

3. We now change the material for just one of the static meshes. Select one of the duplicates, and press F4 to open its properties window. Expand StaticMeshActor, and StaticMeshComponent.

TIP

Try using different DrawScale values in the status bar at the bottom of the UI for precise control over mesh scale!

4. Scroll down under the Rendering category, and locate the Materials property. Click the Add New Item button 🔲 (see **FIGURE 5.59**).

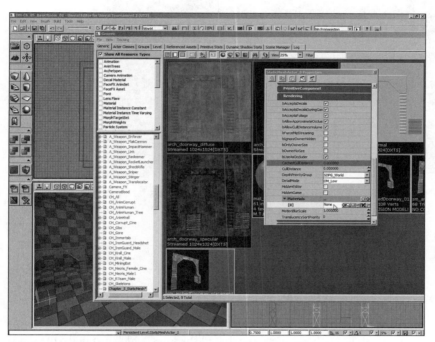

FIGURE 5.59   Clicking the Add New button enables you to assign a new material for the individual mesh.

5. In the new [0] index that appears, use the Generic browser to locate the mat_archedDoorway_alt material included in the SMPlacement package, and then click the Use Current Selection in Browser button 🔲 (see **FIGURE 5.60**).

6. Save your level. Feel free to explore with different placements and lighting schemes for the mesh!

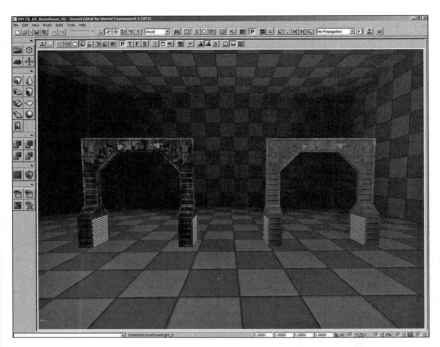

FIGURE 5.60   Placing different materials on your static meshes allows for even more variety in your levels!

END TUTORIAL 5.11

Static Meshes and Shadows

Because of their unmoving nature, static meshes are perfect for receiving pre-calculated shadow maps. By default, a static mesh has only simple vertex-based shadows, which can make the shadows look very soft, to the point of being virtually nonexistent. Setting up a static mesh to receive shadow maps is fairly simple, but does require a few special considerations. For example, if your mesh's UV layout overlaps in any way, then you're going to have a problem with shadow maps. This is because the mapped shadows use your object's UVs to determine how the shadows appear on the surface.

The solution to this problem is to create a separate channel of UVs, essentially an entirely separate layout, whose only purpose is to accommodate shadows. In **TUTORIAL 5.12**, we create a second set of UVs for our archway model so that we can apply them to the object, and tell Unreal Editor to use this second UV channel for the application of shadow maps.

Launch 3ds Max and open the Chapter_05_ShadowUV.max file included with the files for this chapter. This includes our archway mesh, as well as its required collision models. If you want full control over shadows on your mesh, it is sometimes helpful to have a second layout for texture coordinates. In **TUTORIAL 5.12**, we set this up for our archway mesh.

TUTORIAL 5.12: 3ds Max: Creating a Second UV Channel for Shadow Maps

1. Press the H key to bring up the Select by Name window. Click on the archedDoorway and then click the Select button.

2. In the Modify panel, place a new UnwrapUVW modifier onto the object. In the Map Channel group of the modifier's parameters, set the Map Channel field to 2 (see **FIGURE 5.61**).

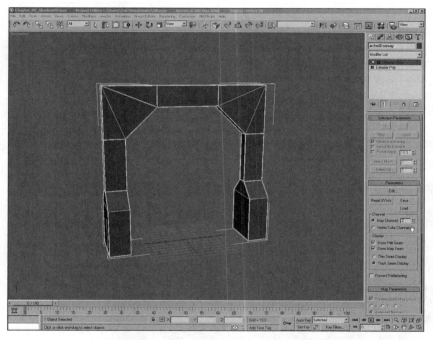

FIGURE 5.61   The Map Channel setting is located in the Parameters rollout.

3. Click the Edit button to bring up the Edit UVWs window. Click the Face Sub-Object Mode button 🔲.

4. Marquee-select all the faces in the Edit UVWs window, and from the Mapping menu, choose Flatten Mapping. Set the Face Angle Threshold to 50 and click OK. This creates a new UV layout that is completely flattened.

5. Close your Edit UVWs window and collapse your object's stack by right-clicking on the stack and choosing Collapse All. Click Yes on the warning box that appears. You have now created a separate layout that is stored on your object's second UV channel.

6. In the viewport, marquee-select all objects and export them in ASE format as archedDoorwayShadows.ase.

END TUTORIAL 5.12

In **TUTORIAL 5.13**, we show how the separate shadow map channel can be activated in Unreal Editor.

TUTORIAL 5.13: Activating Separate Shadow Map Channels in Unreal Editor

1. Launch Unreal Editor and open the Chapter_05_StaticMesh.upk package, and then open the 05_MeshShadows.ut3 map, both included in the files for this chapter. Notice that the static mesh placed in the level has very poor shadowing on it, even though the column should be placing a shadow right down the center (see **FIGURE 5.62**).

> **NOTE**
>
> This is a continuation of **TUTORIAL 5.12**! Please complete it before proceeding!

FIGURE 5.62   The lack of clear shadows is the result of vertex shadowing.

2. In the Generic browser, choose File > Import, and locate the ArchedDoorwayShadows.ase file created in **TUTORIAL 5.12** or the 05_shadowUVs.ase file included in the files for this chapter. Use the following settings in the Import window:

Package: Chapter_05_StaticMesh

Group: Meshes

Name: sm_archwayShadow

Click OK when finished. There will be several warnings about materials. Simply click OK and disregard the messages.

3. Once imported, double-click the mesh to bring up the Static Mesh Editor. Notice that the preview window says that the mesh has two UV channels. In the Properties window, set the following properties:

LightMapCoodinateIndex: 1

LightMapResolution: 128

Close the Static Mesh Editor and save your package when finished.

> **NOTE**
>
> Because the LightMapCoordinateIndex property is 0-based, a value of 1 actually refers to the second UV channel. Also, the value you place in LightMap Resolution becomes squared, so a value of 128 results in a 128×128 shadow map.

4. Use the skills covered in **TUTORIAL 5.7** to apply the mat_arched_doorway material to the mesh. This material can be found in the Chapter_05_StaticMesh package.

5. Select the mesh in the Generic browser, and place a copy behind the second column in the level, so that it is halfway in one of the column shadows. You have to delete the mesh that is already placed there.

6. Double-click the new mesh and expand the StaticMeshActor tab, as well as the StaticMeshComponent category. Near the bottom of the list, under StaticMeshComponent, verify that bOverrideLightMapResolution is set to False (Unchecked). Without this setting, your new shadow map will not work (see **FIGURE 5.63**).

7. Rebuild your lighting, and you will see that the column is applying shadows to the static mesh in the new version (see **FIGURE 5.64**)!

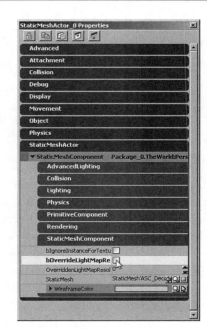

FIGURE 5.63 Verify the bOverrideLightMapResolution setting.

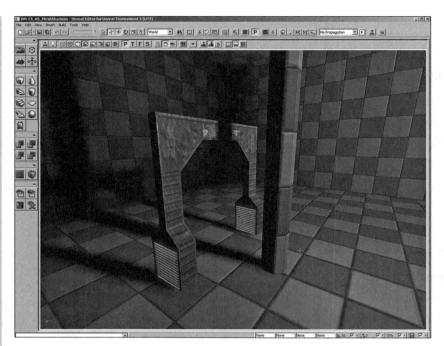

FIGURE 5.64 The new version of the mesh has cleaner shadowing.

8. Save your map.

END TUTORIAL 5.13

Summary

This chapter has covered many of the basics of creating your own static meshes. It's important for you to always remember the vital role that static meshes play in your level, and being able to create your own gives you tremendous power for developing your own levels. From here, you would do well to work on your modeling and texturing skills. We have really only scratched the surface in terms of what you can do with static meshes, as you could easily write an entire book on that subject alone. There are many other avenues to cover, including capturing normal maps from high-resolution geometry, creation of meshes using sculpting applications such as ZBrush, and many more. Our intention here, however, has been to get your feet wet in the process of creating your own 3D content for Unreal, and helping to create levels that are much more your own creation than if you were to only use the assets included with Unreal Tournament 3.

Chapter 6

Introduction to Materials

To get the stunning visual beauty and clarity that Unreal Engine 3.0 can deliver, you need to master materials. They're the single most important factor in the final look of your game. Need a character who's so visually detailed that you can count the pores on her face? Need realistic-looking fire? Want to create a complex interactive machine with number readouts, lighted buttons, knobs, and switches? These all require materials. In fact, materials control the final look of every object you create—whether you're building large-scale environments, interactive objects, playable characters, or the simplest props. In this chapter, we explore materials, what they are, what they're made out of—and most importantly, how you can quickly start creating your own with Unreal Editor's amazingly powerful Material Editor.

What Is a Material?

The very simplest way to think of a material in terms of a game engine is as a paint that is applied to surfaces of objects in your level. However, this is an extreme oversimplification of what a material can do for the look of your objects. Although "paint" typically controls only the color of something, a material can cause an object to look lumpy, shiny, reflective, refractive, and can even give the illusion that the object has fine detail actually modeled into it, such as wrinkles, scars, and pores. Without materials, objects in Unreal Engine 3.0 are only low-polygon representations of real-world objects. Once the material has been applied, these objects come to life. They can look like metal, or wood, or concrete. They can have cracks, dents, lights, buttons, screens with visual readouts, or just about anything else that you can imagine. In **FIGURE 6.1**, you can see an example of a simple polygonal object with and without a material applied.

FIGURE 6.1   A simple chamfered cube, with no material on the left, and with a material on the right

Once you fully understand how materials work and how they are created, you will likely find yourself no longer thinking of them as a simple coating for your objects, but instead think of a material closer to the definition of the word: The substance that makes up an object. For example, you know that concrete is typically dull, gray, and has a slightly pitted surface, whereas car paint can be any color of the rainbow, and tends to be shiny, glossy, and may even have metallic flakes in it. For now, though, let's keep it relatively simple and just think of a material as a coating for your models that controls that object's final appearance in-game.

Materials vs. Textures

Many newcomers to game design can have a difficult time differentiating between materials and textures. Simply put, the difference is that a texture is merely an image, whereas a material is a culmination of a variety of many different elements, including textures. It is easiest to think of a texture as being a component of a material. When you create materials, you use textures to provide color, transparency, glow, and a variety of other effects for your material (see **FIGURE 6.2**).

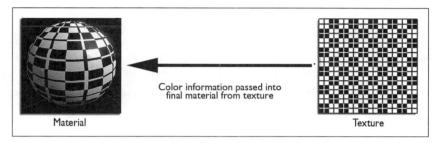

Color information passed into
final material from texture

Material

Texture

FIGURE 6.2   This diagram illustrates the general relationship between materials and textures. Note that the flow of information runs right-to-left, which is the standard for Unreal Editor's Material Editor.

Part of the confusion in knowing the difference between materials and textures is that in versions of Unreal Editor prior to the release of Unreal Engine 3, textures *or* materials could be applied directly to surfaces. This is no longer true. Only materials can be applied to surfaces. Textures are attached to the final material, which is then applied to the given surface.

Texture Coordinates (UVs)

In order to apply a textured material to a surface, you need a way to determine which pixels of the texture to apply to which area of the surface. More precisely, when applying any sort of imagery across the surface of a three-dimensional object, you need a way to control what parts of the image are going to be placed in each location. Because a texture is a two-dimensional object (like a picture), whereas a game object or character is three-dimensional, there must exist some way to "wrap" the 2D image across the 3D object.

This is done through the use of texture coordinates, also called UVs. Starting at the bottom-left corner, the texture being applied to the surface is mapped from 0 to 1 horizontally and from 0 to 1 vertically (see **FIGURE 6.3**). These are the U and V coordinates respectively, sometimes referred to as "tangent space." Each vertex of a surface has values that correspond to the U and V coordinates of the texture that is to be applied to the surface. The texture is then painted onto the surface according to those texture coordinates. Every surface has its own set of UVs, which can be set with the Surface Properties dialog for BSP or by using the appropriate tools in the artist's preferred 3D modeling application for static meshes and skeletal meshes (see **FIGURE 6.4**).

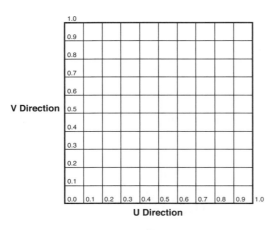

FIGURE 6.3   UV space can be described as a grid that runs from 0 to 1, starting at the lower-left corner.

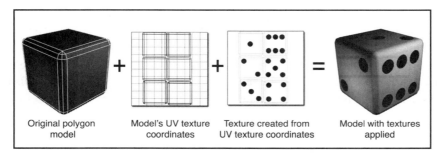

FIGURE 6.4   Here you can see how the UVs of a polygonal object affect how the texture is applied across the object's surface.

In the Material Editor, texture coordinate information can be supplemented through the use of certain Material Expressions. By using some of the expressions described next, you can control the tiling (or repetition) of a texture, change or animate its rotation, pan it in a certain direction, and a variety of other effects. The expressions create such results by changing the values of a material's texture coordinates, either statically or over time.

Material Instructions

Once you start really getting into creating your own materials, you're going to come across the word "instructions." In this case, instructions are commands that are passed to the computer's graphics processor to handle various aspects of the material's behavior. In fact, even when you create a basic material for the first time, you will notice that the Material Editor's Expression window tells you that the material contains many instructions by default, most of which are used to simulate the lighting on the surface of your material.

For our purposes, you can simply use it as an indication of how complex your materials are. The more instructions a material includes, the more complex a material is and, correspondingly, the more expensive it is to render. Because of this, you need to think seriously about which materials in your scene are the most important, and not waste time (or precious processing power) in making a material too complex, only for it to sit in some unseen corner of your level.

Thinking About Color in Unreal

When creating materials, one of the key aspects you deal with is color. As such, it's important for you to know how color is handled internally and how you have to work with it inside of Unreal.

The first thing that is important to realize is that color is stored differently in Unreal than it is in most computer applications. Unreal uses *floating point* values—which generally run from 0.0 to 1.0—to store its colors, whereas many other applications (take Adobe Photoshop, for instance) use values from 0 to 255 for each channel. For example, the color red in most applications would have RGB values of (255, 0, 0). In Unreal, however, the same color would have RGB values of (1.0, 0.0, 0.0).

The upshot to using floating point values is that you can do things that you simply cannot do with the standard 0–255 range. For instance, you *can* have values greater than 1.0, which result in ultra-bright colors. For example, while a standard red would have RGB values of (1.0, 0.0, 0.0), it is completely acceptable to use (2.0, 0.0, 0.0), which would result in an intense, glowing red. This feature is often used to create glowing lights or highlights in a material that simulates the emission of light without actually casting a real, dynamic light.

Another benefit of floating point numbers for colors is the ability to have *negative* values for color channels. This may sound confusing at first, but think of it as a way to *take away* color information. For instance, you could have a negative red channel value (-0.5, 0.0, 0.0) and the new color would *remove* red information from any other color with which it was combined.

The next thing to remember is that each of the three color channels (Red, Green, and Blue) work independently of one another. This means that if you add two colors together, the Red channels get added together, then the Blue channels, and then the Green.

Along with this channel-to-channel behavior comes a certain compatibility issue that must be considered. Only color objects that have the same number of channels can be combined in any way. For instance, you cannot add an RGBA color, which has four channels (Red, Green, Blue, and Alpha), to an RGB color that has three channels (Red, Green, and Blue).

The only exception to this is when you're combining a single value or channel to a color that has multiple channels. For example, you could add the number 0.5 to a color of dark red, which would have RGB values of 0.5, 0.0, and 0.0, respectively. The result would be a coral pink color with RGB values of 1.0, 0.5, and 0.5. What happened was the number 0.5 was added to each channel individually:

R: 0.5			R: 1.0
G: 0.0	+	0.5 =	G: 0.5
B: 0.0			B: 0.5

To work around this behavior, Unreal's Material Editor contains a series of operators called *component masks* that enable you to cancel out certain channels so that the number of channels matches between two colors. For example, say you needed to combine one color that had an Alpha channel (RGBA) to a standard RGB color. You can't by default, because one has four channels and the other has only three. However, you could apply a component mask to the RGBA color, masking out the Alpha channel. Now, both colors have only Red, Green, and Blue channels, and are compatible for combination.

A Quick Word on Lighting

Other than certain special cases, almost all materials need some interaction with a light source to really express themselves. Also, when you really get down to the bare bones of it, materials are all about controlling how a given surface responds to light. Words such as *color*, *shininess*, and *glossiness* all describe how a particular surface is interacting with light that is coming in contact with that surface. Because of this, you will often find that the setup of your level's materials go hand in hand with the placement and control of that level's lights. In fact, once you gain a little more experience, you'll more often than not find yourself working on both lighting and materials simultaneously, or at the very least doing a lot of back-and-forth between your lights and materials. However, for the purposes of clarity, we are currently going to focus strictly on materials and then cover the various aspects of lighting later in Chapter 7, "Introduction to Lighting."

Anatomy of a Material

So, now you know generally what a material *is*; let's take a moment and examine what makes up a material. However, as we progress, you're going to actually get your hands dirty and make a basic material, so that you can see what's involved not only as far as the elements of a material are concerned, but also get a general idea of how they are constructed.

In general, a material is comprised of three primary components that must all work in unison to create the final result. These components are Material Nodes, Material Channels, and Material

Expressions. The three components interact in the manner described in the following diagram (see **FIGURE 6.5**).

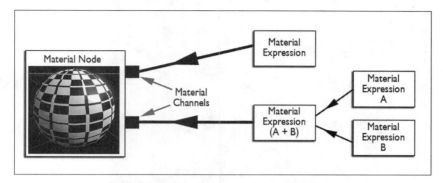

FIGURE 6.5   This diagram illustrates the relationship between Material Nodes, Material Channels, and Material Expressions. Again, notice the right-to-left flow.

Material Nodes

The Material Node is the base object of every material in Unreal Editor. However, rather than simply describe the node or show you a picture, let's begin by making our first material, and you can see one firsthand.

In **TUTORIAL 6.1**, we demonstrate two possible methods for creating a simple material inside Unreal's Generic Browser.

TUTORIAL 6.1: Creating a Basic Material

1. Launch Unreal Editor, and open the Generic browser.

2. There are three primary ways to generate a new material. We look at only two, as the third requires us to import textures; this is a topic we approach later.

   In the File menu of the Generic browser, choose New... (see **FIGURE 6.6**).

3. In the dialog that appears, enter the following information (see **FIGURE 6.7**):

   Package: MyBasicMaterials

   Group: Materials

   Name: mat_simple_1

   Factory: Material

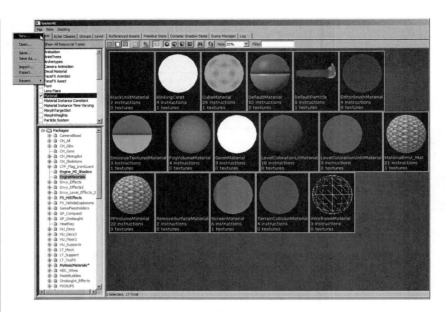

FIGURE 6.6   Choose New from the File menu.

FIGURE 6.7   Fill this information into the New dialog.

Click OK when finished. You'll now see a new package appear in your list called MyBasicMaterials. You'll also notice that this package is expandable (has a little plus sign next to it), and if you expand it, you'll find the Materials group. Within this group, you'll see your new material (see **FIGURE 6.8**).

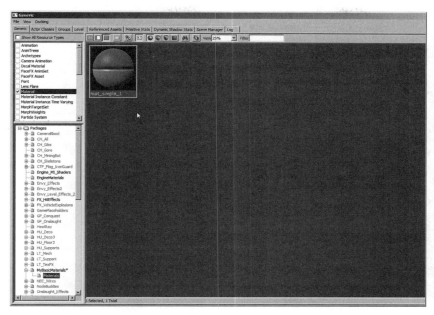

FIGURE 6.8   Your new material now appears.

4. Right-click on your new material and choose Delete from the Context menu. This enables us to re-create our material using the second method for material creation (see **FIGURE 6.9**).

> **NOTE**
>
> Don't be confused into thinking that this is your Material Node. What you see in the Generic browser is just a preview of your material, enabling you to select it for application on a particular object in your level.

> **NOTE**
>
> A couple of things happen when you delete the material. First and most obvious is that you'll see your material disappear. However, because that material was the only thing in our package, you'll also notice that the package itself no longer exists. Without some item to contain (texture, static mesh, material, and so on), a package cannot exist in Unreal Editor. This is useful, as it prevents you from populating your Editor (or your hard drive) with empty packages.
>
> Also of note is that you cannot delete materials (or any other objects for that matter) that are in use by Unreal Editor. If, for example, we had applied our material to an object in our level, or even if we were editing the material the Material Editor, Unreal Editor would not allow us to delete the material. This is also true of any other asset you try to delete from the Generic browser. In such cases, you will see a window showing you all the places in which the asset is referenced.

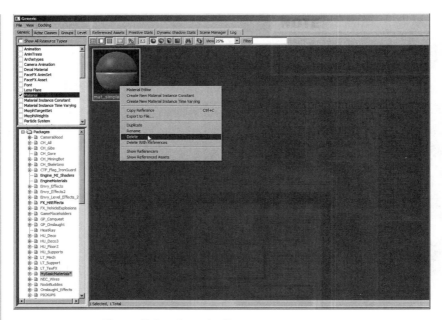

FIGURE 6.9 Choose Delete from the Context menu.

5. Right-click on an empty section of the Generic browser's preview area (that's the big dark gray area that dominates the browser). From the Context menu that appears, choose New Material. The New dialog appears again; reenter the same information you did in Step 3. However, you'll notice that the Factory property is already filled in for you when using this method. Click OK when finished.

6. This time, something different happens when you click OK. You'll notice the Material Editor window appears. Don't get too excited, though; we discuss using the Material Editor a bit later. For now, direct your attention to the large gray window that dominates the center of the area. This is called the Material Expressions window, and it's where all the construction of your materials takes place. Within this window, you can catch your first glimpse of a Material Node (see **FIGURE 6.10**).

   Note that you can navigate the Material Expressions window with the mouse just as you would the orthogonal viewports of your level. Do this now to center the Material Node in the middle of your window. We talk more about this node in the upcoming section.

7. We now need to save this package. If you look at the package list in the lower-left corner of the Generic browser, you will notice that the MyBasicMaterials package has an asterisk next to it, indicating that it needs to be saved. In the Generic browser, make sure that the MyBasicMaterials package is selected, and then choose File > Save from the browser's menubar. You can also right-click the package name and choose 'save'. In the Save dialog that appears, verify that the name of the package is IntroToMaterials.upk, and click Save. The asterisk next to the package in the package list should now disappear (see **FIGURE 6.11**).

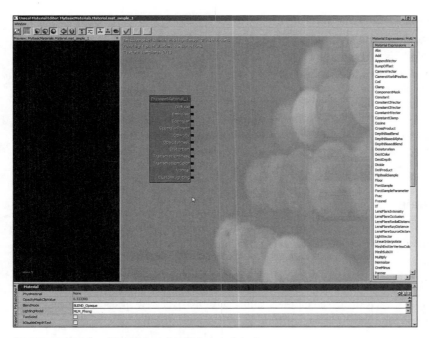

FIGURE 6.10 The Material Editor user interface

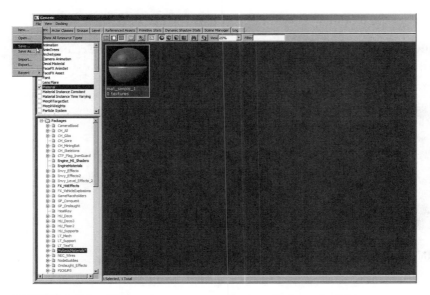

FIGURE 6.11 Be sure to save your package so that you don't lose your new material!

END TUTORIAL 6.1

You've now seen the Material Node, and whether or not you realized it at the time, you got to see some material channels as well, although none of the channels in our material were currently in use. The Material Node is the key object in a material. It's the final point into which all other expressions must pass via the node's channels.

Material Nodes have several properties that you can adjust in order to change the overall behavior of the material itself. These properties can be found in the Properties window of the Material Editor (the long thin window that runs across the bottom of the Editor). However, rather than bog you down with a vast array of settings, we're going to simply change these values as we need them.

Material Channels

When you look at a Material Node, you'll see a list of all the channels available to a material. There are eleven of them in all, and they allow access to individual aspects of a material's behavior. Into each of these channels, you must pass some sort of data. This data comes from Material Expressions, quite often by way of texture samples, which we discuss later.

The following is a list of each of these channels, along with an overview of each channel's purpose. Those of you who come from a background in a 3D animation package, such as 3ds Max or Maya, may recognize several of these channels, and will be happy to note that they function the same way in Unreal Editor as they do in your native 3D application.

Diffuse

Simply put, the Diffuse channel controls the color of your object. It can be a single color or a texture (see **FIGURE 6.12**).

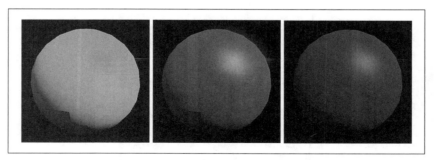

FIGURE 6.12   This is an example of materials with different diffuse values.

Emissive

This channel enables you to create glow effects on your material. Emissive values work independently of any lighting that affects the material, and as such displays identically in an environment with no contribution from lighting as it does when fully lit. This can be used to create fake lights in a material that shows up in complete darkness, or the glow from a window at night, for instance. Values from 0 to 1 in each color channel cause the emission of color, and ramping values above 1 causes a "bloom" effect which causes color to bleed out into surrounding pixels and simulate an overbrightening of the simulated glow. A value of 0,0,0 (Black) results in no glow, as it has an intensity of 0 (see **FIGURE 6.13**).

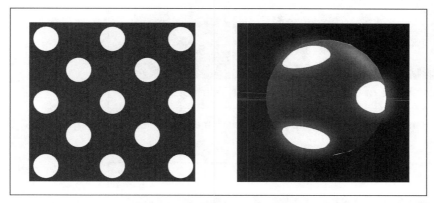

FIGURE 6.13   You can see the result of a texture driving the emissive channel.

Specular

This controls the "hotspot" of light reflection on a surface. The Specular channel controls how light plays across the surface of a material. Consider a shiny car sitting outside on a sunny day. See that spot where the sun is reflecting that looks like a bright white ball? That's the *specular highlight*, which is what this material channel controls.

Like the Emissive channel, the Specular channel accepts an RGB (Color) value as an input. This value determines both the color of the specular highlight as well as its brightness or intensity. Keep in mind, however, that also like the Emissive channel, a value of 0,0,0 (black) results in having no specular highlight, similar to a dull surface such as chalk (see **FIGURE 6.14**).

Specular Power

Where the Specular channel controls the intensity and color of a specular highlight, the Specular Power channel controls the *size and falloff* of the highlight. Unlike Specular and Emissive, however, this channel accepts only a single input value rather than an RGB (color) input. If we *really* wanted to sound technical, we could say that this property simulates the ability to modify the amount of microfaceting of an object's surface, meaning that it creates the illusion of microscopic planes that reflect light back at the viewer. In practical terms, higher values result in smaller (or *tighter*) specular highlights, where lower values result in larger, softer highlights (see **FIGURE 6.15**).

6

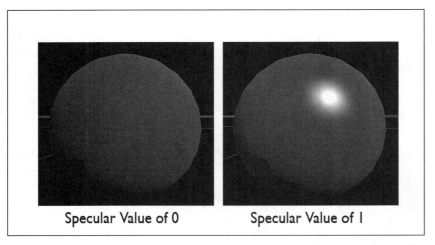

FIGURE 6.14   Here are two materials with vastly different specular values.

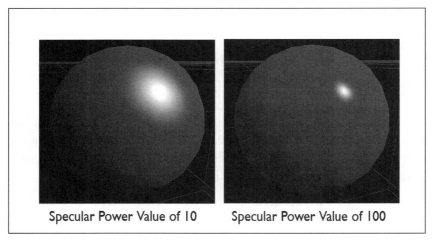

FIGURE 6.15   Notice now differing specular power values tighten or widen the specular hotspot.

Opacity

This channel accepts a single value between 0 and 1 (or black and white, respectively), and controls how opaque or transparent your material is. A value of 0, or black, results in the material being completely transparent.

> **NOTE**
>
> This channel is only functional when the Material Node's LightingModel property is set to MLM_Unlit, and the BlendMode property is set to BLEND_Masked, BLEND_Translucent, BLEND_Additive, or BLEND_Modulate.

Conversely, a value of 1, or white, causes the material to be completely opaque. Values that range in between, such as 0.5 (perfect gray), result in varying degrees of transparency (see **FIGURE 6.16**).

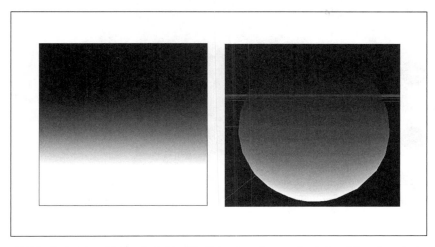

FIGURE 6.16   The material in this figure has its opacity being driven by a texture.

Opacity Mask

This is a simpler version of the Opacity channel that can be used on the default MLM_Phong lighting model (see **FIGURE 6.17**). The primary difference is that it is a binary value, either 1 or 0, on or off. It has no intermediate transparency values. By default, values higher than or equal to 0.5 are opaque, whereas values lower than 0.5 are transparent. However, you can change this by adjusting the Material Node's opacity mask property.

This channel works specifically as a way to mask out individual pixels of a material in an inexpensive fashion that still allows the material to accept lighting. The UnrealEngine does not allow for varying levels of translucency on lit materials, but this technique allows for masking out areas in a material while still letting that material receive lighting information.

> **NOTE**
>
> The Opacity Mask channel can be used in conjunction with the Opacity channel on materials using the MLM_Unlit lighting model along with one of the appropriate blend modes. When doing this, the Opacity Mask is used to limit the scope of the Opacity channel, meaning that its value overrides the Opacity channel.

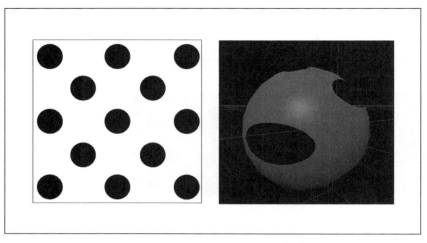

FIGURE 6.17   This MLM_Phong material has the shown texture applied to its opacity mask channel.

Distortion

Simply put, this channel enables you to create a simulated refraction effect, meaning that light bends as it passes through the material. You can use this channel to create distorting glass, heat shimmer effects, or any other effect where refraction may be a factor (see **FIGURE 6.18**). Naturally, because distortion bends light that is passing *through* an object, this channel is only useful on objects that have some level of transparency. It should be noted that at the time of this writing, it is only effective using the MLM_Unlit lighting model.

The intensity of the data passed into the distortion channel is used to give the material a simulated refraction effect. Typically this channel accepts a normal map as an input which determines how the simulated refraction of the surface behaves. The normal map's vector information is used to determine how the rendering engine moves the pixels, which gives an effect similar to refraction.

Transmission Mask/Transmission Color

The Transmission Mask and Transmission Color channels work together to produce an approximation of an effect that is commonly called *sub-surface scattering*. In essence, the channels simulate the scattering of light as it passes through a surface (see **FIGURE 6.19**). For example, if you hold a bright flashlight up to your cheek, you might notice how a large part of your face illuminates to some degree. This is because the light of the flashlight is reflected and refracted in many different directions as it passes through your skin, rather than passing straight through as it would through glass.

FIGURE 6.18   The boxes in this image are being distorted by a cloud of particles, whose material has a texture applied to its distortion channel.

The Transmission Color channel controls the color that the light appears to take on as it passes through the surface. The Transmission Mask channel controls the intensity and placement of the transmission, enabling you to place where you'd like the transmitted light to be visible on the surface.

Normal

The Normal channel is quite possibly the most valuable channel in a material in terms of controlling how detailed your objects appear. If you've been keeping up with buzz words of game design over the past few years, you may have heard the term "normal map." A *normal map* is essentially a texture that describes the

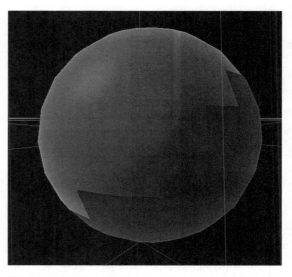

FIGURE 6.19   The lightened area around the rim of this object is due to the simulation of light scattering through its surface.

angles of each part of the surface as the elevation changes. Each pixel of the normal map corresponds to a vector. Good examples of a situation in which you would use a normal map would be wrinkles in skin or cracks in stone. Technically speaking, a normal map perturbs the surface normals (or the direction the surface is pointing) on a pixel-by-pixel basis, allowing for extremely fine control for the addition of minute details (see **FIGURE 6.20**).

FIGURE 6.20   The material on the left has no normal map. The material on the right has a normal map that describes the surface of a brick wall.

The color of the data passed into the normal channel is used to determine the surface normals of the surface to which the material has been applied. The R, G, and B values are used to calculate the vector that actually represents the normal to be used for the corresponding point of the surface. The range of values from 0 to 255 for each color is mapped to a new set of values from -1 to 1. The three values for each pixel are then used to form the vector. By using three separate values, the map is able to describe the angle that each pixel is facing. This allows low-resolution 3d geometry to appear to have tremendous visual detail, as if it had been made of many more polygons than it truly is.

Two important facts should be remembered when using the normal channel. The first is that in nearly every case, you apply a texture sample to it. The second is that the result of a normal map is nothing more than a rendering effect; the polygonal surface itself is no more complex than it was before the map was applied. This is the essence of why normal maps are so important in simulating high levels of detail in your level's surfaces.

Custom Lighting

The custom lighting channel gives you the ability to create your own lighting function. The MLM_Phong lighting model, which is the default setup for controlling how light interacts with the base material, is actually the result of a series of calculations. By attaching networks of

Material Expressions into the Custom Lighting channel, you can create your own simulation of how light should interact with the surface of your material. For this channel to be used, you must set the lighting model to MLM_Custom (see **FIGURE 6.21**).

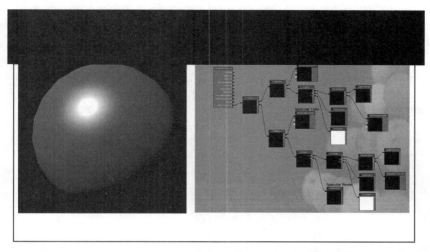

FIGURE 6.21   This example uses the intricate network on the right to approximate the Phong lighting model.

Now that you basically know what channels are available to you, you need to know what you can do with them. This is where Material Expressions come into play. In the next section, we look at Material Expressions and how they are used in your materials.

Material Expressions

Material Expressions are the fundamental building blocks used to create materials. Each expression contains a specific functionality such as providing an interface to a texture, adding two values or vectors, or modifying texture coordinates. By combining these expressions into elaborate networks, many interesting effects can be created, resulting in much more striking visuals for your level. Before we take a close look at each of the available Material Expressions in the Material Editor, we're going to add a few of the simpler expressions into the basic material we created earlier. In **TUTORIAL 6.2**, we demonstrate how to add and connect these material expressions nodes to change its look in some way.

TUTORIAL 6.2: Enhancing Our Basic Material with Material Expressions

1. In Unreal Editor, open the Generic browser, choose File > Open from the menubar, and open the Chapter_05_IntroMaterials package included with the files for this chapter.

   Expand the Materials group, and in the Generic browser's preview window, double click on the mat_simple_1 material created in **TUTORIAL 6.1**. This opens the Material Editor for that material.

2. Let's start by simply changing the color of the material. In the Material Expressions list on the right side of the Material Editor window, scroll down and choose VectorParameter, and then drag and drop it into the Expression window. You should see a new Material Expression icon appear in the Expression window, as shown in **FIGURE 6.22**.

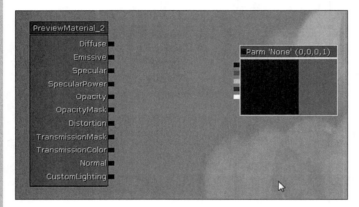

FIGURE 6.22   The VectorParameter expression icon now appears in the Expression window.

3. Before we go any further with creating this material, let's take a quick look at navigating the Expression window. Notice that if you drag in the Expression window with the left mouse button, you can pan your view. You can also zoom in and out using the left and right mouse buttons simultaneously, just as you would in an orthographic viewport. If you would like to relocate an expression icon, hold the Ctrl key and left drag that icon to reposition it.

   Do this now by holding Ctrl, and then left-dragging the VectorParameter icon so that it is even with the top of the Material Node, as shown in **FIGURE 6.23**.

4. We now create our first connection between our expression icon and the main expression node. Take a close look at the VectorParameter icon. Notice that on the left side of the icon, you can see five colored tabs. The topmost tab is black, followed by red, green, blue, and white. These are the multiple outputs that you can use to send information out of this expression. The red, green, and blue tabs are for sending red, green, or blue color information into your material. The white tab is for sending Alpha information, and the black tab is for sending a color comprised of separate R, G, and B values. Keep in mind that on a Material Expression, outputs are always on the left side of the icon, and inputs are always on the right.

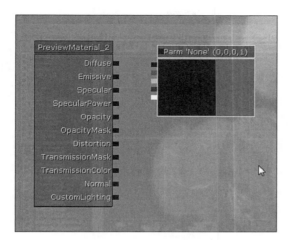

FIGURE 6.23 Practice moving the VectorParameter icon around, and then position it like so.

To make our first connection, drag with the left mouse button from the black tab of the VectorParameter icon. Notice the black wire that extends from the VectorParameter to the location of your mouse's cursor (see **FIGURE 6.24**). Continue dragging the mouse to connect this wire to the tab on the main Material Node corresponding to the Diffuse channel.

5. You have now created an unrealistic material that would be something like black felt. Many of the Material Expressions have properties that an artist can adjust to change the nature of the expression in some way. In the case of the VectorParameter expression, the most important property is the DefaultValue, which is reflected as a color. This is because color information, being in the form of Red, Green, and Blue values, can be thought of as a vector.

> **NOTE**
>
> Provided that you have not yet made any changes to your VectorParameter's properties, your material does not change when you complete this step. This is because by default, a new material is simply flat black.

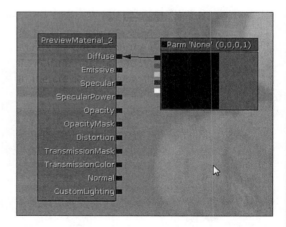

FIGURE 6.24 Notice the wire that denotes a connection from an expression to your material.

Although it is possible to change the overall color of the parameter numerically by expanding the DefaultValue property, we're going to simply use the color picker. Open this now by clicking the black bar next to the DefaultValue property, and then clicking the small magnifying glass button 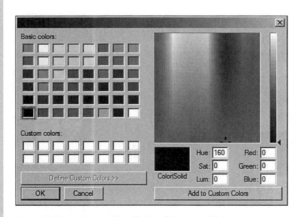 on the right side of the Properties window within the Material Editor (see **FIGURE 6.25**).

In the Color Chooser dialog that opens, choose any color you like, and then click OK. Notice the color of your material changes to reflect your new choice.

6. Let's now take a look at disconnecting Material Expressions. Holding the Alt key, left-click on either end of the wire that connects between the Diffuse channel and the VectorParameter node. You will notice the wire disappear. Keep in mind that the end you choose to Alt-click determines the type of disconnection you receive. If you choose the output end that exits the VectorParameter icon, all wires leaving that output are removed. If instead you choose the input on the main Material Node, then only the wires leading into that particular input are removed (see **FIGURE 6.26**).

> **NOTE**
>
> The individual outputs for R, G, and B on an expression do not actually output those colors. They output single values that reflect how much of that corresponding color is being used to create the final color itself. This means that the individual outputs for R, G, and B appear as various shades along the grayscale spectrum as higher values for that color are used. For example, a color of bright yellow (RGB value 1,1,0) would have an R and G value that appeared white, and a blue value that appeared black.

> **NOTE**
>
> At the time of this writing, the tool tip for this button says "Show Generic Browser." This is an error, as the button opens up the standard Windows color chooser dialog. Also, be aware that next to the magnifying glass button is the Use Mouse to Pick Color From Viewport button , whose functionality is self-explanatory. It works very much like the Eyedropper tool in Photoshop.

FIGURE 6.25   The Color Chooser dialog

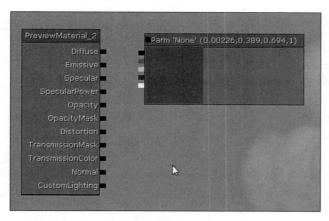

FIGURE 6.26 The connection wire has now been removed.

7. Experiment with reconnecting the output of the VectorParameter into other channels of the material. When finished, reconnect the VectorParameter back to only the Diffuse channel.

8. You now need to commit your changes to the actual material. This is done by clicking the Apply Changes button at the top of the Material Editor ☑, which has a large green checkmark on its face. It's the leftmost of the three such buttons.

9. Save the changes to your package.

> **TIP**
>
> You can force the icon of a VectorParameter expression to reflect the color you have selected by clicking the Realtime Preview box, which appears as a black square in the upper-left corner of every expression icon. If you click it, it turns yellow, indicating that it has been activated. Alternatively, you can check the bRealtimePreview checkbox located in the VectorParameter's properties. The main color of the icon also changes to show the color you have chosen. To save a little bit of processing power, turn this off after you have updated the icon to the currently selected color.

END TUTORIAL 6.2

You've now seen one of the most basic of the Material Expressions, but thus far you've only created a single expression, and used it only in the simplest of examples. However, before we do any more work inside the Material Editor, let's take a moment and look at each of the expressions available to us, along with a brief example of what each one can do. Keep in mind that you may not at first see the value of each of these expressions. Over time, as you begin to construct more and more complex materials, you will begin to find all of these expressions useful in some manner.

The Available Material Expressions

Be aware that this list is almost completely presented in alphabetical order, which is the order in which you will see the expressions while using the Material Editor. However, this may not be the order in which you would like to look at each of the expressions. Because we haven't yet figured out a way to sort lists on paper the way we do with a spreadsheet, we've decided to provide you with some organizational lists that may help you decide which Material Expressions you'd like to read about first, and then you can use the alphabetical listing simply as a reference.

Most Commonly Used Expressions

TextureSample	Constant
VectorParameter	Vector3Constant
ComponentMask	

Mathematical Operation Expressions

Abs	Floor
Add	Frac
Ceil	Multiply
Cosine	OneMinus
CrossProduct	Power
Divide	Sine
DotProduct	Subtract

Texture Coordinate Manipulation

TextureCoordinate	Panner
Rotator	Time

Material Expressions List

Abs

The Abs, or Absolute Value, expression takes in one input and outputs the absolute value of the input. For example, if the expression received an input of -5, the output would simply be 5. This expression has no properties that change its behavior (see **FIGURE 6.27**).

Add

The Add expression takes in two inputs, adds them together, and exposes the result as the output (see **FIGURE 6.28**). Because a mathematical operation is being performed, you must be careful as to the types of data you send this node. The key rule is that in most cases, you want the values added together to have the same number of components.

FIGURE 6.27   Abs expression icon

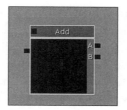

FIGURE 6.28   Add expression icon

For example, if you try to add a Constant3Vector, which has three components (meaning it has three values, such as R, G, and B), to a Constant4Vector, which has four coponents (for R, G, B, and A), you will receive an error. However, it should be noted that the only exception to this rule is a constant, which has only a single component. In such cases, the value of the constant is added to each individual component in the other vector.

AppendVector

An AppendVector expression takes in two components as inputs and combines them to form a vector with more components than the original components (see **FIGURE 6.29**). This means you can take in two single-component constants and append them to form the equivalent of a Constant2Vector, or combine a two-vector and a one-vector constant to form a three-vector, and so on. This can be useful for a variety of procedures, such as creating a texture coordinate from two single-vector Constant expressions,

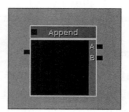

FIGURE 6.29   AppendVector expression icon

or appending an Alpha channel to an existing texture. It can also be used to solve incompatibility issues from one type of data to another.

BumpOffset

A BumpOffset expression takes in two components, Height and UVs, which are used to create a Virtual Displacement Mapping effect. This improves upon the illusion that a surface has physical differences in height over using a normal map alone (see **FIGURE 6.30**).

The Height input acts as a mask for determining where and how much of the displacement to use. The UVs input provides the texture coordinates to use. It has two parame-

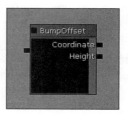

FIGURE 6.30   BumpOffset expression icon

ters as well: HeightRatio and ReferencePlane. HeightRatio is the actual distance the pixels are displaced or, more accurately, it is the ratio between the height of the bumps and the width of the texture. The size of the surface to which the material is applied multiplied by this ratio gives you the actual displacement; thus, larger surfaces appear to have more displacement than smaller surfaces. The ReferencePlane determines how the displacement is applied. A value of 0 applies the displacement toward the camera, resulting in extrusions from the surface, whereas a value of 1 applies the displacement away from the camera, resulting in what appear to be indentations into the surface. Values in between 0 and 1 are used to specify a change in direction. The default value of 0.5, meaning the displacement is applied toward the camera for Height values greater than 0.5 and away from the camera for values less than 0.5, is usually sufficient.

CameraVector

The CameraVector expression gives you access to the vector representing the direction in which the camera is pointing during gameplay (see **FIGURE 6.31**). This is especially useful if you need to perform different effects on a material as it is viewed from different angles, though such an effect would require other expressions as well, such as the ReflectionVector expression, mentioned later.

FIGURE 6.31   CameraVector expression icon

CameraWorldPosition

The CameraWorldPosition expression provides the current location of the camera in 3D space (see **FIGURE 6.32**). An easy way to see its result is to plug it directly into the Emissive channel of a new material, where you can see the color change as you rotate around the sample mesh in the preview window.

FIGURE 6.32
CameraWorldPosition expression icon

Ceil

A Ceil, or Ceiling, expression is a simple rounding expression that takes in one input and rounds its value up to the next integer (see **FIGURE 6.33**). This is different than typical rounding in that values that would typically round downward, such as 3.1282, would actually round upward to 4. The opposite of this expression is the Floor Material Expression.

FIGURE 6.33   Ceil expression icon

Clamp

A Clamp expression takes in three inputs: Input, Min, and Max. The expression then limits (or "clamps") the value of the first input, Input, so that is always between the two values of the Min and Max inputs (see **FIGURE 6.34**).

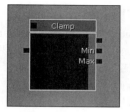

FIGURE 6.34   Clamp expression icon

ComponentMask

A ComponentMask expression takes in one value which can be a vector of any size (see **FIGURE 6.35**). This expression enables you to pick which components of a vector are allowed to pass through it. For example, you could input a Texture Sample, and using the properties of the ComponentMask, output only the R and A values of that texture. The information would then be treated just like a Constant2Vector, in that it would only have two components. This means it could be added, subtracted, multiplied, or divided by a Constant2Vector expression, or any other vector value containing only two components.

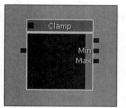

FIGURE 6.35   ComponentMask expression icon

Constant Expressions

The Constant expressions are, in essence, placeholders for static values in your material. These expressions have no inputs—only properties that hold user-inputted values. These values are then outputted to various parts of the expression. There are four different types of Constant expressions, differentiated by the number of components each expression contains, ranging from one component (R), to four components (R, G, B, and A).

Constant

This is the simplest Constant expression, as it can contain only a single value, which is read as R inside the Properties window (see **FIGURE 6.36**).

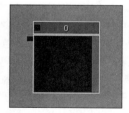

FIGURE 6.36   Constant expression icon

Constant2Vector

This expression contains two constant values, read as components of a two-element vector. These values appear in the Properties window as R and G (see **FIGURE 6.37**).

Constant3Vector

This expression contains three constant values, read as components of a three-element vector. These values appear in the Properties window as R, G, and B (see **FIGURE 6.38**).

Constant4Vector

This expression contains four constant values, read as components of a four-element vector. These values appear in the Properties window as R, G, B, and A (see **FIGURE 6.39**).

ConstantClamp

The ConstantClamp expression works exactly the same way as a regular Clamp (see Clamp entry), but has constant values added as part of its properties, sparing you the time of having to create Constant Material Expressions for the Min and Max inputs. You can instead just change the properties of the ConstantClamp (see **FIGURE 6.40**).

Cosine

A Cosine expression takes only a single input, which is used as the angle (see **FIGURE 6.41**). The expression then takes the cosine of this angle, and the result of this operation is the output. As you may know, taking the cosine of any steadily incrementing or decrementing series results in a waveform. As such, you will in many cases use a Time expression as the input for the Cosine expression, which enables you to create a cosine wave that changes as time progresses. When doing this, the Cosine expression's single parameter, Period, determines the number of seconds required for the waveform to complete one full cycle.

FIGURE 6.37   Constant2Vector expression icon

FIGURE 6.38   Constant3Vector expression icon

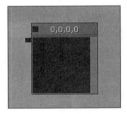

FIGURE 6.39   Constant4Vector expression icon

FIGURE 6.40   ConstantClamp expression icon

CrossProduct

A CrossProduct expression takes in two components, which must be vectors containing the same number of total components, or one must be a single-vector constant and the other a three-component vector. When using this second situation, the single vector is treated as a three-component vector, with each component containing the same value. The output of this expression is the result of a cross-product operation using the inputted vectors (see **FIGURE 6.42**).

FIGURE 6.41   Cosine expression icon

DepthBiasBlend

The DepthBiasBlend expression is intended to help remove the harsh edge that occurs when particles intersect a piece of geometry (see **FIGURE 6.43**). However, this expression is slower and less efficient than the other DepthBias expressions, and it is recommended that you use DepthBiasedAlpha instead.

DepthBiasedAlpha

The DepthBiasedAlpha expression is the first of two expressions (the other being DepthBiasedBlend) whose primary purpose is to help eliminate sharp edges where an object that has this material applied intersects with other geometry (see **FIGURE 6.44**). If you think back to the primer level created in Chapter 3, "Up and Running: A Hands-On Level Creation Primer," you might remember that when we created the steam particles that rose toward the ceiling, there was a sharp line where the sprites passed through the top of the level. DepthBiasedAlpha enables you to solve that problem by providing a bias-based blend between the sprite, and everything that was rendered before it for a given area.

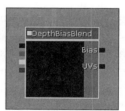

FIGURE 6.42
CrossProduct expression icon

FIGURE 6.43
DepthBiasBlend expression icon

Although the functionality of DepthBiasedAlpha may sound complex, in practice its use is quite simple. You can think of its function as blending between two things: 1) A material including the DepthBiasedAlpha expression, and 2) the current contents of the *destination buffer*.

Simply put, the destination buffer consists of everything that has been rendered in memory to any given pixel. You might as easily say that we are blending between a given particle, and whatever

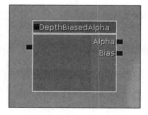

FIGURE 6.44
DepthBiasedAlpha expression icon

object may have already been there. Once again, consider the level we created in Chapter 3 in which we had steam particles lifting up to the ceiling of the level. By using a DepthBiasedAlpha expression, we could have created a bias-based blend between the ceiling (each pixel of which is stored in the destination buffer) and the particles, thereby eliminating the harsh edge that occurs when the particles intersect the ceiling.

The DepthBiasedAlpha expression takes in two inputs: Alpha and Bias. The Bias input handles the actual blend between the contents of the destination buffer and the material. Bias reads black and white values, where a value of 0 (black) blends completely toward the contents of the destination buffer, and 1 (white) blends completely toward the color of our material. The Alpha input is simply passed straight through the expression, with no operations being performed on it. If no Alpha input is passed in, the DepthBiasedAlpha expression outputs a value of 1.

> **NOTE**
>
> This expression is very expensive in terms of instructions. Consider carefully whether the effect is truly worth the cost in processing power! Also, be aware that this expression is preferred over the DepthBiased-Blend expression because of efficiency.

> **NOTE**
>
> It is highly recommended by Epic that you use DepthBiasedAlpha instead of this expression whenever possible, as this expression can sometimes cause sorting issues, meaning you may have problems with what object draws first, among other issues and performance implications.

DepthBiasedAlpha also has two parameters, bNormalize and BiasScale. BiasScale acts as a multiplier to whatever values are passed into the Bias input, thus allowing for a larger blend between the material and the contents of the destination buffer. The bNormalize property maps the depth values from the range of Near to Far to the range of 0 to 1.

DepthBiasedBlend

DepthBiasedBlend is a slightly more complex version of the DepthBiasedAlpha expression, in that it allows for the input of color. This color is then blended with the contents of the destination buffer using the value passed into the Bias parameter (see **FIGURE 6.45**).

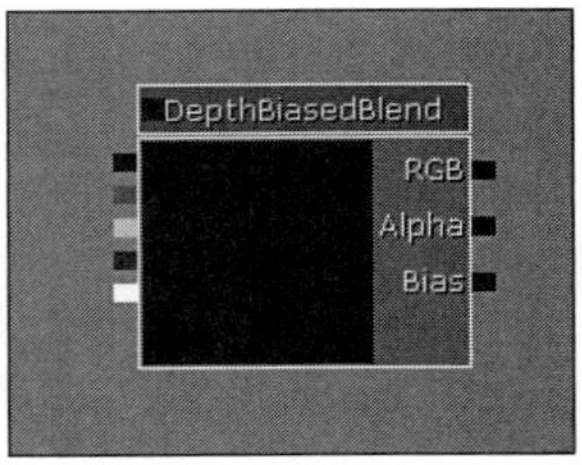

FIGURE 6.45
DepthBiasedBlend expression icon

Desaturation

A Desaturation expression pulls the amount of color out of a material, or *desaturates* it. The overall effect is that it pushes the existing color of a material toward gray. The Desaturation expression takes in two inputs: the first can be a vector with any number of components, whereas the second must be a single-value constant. The first input is desaturated by the percentage specified by the second input. A value of 0 means no desaturation, and a value of 1 means fully desaturated, or rendered in grayscale (see **FIGURE 6.46**).

DestColor

A DestColor expression outputs the color at the current screen position destination. This expression is only used when your material's BlendMode property is set to BLEND_Translucent, BLEND_Additive, or BLEND_modulate. You could, for example, use this material to show objects that are underneath a liquid surface. However, it should be noted that this is a very specific-case expression and is not often used (see **FIGURE 6.47**).

DestDepth

The DestDepth expression outputs what is called "Z-depth," which is how far away a pixel is behind the material. The further away an object behind a pixel being drawn, the higher the Z-depth, hence the higher the value output by the DestDepth expression. It has one parameter, bNormalize, which maps the values from the range of Near to Far to the range of 0 to 1. At the time of this writing, this parameter is nonfunctional. However, the DestDepth expression works just fine. If you need to normalize a particular value, you could always do so using a series of math expressions within the Material Editor (see **FIGURE 6.48**).

Divide

The Divide expression takes in two inputs, divides the first by the second, and outputs the result. Anything can be divided by a one-vector constant in any other case. The inputs for the divisor and the dividend must have an equal number of components (see **FIGURE 6.49**).

DotProduct

A DotProduct expression functions similarly to the CrossProduct expression, but performs a different kind of operation on the vectors. The expression takes in two components, which must be vectors containing the same number of total components, or one

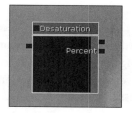

FIGURE 6.46
Desaturation expression icon

FIGURE 6.47   DestColor
expression icon

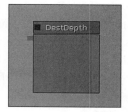

FIGURE 6.48   DestDepth
expression icon

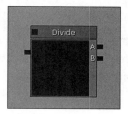

FIGURE 6.49   Divide
expression icon

must be a single-vector constant and the other a three-component vector. When using this second situation, the single vector is treated as a three-component vector, with each component containing the same value. The output of this expression is the result of a dot product operation using the inputted vectors (see **FIGURE 6.50**).

FlipBookSample

A FlipBookSample expression takes in a FlipBook texture as its only parameter. A FlipBook texture is a series of images that are calculated as a single texture, thus enabling you to sample a variety of image series or animation in your materials. Otherwise, it is identical to a TextureSample, described later. The FlipBookSample's outputs are RGB, R, G, B, and Alpha. It also can take in a vector as an input, which is used to determine the texture coordinates used for the texture (see **FIGURE 6.51**).

Floor

The Floor expression is the opposite of the Ceil expression, in that rather than rounding a floating point number upward, it rounds *down* to the next integer. For example, a value of 7.825 would output as 7 when inputted into a Floor expression. This can also be thought of as truncation, as all numbers after the decimal are "cut off" of the value (see **FIGURE 6.52**).

FontSample

The FontSample expression is used to sample in a font and use it in an expression. At the time of this writing, it is only accessible through code (see **FIGURE 6.53**).

FontSampleParameter

See the Parameter expression descriptions at the end of this section.

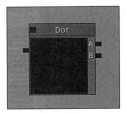

FIGURE 6.50
DotProduct expression icon

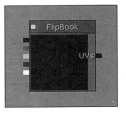

FIGURE 6.51
FlipBookSample expression icon

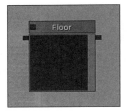

FIGURE 6.52   Floor expression icon

FIGURE 6.53
FontSample expression icon

Frac

The Frac, or Fraction, expression takes in one input and outputs the only portion of its value after the decimal point. For example, an input of 4.356 would output as 0.356 (see **FIGURE 6.54**).

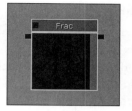

FIGURE 6.54 Frac expression icon

Fresnel

A Fresnel (pronounced freh-NELL) expression is a complex combination of several functions that reads the vector of the pixel's normal, and outputs a value of 0 where that vector aims at the camera, and 1 where the direction of the normal is perpendicular to the direction of the camera. On a perfect sphere, this means that (if directly connected to the Diffuse channel), the center of the sphere would be black, and the outer edges would be white, no matter from what angle the sphere was viewed (see **FIGURE 6.55**).

The Fresnel expression takes in one input, Normal, which can be a three-vector constant or a normal map. It has one parameter, Exponent. This expression computes a falloff based on the normal(s) passed in and the Exponent, which determines the sharpness of the falloff, and outputs the result.

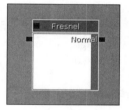

FIGURE 6.55 Fresnel expression icon

If

An If expression provides for conditional decisions to be made on the fly in your material. An If takes in five inputs. The first two, A and B, are the values that are compared against one another. The other three, A>B, A=B, and A<B, are the values that are passed to the output if the condition represented by the name of the input is met (see **FIGURE 6.56**).

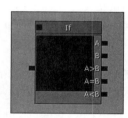

FIGURE 6.56 If expression icon

LensFlare Expressions

The LensFlare expressions are intended for use with the LensFlare system, which is not covered in this book. However, we have included explanations of what these nodes do for your own future reference.

LensFlareIntensity

The LensFlareIntensity expression provides access to the ConeStrength property of a rendered lens flare. This allows the level designer to determine the intensity of the flare with respect to the view's position in relation to the lens flare source (see **FIGURE 6.57**).

FIGURE 6.57
LensFlareIntensity
expression icon

The ConeStrength is 0.0 if the flare source falls outside the radius of the lens flare. If it is inside the radius, the cone strength is 1.0. If the flare uses a directional cone, the ConeStrength ranges between 1.0 and 0.0, where 1.0 occurs when the view is within the inner cone and facing the flare. The value falls off as the view moves through to the outer cone, arriving at zero as the outer cone is reached.

LensFlareOcclusion

The LensFlareOcclusion outputs per-pixel percentage of occlusion of a LensFlare object in the level. For example, if half of a LensFlare object were covered up (occluded) by a tree branch, this node would feed back a value around 0.5. This could be used to make changes to the LensFlare based on how much of it is visible (see **FIGURE 6.58**).

FIGURE 6.58
LensFlareOcclusion
expression icon

LensFlareRadialDistance

The LensFlareRadialDistance works similarly to a dot product, in that it increases as the camera faces directly into the LensFlare. As the LensFlare approaches the sides of the screen, the output value diminishes (see **FIGURE 6.59**).

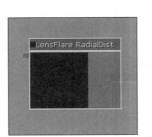

FIGURE 6.59
LensFlareRadialDistance
expression icon

FIGURE 6.60
LensFlareRayDistance
expression icon

LensFlareRayDistance

This gives access to the RayDistance value set within the lens flare object (see **FIGURE 6.60**).

LensFlareSourceDistance

The LensFlareSourceDistance provides the distance of a rendered object from the source of the lens flare (see **FIGURE 6.61**).

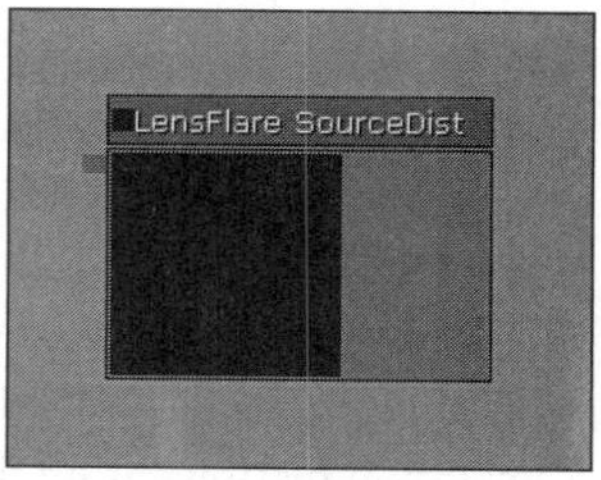

FIGURE 6.61
LensFlareSourceDistance
expression icon

LightVector

The LightVector expression gives you access to the vector representing the direction the current light being used in lighting calculations is pointing. This can be useful when your material is using the MLM_Custom lighting model to calculate your own lighting (see **FIGURE 6.62**).

LinearInterpolate

A LinearInterpolate expression takes in three inputs: A, B, and Alpha. The values of the A and B inputs are blended together based on the value of the Alpha, or mask. The result of this blend is then sent out through the output. A value of 0 in the Alpha causes the expression to blend completely toward the value of the A input is output, whereas a value of 1 means the B input is output. Values in between 0 and 1 blend the inputs accordingly (see **FIGURE 6.63**).

FIGURE 6.62
LightVector expression icon

MeshEmitterVertexColor

The MeshEmitterVertexColor expression is used only with mesh emitter particle systems, which emit instances of static meshes. Every mesh emitted in such a way has a color property, and this expression outputs that color as the vertex color of the entire mesh, avoiding having to access the mesh's vertex color each frame. The expression creates a single color for the entire mesh, rather than on a per-vertex basis (see **FIGURE 6.64**).

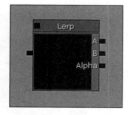

FIGURE 6.63
LinearInterpolate expression
icon

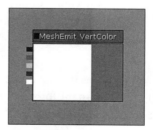

FIGURE 6.64
MeshEmitterVertexColor
expression icon

MeshSubUV

Like the MeshEmitterVertexColor expression, a MeshSubUV is used only with mesh emitter particle systems. The expression takes a multi-frame texture that is to be used for the meshes emitted by the emitter as its only parameter. Otherwise, it is identical to a TextureSample, described later. Using this expression saves calculation by preventing the recalculation of texture coordinates for each mesh particle on each frame (see **FIGURE 6.65**).

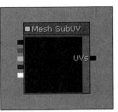

FIGURE 6.65
MeshSubUV expression icon

Multiply

The Multiply expression takes in two inputs, multiplies them, and outputs the result. A one-vector constant may be multiplied by anything, but other vectors of differing sizes cannot be multiplied (see **FIGURE 6.66**).

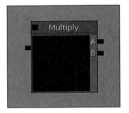

FIGURE 6.66   Multiply expression icon

Normalize

A Normalize expression takes in one vector input and makes its length equal to 1, or "normalizes" it. This means the length of the input is calculated and then each component is divided by that length. The resulting vector is then outputted (see **FIGURE 6.67**).

OneMinus

The OneMinus expression takes in a vector of any size as its input, subtracts the input from one, and outputs the result. For example, an input of 0.15 would have an output of 0.85. This is commonly called "inverting" a value. This can be useful if you have a texture you are using as a mask and you want to reverse the mask, or when you want to invert the colors on a particular texture (see **FIGURE 6.68**).

FIGURE 6.67   Normalize expression icon

Panner

The Panner expression moves the UV coordinates of a texture. It can take in a two-vector constant to override the default texture coordinates and a scalar value representing Time as inputs. It also has two parameters (SpeedX and SpeedY), which are floating point numbers that determine the speed of movement in the X- and Y-axes (see **FIGURE 6.69**).

FIGURE 6.68   OneMinus expression icon

Parameter

See the Parameter expression descriptions at the end of this section.

ParticleSubUV

A ParticleSubUV expression samples an inputted multi-frame texture that is to be used for particles as its only parameter. The different frames of the texture can then be animated in the Cascade Particle Editor. For example, you could have a multi-frame texture that was many different images of flickering flames, and then blend between each of these frames on every individual particle, giving the illusion of animated particles (see **FIGURE 6.70**).

PixelDepth

The PixelDepth expression is similar to the DestDepth expression, but rather than outputting the Z-depth (or distance away) of an object *behind* a given pixel, it instead outputs the Z-depth of the current pixel itself. It has one parameter, bNormalize, which maps the values from the range of Near to Far to the range of 0 to 1 (see **FIGURE 6.71**). At the time of this writing, this parameter is non-functional.

Power

A Power expression takes in two inputs, Base and Exp. The expression then raises the Base value to the power of the Exp value. The result of this operation becomes the output (see **FIGURE 6.72**).

> **NOTE**
>
> When your base value is between 0 and 1 (such as most color values), this expression works as a contrast adjustment, keeping only the brightest values.

FIGURE 6.69   Panner expression icon

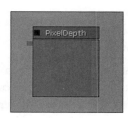

FIGURE 6.70 ParticleSubUV expression icon

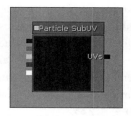

FIGURE 6.71   PixelDepth expression icon

FIGURE 6.72   Power expression icon

ReflectionVector

The ReflectionVector expression gives you access to the vector representing the direction of the CameraVector reflected across the normal of the surface the material is applied to, in tangent space. This can be useful when you want to make changes to a material based on the angle that the surfaces have in relation to the camera (see **FIGURE 6.73**).

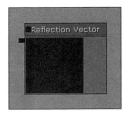

FIGURE 6.73
ReflectionVector
expression icon

Rotator

The Rotator expression rotates the UV coordinates of a texture. It can take in a two-vector constant to override the default texture coordinates and a scalar value representing Time as inputs. It has three parameters, which are each floating point numbers. CenterX and CenterY determine the center of rotation and Speed determines the speed of rotation in revolutions per second (see **FIGURE 6.74**).

FIGURE 6.74   Rotator
expression icon

ScalarParameter

See the Parameter expression descriptions at the end of this section.

SceneDepth

The SceneDepth expression is very similar to the DestDepth expression, but rather than calculating depth for a single pixel, it samples depth across the entire scene. It has one parameter, bNormalize, which maps the values from the range of Near to Far to the range of 0 to 1. At the time of this writing, this parameter is nonfunctional (see **FIGURE 6.75**).

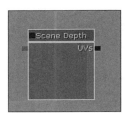

FIGURE 6.75
SceneDepth expression icon

SceneTexture

A SceneTexture expression enables you to sample the texture which represents your current rendered frame, allowing manipulation of your current view as if it were a texture sample (see **FIGURE 6.76**).

FIGURE 6.76
SceneTexture expression icon

ScreenPosition

A ScreenPosition expression outputs the position on the screen of the current pixel being evaluated. The pixel is given a location in screen space between [-1,-1], which would be the lower-left corner, and [1, 1], the upper-right corner. It has one parameter, ScreenAlign, which changes the coordinate range to [0, 0] to [1, 1], which can be useful as a set of texture coordinates for aligning a texture to the screen. To do this, you would need to input the ScreenPosition into a ComponentMask, outputting only the R and G values into the UVs of a given texture (see **FIGURE 6.77**).

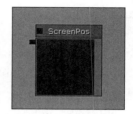

FIGURE 6.77
ScreenPosition expression icon

Sine

The Sine expression is virtually identical to the Cosine expression, aside from the obvious; it performs a sine function on the incoming angle input rather than a cosine function. In most cases, this is connected to a Time expression to cause animation during gameplay. When doing this, the Sine expression's single parameter, Period, determines the number of seconds required for the waveform to complete one full cycle (see **FIGURE 6.78**).

FIGURE 6.78   Cosine expression icon

SquareRoot

A SquareRoot expression takes in one input and outputs the square root of the input. This expression can only receive single-component constants (see **FIGURE 6.79**).

StaticComponentMaskParameter

See the Parameter expression descriptions at the end of this section.

FIGURE 6.79
SquareRoot expression icon

StaticSwitchParameter

See the Parameter expression descriptions at the end of this section.

Subtract

The Subtract expression takes in two inputs, subtracts the second from the first, and outputs the result. A one-vector constant may be subtracted from anything, but other vectors of differing sizes cannot be subtracted from one another (see **FIGURE 6.80**).

FIGURE 6.80   Subtract expression icon

TextureCoordinate

The Texture Coordinate expression has two parameters: CoordinateIndex, which is the UV channel the expression effects, and Tiling, which is the number of times to tile the texture. The output is a two-vector constant (see **FIGURE 6.81**).

FIGURE 6.81
TextureCoordinate expression icon

Polygonal meshes can have more than one set of texture coordinates. These sets are stored in what are called "UV channels." The TextureCoordinate expression provides access to different UV channels of a mesh, as well as allowing for texture repetition, or tiling. Its CoordinateIndex property enables you to choose which UV channel to apply to another expression (such as a TextureSample expression), and the Tiling property controls how many times the texture repeats across the surface. The TextureCoordinate has only one output; a two-component vector that provides a new set of texture coordinates, which then override the texture coordinates of the receiving expression.

TextureSample

The TextureSample expression is probably the most frequently used of all expressions, as it provides access to user-created textures. It takes in a texture as its only parameter and exposes the data stored in the texture as outputs. These outputs are RGB, R, G, B, and Alpha. It also can take in a two-component vector as an input, which is used to determine the texture coordinates used for the texture (see **FIGURE 6.82**).

FIGURE 6.82
TextureSample expression icon

TextureSampleParameter2D

See the Parameter expression descriptions at the end of this section.

TextureSampleParameterCube

See the Parameter expression descriptions at the end of this section.

TextureSampleParameterMovie

See the Parameter expression descriptions at the end of this section.

Time

The Time expression is used to add the passage of time to another expression that is time dependent, such as a Panner, Rotator, Sine, or Cosine, allowing such changes to take place constantly during gameplay. The bIgnorePause property allows time progression to continue even when the game is paused (see **FIGURE 6.83**).

FIGURE 6.83   Time expression icon

Transform

The Transform expression enables you to transform any three-component vector in different coordinate systems, such as world space, view space, and local space (see **FIGURE 6.84**). The expression takes in one input, which must be a three-component vector, which is then transformed from tangent space into the space specified in the TransformType parameter. The options are TRANSFORM_World, TRANSFORM_View, and TRANSFORM_Local. This expression can be useful sampling cubemaps, as it enables you to transform a normal map to world space, rather than tangent space, which exists only across a surface. More information on cubemaps is presented later in this chapter.

FIGURE 6.84   Transform expression icon

TransformPosition

This expression is deprecated and should not be used.

VectorParameter

See the Parameter expression descriptions at the end of this section.

VertexColor

A VertexColor expression functions like a MeshEmitterVertex Color, discussed previously. However, this expression is intended for use on sprite emitters instead of mesh emitters. The VertexColor expression outputs the vertex color for the current fragment being operated on (see **FIGURE 6.85**). This node also allows access to the vertex colors of a static mesh as exported out of a traditional 3d modeling package, for use in your material.

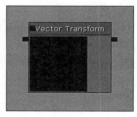

FIGURE 6.85 VertexColor expression icon

Parameter Expressions

The Parameter expressions have been singled out of the preceding list because they are intended for a very special functionality, and it is easiest if we discuss them all in a group. Because materials play such an important role in the final look of your game, it will at some point be just as important for the player to be able to interact with these materials in some way, or for the materials themselves to be able to change in specific ways. For example, maybe all the glowing highlights in a starship's materials change from blue to red as the ship takes damage, or maybe you'd like to blend between a smooth and aged version of a texture over a few seconds to make an object appear to quickly age and corrode.

In Unreal, such actions are performed through the use of material instances, which are special types of materials that reference a parent material. Where standard materials are calculated once and cannot change during gameplay, a material instance can use parameters to change aspects of the material at runtime. The instance itself is applied to an

> **NOTE**
>
> You may be tempted to use parameters where they're not necessary. For example, using a VectorParameter expression gives you access to a Color Chooser window for selecting a color, while the Constant4Vector does not. Even though you don't need external access to the color, it would be easier to use a Color Chooser than to punch in color values manually. However, keep in mind that using parameter expressions does incur a very slight overhead increase, and best practice would be not to use them unless absolutely necessary.

object, and various changes can be made to the instance through parameters. While material instances are not covered in this introduction, the basic idea could be described through the following example.

Say you have a simple material that uses a VectorParameter to drive the Emissive (glow) channel. You could then create a material instance of that initial material, and change the value of the VectorParameter to get different colors of the glow for the material instance. The parameter could also be changed during gameplay using Kismet or Matinee, and any object to which the material instance was applied would be able to change.

The following is a list of the parameter expressions available.

FontSampleParameter

The FontSampleParameter expression is a parameterized version of the FontSample used to sample in a font and use it in an expression. At the time of this writing, it is only accessible through code (see **FIGURE 6.86**).

FIGURE 6.86
FontSampleParameter
expression icon

Parameter

The Parameter expression is a placeholder template for creating your own Material Expressions through code. In and of itself, it has no use (see **FIGURE 6.87**).

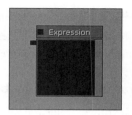

FIGURE 6.87 Parameter expression icon

ScalarParameter

The ScalarParameter expression is the parameter version of a Constant expression. It holds a single floating point number (see **FIGURE 6.88**).

FIGURE 6.87 Parameter expression icon

StaticComponentMaskParameter

The StaticComponentMaskParameter expression behaves just like a ComponentMask, enabling you to cancel out channels of a color as necessary. However, since it is a parameter, it can be accessed or changed as part of a material instance. However, due to its static nature, it cannot be changed during gameplay (see **FIGURE 6.89**).

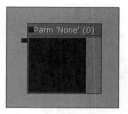

FIGURE 6.88
ScalarParameter expression

StaticSwitchParameter

The StaticSwitchParameter expression enables you to switch between different expression network branches within material instances. The basic idea is that you can have different networks that give completely different results within the same material, and use the switch to select which result you want to use. The expression is static and can therefore not be changed during gameplay (see **FIGURE 6.90**).

FIGURE 6.89
StaticComponentMaskParameter
expression icon

VectorParameter

The VectorParameter expression is the parameter version of a Constant4Vector. It holds four floating point numbers (see **FIGURE 6.91**).

FIGURE 6.90
StaticSwitchParameter
expression icon

FIGURE 6.91
VectorParameter expression
icon

TextureSampleParameter2D

The TextureSampleParameter2D expression is the parameter version of a TextureSample for holding a regular texture (see **FIGURE 6.92**).

TextureSampleParameterCube

The TextureSampleParameterCube expression is the parameter version of the TextureSample expression, but specialized for holding a cubemap (see **FIGURE 6.93**).

TextureSampleParameterMovie

The TextureSampleParameterMovie expression is the parameter version of the TextureSample expression, but specialized for holding a movie (see **FIGURE 6.94**).

FIGURE 6.92
TextureSampleParameter2D
expression icon

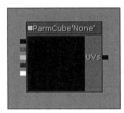

FIGURE 6.93
TextureSampleParameterCube
expression icon

FIGURE 6.94
TextureSampleParameterMovie
expression icon

Material Creation

Now that we've taken a look at the look at all of the available Material Expressions, let's see how we can implement some of them into some simple materials to achieve a variety of effects. Over the next several tutorials, you create some proof-of-concept materials, intended to give you a better idea of what some of these expressions do, and how you will later implement them into your own materials. Think of the following tutorials simply as exercises to help acquaint you with some of the expressions and material network development. Also keep in mind that we construct the material in a progressive manner, meaning that that we demonstrate solutions to problems as they arise, and not simply creating the material with all the necessary expressions at one fell swoop. In this way, you learn a sound method for creating a material one piece at a time.

However, the first thing we're going to need in order to create an interesting material is access to textures. Textures provide us with the actual imagery we use inside a material. We can use them for color, as a modifier to an existing effect, as a way to determine where effects are placed, or mapped, across our material, and for a variety of other uses as well. In order to use a texture, it must first be imported into Unreal Editor. However, even before you import, there are some considerations for texture creation.

Here are some guidelines to consider when creating a texture for Unreal Engine 3.0:

▶ Imported textures should be in Targa (.TGA) format. The Editor accepts other formats, though targas are the preferred format.

▶ Textures do not need to be square, although their pixel dimensions should be in powers of 2, such as 32, 256, 1024, and so on.

▶ As a general rule, textures should be no larger than 2048 pixels. This is a suggestion, but keeping textures down to this size helps speed up processing time.

▶ Just because you *can* have 2048×2048 textures doesn't necessarily mean you *need* them. Always consider how much detail you must have, and choose texture sizes accordingly.

In **TUTORIAL 6.3**, we show how you can bring textures into your Unreal Editor packages for use within your own materials.

TUTORIAL 6.3: Importing Textures into a Package

1. The first thing we need to create a material is a series of textures. In the Generic browser, choose File > Import. There are two textures included in the files for this chapter on your DVD named tex_wall_stone_blocks_dark and tex_wall_stone_blocks_normal. Select both of these textures and click OK (see **FIGURE 6.95**).

> **NOTE**
>
> You may continue from **TUTORIAL 6.2**, but we simply start a new package for this example.

2. The Import dialog appears with two sets of options that you can set. The top area, labeled Info, contains much of the same information we've already seen for specifying package, group, and entity name. Below in the Options area are several settings to control what happens during the import process, such as whether you'd like to make a new material using this texture, and if so, where you'd like it connected.

In the Info area, enter the following information (see **FIGURE 6.96**):

> **Package:** TextureImport
>
> **Group:** Textures

FIGURE 6.95   Choose Import from the Generic browser's File menu.

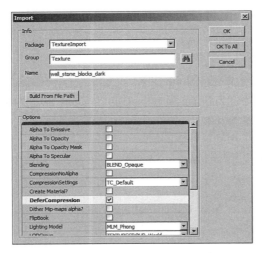

FIGURE 6.96   Fill the preceding information into the Import dialog.

> **NOTE**
>
> It may take a few minutes to bring the textures into Unreal Editor. Be patient!

In the Options area, check the DeferCompression checkbox. This speeds up workflow by not compressing the texture until you save the package.

When finished, click the OK To All button.

3. Your two textures should now appear in your TextureImport package.

   With the TextureImport package selected, choose File > Save to save the changes to your package. You can close the Material Editor at this time.

END TUTORIAL 6.3

Our textures have been loaded into our package, but to use them in our material, we need to sample them using the TextureSample expression before we use them in our material. In **TUTORIAL 6.4**, we demonstrate the creation of a simple brick wall material.

TUTORIAL 6.4: Creating a Brick Wall Material

1. Continue from **TUTORIAL 6.3**, or open the Chapter_06_Materials.upk package included with the files for this chapter. This package already has the textures imported for you.

2. Open the DM-Ch_06_BrickRoom_Start.ut3 level, also included with the files for this chapter. It should contain two cube-shaped rooms connected by a hallway, and should contain some basic lighting.

3. Open the Generic browser, navigate to the Chapter_06_Materials package, right-click on a blank area of the main browser window, and choose New Material from the Context menu. Enter the following values into the New dialog:

Group: Materials

Name: mat_myBrickWall

This opens the Material Editor.

4. We need our texture to be sampled inside of our material. Do this using the following procedure:

    a. Start by dragging a new TextureSample expression from the Expression List on the right side of the Editor and into the Expression window of the Material Editor (the large gray area).

    b. Hold the Ctrl key and drag the TextureSample so that it is just to the right of the Material Node's Diffuse channel (see **FIGURE 6.97**).

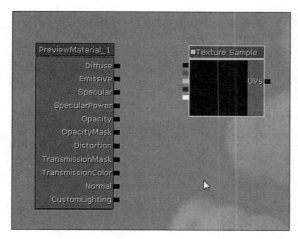

FIGURE 6.97   Position the TextureSample expression like so.

    c. We now need to associate our wall_stone_blocks_dark texture with this new TextureSample expression. Start by making sure that your texture is selected in the Generic browser. You can verify this selection by looking for the pale green border around the texture.

Next, in the Material Editor, select the TextureSample, and in the Properties window of the Material Editor, click the Texture Property, and then click the

> **NOTE**
>
> The texture is very dark. Your TextureSample may appear black. This is normal.

green-arrowed Use Current Selection in Browser button ⬅, located to the right of the property. An image of the texture should now appear in the TextureSample.

5. Repeat the process demonstrated in Step 3 to create a new TextureSample associated to the wall_stone_blocks_normal texture, but place this new TextureSample just to the right of the Material Node's Normal channel (see **FIGURE 6.98**).

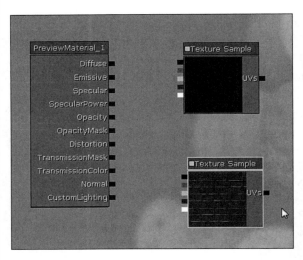

FIGURE 6.98   Position the second TextureSample expression like so.

6. We now need to connect these two textures into our material. Follow these steps:

    a. Drag a wire from the black RGBA tab on the TextureSample that contains the color texture (not the normal map) to the Diffuse channel of the material.

    b. Drag a wire from the black RGBA tab on the TextureSample that contains the normal map to the Normal channel of the material.

7. Click the Apply Changes button ![check], located at the top of the Material Editor interface, and save your package (it's the green check button on the far left).

8. In your Perspective viewport, right-click and choose Select All Surface from the Context menu. Next, in the Generic browser, click on the new mat_BrickWall material, which applies your material to all the surfaces of your level (see **FIGURE 6.99**).

9. Save your current level.

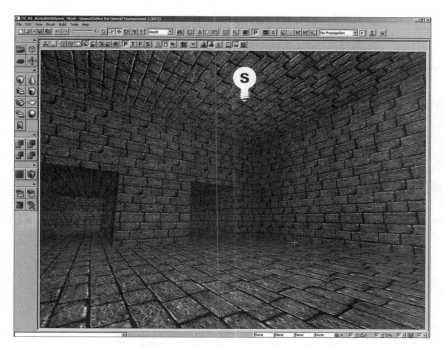

FIGURE 6.99   Your material is now applied to all the surfaces of your level.

END TUTORIAL 6.4

We now have some textures connected to our material, but currently we have a few small problems. The first is that our bricks could be a little shinier, as it would make them look kind of wet. Also, the Diffuse texture is very dark; it would be nice if we could brighten things up a bit. In **TUTORIAL 6.5**, we make some minor adjustments to the look of our material by bringing in some new expressions.

TUTORIAL 6.5: Modifying a Texture with Material Expressions

1. Continue from **TUTORIAL 6.4** or open (double-click) the mat_brickWall_01 material found within the Chapter_06_Materials package, included on your DVD in the package for this chapter. You also need to open the DM-Ch_06_BrickRoom_Start map, and apply the mat_brickWall_01 material to all surfaces. See **TUTORIAL 6.4** if you need help!

2. First, we need to brighten up our texture a bit. We do this by using a Multiply expression. From the Expression List, choose a Multiply and drag it into the Expression window. Position it between the Diffuse TextureSample and the Material Node. This may require that you reposition your TextureSample icon (see **FIGURE 6.100**).

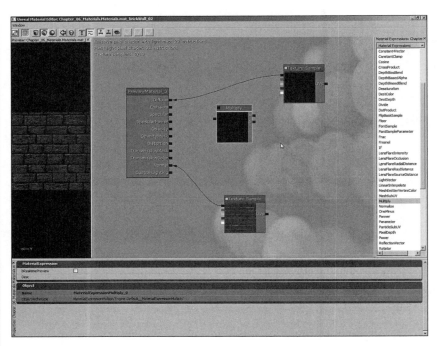

FIGURE 6.100   A new Multiply expression has been added into the Expression window.

3. Connect the RGBA (black) output of the dark brick TextureSample to the B input of the Multiply expression (see **FIGURE 6.101**).

4. Connect the output of the Multiply expression into the Diffuse channel of the material, overriding the existing connection (see **FIGURE 6.102**).

NOTE

As soon as you do this, you're going to get an error. This is because the Multiply expression currently has only a single input.

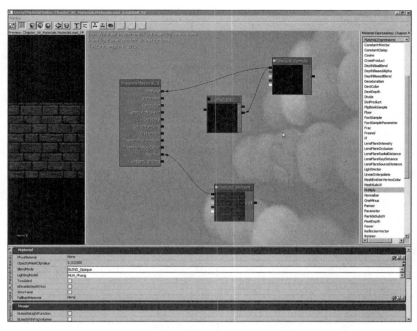

FIGURE 6.101   The RGBA data from the TextureSample is connected to the B input.

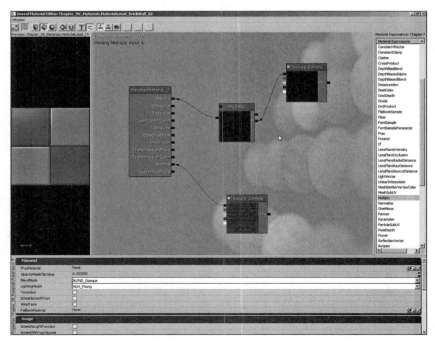

FIGURE 6.102   The Multiply expression is connected to the material.

5. We need a second input to feed into our Multiply expression. This requires a Constant expression, which holds a single floating point value. Create a new Constant expression now by dragging one out of the Expression List. Position it just above your Diffuse TextureSample (see **FIGURE 6.103**).

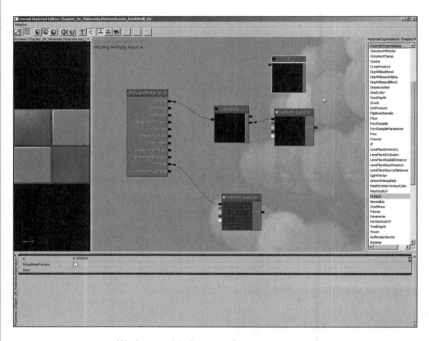

FIGURE 6.103   We have added a new Constant expression.

6. Connect the output of the Constant expression to the A input of the Multiply expression (see **FIGURE 6.104**).

7. With your new Constant expression selected, go to the Properties window and set the R value to a value of 5 or so. This not only brings back your color, but you'll notice that the color is now intensified. Feel free to tweak this value until you are satisfied.

NOTE

Once you complete this step, your error goes away, but your material appears to be flat black. This is because the default value for a new Constant expression is 0, meaning that you are now multiplying the color value of your material by nothing, which causes it to be black.

NOTE

As a reminder, the Diffuse channel can accept values that are greater than 1 for R, G, and B. If you drive the diffuse value high enough, the material actually appears to glow. You can test this by setting the constant's R value to something like 1000. Just be sure to set it back when you're done!

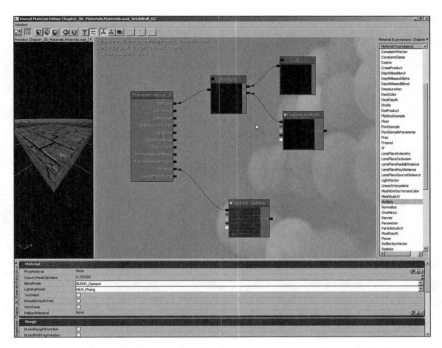

FIGURE 6.104 The Constant's value is now connected into the Multiply.

8. Our material is now looking bright enough to see fairly easily, but it could still be a bit shinier. We can fix this by plugging a dark texture into the Specular channel that lines up with our current brick texture. You could, of course, simply apply a constant value, but using a texture gives you pixel-by-pixel control over which areas are shiny and which ones are not. Our dark brick texture would be perfect for this job, but we don't really need its actual color values.

   Fortunately, the texture artist has stored a black and white version of the texture in the texture's Alpha channel. Connect the white Alpha output of the dark brick TextureSample to the Specular channel of the Material Node. You will now see that the bricks maintain a trace amount of shininess, as if they're damp, but the grout gaps in between each brick are no longer shiny. This is the benefit of using a texture over a simple constant value, which would apply the same level of shininess across the entire surface (see **FIGURE 6.105**).

9. Apply changes to your material (remember, the leftmost green check button!), and save your package.

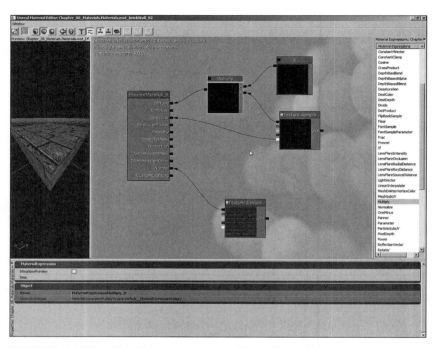

FIGURE 6.105   The Alpha output of our Diffuse TextureSample is now connected into our material's Specular channel.

END TUTORIAL 6.5

Our material is looking much better now, but it would be nice if we could make the bricks look just a little bit larger. There are two ways to handle this problem. The first is within the material itself, by using a TextureCoordinate expression and adjusting the tiling, or repetition of the texture. The second method, which we examine in **TUTORIAL 6.6**, is to control texture placement on a surface-by-surface basis.

> **NOTE**
>
> The following methods apply only to BSP surfaces. Adjusting texture placement on a mesh requires that you adjust the UV texture coordinates in a 3D application or by making simple adjustments in your material, such as using a Panner, Rotator, or TextureCoordinate for tiling.

Surface Properties

Every BSP surface of a level contains a series of information that enables you to control how a material is placed across its surface. This is useful for adjusting the placement of a material without having to open the material and make adjustments to its network. There are two ways to adjust surface properties. One is through the Surface Properties dialog, which offers a great deal of precise functionality. The other is by using Texture Alignment mode, an intuitive widget-based texture placement system.

The Surface Properties Dialog

If you select any BSP surface, you can adjust its texture placement properties by choosing View > Surface Properties. The Surface Properties dialog appears, which gives you an interface-based system for adjusting how textures are placed on your surfaces (see **FIGURE 6.106**).

In **TUTORIAL 6.6**, we take a look at how we can use this window to adjust how textures are positioned on our BSP surfaces. Please note that we do not cover the Lighting options in this chapter, as those are more suited to Chapter 7. **TUTORIAL 6.6** shows how textures can be edited within a material through moving (panning), rotating and scaling them.

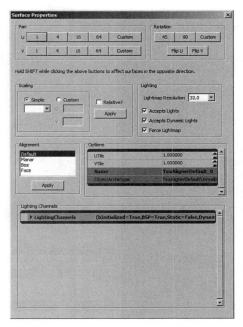

FIGURE 6.106 The Surface Properties dialog in all its texture-tweaking glory

TUTORIAL 6.6: Surface Properties Dialog: Panning, Rotating, and Scaling

1. Continue from **TUTORIAL 6.5** or open (double-click) the mat_brickWall_02 material found within the Chapter_06_Materials package, included on your DVD in the package for this chapter. You also need to open the DM-Ch_06_BrickRoom_Start map, and apply the mat_brickWall_02 material to all surfaces. See **TUTORIAL 6.4** if you need help!

> **NOTE**
>
> As you progress through **TUTORIAL 6.6**, you will misalign your textures. Don't worry about that right now; we fix it in **TUTORIAL 6.7**!

2. Select the floor of one of the rooms in your level, and from the main menubar of Unreal Editor, choose View > Surface Properties. This brings up the Surface Properties dialog. Position this window so that you can still see what's going on with the floor surface in your Perspective viewport (see **FIGURE 6.107**).

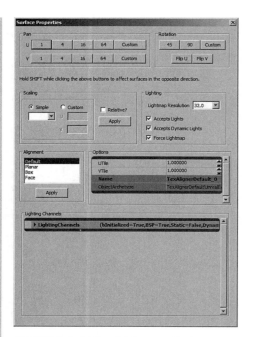

FIGURE 6.107   Make sure that you can see the selected surface, as well as the Surface Properties window.

6

3. We start by taking a look at simple panning of a texture. At the top of the Surface Properties window, you'll see the Pan group, which has a series of buttons you can click to move the texture by the labeled value in Unreal

---

NOTE

These panning movements can only be done in integer values. You cannot pan a texture by values such as 0.4 units.

---

units in either the U or V direction (see **FIGURE 6.108**). Try clicking the buttons a few times and see how the texture moves around either left and right or up and down. If you click the custom button, you'll see a dialog box where you can input a particular number for panning.

Also notice that you can hold the Shift key while clicking to move the textures in the opposite direction.

4. Now let's take a look at rotation. Next to the Pan group, you'll see the Rotation group, which also holds a series of buttons. Clicking these rotates the texture by the given value. The Custom button enables you to punch in your own value. These buttons also move in the opposite direction when the Shift key is held down (see **FIGURE 6.109**).

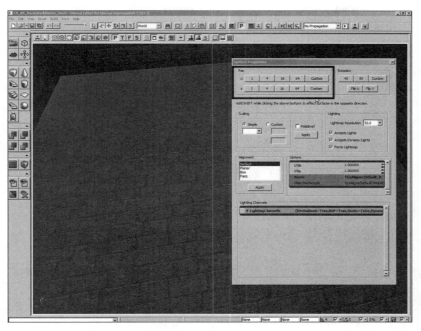

FIGURE 6.108   Pan group

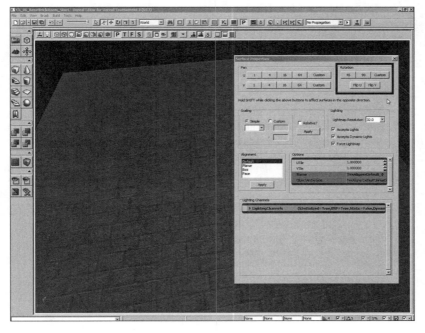

FIGURE 6.109   Rotation group

When you're done experimenting, rotate your floor texture to an interesting angle, such as 45 degrees or so.

> **NOTE**
>
> Unlike the Pan buttons, you can enter floating point values, such as 0.2 into the Custom field.

5. On to the Scaling group. Scaling your texture can be done either uniformly (meaning in both U and V simultaneously) or non-uniformly (scaling in one dimension and not the other). There are also no buttons for scaling, although there is a dropdown list for simple scaling for common scaling sizes (see **FIGURE 6.110**).

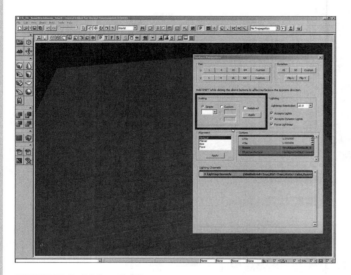

FIGURE 6.110   Scaling group

a. Select one of the walls of your level. In the Surface Properties window, make sure the Simple radio button is checked, and either choose a value for the dropdown list or type in your own value.

> **NOTE**
>
> If you selected 1 as your number, you might have noticed that nothing happened. This is because a value of 1 is analogous to 100 percent. Because your texture was scaled to 100 percent by default, a value of one produces no change. Feel free to choose another value and click Apply again.

Click the Apply button inside the Scaling group when done.

b. Currently, you are scaling in absolute texture space, meaning that all scale measurements are applied considering that the default size of the texture is 100 percent. For example, if you enter a value of 0.5, your texture is always half of its default size.

You can also scale relatively, which means that the current size of your texture is considered to be 100 percent. Test this now by checking the Relative checkbox, entering a value of 0.75 into the Simple scaling field, and clicking Apply a few times. You'll see that each time you click, the texture appears to get smaller. This is because each application is scaling the texture to 75 percent of its current value

Place the scale back to 100 percent by un-checking the Relative checkbox, entering a value of 1 into the Simple scaling field, and clicking Apply.

c. Now set the radio button to Custom instead of Simple. Notice that you can now specify values to scale the texture in only one dimension (either U or V), or by different values in each direction. The Relative checkbox still applies to such scaling.

Try it out by scaling your wall's texture by 2 in U and .5 in V (see **FIGURE 6.111**).

6. These changes are not stored in your material. Instead, they exist inside the surfaces of your BSP. If you were to apply another material to a surface edited in such a way, you'd notice similar placement of the new material.

Save your map's progress.

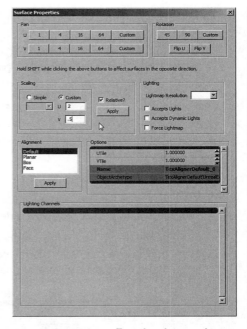

FIGURE 6.111   Test the shown values for the Scaling group.

> **NOTE**
>
> All the operations covered in **TUTORIAL 6.6** can be performed on multiple surfaces simultaneously by selecting all the desired surfaces, and then performing your operation.

END TUTORIAL 6.6

You've now seen how you can adjust the placement of your texture by panning, rotating, and scaling. In **TUTORIAL 6.7**, we look at how you can also align textures to make them appear seamless, provided your texture was designed in a seamless manner. Texture placement can be precisely adjusted with the Surface Properties window.

TUTORIAL 6.7: Aligning Textures with the Surface Properties Window

1. Continue from **TUTORIAL 6.6** or open (double-click) the mat_brickWall_02 material found within the Chapter_06_Materials package, included on your DVD in the package for this chapter. You also need to open the DM-Ch_06_BrickRoom_Start map, and apply the mat_brickWall_02 material to all surfaces. See **TUTORIAL 6.4** if you need help!

2. If you followed along in **TUTORIAL 6.6**, the floor in one of your rooms is probably no longer aligned to all the other textures in your level, meaning that you probably have some seams somewhere. We can fix this using the Alignment group within the Surface Properties window.

   Access this now by choosing View > Surface Properties from the main menubar.

3. Let's start by fixing just the floor. This trick is especially useful when you have multiple adjacent floor surfaces all having different sizes, but using the same texture.

   Click on one of the floor surfaces; then right-click in the Perspective viewport, and from the Context menu, choose Select Surfaces > Adjacent Coplanars. This selects all the floor surfaces that are adjacent to your original selection (see **FIGURE 6.112**).

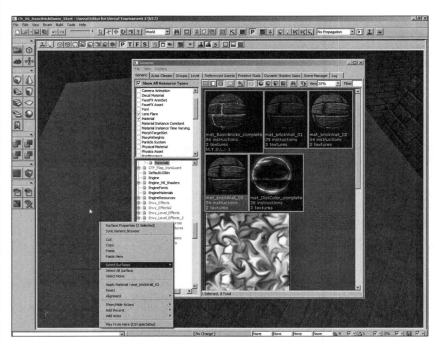

FIGURE 6.112   In this case, selecting Adjacent Coplanars selects all floor surfaces.

4. In the Surface Properties window, go to the Alignment group and choose the Planar; then click the Apply button located in that group. This applies a single planar mapping of your texture across all the selected surfaces. On a texture that has been designed in a seamless manner, this technique eliminates seams between all selected surfaces (see **FIGURE 6.113**).

5. Now let's take a moment and reset all of our texture adjustments to their default settings. Simply right-click in your Perspective viewport, and in the Context menu, choose Select All Surface (see **FIGURE 6.114**).

In the Surface Properties window, choose the Default alignment and click Apply. This resets all texture adjustments to the same values they had when the BSP was first created (see **FIGURE 6.115**).

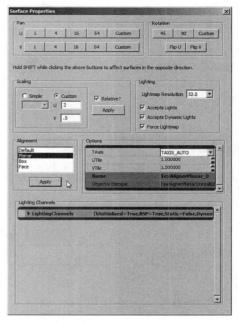

FIGURE 6.113   Select Planar and click Apply.

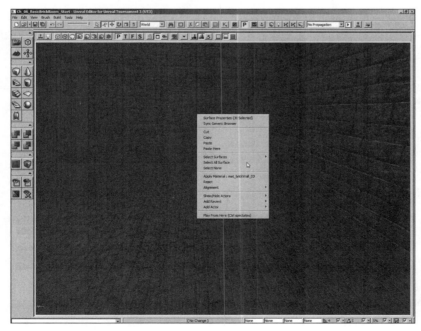

FIGURE 6.114
This selects all surfaces in your level.

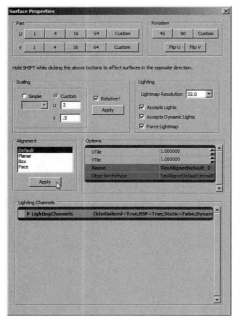

FIGURE 6.115   Apply the Default mapping to all your selected faces.

You also have two other mapping methods in the alignment group: Box, which applies a planar mapping of the texture from six directions, perfect for mapping a cube-shaped room; and Face, which at the time of this writing does not work properly.

6. Save your current map.

END TUTORIAL 6.7

Now that you've seen how to use the Surface Properties window to adjust your texture placement, let's take a brief look at Texture Alignment Mode, which allows for more intuitive (although less precise) adjustment of textures in your map. The Surface Properties window is only one way to adjust your textures. In **TUTORIAL 6.8**, we show how you can also reposition your textures intuitively by using Texture Alignment Mode.

TUTORIAL 6.8: Using Texture Alignment Mode

1. Continue from **TUTORIAL 6.7** or open (double-click) the mat_brickWall_02 material found within the Chapter_06_Materials package, included on your DVD in the package for this chapter. You also need to open the DM-Ch_06_BrickRoom_Start map, and apply the mat_brickWall_02 material to all surfaces. See **TUTORIAL 6.4** if you need help!

2. Select one of the surfaces of your map (it does not matter which one), and click the Texture Alignment Mode button , located just underneath the Geometry Mode button in the Toolbox.

3. You should now see a widget appear on your surface (make sure the Show/Use the Widget button ▭, is active!) that corresponds to whichever transformation widget you currently have selected in the Toolbar (see **FIGURE 6.116**).

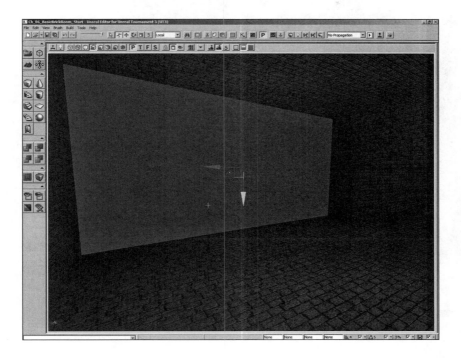

FIGURE 6.116 A special two-dimensional version of the Translation Widget is now visible on the surface.

4. Take a moment and see how using the Translation Widget enables you to move the texture across the surface, the Rotation Widget enables you to rotate the texture, and the Scale Widget (both uniform and non-uniform) enables you to change the size of your texture (see **FIGURE 6.117**).

5. Once finished, remember that you can reset all your changes to the default values by using Default alignment from the Surface Properties window. Do so before going on (see **FIGURE 6.118**).

6. Save the changes to your map when finished.

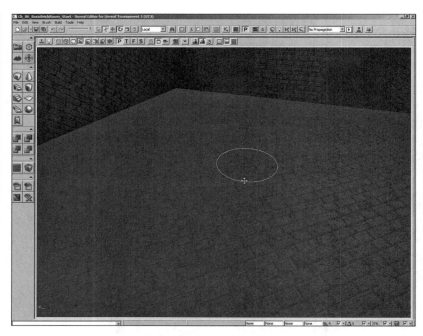

FIGURE 6.117   Here you can see how the rotation widget has been used to rotate the texture.

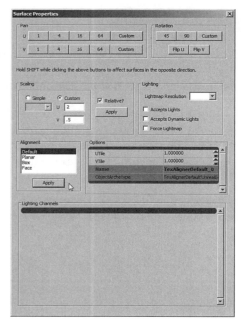

FIGURE 6.118   All surfaces have now been reset.

END TUTORIAL 6.8

You have now seen how to create a basic material, and you've taken a look at some simple texture alignment adjustments using two separate methods. Now let's push things to the next level. In **TUTORIAL 6.9**, we enhance the look of our material by implementing a BumpOffset expression, which supplements the normal map, giving the illusion that the bricks actually protrude from the flat surface of the wall.

TUTORIAL 6.9: Implementing a BumpOffset Expression

1. Continue from **TUTORIAL 6.8** or open (double-click) the mat_brickWall_02 material found within the Chapter_06_Materials package, included on your DVD in the package for this chapter. You also need to open the DM-Ch_06_BrickRoom_Start map, and apply the mat_brickWall_02 material to all surfaces. See **TUTORIAL 6.4** if you need help!

2. Bring in a new BumpOffset expression, and place it somewhere to the right of your Diffuse TextureSample (see **FIGURE 6.119**).

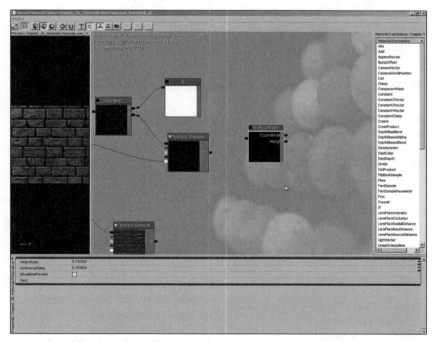

FIGURE 6.119   The BumpOffset expression has now been added to the Expression window.

3. A BumpOffset is intended to offset the UVs of a texture by using the height of the normal map. Connect the output of the BumpOffset into the UVs input of the Diffuse TextureSample expression (see **FIGURE 6.120**).

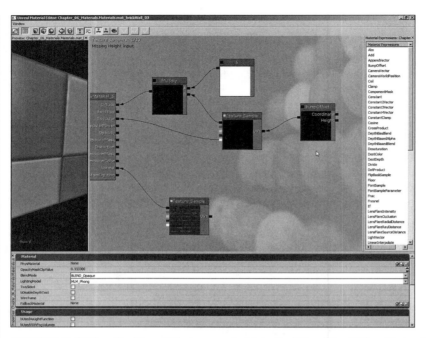

FIGURE 6.120   The BumpOffset connected into the UVs of the Diffuse TextureSample

4. Connect the Alpha output (white tab) of the normal map's TextureSample expression to the Height input of the BumpOffset. We use the Alpha instead of the RGB value because the Height input is looking for a one-component vector parameter, not a three-component vector, which would be supplied through RGB data (see **FIGURE 6.121**).

   Do not apply your changes yet.

5. Before you apply your changes, move the Perspective viewport camera next to one of the walls, looking up at an angle. This helps you see the difference created by the BumpOffset.

> **NOTE**
>
> Your material breaks at this point, feeding back an error. This is because the BumpOffset requires a Height input, which we place in the next step.

> **NOTE**
>
> You will notice after you complete **TUTORIAL 6.9** that your Material Editor has highlighted several of your expressions, and the message "Maximum texture dependency length: 1" has appeared at the top of the Expression window. This is not a concern; it simply has to do with the number of expressions upon which your texture sample has become dependent. In this case, it refers to the BumpOffset expression, which is feeding into the TextureSample.

Once your camera is in position, click the Apply Changes button in the Material Editor, while keeping an eye on the Perspective viewport. You'll suddenly see depth appear in your materials (see **FIGURE 6.122**). Okay, you can admit it—that's pretty awesome, isn't it?

6. Save your package.

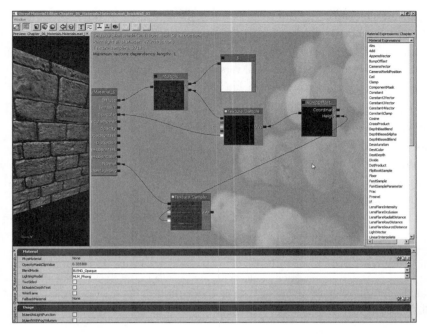

FIGURE 6.121
The normal map's Alpha output is now connected to the BumpOffset.

FIGURE 6.122
If you look carefully, you'll notice that the bricks now appear to have far more depth than before.

END TUTORIAL 6.9

Bump offset a very cool effect for making your materials look more realistic. Now we're going to have a little fun with what's going on in our material. We're going to make it look like there's light coming out from in between the bricks, and then we make that light pulsate based on a sine wave. At the same time, we might want to keep the original version of our brick wall; not every wall we come across has light pouring out between the bricks. So we start by duplicating our current material so that we can create a separate version with our special effect.

In **TUTORIAL 6.10**, we change the look of our brick wall material to cause the mortar to seem to glow. We then use a Sine and a Time expression to cause the glow to pulsate. Many different things are added to our material in this tutorial, so be sure to follow the steps and substeps very carefully! Also, throughout several areas, you will likely need to reorganize the placement of your expression icons to make room. This tutorial assumes that you can do that on your own.

TUTORIAL 6.10: Duplicating and Adding Special Effects to Our Brick Material

1. Continue from **TUTORIAL 6.9** or open (double-click) the mat_brickWall_03 material found within the Chapter_06_Materials package, included on your DVD in the package for this chapter. You also need to open the DM-Ch_06_BrickRoom_Start map, and apply the mat_brickWall_03 material to all surfaces. See **TUTORIAL 6.4** if you need help!

2. First, we duplicate our existing material. Follow these steps:

   a. In the Generic browser, select the mat_BrickWall material (or mat_brickWall_03 if you just opened the file), and right-click it.

   b. From the Context menu that appears, choose Duplicate (see **FIGURE 6.123**).

   c. Change the Name property to mat_GlowBricks. This creates a new version of the brick material (see **FIGURE 6.124**).

3. Open the Material Editor for the mat_GlowBricks material. We start by placing a very simple glow into the crevices of our bricks. Follow these steps:

   a. First, we need a texture map that is dark in the area of the bricks and light in the crevices. We don't have one, but we can make one from our normal map's Alpha channel.

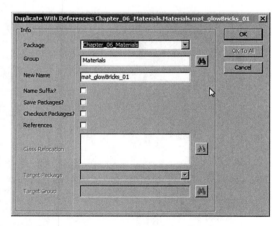

FIGURE 6.123   Duplicating enables us to edit a new version of the material while keeping the original.

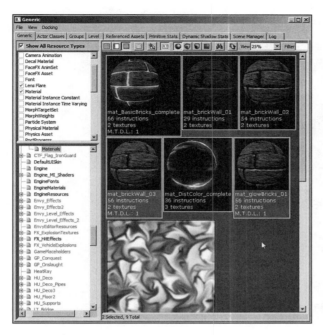

FIGURE 6.124   You can now see both of the materials in the Generic browser.

Unfortunately, the normal map's Alpha is currently in the opposite form; the crevices are dark and the bricks are light.

To fix this, bring in a new OneMinus expression, and connect the output of the normal map TextureSample into the OneMinus's input. If you then connect the output of the OneMinus into the Emissive channel of the material, you can see that the material now glows intensely all over, though the crevices do glow the brightest (see **FIGURE 6.125**).

4. We need to tighten up the focus of the emissive channel. To do this, we use a Power expression.

    a. Bring in a new Power, and connect the output of the OneMinus into the Base input (see **FIGURE 6.126**).

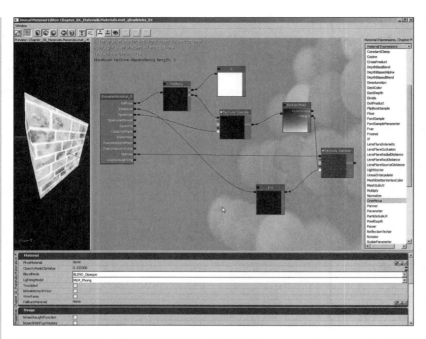

FIGURE 6.125   Here you can see the OneMinus expression connected into the material and the resulting material.

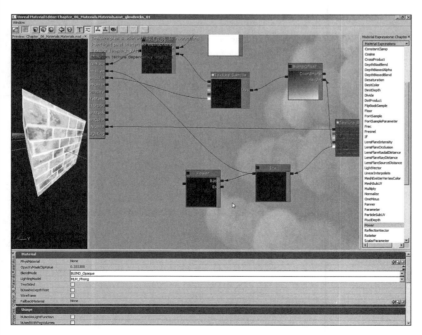

FIGURE 6.126   We have now created a new Power expression.

b. Create a Constant expression and connect its output into the Exp input of the Power (see **FIGURE 6.127**).

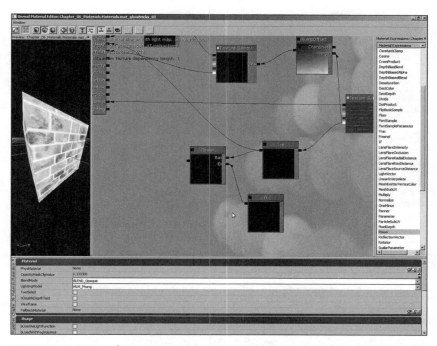

FIGURE 6.127   A new constant is connected into the Exp of the Power.

c. Connect the Power expression to the Emissive channel. Your material temporarily goes black, due to the default 0 value of the constant (see **FIGURE 6.128**).

d. Set the constant's R property to 40. This focuses the emission to only in the crevices (see **FIGURE 6.129**).

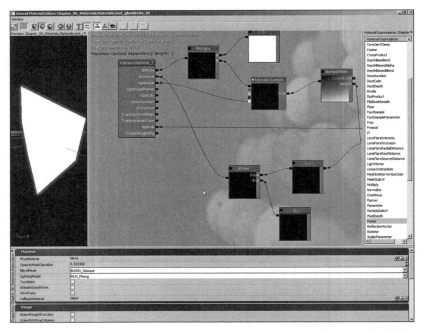

FIGURE 6.128   The Power's output connects to the Emissive channel of the material.

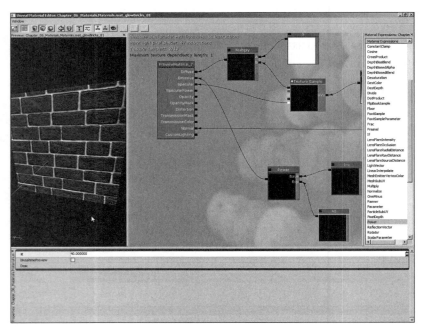

FIGURE 6.129   Once you adjust the value contained in the constant to a value around 40, the bright emission is focused to the crevices only.

5. There is a small problem. If you rotate around the material in the Preview window and look very closely, you'll notice that the glowing crevices appear to "float" just above the crevices of the actual brick. We need to fix this by using our BumpOffset on our normal map. However, we're already using the normal map to create the bump offset effect. This means that if we then connected the BumpOffset expression into the UVs of our normal map's TextureSample, we'd have a cyclic scenario that would feed back an error. Instead, we fix the problem with a new TextureSample. To do this, follow these steps:

   a. Select the TextureSample containing the normal map; then press Ctrl-C and then Ctrl-V to make a duplicate (see **FIGURE 6.130**).

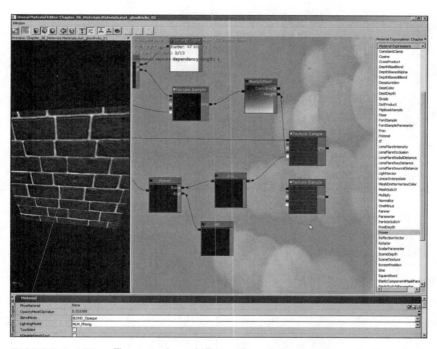

FIGURE 6.130 The normal map's TextureSample has now been duplicated.

   b. Connect the Alpha output of the new TextureSample to the input of the OneMinus expression, overriding the existing connection. This currently has no change on the material (see **FIGURE 6.131**).

   c. Connect the output of the BumpOffset into the UVs output of the new TextureSample. You'll see the glowing crevices appear to snap down into the bump offset crevices (see **FIGURE 6.132**).

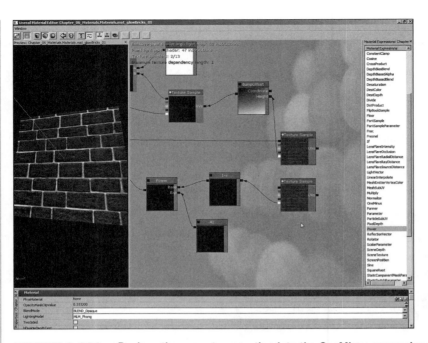

FIGURE 6.131   Replace the current connection into the OneMinus expression with the Alpha from the new TextureSample.

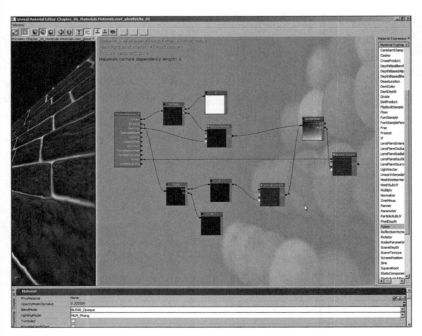

FIGURE 6.132   The glowing crevices are now positioned correctly.

6. We now need to add some color into these glowing crevices. We do so with a Constant3Vector like so:

   a. Create a new Constant3Vector expression. Set its RGB values to create any desired color. We used bright green (0.10, 1.0, 0.10), as shown in **FIGURE 6.133**.

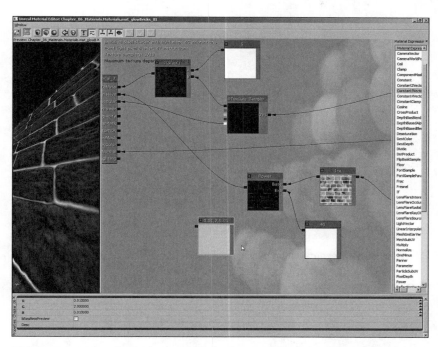

FIGURE 6.133   We have now added a Constant3Vector containing bright green.

   b. Create a new Multiply expression. Connect the output of the VectorParameter into the Multiply's B input (see **FIGURE 6.134**).

   c. Connect the Power's output into the A input of the Multiply (see **FIGURE 6.135**).

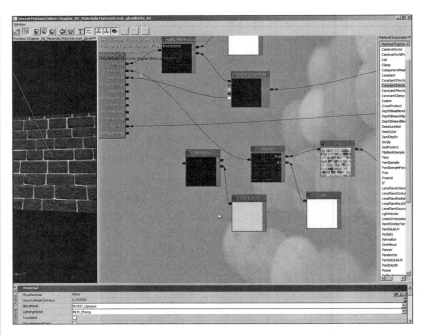

FIGURE 6.134 The new Multiply expression, receiving input B from the new Constant3Vector.

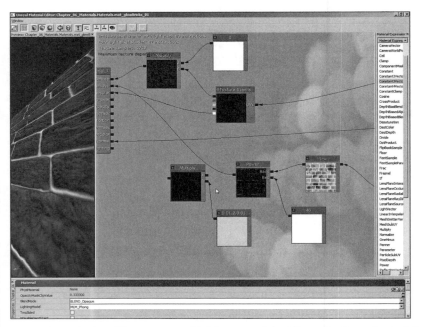

FIGURE 6.135 We are now multiplying our original Power by the output of the new Constant3Vector.

d. Connect the output of the Multiply to the Emissive channel of the material (see **FIGURE 6.136**).

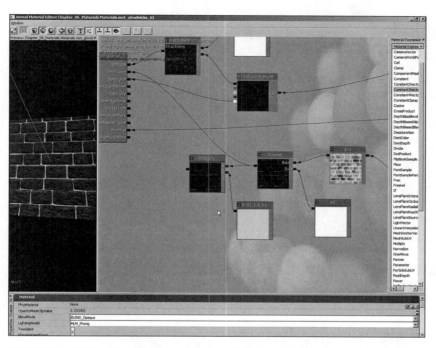

FIGURE 6.136   Finally, connect the new Multiply into the material as shown.

7. The last thing we need to do for our glow effect is to intensify it a bit with another Multiply expression:

a. Select the Multiply expression created in the previous step, and then duplicate it with Ctrl-C, Ctrl-V. Connect the output of the original Multiply expression into the A input of the new Multiply (see **FIGURE 6.137**).

b. Duplicate the Constant expression in the same manner (or create a new one, if you'd like).

c. Connect the new constant's output into the B input of the new Multiply expression (see **FIGURE 6.138**).

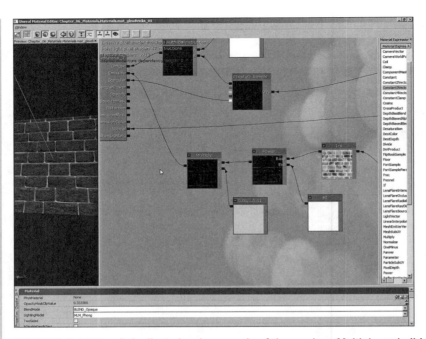

FIGURE 6.137   A duplicate has been made of the previous Multiply, and all icons have been repositioned.

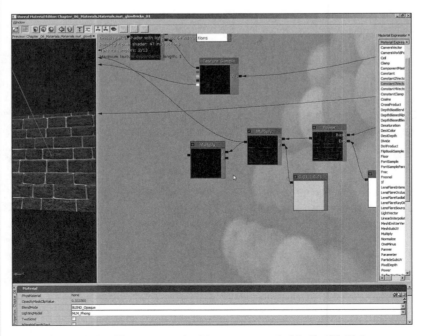

FIGURE 6.138   The new constant is now connected to the Multiply.

d. Connect the new Multiply expression's output into the Emissive channel (see **FIGURE 6.139**).

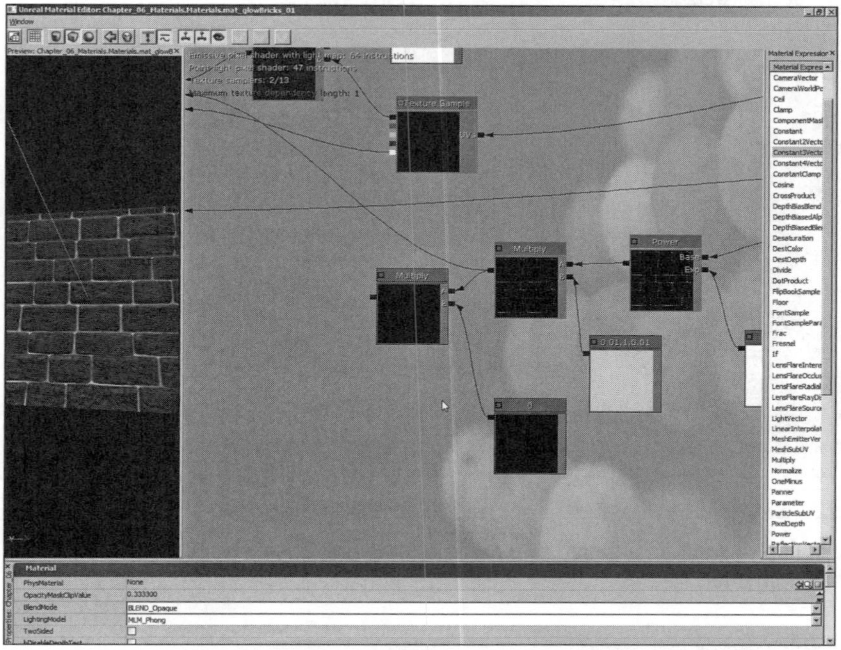

FIGURE 6.139 Our new intensifying Multiply is connected into the Emissive channel of our material.

e. Set your new constant's R property to whatever value gives you a pleasing amount of glow. We used 9 (see **FIGURE 6.140**).

8. Finally, let's create the system that causes our glowing cracks to pulsate over time. This requires the construction of a sine wave. As you may know, a sine wave cycles between 1 and -1, so we're going to need to make mathematical adjustments to the wave so that we are instead cycling between 0.25 and 1. The mathematical expression for this would be as follows:

((Sin(time)) * 0.375) + 0.625

Here's how to construct a network that defines the preceding expression:

a. Create a Sine expression, and then create a Time expression. Then, connect the Time expression's output into the sine's input (see **FIGURE 6.141**).

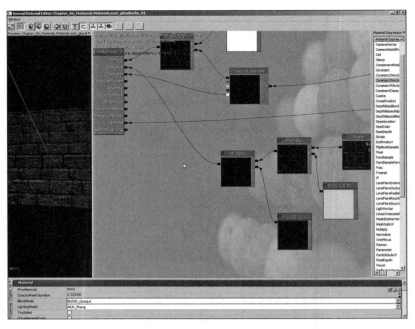

FIGURE 6.140   Multiplying our final output by a factor of around 9 or so causes the glowing crevices to appear much brighter.

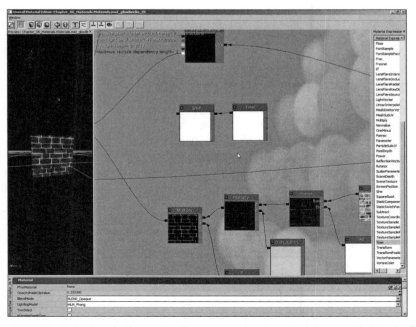

FIGURE 6.141   A Sine and a Time expression have both been added to the Expression window.

b. Create a Multiply expression, and a new Constant expression. Next, set the new constant's R value to 0.375, and connect its output to the new Multiply expression's A input (see **FIGURE 6.142**).

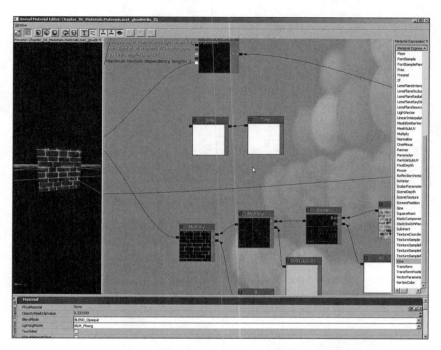

FIGURE 6.142   A 0.375 constant and new Multiply node have been added.

c. Connect the sine's output into the Multiply expression's B input (see **FIGURE 6.143**).

d. You might have noticed that 0.625 is the reverse of 0.375 (1-0.325=0.625). This means that we can simply use a OneMinus expression to get our needed value.

Create a OneMinus expression, as well as an Add expression.

e. Connect the output of the constant (the one holding the value of 0.375) into the input of the OneMinus. Then, connect the OneMinus's output into the A input of the Add, and the output of the Multiply expression into the Add's B input (see **FIGURE 6.144**).

f. We're almost finished. We just need to multiply the result of this new network into our material.

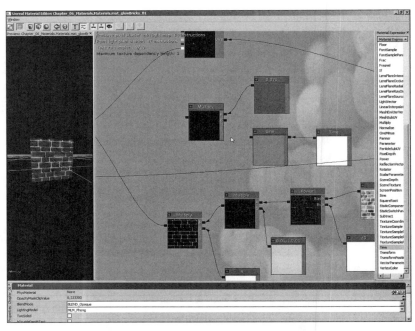

FIGURE 6.143   We are now multiplying the value of the sine by 0.375.

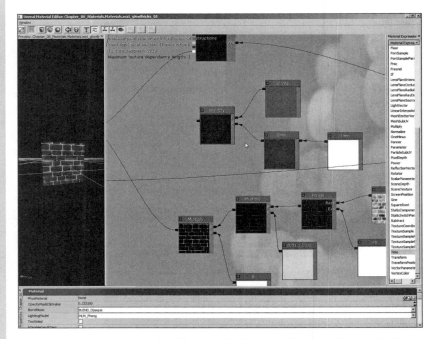

FIGURE 6.144   A new OneMinus and Add expression have been added and connected.

Create a new Multiply expression, connecting the output of the Add into input A and the output of the Multiply that is currently connected to our material's emissive channel into the new Multiply's B input (see **FIGURE 6.145**).

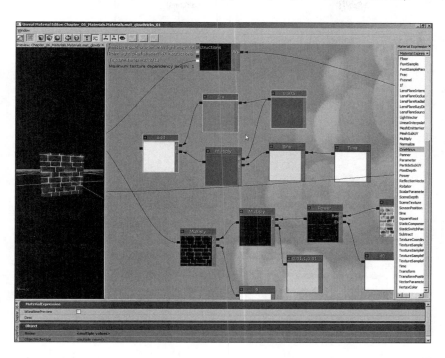

FIGURE 6.145   A new Multiply expression is used to combine this new network into the existing material.

g. Last step, connect the output of the new Multiply expression into the Emissive channel of the material (see **FIGURE 6.146**).

9. Apply changes to your material, and then save your package. If you'd like to see the results, you can open the mat_glowBricks_01 material included in the Chapter_06_Materials package.

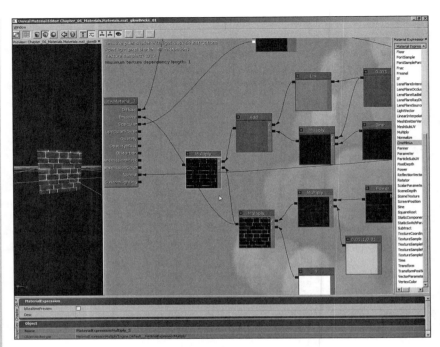

FIGURE 6.146   Finally, everything is connected properly.

END TUTORIAL 6.10

The light in-between your bricks is now pulsating once a second. That's all we're going to do with this example. But feel free to push things further on your own. In the next example, we're going to create a new material using the same textures, but this time with a slightly more technical network, as it is based on pixel depth, meaning our player's distance from a given surface.

In **TUTORIAL 6.11**, we demonstrate how to change the color of a material based on the distance the player is from the surface to which the material has been applied. In short, as the player moves away from the surface, the color shifts.

TUTORIAL 6.11: Color Shift by Distance Material

1. Over the next several tutorials, we start to create a complex material in which we blend from one color to another based on how far we are away from a given object (see **FIGURE 6.147**).

To begin, open the PinwheelLevel.umap included on your DVD in the files for this chapter. It provides us with a series of long hallways we can use to test out our effect. You may need to set the viewport to Unlit mode to see anything (see **FIGURE 6.148**).

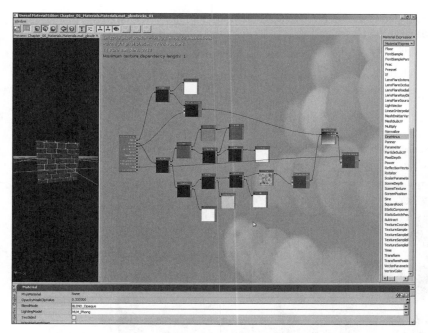

FIGURE 6.147   This is the final texture we are striving to create.

FIGURE 6.148   The PinwheelLevel map contains very long hallways that we can use to show off our material.

2. Open the Generic browser, and then open the Chapter_06_Materials package. Right-click in a blank area of the browser and choose New Material from the Context menu. Enter the following values in the New dialog:

> **Group:** Materials
>
> **Name:** mat_myDistColor

The Material Editor appears (see **FIGURE 6.149**).

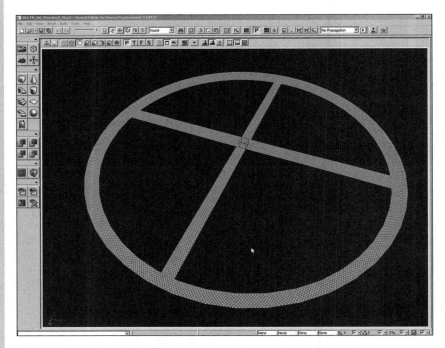

FIGURE 6.149   Make sure your material's properties read as shown.

3. This is where having a plan becomes important in material creation. At this time, all we really know is that we're blending between two colors based on a distance value. Let's start just by establishing our two colors. This time, however, we use a new method for bringing in our appropriate expressions.

> a. Right-click on a blank space of the Expression window, and on the very large Context menu that appears, scroll down and choose New VectorParameter (see **FIGURE 6.150**).

> **NOTE**
>
> We're using the VectorParameter in this case just to get easy access to a color picker for purposes of **TUTORIAL 6.11**. This costs us just a tad bit of extra overhead. In similar circumstances on your own, it would be better to use a Constant3Vector or Constant4Vector instead.

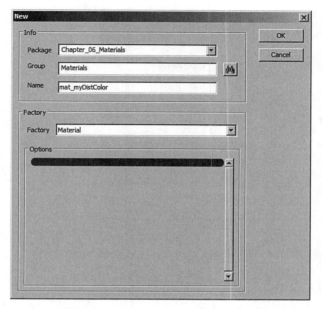

FIGURE 6.150   The New VectorParameter option is near the bottom of the Context menu.

b. Select the VectorParameter icon in the Expression window; then press Ctrl-C, and then Ctrl-V to copy and then paste a duplicate of the expression.

c. Hold the Ctrl key and move this new expression just above the original, and then change its DefaultValue color to any color you like. We used orange (see **FIGURE 6.151**).

d. Click the small black box in the corner of each of the icons to turn on Realtime Preview, enabling you to see which colors are in which expression. You should have one expression containing the color black, and another containing whatever other color you have chosen. Turn off Realtime Preview on each node when finished (see **FIGURE 6.152**).

> **TIP**
>
> As an alternative, you can activate Toggle Realtime Expression in the toolbar, which causes the Expression window to update at all times. This can sometimes bog down your computer on more complex materials, but is a nice way to visualize your changes.

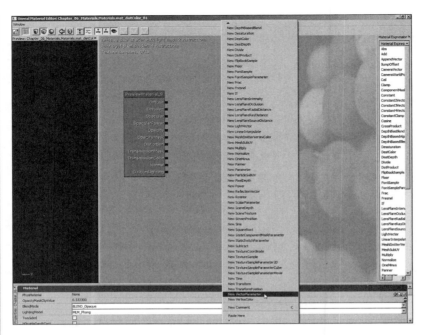

FIGURE 6.151   A copy has been made of the new VectorParameter, and its value has been changed.

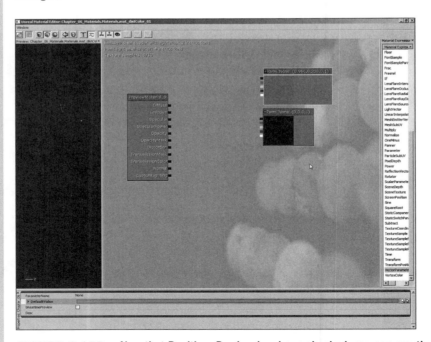

FIGURE 6.152   Now that Realtime Preview has been checked, you can see the colors contained in each of the VectorParameter nodes.

4. Okay, we have our two colors, and now we need a way to blend between them. Depth eventually becomes a factor, but for now we're just going to focus on the blend itself. Follow these steps to bring in and connect the appropriate expression:

    a. Add a LinearInterpolate expression to the Expression window, either using the right-click method or by drag-and-dropping it from the expression list. Place the expression just to the left and slightly below the two VectorParameters. If need be, move all three of the icons away from the main Material Node, which you can do by holding down Ctrl and Alt to perform a marquee-select, and then hold Ctrl and left drag to move all selected items (see **FIGURE 6.153**).

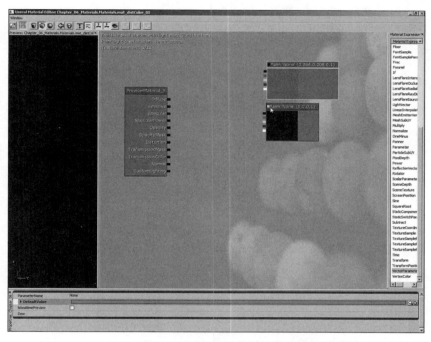

FIGURE 6.153   The new LinearInterpolate should be positioned as shown.

    b. Left-drag from the RGBA output box (it's the only black output box) on the orange VectorParameter to the A input on the LinearInterpolate icon. Next, left drag from the B input on the LinearInterpolate to the RGBA output on the black VectorParameter. As you can see, you can connect a wire in either direction (see **FIGURE 6.154**).

5. The blend is now set up, but does not function properly at this time because we have no inputs connected to the LinearInterpolate's Alpha channel, which is what drives the blend between our two colors. However, we need to control this Alpha based on depth, or to be more precise, on the player's distance from a pixel. Do this now by following these steps:

    a. Add a PixelDepth expression into your Expression window, and position it just below your two VectorParameters. Connect its output to the Alpha of the LinearInterpolate expression, and then connect the output of the LinearInterpolate to the Emissive channel of your material (see **FIGURE 6.155**).

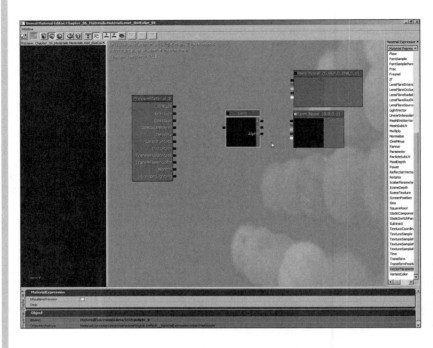

FIGURE 6.154
The two VectorParameters have now been connected to the LinearInterpolate.

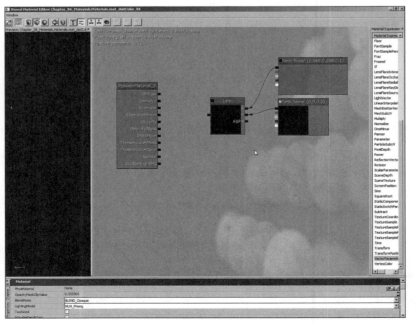

FIGURE 6.155
A new PixelDepth has been added, and the network is connected to the Emissive channel.

The material remains black. The reason for this is that the PixelDepth expression outputs a value between 0 and 16777215. However, our LinearInterpolate's Alpha is looking for a value between 0 and 1. At the same time, we don't really need to normalize a range of 0 to 16 million down to 0 to 1, or else we only get our second color if our surface is 16 million Unreal units away! The solution is to normalize the value to a specified distance, so that we can have a customized depth at which we blend to our second color.

To do this, we first need to determine what our optimum distance is going to be, and then simply divide the depth of any given pixel by that value. In our case, we're going to use 1200 units, at least for the time being.

b. Bring in a Constant expression, and place it just beneath the PixelDepth expression. In the Properties window, set its R value to 1200 (see **FIGURE 6.156**).

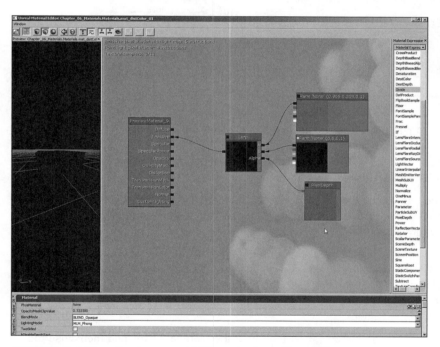

FIGURE 6.156   Create a new 1200 constant, positioned like so.

c. Create a Divide expression, and place it just to the left of the PixelDepth and constant. You may need to move the PixelDepth and the constant to the right just a bit to make room.

d. Connect the PixelDepth's output to the A input of the Divide, and then connect the output of the constant to the B input of the Divide (see **FIGURE 6.157**).

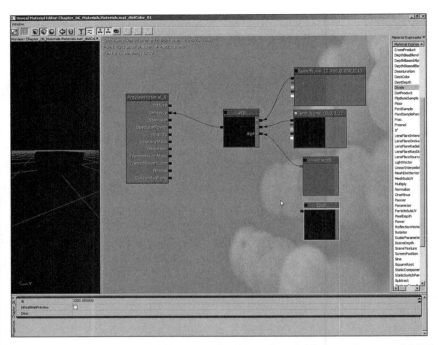

FIGURE 6.157   A new Divide expression is used to divide by a distance of 1200.

    e. Connect the output of the Divide to the Alpha input of the LinearInterpolate (see **FIGURE 6.158**).

       As soon as you do this, you'll notice the material turn orange. If you zoom in and out in the Preview window (right mouse button), you'll see the material turn black as you get far away from it.

6. Select the material's main node, and in the Properties window, set the LightingModel property to MLM_Unlit. We currently have no lighting in our scene, and this saves us some extra calculations. Now, if you drag with the right mouse button in the preview window of the Material Editor, you'll see the sample sphere blend between your two colors based on the proximity of the camera.

7. Click the Apply Changes button ✓, at the top of the Material Editor, and then close the Material Editor for now.

8. Apply your new material to all surfaces of the level. The easiest ways to do this is to right-click on one of the surfaces in your Perspective viewport, and then choose Select all Surface from the Context menu that appears. Once all the surfaces are selected, simply click on your new mat_DistColor material in the Generic browser.

9. Save a copy of your map in a new location, and most importantly, save your package! Testing the level right now does not yield the results we want, as Unreal Tournament does not show the changes in the material.

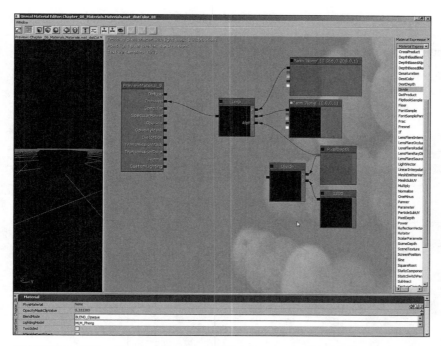

FIGURE 6.158   The new Divide expression is connected into the network.

END TUTORIAL 6.11

If you were to test your level right now, you'd notice that the "color blend by distance" system is definitely working. However, because we currently have no visible texturing on the walls, there's no real way to sense motion until you come to the end of one of the very long hallways. This means that our material is about to get a lot more complicated. Before we take the time to bring in some textures and start connecting them to our material, let's look at how we can keep our materials organized through the use of comments.

Comments enable us to section off parts of our material and label those parts. This is very important once you start getting into more complex materials, and can help you remember what each part of your material is doing, as well as making it much easier for other artists on your team to decipher your networks. In **TUTORIAL 6.12**, we look at how you can keep your materials organized and easy to follow by adding comments.

TUTORIAL 6.12: Placing Comments in a Material

1. Continue from **TUTORIAL 6.11** or open the Chapter_06_Materials package, included on your DVD in the package for this chapter, and open the mat_distColor_01 material by double-clicking it. You also need to open the DM-Ch_06_Pinwheel_01 map.

2. Your network should be organized in a configuration similar to that below. Marquee-select all the expressions of your current material, which should only contain those responsible for our depth-based color blending.

3. With all the expressions selected, right-click anywhere in the Expression window and choose New Comment from the Context menu (or press the "C" key). In the dialog that appears, enter Depth Blender into the Comment Text field (see **FIGURE 6.159**).

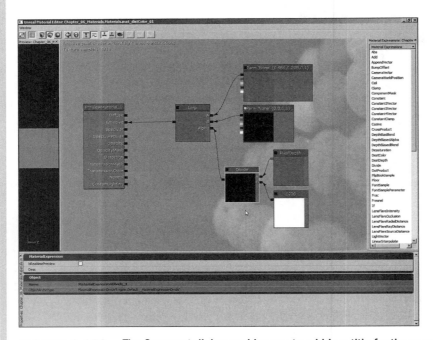

FIGURE 6.159   The Comment dialog enables you to add in a title for the new comment box.

4. You'll see a large yellow box around all of your expressions with your label at the top. This box has some very useful abilities. First off, if you hold Ctrl and move the box, you'll notice that all the enclosed expressions move with it. You can still move each of the expressions individually if you like. Any expressions you place inside the comment box moves along with it (see **FIGURE 6.160**).

You'll also notice a small black triangle in the lower-right corner of the comment box. You can use this to resize the box and encapsulate more expressions or exclude others.

Take a moment and move the comment box around a bit to get used to how it works. When finished, save the changes to your material by clicking the Apply Changes button, and then save your package.

> **TIP**
>
> Another good way to keep your materials organized is to write descriptions for your expressions. All Material Expressions contain a property called Desc, or Description, that you can use to write short comments about what that particular expression does in your network (see **FIGURE 6.161**).

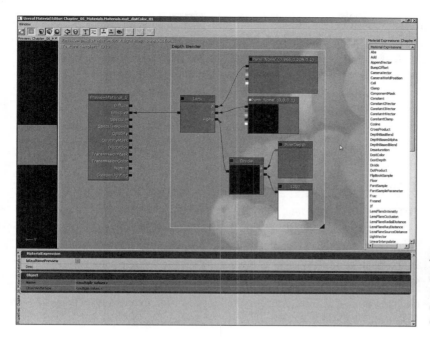

FIGURE 6.160
The selected expressions have now been enclosed in a comment box.

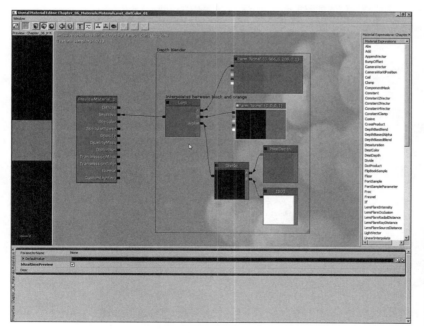

FIGURE 6.161
When you add a description into the Desc property, that description appears just above the expression.

END TUTORIAL 6.12

As mentioned earlier, it is very difficult to detect any motion with our current material. We need some sort of texture on the walls to enable us to see the material passing by as we move. For starters, we simply use the same materials that were used in the brick wall material created earlier in this chapter, although later on it would be very easy for you to exchange them for other textures and get a variety of cool effects. Now that you understand how to change a value—such as color—based on the distance from the player to the surface, we now make things more visually interesting by adding in some textures. In **TUTORIAL 6.13**, we add textures into the depth blend material created earlier.

TUTORIAL 6.13: Connecting Textures into the Depth Blend Material

1. Continue from **TUTORIAL 6.12** or open the Chapter_06_Materials package, included on your DVD in the package for this chapter, and open the mat_distColor_02 material by double-clicking it. You also need to open the DM-Ch_06_Pinwheel_02 map.

2. We need our texture to be sampled inside our material. Do this using the following procedure:

    a. Start by dragging a new TextureSample expression into the Expression window of the Material Editor (see **FIGURE 6.162**).

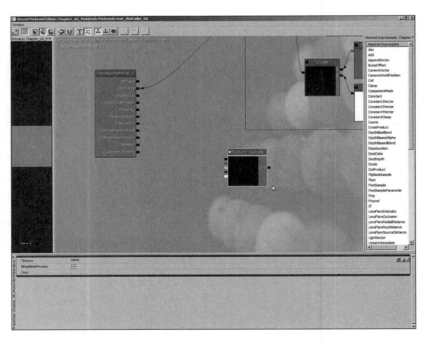

FIGURE 6.162   A new TextureSample expression has been added.

b. We now need to associate our texture with this new TextureSample expression. Start by opening (or fully loading) the Chapter_12_Materials package in the Generic browser.

c. We now need to make sure that the texture is selected in the Generic browser. Click on the wall_stone_blocks texture, found within the Chapter_12_Materials package. You can verify this selection by looking for the pale green border around the texture.

d. Next, in the Material Editor, select the TextureSample, and in the Properties window of the Material Editor, click the Texture Property, and then click the green-arrowed Use Current Selection in Browser button ![button], located to the right of the property. An image of the texture should now appear in the TextureSample (see **FIGURE 6.163**).

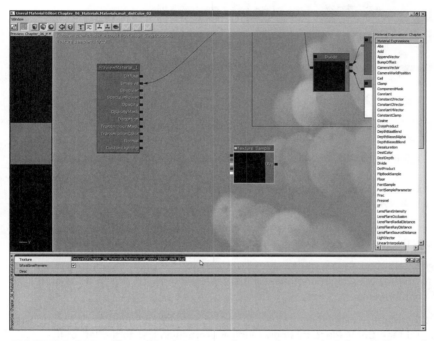

FIGURE 6.163 The appropriate texture has now been assigned to the TextureSample.

3. Our texture is finally ready to be calculated in our material. However, we need it to be connected to our Emissive channel, which is already receiving input from the

> **NOTE**
>
> The texture is very dark. Your TextureSample may appear black. This is normal.

LinearInterpolate expression. Because the texture simply acts as an intensifier for the blend, we multiply the two expressions together. Do this with the following steps:

a. Bring in a new Multiply node (as a shortcut, hold M and left-click), and connect the output of the LinearInterpolate to the Multiply's A input (see **FIGURE 6.164**).

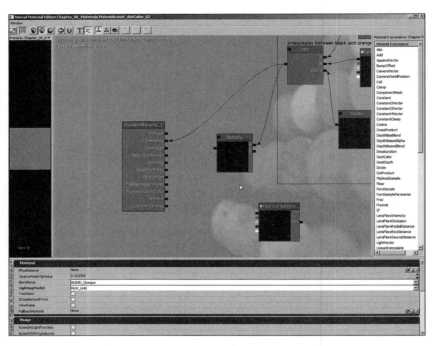

FIGURE 6.164   A Multiply has been added, and the LinearInterpolate has been connected into it.

  b. Connect the RGB (black tab) output of the TextureSample to the B input (see **FIGURE 6.165**).

  c. Connect the output of the multiply to the Emissive channel of the material, which replaces the previous connection from the LinearInterpolate (see **FIGURE 6.166**).

4. Apply changes, and then save your package. Right now the texture appears to be very dark. Let's fix that by bringing in another Multiply expression, and multiplying the current output by a constant value:

  a. Select the Multiply expression in the Expression window and duplicate it by pressing Ctrl-C and then Ctrl-V. Place this new Multiply expression just to the left of the previous one. You may need to do some shuffling of your Material Expressions to make everything fit. Don't forget that you can move your comment box to save time (see **FIGURE 6.167**)!

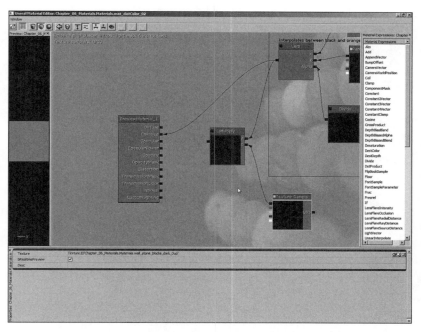

FIGURE 6.165   The TextureSample is also fed into the Multiply expression.

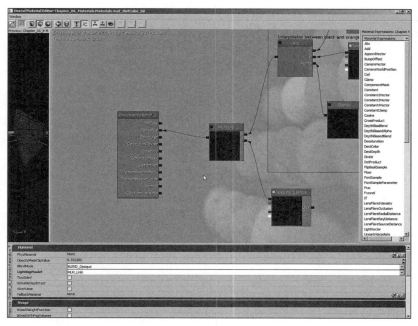

FIGURE 6.166   The Multiply is then connected into the Emissive channel.

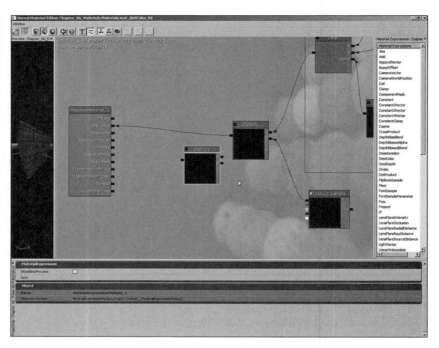

FIGURE 6.167   Duplicate the previous Multiply, and reorganize your expressions.

b. Connect the output of the first Multiply expression into the A input of the second (see **FIGURE 6.168**).

c. Now we need a constant value by which we can intensify our brick texture. From the Expression List, drag in a new Constant expression (or as a shortcut, hold 1 and left click), placing it just to the right of the new Multiply expression, beneath the first Multiply (see **FIGURE 6.169**).

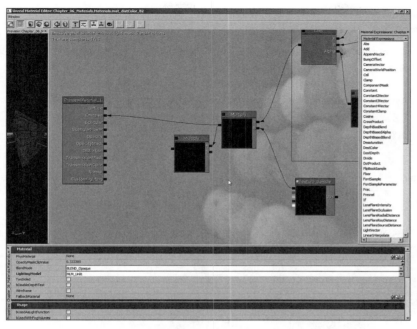

FIGURE 6.168   The new Multiply receives the output of the previous one.

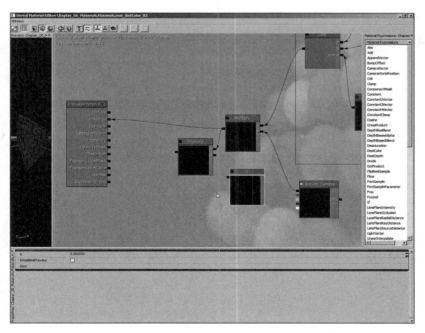

FIGURE 6.169   Create a new Constant expression, positioned like so.

    d. In the properties of the new Constant expression, set the R value to 50, and the Desc property to Glow Intensity.

    e. Connect the output of the constant to the B input of the new Multiply (see **FIGURE 6.170**).

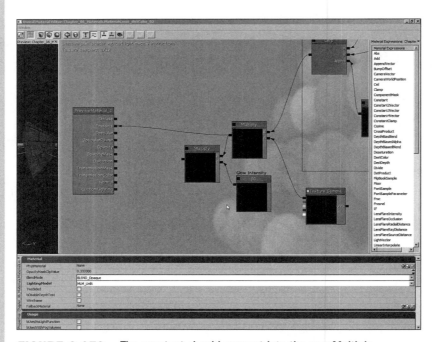

FIGURE 6.170   The constant should connect into the new Multiply.

    f. Connect the new Multiply to the Emissive channel of the material (see **FIGURE 6.171**).

5. Apply changes and save your package. Your bricks now appear to be glowing brightly! However, we have one problem left: If you apply this new material to all the surfaces of your level, you will see that our bricks appear to be very small. We need the texture to appear larger, which means we need it to tile fewer times across the surfaces. Previously, we accomplished this by utilizing the Surface Properties window. You will now see how to do it using a TextureCoordinate expression:

    a. Using the right-click method or the Expression List, create a new TextureCoordinate expression, placing it just to the right of the TextureSample (see **FIGURE 6.172**).

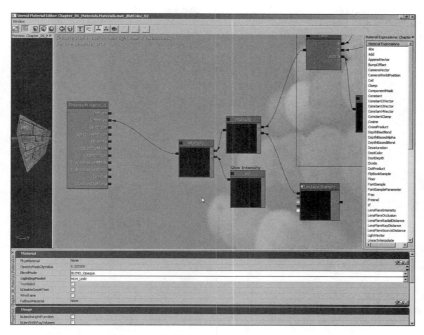

FIGURE 6.171   The new Multiply now feeds your Emissive channel.

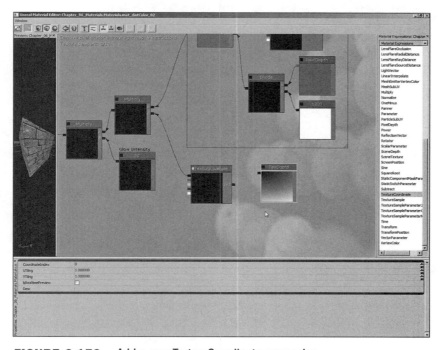

FIGURE 6.172   Add a new TextureCoordinate expression.

b. Connect the TextureCoordinate's output to the UVs input of the TextureSample (see **FIGURE 6.173**).

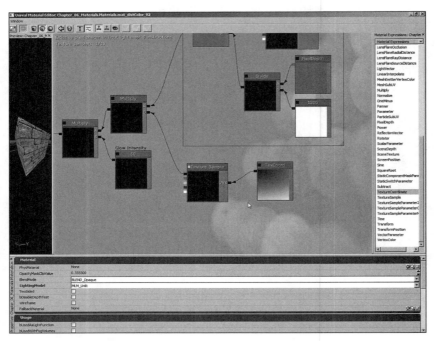

FIGURE 6.173   The TextureCoordinate connects into the UVs input of the TextureSample.

c. Select the TextureCoordinate, and in the Properties window, set the UTiling and VTiling properties to 0.3. This causes the bricks to appear larger, because you are not tiling the texture quite so often (see **FIGURE 6.174**).

6. Apply the changes and save your package.

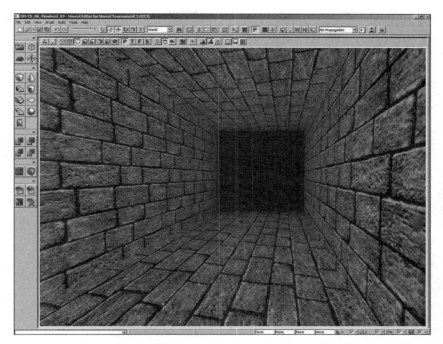

FIGURE 6.174   The bricks now appear larger because of the decreased tiling value.

END TUTORIAL 6.13

The textures that we need are now connected to our material and adjusted, but we have a small problem in that the dark brick texture contains a certain amount of color information. Because we use the texture to drive an intensity value for our two blended colors, this color information is going to become an issue as it slightly offsets our final color. Although the difference may be within acceptable bounds if you were creating this material on your own, we show how you can solve the problem by utilizing a Desaturation expression. In **TUTORIAL 6.14**, we also bring in a Fresnel expression to add a creepy darkening effect to any surface that is angled toward the player.

TUTORIAL 6.14: Desaturating a Texture and Incorporating a Fresnel

1. Continue from **TUTORIAL 6.13** or open the Chapter_06_Materials package, included on your DVD in the package for this chapter, and open the mat_distColor_03 material by double-clicking it. You also need to open the DM-Ch_06_Pinwheel_03 map.

2. We're going to remove the color information from our texture by using a Desaturation expression. Do this now by following these steps:

a. Create a new Desaturation expression. Place it just to the left of the TextureSample icon. As usual, this may require you to reorganize your layout a bit by dragging around some icons (see **FIGURE 6.175**).

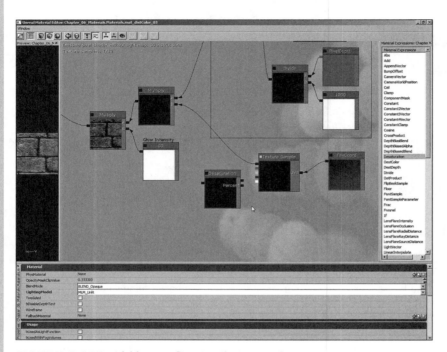

FIGURE 6.175   Add a new Desaturation expression.

b. We're going to connect this Desaturation so that it intercepts the wire that connects the TextureSample to the first Multiply expression. However, to keep our material from feeding back an error, we leave everything connected for as long as we can.

Create a new Constant expression, and connect its output to the Percent input of the Desaturation (see **FIGURE 6.176**).

c. Set the R value of the Constant expression to 1, which is in this case analogous to 100%.

d. Connect the RGBA output of the TextureSample to the unlabeled input of the Desaturation expression (see **FIGURE 6.177**).

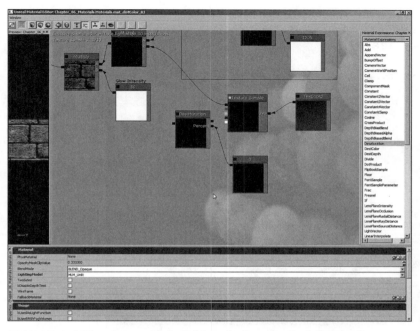

FIGURE 6.176   A new constant drives the Desaturation's Percent input.

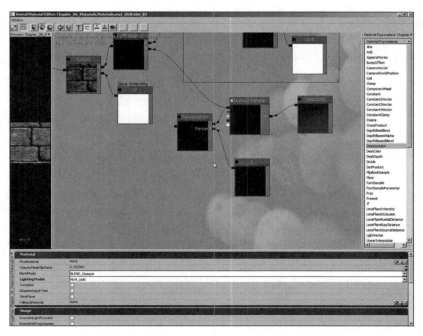

FIGURE 6.177   The TextureSample is now connected to the Desaturation.

e. Finally, connect the output of the Desaturation to the input of the Multiply node currently connected to the TextureSample, replacing the current connection (see **FIGURE 6.178**).

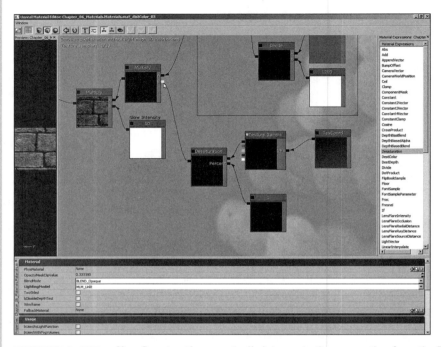

FIGURE 6.178   Your Desaturation eventually intercepts the connection from the TextureSample into the Multiply.

3. You are now getting all your color from your blend system. However, things still look a little drab. We're now going to make the color system a tad more interesting by inserting a Fresnel expression to cause surfaces that are facing us to turn black.

a. Create a new Fresnel expression, placing it just to the right of your Depth Blend comment box. Once again, you may need to reorganize nodes (see **FIGURE 6.179**).

b. The Fresnel is outputting values between 0 and 1, based on the angle a surface is facing relative to the camera. Pixels facing directly at the camera receive a value of 0, whereas pixels facing perpendicularly to the camera's angle receive a 1. This means it is a perfect place to use a multiplier.

Create a new Multiply expression by dragging one in or duplicating an existing one. Set the Desc property of this Multiply to Fresnel Intensity. This expression intercepts the wire that is connecting into the Emissive channel on our material, so adjust the positioning of your expressions accordingly (see **FIGURE 6.180**). However, do not disconnect any of your existing connections!

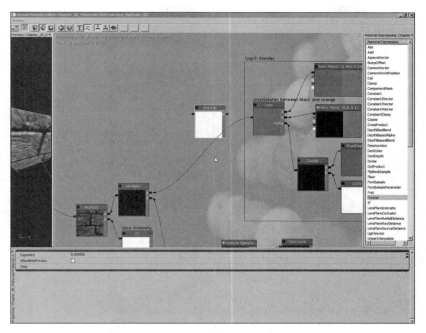

FIGURE 6.179   Add in a new Fresnel expression.

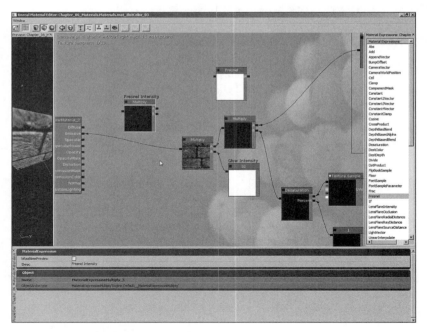

FIGURE 6.180   Create a Multiply expression, either from scratch or through duplication, positioning it like so.

c. Connect the output of the Fresnel into the A input of your new Multiply expression (see **FIGURE 6.181**).

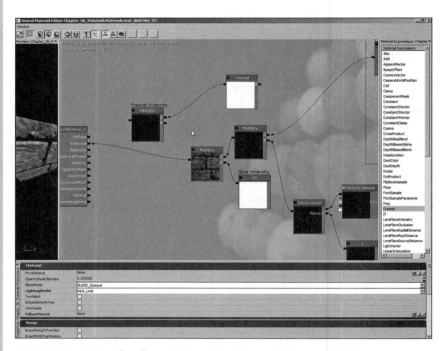

FIGURE 6.181   The Fresnel drives the A input of the new Multiply.

d. *Read this step very carefully!* Connect the output of the Multiply expression that is currently connected to your Emissive channel into the B input of the newly created Fresnel Intensity Multiply expression (see **FIGURE 6.182**).

e. Finally, connect the output of the new Multiply expression to the Emissive channel of your material (see **FIGURE 6.183**).

4. Apply your changes. Your material darkens considerably, and you'll notice that there is now a darkened area that appears to follow the camera. Also, any surface that you are directly facing is also blackened.

Apply the changes and save your package.

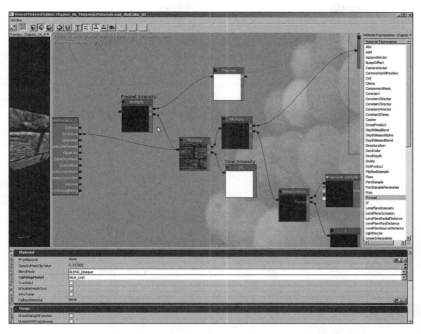

FIGURE 6.182   The Multiply that is currently connected to the Emissive channel now connects into the Input B of the new Fresnel Intensity Multiply, as shown.

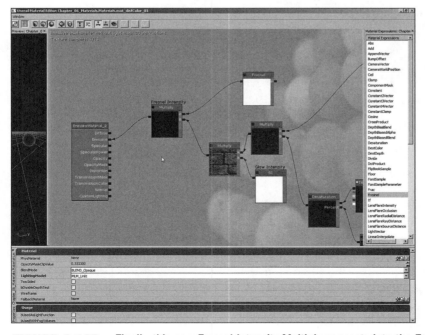

FIGURE 6.183   Finally, this new Fresnel Intensity Multiply connects into the Emissive channel.

5. Your material has likely been darkened too much. You can fix this by adjusting the value of your Glow Intensity constant that you were using to brighten your texture. We originally set it to 50 in **TUTORIAL 6.13**. Let's now increase that value by a factor of 7 or so, bringing it up to 350. This causes your visible bricks to appear to be glowing once again (see **FIGURE 6.184**).

6. Apply your changes and save your package.

> **NOTE**
>
> You could, of course, manage this by inserting another Multiply expression and a new constant. However, this would require further calculations for something we could just as easily calculate on our own! Plus, it makes sense, since the expression was named "Glow Intensity," to increase it whenever we need more glow.

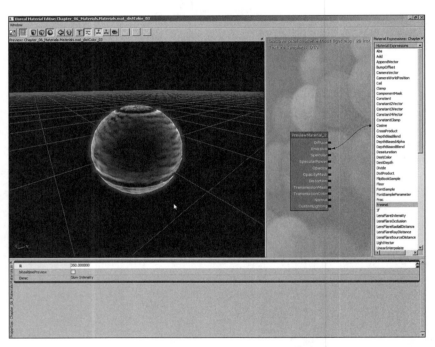

FIGURE 6.184   Increasing the constant value intensifies our glows.

END TUTORIAL 6.14

Our material is really starting to shape up. However, we could use a little more of a "3D" feel in it. At the same time, the fact that we are currently using an unlit material with a strong Emissive channel means that simply attaching a normal map into the Normal channel proves to be ineffective, as we will soon see. Instead, in **TUTORIAL 6.15**, we use a normal map to alter the output of our Fresnel, which causes our bricks to appear to be physically coming out of the wall's surface when viewed from most angles.

TUTORIAL 6.15: Adding a Normal Map to Our Material

1. Continue from **TUTORIAL 6.14** or open the Chapter_06_Materials package, included on your DVD in the package for this chapter, and open the mat_distColor_04 material by double-clicking it. You also need to open the DM-Ch_06_Pinwheel_04 map.

2. We are now going to bring in a normal map for our material. To do this, we need a new TextureSample expression. However, this time, we use a different method for creating the expression, which prevents us from having to go in and associate its texture.

   a. In the Generic browser, select the wall_stone_blocks_normal texture we imported earlier in **TUTORIAL 6.5**.

   b. With the texture selected, hold T and left-click to create a new TextureSample expression. Notice that the texture is already associated to the expression as soon as it is created (see **FIGURE 6.185**).

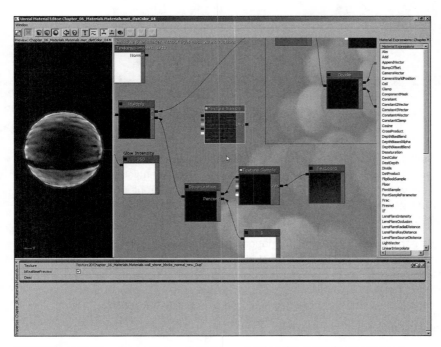

FIGURE 6.185 A new TextureSample containing the normal map appears.

3. Because we have tiled our original texture, we need to tile the normal map as well. Connect the output of our TextureCoordinate expression to the UVs input of the new TextureSample expression (see **FIGURE 6.186**).

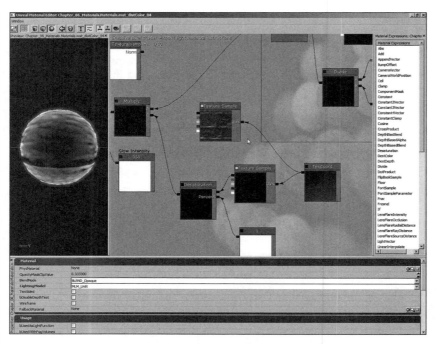

FIGURE 6.186   Connecting the preexisting TextureCoordinate gives us the same tiling amount used previously.

4. As a test, connect the RGBA output of the normal map's texture sample with the Normal channel of our material. Notice that there is no change, even when you apply your changes. This is because any visible change is covered by the strong emission values we are currently using. For our purposes, the Normal channel is ineffective. Disconnect the normal map's TextureSample when done by Alt-clicking its output.

5. We're now going to send this normal information somewhere that it can be useful. Connect the normal map's RGBA output to the Normal input of the Fresnel expression. You'll notice that the material now seems to have much more depth. That is because the new normals are being used to determine whether a pixel is facing the camera, which in turn is driving our colors in such a way that far more detail is visible (see **FIGURE 6.187**).

6. Apply the changes and save your package.

7. There are a few final tweaks that we can make to clean up our effect:

   a. It would be nice if we could have the effect trail out further into the distance. You can manage this by setting the constant that is enclosed in the Depth Blender comment box to 3000 instead of 1200.

   b. We're also going to expand the size of the black area that seems to surround the player. Do this by setting the Fresnel's Exp property to 15 instead of the default 3.

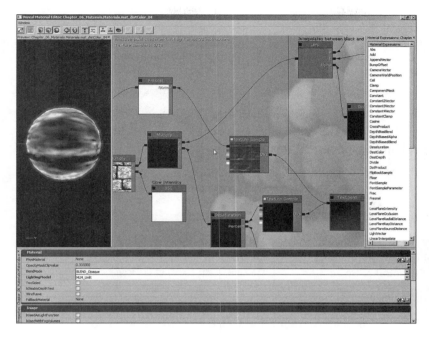

FIGURE 6.187
The normal map's data is used to alter the output of the Fresnel.

8. Apply the changes and save your package (see **FIGURE 6.188**).

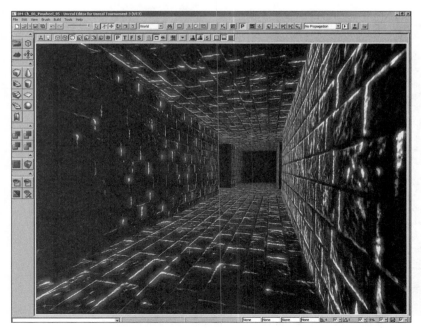

FIGURE 6.188
Our material is finally starting to come together.

END TUTORIAL 6.15

Things are looking pretty cool and spooky on our material. In **TUTORIAL 6.16**, we push the look of our material further by adding in an animated background behind the bricks, giving the illusion of flickering flames. We accomplish this by bringing in a new texture, and using it as a multiplier for our final effect. Throughout several areas, you will likely need to reorganize the placement of your expression icons to make room. This tutorial assumes that you can do that on your own.

TUTORIAL 6.16: Adding an Animated Texture to Our Material

1. Continue from **TUTORIAL 6.15** or open the Chapter_06_Materials package, included on your DVD in the package for this chapter, and open the mat_distColor_05 material by double-clicking it. You also need to open the DM-Ch_06_Pinwheel_05 map.

> **TIP**
>
> Because we're animating this texture, it is a good idea to activate its Realtime Preview checkbox, located in the upper-right corner of the icon.

2. The texture we need can be found in the Chapter_06_Materials package. It is named tex_FlameBase. Select it in the Generic browser.

When finished, go into the Material Editor and bring in a new TextureSample expression associated with your new texture (see **FIGURE 6.189**).

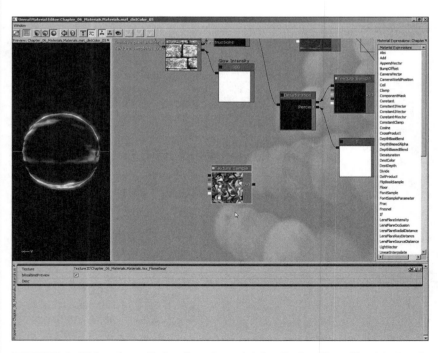

FIGURE 6.189   A new TextureSample containing the tex_FlameSheet texture has been added.

3. We're actually going to use three copies of this texture to create our final result. By using three different tiling sizes along with three different speed values, we get a more randomized-looking effect:

   a. Create a new Panner expression, and connect its output into the UV's of the new TextureSample. Set the following properties inside the Panner (see **FIGURE 6.190**):

   SpeedX: -0.07

   SpeedY: 0.09

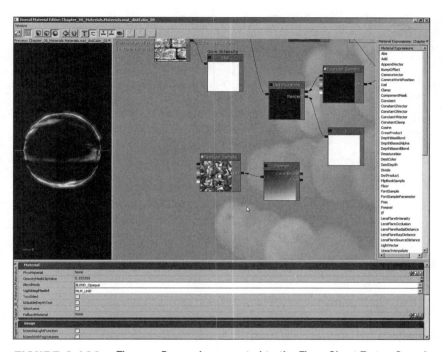

FIGURE 6.190   The new Panner is connected to the FlameSheet TextureSample.

The TextureSample icon now appears to be panning upward and to the right.

   b. Create a new TextureCoordinate expression, and connect its output into the Coordinate input of the Panner. Set the following properties in the TextureCoordinate:

   TilingU: 0.40

   TilingV: 0.35

This makes the texture appear larger (see **FIGURE 6.191**).

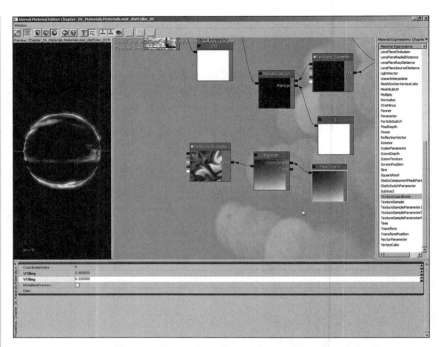

FIGURE 6.191   The new TextureCoordinate changes the size of the flame texture.

c. Select the TextureSample, Panner, and TextureCoordinate icons. Press Ctrl-C and then Ctrl-V to duplicate all three. Move the duplicates just below the originals, and then set the following properties in each of the duplicated expressions:

Panner:

> **SpeedX:** 0.04
>
> **SpeedY:** 0.07

TextureCoordinate:

> **TilingU:** 1.2
>
> **TilingV:** 1.3

This causes the duplicate to be slightly smaller, and moves it upward and slightly to the left (see **FIGURE 6.192**).

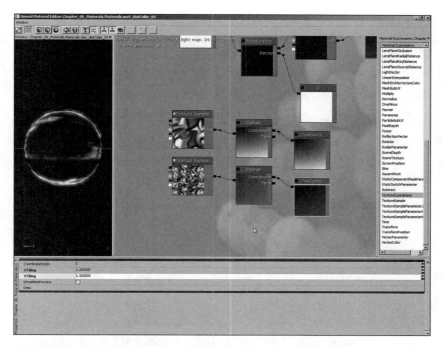

FIGURE 6.192   Here you can see our first duplicate of the TextureSample, Panner, and TextureCoordinate.

  d. Press Ctrl-V again to create a new set of duplicates. Position these duplicates just underneath the previous group, and then set the following properties for the new duplicates:

  Panner:

> **SpeedX:** 0.02
>
> **SpeedY:** 0.05

  TextureCoordinate:

> **TilingU:** 0.08
>
> **TilingV:** 0.06

  This creates a very large copy of the texture that is moving upward and slightly to the left (see **FIGURE 6.193**).

4. We now need to combine all of these textures together:

  a. Bring in a Multiply expression, and connect the output of the topmost TextureSample expression into the Multiply's input A.

  b. Connect the output of the second TextureSample into the Multiply's input B (see **FIGURE 6.194**).

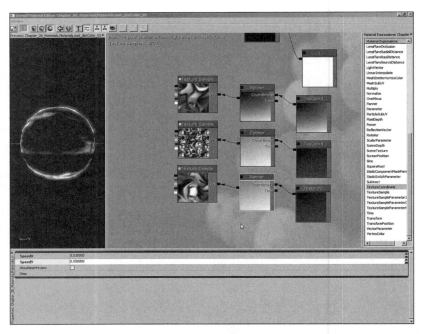

FIGURE 6.193 You now have three copies of the TextureSample, Panner, and TextureCoordinate.

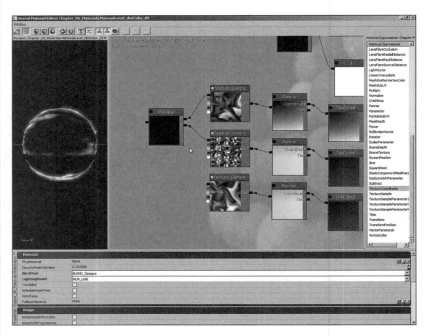

FIGURE 6.194 A Multiply expression is used to combine the data of the first two textures.

c. Create a new Multiply expression, and connect the previous Multiply's output into the new Multiply's input A. Then connect the output of the final TextureSample into the new Multiply's input B (see **FIGURE 6.195**).

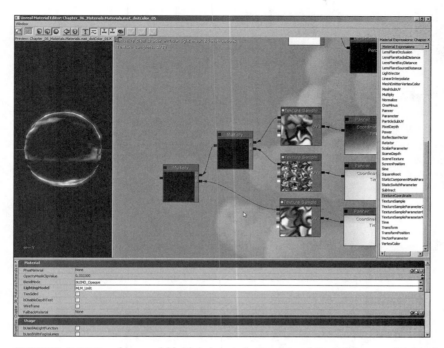

FIGURE 6.195   A second Multiply brings in the data of the third copy of the texture.

5. Next, we're going to intensify the overall combined effect, and then connect the final result into our material.

a. Create a new Multiply expression, set its Desc property to Flame Intensity, and connect the output of the previous Multiply expression into its B input (see **FIGURE 6.196**).

b. Create a new Constant expression, set its R property to 10, and connect it to the Multiply's A input (see **FIGURE 6.197**).

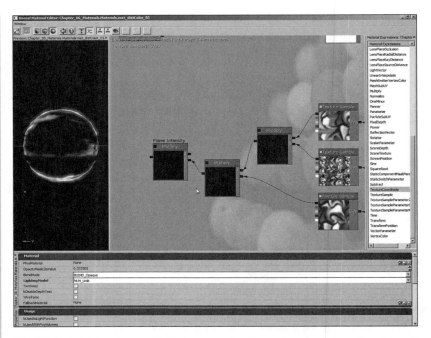

FIGURE 6.196   A new Multiply expression is used as the base of an intensifier system.

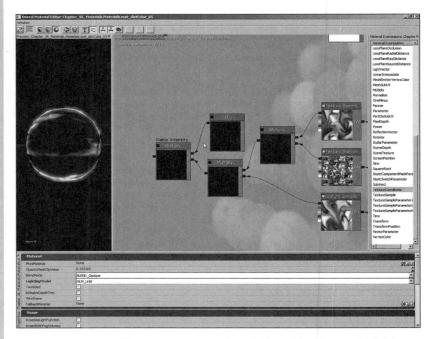

FIGURE 6.197   We use a constant value of 10 to drive the new Multiply expression.

c. Create yet another Multiply expression, and connect its input A to the output of the Multiply expression that is currently connected to the Emissive channel of the material (see **FIGURE 6.198**). (Yes, we're wiring this backward!)

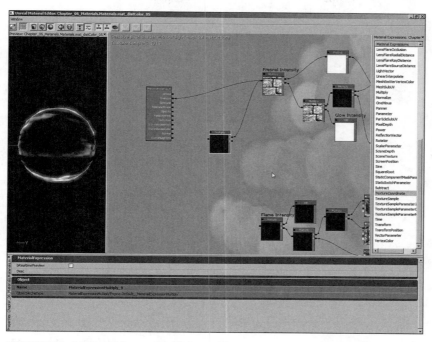

FIGURE 6.198   This new Multiply enables us to combine the animated textures we've just created with the color values already driving our material.

d. Connect the input B of this new Multiply expression to the output of the Multiply material that combines your three flame textures.

e. Connect this final Multiply expression into the Emissive channel, overriding the connection there (see **FIGURE 6.199**).

6. Apply the changes and save your package.

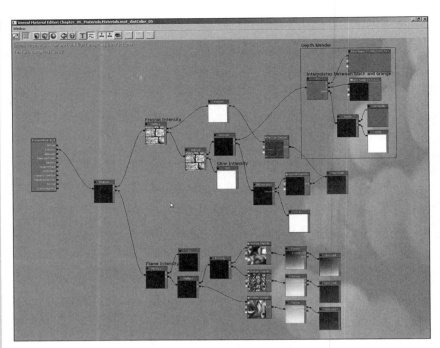

FIGURE 6.199   This is what your final expression should look like.

END TUTORIAL 6.16

Your material now seems to shimmer because of the combination of the three textures. You could, of course, add as many copies as you like, moving in many different directions to help make the effect look more complex. You could even add some rotators into the mix to help change the nature of the motion.

The last effect we're going to add to our material is a subtle color shift that takes place very slowly, almost as if the hallways of our level are alive somehow. In **TUTORIAL 6.17**, we cause the background flicker behind the bricks to slowly shift its color over time.

TUTORIAL 6.17: Adding a Time-Based Blend to Our Material

1. Continue from **TUTORIAL 6.15** or open the Chapter_06_Materials package, included on your DVD in the package for this chapter, and open the mat_distColor_06 material by double-clicking it. You also need to open the DM-Ch_06_Pinwheel_06 map.

2. Focus on the Depth Blender comment box that we created earlier in this chapter. Start off by using the small triangle in the lower-right corner of the box to expand to the right, giving you more room to add expressions (see **FIGURE 6.200**).

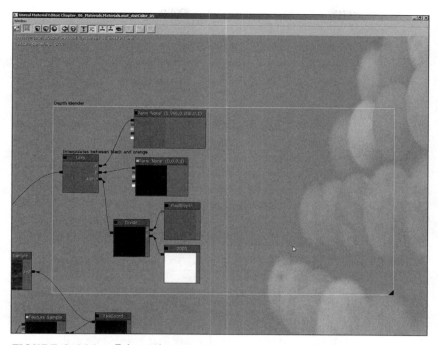

FIGURE 6.200   Enlarge the comment box to make room for some more expressions.

3. We need to set up a system by which we can blend between two colors. Follow these steps:

    a. Select the LinearInterpolate expression inside the Color Blend comment box, as well as the VectorParameter that contains the non-black color of your

        > **NOTE**
        >
        > If you put a description on the Lerp earlier, remove it for the duplicate!

        depth-based blend. Duplicate these two expressions (Ctrl-C, Ctrl-V), and move the duplicates to the right, into the open space you created in the comment box (see **FIGURE 6.201**).

    b. Select the new VectorParameter expression by itself, and duplicate it. Change the duplicate's DefaultValue property to a new color. Because our original color was orange, we chose a dark orange-red. Connect the output of this new VectorParameter to the B input on the new LinearInterpolate (see **FIGURE 6.202**).

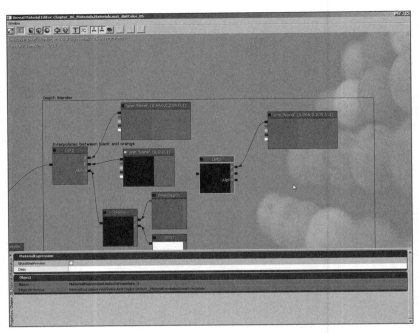

FIGURE 6.201   The LinearInterpolate and orange VectorParameter have been duplicated.

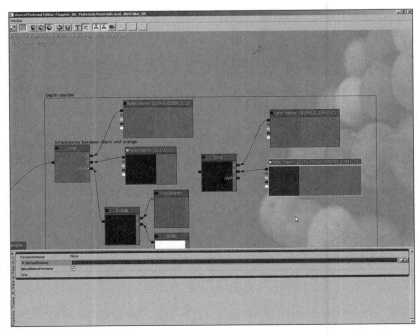

FIGURE 6.202   The original VectorParameter has been duplicated and a new color has been assigned.

4. We now need to set up the time-based system by which we can blend in-between these two colors. This is a very slow blend, cycling every 20 seconds.

    a. Create one of each of the following Material Expressions (see **FIGURE 6.203**):

        Time

        Constant

        Multiply

        Sine

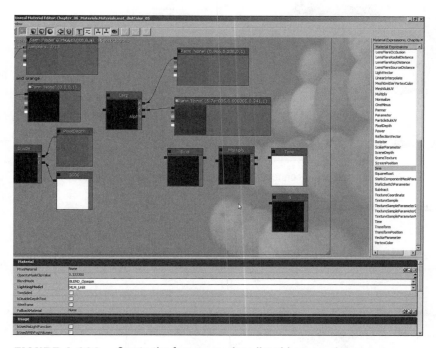

FIGURE 6.203   Create the four expressions listed here, as shown.

    b. Set the value of the constant to 0.05, and connect its output to the B input of the Multiply expression (see **FIGURE 6.204**).

    c. Connect the output of the Time expression into the Multiply's A input (see **FIGURE 6.205**).

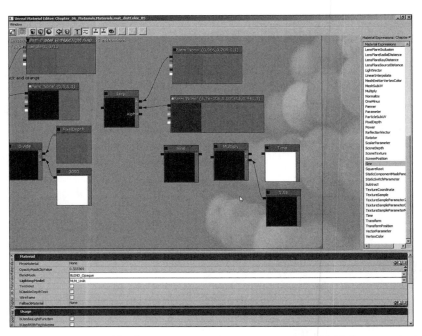

FIGURE 6.204   The Constant expression connects to the Multiply expression's B input.

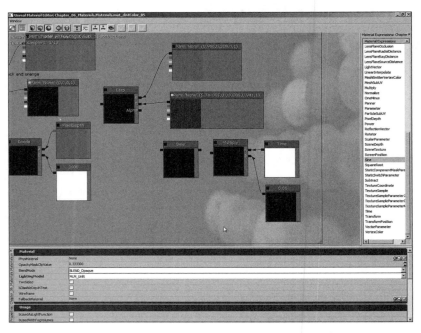

FIGURE 6.205   The Time is also connected to the Multiply. Because we are multiplying time by 0.05, one second from the Time expression is now equal to 20 seconds.

d. Connect the Multiply's output into the input of the sine (see **FIGURE 6.206**).

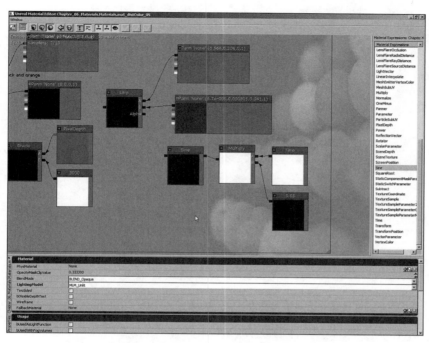

FIGURE 6.206   We are now calculating the sine of (Time*0.05).

    e. Connect the sine's output into the Alpha of the new LinearInterpolate, created in Step 2 (see **FIGURE 6.207**).

5. Now you just need to replace the VectorParameter that is currently driving your color.

    a. Remember that VectorParameter expression that is providing color to your depth-based blend? Select and delete it (see **FIGURE 6.208**).

> **NOTE**
>
> This temporarily breaks your material, feeding back an error. We fix that in the next step.

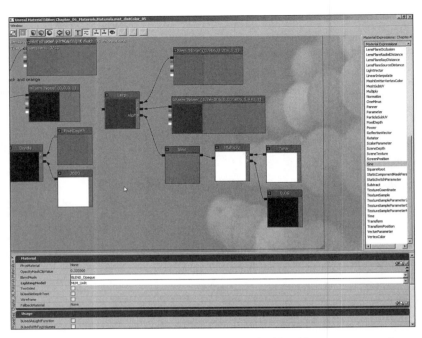

FIGURE 6.207   Our new sine system drives the blend between our newly created colors.

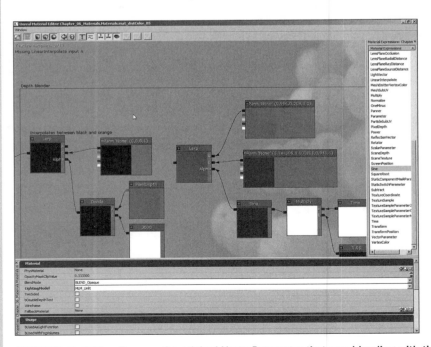

FIGURE 6.208   Remove the original VectorParameter that was blending with the color black on your depth-blend system.

b. Connect the output of the new LinearInterpolate into the input A of the original LinearInterpolate (see **FIGURE 6.209**).

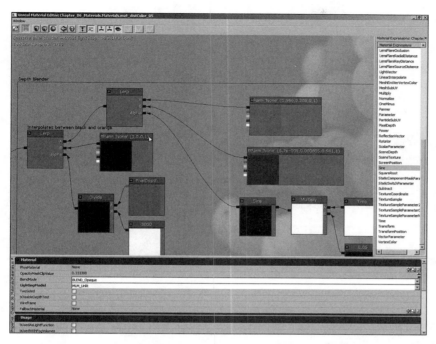

FIGURE 6.209   Replace the original VectorParameter with the new LinearInterpolate.

6. Currently our problem (if you look closely) is that at some point, the blackness in the distance becomes visible and is a different color. This is because the sine wave we've generated is running between 1 and -1, rather than 0 and 1 like we need it to for driving the LinearInterpolate. Fix this with the following steps:

a. After the sine, create the following nodes, and arrange them as shown in **FIGURE 6.210**:

> Constant
>
> Multiply
>
> Add

b. Set the constant's R value to 0.5, and connect it to the A inputs on both the Multiply and Add expressions (see **FIGURE 6.211**)!

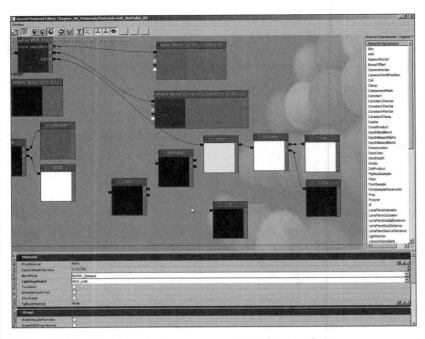

FIGURE 6.210   Arrange the necessary expressions as shown.

6

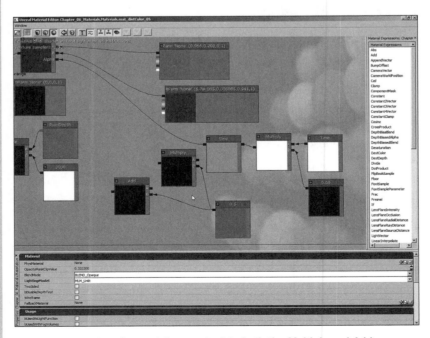

FIGURE 6.211   Connect the constant to both the Multiply and Add.

c. Connect the sine's output to the A input of the Multiply (see **FIGURE 6.212**).

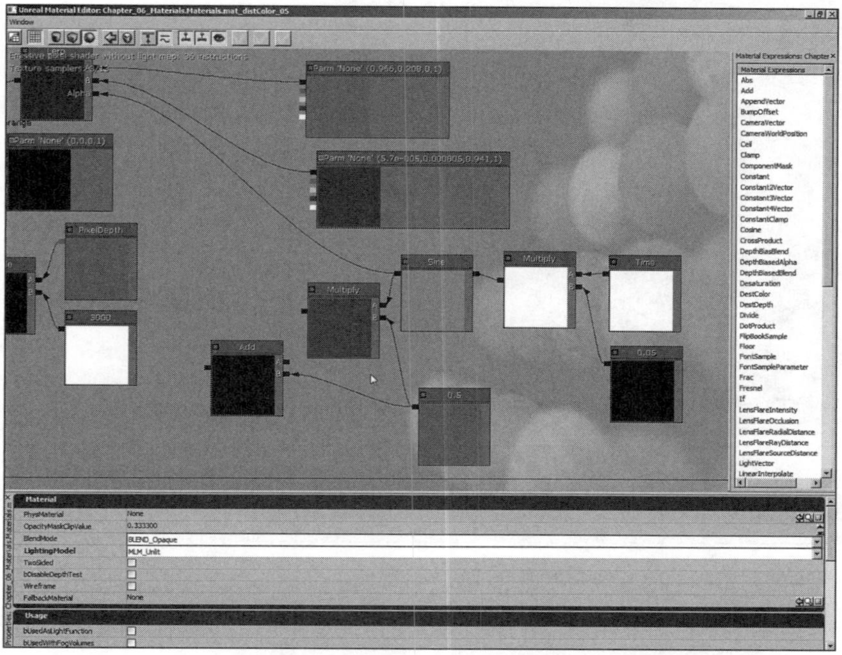

FIGURE 6.212   You're now halving the output of the sine wave.

d. Connect the output of the Multiply to the A input of the Add (see **FIGURE 6.213**).

e. Connect the Add's output to the Alpha of the LinearInterpolate that replaced the initial color (see **FIGURE 6.214**).

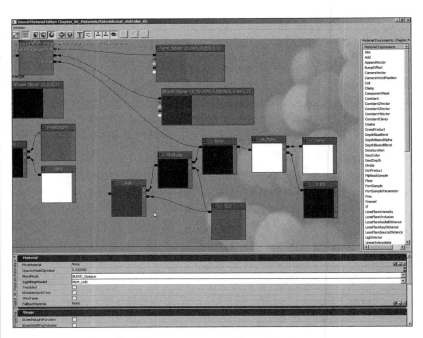

FIGURE 6.213   The sine wave now runs from 0 to 1.

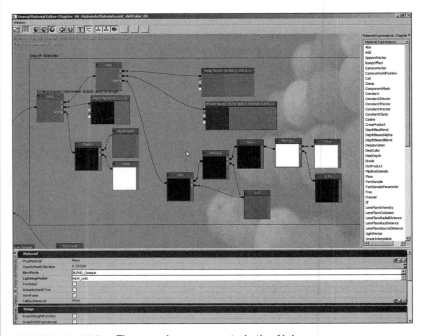

FIGURE 6.214   The new sine wave controls the Alpha.

7. Apply changes and save your package. In the level, you'll now notice the color slowly shifting between your two selected colors over a 20-second interval.

END TUTORIAL 6.17

Your depth-based blend is no longer blending between black and a single color. It should now be blending between black and another blend of two different colors, which are cycling once every 20 seconds. Sounds complex, but it wasn't really that bad, was it?

That wraps things up for this example. There are many different variations you could make on this material. Feel free to experiment and try connecting new expressions or use different settings for some of the values. You'd be amazed at how much you can learn just by a little tinkering!

Summary

That also wraps things up for this introduction to Unreal's material system. There are a great many things that you could explore in the world of materials, but this is about as far as an introductory chapter can take you. At this point, it would be a good idea to spend some time playing with the Material Editor on your own, and see what kind of results you can come up with.

Chapter 7

Introduction to Lighting

Whether you're setting a mood or directing your player's attention, lighting is one of your most powerful tools. When it comes to lighting, Unreal Engine 3.0's revamped tools offer amazing new power and flexibility. The results have blown away folks who used previous versions. You've come along at just the right time: Instead of working around the old system's limitations, your challenge is to master all the power that's built into the new one. A whole lot more fun, wouldn't you say? That's what this chapter is about: understanding the basic principles of lighting and using Unreal's new tools to achieve truly mind-blowing lighting effects.

Light Placement

Placing lights in your level is as simple as holding the L key and left-clicking on a surface in the viewport. However, getting a realistic look from your lighting scenario is not a one-click process. Some considerable thought needs to be put into exactly where lights should be located throughout the level, and how those lights will behave during gameplay. Think about where your lighting should come from. Is there sunlight? Is there a lamp nearby? Try to avoid just placing arbitrary lights around your level.

At the same time, don't think that only placing lights where they would be placed in the real world is the answer, either. The Unreal Engine does not calculate bounced or ambient light, and so you will have to use the tools at your disposal to simulate such effects. As you progress through this chapter, you light a small level that enables you to see the many ways you can use lights to gain a variety of effects (see **FIGURE 7.1**).

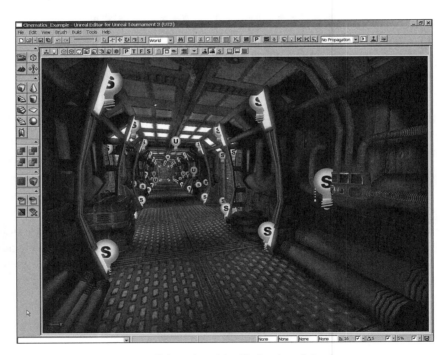

FIGURE 7.1   The many lights placed in this level each have a purpose.

A Word on Building Lights

Even simply placing lights isn't really enough to get your game lit. One of the most important tasks in lighting your level is to build your lighting. Any time you make a change to your level's lighting, whether it's moving a light or simply changing some of its attributes, you usually need to rebuild your level's lighting. Practically, this is as simple as clicking the Build Lighting button  located in the Toolbar of the interface. However, the more complex your lighting scenario becomes, the longer your rebuilding process is going to take. Fortunately, Unreal Engine 3.0 is very good about letting you know when you need to rebuild your lighting, and even directly tells you so when you start the In Editor Game (see **FIGURE 7.2**).

FIGURE 7.2   The In Editor Game gives a warning to rebuild lighting.

Before we really get started with learning about lights and how they work, let's take a look at lighting a simple level. In **TUTORIAL 7.1**, you're going to set up lighting for a single room—a task that looks very simple at first. However, we're going to push things a bit and try to get a reasonably natural result. Please note, however, that we push our result more toward quality than performance. If this were a much larger level, we would use methods that required less overhead on the computer. We focus more on game performance in the next set of tutorials, in which we light a dungeon level. If you've already been working with Unreal's lighting and would like to get into some theory right away, feel free to skip these first five tutorials. We begin this lighting exercise by placing the lights in our scene.

TUTORIAL 7.1   Basic Lighting Primer, Part I: Placement

1. Launch Unreal Editor and open the LampTest level included on the DVD in the files for this chapter. It contains an empty room with a lamp static mesh in the middle. Currently, the Perspective viewport is set to Lit, so all you see is a black field with a lamp shade.

2. With the Perspective viewport selected, press the G key to enter Game Mode. This displays your level in the viewport as it would appear in game. Notice that although the lamp shade appears to glow, it is actually casting no light (see **FIGURE 7.3**).

   Press G again to exit Game Mode when finished.

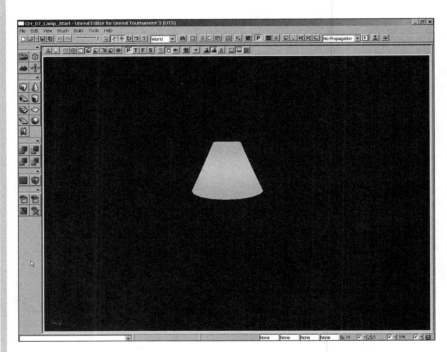

FIGURE 7.3   In Game Mode, you can only see the lamp shade.

3. For starters, let's create a simple light, just to get the hang of doing it. Right-click somewhere in the Perspective viewport and choose Add Actor > Add Light (Point). This places the light at the point where you right-clicked. You'll notice that your level gets some basic lighting in it at this point (see **FIGURE 7.4**).

> **NOTE**
>
> When in Game Mode, only actors that would appear in-game are visible! If you lose your actors while working on a level, try hitting G to see if you're in Game Mode.

FIGURE 7.4   Once the light is off the floor, it illuminates the level.

4. Use the Translation Widget to move around the Light actor. You see the lamp and pedestal cast shadows about the room that update while you move the light. These are called *volume shadows*, which are a type of dynamic (moving) shadow. They are useful for keeping track of where your shadows fall in your level.

5. If you were to test the level right now, you'd get a warning that lighting needs to be rebuilt. Move your Light actor so that you have an interesting shadow on the wall, and click the Build All button located in the Toolbar.

You'll see that your shadows no longer look as good (see **FIGURE 7.5**). This is because they have been converted to precomputed shadows, or shadow maps. These are a different type of

> **NOTE**
>
> You may need to use the Translation Widget to lift the light off the floor to see the effect!

> **NOTE**
>
> The shadow cast by the lamp is only visible when the camera is within a certain distance from the lamp itself. This is an optimization for working in large maps with the lighting not yet built, which would otherwise make moving the camera around very slow. This behavior extends to all shadow volume shadows, whether lighting is built or not. It occurs in-game as well and is controlled by settings in the UTEngine.ini file. For many of the tutorials in this chapter, we have altered these settings to allow shadow volume shadows to be displayed at all times in order to make it possible to show how they work. Keep in mind that creating maps that use shadow volume results in other people seeing the shadows popping in and out unless they have altered their UTEngine.ini file as well.

shadow that, although perhaps not as accurate as the volume shadows you saw earlier, are far more performance-friendly. This is because they are actually just a stored texture, and require no calculations during gameplay.

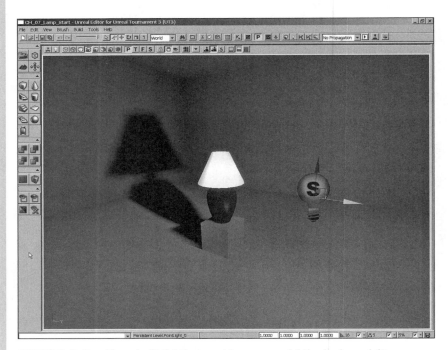

FIGURE 7.5   The rebuilt lighting provides very unsightly shadows right now.

6. Using the Translation Widget, use the front and top viewports to position the Light actor inside the light bulb mesh in the lamp. Use the small red crosshairs in the center of the actor to gauge the position (see **FIGURE 7.6**).

You'll notice that as soon as you move the Light actor, your shadows snap back to shadow volumes, helping you see how your shadows are placed. Once you place the actor inside the light bulb mesh, your level appears to go dark again. This is because you've techni- cally put your light inside a box, and it's casting shadows on the inside of the light bulb! For now, don't worry about this, because we'll be fixing it in **TUTORIAL 7.2**.

7. Save your level.

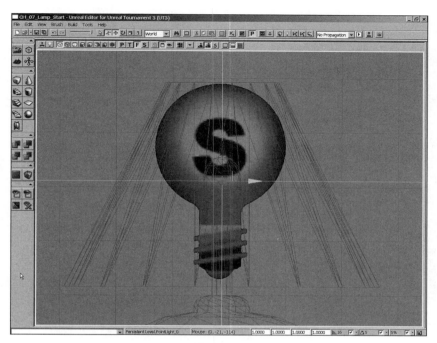

FIGURE 7.6 Place the Light actor inside the bulb like so.

END TUTORIAL 7.1

Continue from **TUTORIAL 7.1**, or open the DM-CH_07_Lamp_01.ut3 map file provided on the DVD in the folder for this chapter. In **TUTORIAL 7.2**, we continue work on our scene by adjusting some of the properties of the light we created previously.

TUTORIAL 7.2 Basic Lighting Primer, Part II: Setting Properties

1. In one of the orthographic viewports, select the PointLight actor you placed earlier. Press the F4 key to open its properties window and expand the Light tab, and then expand the LightComponent category. Within, you will see a large list of properties for the light (see **FIGURE 7.7**).

2. Uncheck the CastShadows property. Because there are no other objects in the room that require cast shadows, turning off this property is the easiest way to allow our light to shine through the mesh of the lamp's light bulb.

   You'll notice that as soon as you do this, the room illuminates once again (see **FIGURE 7.8**).

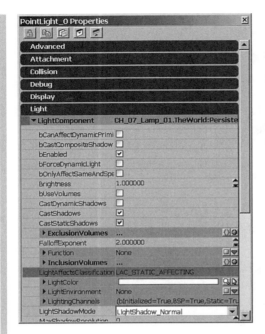

FIGURE 7.7 This is the **Properties window** for the PointLight actor.

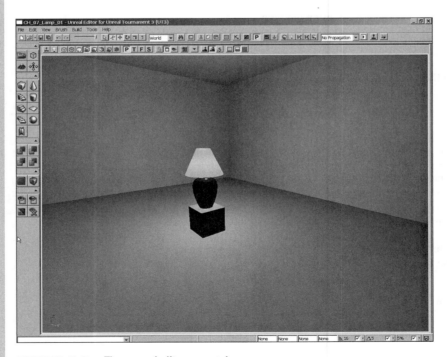

FIGURE 7.8 The room is lit once again.

3. We need to change the color of the light to reflect the color of the lamp shade more accurately. Click on the white bar next to the LightColor property, and you'll see two buttons appear on its right: The first opens the Color Chooser, and the second enables you to pick a color from the viewport.

   Click the small button with the arrow to choose a color from the viewport, and then click on the pale band that runs through the middle of the lampshade in the Perspective viewport. If you like, you can then use the Color Chooser to lighten up the color just a bit for a more realistic result. We used R, G, and B values of 243, 218, and 186, respectively.

4. Set the FalloffExponent value to 3. This creates a more dramatic light decay (see **FIGURE 7.9**).

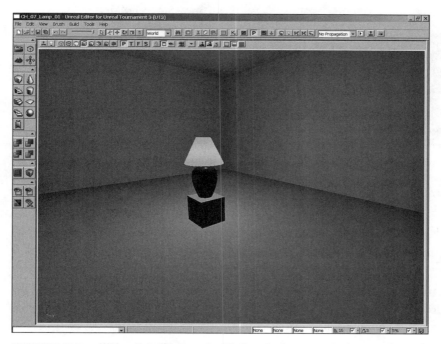

FIGURE 7.9   With a FalloffExponent of 3, the shadows are much more dramatic.

5. For now, we are done editing this light's properties, but it is easier to place other lights within the lamp shade if the icon for the Light actor isn't so big. In the light's Properties window, expand the Display tab, and set the DrawScale to 0.2. This shrinks down the icon to a more manageable size (see **FIGURE 7.10**). Feel free to use another value if you prefer.

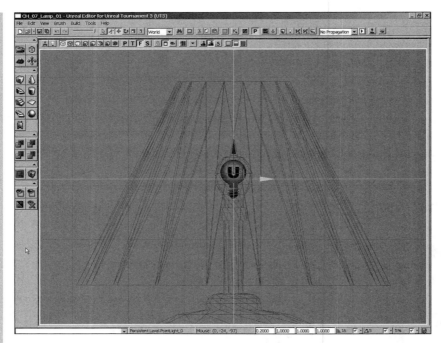

FIGURE 7.10   By adjusting DrawScale, you can make the icon's size much more manageable.

6. Click the Build All button to rebuild your lighting. You'll notice that the shadows in the corners of the room are very chunky and not very clean. We'll fix that a bit later.

7. Save your level.

END TUTORIAL 7.2

Continue from **TUTORIAL 7.2**, or open the DM-CH_07_Lamp_02.ut3 map file provided on the DVD in the folder for this chapter. In **TUTORIAL 7.3**, we create the bright cones of light that come out of the top and bottom of the lamp shade.

TUTORIAL 7.3   Basic Lighting Primer, Part III: Effect Lights

1. Not every light you create is a point light. You have many other types of lights at your disposal, and to get to them, you'll need to use the Actor Classes browser.

   From the main menubar, choose View > Browsers > Actor Classes Browser.

2. Within the Actor Classes browser, locate the Light actor and click the small plus sign next to it to expand it. Within, you will find a list of other types of lights available to you, each of which are discussed later in this chapter. For now, click on the SpotLight actor (don't expand it), and then close the Actor Classes browser (see **FIGURE 7.11**).

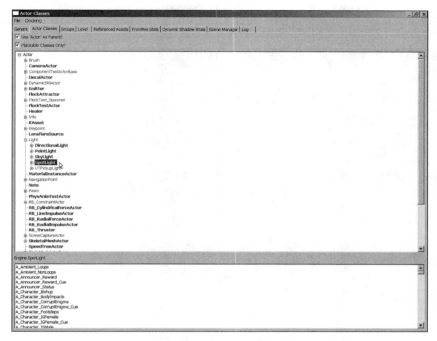

FIGURE 7.11   The Actor Classes browser, showing the SpotLight actor

3. In the Perspective viewport, right-click on the floor of your level and choose Add SpotLight Here from the Context menu. A new SpotLight actor appears on the floor (see **FIGURE 7.12**).

4. Select the new SpotLight, and press F4 to open its Properties window. Set its OuterConeAngle property to 40. Then, set its InnerConeAngle to 22, which widens the light's hotspot. Finally, set its DrawScale property to 0.2 to shrink the size of the icon for easy placement.

5. Use the Translation Widget in the top and side viewports to position the light directly in the center of the lamp static mesh. Once there, move the light upward so that its outer cone just barely fits into the bottom of the lamp shade, as shown. This should place the light very near the top of the lamp shade, well above the bulb, which is important for shadowing purposes (see **FIGURE 7.13**).

6. Set the SpotLights's LightColor property to a cream color, close to that used for the PointLight earlier. We used R, G, and B values of 243, 219, and 188, respectively. Set the FalloffExponent value to 3.

7. In the side viewport, with the SpotLight selected, hold the Alt key and drag down a duplicate of the SpotLight to just above the surface of the light bulb mesh.

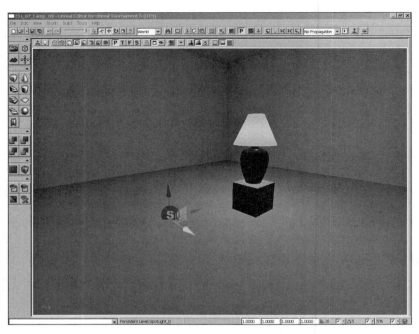

FIGURE 7.12   The new SpotLight actor appears wherever you clicked.

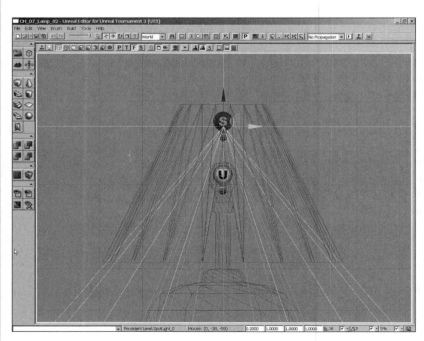

FIGURE 7.13   Place the SpotLight like so in the side viewport.

8. With this new SpotLight selected, press F4 to open the Properties window. Expand the Movement tab, and then expand the Rotation category. Change the Pitch value from –90 degrees to 90 degrees, effectively pointing the light straight up at the ceiling. Then, use the Translation Widget to move the new light vertically along the Z-axis so that its outer cone just barely fits into the top of the lamp shade (see **FIGURE 7.14**).

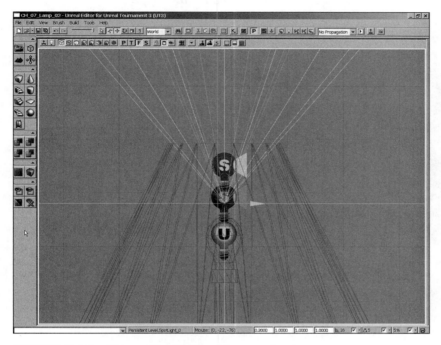

FIGURE 7.14 The new SpotLight points upward.

9. Using the skills you've gained so far, set the following properties on this new SpotLight:

> **CastShadows:** False (Unchecked)
>
> **FalloffExponent:** 5
>
> **InnerConeAngle:** 10

Rebuild lighting and save your level when finished.

END TUTORIAL 7.3

Continue from **TUTORIAL 7.3**, or open the DM-CH_07_Lamp_03.ut3 file provided on the DVD in the folder for this chapter. In **TUTORIAL 7.4**, we add some ambient lighting to help pull our shadows away from being completely black (super-black). This also helps give the illusion that light is bouncing around our level, as it tends to do in the real world.

TUTORIAL 7.4   Basic Lighting Primer, Part IV: Ambient Lighting

1. Open the Actor Classes browser and expand the Light actor. Click SkyLight. Then, in the Perspective viewport, right-click on the floor of the level and choose Place SkyLight Here.

   This immediately washes out your scene. Don't worry; that's normal. Also, be aware that the placement of the SkyLight actor is irrelevant (see **FIGURE 7.15**).

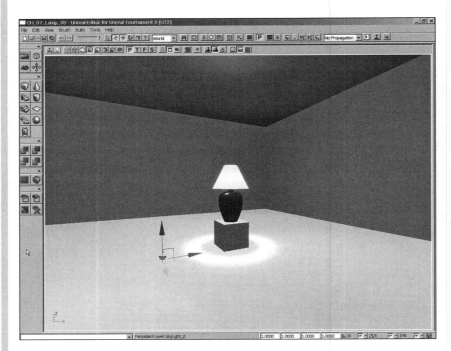

FIGURE 7.15   The initial effect of the SkyLight seems undesirable.

2. Double-click on the SkyLight actor to open the Properties Window. Set the following properties:

   Brightness: 0.15

   LightColor:

   > **R:** 255

   > **G:** 249

   > **B:** 206

3. This fixes the washed-out look, but you'll notice that the lamp mesh still looks very dark. To solve this problem, we're actually going to use a second ambient light using a different lighting channel. We discuss lighting channels in depth later in the chapter (see **FIGURE 7.16**).

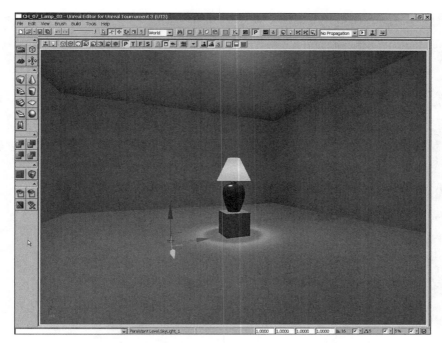

FIGURE 7.16 The room looks much better with the new settings.

Select the SkyLight, and in its Properties Window, expand the LightingChannels category. Uncheck the Static channel. If you watch the lamp mesh very closely, you'll see that it gets a bit darker, since the SkyLight is no longer affecting it.

4. With the SkyLight selected, use the Translation Widget while holding the Alt key to create a duplicate. Again, its placement is irrelevant. Open the Properties window for this new SkyLight, and this time, set the Static channel to True (checked), but set the BSP channel to False (unchecked). This causes the new SkyLight to only affect the lamp mesh (see **FIGURE 7.17**).

Finally, set the brightness value to 1.2, which brightens up the lamp considerably.

5. Now we need to fake some bounced lights coming off the base of our lamp and onto the pedestal. The effect is very subtle but shows you some new techniques for light creation.

Position the Perspective viewport close to the lamp. Then, while holding Ctrl-L, left-click on an area of the lamp's body that is bright red. A new PointLight is created there. This light automatically has the same color as the area you clicked, along with a low brightness and radius, making it a perfect start for a bounce light.

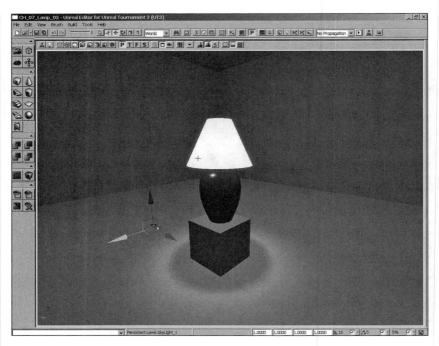

FIGURE 7.17   The second SkyLight affects only the lamp mesh.

6. Select this new PointLight and set the following properties:

> **DrawScale:** 0.2
>
> **Radius:** 64
>
> **Static (LightingChannel):** False (Unchecked)

7. Position this new light above one of the corners of the pedestal, but also in toward the base of the lamp just a bit, as shown. Then, using the Translation Widget and the Alt key, create duplicates of the light in similar positions around the other three corners of the pedestal (see **FIGURE 7.18**). Remember to release the Alt key in between duplications!

8. Rebuild lighting and save your level.

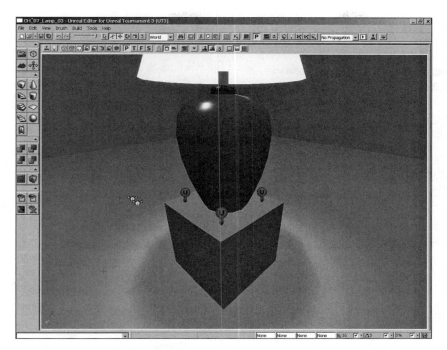

FIGURE 7.18   The bounce lights should be placed at the corners of the pedestal.

END TUTORIAL 7.4

Continue from **TUTORIAL 7.4**, or open the DM-CH_07_Lamp_04.ut3 map file provided on the DVD in the folder for this chapter. In **TUTORIAL 7.5**, we clean up the messy shadows that are being cast around the room.

TUTORIAL 7.5   Basic Lighting Primer, Part V: Cleaning Up Static Shadows

1. In the Perspective viewport, click on the floor of the room to select the surface. Remember that if the surface doesn't appear to be selectable, you're probably in Game Mode, which you can exit by hitting G. Once you have the floor selected, press Shift-B to select all the surfaces of the room.

2. Press F5 to open the Surface Properties window (see **FIGURE 7.19**). Under the Lighting group, you will see Lightmap Resolution, which by default is set to 32. As you may recall from Chapter 4, "A Universe of Brushes: World Geometry In-Depth," setting this to a lower value sharpens up our shadows, at the cost of a longer build time and higher memory usage.

3. Set the Lightmap Resolution value to 4, and then rebuild your lighting. You'll notice a longer build time, but the shadows around the room appear much cleaner. If you like, go ahead and try setting the value to 1, but get it out of your system now; this will probably be the last time you'll ever want to use it. The build times are tremendous!

4. After you've finished experimenting with the Lightmap Resolution, set it back to 4, rebuild lighting, and save your level (see **FIGURE 7.20**).

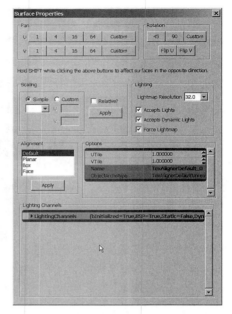

FIGURE 7.19   Here is the Surface Properties window.

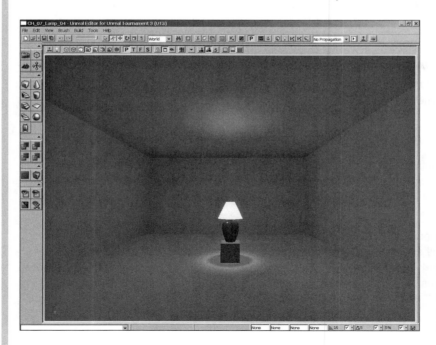

FIGURE 7.20
At a Lightmap Resolution setting of 4, the shadows take longer to rebuild, but look much better.

END TUTORIAL 7.5

Lighting Concepts

Now that you've got your hands dirty in the world of lighting, there are some concepts that you need to understand, as they will help you more fully grasp what is going on beneath the hood of Unreal's lighting system. These are light maps and shadow maps, static and dynamic lighting, and per-vertex lighting and lighting subdivisions.

Light Maps and Shadow Maps

Calculating all lighting and shadowing for your level constantly during gameplay would be crippling to performance. To handle that problem, Unreal generates light maps and shadow maps for all objects and lights that do not move during gameplay. Because those objects are static, the lighting need only be calculated once, and light and shadow maps (which are types of textures) are applied to the objects, meaning that further light calculation is unnecessary.

A *light map* is a texture generated from a calculation of all the lights that are illuminating a particular surface or static mesh. The benefit of this is that multiple lights can strike a single surface, and because the actual calculation is done in advance and "baked" in the form of a light map, there is a minimal drop in performance. Note that normal map information and specularity are still calculated during gameplay, even with light-mapped surfaces (see **FIGURE 7.21**).

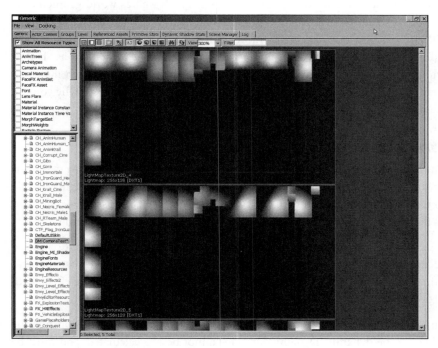

FIGURE 7.21   Here are the light maps of a level's BSP.

A *shadow map* is very similar to a light map, but stores shadowing data instead of illumination data. Shadow maps also bear a distinct difference from light maps in that although a single light map, or set of light maps, can define lighting from many different lights, each light must have its own individual shadow map for a given surface. If many lights strike a single surface, the multiple shadow maps are combined to provide the final result (see **FIGURE 7.22**).

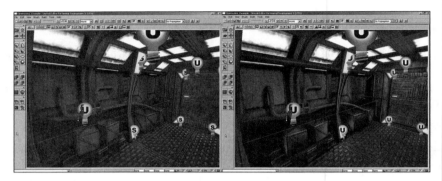

FIGURE 7.22   On the left, a level using light maps. On the right, the same level using shadow maps.

As of Unreal Engine 3.0, static meshes can receive shadow maps as well as world geometry. By default, static meshes are shadowed using lighting subdivision data, as described later in this section. However, although shadow mapping is a far more precise way of handling shadows on static meshes, it should be noted that it does come along with a performance limitation, as shadow mapping is much more memory intensive. Combine this with the fact that for each light that strikes a static mesh, a separate shadow map must be generated, and it is easy to see why you can potentially decrease game performance by relying too heavily on this method.

Static and Dynamic Lighting

When working in Unreal Editor, you often find the words *static* and *dynamic* to mean many different things. For the purposes of this text, however, we consider *static lights* to be lights that do not move during gameplay, meaning that their bMovable property is set to false. *Dynamic lights* are considered as lights that can move, or that have their bMovable property set to true.

When static lights are illuminating a static surface, the lighting is considered to be *static* and can be pre-calculated and stored in light and shadow maps. Static lighting provides the backbone of your level's illumination, as you can use many static lights, resulting in a very lifelike effect, with little concern for overhead.

Conversely, when either a light or object are dynamic (moving) in a lighting relationship, the lighting is considered to be dynamic. Dynamic lighting cannot be pre-calculated, and must be constantly computed during runtime, requiring considerable processing power. As you would expect, dynamic lighting scenarios must be used with caution to avoid serious performance problems.

That is not to say, however, that the use of dynamic lighting is a bad thing. There are times when a dynamic light is absolutely necessary to give you the effect you need. Plus, Unreal also provides special features such as lighting environments and light functions, both of which are covered later in this chapter, to allow optimum efficiency and flexibility when using dynamic lighting (see **FIGURE 7.23**).

FIGURE 7.23   Dynamic lighting (left) tends to be much sharper than static lighting (right), but is much heavier in terms of processing power.

Per-Vertex Lighting and Lighting Subdivisions

This concept pertains only to the lighting of static meshes. In versions of the Unreal Engine prior to version 3.0, the only lighting method available to static meshes was per-vertex lighting. This basically means that a triangle would only appear lit if one or more of its vertices was receiving any light. This would often lead to shadowing anomalies whenever only a single vertex was in shadow. The final result tended to look very generic and would have unsightly results on low-polygon meshes.

As of Unreal Engine 3.0, lighting is calculated across static meshes using lighting subdivisions. This means that each polygon is internally subdivided into multiple parts, and the light striking each part is calculated. The final result is blended together, resulting in the final lighting for the polygon. Naturally, this calculation is more complex, although the performance hit affects level build times much more than gameplay.

The true benefit of lighting subdivisions comes from being able to change the number of subdivisions used to calculate the lighting across each polygon. The higher your subdivisions, the clearer your shadows are, although more calculation is needed to create your shadows (see **FIGURE 7.24**).

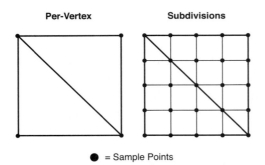

Per-Vertex   Subdivisions

● = Sample Points

FIGURE 7.24   Where per-vertex lighting only looks to see if vertices are illuminated, lighting subdivisions allow for multiple sample points across each polygon for a more accurate result.

Types of Lights

There are many types of lights available for use inside of Unreal Editor. For those of you who have experience in lighting scenes inside of 3D animation software, such as 3ds Max or Maya, you'll feel right at home with the lights available. However, even those who are completely new to the world of lighting will see that the light types available are quite intuitive, and you should have no problem discerning which type to use in a given situation. The four primary types of lights are PointLightsSpotLights, DirectionalLights, andSkyLights, each of which is discussed next.

The first three types of lights (PointLight, SpotLight, and DirectionalLight) each have two subtypes available. These are toggleable lights and moveable lights. This means that you can have a normal PointLight, a toggleable PointLight, or a moveable PointLight. We begin by covering the general differences in these subtypes, and then cover the actual light types individually.

Toggleable Lights

Toggleable lights can be turned on and off during gameplay. This is done through the use of the Toggle sequence object within Kismet. For more information on using Kismet to activate and deactivate lights, please see Chapter 9, "Introduction to Unreal Kismet." Light from a toggleable light cannot be used in a light map.

Moveable Lights

Moveable lights, as the name suggests, are dynamic lights that can move throughout your level. This could be anything from a point light that moves along a path to a spotlight that rotates to point at a target. This motion is handled with Matinee. For more

> **NOTE**
>
> For a moveable light to be animatable in Matinee, the light's Physics property must be set to PHYS_ Interpolating. This property can be found under the light's Movement category.

information concerning Matinee, please see Chapter 10, "Unreal Matinee." As with a toggleable light, the light from a moveable light cannot be used in a light map.

Point Lights

PointLights emit light from a single point in all directions, kind of like a light bulb (see **FIGURE 7.25**). They are the most-often-used type of light, especially in indoor levels. The light has a Radius property that controls how far light travels from the location of the actor. PointLights are available in standard static form (PointLight), toggleable (PointLightToggleable), and moveable (PointLightMovable) (see **FIGURE 7.26**).

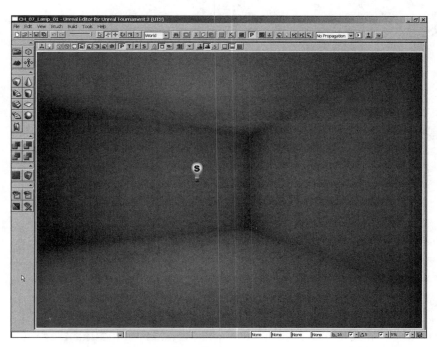

FIGURE 7.25 An example of light being emitted by a PointLight actor. Notice that all walls are lit.

FIGURE 7.26 Icons for a PointLight, a PointLightToggleable, and a PointLightMovable

Spotlights

SpotLights emit light from a single point in a confined cone, like a real-world spotlight or flashlight. This cone can be opened and closed to focus the light via the InnerConeAngle and OuterConeAngle properties.

SpotLights are used whenever you need close-proximity light directed only in a particular direction, such as a searchlight, flashlight, projector, or similar light source. SpotLight actors also use the radius property to determine how far from the actor light will travel (see **FIGURE 7.27**). Just as with the point light, the SpotLight actor is available in its standard form (SpotLight), toggleable (SpotLightToggleable), and movable (SpotLightMovable) (see **FIGURE 7.28**).

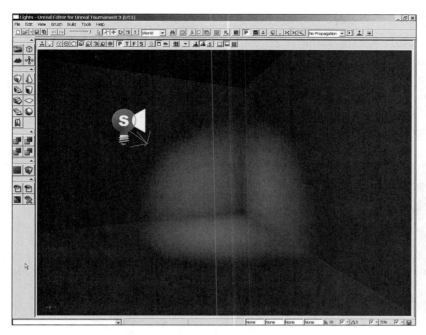

FIGURE 7.27   An example of light being emitted by a SpotLight actor

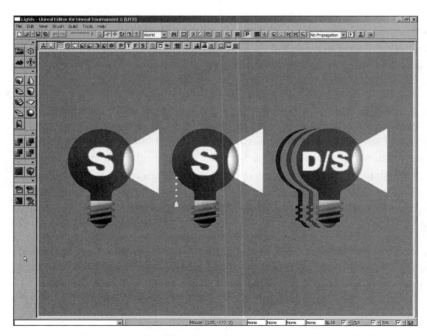

FIGURE 7.28   Icons for a SpotLight, a SpotLightToggleable, and a SpotLightMovable

Directional Lights

DirectionalLights are used when simulating an extremely distant light source, such as the Sun, and are usually only used in outdoor situations. This is because rather than calculating light from a single emissive point, directional lights are calculated as if the light were being emitted from a theoretical plane that is infinitely large and infinitely far away. This means that all rays of light are parallel, resulting in shadows that are also parallel rather than divergent, as they would be if created from a point light (see **FIGURE 7.29**).

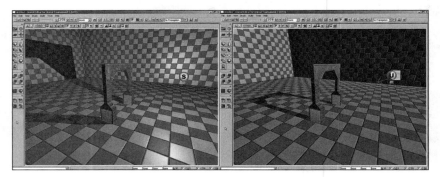

FIGURE 7.29   On the left are shadows created with a point light, and on the right with a DirectionalLight. Notice the parallel nature of the DirectionalLight's shadows.

DirectionalLight actors only come in standard form (DirectionalLight) and toggleable form (DirectionalLightToggleable) (see **FIGURE 7.30**). Because the illuminant surface is infinitely large and infinitely distant, its position is irrelevant. Only its angle matters.

SkyLights

A SkyLight actor emits light from two theoretical hemispheres, upper and lower. These hemispheres are calculated as if they were infinite in size, meaning that there is no way to move an actor "outside" the hemisphere. The purpose of the SkyLight is to provide ambient lighting to a level, thus preventing any shadows from falling into full blackness. Each of the two hemispheres has its own color and brightness values, meaning that you can have brighter light coming from above with dimmer coming from below, simulating the effect of diffused light coming from many surfaces at once. SkyLights do not have a toggleable or movable form (see **FIGURE 7.31**).

SkyLight actors only come in standard form (SkyLight) and toggleable form (SkyLight Toggleable). Because the illuminant surface is infinitely large and infinitely distant, its position is irrelevant. Only its angle matters (see **FIGURE 7.32**).

FIGURE 7.30   Icons for a DirectionalLight and a DirectionalLightToggleable

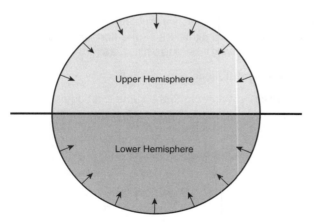

FIGURE 7.31   Diagram demonstrating how SkyLights behave

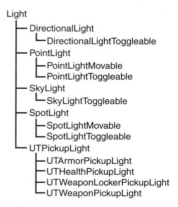

FIGURE 7.32   A diagrammatic breakdown of the types of lights available, along with their subtypes

Pickup Lights

Pickup lights are special versions of point lights that are used solely with certain pickups that can be placed in a map. Each type of pickup light is designed to be used with a specific pickup and is named accordingly. The base pickup light is the UTPickupLight. This particular type, much like the base light, is never used directly. The types of pickup lights that are used are the UTArmorPickupLight, the UTHealthPickupLight, the UTWeaponLockerPickupLight, and the UTWeaponPickupLight. These lights are not placed manually, as is the case with other lights. Once a pickup is placed in the map, the Add Pickup Lights command is chosen from the Tools menu, which places the appropriate pickup light, if any is necessary.

We now begin our second series of tutorials, in which we light a more game-like scene of a small dungeon. It is highly recommended that unless you already have some experience working with lights, you complete the primer tutorials at the beginning of this chapter.

In **TUTORIAL 7.6**, we begin lighting a new scene depicting a dark and dank dungeon. To begin, we place the necessary lights.

TUTORIAL 7.6   Lighting the Dungeon, Part I: Light Placement

1. Launch Unreal Editor and open the Light_Demo map included on the DVD in the files for this chapter. We start by placing our initial lights in the scene. Your Perspective viewport appears almost completely black, as it is currently in Lit mode. Switch it to Unlit before continuing.

2. Open the Actor Classes browser and expand Light > PointLight, and select PointLightMovable. Then, in the Perspective viewport, right-click on the floor and choose Place PointLightMovable Here from the Context menu (see **FIGURE 7.33**).

   When finished, set your Perspective viewport to Lit mode.

3. Use the Translation Widget to move the PointLightMovable to the same location as the particle emitter just above the torch mesh. From now on, this light is referred to as the Torch Light (see **FIGURE 7.34**).

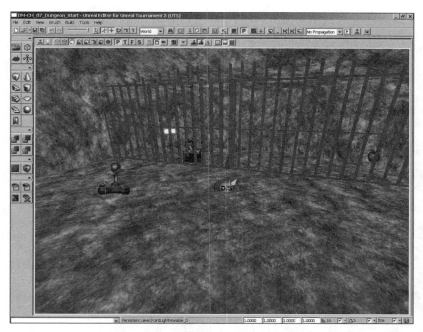

FIGURE 7.33   The PointLightMovable should appear where you right-clicked.

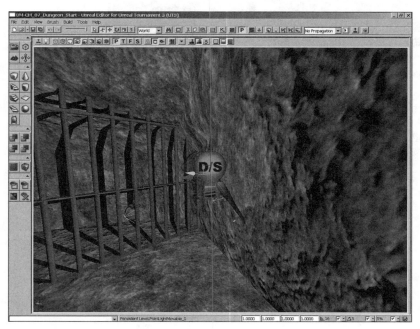

FIGURE 7.34   The Torch Light should be placed just above the torch static mesh.

4. Back in the Actor Classes browser, expand 'Light' and select the SpotLight actor. Right-click and place one on the floor, then use the Translation Widget to position it just underneath the grate in the ceiling. From now on, this is referred to as the Overhead Light (see **FIGURE 7.35**).

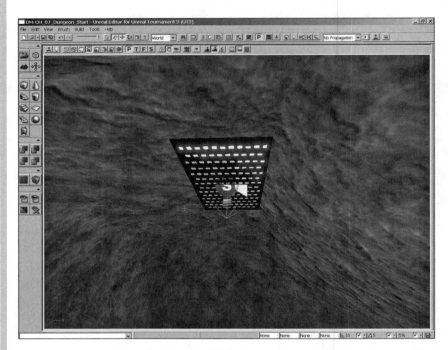

FIGURE 7.35 Place the Overhead Light just underneath the grate in the ceiling.

5. For our third light, hold the L key and click on the floor of the cell to place a new PointLight actor. Use the Translation Widget to move this light just in front of the white light that is set into the wall of the cell. This is referred to as the Wall Light from now on (see **FIGURE 7.36**).

6. Rebuild your lighting and save your level

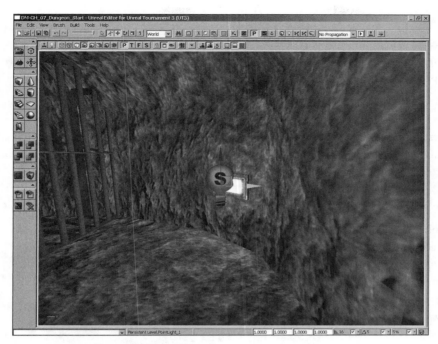

FIGURE 7.36 The Wall Light should be just in front of the lamp in the cell.

END TUTORIAL 7.6

Light Properties

As you work with lighting more and more in Unreal Editor, you're going to quickly discover that there are a great many properties available for editing the look and behavior of your lights. This section is designed to show you those that are most frequently used, rather than to bombard you with every nuance of every single parameter. Once you become more comfortable lighting your scenes, you may start to use some of the other properties on your own.

We begin by taking a look at some generic properties that exist on some level within all lights. From there, we look at some exclusive properties that pertain only to a particular light type.

General Properties

No matter what type of light you use, there are some common properties that you will often need to adjust to get the effect you want. In this section, we cover those properties and how they alter the look of your lights.

bEnabled

The bEnabled property determines whether the light is actually on or off. Think of it as a switch for your light. Unless your light is toggleable, this property is typically set to True. On toggleable lights, this is the property that is being activated and deactivated to switch the light on and off.

Brightness

As its name suggests, this property controls the intensity of the light. Beware of using values that are too high, because you will start to "wash out" your levels. This value can be animated through Matinee to have a light that fades or pulsates.

LightColor

Another rather obviously named property, LightColor enables you to change the hue, saturation, and value of the emitted light. It is set using a standard Windows Color Chooser window, such as the one shown in **FIGURE 7.37**. This can also be animated using Matinee.

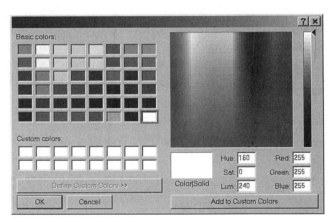

FIGURE 7.37   The Color Chooser is used to change a light's color.

Radius

The Radius property controls the distance from the light at which the intensity reaches a value of 0. To put it another way, it changes the radius of a theoretical sphere that controls the extents of the light. Objects within the radius are affected by the light on some level; objects without receive no light. Directional lights and skylights do not use this property (see **FIGURE 7.38**).

FalloffExponent

The FalloffExponent property controls how quickly the intensity of the light reaches 0 as light travels closer to the extents of the radius. This is set to 2 by default, resulting in square falloff. A setting of 3 results in cubic falloff, and so on. A value of 0

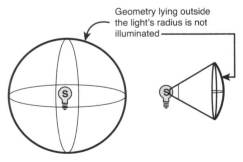

FIGURE 7.38   The radius of pointlights and spotlights

results in no falloff whatsoever, and the light retains its full intensity to the extents of the radius. Directional lights and skylights do not use this property.

Exclusive SpotLight Properties

This section is dedicated to the primary properties that exist only for SpotLight actors. Generally, these only include the necessary controls for the shape of the SpotLight's cone.

InnerConeAngle and OuterConeAngle

There are two cones in a SpotLight to control the angle of the light being emitted. The area within the inner cone receives 100% illumination, with a gradual falloff as you move outward to the outer cone, beyond which there is no illumination (see **FIGURE 7.39**).

By default, the InnerConeAngle property is set to 0, meaning that there is practically no "hot spot" at which the light receives full 100 percent intensity.

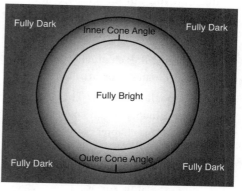

FIGURE 7.39   Inner and outer cone angles

Exclusive DirectionalLight Properties

This section includes any properties that exist only on DirectionalLight actors. At the time of this writing, the only one of these is TraceDistance.

TraceDistance

The TraceDistance property controls how far away one object can be from another and still cast shadows on it. By default, this is set to 100,000. This means, for example, that if you had a platform that was 150,000 units above the ground, it would not cast a shadow on the ground. However, if you then moved it to 90,000 units, a shadow would appear.

Exclusive SkyLight Properties

As with the other types of lights, SkyLights have some properties that are exclusive to them. This includes the LowerBrightness and LowerColor, which parallel the original Brightness and Color properties.

LowerBrightness and LowerColor

As mentioned earlier, a SkyLight has two hemispheres. Each of these hemispheres can be controlled independently to achieve the desired effect. LowerBrightness and LowerColor provide access to the intensity and color of the lower hemisphere.

Lighting Channels

In the real world, turning on a light in a dark room illuminates every surface within range of the light, and within its line of sight. In Unreal, however, you have the power to control whether or not a particular light can affect a given object. This is done through the use of light channels. Think of them as channels of a television. The light broadcasts on a particular channel or channels, and as long as an object is receiving at least one of those channels, the object is illuminated. In this way, you can set certain objects to receive no light from certain lights, or instead create lights that only illuminate particular objects. There are many lighting channels available; the following are some of the most common:

▶ **BSP:** The BSP channel is used by all BSP brushes. If this channel is activated in your light, it illuminates your brushes.

▶ **CompositeDynamic:** The CompositeDynamic channel is used in conjunction with light environments, and is covered more thoroughly within the "Light Environments" section later in this chapter.

▶ **Dynamic:** The Dynamic lighting channel is for any objects that move or change during play. Without this channel checked, your light will not fall on players, movers, or any other dynamic surface. However, don't think you *must* activate this channel to light dynamic objects. You also have the option of using Light Environments through the CompositeDynamic channel mentioned above. We discuss light environments in the "Light Environments" section later in this chapter.

▶ **Static:** The Static lighting channel applies to all objects that do not move or change during gameplay, such as static meshes.

▶ **Cinematic/Gameplay/Unnamed:** There are several other channels within a light as well. These are provided as user-controlled channels. For instance, you can turn off all channels except for Unnamed_1, and only other objects in which the Unnamed_1 channel has been activated are illuminated. These channels are broken up into three groups simply for organizational purposes. The Cinematic channels naturally are meant to be used for lights used in cinematic sequences, possibly as rim lighting. The Gameplay channels can be used for lights that are part of some gameplay event. The Unnamed channels are provided for any miscellaneous usage (see **FIGURE 7.40**).

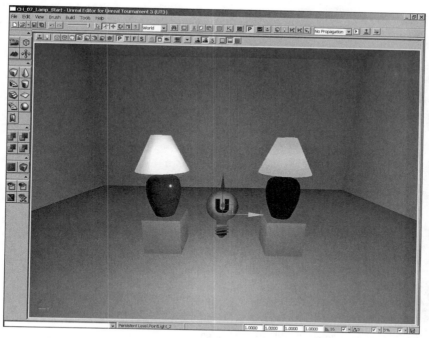

FIGURE 7.40   In this image, the light is only using the BSP and Unnamed_1 channel. The mesh on the left has Unnamed_1 activated; the mesh on the right does not.

Continue from **TUTORIAL 7.6**, or open the DM-CH_07_Dungeon_01.ut3 map file provided on the DVD in the folder for this chapter. In **TUTORIAL 7.7**, we establish the necessary properties for the lights we placed in **TUTORIAL 7.6**.

TUTORIAL 7.7   Lighting the Dungeon, Part II: Light Properties

1. Select the Wall Light and press F4 (or double-click the actor) to open its Properties window. Set the following properties (see **FIGURE 7.41**):

   FalloffExponent: 8.0

   Radius: 960.0

   LightColor:

   R: 255

   G: 255

   B: 185

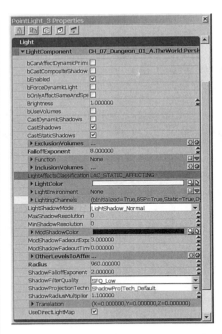

FIGURE 7.41   The Properties window should appear like so.

2. Expand the "Lighting Channels" section and verify that *only* the following channels are active:

    BSP

    CompositeDynamic

    Dynamic

    Static

> **NOTE**
>
> Do not change the color of the Torch Light! We control its color with a light function later.

3. Select the Torch Light and set the following properties in its Properties window:

    FalloffExponent: 8.0

    Radius: 860.0

4. Expand the Torch Light's lighting channels and verify that *only* the following channels are active:

    BSP

    CompositeDynamic

    Dynamic

    Static

5. Select the Overhead Light and set the following properties:

>   **Brightness:** 6.0
>
>   **FalloffExponent:** 12.0
>
>   **OuterConeAngle:** 85.0
>
>   **Radius:** 960.0

6. Verify that the following lighting channels are active for the Overhead Light:

>   BSP
>
>   CompositeDynamic
>
>   Dynamic
>
>   Static

7. Rebuild lighting and save your level (see **FIGURE 7.42**).

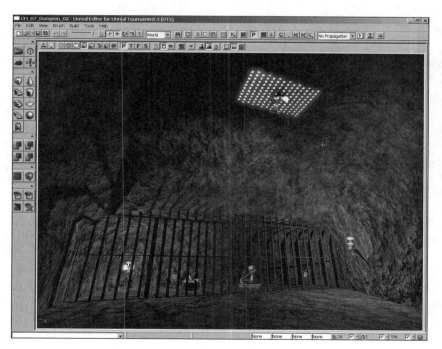

FIGURE 7.42   Your final level should look something like this.

END TUTORIAL 7.7

Lighting Volumes

Lighting volumes are another method of determining what objects a light affects, aside from lighting channels. They work by enabling you to designate a list of volumes: inclusion volumes or exclusion volumes. Simply put, objects that are within any of the volumes listed in the InclusionVolumes list are illuminated, whereas any objects that are within volumes listed in the ExclusionVolumes list are not (see **FIGURE 7.43**).

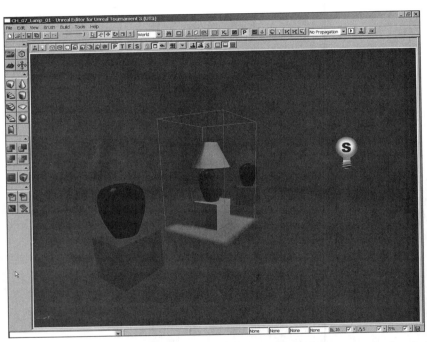

FIGURE 7.43   The volume shown is within the InclusionVolumes list. Notice that objects outside of the volume are unlit.

Lighting volumes are activated through the bUseVolumes property. Typically, you then add volumes to one of the arrays for InclusionVolumes or ExclusionVolumes. You can use both if you like; however, keep in mind that in such cases, any objects that fall into both an inclusion and exclusion volume are unlit, and so are any objects that are not within any volumes.

Shadows

Shadows play a key role in the look of your level's lighting. In Unreal Engine 3.0, there are three different types of shadows available: Precomputed shadows, shadow buffer shadows, and shadow volume shadows. The type that you use is not set manually, but instead depends on the lighting situation, whether either the light and/or the object are static or dynamic.

All three types of shadow are seamlessly integrated into the lighting system. The only noticeable difference to the player would be the amount of fuzziness surrounding the edges of the shadows. Although precomputed shadows can be very fuzzy depending on their resolution, shadow volume shadows are very crisp.

No matter which technique is employed, the shadows function independently of all other lighting effects, such as bump mapping and specularity, meaning that different types of shadow do not alter such effects.

Precomputed Shadows (Shadow Maps)

Precomputed shadows are created during light building and stored within shadow maps. They are used when static lights are illuminating static geometry. These shadows are ray-traced, meaning that the individual rays of light are calculated from the illumination source to the illuminated object. Precomputed shadows do not take a material's alpha into account, as shown in **FIGURE 7.44**.

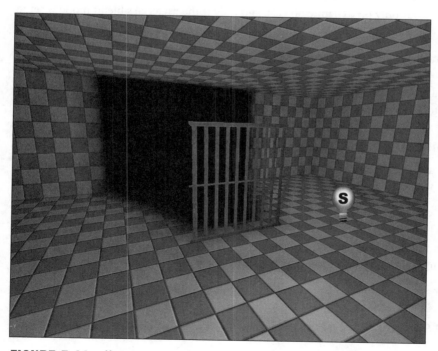

FIGURE 7.44   Here you see a sheet brush with an alpha-masked material. Notice that the object still casts a solid shadow.

In order for a light to be considered in the creation of precomputed shadows, its UseDirectLightMap property, located under its LightComponent category, must be set to True, which is the default setting for static lights.

For information on using mapped shadows with BSP-based geometry, please see Chapter 4. For information on mapped shadows with static meshes, please see Chapter 5, "Static Meshes."

Shadow Buffer Shadows

Shadow buffer shadows are used only when a static light illuminates dynamic geometry, such as characters, movers, and so on.

Shadow buffer shadows have a blurred, or softened, outer edge. There are several different algorithms to control this softening effect available within the ShadowFilteringTechnique property. Within, you will find a list of different methods used to filter shadow buffer shadows, based on whether you're looking for quality or performance. As an example, the game *Gears of War* uses the BCF_Low setting for its shadow buffer filtering, which is the lowest-quality setting, but also provides the best performance.

Shadow buffer shadows can take alpha information from an alpha-masked material into the shadow calculation, but only on dynamic objects, and only if the material's blend mode is set to BLEND_Masked (see **FIGURE 7.45**).

There is a performance consideration with shadow buffer shadows when used with point lights. If an object cannot fit within a 90 degree field of view from the light, the engine switches over to a much slower cubemap buffer-filtering system. Put simply, you typically want players and other dynamic objects to be kept away from shadow-casting point lights.

Shadow Volume Shadows

Shadow volumes are used only when a dynamic light illuminates dynamic geometry or static geometry.

Shadow volumes are most often seen when moving lights around inside of Unreal Editor. They are characterized by having very crisp edges with no softening, and remain accurate no matter the distance between the light and the occluding object. Shadow volumes do not take a material's alpha channel into account at all, meaning that all alpha masks are ignored.

As mentioned previously, you see shadow volumes whenever you move a light inside the editor (see **FIGURE 7.46**). The shadow volumes remain until lighting is built, at which point the appropriate type of shadow takes over. Shadow volumes are used in-game only when the light source is in motion.

FIGURE 7.45
Notice the mover on the left casts accurate alpha-based shadows, whereas the static mesh on the right does not.

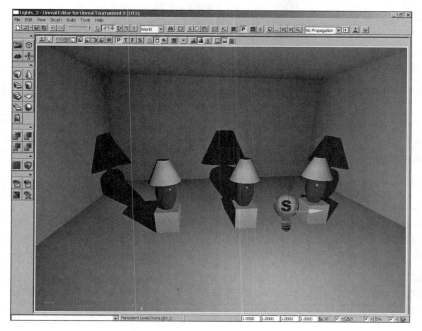

FIGURE 7.46
As soon as you move a light within the editor, shadow volumes appear to help with light and shadow placement.

You can force a light to create shadow volumes at all times by setting its bForceDynamicLight property to true.

Shadow Modulation

Modulated shadows are not actually a type of shadow, but are instead a mode that can be used when calculating dynamic shadows. Simply put, modulated shadows provide you with direct access to the shadow's color (see **FIGURE 7.47**). This is beneficial when multiple lights start to wash out your shadow, making it hard to see. In such cases, you can set your LightShadowMode property to LightShadow_Modulate and then use the ModShadowColor property to change the color of the shadow itself.

It should be noted that using modulated shadows has no effect on shadows cast from static objects by static lights, unless the bForceDynamicLight property is set to true. In such instances, you will use volume shadows, which can use modulation.

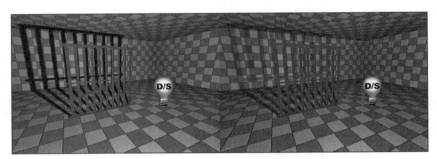

FIGURE 7.47   Here you can see the difference between normal shadows and modulated shadows.

Continue from **TUTORIAL 7.7**, or open the DM-CH_07_Dungeon_02.ut3 map file provided on the DVD in the folder for this chapter. **TUTORIAL 7.8** demonstrates the setup of the necessary shadow properties for our lights.

TUTORIAL 7.8   Lighting the Dungeon, Part III: Shadow Properties

1. Select the Wall Light, and in its Properties window, activate the CastDynamicShadows property. This causes the light to cast shadows from the cell door as it opens and closes, as well as cast shadows from the player and the pawn (see **FIGURE 7.48**).

2. While still viewing the Wall Light's properties, locate the LightShadowMode property, and set it to LightShadow_Modulate. This causes the shadows to appear a bit lighter, and give you the ability to edit their color if so desired.

3. Select the Overhead Light, and in its Properties window, deactivate the CastShadows, because it is not important for this light to shadow our level (see **FIGURE 7.49**).

FIGURE 7.48 The Wall Light casts shadows through the bars of the cell door.

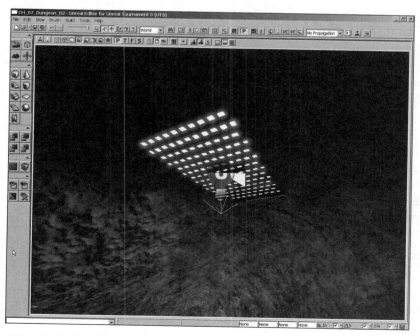

FIGURE 7.49 The Overhead Light does not need to cast shadows.

4. Rebuild lighting and test your level. You should now see dynamic shadows being cast by the door, the prisoner, and by your own character!

END TUTORIAL 7.8

Continue from **TUTORIAL 7.8**, or open the DM-CH_07_Dungeon_03.ut3 map file provided on the DVD in the folder for this chapter. Please note that this chapter uses Kismet and Matinee. For more information about these topics, please see Chapters 9 and 10, respectively. In **TUTORIAL 7.9**, we move our lights around to enhance the realism of the fire effect.

TUTORIAL 7.9   Lighting the Dungeon, Part IV: Animating Lights

1. Our first step is to ensure that our light can indeed be animated. Select the Torch Light, and in its Properties window, expand the Movement tab. Set the Physics property to PHYS_Interpolating (see **FIGURE 7.50**).

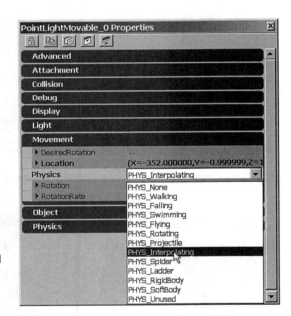

2. Click the Open Kismet button **K** to open the Kismet Editor. You will see a Matinee sequence connected to the Level Startup event, labeled "playing animation" (see **FIGURE 7.51**).

3. The current Matinee sequence object is causing the particle emitter for the torch's flame to wave around. We're now going to duplicate that object and use it as a basis to make the light wave as well. Follow these steps:

FIGURE 7.50   Setting the Physics property is required to make the light mobile through Matinee.

   a. Select the Matinee sequence object, as well as the Matinee data object connected to it. Duplicate the pair by pressing Ctrl-C and then Ctrl-V (see **FIGURE 7.52**).

   b. Select the new Matinee sequence object. In the Properties area at the bottom of the Kismet window, set the ObjComment property to animating light.

   c. Alt-click the small box labeled InterpGroup at the bottom of the new Matinee sequence object to break the wire to the emitter object variable.

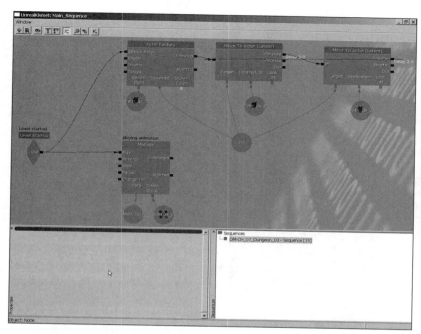

FIGURE 7.51   This shows the level's Kismet sequences.

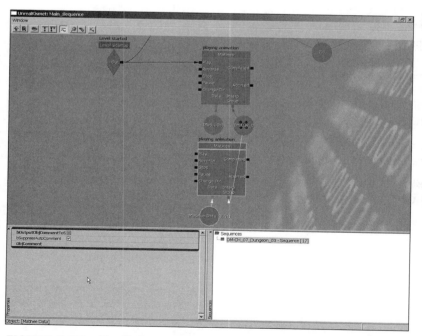

FIGURE 7.52   The Matinee sequence and data object have been duplicated.

d. Drag a new wire from the Play input of this new Matinee sequence object to the Out of the Level Startup event (see **FIGURE 7.53**).

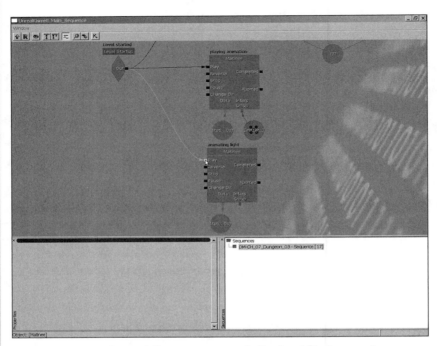

FIGURE 7.53   Connect the new sequence to the Level Startup event.

e. In the Perspective viewport, select the Torch Light. Then, back in the Kismet Editor, right-click on the InterpGroup input box on the bottom of the Matinee sequence object and choose New Object Variable using PointLightMovable_0 (see **FIGURE 7.54**).

4. If we tested the level right now, the light would appear to have a slight wavering motion to it. However, we accentuate the effect by animating the brightness of the light as well:

a. In the Kismet Editor, right-click on the new Matinee sequence you duplicated and choose Open UnrealMatinee from the Context menu (see **FIGURE 7.55**).

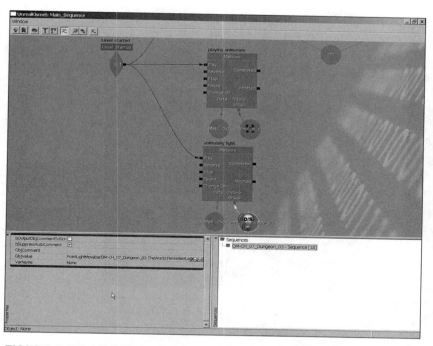

FIGURE 7.54   The Matinee sequence now affects the Torch Light.

b. Right-click on the InterpGroup track and choose New Float Property Track. From the dialog that appears, select PointLightComponent0.Brightness from the dropdown and click OK (see **FIGURE 7.56**).

FIGURE 7.55   Open Matinee from the Context menu.

c. With the Brightness track selected, click the Stop button twice just to make sure that the time slider is set to 0.00. Then, click the Add Key Button ⏻ to set the first key.

d. The time slider can be seen as a small black line on the number-ruled gray bar that runs along the bottom of the Matinee window. Drag this to 1.00, and then click the Add Key ⏻

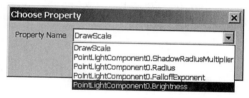

FIGURE 7.56   Choose the PointLightComponent0.Brightness property.

button again. Finally, move the time slider to 2.00, which should be the end of the sequence, and add one more key (see **FIGURE 7.57**).

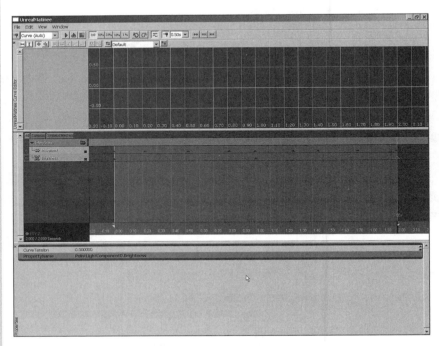

FIGURE 7.57   Keys for 0.00, 1.00, and 2.00 have been added.

e. Move the time slider to three different arbitrary locations within the 0.00 to 1.00 range, and click the Add Key button [img] on each one.

f. Right-click on each of these three new keys in turn, and choose Set Value from the Context menu. Into each key, input any random value between 0.5 and 1.2. **Do not change the keys at 0.00 and 1.00.** This creates a change in brightness that begins and ends in a value of 1.0, meaning it can cleanly repeat indefinitely. Repeat this same process between the keys at 1.00 and 2.00 (see **FIGURE 7.58**).

5. Rebuild your lighting and save your progress. Feel free to test the level, and you will see that the light is not only moving about, it is also flickering based on the animation you just created.

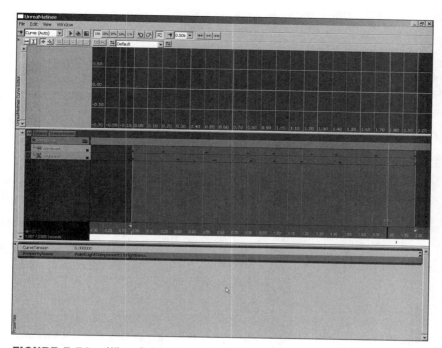

FIGURE 7.58   When finished, you should have nine keys that fluctuate between the times of 0.00 and 2.00.

END TUTORIAL 7.9

Light Environments

Performance is a major concern with dynamic lighting. When casting dynamic shadows, you always want to take performance into account by making sure that you don't have too many dynamic shadow casting lights in one area (see **FIGURE 7.59**). However, what happens when your player enters an area that uses many obviously placed lights, and you need them all to cast dynamic shadows? You could set up a second set of lights just to cast those shadows, but you would likely destroy your overall lighting in the process, not to mention take a substantial hit in performance.

Enter the light environment. Light environments provide a simple way for level designers to use a single set of lights to affect both static and dynamic objects through the use of some very clever techniques, without having to worry about the severe performance hit of having many different dynamic-shadows casting lights. The only noticeable drawback is that light environments only allow for a single dynamic shadow per object at a time (see **FIGURE 7.60**). However, the performance benefit is so great compared to using multiple dynamic-shadow casting lights that this drawback is practically moot.

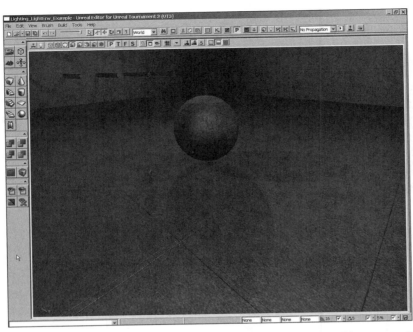

FIGURE 7.59   Although the three dynamic lights striking this object are casting pleasant shadows, a lighting setup such as this would cause a major performance hit.

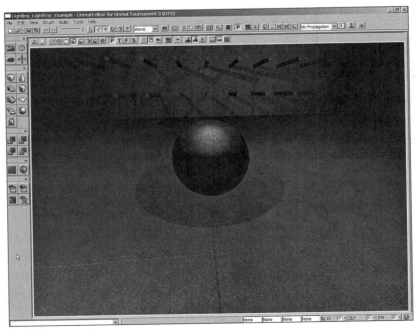

FIGURE 7.60   The actor in this scene is being lit solely by a light environment.

Light environments work by internally creating a skylight and a directional light. Note that these objects do not actually exist in your level, nor do you need to create them. The skylight is used to control the color of the ambient light that is illuminating the dynamic object, and the directional light is used to cast a single dynamic shadow.

For color, the engine calculates a weighted average color of all the lights currently affecting the object. The "weight" is based on the brightness of each light, meaning that brighter lights have more effect over the average color. The direction of the shadow is calculated by proximity of the relevant lights—by "relevant," we mean lights that you've specifically told to be a part of the light environment calculation. We'll cover how to do that in a moment.

Activating a light environment is actually a two-stage process. The first stage requires that you activate the bCastCompositeShadow shadow in your light's properties, and make sure that the light has its CompositeDynamic channel active. You would need to do this for all lights that you want to be calculated as a part of the light environment.

The second stage to activate a light environment takes place on the object itself. Within any dynamic object's properties, you will find the LightEnvironmentComponent category, within which you'll see the bEnabled property. Once you set bEnabled to True (default value is False), the object is no longer considered to be in the Dynamic channel, and is now in the CompositeDynamic channel, meaning that it is now receiving lights from a light environment.

Light environments are the method of choice for handling dynamic lighting from multiple sources with minimal overhead. In fact, all pawns in the game *Gears of War* were lit using light environments!

Let's take a quick break from our dungeon level, and have a look at light environments in a specially designed level, just to show how useful they can be! **TUTORIAL 7.10** functions as a simple exercise to show you how to set up a basic light environment.

TUTORIAL 7.10 Your First Light Environment

1. Launch Unreal Editor and open the DM-CH_07_LightEnv_Start.ut3 map included on the DVD in the files for this chapter. Within, you find a room illuminated by four multicolored lights, along with a dynamic physics actor in the middle of the room. Currently, none of the lights are emitting on the Dynamic channel, so the physics actor appears to be unlit (see **FIGURE 7.61**).

2. Select all four of the lights, and open the Properties window. Check the CastDynamicShadows property; then expand LightingChannels and activate the Dynamic channel. Suddenly, the dynamic sphere actor becomes lit.

3. Still in the Properties window, set the LightShadowMode property to LightShadow_Modulate.

FIGURE 7.61   Because it is unlit, the ball in the scene appears to be black.

4. Rebuild lighting and test the level. Play with the dynamic actor in the level by clicking it and right-dragging it around. Notice the high quality of the lighting, and the fact that all four of the lights are casting independent shadows and specular highlights on the ball. It looks great, but there's a drawback in performance.

   While in the In Editor Game window, press the Tab key to bring down the console. Type the command **stat fps** to show the game frames per second. Press Enter, and then hide the console with the Tab key. Take note of your current frames per second. On our machines, we were averaging somewhere between 40 and 80 (see **FIGURE 7.62**).

   Exit the In Editor Game when finished.

5. Now, select all four lights and open their properties window once again. This time, uncheck CastDynamicShadows, and under LightingChannels, deactivate Dynamic.

6. Select the sphere rigid body in the middle of the level, and open its Properties window. Expand the DynamicSMActor tab, and then expand the LightEnvironment category. Under LightEnvironmentComponent, check bEnabled. This causes the actor to be lit by the light environment (see **FIGURE 7.63**).

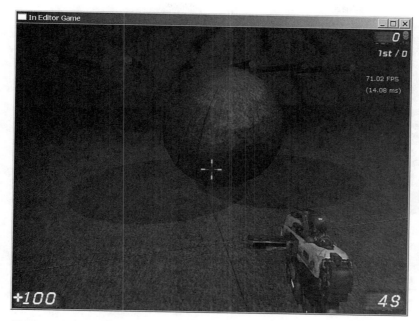

FIGURE 7.62 Take note of your frames per second.

7. Rebuild lighting and test the level again. Notice that you now only see a single specular highlight on the ball that blends its color based on the closest light. Also, you are only casting one shadow.

However, take a glance at your frames per second now. They should be much higher. On our machines, we saw results as high as 170. You might notice that the shadow is not always extremely accurate. But with the obvious boost in performance, this would be a much better choice for playability (see **FIGURE 7.64**)!

8. Save your level.

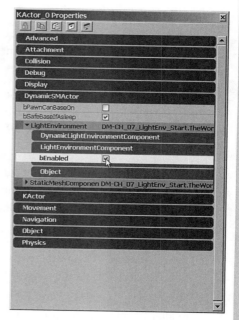

FIGURE 7.63 The bEnabled property is located beneath the LightEnvironmentComponent category.

FIGURE 7.64   The level is much more efficient when using a light environment.

END TUTORIAL 7.10

Light Functions

Light functions provide a way for you to control the color and intensity of a light through a material, or even have a light project a texture onto a surface. This can be used to achieve a wide variety of results, from movie projectors to light streaming through a stained glass window and many more.

A light function reads the Emissive channel of the assigned material, and uses it to drive the brightness and color of the light. The projection direction depends on the type of light used; point lights project in all directions, spotlights project in a cone, and directional lights project from a plane (see **FIGURE 7.65**).

A key thing to remember about light functions are that once activated, the UseDirectLightMap property is automatically disabled, meaning that lights using light functions cannot be used in the calculation of precomputed (mapped) shadows.

There are two main properties used in light functions, as follows:

▶ **SourceMaterial:** This property contains the material that is being used in the light function, as selected from the Generic browser.

▶ **Scale:** This property controls the size of the texture of the source material, enabling you to alter the projection without having to go into the material and adjust your tiling.

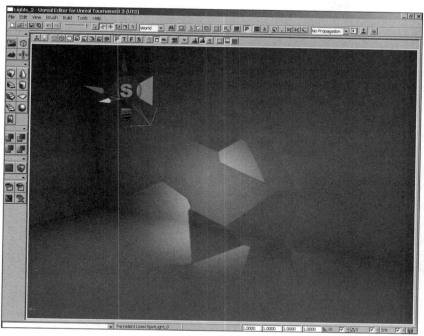

FIGURE 7.65   Here you can see a light function applied to a spotlight.

Continue from **TUTORIAL 7.9**, or open DM-CH_07_Dungeon_04.ut3 map file provided on the DVD in the folder for this chapter. In **TUTORIAL 7.11**, we apply a light function to the Torch Light to control its color.

TUTORIAL 7.11   Lighting the Dungeon, Part V: Adding a Light Function

1. Open the Generic browser and locate the mat_TorchLight material located in the level's package. Double-click it to open the Material Editor.

2. In the Material Editor's Properties area, check the bUsedAsLightFunction property (see **FIGURE 7.66**).

3. Select the Torch Light and locate the Function property. To the right, two buttons are visible: Clear All Text and Create A New Object. Click the Create A New Object button, and choose LightFunction from the Context menu that appears.

4. The new light function expands. Locate the SourceMaterial property and use the Generic browser to set it to the mat_TorchLight material (see **FIGURE 7.67**).

5. Rebuild your lighting. You'll now notice that the light's color is driven by the material.

6. Save your level.

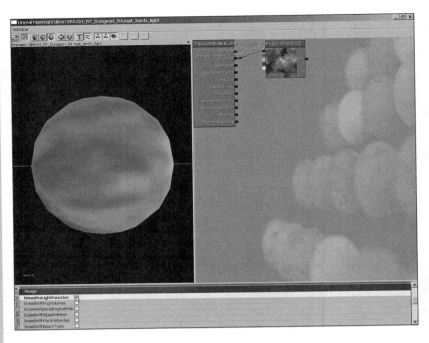

FIGURE 7.66
Make sure the
bUsedAsLightFunction
property is checked.

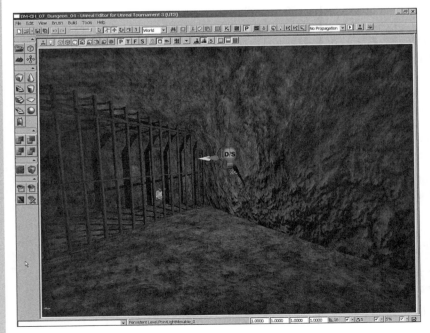

FIGURE 7.67
Once the
mat_TorchLight
material is added,
your lighting
changes color.

END TUTORIAL 7.11

Continue from **TUTORIAL 7.10**, or open DM-CH_07_Dungeon_05.ut3 map file provided on the DVD in the folder for this chapter. Our goal in **TUTORIAL 7.12** is to create some lights whose sole purpose is to illuminate the torch static mesh.

TUTORIAL 7.12   Lighting the Dungeon, Part VI: Lighting the Torch Mesh

1. In the Perspective viewport, click the Real Time button ![real time button] to show some particles. Once some are visible, click the Real Time button ![real time button] again to stop playback (see **FIGURE 7.68**).

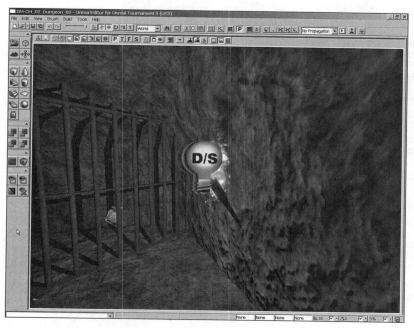

FIGURE 7.68   Get some particles visible in your level.

2. Hold Ctrl-L and click in one of the most deeply orange areas of the flame. This created a new light using the color you were clicking, although you will not see the light.

3. Press the Home key to snap the viewport to the location of the light, which should be near the center of the room. Use the Translation Widget to move this light to one side of the torch static mesh, very close to the surface (see **FIGURE 7.69**).

4. Tweak the color of the light to a deeper orange if you like, and then set the following properties:

Brightness: 3   **CastShadows:** False (Unchecked)

FalloffExponent: 20   **Radius:** 64

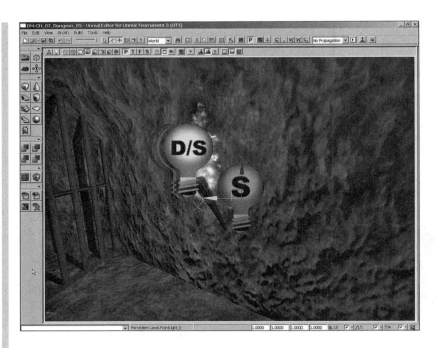

FIGURE 7.69   Move the new light next to the torch mesh.

5. Expand the LightingChannels category, and deactivate all channels. Then, check the Unnamed_1 channel (see **FIGURE 7.70**).

6. Select the torch static mesh. In its Properties window, expand the StaticMeshActor tab, and then expand the StaticMeshComponent category. Locate the Lighting tab, and then expand the LightingChannels category.

   Check the Unnamed_1 channel, so that the light can affect the mesh.

7. Duplicate the light twice and place the duplicates around the mesh, forming a triangle (see **FIGURE 7.71**).

8. Rebuild lighting and save your level.

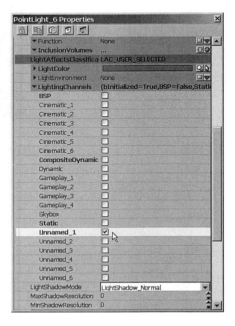

FIGURE 7.70   Only Unnamed_1 should be active.

FIGURE 7.71   The three lights are used only to illuminate the mesh.

END TUTORIAL 7.12

Workflow Tips

The following are some simple performance-friendly guidelines to keep in mind when lighting your levels:

- ▶ Keep the amount of dynamic shadows, either cast by dynamic lights or by static lights on dynamic geometry, to an absolute minimum.

- ▶ Light environments should be used whenever possible in place of dynamic lighting and shadowing.

- ▶ If a light has no potential to cast shadows, disable shadow casting on the light by setting its CastShadows property to False.

- ▶ If an object has no potential to cast shadows, disable shadow casting on the object by setting its CastShadows property to False.

- ▶ Use subtle ambient or bounce lighting (using skylights or multiple point lights) and/or modulated shadows to avoid super-black shadows.

▶ All lights, other than ambient or bounce lighting, should have a visual source, such as a static mesh, in the world. Always ask yourself: "Where is the light coming from?"

▶ When necessary, add lights for emissive surfaces—they only give the appearance of emitting light, but do not actually emit light themselves.

▶ When using shadow maps, make sure to only use a resolution high enough to give the necessary detail.

▶ Enable UseLightMap whenever possible, such as when static lights are affecting static objects, to force lighting to be baked into light maps.

▶ Avoid light functions when possible because they cannot be stored in light maps, even when they are static. However, at the time of this writing, there is potential that the ability for static light function lights being calculated in the light map are added in a future release of the engine.

▶ Keep shadow buffer casting meshes out of immediate proximity of point lights.

▶ Use the minimum amount of lighting subdivisions to get the desired lighting in order to decrease build times.

Summary

In this chapter, you learned how various types of lighting and shadows work together in Unreal Engine 3 to help you create levels that look and feel lifelike. Lighting an environment may seem fairly simple when examining real life. After all, you can simply place a single lamp in your living room, and the room gets lit perfectly with bounce lighting and nice soft shadows. Creating realistic-looking levels in Unreal Engine 3, however, requires the placement of multiple lights of different types and settings to achieve the same effect.

When viewing the levels of professional designers, it can often seem that they are employing some sort of black magic to obtain the amazing mood and feel their levels possess. In reality, it is nothing more than a solid understanding of the types of lights available and how they will interact with the geometry in the level mixed with a great deal of practice. Now that you should have this same understanding of the lighting within Unreal Engine 3, you can begin to put your knowledge into practice by creating stunning levels that rival those seen in Gears of War or Unreal Tournament 3.

Chapter 8

Terrain

Feeling claustrophobic? Enough with the rooms and corridors already—get outside! Many of the most stunning levels you'll ever play or build will have vast landscapes and outdoor areas. To build great outdoor levels, you need to create terrain. Thankfully, Unreal Editor contains a state-of-the-art terrain generation system—everything you need to sculpt, paint, and decorate even the most massive landforms. Want your own mountain or continent? This chapter will show you exactly how to build it.

What Is Terrain?

Terrain is, like virtually everything else in Unreal, just an actor. The Terrain actor is used to create a realistic landscape surface for outdoor levels (see **FIGURE 8.1**). More specifically, the actor is a piece of geometry whose shape is controlled through a height map, which is simply a grayscale image used to determine elevation much like a topographical map (see **FIGURE 8.2**).

FIGURE 8.1   Terrain can make your outdoor levels much more interesting.

FIGURE 8.2   On the left, you can see the height map used to generate the terrain on the right.

The geometry of a Terrain actor is dynamically tessellated during gameplay. This means that the number of polygons—and therefore the amount of physical detail—in the terrain is in constant change. This change is dependent upon the player's proximity to a certain section of terrain. If a player is near to a section, the amount of tessellation is increased, giving the terrain a very detailed look. As the player moves away from that section, the amount of tessellation is reduced, meaning that the physical detail is reduced. This saves considerable processing power, because the terrain becomes physically simpler as it recedes into the distance.

Accessing Terrain

Creating terrain within a map is a very straightforward process, although editing the terrain to get the desired look for your landscape is a bit more involved. Located in the Tools menu, Unreal Editor provides a New Terrain…dialog that walks you through the creation of a terrain using a wizard-style interface. This makes the creation of a new terrain quite painless. However, if you would like to create your terrain manually, you can simply place a Terrain actor, which can be located within the Actor Classes browser under Actor > Info > Terrain. Once placed, you can make changes to the terrain properties just as you would with any other actor by using the Properties window, accessible through the F4 key (see **FIGURE 8.3**).

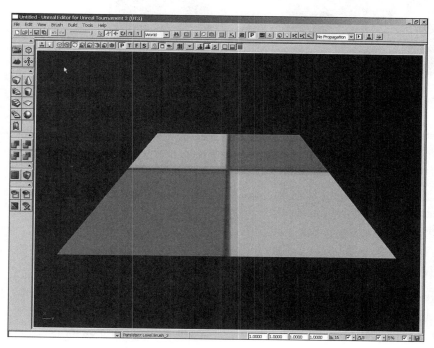

FIGURE 8.3   Terrain looks like a single flat sheet when created.

To edit your terrain by changing its physical shape, you must make adjustments to the terrain's height map by using the Terrain Editing dialog. This dialog is accessed by clicking the Terrain Editing Mode button ![button] in the toolbox. The Terrain Editing dialog is discussed in detail later in the "Terrain Editor Dialog" section (see **FIGURE 8.4**).

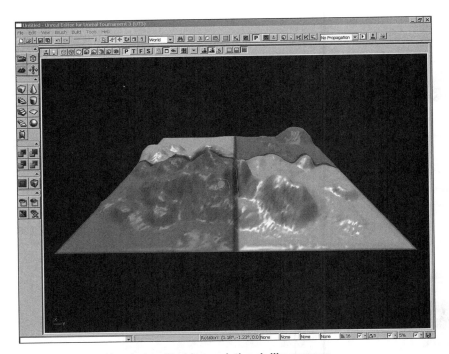

FIGURE 8.4   Terrain is edited in a paintbrush-like manner.

The shape of a terrain can also be created by importing height maps made in exterior applications (such as Adobe Photoshop, Terragen, World Machine, and so on). This method is covered later in this chapter.

In **TUTORIAL 8.1**, you create the initial Terrain actor, as well as adding in the DirectionalLight actor that serves as a work light while creating the terrain. This light can be thought of as a simple sunlight generator.

TUTORIAL 8.1: Creating Your First Terrain

1. Launch Unreal Editor and open the DM-CH_08_FirstTerr_Start.ut3 map file provided on the DVD in the folder for this chapter.

2. Open the Actor Classes browser. Select Actor->Info->Terrain in the Actor browser (see **FIGURE 8.5**).

3. Right-click in the top viewport, and choose Add Terrain Here to place a new terrain in the map (see **FIGURE 8.6**).

8

FIGURE 8.5 The Terrain actor is located under Info.

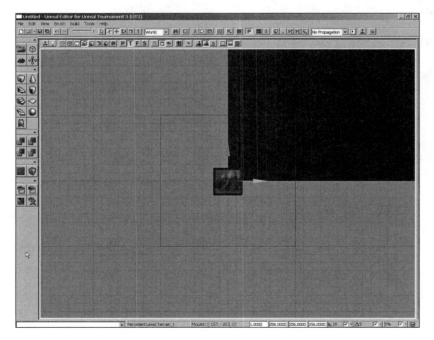

FIGURE 8.6 Notice the terrain icon that appears.

4. With the terrain selected, press F4 to open its Properties window. Under the Terrain section, set the NumPatchesX and NumPatchesY properties to 128 (see **FIGURE 8.7**).

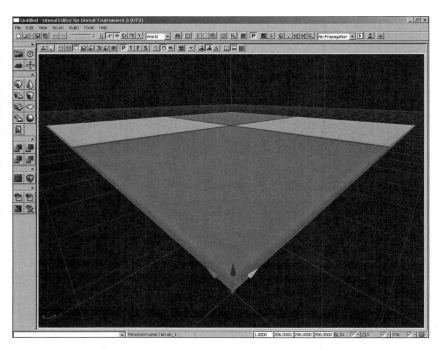

FIGURE 8.7   The terrain becomes much larger once the patches are added.

5. Back in the Actor Classes browser, select Actor->Light->DirectionalLight in the Actor browser, right-click on the terrain in the viewport, and choose Add DirectionalLight Here to place a directional light in the map. Rotate the directional light about 20 degrees around the Y-axis to point it down at the terrain (see **FIGURE 8.8**).

6. Save your level. At this time, your terrain is rather boring. In **TUTORIAL 8.2**, we introduce you to Terrain Editing Mode and show you the basics of shaping your terrain.

> **NOTE**
>
> You may need to switch the View mode to Wireframe or Unlit to see the terrain in order to right-click on it. Make sure to turn the view mode back to Lit after creating the directional light.

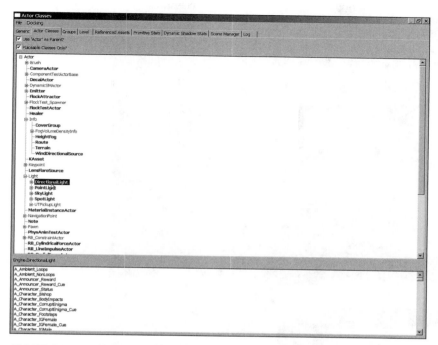

FIGURE 8.8   Adding a directional light helps us see the contours of the terrain.

END TUTORIAL 8.1

Please complete **TUTORIAL 8.1** before attempting **TUTORIAL 8.2**, or open the DM-CH_08_FirstTerr_01.ut3 map file provided on the DVD in the folder for this chapter. Follow the steps to sculpt some simple detail into your terrain surface.

TUTORIAL 8.2: Editing Your First Terrain

1. Press the Terrain Editing Mode button ⚓ in the toolbox to open the Terrain Editor. This opens the Terrain Editing dialog, which provides you with access to all the editing functions for terrain (see **FIGURE 8.9**). We discuss this dialog in-depth later in this chapter.

2. In the Generic browser, open the Chapter_08_TerrainDemo package included on the DVD in the files for this chapter. Select the tls_base TerrainLayerSetup. This is a very basic layer setup containing three materials that are used based on the slope of the terrain.

3. In the Terrain Editor dialog, right-click in the Terrain Browser area, seen as a wide gray box near the bottom the Terrain Editing dialog. Choose Add Selected Layer, and enter the name Layer0 when prompted (see **FIGURE 8.10**). This adds the selected TerrainLayerSetup in the Generic browser to this terrain. The terrain should now be rendered with a grass material.

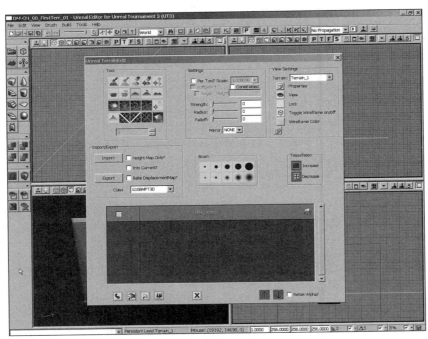

FIGURE 8.9   The Terrain Editing dialog appears when you enter Terrain Editing Mode.

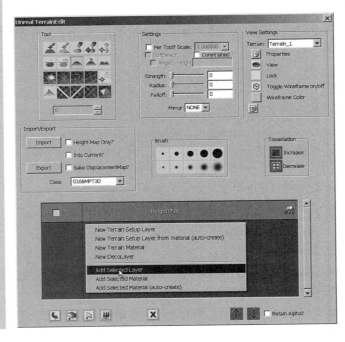

FIGURE 8.10   Choose Add Selected from the Context menu of the Terrain Browser area.

4. In the Terrain Editing dialog's Browser
area, click the HeightMap layer. Select
the Paint tool ![paint icon] from the Tool section
of the Terrain Editor. In the Settings
area, set the Radius and Falloff to 512

> **NOTE**
>
> You may have to move the mouse over the perspective
> viewport to get the terrain to update and show the
> newly assigned materials.

and 384 respectively. Holding down Ctrl, click the left or right mouse buttons and drag the
mouse to raise or lower the vertices of the terrain within the radius (see **FIGURE 8.11**).
Use this tool with varying radius and falloff settings to build up some mountains on your
terrain. Notice the texture change as you paint in the mountains.

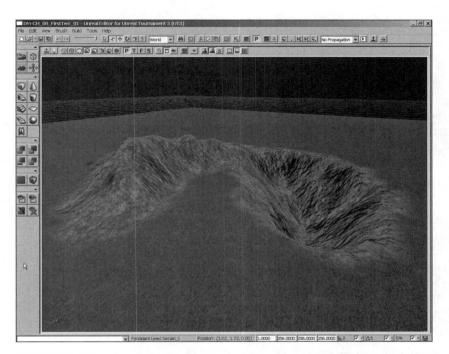

FIGURE 8.11   You can paint down as well as up by using the left and right mouse buttons.

5. Switch to the Flatten tool with a radius and falloff of 512 and 384, respectively. Place
the cursor about halfway up the side of the mountains, hold down Ctrl, and press the
left mouse button. This should create a plateau on the side of the mountain (see
FIGURE 8.12).

6. The Flatten tool can create drastic changes in the height of adjacent vertices, which is
most noticeable because of the stretching of the texture applied to the terrain. To fix this,
select the Smooth tool ![smooth icon] and, while holding Ctrl, press the left mouse button and drag
the mouse around the edges of the plateau. You most likely need to adjust the radius and
falloff to limit the smoothing to a small enough area so that you are only smoothing the
edges of the plateau while allowing it to keep its overall shape (see **FIGURE 8.13**).

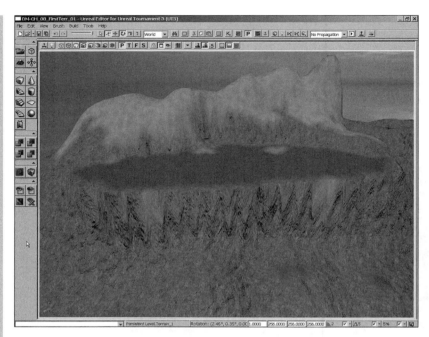

FIGURE 8.12   The Flatten tool creates a plateau like this.

FIGURE 8.13   Use the Smooth tool to smooth out the edges of your plateau.

7. At this point, you have created a basic terrain that you can now test out. Rebuild the map and use the Play In Editor function to test out your new terrain. Feel free to experiment with the other terrain editing tools, as well as the Strength, Radius, and Falloff settings.

END TUTORIAL 8.2

Terrain Anatomy and Properties

There are a variety of terms and properties that must be understood before you can hope to reap the full benefit of the terrain creation system. In this section, we cover the important components of terrain, as well as the key properties that you must know to efficiently work with terrain.

Terrain Anatomy (Terminology)

This list contains a variety of different terms that you will come across while working with Unreal's Terrain system.

Patches—Terrain geometry is actually comprised of a series of rows of triangles. Every pair of these triangles forms a quad (four-sided shape). These quads are referred to as patches.

Components—Components are groups of patches that are considered as a single entity when calculating collision and occlusion.

Height Map—A height map is a grayscale image whose pixel values are mapped to the height of the corresponding vertices of the terrain geometry. Because the number of vertices is always one greater than the number of patches in each direction (consider that it takes four fingers on your hand to create three gaps between them), the dimensions of a height map will always be NumPatchesX+1 by NumPatchesY+1.

Tessellation—In terms of using terrain, tessellation refers to a change in the number of faces of the terrain surface as the player gets closer to it or farther away. Put basically, terrain loses polygons—or becomes geometrically simpler—the farther you get away from it.

This change in detail occurs over five separate distances, each subsequent distance resulting in greater reduction in overall tessellation (see **FIGURE 8.14**). Although the properties of the terrain, described next, control exactly how much tessellation takes place, the default values for these ranges are as follows (measured in Unreal units):

0–1024

1024–2048

2048–4096

4096–8192

8192+

> **NOTE**
>
> These are the default ranges for tessellation. These ranges can be adjusted by changing the TessellationDistanceScale property.

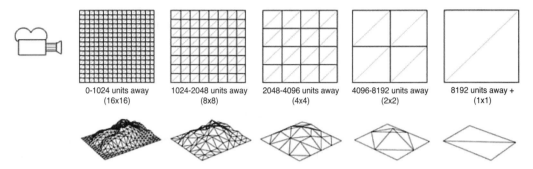

This diagram assumes that MacTessellationLevel is set to 16, MinTessellationValue is set to 1, and TessellationDistanceScale is set to 1.

| 0-1024 units away (16x16) | 1024-2048 units away (8x8) | 2048-4096 units away (4x4) | 4096-8192 units away (2x2) | 8192 units away + (1x1) |

FIGURE 8.14   This diagram illustrates the change in tessellation over distance.

Terrain Properties

This section contains the various properties that belong to the Terrain actor, explaining what each one does and how it might be used. For convenience, the different types of properties have been grouped together by common function. The property types include general properties, lighting properties, and collision properties.

General Properties

For the purposes of this text, we consider the general properties to be located underneath the Terrain category in the Properties window. The following list includes the key properties in this area:

bShowWireframe—This overlays a wireframe on the terrain in the viewport.

WireframeColor—This enables you to set the color used to display the wireframe when bShowWireframe is set to True.

DecoLayers—This property is an array of all the DecoLayers applied to the terrain. DecoLayers are explained later in the "DecoLayers" section.

Layers—This property is an array of all the layers of the terrain. Layers are described in more detail in the "Terrain Layers" section.

NumPatchesX—This property determines the number of patches (or quads) at the highest level of tessellation (detail) for the terrain in the X direction.

NumPatchesY—This property determines the number of patches (or quads) at the highest level of tessellation (detail) for the terrain in the Y direction.

MaxComponentSize—This property sets the number of patches in a single row (along both the X and Y directions) of the terrain's components. This means that if set to a value of 4, each component would be 4 patches by 4 patches.

Keep in mind that components are used to determine occlusion culling. In order for a section of terrain to be culled from the render, the entire component must be completely occluded. If your component size is too big, it is harder to completely occlude your components, meaning that sections of your terrain remain visible, even when they are behind another object. At the same time, if your component size is too small, the amount of processing power used to calculate the occlusion and culling becomes inefficient.

Working with MaxComponentSize is a balancing act that is based primarily on how likely it is that any part of your terrain is occluded at any given time.

MaxTessellationLevel—This property serves as the maximum number of patches (squared) at the highest level of tessellation that can be condensed down to a single patch at the lowest level of tessellation. This number must be a power of 2 between 1 and 16, allowing only for the values 1, 2, 4, 8, and 16. The default value is 4.

As described previously in the definition of tessellation, Unreal downscales the amount of detail in a terrain based on five distances from the player. At 1024 units from the player (by default) the first of these downscales occurs such that every 2×2 square of patches becomes a single patch. At 2048 units, every 2×2 square of these new patches also becomes condensed to a single patch. This continues until the difference between the original number of patches condensed equals the MaxTessellationLevel.

Or, put another way, if this value is set to 8, then 64 patches at the highest level of detail become a single patch at the lowest level of detail, provided that the MinTessellationLevel is set to 1. A good rule of thumb is that the flatter your landscape, the higher you can set this value.

MinTessellationLevel—This is the minimum number of patches in each direction to which the MaxTessellationLevel can be collapsed. Therefore, if MaxTessellationLevel is set to 8 and MinTessellationLevel is set to 2, then an 8×8 group of patches can be collapsed down to a 2×2 group of patches once all de-tessellation has occurred. If this value is equal to the MaxTessellationLevel, no detail will be tessellated out, so the terrain will always be at the highest level of detail. This value must be a power of 2 from 1 to 16 and less than or equal to the value set in MaxTessellationLevel.

EditorTessellationLevel—This property sets the tessellation level that will be used in the Editor's viewports. This value must be a power of 2 from 1 to 16 and between the MinTessellationLevel and the MaxTessellationLevel. A value of 0 means that the Editor's viewports use the tessellation algorithm used in game to dynamically tessellate the terrain.

TessellationDistanceScale—This property serves as a divisor for the tessellation algorithm to determine how close to the player geometry will be tessellated out. Higher values mean geometry is de-tessellated closer to the player. For instance, a TessellationDistanceScale of 2 results in the first stage of de-tessellation occurring at 512 units from the player, rather than the default 1024.

TessellationCheckDistance—This enables you to specify a maximum distance from the camera's location that terrain components must be within in order to have tessellation checks performed. If this value is less than 0, the default value set in the UTEngine.ini is used. If the value of this property is 0, all components are checked each frame.

bMorphingEnabled—This causes the terrain to interpolate when changing between tessellation levels limiting the visual popping that is often associated with this transition. Enabling this option can cause performance issues as this process is very expensive to perform.

bMorphingGradientsEnabled—This is an enhanced version of the morphing process described previously. Its effects are usually not noticeable, and it is even more expensive than the basic morphing. As such, enabling this option should probably be avoided in most cases. bMorphingEnabled must be set to True for this property to have any effect.

NormalMapLayer—This enables you to specify an index (0 based) to a layer, and the normal maps from the various materials within that layer are blended together and used as the normal for the entire terrain. If this value is -1, the normal maps of all materials in all layers are blended together and used as the normal for the entire terrain.

Lighting Properties

The following properties can be found underneath the lighting category in the Properties window. These properties control how the terrain surface deals with lighting in your levels.

bIsOverridingLightResolution / StaticLightingResolution—These properties work in conjunction to enable you to have precise control over static shadows on your terrain. The bIsOverriding LightResolution un-restricts (or overrides) the terrain's StaticLightingResolution, or the number of texels (texture pixels) to use per patch for the shadow maps of the terrain.

One shadow map is used for each component of the terrain, meaning that you must keep the MaxComponentSize property in mind as it controls the number of patches in each component. The larger your components, the more area each shadow map has to cover.

When bIsOverridingLightResolution is False, StaticLightingResolution must be a power of 2 from 1 to the value of the MaxTessellationLevel property. If bIsOverridingLightResolution is True, then StaticLightingResolution must be a power of 2 greater than or equal to 1, but is not limited by an upper bound. You must be extremely careful when using this as you could potentially have a large number of very large shadow maps for your terrain, causing a significant drop in performance.

Collision Properties

Under the Collision category, you will find any properties that control how the terrain surface deals with collisions.

CollisionTessellationLevel—This property sets the tessellation level of each component for use in collision calculations. This value must be set to a power of 2 ranging from 1 to the value of the MaxTessellationLevel property.

In **TUTORIAL 8.3**, we create the initial terrain actor for editing later.

TUTORIAL 8.3: Creating an Outdoor Environment, Part I: Initial Terrain Creation

1. Launch Unreal Editor and open the terrain_demo_start map included on the DVD in the files for this chapter.

2. In the Actor Classes browser, select Actor->Info->Terrain in the Actor browser, right-click in the top viewport, and choose Add Terrain Here to place a new terrain in the map (see **FIGURE 8.15**).

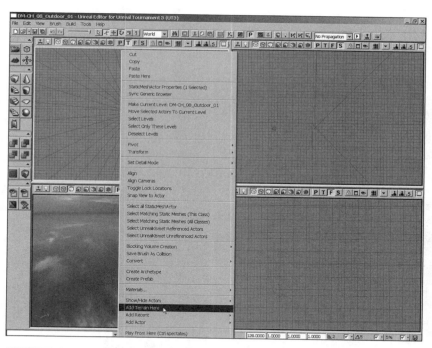

FIGURE 8.15   Add the new terrain to your level.

3. Position the terrain so it is centered on the sky mesh in the top viewport and even with the bottom of the sky mesh in the side viewport.

4. With the terrain selected, press F4 to open its properties. Under Movement, set the Location.Z property to 0. This is necessary for setting up a TerrainLayerSetup (which we get to in subsequent tutorials) to use minimum and maximum heights for its TerrainMaterials. If the terrain is not located at Z=0, then adjustments would need to be

made in the values of the TerrainLayerSetup to compensate, as materials that were supposed to appear at particular elevations would not appear at those elevations.

> **NOTE**
>
> This is a fairly high number of patches for a terrain. We are using this value to make seeing the effects of the tools more easily visible. Usually, values of 128 or 256 are sufficient to provide the necessary detail in medium- to large-sized maps.

5. Under the Terrain section, set the following properties:

   NumPatchesX: 512

   NumPatchesY: 512

6. Under Display, set the DrawScale3D (this is the same as setting the DrawScale3D in the main editor window) of the terrain to the following values (see **FIGURE 8.16**):

   X: 64

   Y: 64

   Z: 256

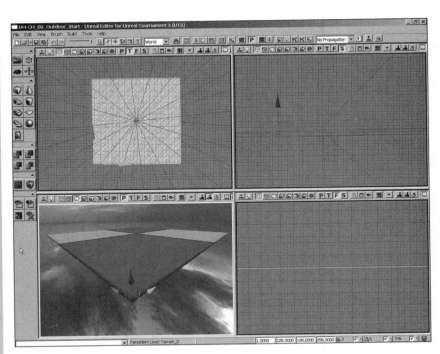

FIGURE 8.16   Your terrain is now much smaller.

7. Save your level so that we can continue work on it in later tutorials in this chapter.

END TUTORIAL 8.3

TerrainMaterials and Layers

Materials are applied to a terrain through the use of TerrainMaterials. A TerrainMaterial is essentially a pass-through for a standard material, adding in some extra terrain-centric functionality. This includes control over displacement, the addition of foliage, or adjustment for the material's scaling on the surface of the terrain. TerrainMaterials are created in the Generic browser by choosing File > New > TerrainMaterial, or by right-clicking in an empty area of the Generic browser and choosing New TerrainMaterial from the Context menu. We discuss the use of TerrainMaterials as we progress through this chapter.

TerrainMaterial Properties

Following are the properties found within a TerrainMaterial, along with their corresponding descriptions:

DisplacementMap—This property enables you to assign a grayscale texture to be used by the engine to move the vertices of the terrain wherever this TerrainMaterial is exposed on the terrain. This movement takes place along the surface normal of the terrain geometry, rather than just vertically as with a height map.

DisplacementScale—This number serves as a multiplier for the amount of displacement to perform using a displacement map.

Foliage—The Foliage array enables you to assign static meshes—such as models of grass and shrubbery—to be used to populate the terrain wherever the corresponding material is applied. This is similar to DecoLayers, and is discussed later in the "DecoLayers" section.

MappingPanU—This property is an offset for the placement of the material upon the surface of the terrain in the U texture coordinate direction.

MappingPanV—This property is an offset for the placement of the material upon the surface of the terrain in the V texture coordinate direction.

MappingRotation—This is an offset for the rotation of the material.

MappingScale—This property is a multiplier for the texture coordinates of the material.

MappingType—This property enables you to choose a particular mapping plane to which to align the material when it is applied to the terrain, or to simply have the plane chosen for you automatically. This property includes the following options:

- ▶ **TMT_Auto**—This allows the engine to choose the "best" plane to use.
- ▶ **TMT_XY**—This aligns the material along the XY plane.
- ▶ **TMT_XZ**—This aligns the material along the XZ plane.
- ▶ **TMT_YZ**—This aligns the material along the YZ plane.

Material—This property contains the regular material that is used for this TerrainMaterial.

Terrain Layers

TerrainMaterials can be divided into groups known as *layers*. Layers provide the level designer with a way to set up groups of materials that can be exposed on the terrain and blended together based on a variety of circumstances, such as elevation of the terrain or its slope along a hill or mountain. For example, you could have a layer that contains materials for a jungle environment, including grassy areas for flatland, deep brown rocky crags for steep slopes, and dense swamp for valleys. You could then have another layer with a snowy environment with icy rock cliffs, and snow and ice as the base. You can then blend between these layers to seamlessly flow from one type of environment to another (see **FIGURE 8.17**).

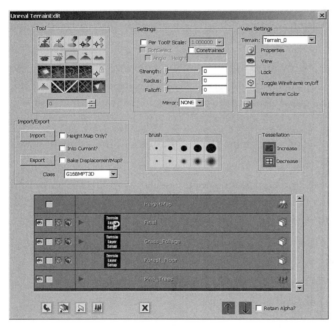

FIGURE 8.17   Layers are visible within the Terrain Editing dialog Browser area.

Weight Maps

Terrain layers use weight maps to determine the exact placement of each material on the terrain surface. These weight maps are simply RGBA textures, with each of the four channels representing the alpha of a particular material. These alphas are created automatically using four settings of a TerrainLayerSetup, discussed next, and are used to expose certain materials under certain conditions, such as at a particular elevation or a given slope.

The reason that weight maps are condensed from multiple grayscale alpha maps into RGBA textures is that shaders are limited in the number of textures they can contain. A terrain that held many different layers could use up this limit very quickly if each layer's alpha map counted as one texture. Using the four channels of a single RGBA texture allows the number of total textures to be cut by a factor of four, allowing more layers per terrain.

Although weight maps are generated automatically, they can be found within the Generic browser. To view a weight map, look in the level's package. Note that these weight maps cannot be exported.

TerrainLayerSetup

Each material within a layer can be assigned to a particular slope or elevation using a TerrainLayerSetup. A *TerrainLayerSetup* is a collection of TerrainMaterials along with a series of properties that control how each material is exposed and rendered on the terrain (see **FIGURE 8.18**).

FIGURE 8.18   The patches of different materials in this image are the result of a TerrainLayerSetup.

TerrainMaterials are assigned to an array named Materials. Each entry of this array holds a reference to one TerrainMaterial along with a series of properties to control the circumstances under which the material displays on the terrain surface. The Materials array can have as many slots as desired, but keep in mind that the materials render from bottom to top, meaning that array entry [0] is rendered on top of array entry [1] and so on. This is important, because whenever the setup for two materials should cause them both to render in the same location, their placement in the Materials array determines which one is rendered on top of the other.

TerrainMaterial Properties

Each entry in the Materials array contains the following properties:

UseNoise—This tells the entry whether to use the noise settings for Min and MaxHeight and Min and MaxSlope or to just ignore noise altogether.

NoiseScale—This serves as a multiplier for the noise values.

NoisePercent—This controls how much of the overall noise effect is applied to the material.

MinHeight—MinHeight enables you to set a minimum height for this material to be rendered. For example, if this value was set to 256, the material is only placed on the terrain in areas where the terrain's elevation is 256 units high or higher. Values are in absolute world coordinates.

Base—This is the actual value used for the minimum height calculation.

NoiseScale—This property controls the frequency of the noise applied to the MinHeight Base. The smaller the value, the less total noise there will be.

NoiseAmount—This property sets the amount of noise variance above and below the Base value.

MaxHeight—MaxHeight enables you to set a maximum height for this material to be rendered. For example, if this value was set to 256, the material will only be placed on the terrain in areas where the terrain's elevation is 256 units or lower. Values are in absolute world coordinates.

Base—This is the actual value used for the maximum height calculation.

NoiseScale—This property controls the frequency of the noise applied to the MaxHeight Base. The smaller the value, the less total noise there will be.

NoiseAmount—This property sets the amount of noise variance above and below the Base value.

MinSlope—MinSlope enables you to set minimum slope, or angle of the terrain surface, for the material to be visible. The values for this property are a bit interesting: 0 equals a flat surface (no slope), 1 equals a 45-degree incline, and infinity equals 90 degrees (vertical). Obviously, you cannot achieve infinity in your value, which is acceptable as neither terrain can achieve a vertical slope in and of itself. For MinSlope, any slopes greater than the one defined by the property can contain the assigned material.

Base—This is the actual value used for the maximum height calculation.

NoiseScale—This property controls the frequency of the noise applied to the MaxHeight Base. The smaller the value, the less total noise there will be.

NoiseAmount—This property sets the amount of noise variance above and below the Base value.

MaxSlope—MaxSlope enables you to set minimum slope, or angle of the terrain surface, for the material to be visible. The values for this property are a bit interesting: 0 equals a flat surface (no slope), 1 equals a 45-degree incline, and infinity equals 90 degrees (vertical). You cannot achieve infinity in your value, which is acceptable as neither terrain can achieve a vertical slope in and of itself. For MaxSlope, any slopes less than the one defined by the property can contain the assigned material.

Base—This is the actual value used for the maximum height calculation.

NoiseScale—This property controls the frequency of the noise applied to the MaxHeight Base. The smaller the value, the less total noise there will be.

NoiseAmount—This property sets the amount of noise variance above and below the Base value.

Alpha—This property controls the opacity of the material. 0 is equal to completely transparent, and 1 is equal to completely opaque. If any entry in the Materials array has an alpha value of 1, then all materials beneath it will not be rendered because of the sorting order used.

Material—This is a reference to the TerrainMaterial used for this entry in the Materials array.

As a level designer in a real-world game development environment, it is likely that you will not have the actual textures and materials for your terrain when you are ready to begin editing and shaping it. In such a situation, you need a way to begin editing the terrain while still having a good idea of how it will look with the finished materials applied to it. To accomplish this, we are going to create a TerrainLayerSetup and some placeholder materials that will give us a general idea of how the terrain will look.

First, we need to know what type of environment we are creating. For these tutorials, we are going to be creating a snow-capped, mountainous area with grassy valleys. As such, we at the very least need some grass, rock, and snow materials. It is a good idea to use the Internet, or a camera if you happen to be near a similar environment, to gather reference photos of the type of environment you are going to be creating. They can be used throughout the editing process to help you achieve a much more life-like result.

Please make sure you have completed **TUTORIAL 8.3** before beginning, or open the CH_08_ Outdoor_01.ut3 map file that is provided on the DVD in the folder for this chapter. In **TUTORIAL 8.4**, we create the materials that will be painted onto the surface of our terrain.

TUTORIAL 8.4: Creating an Outdoor Environment, Part II: Terrain Editing Materials

1. In the Generic browser, select the package with the same name as your map. Right-click on the background and choose New Material. Name the material mat_editing_grass and click OK to create the material. The Material Editor opens with the new material in it (see **FIGURE 8.19**).

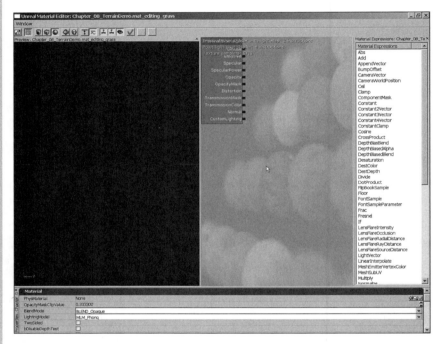

FIGURE 8.19   Your new material appears.

2. In the Generic browser, select the EngineMaterials package and select the DefaultDiffuse texture (see **FIGURE 8.20**). The reason we are using this specific texture is that its grid-like design enables us to see any stretching of the materials on the terrain as we are editing. This is much like using a checker texture in a 3D modeling application when laying out UVs. Back in the Material Editor, hold the T key and left-click in the workspace to add a TextureSample using the selected texture.

3. Hold the 3 key and left-click in the workspace to add a Constant3Vector. Set the R, G, and B properties to 0, 1, and 0, respectively (see **FIGURE 8.21**).

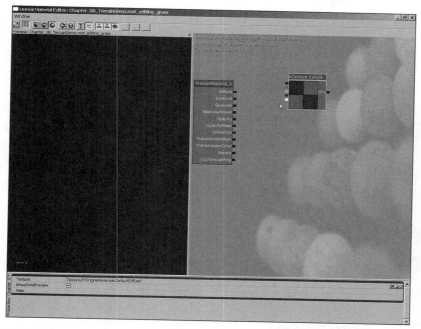

FIGURE 8.20   Add the DefaultDiffuse texture to your new material.

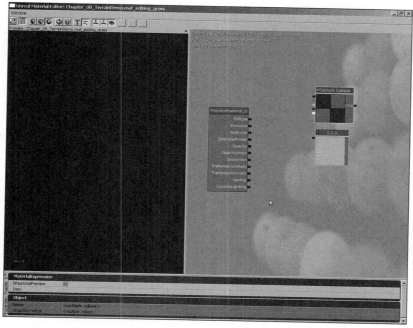

FIGURE 8.21   The Constant3Vector is used to change the color of the texture.

4. Hold the M key and left-click in the workspace to add a Multiply expression and connect the RGB output of the TextureSample to the A input and the output of the Constant3Vector to the B input (see **FIGURE 8.22**).

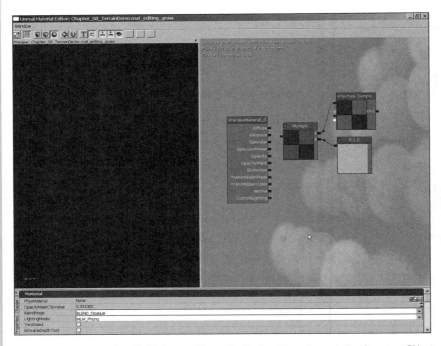

FIGURE 8.22   The Multiply combines the TextureSample and the Constant3Vector.

5. Connect the output of the Multiply to the Diffuse channel of the material node.

6. Hold the 1 key and left-click in the workspace to add a Constant expression. Set its R property to 1 and connect its output to the Specular channel of the material node.

7. Duplicate the Constant expression (Ctrl+C and Ctrl+V) and set the new expression's R property to 20. Connect its output to the SpecularPower channel of the material node, press the Apply Changes button ![button], and close the Material Editor (see **FIGURE 8.23**).

8. Duplicate the mat_editing_grass material (right-click and choose Duplicate) and name the new material mat_editing_rock. Double-click the new material to edit it in the Material Editor and change the R, G, and B properties of the Constant3Vector to 0.5, 0.4, and 0.35, respectively. Click Apply Changes and close the Material Editor (see **FIGURE 8.24**).

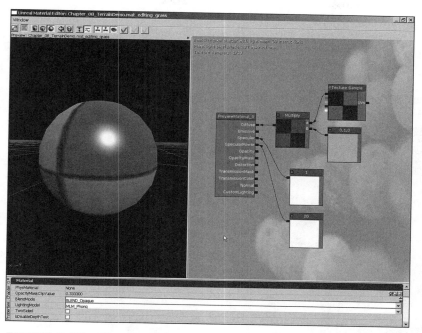

FIGURE 8.23 The network is now driving the Diffuse color and specularity of the material.

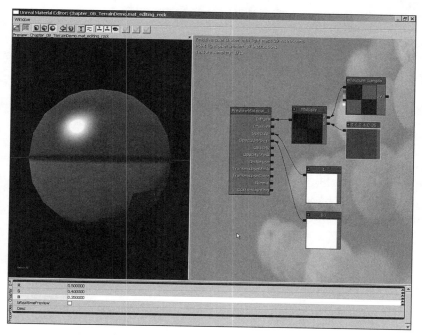

FIGURE 8.24 Duplicate and change the color of the material.

9. Duplicate the mat_editing_rock material and name the new material mat_editing_snow. Double-click the new material to edit it in the Material Editor and change the R, G, and B properties of the Constant3Vector to 2.0, 2.0, and 2.0, respectively. Click Apply Changes and close the Material Editor (see **FIGURE 8.25**).

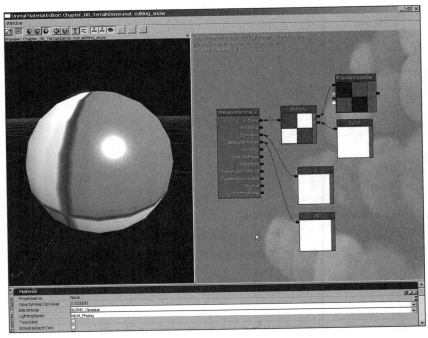

FIGURE 8.25 Duplicate and change the color again.

10. Save your map to ensure that you don't lose your changes.

END TUTORIAL 8.4

Please make sure you have completed **TUTORIAL 8.4** before beginning, or open the CH_08_ Outdoor_02.ut3 map file that is provided on the DVD in the folder for this chapter. In **TUTORIAL 8.5**, we create the TerrainMaterial object that enables us to paint the material created previously onto the surface of the terrain.

TUTORIAL 8.5: Creating an Outdoor Environment, Part III: Terrain Editing TerrainMaterials

1. In the Generic browser, select the package with the same name as your map. Right-click on the background of the Generic browser and choose New TerrainMaterial. Name the new TerrainMaterial tmat_editing_grass (see **FIGURE 8.26**).

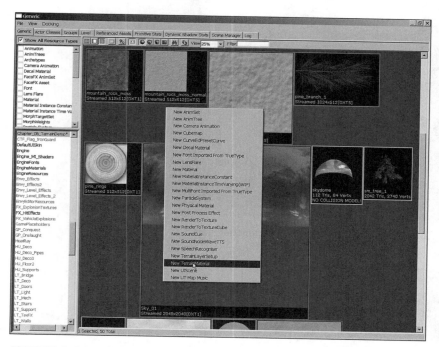

FIGURE 8.26   Create a new TerrainMaterial.

2. Duplicate this TerrainMaterial and name the duplicate tmat_editing_rock.

3. Duplicate tmat_editing_rock and name the duplicate tmat_editing_snow (see **FIGURE 8.27**).

4. Double-click the tmat_editing_grass TerrainMaterial to open its properties and assign the mat_editing_grass Material to its Material property.

5. Double-click the tmat_editing_rock TerrainMaterial to open its properties and assign the mat_editing_rock Material to its Material property.

6. Double-click the tmat_editing_snow TerrainMaterial to open its properties and assign the mat_editing_snow Material to its Material property (see **FIGURE 8.28**).

7. Save your map. The TerrainMaterials are now ready to be added to a TerrainLayerSetup.

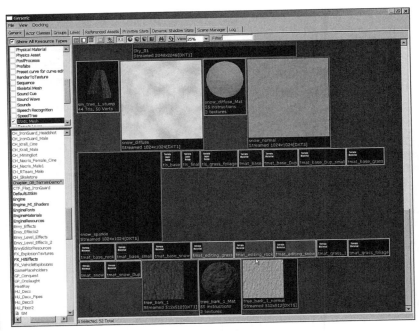

FIGURE 8.27   You should now have three new TerrainMaterials.

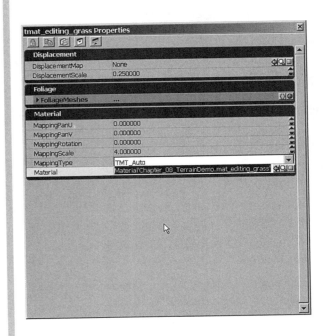

FIGURE 8.28   Each TerrainMaterial now has its appropriate material applied.

END TUTORIAL 8.5

Please make sure you have completed **TUTORIAL 8.5** before beginning, or open the CH_08_
Outdoor_03.ut3 map file that is provided on the DVD in the folder for this chapter. In **TUTORIAL
8.6**, we create the TerrainLayerSetup object that houses our TerrainMaterials.

TUTORIAL 8.6: Creating an Outdoor Environment, Part IV: Terrain Editing TerrainLayerSetup

1. In the Generic browser, select the package with the same name as your map. Right-click
   on the background of the Generic browser and choose New TerrainLayerSetup. Name the
   TerrainLayerSetup tls_editing (see **FIGURE 8.29**).

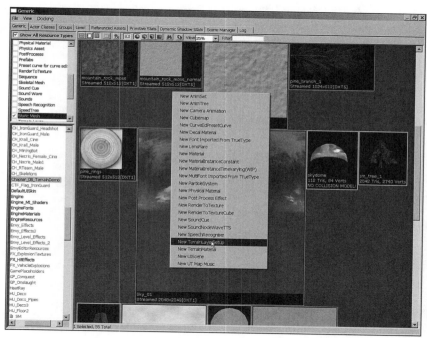

FIGURE 8.29   Create a new TerrainLayerSetup.

2. Double-click tls_editing to open its properties if they do not appear automatically. Create
   three slots in the Materials array by clicking the Add New Item button ⬜ three times (see
   FIGURE 8.30).

3. Select tmat_editing_snow in the Generic browser and assign it to the Material property
   of slot [0] by clicking the Use Selection from Generic Browser button ⬜ (see
   FIGURE 8.31).

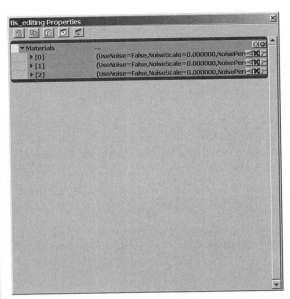

FIGURE 8.30   Add the three slots to hold the TerrainMaterials.

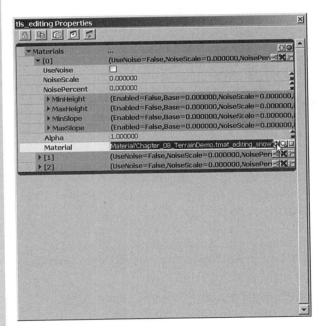

FIGURE 8.31   The snow TerrainMaterial has now been added.

4. Set UseNoise to True by checking its checkbox, and set NoiseScale and NoisePercent to 2.0 and 1.0, respectively.

Because we want our snow to mainly be used as snowcaps to our mountains, we need to use the MinHeight section to limit the altitudes at which snow can be rendered. We also use some noise to break up the snow. Note that the values we are using for the noise were settled upon after some trial and error using the reference photos as a guide.

5. Expand the MinHeight section and set the following properties:

> **Enabled:** True
>
> **Base:** 4096.0
>
> **NoiseScale:** 10.0
>
> **NoiseAmount:** 4096.0

6. Select tmat_editing_rock in the Generic browser and assign it to the Material property of slot [1] by clicking the Use Selection from Generic Browser button ![button].

The rock material should be used on protruding surfaces or surfaces with some slope to them. We use the MinSlope section for this. A value of 0.0 is a flat surface, and 1.0 is a 45-degree slope; as the value increases, the slope approaches straight up and down.

7. Expand the MinSlope section and set the following properties:

> **Enabled:** True
>
> **Base:** 0.2

8. Select tmat_editing_grass in the Generic browser and assign it to the Material property of slot [2] by clicking the Use Selection from Generic Browser button ![button].

We want the grass material to only be rendered on relatively flat surfaces, which will be our valleys and any plateaus. This is accomplished using the MinSlope and MaxSlope sections with the MaxSlope equal to the MinSlope of the rock.

9. Expand the MinSlope section and set the following properties:

> **Enabled:** True
>
> **Base:** 0.0

10. Expand the MaxSlope section and set the following properties:

> **Enabled:** True
>
> **Base:** 0.2

11. Save your map.

END TUTORIAL 8.6

Please make sure you have completed **TUTORIAL 8.6** before beginning, or open the CH_08_Outdoor_04.ut3 map file that is provided on the DVD in the folder for this chapter. In **TUTORIAL 8.7**, we create the editing layer for our terrain.

TUTORIAL 8.7: Creating an Outdoor Environment, Part V: Terrain Editing Layer

1. Select the Terrain actor, press F4 to open its properties, and expand the Terrain section. You should see the Layers array, but if you try to expand it, it does not expand because it is empty at this point.

2. On the right side of the Layers property, click the Add New Item button 🔲. Now there should be one slot in the Layers array (see **FIGURE 8.32**).

3. Expand slot [0] and set the Name property to Editing. This is the name that will be used to identify the layer later on in the Terrain browser.

4. In the Generic browser, select the tls_editing TerrainLayerSetup. Then, press the Use Current Selection in Generic Browser button 🔳 of the Setup property to assign the TerrainLayerSetup to that layer. There should be a little pause while it is calculating, and then you should see the terrain being rendered using the grass material because everything is flat at this point (see **FIGURE 8.33**).

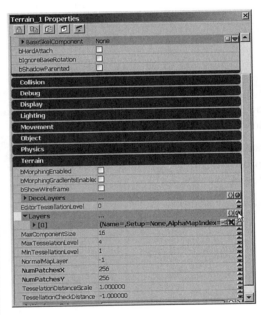

FIGURE 8.32 You have now added a new slot for the layers.

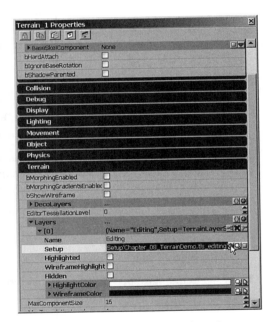

FIGURE 8.33 The tls_editing layer has now been added.

This should give us a nice approximation of the finished layer setup so we can get a head start on outlining the basic shape of our terrain, all without having to have our final textures in place.

5. Save your map.

END TUTORIAL 8.7

Terrain Editor Dialog

The Terrain Editor dialog is the central interface for the creation of your terrain's final look (see **FIGURE 8.34**). It is accessed by clicking the Terrain Editing Mode button 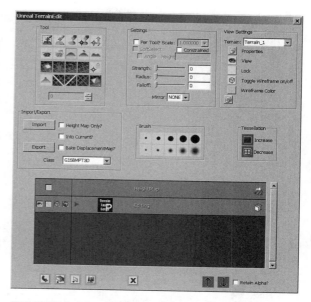 in the toolbox. Very similar to Geometry Mode for editing BSP brushes, Terrain Editing Mode gives access to the Terrain Editing dialog and a wide variety of terrain tools. In this section, we focus primarily on the interface for the Terrain Editing dialog, while the actual tools for editing terrain are covered later in the "Terrain Editing Tools" section.

FIGURE 8.34 Terrain Editing dialog

The Terrain Editing Dialog Interface Overview

The Terrain Editing dialog consists of eight key areas, each with its own specific application. However, it should be known in advance that working with terrain is a brush-based painting and sculpting system. In this case, we use the word "brush" more in a paintbrush-like sense than when discussing BSP. As such, many of the tools and settings available in the Terrain Editing dialog refer in some way to the use of brushes. Following is each of the key areas of the interface, along with the functionality you will find in each of them, except for in-depth functionality of the tool area, because that has its own dedicated section.

Tool Area

As mentioned previously, the Tool area is covered in a more thorough fashion in the "Terrain Editing Tools" section. However, in short, the area contains all the various tools needed to edit the shape and materials of your terrain (see **FIGURE 8.35**).

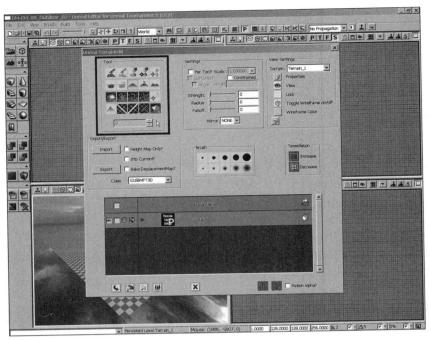

FIGURE 8.35   Tool area of the Terrain Editing dialog

Settings Area

The Settings area includes a variety of settings for your tools (see **FIGURE 8.36**). The settings are as follows:

▶ **Per Tool?**—This option causes the Strength setting to be applied to the currently selected tool only, enabling you to have individual and separate strengths for each tool.

▶ **Scale**—This value is multiplied by the Strength setting when using the Vertex Paint tool, allowing for finer control over painting.

▶ **SoftSelect**—This causes the Vertex Paint tool to use soft selection. At the time of this writing, the Vertex Paint tool is non-functional.

▶ **Constrained**—This setting causes any terrain editing operations to only affect vertices that would be present at the tessellation level specified by the EditorTesselationLevel setting. Any vertices that would only be present at higher levels of tessellation are set to match the surrounding vertices. This requires EditorTessellationLevel to be set to a value other than 0.

▶ **Angle**—This setting allows the Flatten tool to flatten the terrain at an angle rather than along the XY plane. The actual angle is acquired based on the angle of the terrain directly underneath the cursor when the tool is engaged.

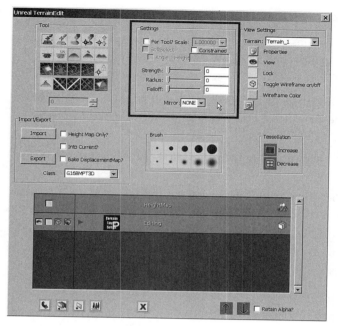

FIGURE 8.36 Settings area of the Terrain Editing dialog

▶ **Height**—This setting causes the Flatten tool to flatten the terrain at the height specified here rather than using the height of the terrain directly underneath the cursor when the tool is engaged.

▶ **Strength**—This is the amount of influence the current tool will impart once engaged.

▶ **Radius**—This setting controls the distance from the cursor that the tool influences at 100% of the Strength value.

▶ **Falloff**—This is the distance from the edge of the radius that the tool's influence fades out to 0.

▶ **Mirror**—This setting enables you to mirror your editing about specific axes. The options for this setting are as follows:

> **NONE**—No mirroring is performed.
>
> **X**—Editing is mirrored about the X-axis.
>
> **Y**—Editing is mirrored about the Y-axis.
>
> **XY**—Editing is mirrored about the XY-axis (or the diagonal line defined by the equation X=Y).

View Area

This area contains an assortment of buttons (and one dropdown) that perform a variety of functions pertaining to terrain visibility and function (see **FIGURE 8.37**). The functionality of these is as follows:

- ▶ **Terrain (Dropdown)**—This dropdown list enables you to select any of the terrain objects available in the map and make them active. Only the terrain selected in this list is available for editing.

- ▶ **Properties**—Clicking this button displays the Properties window for the currently active terrain.

- ▶ **View**—This button toggles the visibility of the active terrain. It displays the eye icon when the terrain is visible and is blank when the terrain is not visible.

- ▶ **Lock**—Toggling this button locks and unlocks the active terrain, making it able or unable to be edited with the editing tools.

- ▶ **Toggle Wireframe on/off**—This button renders the terrain with a wireframe overlay.

- ▶ **Wireframe Color**—This allows the color the wireframe is displayed with to be set.

- ▶ **Recompile Materials**—This button forces all the materials applied to the active terrain to be recompiled after making changes to them so the changes are visible.

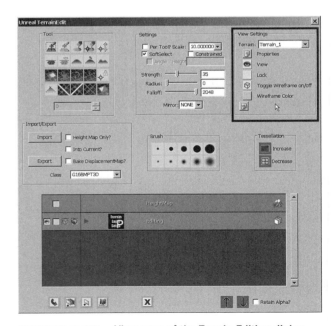

FIGURE 8.37   View area of the Terrain Editing dialog

Import/Export Area

This area provides functionality for importing/exporting terrains, height maps, and alpha maps (see **FIGURE 8.38**). The options and operations within include the following:

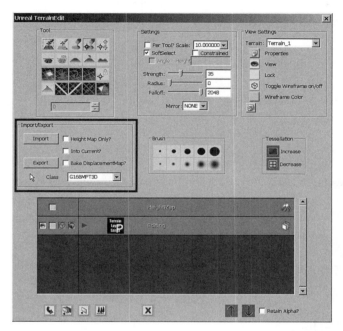

FIGURE 8.38   Import/Export area of the Terrain Editing dialog

▶ **Import**—This opens a file browser for you to select the terrain (.t3d format), height map (G16 .bmp), or alpha map (G16 .bmp) you want to import. You can then import it and create a new

> **NOTE**
>
> The term "G16.bmp" refers to a grayscale, 16-bit bitmap image.

terrain from the .t3d file or assign the map to the currently selected terrain or layer accordingly. The function performed is reliant on the Height Map Only, Into Current, and Class settings.

▶ **Export**—This exports the terrain (to .t3d), height map (to G16 .bmp), or alpha map (to G16 .bmp) of the currently selected terrain or layer, respectively. The function performed is reliant on the Height Map Only and Class settings.

▶ **Height Map Only?**—If this is checked, only the height map of the terrain or alpha map of a layer is imported or exported, depending on which was selected.

▶ **Into Current?**—If this is checked and Height Map Only? is also checked when importing a height map, the height map is used for the currently selected terrain, effectively replacing its height map.

▶ **Bake Displacement Map?**—This functionality is not currently implemented.

▶ **Class**—This dropdown list enables you to select the type of importer or exporter to use. The options are as follows:

G16BMPT3D—This imports or exports G16 .bmp files and is used when dealing with height maps or alpha maps.

TextT3D—This imports or exports .t3d files and is used when dealing with importing or exporting whole terrains.

Brush Area

This area contains a variety of presets for quickly accessing and saving commonly used brush settings (see **FIGURE 8.39**). Current brush settings can be saved to one of the slots by right-clicking and choosing Save Preset. The settings of the preset can be seen as a tool tip by mousing over the preset.

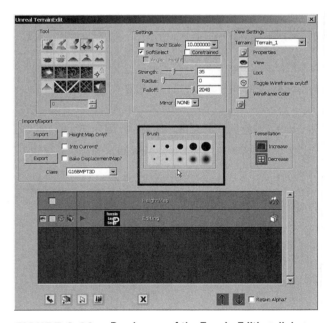

FIGURE 8.39   Brush area of the Terrain Editing dialog

Tessellation Area

This area contains buttons that enable you to increase or decrease the tessellation of the terrain (see **FIGURE 8.40**). Each of these buttons are described as follows:

- ▶ **Increase**—This button increases the NumPatchesX and NumPatchesY by a factor of two. It also *decreases* the DrawScale3D.X and DrawScale3D.Y by a factor of two. This is done so that the increase in tessellation does not make the terrain twice as large as it was previously.

- ▶ **Decrease**—At the time of this writing, this button is non-functional.

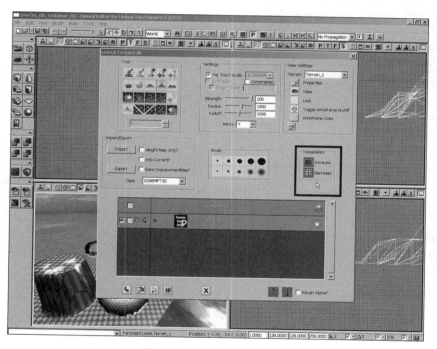

FIGURE 8.40   Tessellation area of the Terrain Editing dialog

The Browser Area

This is a graphical listing of the various terrain components such as height maps, layers, TerrainMaterials, foliage, DecoLayers, and decorations (see **FIGURE 8.41**).

> **NOTE**
>
> The availability of these buttons changes based on what objects are listed within the Browser area. For example, a height map only has the Lock button available, whereas a layer has all four of the buttons listed next.

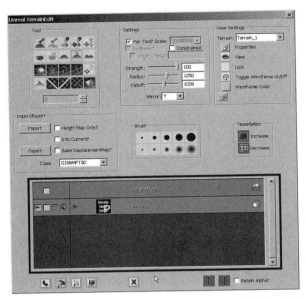

FIGURE 8.41   Browser area of the Terrain Editing dialog

The left column provides buttons for the following functions:

▶ **View**—This toggles the visibility of the layer or DecoLayer.

▶ **Lock**—This locks the height map, layer, or DecoLayer so it cannot be edited.

▶ **Wireframe Overlay**—This button overlays the terrain with a representation of its wireframe. Right-clicking on this button enables you to change the color used for the overlay. At the time of this writing, this button is non-functional.

▶ **Solid Overlay**—This button overlays the layer with a solid color. Right-clicking on this button enables you to change the color used for the overlay.

Context Menu

By right-clicking on various objects in the Browser area, you gain access to a Context menu. This contains many common terrain and layer creation functions. Keep in mind that the functions available in the Context menu change based on the object being right-clicked. These functions are as follows:

Generic Functions

▶ **Rename**—This enables you to rename the item. This can be used with layers and DecoLayers.

- ▶ **Create New**—This enables you to create and assign a new TerrainLayerSetup or TerrainMaterial. This can be used with layers and materials.

- ▶ **Delete**—This deletes the item. This can be used with layers, materials, foliage, DecoLayers, and decorations.

- ▶ **Use Selected**—This assigns the asset that is selected in the Generic browser provided that type of asset can be assigned to the given item. This can be used with layers, materials, foliage, and decorations.

Layer-Specific Functions

- ▶ **New Terrain Setup Layer Before This Item**—This adds a new, empty layer before the current layer.

- ▶ **New Terrain Setup Layer**—This adds a new, empty layer after the last layer in the array.

- ▶ **New Terrain Setup Layer After This Item**—This adds a new, empty layer after the current layer.

- ▶ **New Terrain Setup Layer from Material (Auto-Create)**—This creates a new layer including a TerrainLayerSetup and a TerrainMaterial from a regular material selected in the Generic browser and adds the layer after the last layer in the array.

- ▶ **Add Selected Layer Before This Item**—This creates a new layer using the TerrainLayerSetup selected in the Generic browser and adds it before the current layer.

- ▶ **Add Selected Layer**—This creates a new layer using the TerrainLayerSetup selected in the Generic browser and adds it after the last layer in the array.

- ▶ **Add Selected Layer After This Item**—This creates a new layer using the TerrainLayerSetup selected in the Generic browser and adds it after the current layer.

Material-Specific Functions

- ▶ **New Terrain Material Before This Item**—This adds a new, empty TerrainMaterial before the current material.

- ▶ **New Terrain Material**—This adds a new, empty TerrainMaterial after the last material in the array.

- ▶ **New Terrain Material After This Item**—This adds a new, empty TerrainMaterial after the current material.

- ▶ **Add Selected Material Before This Item**—This creates a new material using the TerrainMaterial selected in the Generic browser and adds it before the current material.

- ▶ **Add Selected Material**—This creates a new material using the TerrainMaterial selected in the Generic browser and adds it after the last material in the array.

▸ **Add Selected Material After This Item**—This creates a new material using the TerrainMaterial selected in the Generic browser and adds it after the current material.

▸ **Add Selected Displacement**—This assigns the selected texture in the Generic browser to DisplacementMap property of the current material.

▸ **Add Selected Foliage**—This creates new foliage using the static mesh selected in the Generic browser and assigns it to the current material.

DecoLayer-Specific Functions

▸ **New DecoLayer Before This Item**—This adds a new, empty DecoLayer before the current DecoLayer.

▸ **New DecoLayer**—This adds a new, empty DecoLayer before the current DecoLayer.

▸ **New DecoLayer After This Item**—This adds a new, empty DecoLayer after the current DecoLayer.

▸ **Add Selected Decoration Before This Item**—This creates a new decoration using the static mesh selected in the Generic browser and assigns it before the current decoration.

▸ **Add Selected Decoration**—This creates a new decoration using the static mesh selected in the Generic browser and assigns it after the last decoration in the array.

▸ **Add Selected Decoration After This Item**—This creates a new decoration using the static mesh selected in the Generic browser and assigns it after the current decoration.

Bottom Row Area

The buttons found along the bottom row perform the following tasks (see **FIGURE 8.42**). Note that the first five buttons, although visible at the time of this writing, are likely to be removed in favor of using the Context menu because their functions are redundant:

▸ **Use Selected**—This assigns the currently selected asset in the Generic browser to the layer, TerrainMaterial, DecoLayer, and so on that is selected in the Terrain browser. It requires the correct type of asset to be selected in the Generic browser for the type of object selected in the Terrain browser.

▸ **New Layer**—This creates a new (empty) layer and adds it to the current terrain.

▸ **New Material**—This creates a new (empty) TerrainMaterial and adds it to the selected layer in the Terrain browser.

▸ **New DecoLayer**—This creates a new (empty) DecoLayer and adds it to the current terrain.

▸ **Delete**—This deletes the currently selected object in the Terrain browser. This does not work on the height map.

▶ **Move Up**—This moves the selected object in the Terrain browser up one slot. This movement is limited to occurring within its own hierarchy. At the time of this writing, this is only effective for layers and materials.

▶ **Move Down**—This moves the selected object in the Terrain browser down one slot. This movement is limited to occurring within its own hierarchy. At the time of this writing, this is only effective for layers and materials.

▶ **Retain Alpha?**—At the time of this writing, this button is non-functional.

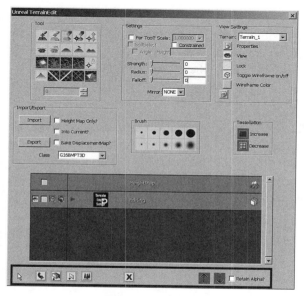

FIGURE 8.42 Bottom row of the Terrain Editing dialog

Terrain Editing Tools

The terrain editing tools are your key for adjusting the look of your terrain. They enable you to sculpt the shape, paint locations for materials, and much more. In this section, we cover each of the available tools and their inherent functions.

> **NOTE**
>
> Most of the terrain editing tools have opposing functions built into them through the use of the left and right mouse buttons. The positive function (such as adding or moving the terrain up) is performed by holding Ctrl + left-clicking the mouse. The negative function (such as subtracting or moving the terrain downward) is performed by holding Ctrl + right-clicking the mouse.

Add/Remove Sectors

This tool adds or removes rows and/or columns of patches to the current terrain. The number of rows or columns added or removed is determined by how far and in which direction the cursor is moved while using the tool. The rows or columns are added or removed in groups the size of the value specified in MaxTessellationLevel. If MaxTessellationLevel is set to 4, then 4 rows or columns of patches are added or removed at a time when the tool is used. This tool has opposing functions when using the left and right mouse buttons.

Add/Remove Polygons

This is not implemented at the time of this writing.

Paint

This tool raises or lowers the vertices located within the influence of the brush at a constant rate while the tool is used. The distance the vertices are moved is dependent on the Strength setting of the brush. This tool has opposing functions when using the left and right mouse buttons.

Vertex Paint

This tool is somewhat like the Paint tool, but it lets you select specific vertices to affect and move them manually with the mouse. Ctrl + left-clicking adds vertices within the brush's radius to the selection and Ctrl + right-clicking removes vertices within the brush's radius from the selection. Ctrl + Alt + Shift + right-clicking clears the selection completely. Ctrl + Alt + left-clicking and moving the mouse up or down moves the selected vertices.

At the time of this writing, this tool is nonfunctional.

Manual Edit

This is not implemented at the time of this writing.

Flatten

This tool flattens all vertices within the brush's radius to the same level when used. The height of the vertices after flattening is the height of the terrain under the cursor when the tool was first engaged. This tool works in conjunction with the Angle and Height settings described in the "Terrain Editor Dialog" section.

Flatten Specific

This tool does nothing and, at the time of this writing, is scheduled to be removed.

Smooth

This tool has multiple uses depending on whether the height map or a layer is selected in the Terrain browser.

If a height map is selected, the vertices within the brush's influence are raised or lowered at a constant rate in an attempt to bring each vertex's height closer to the height of its surrounding vertices, resulting in a smoother surface. The rate at which the vertices are smoothed is dependent on the strength of the brush.

If a layer is selected, the values of the pixels of the alpha map of that layer are raised or lowered at a constant rate in an attempt to bring each pixel's value closer to the values of the surrounding pixels, resulting in a smoother alpha map. The rate at which the pixels are smoothed is dependent on the strength of the brush.

Average

This tool moves the vertices within the brush's influence to the average height of all the affected vertices. This tool has opposing functions when using the left and right mouse buttons.

Noise

This tool moves the vertices within the brush's influence to random heights. The upper and lower bounds of the amount of movement are dependent on the Strength setting of the brush.

Visibility

This tool hides or unhides patches of the terrain within the brush's influence. To avoid problems with tessellation, the tool works by hiding groups of patches the size of the value specified in MaxTessellationLevel in each direction. So, if MaxTessellationLevel is set to 4, 4×4 groups of patches are hidden at a time.

Texture Pan

This tool enables you to pan all the materials of the selected layer or a single selected material of the terrain in the direction the mouse is dragged while holding down Ctrl + left or right mouse button. This functionality is identical to changing the MappingPanU and MappingPanV properties of the TerrainMaterials themselves, except that propagation to the material is not automatic, meaning that you have to recompile the terrain's materials manually using the Recompile Materials button in the View Settings section.

Texture Rotate

This tool enables you to rotate all the materials of the selected layer or a single selected material of the terrain in the direction the mouse is dragged while holding down Ctrl + left or right mouse button. This functionality is identical to changing the MappingRotation property of the TerrainMaterials themselves, except that propagation to the material is not automatic, meaning that you have to recompile the terrain's materials manually using the Recompile Materials button in the View Settings section.

Texture Scale

This tool enables you to scale all the materials of the selected layer or a single selected material of the terrain in the direction the mouse is dragged while holding down Ctrl + left or right mouse button. This functionality is identical to changing the MappingScale property of the TerrainMaterials themselves, except that propagation to the material is not automatic, meaning that you have to recompile the terrain's materials manually using the Recompile Materials button in the View Settings section.

Lock Vertex

At the time of this writing, this tool is non-functional.

Mark Unreachable

At the time of this writing, this tool is non-functional.

Split Terrain X

This tool enables you to split the selected terrain into multiple terrains along the X-axis. The line along which the splitting occurs will be marked in yellow, and Ctrl + left-clicking will perform the split.

Split Terrain Y

This tool enables you to split the selected terrain into multiple terrains along the Y-axis. The line along which the splitting occurs will be marked in yellow, and Ctrl + left-clicking will perform the split.

Merge Terrain

This tool enables you to merge two terrains into one single terrain. The line along which the terrains will be merged, assuming they are able to be merged, will be marked in yellow. The requirements for two terrains to be merged are as follows:

- The heights of each Terrain actor must be within .0001 units of each other.
- The two adjacent edges of the terrains to be merged must be less than .0001 units apart.
- The number of patches of each terrain along the two adjacent sides must be equal.

Orientation Flip

This tool flips the edge dividing each patch into two triangles to the opposite direction of the default orientation. The opposing function using the right mouse button flips the edge back to the default orientation. This tool only works on patches that are present when the terrain is fully tessellated, meaning you need to be viewing the terrain at the highest level of detail to properly use this tool.

Please make sure you have completed **TUTORIAL 8.7** before beginning, or open the CH_08_Outdoor_05.ut3 map file provided on the DVD in the folder for this chapter. In **TUTORIAL 8.8**, you sculpt the shape of your terrain surface using the terrain editing tools.

TUTORIAL 8.8: Creating an Outdoor Environment, Part VI: Basic Terrain Editing

1. Enter Terrain Editing Mode if not already in it and select the Paint tool . Set the following brush settings (see **FIGURE 8.43**):

   Strength: 75

   Radius: 1024

   Falloff: 512

FIGURE 8.43   Your Settings area should appear like so.

2. Make sure that you have the height map selected in the Browser area.

3. Hold down Ctrl and the left mouse button while making back and forth strokes around the perimeter of the terrain, making an indention on one side so that the valley takes on a

U-shape when viewed from above. Don't ever keep the mouse in one place for too long to begin with because we want a fairly even build-up at this point (see **FIGURE 8.44**).

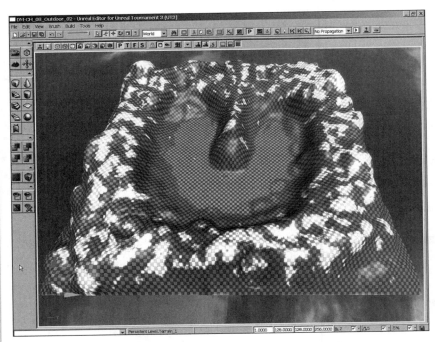

FIGURE 8.44   Turn your terrain into a valley by lifting the perimeter.

4. Continue with this process until you get the entire perimeter built up to where the top is beginning to be mostly covered in the snow material. At this point, you can start focusing on smaller areas and shortening your strokes to build up peaks in the mountains.

Feel free to adjust your brush settings at any time. Just remember that we are only building up the basic shape at this point (see **FIGURE 8.45**). Fine details are added in later on. Don't forget to use your reference photos as a guide!

If you make a mistake or don't like the way something turned out, you can use the Undo button ↩ or Ctrl + Z to undo the last action. You can also use the other tools to fix problem spots. For instance, if you paint the terrain too far up in one spot, you can use the smooth tool to even it out instead of trying to paint it back down. All the tools are there for a reason, so make sure to use them if you need to.

It is also a good idea to check the Per Tool? checkbox and the Brush presets because they enable us to have specific brush settings for each tool. This makes it easy to switch back and forth from painting and smoothing, for example, and not have to manually set the individual brush settings each time.

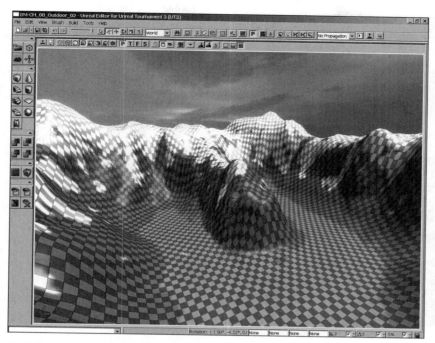

FIGURE 8.45   Carefully sculpt mountains into the surrounding terrain.

5. Once you have some basic mountains you are happy with, you can start adding detail to them. To do this, start by selecting the Paint tool and setting the brush settings as follows:

> **Strength:** 15
>
> **Radius:** 192
>
> **Falloff:** 96

6. Using small strokes, paint the terrain up and down in somewhat random areas to break up the smoothness of the mountains. Because of the low strength of the brush, the terrain does not change much from a single stroke. This enables you to have much finer control over the editing. You will have to go over the same area with multiple strokes to really build it up, but each stroke makes a subtle change, which has a nice result when using random strokes (see **FIGURE 8.46**).

As before, make sure to use your reference photos to guide your editing. Keep in mind the environment you are trying to re-create. Be sure to look for things like how the snow is caught by flat surfaces or crevasses so areas where there is snow on your terrain would be prime areas to add those features. Of course, we can always go back and make use of extra layers to precisely add snow or rock materials later on so you don't have to follow the base layer's material placement exactly.

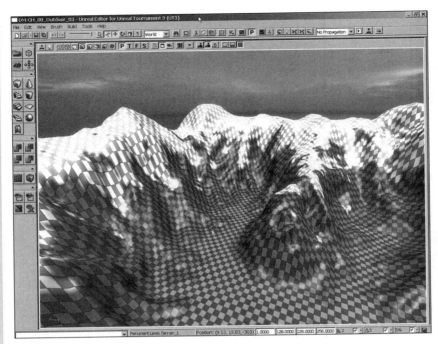

FIGURE 8.46   The smaller brush size makes detailing much easier.

7. After you have the mountains looking the way you want them, you can focus on the transition from the mountains to the valley. You don't necessarily want perfectly flat ground transitioning into steep mountain sides too abruptly, although similar situations do occur in nature, so it is a legitimate feature if used appropriately.

Use the Paint tool with the following settings:

> **Strength:** 15
>
> **Radius:** 192
>
> **Falloff:** 192

Build up the area around the base of the mountains so that it is a more gradual incline. You can also use the technique from the last step to add detail to the base of the mountains while you are at it. You can break up the flatness of the grassy area by painting up and down randomly over the same area. This can also be achieved with a combination of the Noise tool and Smooth tool if that method is preferable to you. The first method provides a little more control over the final result, though (see **FIGURE 8.47**).

8. Save your map. Your terrain should be shaping up nicely at this point and all through the use of only a few basic tools. In **TUTORIAL 8.9**, we take a look at using additional tools to add very specific features to the terrain.

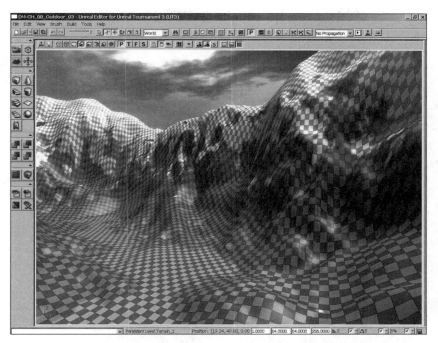

FIGURE 8.47 Smooth out the change between the mountains and the valley.

END TUTORIAL 8.8

Please make sure you have completed **TUTORIAL 8.8** before beginning, or open the CH_08_Outdoor_06.ut3 map file that is provided on the DVD in the folder for this chapter. In **TUTORIAL 8.9**, we make further edits on the shape of the terrain surface by utilizing more advanced tools.

TUTORIAL 8.9: Creating an Outdoor Environment, Part VII: Advanced Terrain Editing

1. Select the Flatten tool in the Terrain Editing dialog and set the following brush settings:

    Strength: 100

    Radius: 128

    Falloff: 128

2. Now pick a place in the side of one of the mountains where you would like to place a plateau and begin flattening an area of the terrain by holding Ctrl and left clicking (the side of the mountain you choose should be parallel to one of the outer edges of the terrain; the reason for this is apparent later). You will notice that the flattened area has very hard

edges, and they are jagged because of the way the edges are aligned (see
FIGURE 8.48).

FIGURE 8.48   The new plateau has a very hard edge.

3. Select the Orientation Flip tool ![icon] and set the following brush settings:

> **Strength:** 100
>
> **Radius:** 64
>
> **Falloff:** 0

Begin Ctrl + left clicking around all the hard edges created when you carved out the
plateau. This includes not only the edges around the surface of the plateau, but also the
edges around the bottom of the plateau and the top edge where it was carved out of the
mountain. If you notice that you flip an edge the wrong way, simply use Ctrl + right mouse
button to flip it the opposite direction. You need to use a combination of flipping with
the left mouse button and the right mouse button to smooth out all the edges (see
FIGURE 8.49).

FIGURE 8.49   Using the Orientation Flip tool can help with smoothing by adjusting the flow of your topology.

4. Now that the edges are as smooth as it is possible to make them using the Orientation Flip tool, select the Smooth tool and set the brush settings to the following values:

> **Strength:** 100
>
> **Radius:** 192
>
> **Falloff:** 192

Begin smoothing around the edges of the plateau, being careful not to smooth too much of the actual surface so it keeps its flat shape for the most part. This is partly to smooth out the edges of the plateau and partly to ease the stretching of the UVs of the vertical faces of the plateau (see **FIGURE 8.50**).

If you need to adjust the brush settings at any time, feel free to do so. The values provided are just guidelines to give you a place to start from. The whole terrain editing process consists of continually adjusting brush settings to give the desired effect.

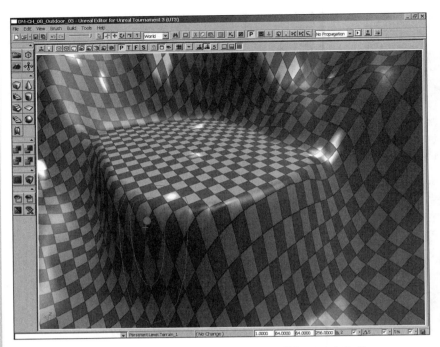

FIGURE 8.50   The Smooth tool pushes your smoothing much further.

5. Now we are going to add an opening to a cave or base, or whatever you can imagine might be located inside a mountain. Select the Visibility tool ▨ and set the following brush settings:

> **Strength:** 100
>
> **Radius:** 128
>
> **Falloff:** 0

6. Hide some of the patches of the side of the mountain just above the plateau by holding Ctrl and clicking the left mouse button. Notice that this tool hides patches (or quads) and not just individual triangles. This is the reason the side of the mountain needed to be parallel to the edge of the terrain when we chose where to make the plateau (see **FIGURE 8.51**).

This gives us flat edges around the hole in the terrain instead of jagged edges. Of course you could have these jagged edges, but you would need to cover them up with static meshes so that the player did not see them or collide with them. In fact, most caves are either be static meshes themselves, or a separate pair of terrains: one for the floor and another one rotated upside down for the ceiling. This technique would give you tremendous control over the look of your cave, as well as the ability to sculpt such things as stalactites.

FIGURE 8.51   Patches of the terrain have been hidden, making way for a cave or mountain base of operations.

7. The next thing we want to do is make the bottom of the opening level with the plateau's surface. We can do this using the Flatten tool (assuming that the opening is currently higher than the plateau's surface...which it probably is, according to the previous instructions). Start flattening from the plateau's surface and slowly make your way toward the opening. Go slowly and stop when you get the opening level with the surface (see **FIGURE 8.52**). This should make it easier to create and place the mesh or meshes that form the entrance to the cave, base, and so on.

8. As an optional step, you can place the base_entrance static mesh in the hole you have created. You need to adjust its scale and rotation, and likely paint your height map slightly to fit around the edges, but it enables you to have an actual cave entrance in the side of your mountain (see **FIGURE 8.53**)!

9. Save your map. At this point, you should have a mostly finished terrain in terms of editing the height map. Of course, you can continue adding detail and editing the terrain on your own if you want. Plus, there may be further editing and touching up after the finished materials and layers are created and applied.

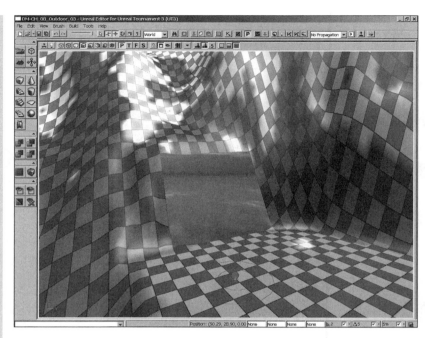

FIGURE 8.52
Flatten out the bottom of the opening.

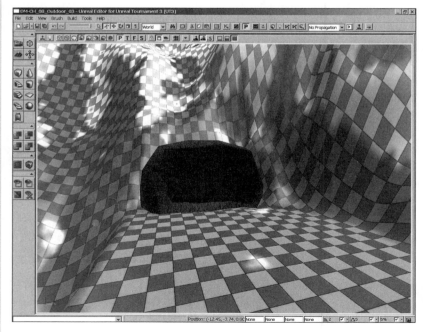

FIGURE 8.53
The cave mesh has been added.

END TUTORIAL 8.9

Please make sure you have completed **TUTORIAL 8.9** before beginning, or open the CH_08_ Outdoor_07.ut3 map file that is provided on the DVD in the folder for this chapter.

TUTORIAL 8.10: Creating an Outdoor Environment, Part VIII: Final Base Layer Materials

1. Make sure you have the package with the same name as your map in the Generic browser. Right-click in the Generic browser and choose New TerrainMaterial to create a new TerrainMaterial and name it tmat_grass (see **FIGURE 8.54**). The Properties window for tmat_grass should open up automatically.

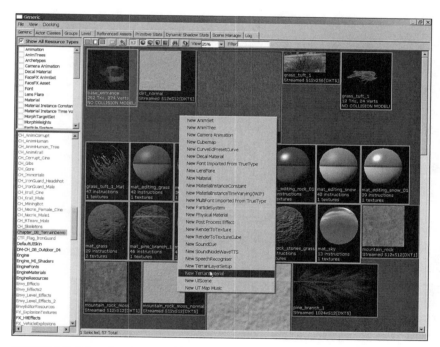

FIGURE 8.54   Create a new TerrainMaterial.

Select the mat_grass material already created and assign it to the Material property of the tmat_grass TerrainMaterial. That finishes off for the grass material (see **FIGURE 8.55**).

2. We are going to create two versions of the rock material: one with a small MappingScale and one with a larger MappingScale. The two are then blended together in the TerrainLayerSetup. This allows the material to keep its detail with no obvious tiling, whether viewed up close or far away.

Create another new TerrainMaterial by right-clicking in the Generic browser and choosing New TerrainMaterial. Name this one tmat_rock. Again, its properties should open up auto- matically (see **FIGURE 8.56**).

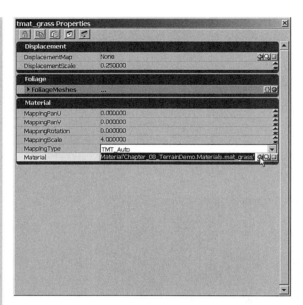

FIGURE 8.55   The final grass is now in place.

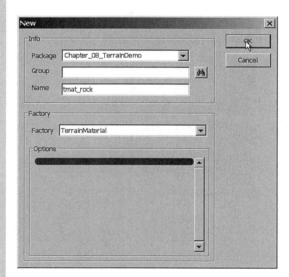

FIGURE 8.56   Create a new TerrainMaterial for the rock material.

3. Select the mat_rock material and assign it to the Material property of tmat_rock. Also, set the following properties:

       MappingScale: 48.0

       MappingRotation: 60.0

4. Now, duplicate (select, right-click, and choose Duplicate) the tmat_rock TerrainMaterial and name the new version tmat_rock_detail. This is the up-close version of the rock TerrainMaterial. Set the following properties on the detail rock material (see **FIGURE 8.57**):

> **MappingScale:** 16.0

> **MappingRotation:** -45.0

5. We are also going to add in a mossy, ground cover-type material to break up the rock material. This is done using the noise feature of the TerrainLayerSetup and keeps the mountain sides from being too bland.

Create another new TerrainMaterial by right-clicking in the Generic browser and choosing New TerrainMaterial. Name this one tmat_moss. Again, its properties should open up automatically (see **FIGURE 8.58**).

6. Select the mat_moss material and assign it to the Material property of tmat_moss. Also, set the following properties:

> **MappingScale:** 48.0

> **MappingRotation:** 30.0

7. Now, duplicate the tmat_moss TerrainMaterial and name the new version tmat_moss_detail. This is the up-close version of the rock TerrainMaterial. Set the following properties on the detail rock material (see **FIGURE 8.59**):

> **MappingScale:** 16.0

> **MappingRotation:** -50.0

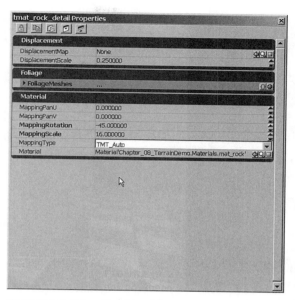

FIGURE 8.57   The "detail" version of the rock TerrainMaterial has a smaller mapping scale and a different rotation.

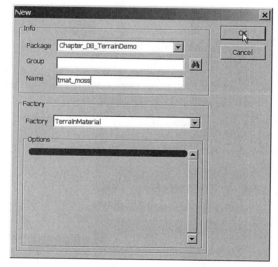

FIGURE 8.58   Create a new TerrainMaterial for the moss.

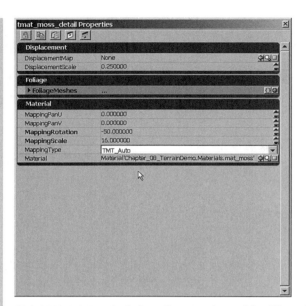

FIGURE 8.59   As before, the moss has a "detail" version for up-close viewing.

8. As with the rock material, we are going to use two versions of the snow material with differing scales to allow for up-close detail, but reduce any visible tiling when viewed from far away.

Create another new TerrainMaterial by right-clicking in the Generic browser and choosing New TerrainMaterial. Name this one tmat_snow. Again, its properties should open up automatically.

9. Select the mat_snow material and assign it to the Material property of tmat_snow. Also, set the following properties:

    MappingScale: 16.0

    MappingRotation: 45.0

10. Now, duplicate the tmat_snow TerrainMaterial and name the new version tmat_snow_detail. This is the up-close version of the rock TerrainMaterial. Set the following properties on the detail rock material (see **FIGURE 8.60**):

    MappingScale: 8.0

    MappingRotation: -60.0

11. Save your map.

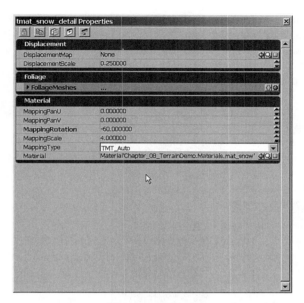

FIGURE 8.60   There should be two versions of the snow as well.

END TUTORIAL 8.10

Please make sure you have completed **TUTORIAL 8.10** before beginning, or open the CH_08_Outdoor_08.ut3 map file that is provided on the DVD in the folder for this chapter.

TUTORIAL 8.11: Creating an Outdoor Environment, Part IX: Final Base Layer Setup

1. We are going to use our "editing" TerrainLayerSetup as a starting point for our final TerrainLayerSetup. It needs additional slots added to it, of course, but it saves us a little work as opposed to creating an entirely new one.

   In the Generic browser, select tls_editing, right-click on it, and choose Duplicate. Name the new version tls_final. Notice that the properties do not open up when duplicating as they do when creating a completely new object (see **FIGURE 8.61**).

2. Find tls_final and double-click on it to open its properties. Expand the

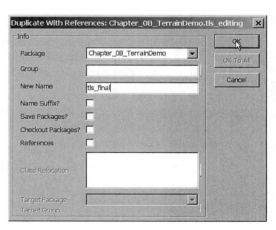

FIGURE 8.61   Duplicate the tls_editing layer to create the final version.

Materials array, and you should see the three existing slots. We now have two snow materials, so we need an extra slot for the extra snow material. Click on the right side of the [0] slot, which is the snow material, and you should see three buttons appear. The first button is labeled Duplicate This Item. Click that button to make a copy of this slot just below the current slot (see **FIGURE 8.62**).

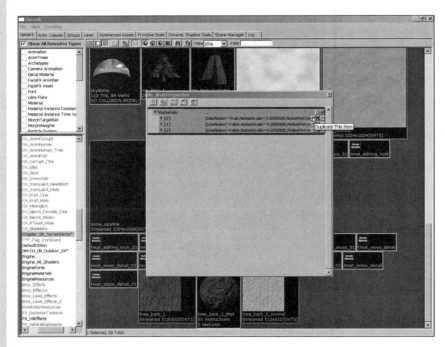

FIGURE 8.62   Make a duplicate of the existing snow slot.

3. Now, we need to assign our final snow materials to their slots in the TerrainLayerSetup. Expand the first two slots so you can see their Material properties. In the Generic browser, select tmat_snow_detail and assign it to the Material property of the [0] slot. Next, select tmat_snow and assign it to the Material property of the [1] slot (see **FIGURE 8.63**).

4. Even though we have slots for both our snow materials, and they both have the correct material assigned, we still would only be able to see one of them, the first one in the list, rendered on the terrain at this point. We need to lower the alpha of the [0] slot in order to let the other snow material show as well.

   Set the alpha of slot [0] to 0.5 (see **FIGURE 8.64**).

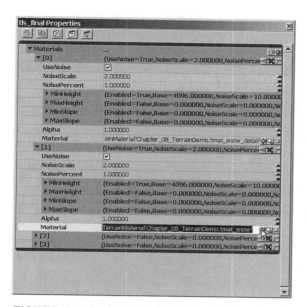

FIGURE 8.63 Remember that the detail version should go on top of the regular version.

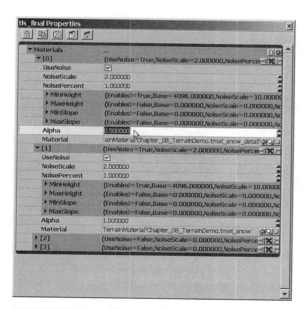

FIGURE 8.64 Changing the alpha of the detail snow is necessary to see the other version.

5. Slot [2] holds our rock material, but we now have two rock materials. As before, click on the right side of the slot and click the Duplicate This Item button to create a copy of the slot (see **FIGURE 8.65**).

6. We need to assign our final rock materials to their slots in the TerrainLayerSetup. Expand the first two slots so you can see their Material properties. In the Generic browser, select tmat_rock_detail and assign it to the Material property of the [2] slot. Next, select tmat_rock and assign it to the Material property of the [3] slot.

7. Again, we will not be able to see the second rock material unless we adjust the alpha property of slot [2] to allow it to show through. A value of 0.5 should work well (see **FIGURE 8.66**).

8. Save your map at this point. We finalize the new TerrainLayerSetup in **TUTORIAL 8.12**.

FIGURE 8.65   Once again, we duplicate the existing slot to make way for the two new materials.

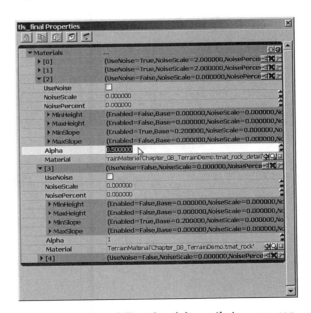

FIGURE 8.66   Adjust the alpha so that we can see through the detail material.

END TUTORIAL 8.11

Please make sure you have completed **TUTORIAL 8.11** before beginning, or open the CH_08_Outdoor_09.ut3 map file that is provided on the DVD in the folder for this chapter.

TUTORIAL 8.12: Creating an Outdoor Environment, Part X: Final Base Layer Setup, Continued

1. Select the package with the same name as your map in the Generic browser, and double-click the tls_final TerrainLayerSetup to open its properties. We are now ready to move on to the other materials.

2. Before we move on to the grass material slot, we added two mossy materials that weren't accounted for in the "editing" TerrainLayerSetup. Because of the way these are going to be used, they need to be above the rock materials in the list. To insert a new slot, click on the right side of slot [2] as before, but this time click the last button, which is labeled Insert New Item Here. This creates a new, empty slot [2] and moves everything else down (see **FIGURE 8.67**).

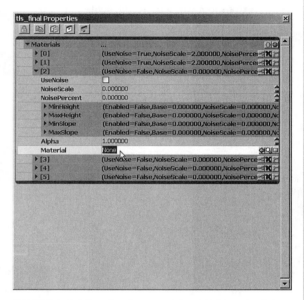

FIGURE 8.67   You have now inserted a new slot for the moss.

3. Select tmat_moss_detail in the Generic browser and assign it to the Material property of slot [2].

4. Now, we need to add some noise to the moss material so that it only overlays the rock material in random areas. Set the following properties for slot [2]:

> **UseNoise:** True
>
> **NoiseScale:** 10.0
>
> **NoisePercent:** 0.75
>
> **MinSlope:**
>
> > ▶ **Enabled:** True
> >
> > ▶ **Base:** 0.2
> >
> > ▶ **NoiseScale:** 2.0
> >
> > ▶ **NoiseAmount:** 5.0

That should give a nice random placement of the material on the mountain sides. Feel free to play with the noise settings to get a different result.

5. That takes care of the detail moss texture, but we need to duplicate slot [2] for the other moss material now. Click the Duplicate this Item button of slot [2]. Select tmat_moss in the Generic browser and assign it to the Material property of slot [3]. The rest of the settings remain the same for this slot (see **FIGURE 8.68**).

Now we need to adjust the alpha properties of these two slots to allow the second rock materials to show through a bit. Set slot [2]'s alpha property to a value of 0.125. Then, set slot [3]'s alpha property to .375.

6. The last slot we need to set up is the grass material slot. This is simply a matter of selecting tmat_grass in the Generic browser and assigning it to the Material property of slot [6] (see **FIGURE 8.69**).

7. Now, you can apply tls_final to the terrain. Make sure tls_final is selected in the Generic browser and open the Terrain Editing dialog. In the Terrain browser, select the Editing layer. Right-click on it and choose Use Selected from the Context menu. This might take a few minutes as the Editor does some calculating and caches the terrain material. Once it finishes, the final material should be

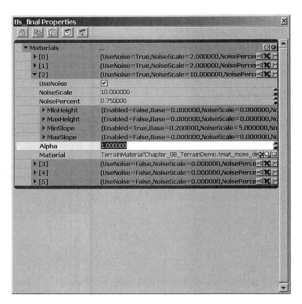

FIGURE 8.68   Duplicate the moss material to make way for the non-detail version.

FIGURE 8.69   The grass material is now in place.

applied to your terrain. The last thing you should do it right-click on the Editing layer in the Terrain browser and choose to rename it to Final.

8. Save your level.

END TUTORIAL 8.12

Decorating Your Terrain: Foliage and DecoLayers

One of the key methods in making your terrains more believable is to decorate them with objects such as grass, bushes, trees, rocks, and other such items one might find on an open landscape. In Unreal's terrain system, this can be handled through the use of foliage and DecoLayers. The two systems are very similar, yet have key differences. Both essentially provide a way to populate your terrain with decorative static meshes. Foliage is actually a part of a TerrainMaterial, whereas DecoLayers are actually a separate system that can be added to terrain (see **FIGURE 8.70**).

FIGURE 8.70   Foliage and DecoLayers can add a nice amount of realism to your levels.

There are other differences as well in how the two systems behave in-game. Foliage fades away and scales down to 0 percent of its original size as the player moves away from it. DecoLayer objects (called decorations) are always visible unless occluded.

Foliage

Foliage is added through the Foliage array, which can be found within the properties of a TerrainMaterial. This array enables you to assign static meshes—such as models of grass and shrubbery—to be used to populate the terrain wherever the corresponding material is applied. This is similar to DecoLayers, although different in that meshes assigned in the Foliage array are only visible within a specified distance of the player, whereas DecoLayer meshes are always rendered, provided they are not being occluded.

Foliage-Specific Properties

Once foliage has been applied to your terrain system, it can be controlled via the following properties:

StaticMesh—This property contains the static mesh to be used for the individual entry of the array. Separate static meshes require a separate array entry.

Material—This property enables you to override the material that is assigned to the static mesh. Please note that you can only override the first material applied to the mesh, not subsequent materials.

Density—This property is the number of meshes to place per terrain patch.

MaxDrawRadius—This property is the farthest distance from the player that the mesh is made visible and will then begin fading and scaling into the player's view.

MinTransitionRadius—This is the distance from the player at which the mesh finishes fading and scaling and is completely visible and full scale.

MinScale—This provides the lower bound that is used when calculating the random scales for the multiple copies of the static mesh.

MaxScale—This provides the upper bound that is used when calculating the random scales for the multiple copies of the static mesh.

Seed—This is the base value used to calculate the random distribution of static meshes. Changing this value gives you a different random placement of meshes.

SwayScale—This value controls the movement of vertices of foliage meshes due to WindPointSource or WindDirectionalSource actors placed in the map.

AlphaMapThreshold—This sets a threshold based on the weight map for the material. Beneath the value of this threshold, foliage does not appear. This means that if you have an area where, for example, a particular material is not yet completely visible, you can prevent foliage from showing through.

SlopeRotationBlend—This is the percentage of the terrain's slope that is applied to the foliage.

Please make sure you have completed **TUTORIAL 8.12** before beginning, or open the DM-CH_08_Outdoor_10.ut3 map file provided on the DVD in the folder for this chapter.

At this point, we have a nice-looking terrain, and we have seen how to use a TerrainLayerSetup to determine which materials get placed where on the terrain. In **TUTORIAL 8.13**, we take it even further by creating a layer that can be painted anywhere on the terrain using the editing tools. The material used in this layer also has foliage associated with it, which gives the terrain a more realistic look.

TUTORIAL 8.13: Creating an Outdoor Environment, Part XI: Grass Foliage Layer

1. In the Generic browser, select the Chapter_08_TerrainDemo package and select mat_grass. Finally, enter Terrain Editing Mode.

2. Right-click on the Final layer in the Terrain browser and choose New Layer from material (auto-create). This creates a TerrainMaterial and TerrainLayerSetup using the material that was selected in the Generic browser and assigns the TerrainLayerSetup to a new layer on the terrain. This is a very fast and easy way of creating a new layer.

   Name the TerrainLayerSetup tls_grass_foliage and name the TerrainMaterial tmat_grass_foliage. After the layer is created, right-click on it and choose to rename it to Grass_Foliage (see **FIGURE 8.71**).

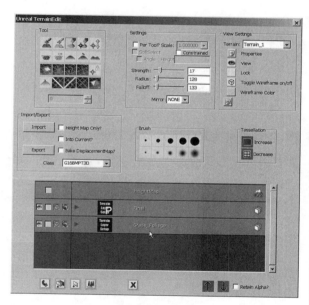

FIGURE 8.71   The new grass material layer holds our foliage.

3. In the Generic browser, navigate to your map's package, and find the tmat_grass_foliage TerrainMaterial that was just created. Double-click it to open its properties. Under Foliage, there is an array named FoliageMeshes. Click the Add New Item button ![icon] to create a slot in the array (see **FIGURE 8.72**).

4. Expand slot [0] so you can see all of its properties. Select the grass_tuft_1 static mesh in the Chapter_08_TerrainDemo package in the Generic browser and assign it to the StaticMesh property using the Use Current Selection in Generic Browser button ![icon] (see **FIGURE 8.73**).

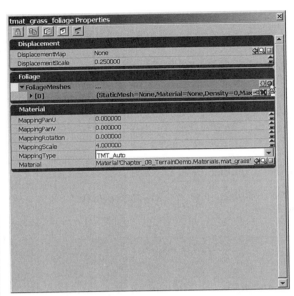

FIGURE 8.72   You must add a new slot to use the FoliageMeshes property.

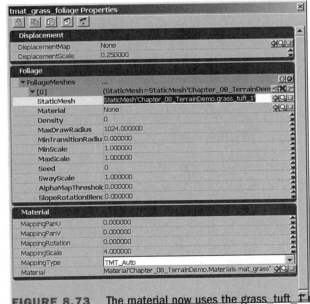

FIGURE 8.73   The material now uses the grass_tuft_1 mesh as its foliage.

5. Set the following properties to their corresponding values:

> **Density:** 1
>
> **MaxDrawRadius:** 10240
>
> **MinTransitionRadius:** 7680
>
> **MinScale:** 0.75
>
> **MaxScale:** 1.25
>
> **SlopeRotationBlend:** 1.0

6. Back in the Terrain Editor dialog, select the Paint tool 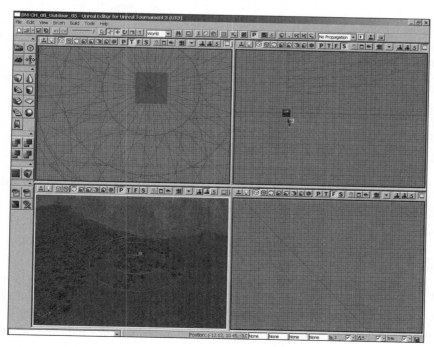 and set your brush to the following settings (or feel free to adjust them if you prefer):

> **Strength:** 30
>
> **Radius:** 256
>
> **Falloff:** 160

7. Make sure the Grass_Foliage layer is selected in the Terrain browser and begin painting over the areas where the grass material is currently on the terrain, or any areas where the automatic placement of the materials doesn't quite match what you'd like, and it feels like there should be grass there (see **FIGURE 8.74**).

FIGURE 8.74 Grass meshes appear as you paint.

Adjust your brush settings as needed. You don't want to overdo foliage because each instance of the mesh used is going to need to be rendered. The number of polygons can add up quickly. Lower brush strengths cause fewer instances of the foliage to be placed with each stroke.

8. Save your level.

END TUTORIAL 8.13

DecoLayers

DecoLayers, like the Foliage system, allow for a way to populate a terrain with static meshes. However, DecoLayers also provide the ability to populate a terrain with SpeedTrees, which are a special kind of asset for providing realistic trees and plants. DecoLayers are independent of TerrainMaterials, and are placed on the terrain based on their own alpha map that can be painted by the designer without concern for the placement of any materials.

Unlike the Foliage system, the meshes placed through DecoLayers have no dynamic visibility based on the proximity of the player. As such, one must be very careful about the usage of DecoLayers. Overdoing it could easily result in a performance hit.

DecoLayers are very useful for randomly placing large meshes that should be visible at all times, such as random cityscape generation or the trees of a forest. Each DecoLayer has the following properties.

DecoLayer-Specific Properties

The following list contains the properties found within a DecoLayer:

Name—This is a name for the layer that is used in the Terrain Editor's browser.

Decorations—This is an array of the decorations (or meshes) that is used for this DecoLayer. If multiple decorations are used in a single DecoLayer, one is picked at random each time a mesh is placed.

Factory—This is where you set up the static mesh properties to be used for the decoration. You must first create either a new StaticMeshComponentFactory or SpeedTreeComponentFactory here using the Create A New Object button. A *StaticMeshComponentFactory* is a template for creating static mesh actors during play or a runtime, whereas a *SpeedTreeComponentFactory* is for creating SpeedTree actors. Once created, you have access to the following properties:

StaticMeshComponentFactory Properties

- ▶ **StaticMesh**—This is the static mesh to use for this decoration.
- ▶ **Materials**—This is an array of materials for overriding the materials of the static mesh specified in the StaticMesh property.

SpeedTreeComponentFactory Properties

▶ **SpeedTreeComponent**—This is a collection of properties that allows a SpeedTree to be specified for this DecoLayer, as well as a great deal of other properties dealing with the display and behavior of the SpeedTree.

Shared Factory Properties

▶ **CollideActors**—This determines whether the meshes spawned by this factory should collide with actors or not. However, in this case, the word "collide" means that collision notifications (such as Touch events) are triggered, but the mesh does not actually stop the actors that come into contact with it.

▶ **BlockActors**—This determines whether actors that are colliding with the meshes spawned by this factory are stopped or not.

▶ **BlockZeroExtent**—This determines whether the meshes spawned by this factory block zero extent traces such as weapon fire.

▶ **BlockNonZeroExtent**—This determines whether meshes spawned by this factory block non-zero extent traces, such as player collision checks.

▶ **BlockRigidBody**—This determines whether meshes spawned by this factory block objects using rigid body physics.

▶ **HiddenGame**—This determines whether the meshes spawned by this factory are visible during play.

▶ **HiddenEditor**—This determines whether meshes spawned by this factory are visible in the Editor.

▶ **CastShadow**—This determines whether meshes spawned by this factory cast shadows or not.

▶ **MinScale**—This is the lower bound used when calculating a random scale for this decoration.

▶ **MaxScale**—This is the upper bound used when calculating a random scale for this decoration.

▶ **Density**—This is a multiplier that determines how many instances of this decoration are placed on the terrain. The maximum number of instances is equal to: Density*NumPatchesX*NumPatchesY. This is only a theoretical maximum and not the actual number of meshes that are placed on the terrain—instances are only placed where the alpha map of the DecoLayer is not black and on visible patches of the terrain.

▶ **SlopeRotationBlend**—This is the percentage of the terrain's slope that is used for the decoration.

▶ **RandSeed**—This is the base value from which to calculate the random distribution of meshes. Changing this value gives you a different random placement of meshes.

Please make sure you have completed **TUTORIAL 8.13** before beginning, or open the DM-CH_08_Outdoor_11.ut3 map file provided on the DVD in the folder for this chapter. In **TUTORIAL 8.14**, we add some decoration meshes for the forest.

TUTORIAL 8.14: Creating an Outdoor Environment, Part XII: Forest Decorations

1. In the Generic browser, select the Chapter_08_TerrainDemo package and select the sm_tree_1 static mesh. You may have to fully load the package to see the static mesh asset.

2. Open the Terrain Editor dialog and click the New DecoLayer 🔲 button below the Terrain browser (see **FIGURE 8.75**).

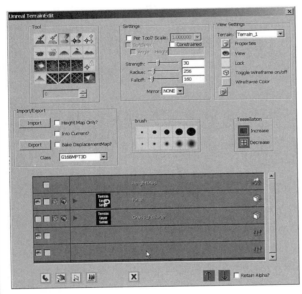

FIGURE 8.75   This new DecoLayer supports our trees.

3. Right-click on the new DecoLayer and choose Add Selected Decoration. Right-click on the DecoLayer again and choose to rename it to Pine_Trees (see **FIGURE 8.76**).

4. Select sm_tree_1_stump in the Generic browser. Right-click on the Pine_Trees DecoLayer again and choose Add Selected Decoration once again.

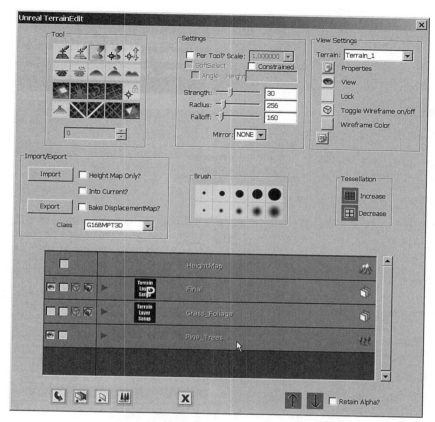

FIGURE 8.76   You have now renamed the layer and added a mesh.

5. Next, open the terrain's properties by pressing the Properties button [image] in the View Settings section of the Terrain Editor. Expand the Terrain section, expand the DecoLayers property, expand slot [0], and expand decorations. Set the following properties:

[0]:

   MinScale: 0.75

   MaxScale: 1.25

   Density: 0.25

   SlopeRotation: 1.0

   RandSeed: 0

[1]:

>   **MinScale:** 0.25
>
>   **MaxScale:** 1.0
>
>   **Density:** 0.075
>
>   **SlopeRotation:** 1.0
>
>   **RandSeed:** 1

6. Make sure the Pine_Trees DecoLayer is selected. Then, select the Paint tool  and set your brush to somewhere around the following settings:

>   **Strength:** 100
>
>   **Radius:** 256
>
>   **Falloff:** 160

7. Begin painting the area at one end of the U shape of the valley to place trees there (see **FIGURE 8.77**).

FIGURE 8.77   As you paint, trees and stumps appear.

As with foliage, do not go overboard. Each tree is quite a few polygons that need to be rendered so try to use as few as possible to get the desired result.

You can always go into the Decorations' properties and adjust the Seed property to change the random placement of the meshes on the terrain to get the distribution that suits the terrain best. Just make sure you set the seed of each decoration to a different value or they are placed on top of one another.

8. Select mat_forest_floor in the Generic browser and open the Terrain Editor dialog. Right-click on the Grass_Foliage layer in the Terrain browser and choose New Layer from material (auto-create).

   Name the TerrainLayerSetup tls_forest_floor and name the TerrainMaterial tmat_forest_floor. After the layer is created (which may take a moment), right-click on it and choose to rename it to Forest_Floor.

9. Select the Paint tool  and set your brush to somewhere around the following settings:

   > **Strength:** 30
   >
   > **Radius:** 256
   >
   > **Falloff:** 160

10. Now, make sure the Forest_Floor layer is selected in the Terrain browser and begin painting the terrain beneath the tree decorations (see **FIGURE 8.78**).

FIGURE 8.78 Paint in the Forest Floor material underneath the trees.

11. Save your package.

END TUTORIAL 8.14

Terrain Workflow Considerations

Following are some useful tips to remember when working with Unreal's terrain system:

▶ Keep materials used on a terrain as simple as possible because they most likely cover a great deal of the screen.

▶ Try to limit the number of different materials used on a terrain to three or four. This is more about the number of textures than about the number of materials. All the materials applied to a terrain are actually combined into one overall material that is limited in the number of textures it can use just as any other material is.

▶ Whether you use multiple-material, procedural layer setups, or multiple single-material layer setups should be determined by which method is more comfortable and gives the best visual results.

▶ Using the same material in multiple TerrainMaterials with differing scales and rotations can break up any tiling effects that may be present.

▶ Changes made to TerrainMaterials or the materials they contain require recompiling the terrain shader in order to see their effects. Using simpler materials and fewer layers reduces the time it takes to recompile and increase iteration time.

▶ Be very careful with the values used for the StaticLightingResolution property. You can easily increase build times and the amount of memory needed for the light maps created to very undesirable levels.

▶ If the results of using an editing tool are not desirable, the undo command (Ctrl + Z) is usually able to revert the terrain to the previous state.

▶ Always name your layers so they are easily identifiable in the Terrain browser.

▶ Use the brush presets and the Per Tool settings to keep from having to constantly adjust the brush settings individually.

▶ Remember that you can create other objects than just walkable surfaces. You could, for example, rotate terrain 180 degrees around its Y-axis to create the ceiling of a cave!

▶ Sometimes Terrain is not the tool for the job. Vertical cliffs, overhangs, and certain other geologic features are often best suited to be made with static meshes instead of terrain.

Summary

In this chapter, you learned about the intricacies of Terrain and saw how it can be used to create interesting outdoor environments. As you have seen, the terrain system in Unreal Engine 3 is quite complicated, and mastering its use can take a great deal of patience and practice. Once you do, though, you will notice your maps beginning to take on a more polished and believable look and feel. How polished and believable is completely in your hands, as you now have the tools and the understanding of how they work at your disposal. The only limit to what environments you might create is your own dedication and imagination.

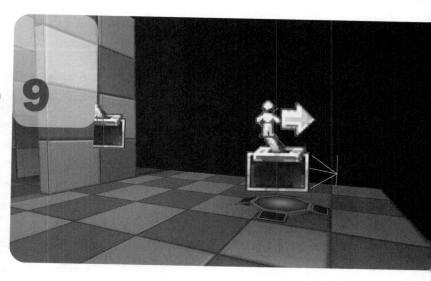

Chapter 9

Introduction to Unreal Kismet

"Kismet is a visual scripting system you can use to create complex scripted sequences quickly and easily, with surprisingly little programming knowledge." That marketing-speak is true enough, but it doesn't even begin to describe how vital Kismet is to your gameplay. Virtually every interesting thing your game needs to do during gameplay will need to use Kismet in some way. This includes tasks as simple as opening a door and as complex as launching just the right event when a player holds a specific object at a critical location in your level. This chapter reveals Kismet's immense power and shows how you can use it in your own levels.

Kismet: The Big Picture

In form, Kismet appears as a network of modules, known as sequence objects, connected by wires (see **FIGURE 9.1**). Each one of the sequence objects performs a specific function, and the wires connecting them are used to transmit information from one sequence object to another. Although these networks can appear to be very complex, you will quickly discover that their creation can be quite simple.

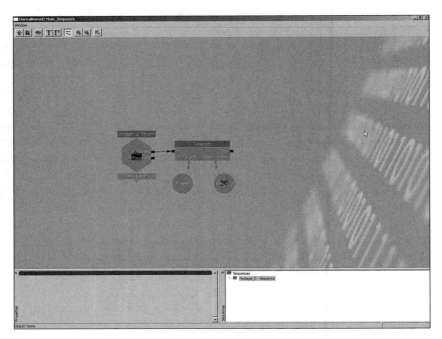

FIGURE 9.1   This simple Kismet sequence would teleport a player when he comes in contact with the trigger.

The sequence shown in Figure 9.1 could be written out in English as follows:

When the player touches Trigger_0, teleport the player to the location of Teleporter_0.

Kismet is the backbone of level interactivity, as it provides a way for artists (the non-programming type, that is) to create complicated scripts to power the levels that they have designed. The purpose of this chapter is to get you quickly in tune with how Kismet works, and enable you to create a series of gameplay-based sequences. As we progress, the tutorials you complete become more and more complex, enabling you to see how to create sequences ranging from extremely simple to moderately elaborate.

Accessing Kismet

Now that you know essentially what Kismet is, let's take a brief look at where you're going to find it in Unreal Editor, along with a quick look at its interface (see **FIGURE 9.2**).

Kismet is most directly accessed by clicking the Open Kismet button [K] located in the middle of the toolbar. You will also be able to access Kismet from within the UI Editor system, which we do not cover in this introductory text.

Main
Sequence
window

Menubar   Toolbar

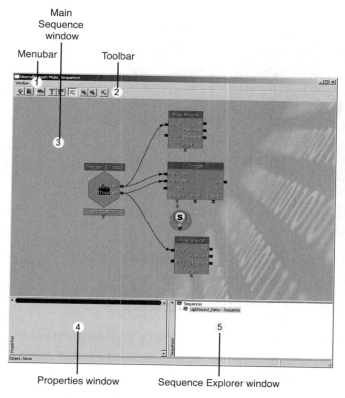

Properties window   Sequence Explorer window

FIGURE 9.2   The Kismet interface

Okay, you know generally what it is, where to find it, and a bit of what it looks like, so let's get our hands dirty and create an actual Kismet sequence! In **TUTORIAL 9.1**, you create a simple light switch using Kismet.

TUTORIAL 9.1: Triggering Lights with Kismet

1. Open Unreal Editor and launch the DM-Ch_09_KLightSound_Start.ut3 map file included with the files for this chapter. This is a simple platform level that includes only a single dim light for navigation (see **FIGURE 9.3**). We now set up a system by which we can turn on a second light and eventually play a sound.

2. In the Perspective viewport, right-click near a corner (any corner will do) of the level's main platform and choose Add Actor > Add Trigger from the Context menu.

   Immediately open the Properties window for this new actor (by double-clicking it or pressing F4). Within the Display category, set the bHidden property to False by unchecking its checkbox. This enables us to see the trigger while play testing the level (see **FIGURE 9.4**).

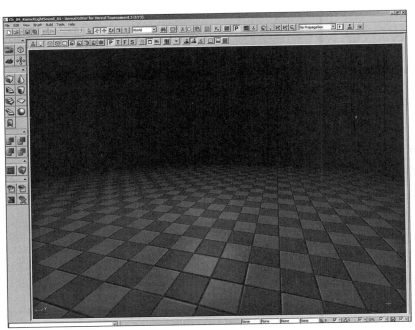

FIGURE 9.3   The DM-Ch_09_KLightSound_Start.ut3 level appears to be only a blank platform.

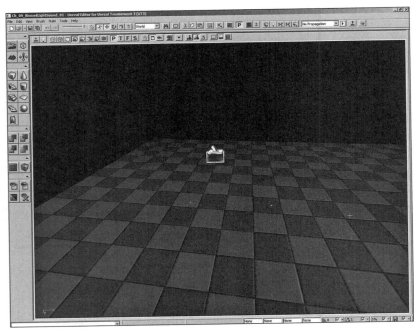

FIGURE 9.4   Here you can see the trigger placed on the corner of our level.

3. We now need a toggleable light. Follow these steps to create one:

    a. From the Unreal Editor main menubar, choose View > Browser Windows > Actor Classes.

    b. From within the Actor Classes browser, expand Light > Point Light and select PointLightToggleable (see **FIGURE 9.5**).

FIGURE 9.5   The pertinent classes have been expanded to show the PointLightToggleable actor.

    c. In the Perspective viewport, right-click on the opposite corner of your level away from the trigger, and choose Add PointLightToggleable Here.

    d. Use the Translation Widget to move the light up from the floor of the level (see **FIGURE 9.6**).

    e. Open the Properties window for the light, and under the Light category, expand LightComponent and uncheck the bEnabled property. This causes the light to be switched off when the level starts.

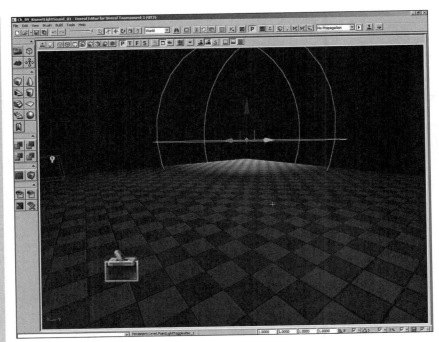

FIGURE 9.6   Place the light above the opposite corner from the trigger.

4. Click the Open Kismet button ![K] to open the Kismet Editor. We now create a simple sequence to turn our light on and off when our player comes in contact with the trigger.

5. We begin by establishing our event, which keeps track of when the player touches the trigger. In the Perspective viewport, select the trigger actor. Then, in the Kismet window, right-click on a blank area of the Sequence window and choose New Event Using Trigger_1 > Touch from the Context menu. This creates a new Touch event, enabling us to initiate actions when the player comes within the contact radius of the trigger (see **FIGURE 9.7**).

6. We now need to establish the action that takes place when the trigger is touched. In a blank area of the Sequence window, somewhere to the right of the Touch event, right-click and choose New Action > Toggle > Toggle. You can reposition the Toggle sequence object by Ctrl-dragging it, just as you move objects in the Material Editor (see **FIGURE 9.8**).

9

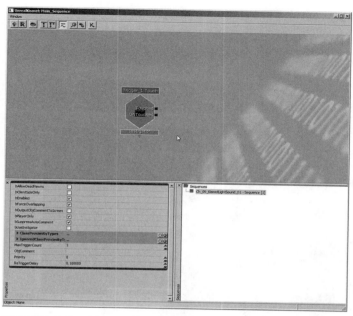

FIGURE 9.7 The new Touch event has been created.

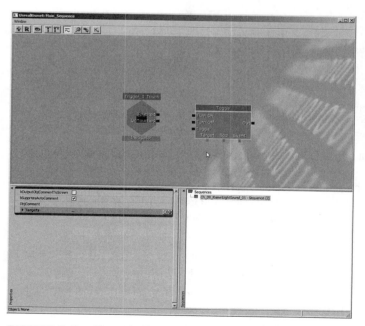

FIGURE 9.8 Place the Toggle action sequence object just to the right of the Touch object.

7. Creating the Toggle sequence object is not enough. We need to tell Kismet exactly which object we are toggling. To do this, follow these steps:

   a. In the Perspective viewport, select the PointLightToggleable created earlier.

   b. Back in the Kismet window, right-click in a blank area of the Sequence Window beneath the Toggle object and choose New Object Var Using PointLightToggleable_1. This creates a variable that is tied directly to the PointLightToggleable actor in your level (see **FIGURE 9.9**).

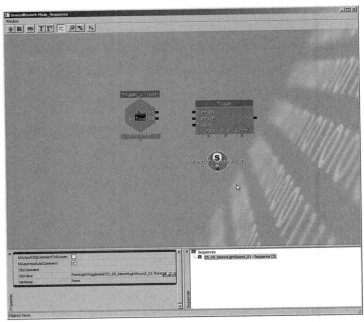

FIGURE 9.9   You now have a new object variable that designates the PointLightToggleable actor.

   c. On the Toggle object, you see a small pink input box underneath the word "Target." Drag a wire from that input and connect it to the PointLightToggleable_1 variable. The Toggle object is now connected to the light, and is able to turn it on and off (see **FIGURE 9.10**).

8. The last thing left to do is connect our Touch event to our Toggle action, which tells Kismet to Toggle the status of the light when the player comes into contact with the trigger.

   Drag a wire from the Touch output of the Touch object, and connect it to the Turn On input on the Toggle object (see **FIGURE 9.11**).

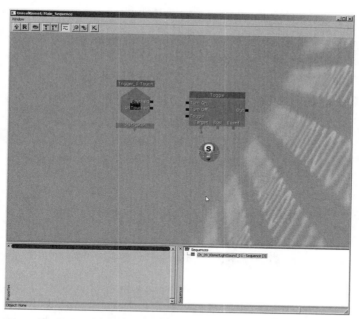

FIGURE 9.10 With the new object variable connected to the target of the Toggle, Kismet can now use the Toggle to affect PointLightToggleable_1.

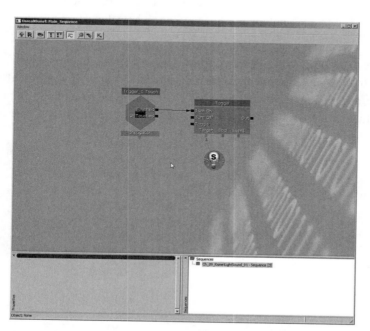

FIGURE 9.11 Once we have connected the two sequence objects together, Kismet knows to "fire" the Toggle sequence object as soon as the player touches the trigger.

9. Click the Build All button [K] and save the current level.

Try out your new trigger by testing the level. You may click the Play In Editor button located on the right side of the toolbar (we've already placed a PlayerStart for you), or right-click on the floor and choose Play From Here.

Your level begins with very dim lighting. When you run your character into the trigger, the light switches on. However, at this time, the light only turns on once and remains on indefinitely. Later, in **TUTORIAL 9.2**, we change the Touch event so that it can be fired multiple times, as well as reprogram the sequence to turn off the light when we are no longer in contact with the trigger. We also take a look at triggering sound effects when our trigger is touched and "un-touched."

END TUTORIAL 9.1

Anatomy of a Sequence Object

Now that you've created a simple sequence, let's analyze sequence objects for a moment. First, along the sides of a sequence object, you generally find a series of inputs and outputs, with inputs being on the left and outputs on the right. The inputs on the left side of a sequence object are intended to receive a signal from another sequence object. This signal activates the sequence object in some way. Some sequence objects have only a single input on the left, typically named In. Other sequence objects, such as a Toggle, contain many depending on how the sequence object functions (see **FIGURE 9.12**).

Sequence objects can also have many outputs along their right side as well. Such sequence objects typically handle different sets of sequences, and the multiple outputs enable you to choose which sequence is fired. For example, a Condition sequence object can compare two values, and use one output if Value A is greater than Value B, or another output if Value B is greater than A (see **FIGURE 9.13**).

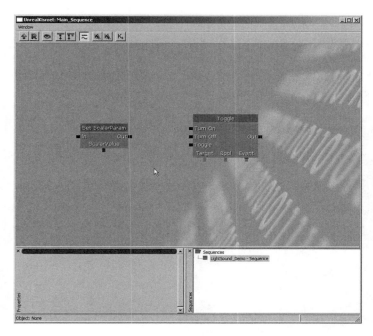

FIGURE 9.12 On the left, the Set ScalarParam sequence object has only one input, whereas the Toggle on the right contains many.

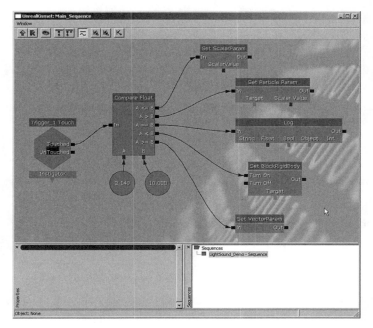

FIGURE 9.13 Here you can see a Condition sequence object, with its multiple outputs each connected to different sequences.

Along the bottom of a sequence object, you can also find a series of inputs and outputs. However, the inputs and outputs found along the bottom of a sequence object allow for interaction with variables, not with other sequence objects. These inputs and outputs can be differentiated from one another by the shape of the connector. An *input* always has a square-shaped connector, whereas an *output* has a triangular shape (see **FIGURE 9.14**).

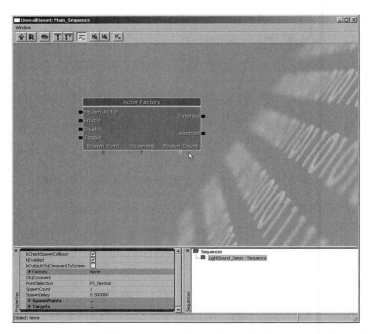

FIGURE 9.14   The sequence object shown in the picture has both inputs and outputs along the bottom, for receiving data from and sending data to different variables.

Types of Sequence Objects

There are five types of sequence object available in Kismet. They are events, actions, variables, conditions, and Matinee objects. In this section, we give a brief description of all five, starting with the three most frequently used.

Events

Events are the beginning of every Kismet sequence. An *event* is, simply put, something that happens inside your level. This can be when a player touches an object, uses a trigger, damages or destroys another actor, or a variety of other occurrences. There are also remote events, which you can fire as a part of an existing sequence. The most important thing to keep in mind is that events are the first step in a sequence, in that they "send the initial signal" (see **FIGURE 9.15**).

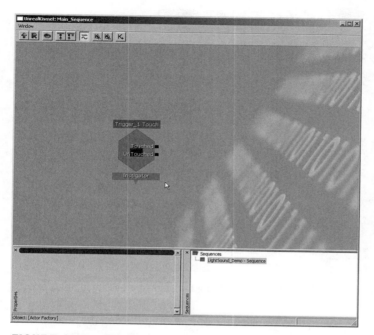

FIGURE 9.15 This Touch event has two different outputs—one for when the trigger is touched, and another for when the player breaks contact with the trigger.

Actions

Actions are the counterpart to events, and are the most frequently used type of sequence object. An action can take on many forms. In general, an action object performs a specific task when it receives a signal from an event or other sequence object. The tasks are too many to be listed here, but can include such things as changing a material instance parameter, teleporting the player to a new location, changing the value of a variable in the sequence, and many more. By stringing together a series of different actions, you can create very intricate networks (see **FIGURE 9.16**).

Variables

Just as in code scripting, *variables* are used to store certain types of data. You can store Boolean values, integers, floating point values, strings, vectors, and objects in variables. Variables are read by actions in your sequences, allowing for data input to control how the actions work. For example, if you need to teleport a player to the location of Teleporter_1, you would need one variable to represent the player and another to represent the Teleporter_1 actor.

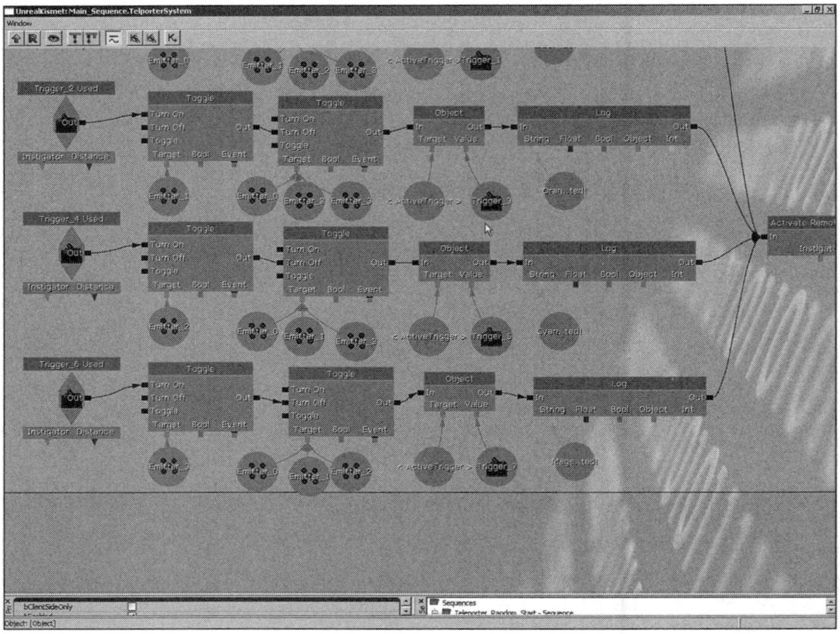

FIGURE 9.16   Here you can see a series of actions all strung together to create a complex effect.

Variables can also be written to in a sequence. By using the outputs found along the bottom of an action or event, you can store a given value in a variable for use later. Variables are color-coded as to what types of data they can store (see **FIGURE 9.17**). The color-coding is as follows:

> Boolean values: Red
>
> Integers: Cyan
>
> Floats: Blue
>
> Objects: Pink
>
> Strings: Green
>
> Vectors: Yellow
>
> Union (typeless): White

Conditions

Conditions are simply testing objects. You can use them to test whether one value is greater than or less than another, whether one object variable is equal to another, and much more. Conditions do not directly affect your level, but instead control the flow of your Kismet sequence, enabling you to trigger one part of a sequence or another based on a certain condition (see **FIGURE 9.18**).

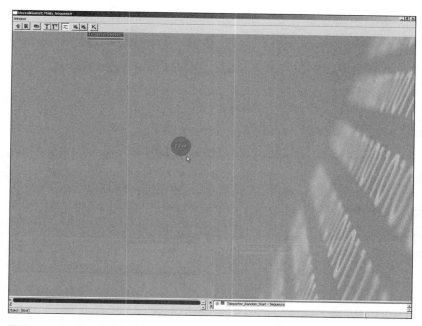

FIGURE 9.17 Variables appear as small circles containing some sort of label.

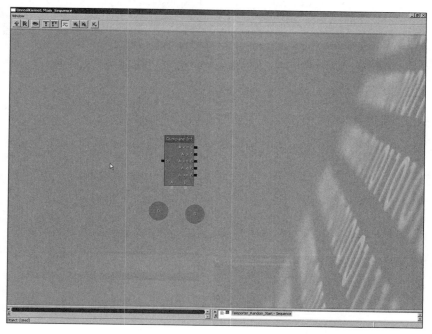

FIGURE 9.18 This condition object is testing the value of two integers.

Matinee

Matinee objects are used to control matinee sequences in game. Although it is true that Matinee and Kismet are inexorably intertwined in Unreal Engine 3.0, we do not go into great detail on using Matinee until Chapter 10, "Unreal Matinee."

Kismet Sequence Flow

Although working with Kismet is fairly simple, there are a few things that you must understand about how data is passed along its networks. First and foremost, with a few exceptions, Kismet relies on two main things: events and actions. An event calls on an action, which can then call on other actions, trigger remote events, and so on.

The most important aspect to understand about Kismet sequence flow is that all actions must be "fired" by something, usually by an event. An action sitting by itself is never activated, and therefore never affect the level. This demonstrates the vital importance of the In and Out connections on the left and right side of actions and events.

As a fun little analogy, you can think actions as explosives, events as detonators, and the lines connecting them as the wiring between the two. By itself, an action, or explosive, does nothing. When you wire it to an event, or detonator, you get an interesting effect. When you wire a detonator to a series of explosives that in turn ignite other detonators and explosives, you get a glorious effect that can truly bring the house down (see **FIGURE 9.19**)!

In **TUTORIAL 9.2**, we see how we can supplement our original sequence we created in **TUTORIAL 9.1** by simultaneously playing a sound when we toggle the light on and off.

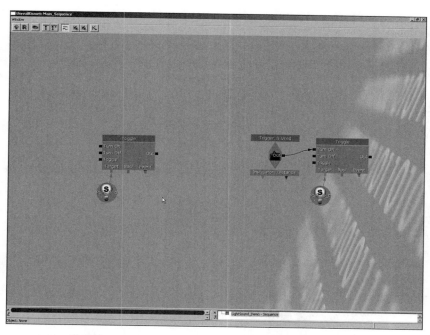

FIGURE 9.19   The sequence on the right has only an action, meaning that it is not activated. The sequence on the left is activated via a Used event, meaning that it fires when a player uses a particular trigger actor.

TUTORIAL 9.2: Repeated Triggers and Firing Simultaneous Actions; Playing Sounds While Toggling Lights

1. Continue from **TUTORIAL 9.1** by opening the DM-Ch_09_KLightSound_Start.ut3 level you saved. If you have not yet completed **TUTORIAL 9.1**, you can open Ch_09_KLightSound_01.ut3 map included with the files for this chapter.

2. We need to set up our trigger system so that it can be initiated an infinite number of times. However, this does us no good unless we take into account the ability to also switch the light back off. Follow these steps to reprogram our sequence so that the light can be turned on and off based on whether or not the player is touching the trigger:

   a. Click the Open Kismet button K, to open the Kismet Editor.

   b. Select the Touch event. In the Properties window of the Kismet Editor, set the MaxTriggerCount property to 0 (you may have to scroll the properties area down to see it). This effectively removes the maximum number of times the event can be fired (see **FIGURE 9.20**).

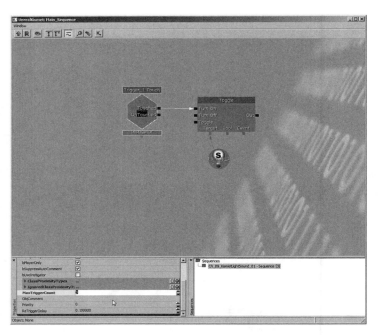

FIGURE 9.20   Here you can see the Properties window of the Kismet Editor. Notice that the MaxTriggerCount for the Trigger object has been set to 0.

    c. Drag a wire from the UnTouched output of the Touch event to the Turn Off input on the Toggle object. This means that when our player is no longer in contact with the trigger, the light automatically switches off (see **FIGURE 9.21**).

3. Save your progress and test your level. You'll now notice that the light turns on when the trigger is touched, and turns back off when you step away from the trigger. Exit the Play In Editor window by pressing Esc when finished.

4. We now enhance our example to play sounds. In the Generic browser, open the Chapter_09_KismetContent.upk package included on the DVD with the files for this chapter. Inside this package, you will find a group named SoundCues (see **FIGURE 9.22**).

> **TIP**
>
> As an alternate method to achieve a very similar result, you could connect both the Touch and UnTouch outputs to the Toggle input of the Toggle object!

9

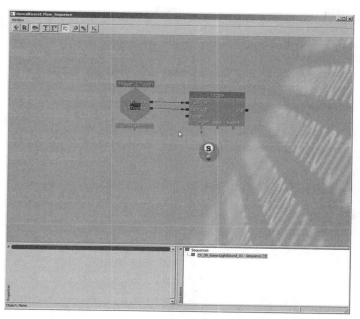

FIGURE 9.21 Now that we have wired UnTouched to Turn Off, Kismet disables the light as soon as the player steps away from the trigger.

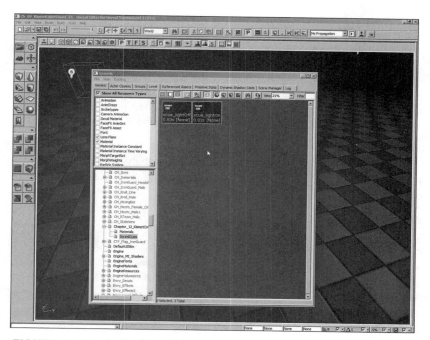

FIGURE 9.22 In the Generic browser, open the KismetSounds package and expand the SoundCues group. Make sure you see the sCue_lightOn and sCue_lightOff objects.

5. Time to bring these sounds into our Kismet sequence:

a. In the Kismet Editor, right-click on a blank area of the sequence window directly above the Toggle object. In the Context menu, choose New Action > Sound > Play Sound. This creates a new Play Sound sequence object (see **FIGURE 9.23**).

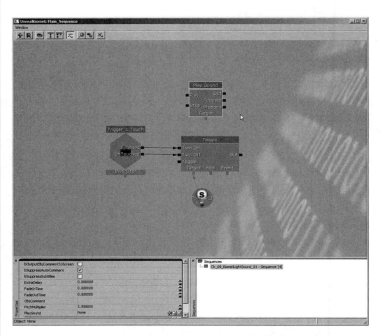

FIGURE 9.23   Place this first Play Sound object just above the Toggle object.

b. Go to the Generic browser, and within the Chapter_09_KismetContent.upk package, expand the SoundCues group. Select the scue_lightOn sound cue object.

c. Back in the Kismet Editor, select the top Play Sound object. In the Properties window of the Kismet Editor, click on the Play Sound property and then click the Use Current Selection in Browser button [K]. This should place the scue_lightOn sound cue into the property.

d. Drag a wire from the Play input of the upper Play Sound object to the Touched output of the Touch event. The lightOn sound now plays when we touch the trigger. Note that we did the wiring backwards this time (see **FIGURE 9.24**).

> **NOTE**
>
> When playing sounds using Kismet, you can only use SoundCue objects—not WAV files.

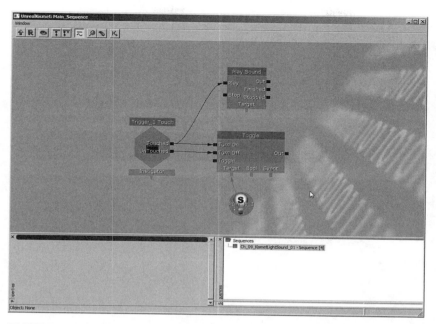

FIGURE 9.24   The Play Sound object has been wired into the Touch object.

    e. Using the same process described previously, create a new Play Sound object, placed below the Toggle object. Connect the scue_lightOff sound cue to this Play Sound object, and connect its Play input to the UnTouched output of the Touch event. This causes the lightOff sound to play when we break contact with the trigger (see **FIGURE 9.25**).

6. Save and test your level. Notice that one sound plays when the light comes on, and another sound plays when the light goes off.

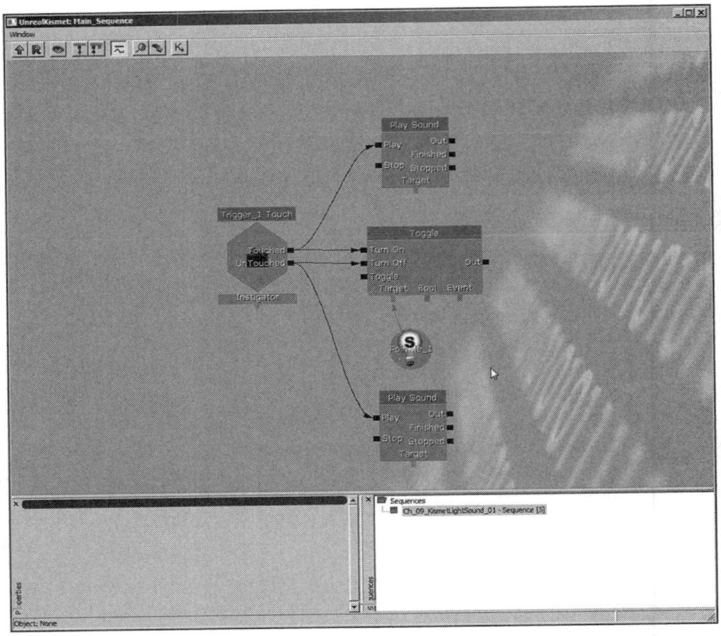

FIGURE 9.25   Here you can see the second Play Sound object below the trigger, connected to the UnTouched output of the Touch object.

END TUTORIAL 9.2

You've now seen how you can branch off a sequence so that you can perform many different actions in unison. Throughout the rest of the chapter, you will see a variety of other gameplay-oriented sequences, with each getting more intricate than the last.

We start by showing how you can change a material parameter during gameplay through the use of Material Instances. Although this example is fairly simple, you can use it in conjunction with what you learned in the chapters over materials to control a variety of different material effects. For more information on materials, please see Chapter 6, "Introduction to Materials."

In **TUTORIAL 9.3**, we show how to use Kismet to affect materials in your levels during gameplay.

TUTORIAL 9.3: Using Kismet with Simple Material Instances

1. Launch the Unreal Editor and open the DM-Ch_09_KMatInst_Start.ut3 map included with the files for this chapter. You see a small, glowing, red sphere. The material on this sphere is connected to a material instance, which gives us access to change its color from red to blue (see **FIGURE 9.26**).

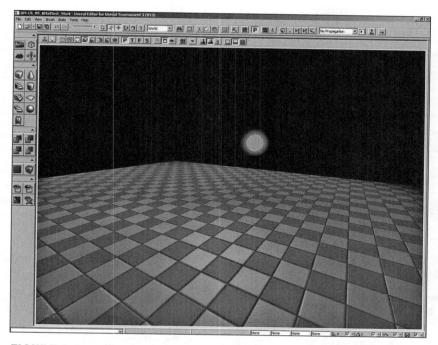

FIGURE 9.26   The MaterialInstance_Demo shows a simple level in which we change the color of a glowing sphere by affecting its material instance with Kismet.

2. Add in a new Trigger object just across the level from the sphere, and uncheck its bHidden property (remember, it's under the Display category) so that it is visible during gameplay (see **FIGURE 9.27**).

3. Select the trigger and open the Kismet Editor. Right-click and choose New Event Using Trigger_1 > Used from the Context menu. This initiates the sequence whenever the player walks up to the trigger, looks at it, and presses the Use button (E key by default).

Set the MaxTriggerCount property for this event to 0. Then, uncheck bAimToInteract. This keeps players from having to look directly at the trigger when it is used, enabling them to watch the sphere instead (see **FIGURE 9.28**).

BEGIN NOTE

This level requires the Chapter_09_KismetContent. upk package, included with the files on the DVD for this chapter. If the sphere appears gray instead of red, locate and open this package, and then reload the level.

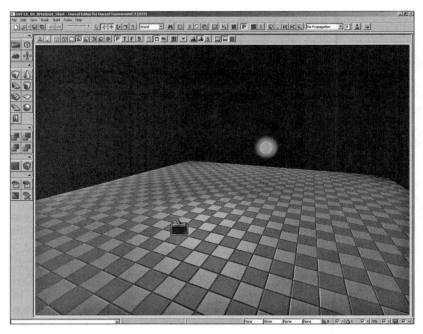

FIGURE 9.27   The new trigger has been placed just across from the sphere.

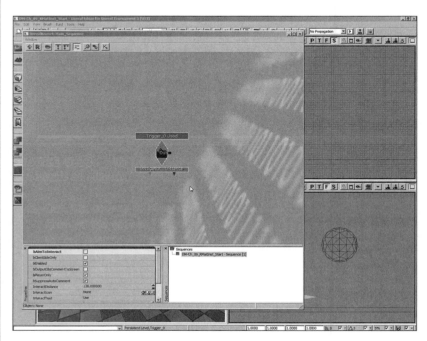

FIGURE 9.28   We have now created a new Used event in the Kismet Editor.

4. What we want to have happen is that when the player uses the trigger, the ball changes from red to blue, and then back to red after a delay of about 2 seconds. More precisely, we want to change the value of the RedBlue scalar parameter within the material from 0 to 1, and then back to 0. We start just by changing the color to red:

  a. Right-click in the Sequence window to the right of the Used event, and choose New Action > Material Instance > Set ScalarParam from the Context menu (see **FIGURE 9.29**).

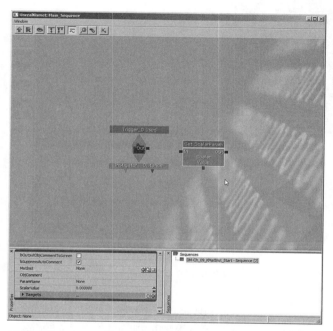

FIGURE 9.29   Place the new Set ScalarParam object just to the right of the Used object.

  b. In the Generic browser, open the Chapter_09_KismetContent.upk package and select the mat_RedBluePulsar_inst material instance constant. Once selected, you can close the Generic browser.

  c. Select the new Set ScalarParam object, and in the Properties window of the Kismet Editor, select the MatInst parameter and click the Use Current Selection in Browser button **K**.

  d. Click on the ParamName property, and type **redblue** for its value. You will notice its case change to say RedBlue. This is an indication that Unreal recognized the parameter's name (see **FIGURE 9.30**).

> **NOTE**
>
> If nothing appears when you click the Use Current Selection in Browser button, it is possible that you selected the parent material instead of the material instance. If this is the case, make sure to go back into the Generic browser and open up the material instance constant.

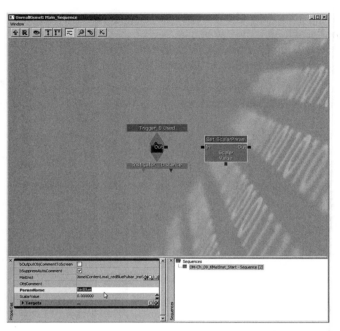

FIGURE 9.30   Here you can see that the RedBlue parameter has been entered into the ParamName property.

e. Set the ScalarValue property to 1.

f. Drag a wire from the Out output of the Used event to the In input on the Set ScalarParam object (see **FIGURE 9.31**).

5. If we were to test the level at this point, all we could do is turn the light to blue. We now need to put in the delay system that sets the color back to red. Exit the Play In Editor window (Esc) and open the Kismet Editor.

a. Duplicate the existing Set ScalarParam object by using Ctrl-W.

b. Move this duplicate to the right of the original, leaving enough room for another sequence object to be placed in between (see **FIGURE 9.32**).

c. Set the ScalarValue property of this new Set ScalarParam to 0, which changes the color back to red.

> **NOTE**
>
> You may test the level at this point, but remember to stand close to the trigger before hitting the Use (E) key.

> **TIP**
>
> Kismet objects may be duplicated by using Ctrl-W, but you can also copy/paste them with Ctrl-C, Ctrl-V!

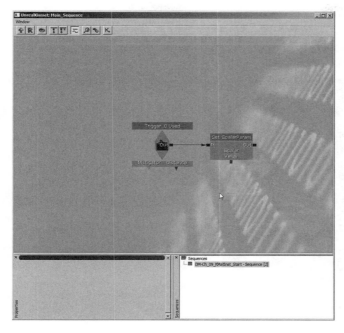

FIGURE 9.31   The Used object has now been wired to the new Set ScalarParam object, enabling us to change the color of the material.

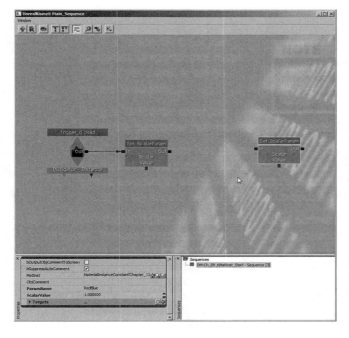

FIGURE 9.32   You can now see the duplicate of the Set ScalarParam. We use this new object to set the color of our material back to red.

d. Right-click between the two Set ScalarParam objects and choose New Action > Misc > Delay from the Context menu. Place this new object directly in-between the two Set ScalarParams (see **FIGURE 9.33**).

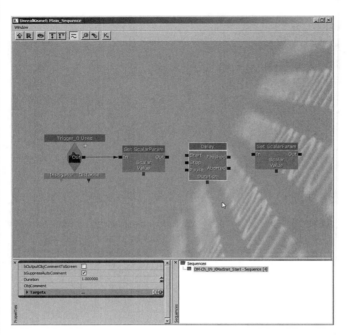

FIGURE 9.33   The new Delay object causes a timed delay to take place between when the material is changed to blue and when it automatically resets to red.

e. Select the new Delay object, and in the Properties window of the Kismet Editor, set the Duration property to 2.

f. Drag a wire from the Out of the first Set ScalarParam object into the Start input of the delay. Then, drag another wire from the Finished output of the delay in to the In input of the second Set ScalarParam (see **FIGURE 9.34**).

6. If you test your level now, you will see that if you use the trigger, the color of the sphere changes to blue, then hold for two seconds, and then switch back. However, we have one more problem. If you exit the level while the sphere is blue, it is still blue when you re-enter the level. Let's fix this now:

> **TIP**
>
> A simpler way to achieve the delay effect would be to simply connect the duplicated Set ScalarParameter to the Out of the first, and then right-click on either connection point and choose Set Activate Delay from the Context menu. This enables you to set a timed delay for that input or output. The Delay node is used in this example merely for the sake of practice!

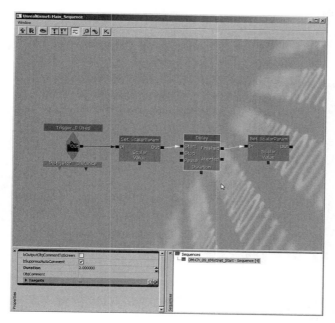

FIGURE 9.34 The delay has now been wired into the sequence.

a. Right-click on a blank area of the Sequence window and choose New Event > Level Startup (see **FIGURE 9.35**).

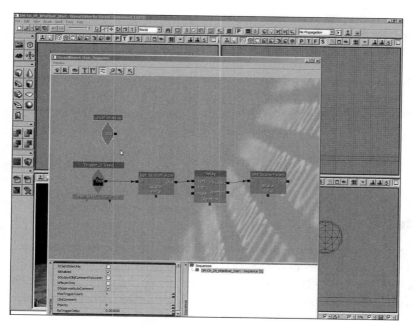

FIGURE 9.35 Place this new Level Startup object above the main sequence.

b. Drag a wire from the Out output of this event into the In input of the second Set ScalarParam, which is currently at the end of your previous sequence (see **FIGURE 9.36**).

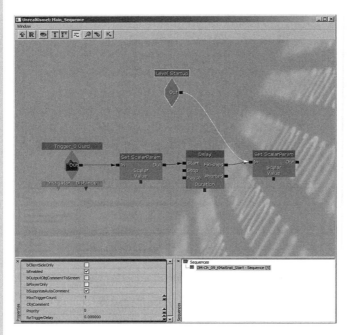

FIGURE 9.36   Connect the Level Beginning's output to the input of the second Set ScalarParam object.

In this way, you are reusing an existing sequence object to reset your color, rather than creating a new one. You are, of course, welcome to use a new Set ScalarParam object if you like, which may help with readability of the sequence.

7. Save and test your level.

END TUTORIAL 9.3

Simple Kismet Sequences

Another important operation you may need to perform in your levels is the spawning of actors. As an example, perhaps you need a series of objects to spawn when your player enters a specific room. In this next proof-of-concept level, we spawn rigid bodies whenever a player uses a trigger. We also place a second trigger that enables the player to delete all rigid bodies in the level, through the use of an object list.

An *object list* is a type of object variable that, instead of storing a single object, contains a list of many objects. You can use a series of actions to populate, control, and clear this list throughout your sequence. Using an object list can have great advantages over creating many different object variables, especially when spawning new objects into the level.

TUTORIAL 9.4 demonstrates two important concepts for using Kismet. The first is the spawning of actors, which enables the designer to add objects into a level during gameplay. We also show how to log information during a Kismet sequence, which can be crucial when trying to debug errors in your Kismet sequences.

TUTORIAL 9.4: Spawning Actors with Kismet and Logging Sequences

1. Launch the Unreal Editor and open the DM-Ch_09_KSpawn_Start.ut3 map included with the files for this chapter. This is a tall level with a series of pegs against one wall. You notice some simple placeable actors near the top of the level, and two triggers near one corner.

2. In the Front viewport, select the leftmost trigger (Trigger_0), and in the Kismet Editor, right-click and choose Create New Event using Trigger_0 > Used to create a new Used event with this trigger.

   Set the MaxTriggerCount property to 0, and uncheck bAimToInteract.

3. Repeat all of Step 1 to create a second Used event for Trigger_1, and move it somewhere below the first. Don't forget the MaxTriggerCount and bAimToInteract properties (see **FIGURE 9.37**)!

> **NOTE**
>
> This level requires the Chapter_09_KismetContent. upk package, included with the files on the DVD for this chapter. If necessary, locate and open this package, and then reload the level.

4. The first thing we need to do is spawn our actor. The TestPlaceableActors located near the top of the level serve as spawn points so that we can get some level of randomization in spawn positions. Follow these steps to get the proper actor in place:

   a. Right-click in a blank area to the right of the Used event for Trigger_0, and choose New Action > Actor > Actor Factory.

   b. Connect the Out output of the Used event for Trigger_0 to the Spawn Actor input of the Actor Factory. This causes a new actor to be spawned every time the player uses the trigger (see **FIGURE 9.38**).

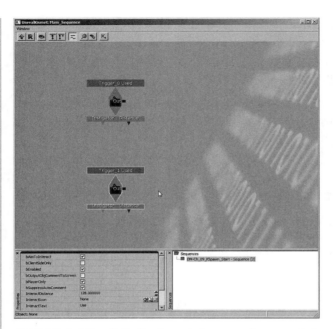

FIGURE 9.37   Both Used events have now been created.

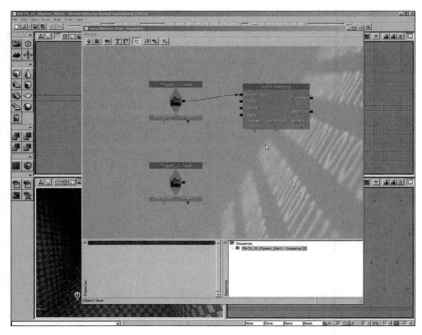

FIGURE 9.38   The actor factory has now been attached to the Used event for Trigger_0.

5. Next, we establish the kind of actor we want to spawn.

    a. Select the Actor Factory, and in the Properties window, locate the Factory property, and click the Add New Object button ![icon]. From the Context menu, choose ActorFactoryRigidBody. A list of new properties appears for the rigid body (see **FIGURE 9.39**).

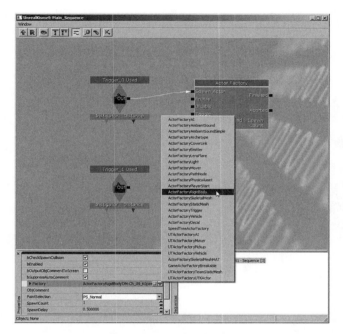

FIGURE 9.39   Here you can see the Context menu that appears when you click the Add New Object button.

    b. Locate the StaticMesh property, and use the Generic browser to set the property to the sm_simpleSphere mesh, included in the KismetSpawn package.

6. Now we need to set up where we want the rigid bodies to spawn.

    a. With the Actor Factory selected, go to the Properties window and find the SpawnPoints property.

    b. Click the blank area next to the property, and then click the Add New Item button ![icon] ten times to create ten different spawn points.

    c. Enter the following information into each index for the spawn points (see **FIGURE 9.40**):

    [0]: TestPlaceableActor_0

    [1]: TestPlaceableActor_1

[**2**]: TestPlaceableActor_2

[**3**]: TestPlaceableActor_3

[**4**]: TestPlaceableActor_4

[**5**]: TestPlaceableActor_5

[**6**]: TestPlaceableActor_6

[**7**]: TestPlaceableActor_7

[**8**]: TestPlaceableActor_8

[**9**]: TestPlaceableActor_9

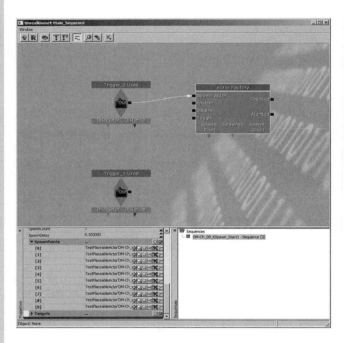

FIGURE 9.40   Your fully populated spawn points list should appear like so.

7. Our spawn points are in place, and at this point, we can effectively spawn a new rigid body each time we use Trigger_0. However, it would be nice if we could keep all of our rigid bodies in a list, so that we can destroy them all at once using Trigger_1. Use the following steps to use Kismet to create the list during gameplay:

   a. Right-click to the right of the Actor Factory object and choose New Action > Object List > Modify ObjectList from the Context menu.

b. Connect the Finished output of the Actor Factory to the Add To List input of the Modify ObjectList sequence object (see **FIGURE 9.41**).

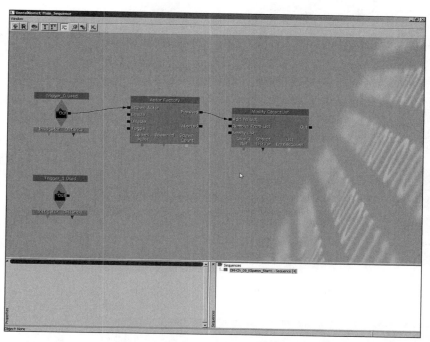

FIGURE 9.41   The Modify ObjectList is now attached to the Actor Factory sequence object.

c. We now create the list itself. Right-click beneath the Modify ObjectList sequence object and choose New Variable > Object > Object List from the Context menu. Connect the ObjectListVar output to this new variable (see **FIGURE 9.42**).

d. We now need to provide an object that we can place into the list. Right-click beneath the Actor Factory object and choose New Variable > Object > Object. Connect the Actor Factory's Spawned output to this new variable, and connect the Modify ObjectList's ObjectRef input to it as well (see **FIGURE 9.43**).

> **NOTE**
>
> You'll see three question marks (???) located within the new object variable. This is because we have yet to assign it a value in Kismet. However, you'll also notice that the Spawned output uses a triangle instead of a square, meaning it is outputting a value. The result of all of this is that the Actor Factory actually *sends* the name of the object into the blank object variable, and the Modify ObjectList object then *reads* that name and applies it to the list.

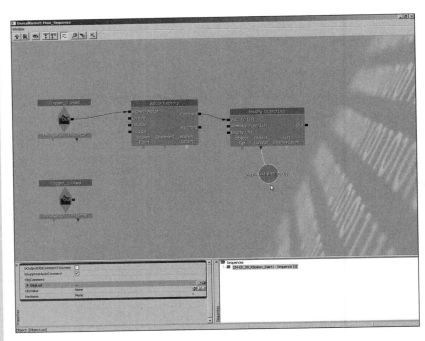

FIGURE 9.42   Our object list variable is now in place.

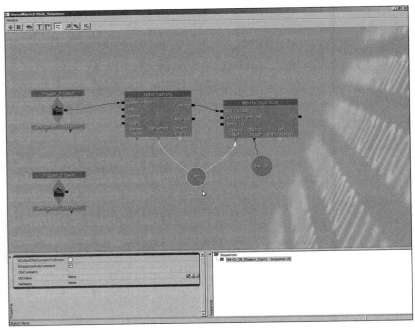

FIGURE 9.43   We now pass the current value of the Object variable into an entry of our object list.

8. We now need to log to the screen how many rigid bodies are in the level at any given moment.

   a. Right-click in a blank area to the right of the Modify ObjectList sequence object, and choose New Action > Misc > Log.

   b. Connect the Out output of the Modify ObjectList sequence object to the In input of the Log (see **FIGURE 9.44**).

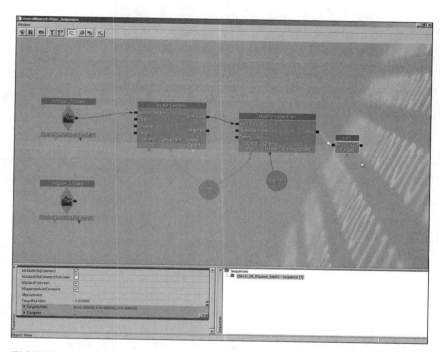

FIGURE 9.44   The Log object sends information to the screen during gameplay. It is most often used for debugging purposes.

   c. We need to create a new Int variable to store the number, but this time we're going to use a shortcut. Right-click on the small teal triangle beneath the List EntriesCount output of the Modify ObjectList sequence object. From the Context menu that appears, choose Create New Int Variable. You can do this with any color-coded output!

   d. Now we need to send this information to our Log. However, if you look closely, you will notice that the Log currently has no inputs that accept Int data. We need to expose it.

      Right-click on the Log and choose Expose Variable > Int – Int* from the Context menu. You will see an Int input appear on the bottom of the Log.

> **e.** Connect this new Int input into the Int variable (see **FIGURE 9.45**).

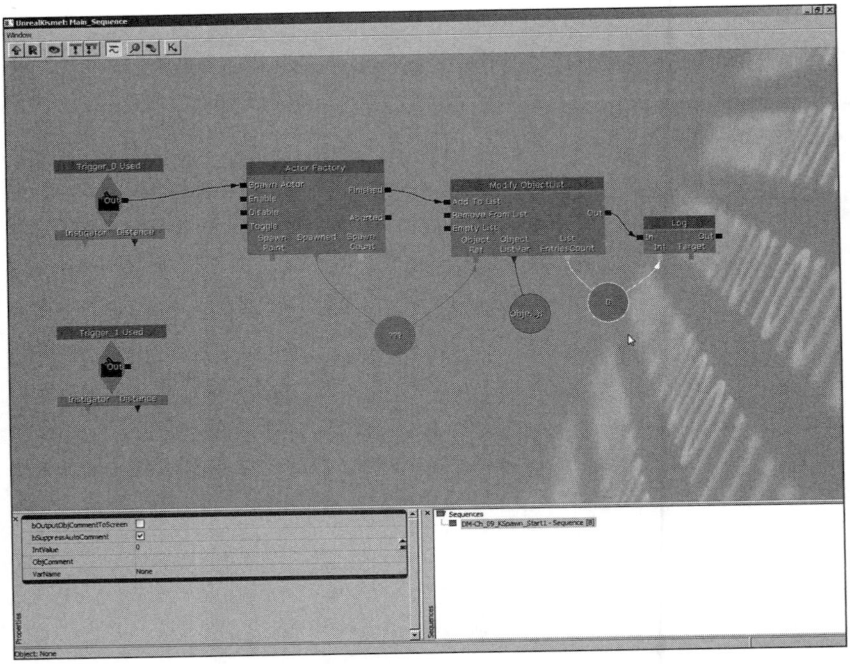

FIGURE 9.45   With our variables in place and connected, we can now output the number of rigid bodies in the list to the screen.

> **9.** We're almost finished. Now, all we need to do is use the objects contained in the object list to destroy all the rigid bodies in the level.
>
> > **a.** Right-click to the right of the Used event for Trigger_1. In the Context menu, choose New Action > Actor > Destroy.
> >
> > **b.** Connect the Out output of the Trigger_1 Used event to the Destroy's In input.
> >
> > **c.** Connect the Destroy's Out output to the Empty List input on the Modify ObjectList sequence object.
> >
> > **d.** Connect the Destroy's Target input to the object list variable (see **FIGURE 9.46**).
>
> **10.** If you test the level right now, you'd see that the spheres were all just a little big. Fix this with the following steps:
>
> > **a.** In the Kismet Editor, select the Actor Factory and look under the Factor properties. Find the DrawScale3D properties and set the following:
> >
> > > **X:** 0.5
> > >
> > > **Y:** 0.5
> > >
> > > **Z:** 0.5

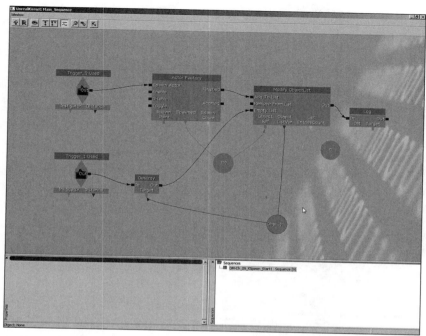

FIGURE 9.46   Your completed network should look something like this.

11. Save and test your results. You should now be able to use Trigger_0 to create as many rigid bodies as you like (until you overstress your computer, that is) and then simply delete them all by using Trigger_1.

END TUTORIAL 9.4

Commenting Kismet Sequences

Before we move on and take a look at more complex sequences, let's take a look at commenting. Just as in code-based scripting, commenting can play a vital role in enabling you to easily read what each sequence object is doing in your Kismet sequence. Comments in Kismet work very similarly to the Material Editor, in that you may create comment boxes that contain a series of objects.

However, you need not always draw a box for a comment. If you like, you can create a free-floating comment in your sequence that you can place anywhere. Each comment is an object in itself, and you can activate and deactivate its box using the bDrawBox property.

Each sequence object can also hold its own comment, without having to use a separate comment object. Every Kismet sequence object has an ObjComment property, into which you can input any string (word or phrase of alphanumeric characters) to describe what the object is doing in your sequence (see **FIGURE 9.47**).

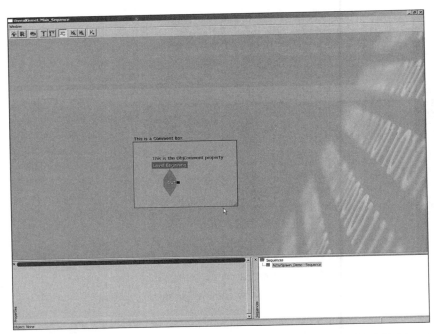

FIGURE 9.47   This figure shows a comment box, enclosing an object that is using its own ObjComment property.

Intermediate Kismet Sequences

In **TUTORIAL 9.5**, we begin a complex sequence by creating a list of comments. As we progress, you can activate the boxes for these, and use them to enclose the sequence objects that are associated to each comment. In this way, you can essentially write out your sequence in English before you even begin. This means that comments can function both as a to-do list, and as a way to keep your sequence organized while you work.

You will be creating an effect that should be fairly familiar to fans of the Unreal game series. We touch a trigger, which turns off all the lights in a hallway. Then, a few seconds later, the lights all come back on, one at a time, but they will be red instead of white.

We change the color of the lights by using a material applied as a light function. This process is already completed when you open the level. For more information on using light functions, please see Chapter 7, "Introduction to Lighting."

When we launch the level, you will notice that we are using interpolation actors for the light meshes. This is because we toggle their visibility in the level. If a mesh needs to change dynamically during gameplay, you need to use an interpActor instead of a static mesh, which cannot change.

When writing programming code, adding comments can help keep you on track and prevent confusion. Kismet is no different. In **TUTORIAL 9.5**, we create a list of comments to use as guidelines to construct the sequence.

TUTORIAL 9.5: Constructing Intermediate Lighting Sequences, Part I: Commenting

1. Launch the Unreal Editor and open the DM-Ch_09_KUnrealOne_Start.ut3 map included with the files for this chapter. This level shows a hallway lit by a series of simple light fixtures. You'll also see that a trigger and a PlayerStart actor have been added at one end, and a Note actor added at the other. In **TUTORIAL 9.5**, we focus solely on the creation of the sequence, not the assets involved.

2. As stated earlier, it's a good idea to have your sequence planned out before you dive into Kismet. We're going to start by creating a series of comments, and using the structure of those comments to guide the sequence creation process. In this way, we can work with Kismet very much like a programmer.

> **NOTE**
>
> This level requires the Chapter_09_KismetContent. upk package, included with the files on the DVD for this chapter. If necessary, locate and open this package, and then reload the level.

Open the Kismet Editor and right-click a blank area. Choose New Comment from the Context menu, and type the following for the comment: **Hide light meshes and turn off all lights** (see **FIGURE 9.48**).

3. Repeat step 2 to create separate comments for each of these statements as well, forming a list within the Kismet Editor (see **FIGURE 9.49**):

   ▶ Wait three seconds before continuing.

   ▶ Change the color of lighting objects while the lights are off.

   ▶ Show lighting objects in sequence.

   ▶ Spawn a bad guy.

   ▶ Initial level conditions.

> **NOTE**
>
> If you have a comment selected when you create another, Kismet creates the subsequent comment with its comment box active, thinking that you wanted to create a comment box around the original comment object. If this happens, just uncheck the bDrawBox property on the comment object.

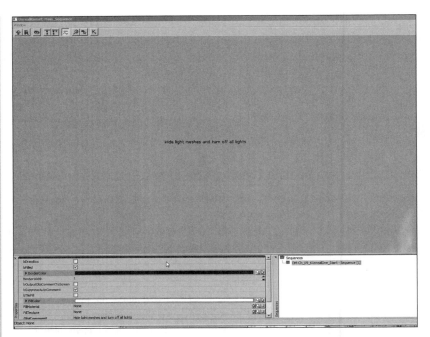

FIGURE 9.48   Your new comment appears like so in the Kismet Editor.

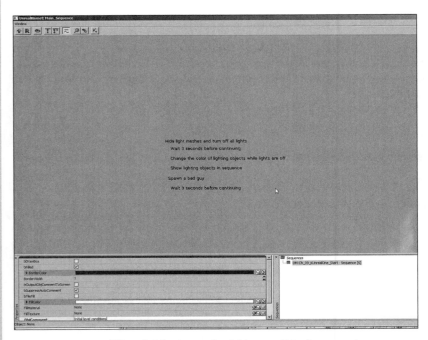

FIGURE 9.49   When finished, you should have a list of comments.

4. In the Perspective viewport, select the Trigger object located at the end of the hallway.

5. Back in the Kismet Editor, create a new Touch sequence object using the selected trigger. Position this object above your list of comments (see **FIGURE 9.50**).

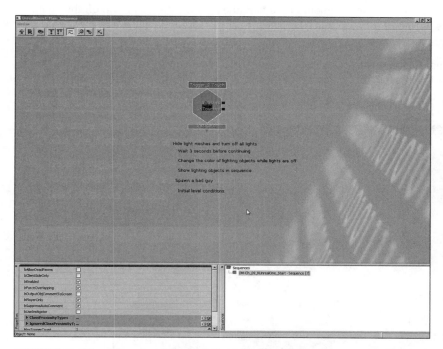

FIGURE 9.50 Wrap up by creating the initial Touch event for your level's trigger.

6. Save your map progress. Although we have not yet created a functioning part to the sequence, we now have a "to do" list that we can follow, making the remainder of the production much easier. When creating complex sequences on your own, using this method can help you and others on your team keep your sequences and their production far more organized.

END TUTORIAL 9.5

Now that we have our comments in place, we can use them to determine what it is that we will do next in our sequence. We start by creating an object list that contains all our lights, and use it to turn all the lights off when we touch the trigger.

Our comments are now in place. In **TUTORIAL 9.6**, we establish a list of objects that will be affected by the sequence. We do this using an Object List, which can contain multiple objects, rather than using individual object variables.

TUTORIAL 9.6: Constructing Intermediate Lighting Sequences, Part II: Object Lists

1. Continue from **TUTORIAL 9.5**, or open the DM-Ch_09_KUnrealOne_01.ut3 map included with the files for this chapter.

2. The first thing in our list of comments is to hide the light meshes and turn off the lights. For starters, we need to make sure the player does not see the light fixture meshes when the lights go out.

   In the Kismet Editor, right-click a blank area of the Sequence window somewhere to the right of the Touch event and choose New Action > Toggle > Toggle Hidden. Place this object to the right of the Touch object created in **TUTORIAL 9.5** (see **FIGURE 9.51**).

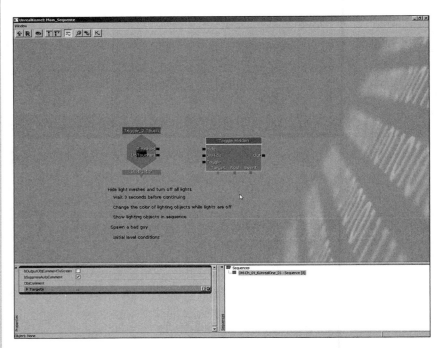

FIGURE 9.51   Place the Toggle Hidden object in your sequence like so.

3. We now need a way to tell this object that it hides all the light meshes. Although we could select all the meshes and create object variables from all of them at once from the right mouse menu, it is easier to read and manage later if we simply use an object list.

   Right-click beneath the new Toggle Hidden object and choose New Variable > Object > Object List (see **FIGURE 9.52**).

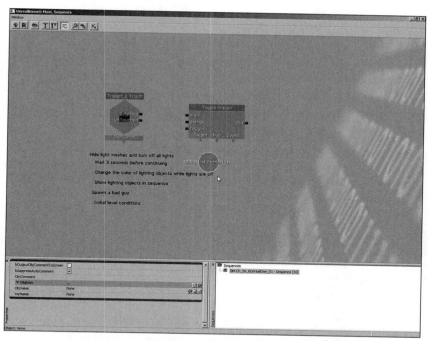

FIGURE 9.52   The object list should be created just beneath the Toggle Hidden object.

4. The object list is a single variable that contains a list of objects. In this case, it contains all of our light meshes. Populating the list is easy; just follow these steps:

    a. In the top viewport, select one of the light mesh InterpActors (any one will do).

    b. Right-click on the mesh after it is selected and choose Select All InterpActor.

    c. In the Kismet Editor, right-click on the object list and choose Insert Selected Actors into Object List (see **FIGURE 9.53**).

5. Connect the Target input of the Toggle Hidden to this new object list. Then, connect the Touch output of the Touch object to the Hide input of the Toggle Hidden (see **FIGURE 9.54**).

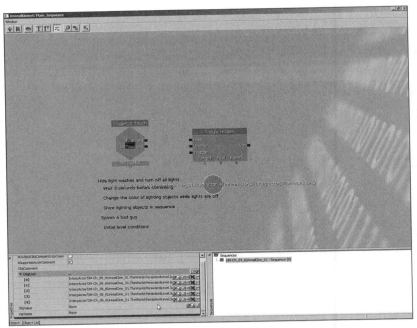

FIGURE 9.53   Your final object list properties should appear as shown.

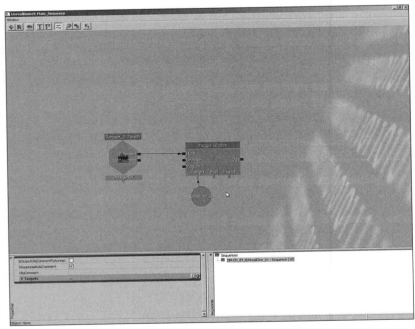

FIGURE 9.54   The Toggle Hidden and object list are now wired into the sequence.

6. We now need to create a way to turn off the lights. Follow these steps:

> **a.** Right-click a blank area to the right of the Toggle Hidden object, and choose New Action > Toggle > Toggle from the Context menu (see **FIGURE 9.55**).

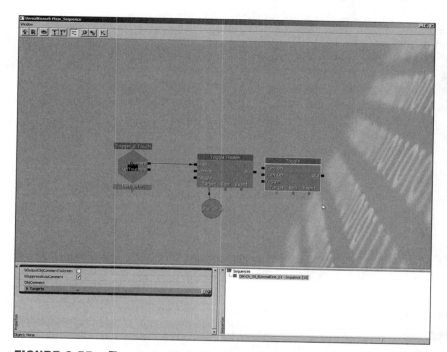

FIGURE 9.55   The new toggle is placed just to the right of the previous Toggle Hidden sequence object.

> **b.** This time, we populate the list just after we create it. In the top viewport, select all five of the lights across the top of the hallway.
>
> **c.** In the Kismet Editor, right-click underneath the toggle and choose New Variable > Object > Object List from the Context menu.
>
> **d.** Immediately right-click on the new object list and choose Insert Selected Actors into Object List (see **FIGURE 9.56**).
>
> **e.** Connect the Target input of the toggle to this new object list variable.
>
> **f.** Connect the Out output of the Toggle Hidden object to the Turn Off input of the Toggle object (see **FIGURE 9.57**).

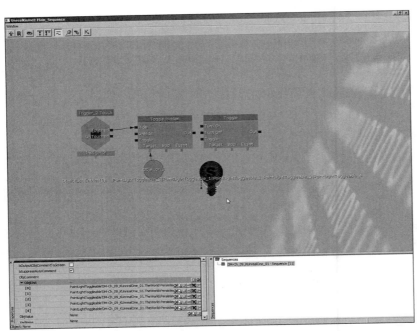

FIGURE 9.56   Your new object list contains all the pointLightToggleable actors in the level.

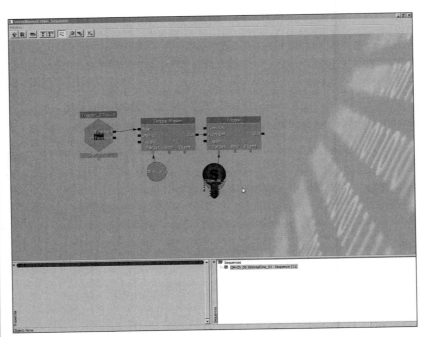

FIGURE 9.57   The toggle has now been connected into the sequence to turn off all the lights.

7. Finally, let's put our first comment in place.

    a. Select the Hide light meshes and turn off all lights comment (it will not highlight, but it will be selected if you click on it), and Ctrl-drag it above the Toggle Hidden and Toggle objects.

    b. With the comment selected, check the bDrawBox property. This displays a box with which you can surround all objects involved with the comment.

    c. You likely need to expand this box's size. However, the triangle handle used to resize it may be hidden from view behind one of your sequence objects. Set the SizeX property to some size large enough to expose the handle. We used a value of 600.

    d. Once the handle is exposed, use it to resize the box to surround the Toggle Hidden and Toggle objects, along with their associated variables (see **FIGURE 9.58**).

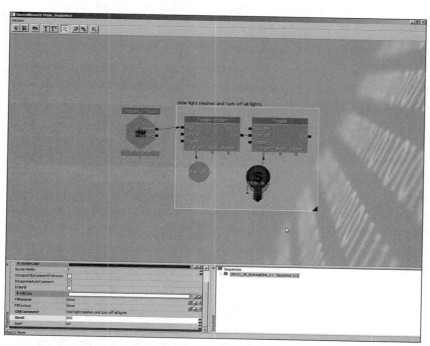

FIGURE 9.58 When finished, your comment box should surround all the sequence objects involved with turning off the lights and hiding the light meshes.

8. Save and test the level. The only effect we have so far is that all lights go out when we touch the trigger.

END TUTORIAL 9.6

So, now all the lights go off when we touch the trigger. However, when they come back on, we need them to be a different color. This means that we need to perform a few actions simultaneously. First, we need to start a delay of about two to three seconds before the lights come back on, and during that delay, we need to change the color of the material that is applied to our lights and to our meshes. It's all a bit like sleight of hand; while the lights are off, we're doing something behind the player's back to change the final effect.

In **TUTORIAL 9.7**, we look at how we can set up this system, using a Delay object and a Set VectorParam object at the same time. We show how to use Kismet to change the color of the lights in the corridor while they are off. This means that when they are eventually switched back on, they are not the same color as they were at the beginning of the sequence.

TUTORIAL 9.7: Constructing Intermediate Lighting Sequences, Part III: Changing Light Color

1. Continue from **TUTORIAL 9.6**, or open the DM-Ch_09_KUnrealOne_02.ut3 map included with the files for this chapter.

   Next up on our list of comments is Wait 3 seconds before proceeding. However, let's worry about the delay in a moment, and focus on our next operation, which is to change the color of lighting objects while lights are off. There are two parts to this: change the color of the actual lights, and change the color of the material instance applied to the lights.

2. We handle the material instance first, because that's a bit easier. To do this, we need a Set VectorParam object. Follow these steps to set one up:

   a. Right-click on a blank area to the right of the Toggle object but outside the comment box and choose New Action > Material Instance > Set VectorParam from the Context menu (see **FIGURE 9.59**).

   b. In the Generic browser, within the KismetLightSequence package, choose the mat_lightColor_inst material instance.

   c. Back in the Kismet Editor, select the Set VectorParam object. In the Properties window, click the MatInst property and then click the Use Selection in Browser button [K].

   d. For the ParamName property, enter LightColor.

> **NOTE**
>
> If nothing appears when you click the Use Current Selection in Browser button, it is possible that you selected the parent material instead of the material instance. If this is the case, make sure to go back into the Generic browser and open up the material instance constant.

9

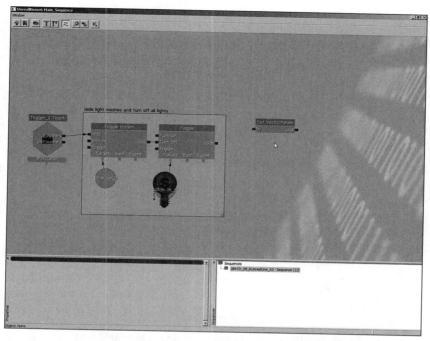

FIGURE 9.59   The Set VectorParam object enables us to change the material that is currently applied to our lights.

e. Click the small black triangle next to the VectorValue property and set the following values:

> **B:** 0.13
>
> **G:** 0.13
>
> **R:** 1.00

Or, if you were to input the colors into the Color Chooser window instead (see **FIGURE 9.60**):

> **R:** 255
>
> **G:** 100
>
> **B:** 100

f. Drag a wire from the Out output of the Toggle to the In input of the Set VectorParam (see **FIGURE 9.61**).

> **NOTE**
>
> In the Properties window of the Set VectorParam node, you'll notice that RGB are listed *backward* from the conventional order! Don't overlook this, or your color will be wildly different than ours!

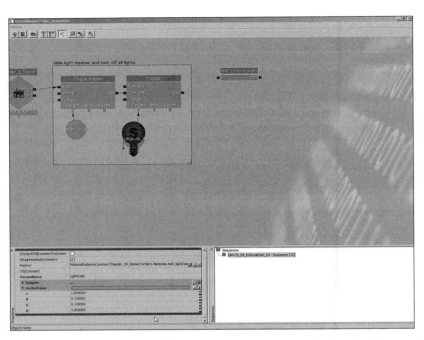

FIGURE 9.60   Your Properties window for the Set VectorParam should appear like so.

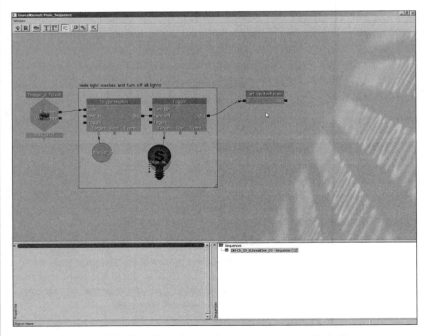

FIGURE 9.61   The Set VectorParam has now been wired into the sequence.

3. The first part of the color change is done, in that we've changed the color of the mesh. Now, however, we need to change the color of the lights as well. The easiest way to handle this is with a simple Matinee sequence. We keep things straightforward, as Matinee is covered in much greater detail in Chapter 10. For now, however, follow these steps:

   a. Right-click just underneath the Set VectorParam object and create a new Matinee (see **FIGURE 9.62**).

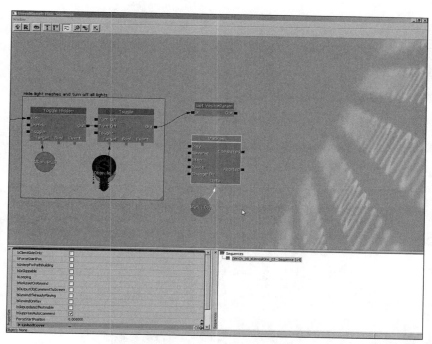

FIGURE 9.62 A new Matinee object and its requisite Data node appear.

   b. Double-click this new Matinee object to open the Matinee Editor (see **FIGURE 9.63**).

   c. Right-click in the wide gray bar on the left side of the Editor (the Group/Track list). From the Context menu that appears, choose Add New Empty Group (see **FIGURE 9.64**).

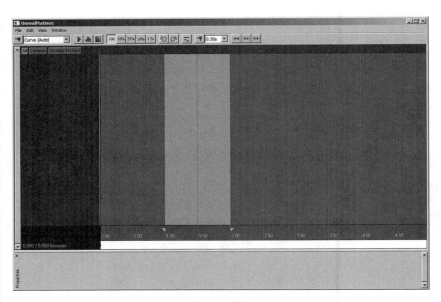

FIGURE 9.63   Welcome to the Matinee Editor.

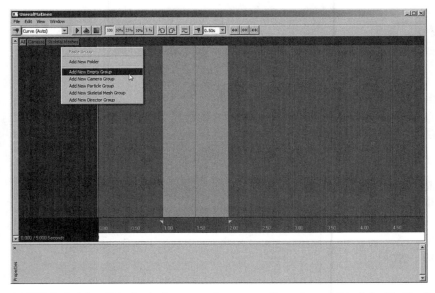

FIGURE 9.64   This Context menu only appears if you have right-clicked in the Group/Track list.

    d. In the New Group Name window, enter ChangeLightColor and click OK (see **FIGURE 9.65**).

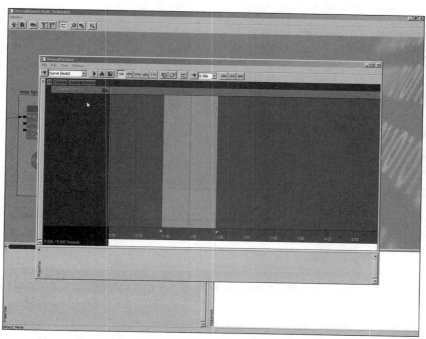

FIGURE 9.65   The new ChangeLightColor group appears.

    e. Close the Matinee Editor.

4. We have created our Matinee, but we need to do two more things: 1) we need to associate our lights to it, and 2) we need to establish the animation that actually changes the color of our lights. These are both fairly simple tasks. Just follow these steps:

    a. First, you'll notice the Matinee has a new input along the bottom named ChangeLightColor. Select the object list containing your lights (it has a big purple light bulb in it) and duplicate it with Ctrl-C, Ctrl-V (see **FIGURE 9.66**).

    b. Move the duplicate just underneath the ChangeLightColor input of the Matinee, and drag a wire from the input to the duplicated object list (see **FIGURE 9.67**).

    c. Double-click the Matinee to open the Matinee Editor.

    d. Click on the ChangeLightColor group on the left side of the Editor to select it. It turns orange to indicate selection.

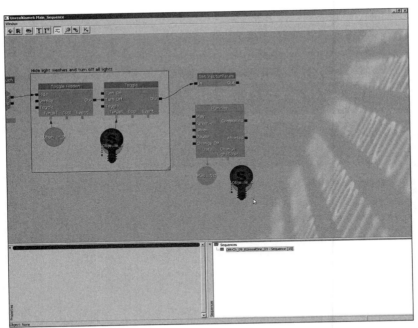

FIGURE 9.66   Make a duplicate of the object list containing all the toggleable lights in the level.

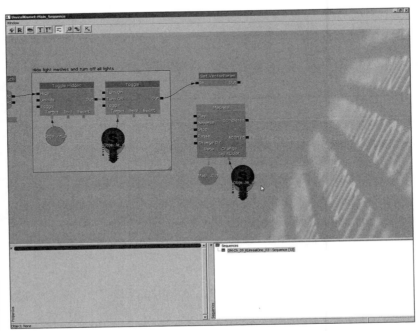

FIGURE 9.67   The ChangeLightColor group now affects all lights within the object list.

e. Right-click on the group and choose New Color Property Track from the Context menu. A window appears in which you can choose which color property you'd like to animate. The LightColor property should be selected by default, so just click OK (see **FIGURE 9.68**).

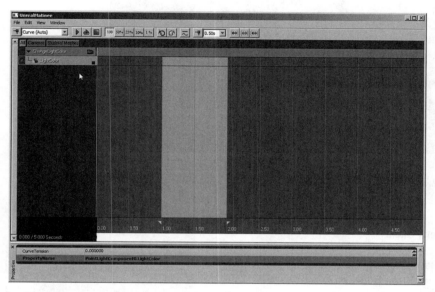

FIGURE 9.68   You now have a Color Property track that we can use to change the color of the lights.

f. Let's make sure our time slider is at 0.0. There is a gray rule of numbers along the bottom of the Editor. Click within it and drag as far as you can to the left.

g. Press the Enter key to add a keyframe. This keyframe appears as a small orange tri-angle, right at the beginning of the timeline (0.0), as shown in **FIGURE 9.69**.

h. Select this keyframe; then right-click on it and choose Set Color from the Context menu. Enter the following values (see **FIGURE 9.70**):

> **R:** 255
>
> **G:** 100
>
> **B:** 100

i. Close the Matinee Editor.

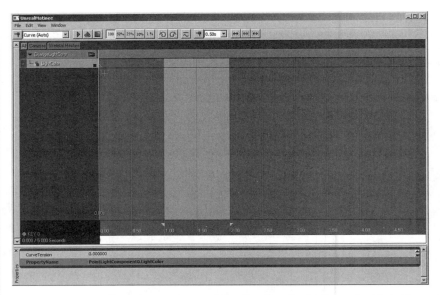

FIGURE 9.69   If you have not moved the timeline, the keyframe is only halfway visible, right next to the Color Property track.

5. That may have seemed like a lot, but that's actually a pretty easy setup once you get the hang of it. Next, let's connect a wire from the Out of the Toggle to the Play input of the Matinee, which triggers the animation (see **FIGURE 9.71**).

6. The next thing we should do is set up our comment for this section of our sequence. Select the Change the color of the lighting... comment from the list of comments and move it above the Set VectorParam and the Matinee. As done in **TUTORIAL 9.6**, show the box and adjust it to surround the nodes (see **FIGURE 9.72**).

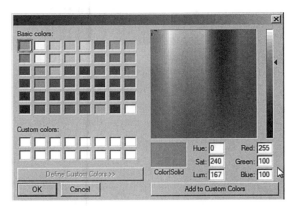

FIGURE 9.70   These settings change the color of the lights to orange red.

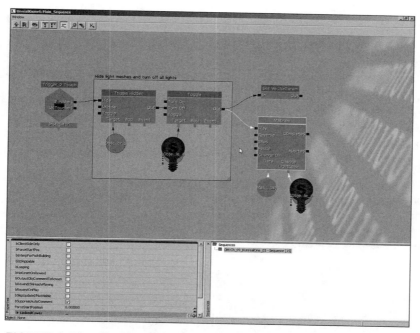

FIGURE 9.71   The Matinee is now connected to the sequence.

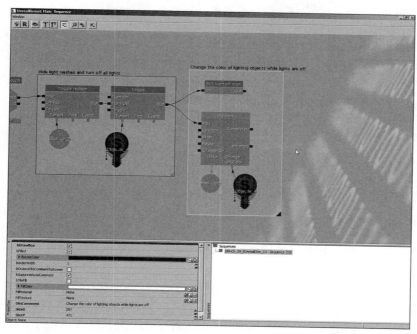

FIGURE 9.72   The new section of our visual script has been commented.

7. The last thing we need to tend to is that delay. This one's easy. Just right-click on the Out of the Set VectorParam node, and choose Set Activate Delay from the Context menu. In the window that appears, enter 3.0 and press Enter (see **FIGURE 9.73**). Done.

FIGURE 9.73 There will now be a 3.0-second delay on the output from the Set VectorParam.

8. Finally, select the Wait 3 seconds... comment from the list, and move it near the Out of the Set VectorParam node, just so we can see what the wait is all about. There is no need to show the box for the comment (see **FIGURE 9.74**).

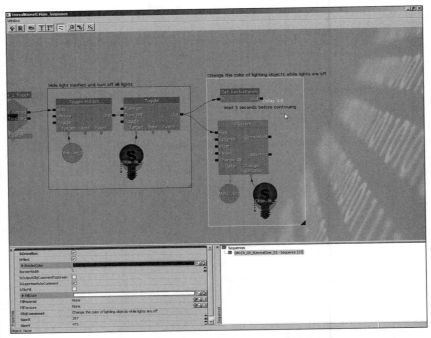

FIGURE 9.74 The comment will now alert an artist that there is a reason that we are waiting.

9. Save your level. At this time, testing the level yields no changes viewable by the player.

END TUTORIAL 9.6

Okay, the light color has been changed, but now we need to turn the lights back on. The final effect we're going for is that the lights should come on starting at the front and moving forward, with a new light coming on about every 0.75 seconds. To do this, we use a Delayed switch. This is different than a delay, in that where a delay simply waits to activate its output for a certain amount of time, the Delayed switch cycles through a series of outputs based on a timed interval.

In **TUTORIAL 9.8**, we add a Delayed switch into our sequence that activates each of the lights in turn, rather than all at once.

TUTORIAL 9.8: Constructing Intermediate Lighting Sequences, Part IV: Delayed Switches

1. Continue from **TUTORIAL 9.6**, or open the DM-Ch_09_KUnrealOne_03.ut3 map included with the files for this chapter.

2. As our next comment suggests, we're going to bring our lights back on in sequence. We start at the far end of the hallway, and turn on another light every 0.75 seconds until all five lights are back on. Although we could simply insert a series of toggles and Toggle Hiddens with Delay objects in between, it is much easier and more efficient (not to mention just plain *cooler*) to use a Delayed switch object instead.

   To create one, right-click in a blank area to the right of the Set VectorParam—outside the comment box—and choose New Action > Switch > Delayed (see **FIGURE 9.75**).

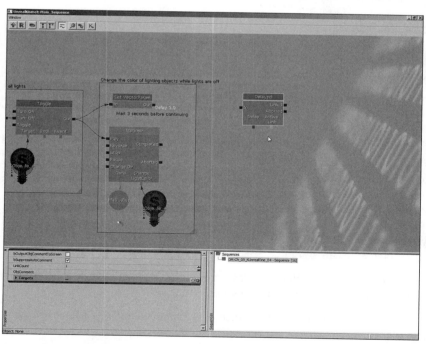

FIGURE 9.75   We have now created a Delayed switch, which we use to turn the lights back on in succession.

3. Wire the Out of the Set VectorParam object (the one that has the Activate Delay on it) to the In input of the Delayed switch object. Then, select the Delayed switch and set its LinkCount property to 5 (see **FIGURE 9.76**).

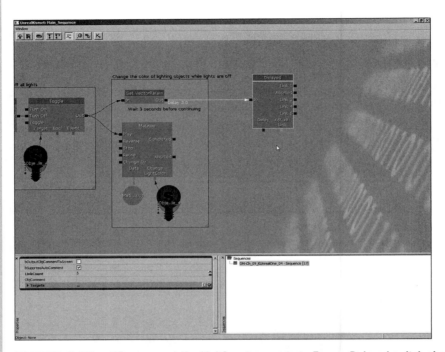

FIGURE 9.76   When you set the LinkCount property to 5, your Delayed switch should look like this.

4. We need to establish the duration of the delay in the Delayed switch object. Right-click on the blue input box just under the Delayed switch's Delay input and choose Create New Float Variable. Select this variable, and in the Properties window, set its FloatValue property to 0.75 (see **FIGURE 9.77**).

> **NOTE**
>
> At the time of this writing, the output link named Aborted counts as Link 2, meaning your numbering system should go something like Link 1, Aborted, Link 3, Link 4, Link 5. We use the Aborted link as if it were named Link 2.

5. We now need to create the Toggle Hidden objects that turn our meshes back on, starting at the back and working forward. Follow these steps:

   a. Right-click to the right of the Delayed switch object and choose New Action > Toggle > Toggle Hidden.

   b. Connect the UnHide input of this Toggle Hidden to the Link 1 output of the Delayed switch object (see **FIGURE 9.78**).

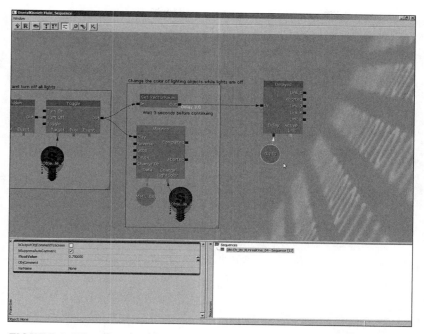

FIGURE 9.77   You should now have a Float variable connected to the Delayed switch to create the timing for your delay.

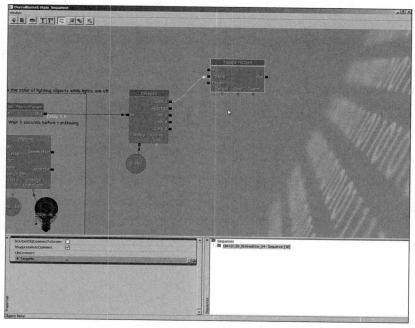

FIGURE 9.78   You need to connect the new Toggle Hidden to Link 1 of the Delayed switch.

c. In the Perspective viewport, select the light mesh at the back of the hallway (InterpActor_5). In the Kismet Editor, right-click on the Target input of the new Toggle Hidden and choose New Object Var using InterpActor_5 (see **FIGURE 9.79**).

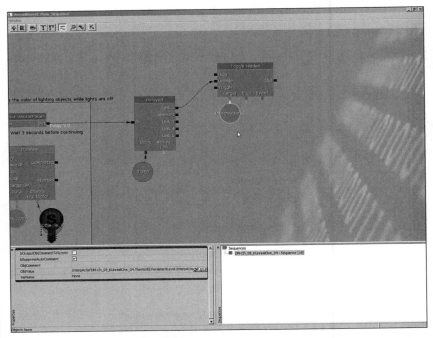

FIGURE 9.79   With the target object variable connected, you now unhide the InterpActor mesh.

d. Create four more Toggle Hidden objects in a column beneath the one you just created. For each new copy, set the target to a new object variable, using the next subsequent light mesh, working your way toward the front of the hallway. Remember that the Aborted link on the Delayed switch counts as Link 2 (see **FIGURE 9.80**).

6. Almost there; now all we need to do is also turn our lights back on. Using the techniques covered previously in Step 4, create five new Toggle objects (New Action > Toggle > Toggle), connecting the Turn On input of each to the Out output of one of the Toggle Hidden objects.

> **TIP**
>
> When creating object variables, you can select all the objects that you need variables for at the same time. Then, when you right-click in the Kismet Editor, you see Create New Object Vars From X, which creates separate variables for each object you have selected!

9

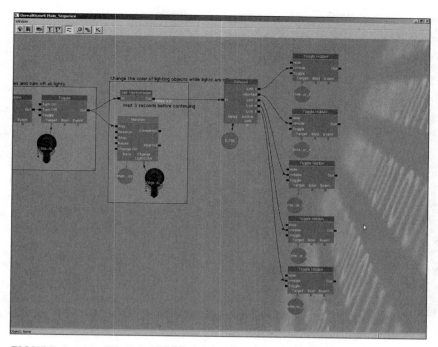

FIGURE 9.80   When finished, your network should look something like this.

7. Create object variables for your five PointLightToggleable actors, and associate them to their corresponding Toggle objects. Remember that the result you're looking for is for the lights and light objects to reappear one at a time, starting at the back and working forward (see **FIGURE 9.81**).

8. Select the "Unhide light meshes and turn lights back on in sequence" comment and move it above the Delayed switch and all the Toggle Hidden and Toggle objects. Activate its bDrawBox property, and adjust the size of the box to encompass all of these objects and their associated variables (see **FIGURE 9.82**).

9. Save and test your level. If you connected any of your lights out of order, simply go back into Kismet and adjust your connection wires and object layout.

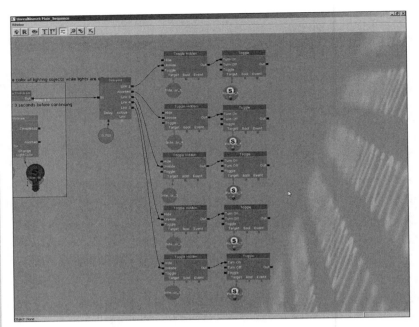

FIGURE 9.81
The final network for turning on the lights and meshes looks like this. Notice that the Toggle Hiddens and toggles are in sequence for each light.

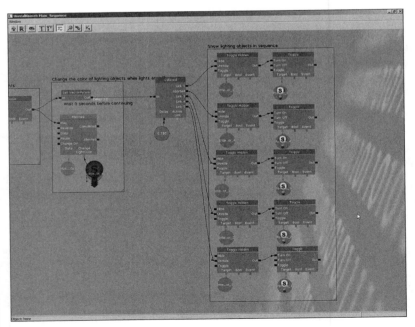

FIGURE 9.82
When finished, apply your comment box so that you can understand the network later.

9

END TUTORIAL 9.8

All our lights are coming back on, but we still have a problem. If you run the level and try the effect, everything looks great…the first time you run it. After that, the lights are red when the level begins. That's no good.

What we need to do is have Kismet reset all the lights back to their original settings when the level begins. That way, no matter when we exit the level, the effect is reset when we restart it, kind of like priming the system.

In **TUTORIAL 9.9**, we set up our level's initial conditions, which handle setting the lights back to their original color.

TUTORIAL 9.9: Constructing Intermediate Lighting Sequences, Part IV: Setting Initial Level Conditions

1. Continue from **TUTORIAL 9.6**, or open the DM-Ch_09_KUnrealOne_04.ut3 map included with the files for this chapter.

2. Our final comment says that we need to set the initial conditions for the level. Right-click on a blank area of the Kismet Sequence Window and choose New Event > Level Startup (see **FIGURE 9.83**).

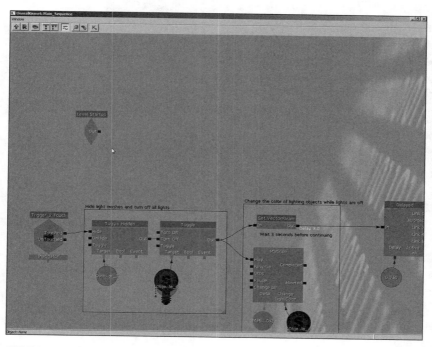

FIGURE 9.83   The Level Startup event is fired at the start of each level. We use it to turn all the lights and light meshes on and back to their normal color when the level starts.

3. Select the Toggle Hidden and Toggle objects within the Hide light meshes and turn off all lights' comment boxes, along with their associated object list variables. Then, while holding Ctrl, select the Set VectorParam object as well.

Duplicate these objects using Ctrl-C, Ctrl-V, and move the duplicates to the right of the Level Beginning object.

4. Alt-click the Out output box on the new Toggle object, and then rewire it to the In input of the new Set VectorParam.

Next, Alt-click the wire leading from the Toggle Hidden to the Toggle, and create a new wire leading from the Out output of the Toggle Hidden to the Turn On input of the Toggle (see **FIGURE 9.84**).

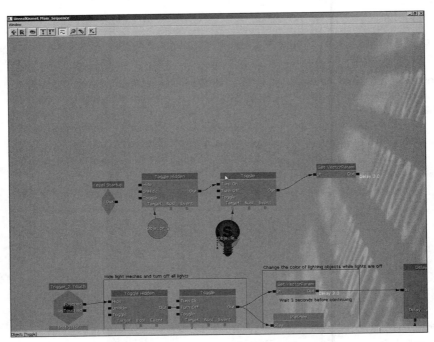

FIGURE 9.84   Reconnect the wire so that the Toggle Hidden attaches to the Turn On input, instead of Turn Off.

5. Drag a wire from the Out output of the Level Beginning to the UnHide input of the Toggle Hidden.

6. Select the Set VectorParam object. In the Properties window, expand the VectorValue property, and set the color to whatever color you'd like the lights to be when the level begins. We used the following:

A: 1.0	**G:** 0.98
B: 0.98	**R:** 0.46

9

Or if you were to input the color using the Color Chooser window, use the following:

R: 179

G: 252

B: 252

7. Adjust the Initial level conditions comment so that its comment box surrounds all of these new objects (see **FIGURE 9.85**).

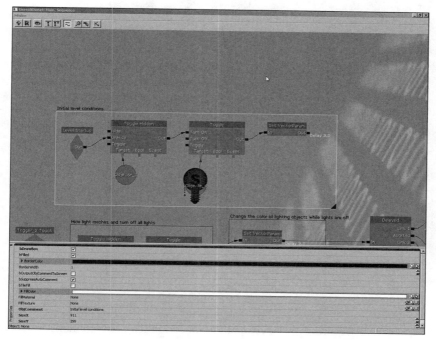

FIGURE 9.85   Your final Initial level conditions network should appear like so.

8. Save and test your level. Your lights should now reset when the level starts.

END TUTORIAL 9.9

So now you've got the effect completed, but that's no reason to stop. You could take a look at some of the things you've learned throughout this chapter and really spruce up this effect through the use of sound effects, the spawning of new actors, and so on. Take some time to experiment and see what you can come up with!

Over the next series of tutorials, we're going to create the most complex example in this chapter: a randomized teleportation system. However, before we begin, it is a good idea to go over how it's supposed to work.

We start with a preconstructed simple level. In four separate locations, you find a teleporter station, consisting of a teleporter pad mesh, next to a wall-mounted control panel. One of these is on the ground level, next to a PlayerStart actor, the others are on elevated platforms, which are color-coded through the use of lights (see **FIGURE 9.86**).

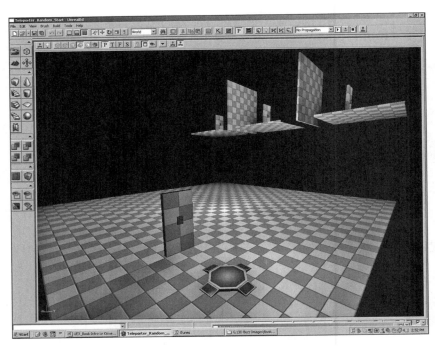

FIGURE 9.86   Here you can see the level we use in **TUTORIAL 9.10**.

The meshes for these objects have already been created for you, and each mesh contains a material instance, which enables you to switch between an active (powered-up) state, and an inactive (powered-down) state. The idea is that a player walks up the very first teleporter, and uses the control pad to activate it. The teleporter then comes to life with particles (also preconstructed), as shown in **FIGURE 9.87**.

Once players step into the first teleporter, they are sent at random to one of the color-coded platforms. There, they can activate the teleporter located on the platform, which in turn sends them back to their starting point.

This sequence is relatively complex, so we're going to take it a step at a time. During the first few tutorials, we go slowly, showing each thing you should be connecting. However, as we progress toward the end, we begin taking a few liberties, enabling you to use your Kismet experience to create the remaining sequence, without an instructor holding your hand. Don't worry—it is pretty easy once you get into it.

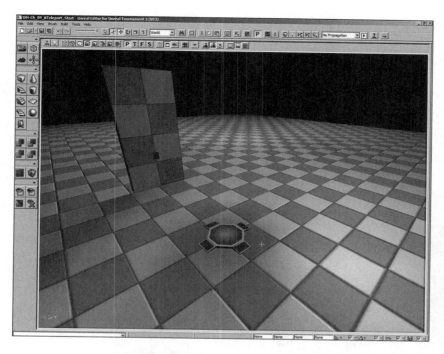

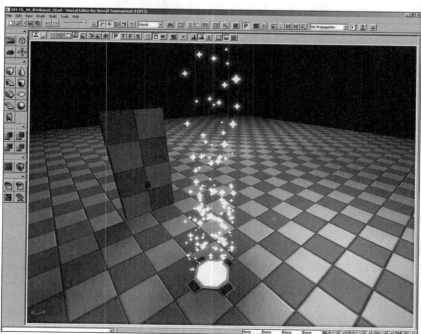

FIGURE 9.87 When powered down, the teleporter pad appears as on top. When activated, it appears as at bottom.

In **TUTORIAL 9.10**, we start with a simple setup for the complex teleportation system, in which you place your actors and create a list of comment boxes to be used throughout the rest of the sequence construction. Specifically, we add in the Trigger and Teleporter actors necessary for the sequence.

TUTORIAL 9.10: Creating Complex Teleportation Systems, Part I: Setup

1. Launch the Unreal Editor, or, if it is running, restart it. Open the DM-Ch_09_KTeleport_Start map included with the files for this chapter (see **FIGURE 9.88**).

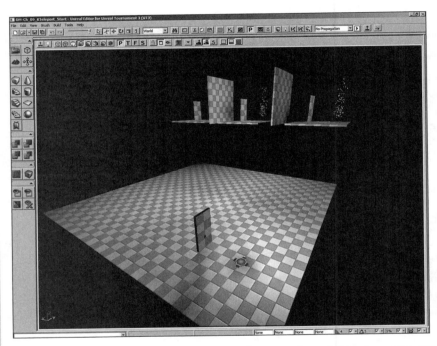

FIGURE 9.88   The DM-Ch_09_KTeleport_Start map has a teleporter on the ground floor, and three more on elevated platforms.

2. Our first step is to establish all the "behind the scenes" actors we need for our sequence. In this case, this includes triggers and teleporters. We start by placing all of our necessary triggers.

> **NOTE**
>
> We are restarting the Unreal Editor so that all actor numbering is accurate between **TUTORIAL 9.10** and what you see on the screen. Also, this level requires the Chapter_09_KismetContent.upk package, included with the files on the DVD for this chapter. If necessary, locate and open this package, and then reload the level.

9

a. Place a trigger directly in front of the small command panel on the Ground Floor. It should be named Trigger_0 (see **FIGURE 9.89**).

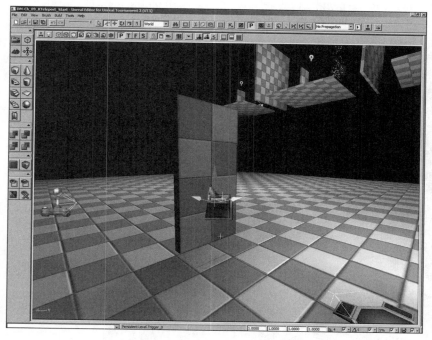

FIGURE 9.89   The first trigger should be placed in front of the Ground Level control pad.

b. Place a trigger in the center of the teleporter pad mesh on the Ground Floor. It will be named Trigger_1.

c. Place a trigger in front of the small command panel on the Orange Level. It should be named Trigger_2.

d. Place a trigger in the center of the teleporter pad mesh on the Orange Level. It will be named Trigger_3.

> **NOTE**
>
> If this first trigger is not named Trigger_0, please close the Unreal Editor without saving, re-launch it, and reopen the DM-Ch_09_KTeleport_Start map. Also, if during the placement of these triggers, you should accidentally delete one or your numbering should be thrown off for some reason, simply delete all triggers that are out of order, save your level, and restart the Unreal Editor. Numbering is very important later. Of course, if you're pretty confident that you can keep track if your numbers are different than ours, then by all means continue *at your own risk*.

e. Place a trigger in front of the small command panel on the Cyan Level. It should be named Trigger_4.

f. Place a trigger in the center of the teleporter pad mesh on the Cyan Level. It will be named Trigger_5.

g. Place a trigger in front of the small command panel on the Magenta Level. It should be named Trigger_6.

h. Place a trigger in the center of the teleporter pad mesh on the Magenta Level. It will be named Trigger_7 (see **FIGURE 9.90**).

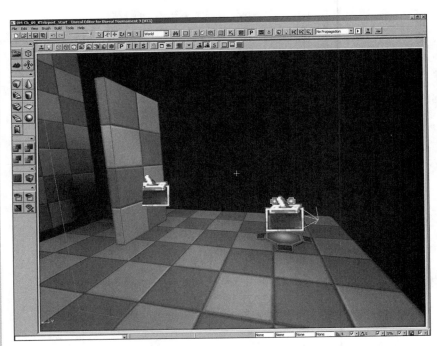

FIGURE 9.90   When finished, all of your control panels should have a trigger in front of them, and all teleporter pads should have a trigger floating above them.

3. We now need to place our Teleporter actors. These serve as points of destination for our teleportation. The benefit of using these actors is that they can designate not only a position, but also an orientation for our player.

a. Open the Actor Classes browser (View > Browser Windows > Actor Classes). Expand NavigationPoint, and choose Teleporter.

b. Place a Teleporter actor just above the teleporter pad mesh on the Ground Level. It will be named Teleporter_0 (see **FIGURE 9.91**).

c. Place a Teleporter actor just above the teleporter pad mesh on the Orange Level. It will be named Teleporter_1.

> **NOTE**
>
> If your Teleporter actor is too close to the ground, your icon will change to a label reading "Bad Size." If this happens, simply move the icon away from the nearest surface. As a shortcut, you can just press the End key to realign the teleporter!

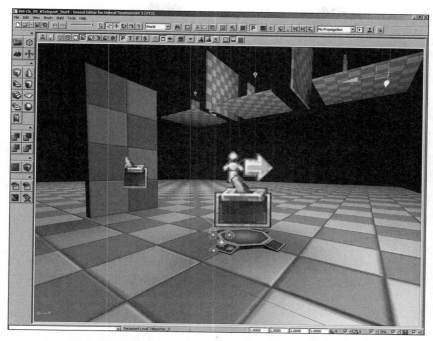

FIGURE 9.91   The Teleporter actor appears just above the trigger.

d. Place a Teleporter actor just above the teleporter pad mesh on the Cyan Level. It will be named Teleporter_2.

> **NOTE**
>
> It's best to avoid rotating the Teleporter actor around any axis other than Z (Yaw). Doing so may cause strange results during gameplay.

e. Place a Teleporter actor just above the teleporter pad mesh on the Magenta Level. It will be named Teleporter_3.

f. Each Teleporter actor has a small blue wire arrow pointing out of it, designating the orientation of the player upon teleporting to that location. Make sure that these arrows all point to each teleporter pad's respective control panel (see **FIGURE 9.92**). (They should be, but it's best to double-check!)

4. Open the Kismet Editor. We start with a list of comments that we can use to keep our progress focused throughout the setup of our sequence. Create a separate comment for each of the following statements:

   ▶ Phase One: All emitters off when level starts.

   ▶ Phase Two: Activate nearest emitter while deactivating all others.

   ▶ Phase Three: Send player from Ground Level to random platform.

   ▶ Phase Four: Send player from activated platform back to Ground Level.

   ▶ Phase Five: Activate/deactivate material instances (see **FIGURE 9.93**).

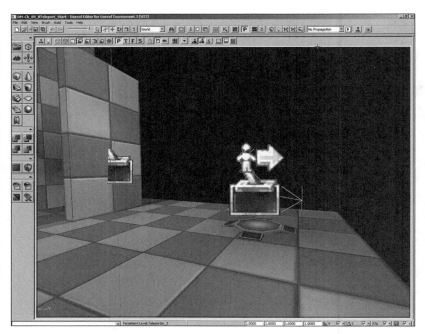

FIGURE 9.92   When finished, all teleporter pad meshes should have a Teleporter actor over them.

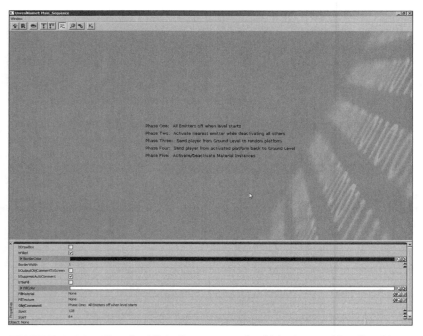

FIGURE 9.93   Your final list of comments should look something like this.

5. For all of these comments, activate the bDrawBox property, and space the comments out from one another. Throughout this sequence, you resize these boxes to contain all the sequence objects associated with each comment. The steps of these tutorials assume that you are resizing and rearranging the boxes on your own!

6. Let's also go ahead and bring in the Object Variables we need for our sequence. This includes all of our triggers and teleporters. This enables you to have the object variables on hand, rather than having to go into a level and select them.

   a. Click the Search for Actors ⬇ button located in the Unreal Editor toolbar. In the Search For line, type the letter T. You will notice that your list focuses down to only those actors whose name start with T—in this case, the triggers and teleporters (see **FIGURE 9.94**).

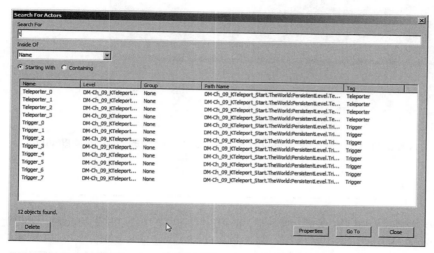

FIGURE 9.94   Once you press the T key, you should see all of your triggers and teleporters.

   b. In the Search for Actors window, click Teleporter_0. Then, while holding Shift, click Trigger_7. This should select all actors in the list.

   c. In the Search for Actors window, click the Go To button; then click Close.

   d. With all your objects selected, open the Kismet Editor. Right-click on a blank area of the sequence window away from all comment boxes and choose Create New Object Vars using Trigger_0,... from the Context menu (see **FIGURE 9.95**).

7. Using the same technique, create object variables for Emitter_0, Emitter_1, Emitter_2, and Emitter_3.

8. Save your progress.

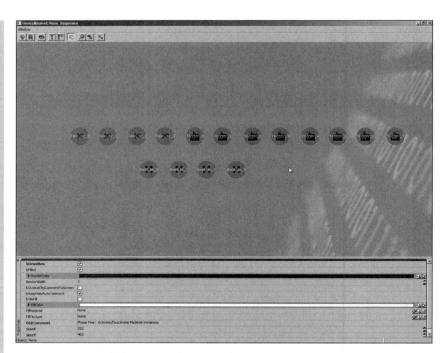

FIGURE 9.95   This is a quick method for creating multiple object variables for a large group of selected objects.

END TUTORIAL 9.10

With all the actors in place and our comments set up inside Kismet, we're ready to begin taking a look at our sequence. We actually start with Phase Two, since Phase One simply sets our level's initial conditions. For now, we're simply going to focus on the emitters rather than teleportation. After all, from a player's perspective, the particles are what make the teleporter active or inactive, since the actors involved in teleportation are invisible in-game. In **TUTORIAL 9.11**, we activate the particle emitter on the nearest teleportation pad and create the sequence objects for our level's initial conditions.

TUTORIAL 9.11: Creating Complex Teleportation Systems, Part II: Activating the Nearest Emitter and Establishing Initial Level Conditions

1. Continue from **TUTORIAL 9.10**, or open the DM-Ch_09_KTeleport_01.ut3 map included with the files for this chapter.

2. The first thing we need to do is set up the events for each of our control triggers. Please open the Kismet Editor and perform the following:

a. Select all the control panel triggers. These should be Trigger_0, Trigger_2, Trigger_4, and Trigger_6 (see **FIGURE 9.96**).

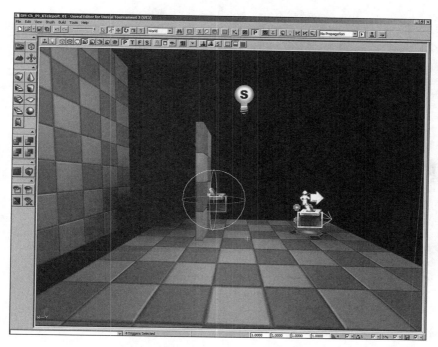

FIGURE 9.96 Make sure to select only the triggers in front of the control panels, not those above the teleporter pad meshes.

b. In an open area of the Kismet Editor, right-click and choose Create New Events Using... > Used. This creates a new Used event for each trigger.

c. Position all these events inside the Phase Two comment box, arranging them vertically with Trigger_0's Used event at the top, and then Trigger_2, Trigger_4, and Trigger_6 (see **FIGURE 9.97**).

d. Select all of these new Used events, and set their MaxTriggerCount property to 0.

3. We begin by turning on the emitter nearest to each trigger.

a. Right-click just to the right of the Trigger_0 Used event and choose New Action > Toggle > Toggle from the Context menu.

b. Locate the Emitter_0 object variable created earlier. Make a duplicate of it (Ctrl-C, Ctrl-V), and move it just beneath this new Toggle. Connect this duplicate to the Target input of the Toggle (see **FIGURE 9.98**).

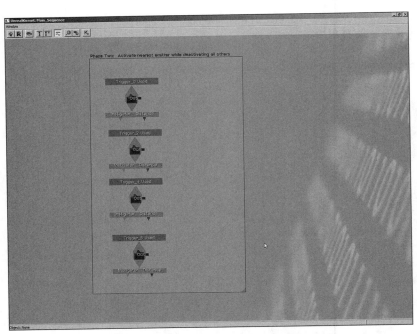

FIGURE 9.97   The four events should be arranged in your comment box like so.

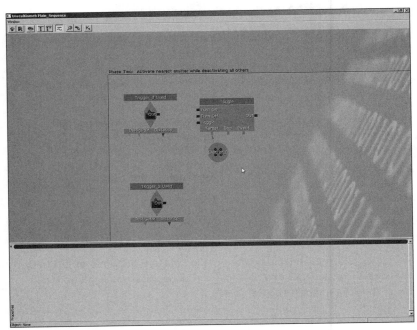

FIGURE 9.98   Use a duplicate of the Emitter_0 object variable to connect to the Toggle.

c. Connect the Trigger_0 Used output to the Turn On input on the Toggle.

d. Repeat this process for the remaining three triggers such that Trigger_2 turns on Emitter_1, Trigger_4 turns on Emitter_2, and Trigger_6 turns on Emitter_3 (see **FIGURE 9.99**).

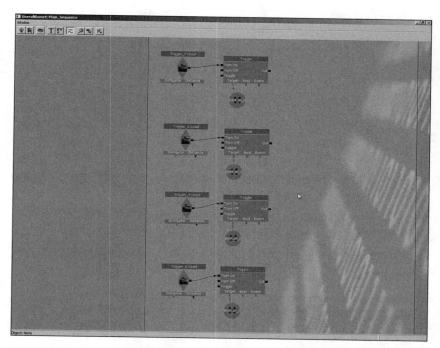

FIGURE 9.99   When finished, your first network should look something like this.

4. We now need to establish sequence objects such that when one emitter is turned on, all others are turned off:

a. Create a new Toggle sequence object, positioned just to the right of the Trigger_0 Used event sequence, like so (see **FIGURE 9.100**).

b. Connect the Turn Off input of this new Toggle to the Output of the previous Toggle.

c. Create duplicates of the object variables for Emitter_1, Emitter_2, and Emitter_3. Position these duplicates underneath the new Toggle and connect them all to the Target input (see **FIGURE 9.101**).

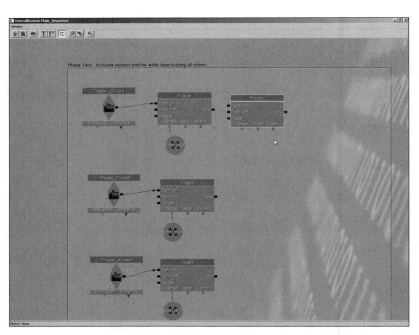

FIGURE 9.100   Position your next Toggle sequence object to the right of the first Toggle that is connected to the Trigger_0 Used sequence.

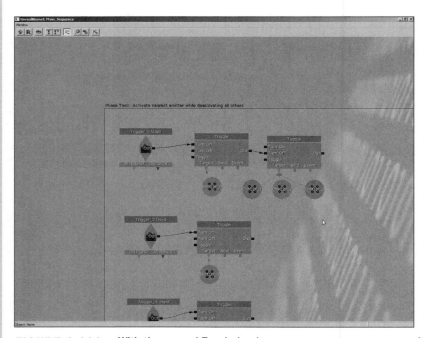

FIGURE 9.101   With the second Toggle in place, your sequence turns on emitter 0, while turning off Emitters 1, 2, and 3.

d. Repeat this process for the remaining event sequences to create the following circumstances (see **FIGURE 9.102**):

 ▶ When Emitter_1 is turned on, Emitters 0, 2, and 3 turn off.

 ▶ When Emitter_2 is turned on, Emitters 0, 1, and 3 turn off.

 ▶ When Emitter_3 is turned on, Emitters 0, 1, and 2 turn off.

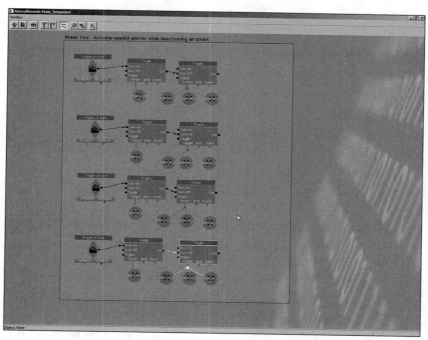

FIGURE 9.102   Your final network should look something like this when completed.

5. Inside the Phase One comment box, right-click and choose New Event > Level Startup from the Context menu.

6. Create a new Toggle, and connect its Turn Off input to the Out output of the Level Beginning sequence object.

7. Create duplicates of all four of the Emitter object variables, and connect them to the target of this new Toggle (see **FIGURE 9.103**).

8. Save your progress. If you test the level now, you will see that the emitters begin the level deactivated, but you can turn each one on if you use the control panel located next to them.

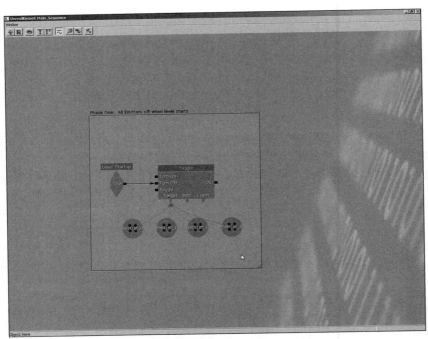

FIGURE 9.103   Your Phase One comment box should appear like so, turning off all emitters when the level begins.

END TUTORIAL 9.11

We're now ready to begin teleportation. First, though, we need to check and see which of the teleporters is active. We don't want the player to be able to teleport from a teleporter that isn't activated, do we? Therefore, our sequence needs to check and see whether or not the teleporter that the player is touching has indeed been activated. If it has, Kismet continues with the sequence and teleports the player. If not, nothing happens.

The first step in creating this system is to store the name of the activated teleporter trigger in a variable. Later on, we can compare that variable against the name of the trigger that the player is touching and use the result to decide whether or not the player should be teleporting.

In **TUTORIAL 9.12**, we begin this setup by creating a variable that contains the name of the activated teleporter trigger. We also create a system that logs to the screen the name of the activated teleporter, which can help in debugging should we have problems down the road. We create a system within Kismet that allows us to keep track of which teleporter is currently active, preventing the player from teleporting from a teleporter that has not yet been enabled.

TUTORIAL 9.12: Creating Complex Teleportation Systems, Part III: Establishing the Active Trigger for Each Teleporter

1. Continue from **TUTORIAL 9.11**, or open the DM-Ch_09_KTeleport_02.ut3 map included with the files for this chapter.

2. We start by setting up a system by which we can store the name of the active teleportation trigger, so that we can use it later to determine whether a teleporter is active or not:

   a. In a blank area of the Sequence window, create a new comment box labeled Named Variable Sources.

   b. Inside this comment box, right-click and choose New Variable > Object > Object.

   c. Select this new object variable and set its VarName property to ActiveTrigger. We use this name to change the value of the variable later, via a Named Variable sequence object (see **FIGURE 9.104**).

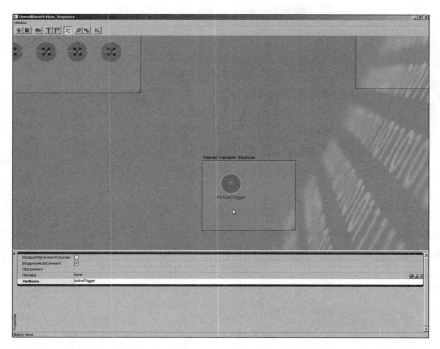

FIGURE 9.104   Notice that when you assign the VarName property, the name you choose appears underneath the variable in Kismet.

3. Return your attention to the Phase Two comment box. We now set up the proper sequence to store the active Trigger in the ActiveTrigger variable:

a. Right-click to the right of the top row of sequence objects and choose New Action > Set Variable > Object. Connect the In of this object to the Out of the previous Toggle object (see **FIGURE 9.105**).

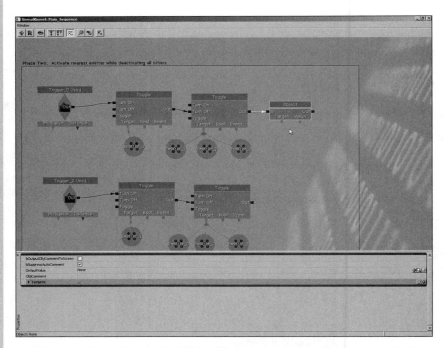

FIGURE 9.105   The new Set Object Variable sequence action is connected to your sequence, as shown here.

b. Duplicate the object variable for Trigger_1 (the trigger on the Ground Floor teleportation pad), and position it below this new Set Object Variable sequence object.

c. Connect the Trigger_1 object variable to the Value input, as shown in **FIGURE 9.106**.

d. Right-click to the left of the Trigger_1 object variable and choose New Variable > Named Variable from the Context menu.

> **NOTE**
>
> Once you assign the ActiveTrigger name to the named variable, its icon changes from a red X to a green checkmark. However, you may need to close and reopen the Kismet Editor to see the change!

e. Select the new named variable, and set its FindVarName property to ActiveTrigger. This invisibly connects it to the ActiveTrigger object variable created earlier.

f. Connect the target of the Object action to the new named variable. The sequence is now set up so that when Trigger_0 is used, the ActiveTrigger variable is set to Trigger_1 (see **FIGURE 9.107**).

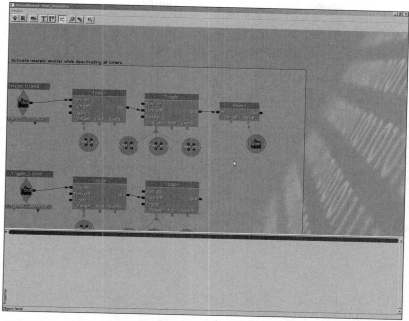

FIGURE 9.106   Connect the duplicated Trigger_1 object variable to the Value input of the Object sequence object.

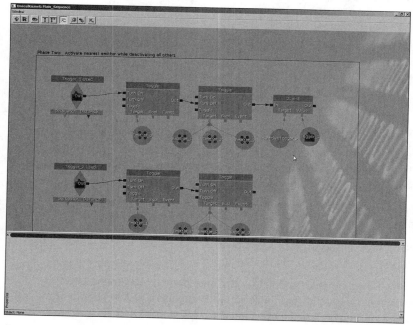

FIGURE 9.107   The named variable is now receiving the value from the Object sequence object.

g. Repeat the preceding steps to establish the following circumstances (see **FIGURE 9.108**):

- ▶ Using Trigger_2 sets the ActiveTrigger variable to Trigger_3.
- ▶ Using Trigger_4 sets the ActiveTrigger variable to Trigger_5.
- ▶ Using Trigger_6 sets the ActiveTrigger variable to Trigger_7.

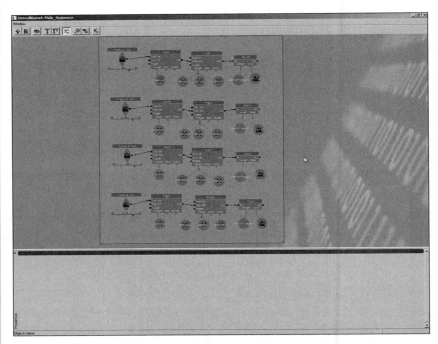

FIGURE 9.108   Your final network should appear something like this.

4. We now log to the screen the teleporter we have just activated.

a. Inside the Phase Two comment box, you currently have four event sequences. Right-click at the end of each one, and choose New Action > Misc > Log from the Context menu, thus placing a Log sequence object at the end of each sequence.

b. Connect each of the four Log objects to their respective sequences, like so (see **FIGURE 9.109**).

c. Right-click on each of the Log sequence objects and choose Expose Variable > String – String*. This enables you to attach a String variable to the log.

d. Create a new String variable, and set its StrValue property to Ground Level Teleporter Active. Connect this variable to the String input on the bottom of the log connected to the Trigger_0 sequence (see **FIGURE 9.110**).

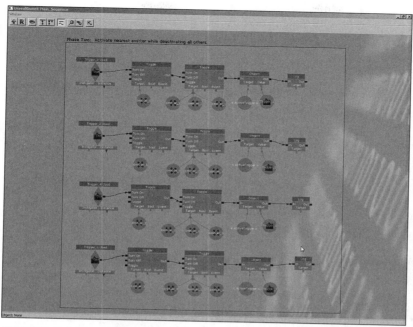

FIGURE 9.109 Connect a separate Log sequence object to each of the four sequences.

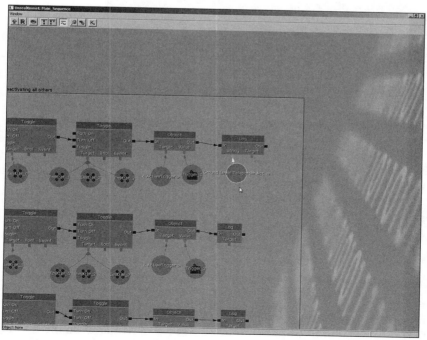

FIGURE 9.110 The new string is attached to the log for the Trigger_0 sequence.

> **e.** For Trigger_2's log, attach a new string variable set to Orange Level Teleporter Activated.
>
> **f.** For Trigger_4's log, attach a new string variable set to Cyan Level Teleporter Activated.
>
> **g.** For Trigger_6's log, attach a new string variable set to Magenta Level Teleporter Activated (see **FIGURE 9.111**).

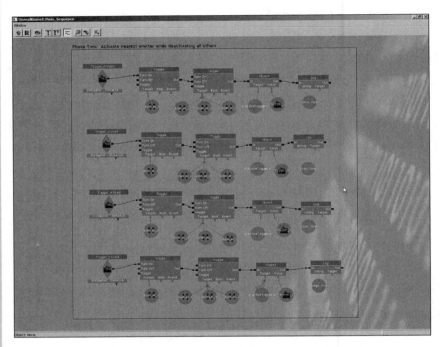

FIGURE 9.111   When finished, all four of the sequences should have their own log and string variable.

> **5.** For cleanliness, right-click on each log in turn and choose Hide Unused Connectors. You can use this whenever you don't want to have to see excess connectors on your nodes. It can dramatically shrink the necessary space for some networks, although care should be used because you may find yourself needing to re-expose those connections later.
>
> **6.** Save your progress. If you test the level now, using a control panel reports to the screen which teleporter you've activated.

END TUTORIAL 9.12

Now that we have a system in place that will activate the teleporters, we are ready to send off the player to one of the random platforms when they touch the activated teleporter on the ground level. Keep in mind that this system will be separate from the sequence that sends us back to the Ground Level. That is because only this teleportation has a random factor, in that the player will be randomly sent to one of the platforms. Once on a platform, the local teleporter will only send them back to the Ground Level.

In **TUTORIAL 9.13**, we establish the necessary sequence objects to cause the player to teleport to any of the available raised teleportation pads.

TUTORIAL 9.13: Creating Complex Teleportation Systems, Part IV: Sending the Player to a Random Platform

1. Continue from **TUTORIAL 9.12**, or open the DM-Ch_09_KTeleport_03.ut3 map included with the files for this chapter.

2. Select Trigger_1 (it's the one on the Ground Floor teleportation pad), and create a new Touch event in the Phase Three comment box. Be sure to set its MaxTriggerCount to 0 (see **FIGURE 9.112**).

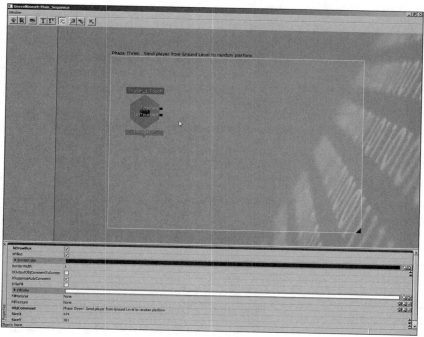

FIGURE 9.112   Create a new Touch event from Trigger_1, and place it in the Phase Three comment box.

3. We first need to check and see if the Ground Level teleporter (or more precisely its trigger) is active before we teleport the player.

a. Right-click to the right of the new Touch event and choose New Condition > Comparison > Compare Objects. Connect this new condition object to the Touched output of the Touch event (see **FIGURE 9.113**).

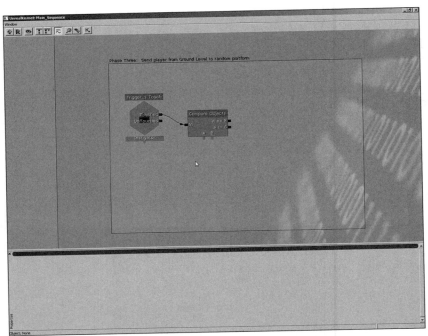

FIGURE 9.113   Create and connect the new Compare Objects sequence object like so.

b. Locate the object variable for Trigger_1. Duplicate it, and connect the duplicate to the B input of the Compare Objects.

c. Duplicate one of the named variables and connect it to the A input of the Compare Objects (see **FIGURE 9.114**).

4. We now create a random switch to control the teleporter to which the player is sent.

a. Right-click to the right of the Compare Objects and choose New Action > Switch > Random. Connect its In input to the A == B output of the Compare Objects.

b. Select the random switch and set its LinkCount property to 3 (see **FIGURE 9.115**).

> **NOTE**
>
> You may have already realized it, but the order of the objects connected to the A and B inputs for the Compare Objects is irrelevant.

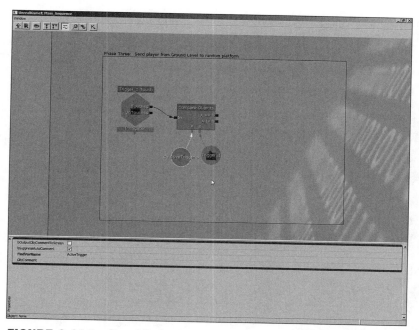

FIGURE 9.114   To put it simply, you are now checking to see whether Trigger_1 is currently being stored in the ActiveTrigger variable.

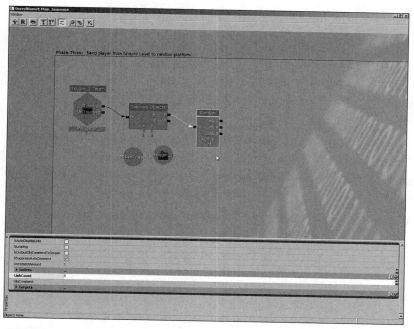

FIGURE 9.115   Your new random switch has three separate links. A link is selected randomly each time the switch is activated.

5. Inside the Named Variable Sources comment box, create a new Object variable, and set its VarName property to DestinationPoint (see **FIGURE 9.116**).

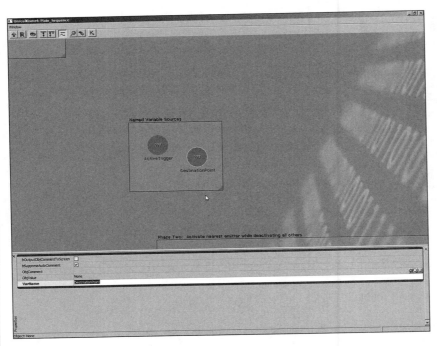

FIGURE 9.116   The new DestinationPoint variable stores the name of the teleporter to which we are sending the player.

6. We now create the sequence objects that fire from our random switch to instruct our sequence as to which platform to send the player. Go back to the Phase Three comment box.

    a. Create a new Set Object Variable action (New Action > Set Variable > Object), and connect it to Link 1 of the random switch (see **FIGURE 9.117**).

    b. To the Target input, connect a new named variable, setting the FindVarName property to DestinationPoint.

    c. To the Value input, connect a duplicate of the Teleporter_1 object variable (see **FIGURE 9.118**).

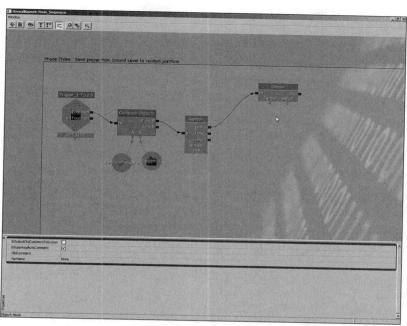

FIGURE 9.117   The new Object sequence object connects to Link 1.

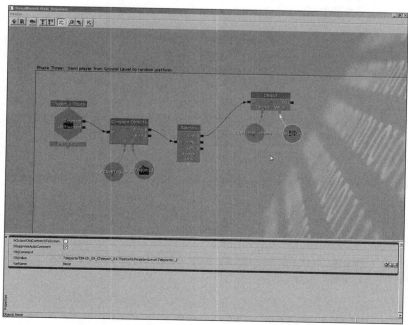

FIGURE 9.118   You are now setting the DestinationPoint variable to Teleporter_1 if this link is chosen by the random switch.

   d. Create a second Set Object Variable action, placed below the first. Set its target to a duplicate of the DestinationPoint named variable, and set its Value to a duplicate of the Teleporter_2 object variable (see **FIGURE 9.119**).

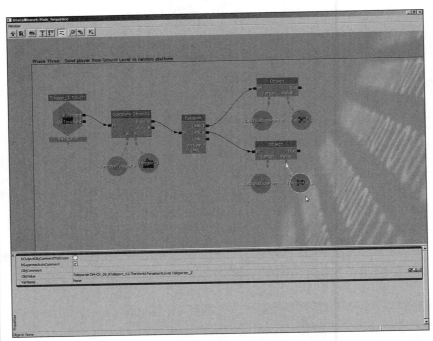

FIGURE 9.119   The Set Object Variable action connected to Link 2 sets the DestinationPoint variable to Teleporter_2.

   e. Create a third Set Object Variable action, placed below the second. Set its target to a duplicate of the DestinationPoint named variable, and set its value to a duplicate of the Teleporter_3 object variable (see **FIGURE 9.120**).

7. Finally, it's time to set up our Teleport object, as follows:

   a. Right-click to the right of the three Object sequence objects, and choose New Action > Actor > Teleport.

   b. Connect the In input of the Teleport object to all the Out outputs of the Object sequence objects (see **FIGURE 9.121**).

   c. For the target, right-click and choose New Variable > Object > Player. Connect this new variable to the target.

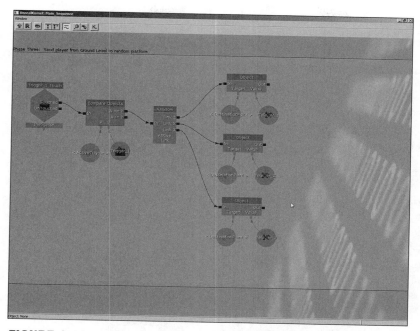

FIGURE 9.120 With the third Set Object Variable in place, we can now randomly choose between our three teleporters.

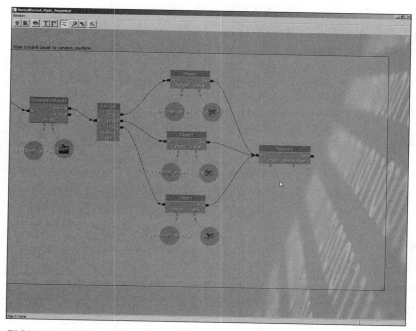

FIGURE 9.121 Notice that all three Object sequence objects are connected to the teleporter, meaning that each one activates the teleporter if selected by the random switch.

    d. For the destination, create a duplicate of the DestinationPoint named variable (see **FIGURE 9.122**).

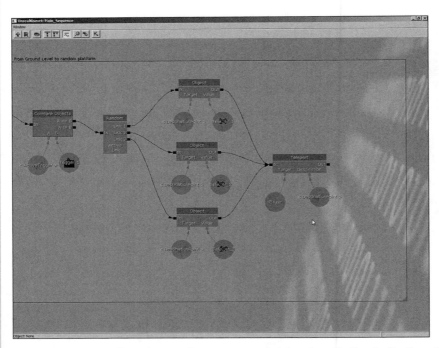

FIGURE 9.122   The teleporter is now set to send the player to the destination of the actor currently stored in the DestinationPoint variable.

8. Save your progress. Feel free to test the level at this point. You will randomly be sent from the Ground Level up to one of the platforms when you activate the Ground Level teleporter and step into it. However, at this time, we don't yet have a way to teleport home.

END TUTORIAL 9.13

We are now able to send the player to one of the three platforms. However, we need to improve on things a bit before we can call this part of the system complete. First, for debugging purposes (and as a skill exercise), it would be nice if we could log to the screen the platform to which we just sent the player. Also, we need to deactivate the emitter from our departure point once the teleportation is complete.

To perform this deactivation, we have a few choices. We could, for instance, attach a Toggle to the end of all of our teleportation sequences, which turned off the emitter located at the departure point. However, we're going to get a little more sophisticated than that by implementing a remote event.

You can think of a remote event kind of like a wireless receiver. It simply waits until it receives a signal, and then it activates just like any other event. However, in order for it to be useful, you need to use an Activate Remote Event sequence object, which sends out the signal to the remote event (see **FIGURE 9.123**).

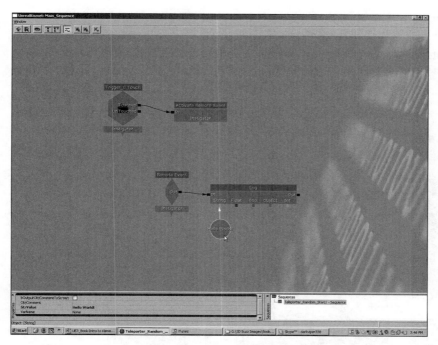

FIGURE 9.123   In this simple example, touching the trigger activates the remote event, which logs Hello World to the screen.

For remote events to work, they must have a name, located in their EventName property. You can then use that name in the EventName property of an Activate Remote Event sequence object to fire off the remote event.

In **TUTORIAL 9.14**, we log our destinations to the screen, and then set up our first remote event to turn off all the emitters, rather than having to turn each one off individually.

Debugging and testing this sequence could prove tricky if we don't log some information regarding what's going on with the data. In **TUTORIAL 9.14**, we establish a logging system for this purpose, as well as demonstrate remote events.

TUTORIAL 9.14: Creating Complex Teleportation Systems, Part V: Logging Destination Arrivals and Implementing Remote Events

1. Continue from **TUTORIAL 9.12**, or open the DM-Ch_09_KTeleport_04.ut3 map included with the files for this chapter.

2. We need to determine the destination where the player arrived in order to log the proper phrase to the screen. Return to the Phase Three comment box.

   a. Create a new Compare Objects condition and connect it to the Out output of the Teleport object (see **FIGURE 9.124**).

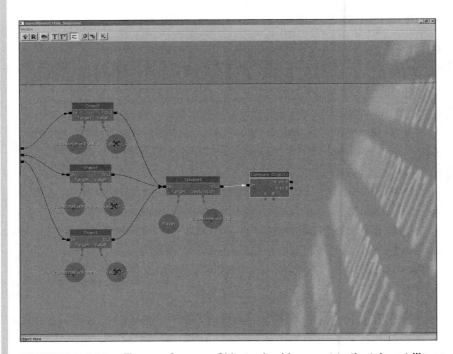

FIGURE 9.124   The new Compare Objects should connect to the teleport like so.

   b. Set A to a duplicate of the DestinationPoint named variable.

   c. Set B to a duplicate of the Teleporter_1 object variable (see **FIGURE 9.125**).

   d. Create a new log by holding the L key and clicking in a blank area of the workspace (neat, isn't it?), and then wire it to the A==B output of the Compare objects.

   e. Right-click on the new log and expose the String variable input.

   f. Create a new String variable with a value of Transmission to Orange Level Successful. Connect this variable to the String input of the log (see **FIGURE 9.126**).

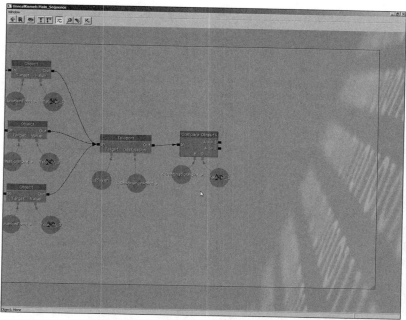

FIGURE 9.125   The Compare Objects now checks to see if the DestinationPoint variable contains the Teleporter_1 actor.

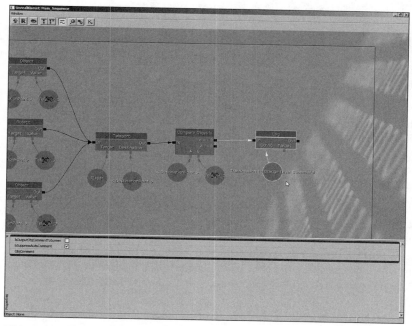

FIGURE 9.126   If the Compare Objects finds that the DestinationPoint is equal to Teleporter_1, then it logs that we were successfully sent to the Orange Level.

3. We now log into the screen's other phrases, depending on where we were just sent.

> **NOTE**
>
> As a point of trivia for all the non-programmers reading this book, A==B is actually read, "A is equal to B," while A!=B is read, "A is *not* equal to B."

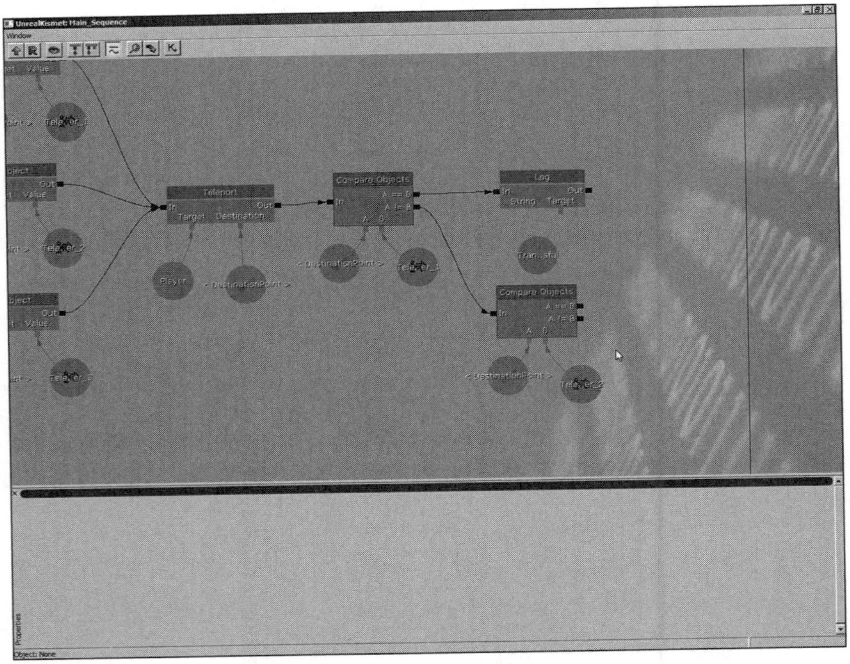

    a. Create a second Compare Objects, connect its In input to the A!=B output of the first. It should compare the DestinationPoint named variable in A against the Teleporter_2 object variable in B (see **FIGURE 9.127**).

FIGURE 9.127   Now, if our sequence discovers that DestinationPoint is not equal to Teleporter_1, it then checks to see if DestinationPoint is instead equal to Teleporter_2.

    b. This second Compare Objects should connect to a new log, which is reading a String variable with a value of Transmission to Cyan Level Successful (see **FIGURE 9.128**).

    c. We don't need a third Compare Objects for the last teleporter. Naturally, the process of elimination dictates that if it's not Teleporter 1 or Teleporter 2, it must be Teleporter 3. Save yourself a comparison by just creating a new log, which reads a new string of Transmission to Magenta Level Successful. Connect the log directly to the A!=B output of the second Compare Objects, as shown in **FIGURE 9.129**.

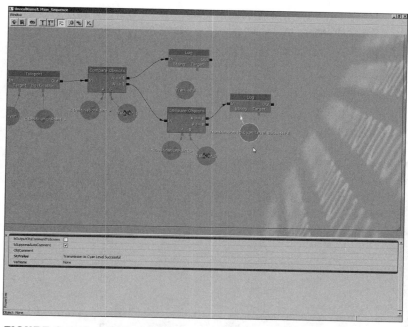

FIGURE 9.128 If the sequence finds that the DestinationPoint is equal to Teleporter_2, it logs that we were sent to the Cyan Level.

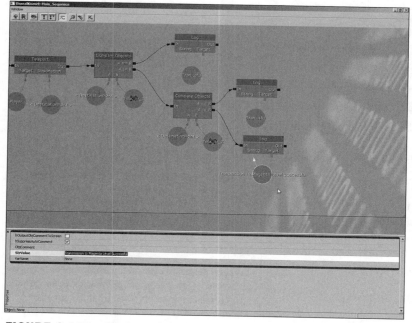

FIGURE 9.129 We know that if we didn't send the player either of the first two teleporters, we're safe in saying that they were sent to the third.

4. Next, we're going to set up a system that deactivates all of our teleporters as soon as the player is teleported. We could figure out which one is on and turn that one off directly, but it is far easier if we just send a command to shut them all down. The really cool part is that the work for this is already almost done. As you might recall, we turned off all the emitters in Phase One of the sequence. If we want to turn them off again, all we need is a way to activate Phase One once more. To do this, we use our first remote event.

   a. In the Phase One comment box, right-click and choose New Event > Remote Event (see **FIGURE 9.130**).

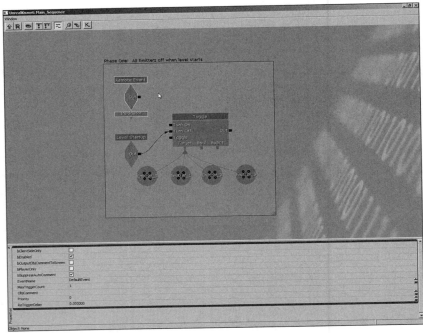

FIGURE 9.130   The new remote event should be placed inside the Phase One comment box.

   b. Set the EventName property to DeactivateTeleporters.

   c. Connect the Out of this event to the Turn Off of the Toggle (see **FIGURE 9.131**).

   d. In order to fully deactivate the teleporter, we need to set the ActiveTrigger variable to something else. If we do not, we can still jump down and walk into the Ground Level teleporter (even though it is not emitting particles), and it still sends us to our previous destination.

> **TIP**
>
> It may be helpful to also set the ObjComment property to DeactivateTeleporters as well, so that you do not have to select the event to see what its name is.

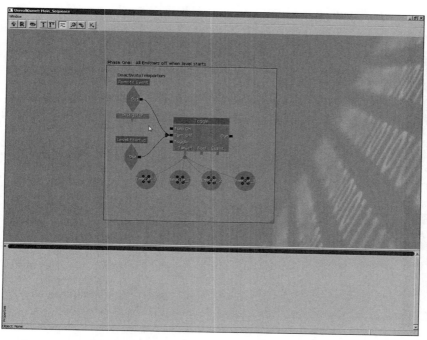

FIGURE 9.131   The DeactivateTeleporters remote event is reusing the Toggle found in the Phase One comment box to kill off all emitters.

Create a new Set Object Variable object, and use it to set ActiveTrigger to the player. You need a new Player object variable, and a duplicate of the ActiveTrigger named variable. Take a look at **FIGURE 9.132** if you need help.

When finished, connect this Object sequence object to the Out of the Toggle.

e. Let's go back to the Phase Three comment box. Underneath the first Compare Objects sequence object, and just to the right of the teleport, right-click and choose New Action > Event > Activate Remote Event.

> **NOTE**
>
> It doesn't really matter what object you use as your value. We're simply using the player as a matter of choice. The important thing is that the ActiveTrigger variable gets set to anything other than one of the teleportation pad triggers.

f. Set the EventName property of the new Activate Remote Event object to DeactivateTeleporters, and then connect its In input to the Out of the teleport (see **FIGURE 9.133**).

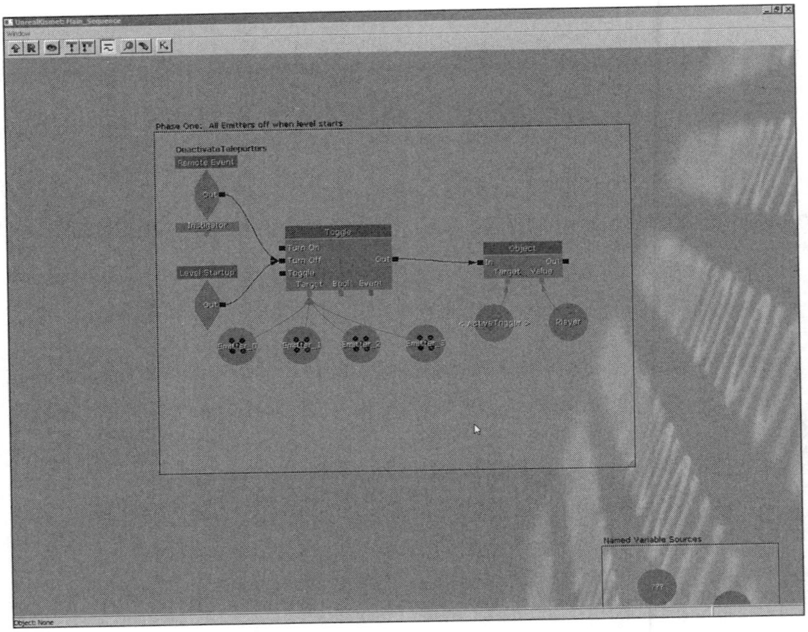

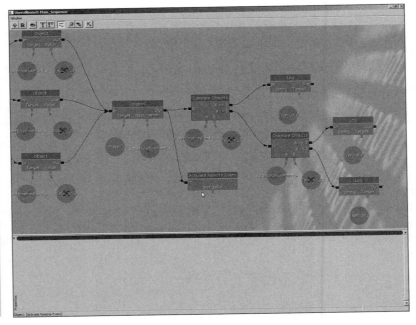

FIGURE 9.132
The Phase One sequence now sets the ActiveTrigger variable to contain the player. Doing so causes all of our condition sequence objects that are currently reading ActiveTrigger to return a value of False, thereby deactivating all teleporters.

FIGURE 9.133
Now, once your player is teleported, the sequence activates the DeactivateTeleporters remote event, turning off all emitters and deactivating teleporter triggers.

9

5. Save and test your progress. Kismet should now log to the screen which level the player is sent. Also, when you teleport up to a platform, the Ground Floor teleporter deactivates.

END TUTORIAL 9.14

Well, you should be happy to note that at this point, the hard part of the sequence is over. Now, all we need to do is to send the player back to the Ground Level from whatever platform he is located. However, we're going to pick up the pace a little bit by creating the sequences for each of the three platforms simultaneously. Don't worry; we're not doing anything to which you shouldn't already be accustomed by now!

Once the player has arrived at one of the upper teleportation pads, he needs a way to be sent back to the ground floor. In **TUTORIAL 9.15**, we create the necessary Kismet sequence objects to handle this.

TUTORIAL 9.15: Creating Complex Teleportation Systems, Part VI: Sending the Player Back to the Ground Level

1. Continue from **TUTORIAL 9.12**, or open the DM-Ch_09_KTeleport_05.ut3 map included with the files for this chapter.

2. Select Triggers 3, 5, and 7 (they're the ones above the teleportation pads on each of the three platforms). In the Phase Four comment box of the Kismet Editor, right-click and choose Create New Events using… > Touch.

Set the MaxTriggerCount for each of these new events to 0, and arrange them in the comment box from top to bottom in the order of 3, 5, and 7 (see **FIGURE 9.134**).

3. To the Touched output of each one of these events, connect a separate Compare Objects sequence object, using a duplicate of the ActiveTrigger named variable for A, and whichever trigger is associated with the Touch event for B.

For example, Trigger_3's Compare Objects compare against the ActiveTrigger named variable and Trigger_3, while Trigger_5's compares against ActiveTrigger and Trigger_5 (see **FIGURE 9.135**).

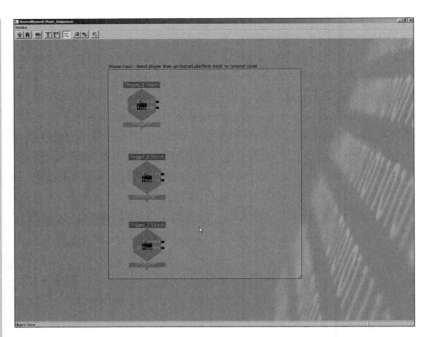

FIGURE 9.134   Your three new Touch events should be placed within the Phase Four comment box.

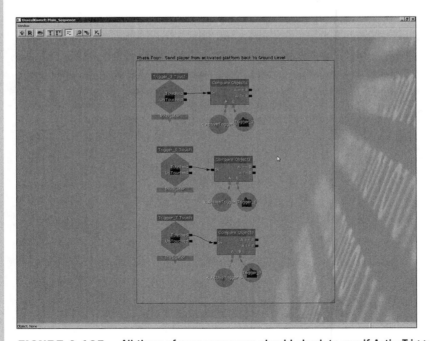

FIGURE 9.135   All three of your sequences should check to see if ActiveTrigger currently contains the trigger that was just touched. The appropriate network is shown here.

4. Connect the A==B output of all three of these Compare Objects to a single new Teleport object, which uses the player as the target and Teleporter_0 as the destination (see **FIGURE 9.136**).

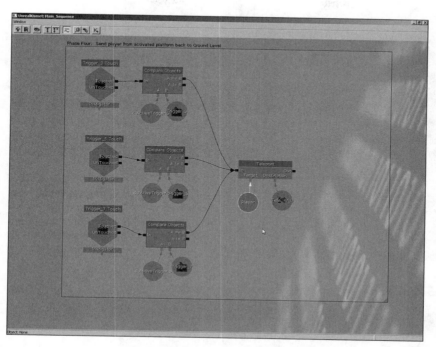

FIGURE 9.136   We don't need to do anything fancy with the teleporter's destination, because all three of these teleporters should be sending the player back to the Ground Level.

5. Connect the output of the teleport to a new log, which is using a string containing a value of Transmission to Ground Level Successful (see **FIGURE 9.137**)!

6. Finally, connect the Out of the Log to a new Activate Remote Event object, whose EventName property is set to DeactivateTeleporters. Of course, you could always duplicate the existing one (see **FIGURE 9.138**).

7. Save and test your level. You should now be able teleport from the Ground Level to any platform and back again, with Kismet logging the destinations all the while.

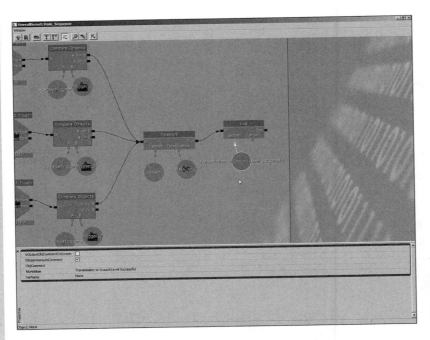

FIGURE 9.137
Your sequence now logs to the screen that the player has been sent to the Ground Level.

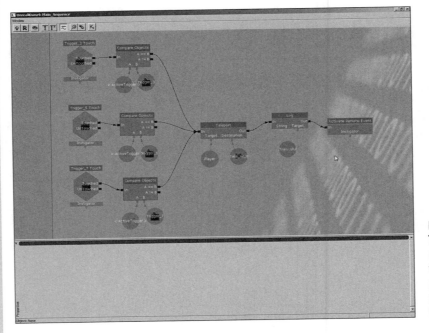

FIGURE 9.138
The new Activate remote event deactivates all the teleporters once the player is sent back to the Ground Level.

END TUTORIAL 9.15

Good work so far! What we need to do from here is to change the states of our materials from inactive to active. However, it should be noted that in this example, we are cheating in a sense in that we are changing all the materials for all the meshes simultaneously. For instance, if you activate the teleporter for the Orange Level, and then look back down at the Ground Floor, you see that the teleporter pad has lit up, even though you did not activate the Ground Floor. If, in your game, you needed each of the pads to light up individually, you would need a separate material instance applied to each one. For simplicity's sake, we're doing all four at the same time, assuming that you'd be using this in an instance where you couldn't necessarily see all four pads at once.

In **TUTORIAL 9.16**, we adjust the state of our materials using remote events. We add the initial Kismet sequence objects to allow the materials on the teleportation pads and the keypads to be altered during gameplay.

TUTORIAL 9.16: Creating Complex Teleportation Systems, Part VII: Creating Remote Events to Affect Our Materials

1. Continue from **TUTORIAL 9.12**, or open the DM-Ch_09_KTeleport_06.ut3 map included with the files for this chapter.

2. In the Phase Five comment box, right-click and choose New Event > Remote Event. Set the EventName property to ActivateMaterials, and set the MaxTriggerCount to 0 (see **FIGURE 9.139**).

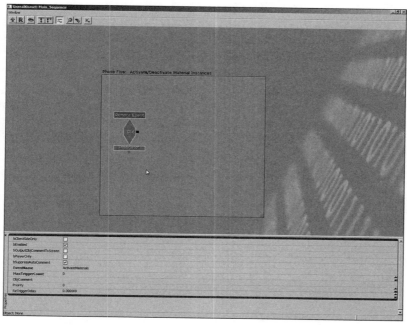

FIGURE 9.139   Our first remote event sets all the materials to their active state.

3. To the right of this event, right-click and choose New Action > Material Instance > Set ScalarParam. Connect this to the Out of the remote event (see **FIGURE 9.140**).

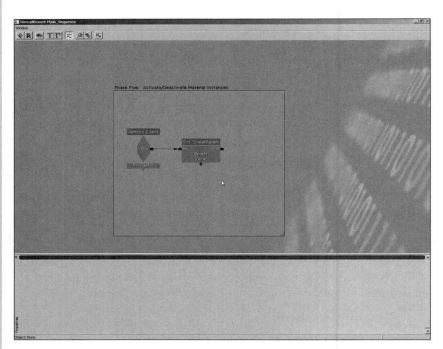

FIGURE 9.140   The new Set ScalarParam changes the state of the control panels.

4. With this new Set ScalarParam selected, set the following properties:

MatInst: matInst_teleporterButton

ParamName: ActiveButton

ScalarValue: 1.0

5. Create a second Set ScalarParam object, connected to the first, and set the following properties (see **FIGURE 9.141**):

MatInst: matInst_simpleTeleportPad

ParamName: Activated

ScalarValue: 1.0

> **NOTE**
>
> The names of these material instances, as well as their associated parameters, can be verified in the Generic browser by looking through the Chapter_09_ KismetContent.upk package.

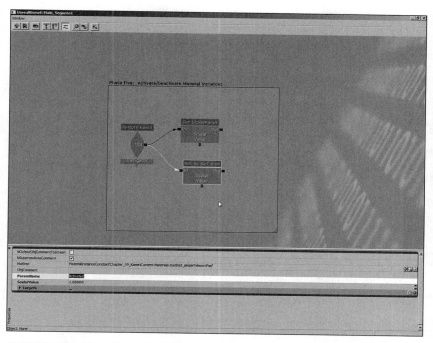

FIGURE 9.141 The second Set ScalarParam changes the material state of the teleporter pad meshes.

6. Select the remote event and both Set ScalarParam objects, duplicate them, and move them just beneath the original (see **FIGURE 9.142**).

7. Select the newly duplicated remote event and set its EventName property to DeactivateMaterials.

8. Select each of the two duplicated Set ScalarParam objects and set their ScalarValue properties to 0.

9. Save your level. There are no playable changes at this time.

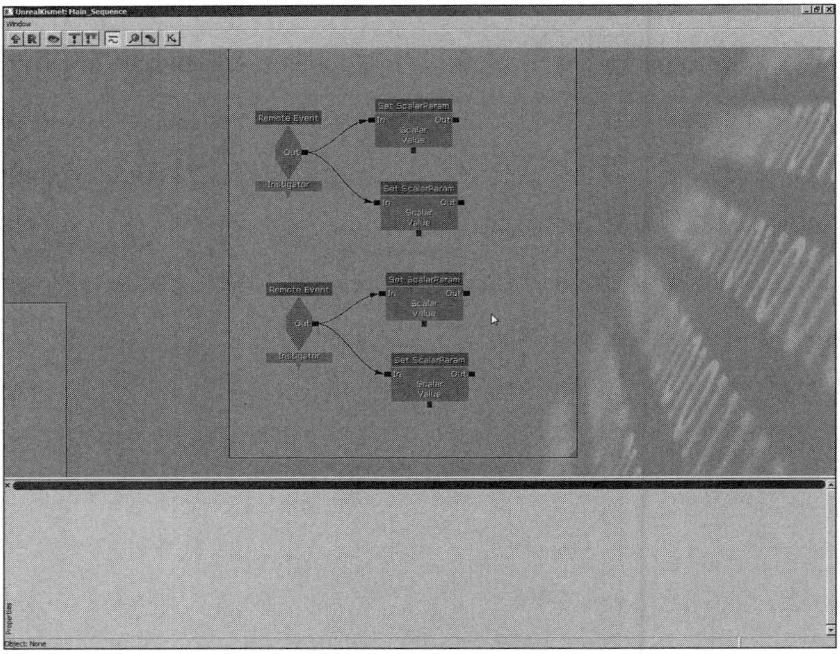

FIGURE 9.142   We have now duplicated the remote event and both of the Set ScalarParam objects. The second set sets the materials to their inactive state.

END TUTORIAL 9.16

We're almost done. The last thing we need to do is trigger off some final remote events to adjust our materials properly, and then delete out any remaining object variables that are not currently in use. However, be sure when doing this that you do not accidentally delete the Named Variable Sources created earlier. Those variables appear not to be connected to anything, although they are indeed being used by the sequence.

In **TUTORIAL 9.17**, we wrap up the sequence by finalizing the material adjustment system and clearing out any unused nodes that might be left behind.

TUTORIAL 9.17: Creating Complex Teleportation Systems, Part VIII: Connecting Final Remote Events and Cleanup

1. Continue from **TUTORIAL 9.12**, or open the DM-Ch_09_KTeleport_07.ut3 map included with the files for this chapter.

2. In the Phase One comment box, create a new Activate Remote Event action (New Action > Event > Activate Remote Event), and connect it to the Out output of the Object sequence object. Set its EventName to DeactivateMaterials (see **FIGURE 9.143**).

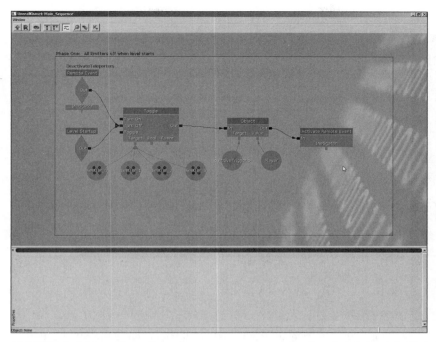

FIGURE 9.143   Phase One of our sequence now sets all materials back to their inactive state.

3. In the Phase Two comment box, create a new Activate Remote Event action to the right of the four Log objects. Connect all four logs into it, and then set its EventName to ActivateMaterials (see **FIGURE 9.144**).

4. Delete all unused object variables, but be sure not to delete those contained in the Named Object Sources comment box, as they are tied to named variables (see **FIGURE 9.145**).

> **NOTE**
>
> If you hid all the unused connectors of the logs, you may not see their Out outputs. You can reveal them by right-clicking on each log in turn and choosing Expose Output > Out from the Context menu!

5. One final thing we could do is make sure that the teleporters don't fire any stray particles into the level on startup. An easy and foolproof way to do that is to deactivate them by default. Do this now using the following steps:

a. In a viewport, select one of the emitters (it does not matter which).

b. Right-click on it and choose Select All Emitters from the Context menu.

c. Press F4 to go to the Properties window. Expand Emitter > ParticleSystemComponent > ParticleSystemComponent, and set bAutoActivate to False (unchecked).

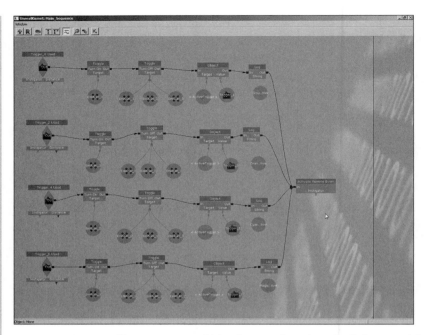

FIGURE 9.144 Now, no matter which teleporter is activated, all the materials are set to active.

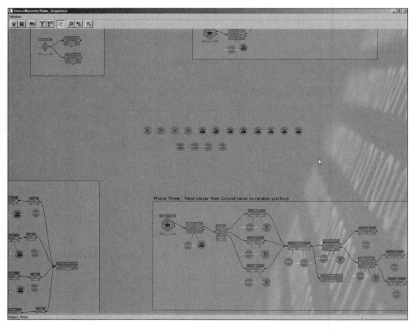

FIGURE 9.145 If you have any original object variables lying around your sequence, select and delete them.

6. Finally, back in the Kismet Editor, select each of your comment boxes along with their contents and carefully arrange them for maximum readability later. In our case, we positioned them by phase from left to right, but feel free to use your own layout.

7. Save and test your level. You will now notice the material change on the control panels when a teleporter is activated, as well as the pad itself lighting up. You can see the final setup by opening the kismetTeleport_demo map included with the files for this chapter.

END TUTORIAL 9.17

Summary

This chapter has covered a lot in terms of the basics of Kismet. There's still much you can learn. In fact, we've really only scratched the surface. An experienced scripter can create entire games using Kismet! Still, we are certain that you will find this foundation extremely useful as you start to create your own levels and worlds with Unreal Technology. Be sure to practice and take time to work with your sequences, making them as efficient as they can be. Kismet really is the heart of Unreal Engine 3's gameplay, and those who master it will be able to create many more memorable gaming experiences than those who fail to recognize its power.

Chapter 10

Unreal Matinee

This chapter will get you up-and-running with Matinee, Unreal Engine 3.0's complete, built-in animation system. Using the skills you'll master here, you can create all manner of animated assets—from doors and lifts to animated materials.

What Is Matinee?

Matinee is a tool within Unreal Editor that is used to change properties of actors over time, or to animate them. These properties could include location, rotation, size, or even properties specific to a particular actor, such as the brightness or color of a light. Matinee can also be used to activate events within Kismet, to play sound effects, and to play skeletal animation for characters, including facial animations with Unreal Editor's FaceFX system.

Matinee is fully integrated into Kismet, providing for a wide range of animation control based on events and actions throughout your sequence. This means that you can use actions and events in your level's Kismet to fire off a Matinee animation, or allow Matinee to be a driving force of your sequences, triggering actions and other events at certain intervals (see **FIGURE 10.1**).

Matinee is also used to create animated cutscenes in your games. The creation of movies using game engines, also known as *machinima*, is handled entirely within the Matinee system. You can use it to create dramatic sequences that support and enhance the gameplay experience, or create your own entire film using the game engine as your renderer!

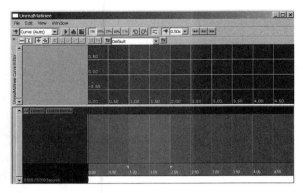

FIGURE 10.1   The Matinee Editor can be accessed through Matinee Kismet sequence objects.

Matinee Terminology

Before you get too far into the world of Matinee, there is some basic terminology you need to understand. Knowing what the following terms mean give you a much easier time while learning to use the Matinee system:

▶ **Animation**—Many people who begin learning about computer animation immediately associate the word with motion. However, *animation* is more precisely thought of as the change in a property value over time. Even the movement of an object is really no more than the gradual change of an object's location properties. However, there are many more properties that can also be animated, such as emission rates, light brightness and color, and many more.

▶ **Keys**—*Keys* are the basis for animation in a computer. Keys store the value of a property at a given time. The Matinee system then interpolates the change in time from one key to the next, resulting in animation. Animation of any sort requires at least two keys. Keep in mind that keys are sometimes referred to as *keyframes*.

▶ **Curves**—In terms of using Matinee, *curves* are considered to be graphical representations of the interpolation between one key and the next (see **FIGURE 10.2**). In the Matinee Editor, you have access to the Curve Editor, which enables you to change the shape of these curves, and thereby change the nature of your animation, without having to add new keys. For example, a curve that travels in a straight line from one key to the next defines linear animation, which moves at a constant rate, while a curve that had an ease-in and ease-out shape (S-curve) would define animation that accelerates from zero and then decelerates to zero again. The shape of these curves is controlled through Bezier tangent handles. For more information on using the Curve Editor, please see Appendix B, "The Curve Editor."

10

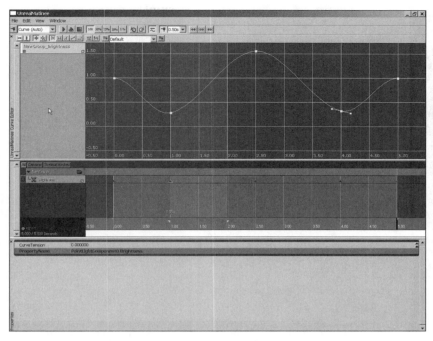

FIGURE 10.2   Curves graphically represent the change in a property value over time.

▶ **Tangents**—*Tangents* are small handles that can be used to change the shape of a curve as it enters and exits a key (see **FIGURE 10.3**). They use a Bezier style of control, which may be familiar to readers who have any experience in working with function curves in popular animation packages. Each key has two tangents: one for the incoming curve and one for the outgoing. These can be edited in unison so that they always remain contiguous, or broken as to create a sharp angle, which results in a drastic change in animation rate. At the time of this writing, tangents cannot have their weight adjusted.

▶ **Tracks**—*Tracks* are a set of keys that are tasked with performing a specific operation. There are several types of track, each designed for a different purpose. Movement tracks hold positional data, allowing for animation of location, whereas an event track is designed to allow for the activation of Kismet events at specific time intervals throughout the animation. Tracks are contained within groups.

▶ **Groups**—*Groups* are simply containers that hold tracks. They can be used for organization, but are also used to designate actors in the scene that is associated with the tracks contained in the group. This is because each group that is created in the Matinee sequence receives its own variable input on the sequence object in Kismet. Object variables containing various actors, such as InterpActors, can be attached to the variable input. All actors attached to that group input receive animation based on the tracks contained within the group.

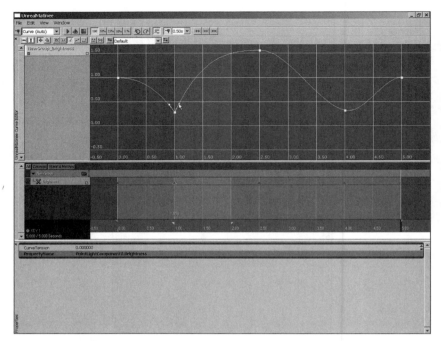

FIGURE 10.3   Tangents allow for curve shape to be altered.

▶ **Director Group**—This is a special type of group that is designed for handling camera-specific actions, such as cuts, slow-motion effects, fades, and color scaling. There can be only one director group in each Matinee sequence. The group is most effectively used in creating cinematic sequences and machinima features.

In **TUTORIAL 10.1**, we walk you through the creation of a very simple InterpActor that moves back and forth to transport the player over a gap. We're going to keep things very basic, essentially just giving you a chance to see several parts of the Matinee process so that they are familiar as we discuss them later. **TUTORIAL 10.1** assumes a basic knowledge of the Kismet system. For more information on using Kismet, please see Chapter 9, "Introduction to Unreal Kismet."

TUTORIAL 10.1: Your First Matinee Sequence, Part I: Initial Setup

1. Launch Unreal Editor and open the DM-CH_10_Mover_Start.ut3 map file and the Chapter_10_MatineeDemo package included on the DVD in the files for this chapter. Open the Generic browser and locate and select the sm_grate static mesh located in the Matinee_Demo package (see **FIGURE 10.4**).

> **NOTE**
>
> Make sure your Drag Grid is set to 8.

10

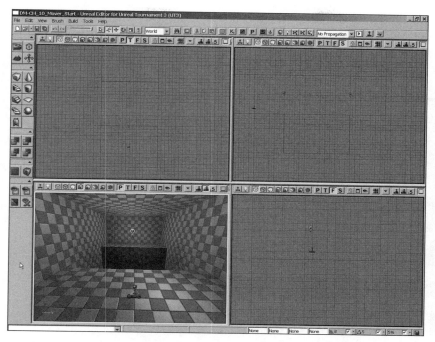

FIGURE 10.4 The Mover_Demo map is a simple room with a large gap separating it.

2. We now place the mesh in the level as an InterpActor and establish some initial properties:

   a. Right-click in the Perspective viewport on the floor of the level and choose Add InterpActor:StaticMesh MatineeDemo.sm_grate to place the InterpActor in the level (see **FIGURE 10.5**). If done properly, the new mesh should have a pink wireframe, instead of the usual teal sported by static meshes.

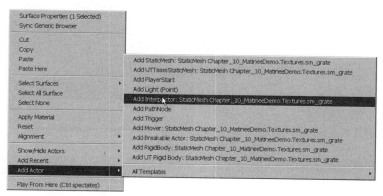

FIGURE 10.5 Place the mesh in the level as an InterpActor.

> **b.** In the top viewport, position the mesh so that it is flush with the north side of the gap, or the side that is nearest to the top of the viewport (see **FIGURE 10.6**). Center the grate evenly in the Y-axis, and then switch the side viewport and make sure that the grate is even with the top of the gap in the Z-axis.

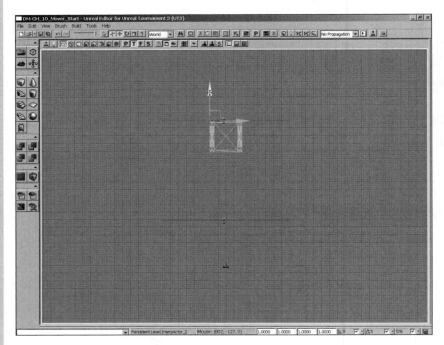

FIGURE 10.6   The grate should be positioned in the top viewport against the north edge of the gap.

> **c.** With the grate selected, press F4 to open the Properties Window. Expand the Collision tab, and verify that the CollisionType property is set to COLLIDE_BlockAll.

3. With the InterpActor selected, open Kismet and create a new Level Startup event (New Event > Level Startup). Next, create a new Matinee sequence object (New Matinee) and link its Play input to the Out output of the Level Startup (see **FIGURE 10.7**).

4. Double-click the Matinee sequence object to access the Matinee Editor (see **FIGURE 10.8**).

10

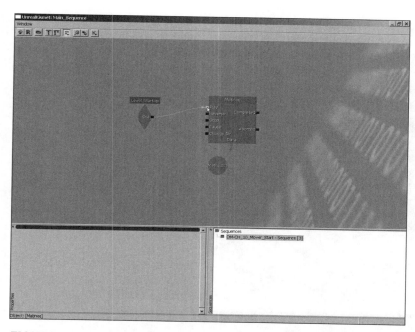

FIGURE 10.7 Create and connect the sequence objects as shown.

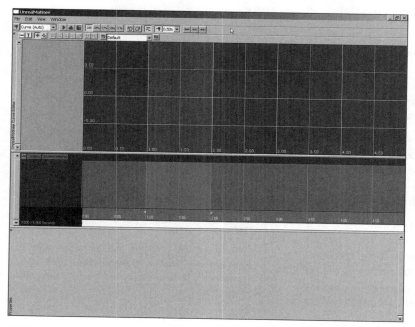

FIGURE 10.8 Double-clicking the Matinee object opens the Matinee Editor.

5. Right-click in the pale gray column on the left side of the Matinee Editor and choose Add New Empty Group from the Context menu. A text box appears, asking for a name for the new group. Enter Platform and press Enter (see **FIGURE 10.9**).

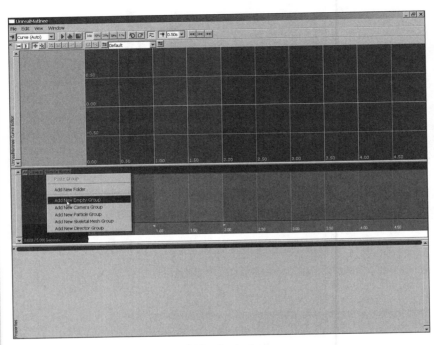

FIGURE 10.9   The Group/Track List Context menu

6. The new group appears as a bar in the Matinee Editor's timeline. Right-click on this new group and choose Add New Movement Track from the Context menu. This creates the track that holds the actual animation keys (see **FIGURE 10.10**).

7. The first key in our sequence has already been created at time 0.00. This is the default behavior for movement tracks. We now need to create the other keys so that we can have animation. Across the bottom of the main window of the Matinee Editor is a gray bar with many numbers running across it. This is the time slider. If you left drag within this bar, you are adjusting the current time for the animation.

Drag the time slider, indicated by a thick black bar with a thin white bar extending out of it, to set the current time to 1.00. You can verify the current time using the green numbers in the lower-left corner of the Matinee Editor (see **FIGURE 10.11**).

> **TIP**
>
> If you need added precision, use the mouse wheel to zoom into the timeline. However, know that slight discrepancies in time values are typically not problematic.

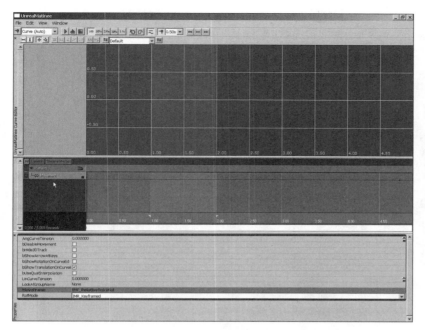

FIGURE 10.10   The new movement track has now been added.

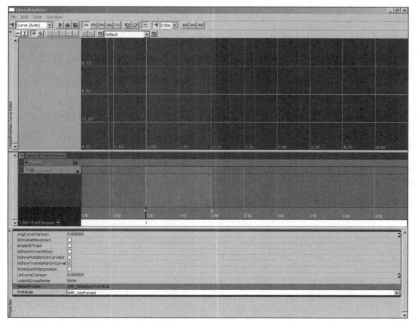

FIGURE 10.11   Use the green numbers in the lower-left corner to gauge the time.

8. Once the time slider is at a value of 1.00, press the Add Key button ![Add Key icon], located in the Matinee Editor's toolbar at the top of its interface. This creates a key at the time 1.00 (see **FIGURE 10.12**).

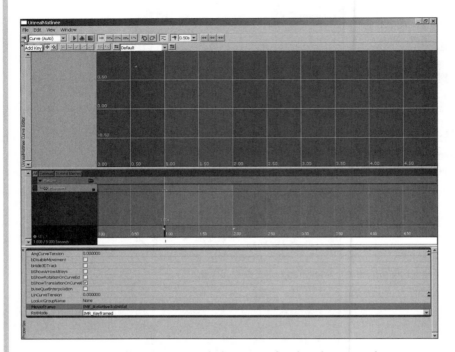

FIGURE 10.12   Keys appear as dark orange triangles along a track.

9. Close the Matinee Editor, and save your level's progress.

END TUTORIAL 10.1

Continue from **TUTORIAL 10.1**, or open the DM-CH_10_Mover_01.ut3 map file provided on the DVD with the files for this chapter. In **TUTORIAL 10.2**, we create the remaining keys for our sequence, and explore Interpolation Mode, which enables us to interactively edit the position of InterpActors in our level for animation.

TUTORIAL 10.2: Your First Matinee Sequence, Part II: Interpolation Mode

1. Open the Kismet Editor and double-click on the Matinee sequence object to access Matinee Editor.

2. Click and drag on the time slider, and move it to a time of 4.00. If you are not precisely on the 4.00, don't worry; we fix that in a moment. Once the time slider is in position, make

sure the movement track is selected and click the Add Key button 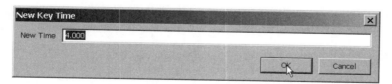 to create a new key (see **FIGURE 10.13**).

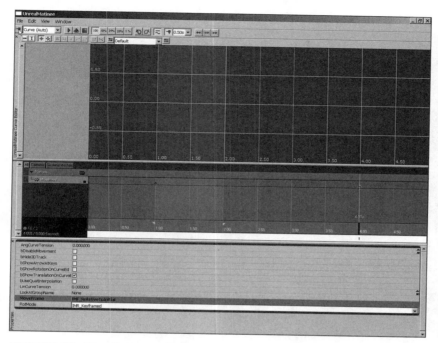

FIGURE 10.13   Set a new key at or near 4.00.

3. We want this new key to move our grate mesh across the gap over the three-second interval between the key at 1.00 and the new key at 4.00. But first, let's make sure that the new key is exactly at a time value of 4. In the movement track along the timeline, you see a dark orange triangle, which signifies the key.

Right-click on this triangle, and choose Set Time from the Context menu. In the window that appears, set the time value to 4 and press Enter (see **FIGURE 10.14**).

FIGURE 10.14   The Set Time window

4. We now need to create the actual motion that takes place between times 1.00 and 4.00. The first step is to designate exactly which key will hold this information. Click on the triangle icon for the key at time 4.00.

5. Move the Matinee Editor out of the way, but do not close it. In the Perspective viewport, notice the words ADJUST KEY 2. This tells you that you are in Interpolation Mode, which enables you to edit the value of keys (see **FIGURE 10.15**).

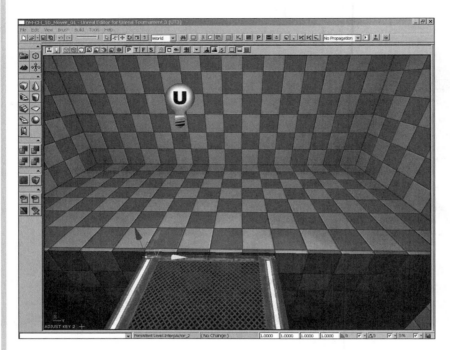

FIGURE 10.15   Note the ADJUST KEY message in the viewport.

Using the Translation Widget in the top viewport, move the grate mesh downward in the X-axis so that it is flush with the southern lip of the gap (see **FIGURE 10.16**).

> **NOTE**
>
> When Matinee is open, you cannot hold Shift while moving objects to move the camera in tandem.

6. Let's take a moment and test out what we've done. Navigate back to the Matinee Editor, and position it so that you can see the Perspective viewport. Drag the time slider back and forth across the bottom of the timeline.

You should notice that your grate is moving back and forth across the gap as you drag, but that the animation is a little off. The grate actually goes through the edge of the gap at one point, but this is normal and will be fixed later.

10

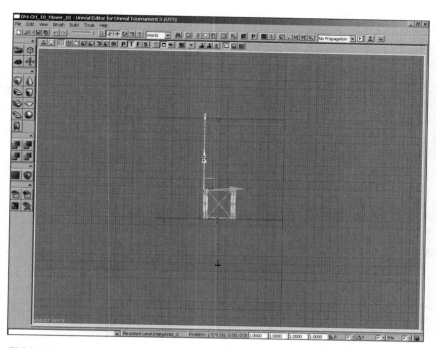

FIGURE 10.16   Move the grate to the opposite side of the gap.

7. Drag the time slider to time 5.00, which is also the end of the sequence, and click the Add Key button ⏺. This creates a key that holds the platform at the southern side of the gap for one second (see **FIGURE 10.17**).

8. Close the Matinee Editor and save your level's progress.

> **NOTE**
>
> If you do not have motion at this point, make sure the viewport has Realtime enabled and that the InterpActor is connected to the Platform group in Kismet.

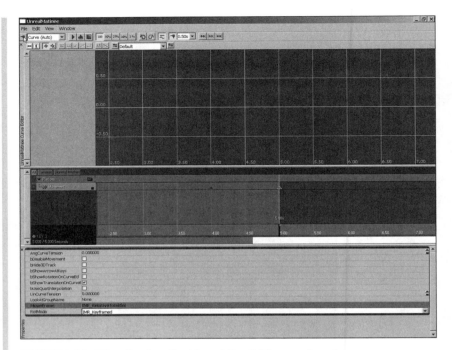

FIGURE 10.17   Create a final key at the 5.00 second mark.

END TUTORIAL 10.2

Continue from **TUTORIAL 10.2**, or open the DM-CH_10_Mover_02.ut3 map file provided on the DVD with the files for this chapter. **TUTORIAL 10.3** focuses on editing the animation that we have created through tweaking our curves.

TUTORIAL 10.3: Your First Matinee Sequence, Part III: Editing Curves

1. Open the Kismet Editor and double-click the Matinee sequence object to access the Matinee Editor.

2. In the Matinee Editor, the Curve Editor should be visible by default. If it is not, click on the Toggle Curve Editor button ⇌. The Curve editor appears. At first, you will not be able to see the curves for the movement track. To solve this, click on the small black square in the lower-right corner of the movement track's label. The curves suddenly become visible (see **FIGURE 10.18**).

> **NOTE**
>
> The curves may not fit in the visible area of the Curve Editor by default. You can click the Fit Horizontally ↔ and Fit Vertically ↕ buttons on the toolbar to make the curve fit in the visible area.

10

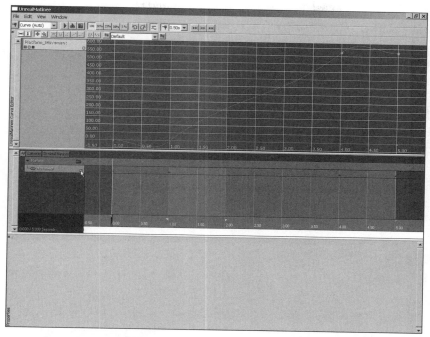

FIGURE 10.18 Once you click the small black square on the movement track, you can see the curves in the curve editor.

3. Currently, there are actually three curves available in the Curve Editor—one for each of the three axes. We have only animated our platform on the X-axis, so we only need to see the curve for X. On the Platform Movement label on the left side of the Curve Editor, you will see three small square buttons: one red, one blue, and one green.

   Click on the red and blue squares. This turns them black, which hides the curves for X and Z. Remember that RGB color coding is analogous to XYZ.

4. You now only see the Y curve. You might notice that in the viewports, the InterpActor appears to be moving along the X-axis, but the movement information is stored in the Y-axis within the movement track. The reason for this is that movement tracks use the Relative To Initial movement type. We discuss this in greater detail later, but it has to do with the fact that we had to rotate the InterpActor from its initial orientation. For now, just accept that the movement being stored in the Y-axis is correct, even though the mover actually moves in the X-axis.

   At time intervals 0, 1, 4, and 5, you will see keys. Notice that the curve arcs upward between the first and second keys, and then arcs downward between the third and fourth. This behavior is known as *overshoot*, and is the cause of the platform moving into the edges of the gap instead of stopping when it hits them (see **FIGURE 10.19**).

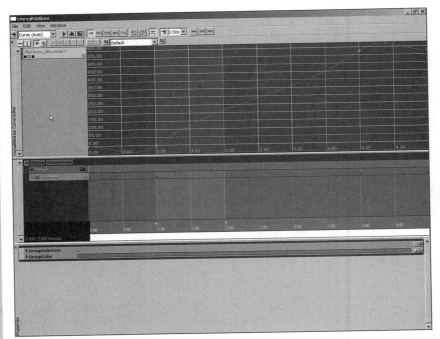

FIGURE 10.19   Notice the overshoot at the beginning and end of the curve.

We can fix the first key (Key 0) by selecting it, and clicking the Linear button ![button], located in the Curve Editor's toolbar. Notice as you click this button that the segment of curve between the first and second key flattens out (see **FIGURE 10.20**).

5. The next section of the curve, between Key 1 and Key 2, slants downward, which graphically represents motion in the negative direction. However, you will notice that there is a sharp angle where the new flat segment reaches Key 1. This sharp angle results in an immediate change in speed, with no acceleration. To fix this, we use the key's Bezier tangent handle to smooth out the angle (see **FIGURE 10.21**).

> **NOTE**
>
> Keys are numbered using a 0-based system. This means that the first key is Key 0; the second is Key 1, and so on.

10

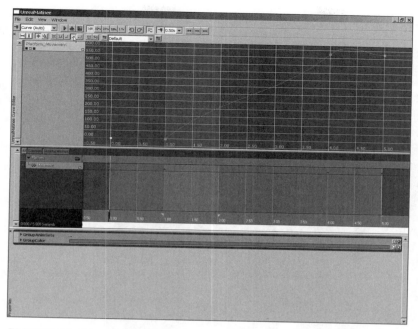

FIGURE 10.20   Setting the first key to Linear flattens out the beginning of the curve.

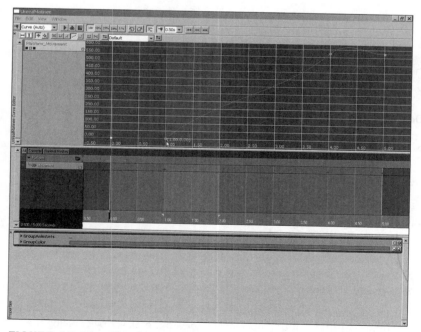

FIGURE 10.21   The sharp angle of the curve creates a dramatic change in speed, which we want to soften.

Click on Key 1, and notice the small white handle coming out of it. This is its Bezier tangent handle. Dragging on the small knob on the end of this handle enables you to edit how the shape of the curve changes as it leaves a keyframe. Drag out this handle perfectly horizontal to the right of the key. This creates a smooth transition—and therefore smooth acceleration—from the flat area of the curve to the second segment (see **FIGURE 10.22**).

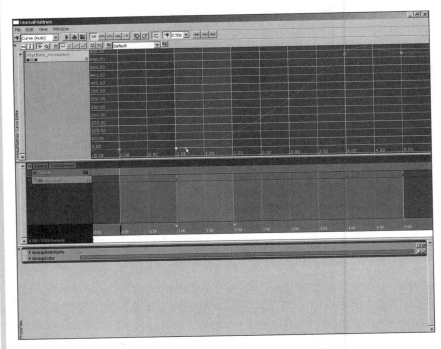

FIGURE 10.22   Drag out the tangent horizontally from Key 1.

6. Click on Key 2, and then click on the Linear button 🖉 once again to flatten out the end of the animation (see **FIGURE 10.23**). This stops the motion. Remember that a flat line on a curve indicates no change over time, or that animation has stopped.

7. Select the tangent on the left side of Key 2, and drag its handle so that it extends flat out to the left of the key. This creates a smooth transition from the area of motion to the newly flattened area (see **FIGURE 10.24**).

Your animation can now be defined as ease-in and ease-out. It starts with no motion, and then accelerates toward the other side of the gap. It slows down as it approaches the other side of the gap, and gradually comes to a graceful stop at the other side.

8. Close the Matinee Editor and the Kismet Editor. Save your level, and test it out by clicking the Play In Editor button 👤. The platform now moves toward the player by crossing the gap. However, it makes no return trip! We fix this in **TUTORIAL 10.4**.

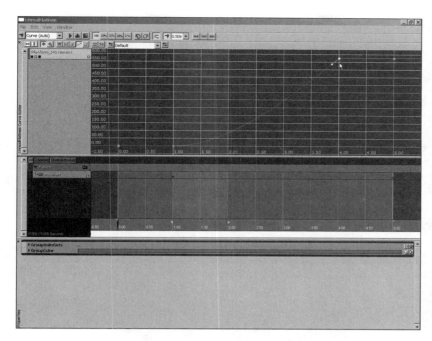

FIGURE 10.23
The second area of overshoot is now flattened.

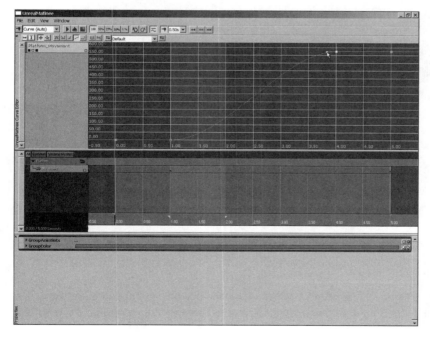

FIGURE 10.24
Flatten the tangent on the left side of Key 2.

END TUTORIAL 10.3

Continue from **TUTORIAL 10.2**, or open the DM-CH_10_Mover_02.ut3 map file provided on the DVD with the files for this chapter. In this final section for your first Matinee sequence, we adjust the sequence object so that the animation constantly plays back and forth, enabling the player to freely cross the gap in either direction.

TUTORIAL 10.4: Your First Matinee Sequence, Part IV: Constant Back and Forth Playback

1. Open the Kismet Editor. Take a moment and acquaint yourself with the sequence. Notice that the Matinee sequence object now has a Platform input on the bottom, corresponding with our Platform group created earlier in the Matinee Editor (see **FIGURE 10.25**).

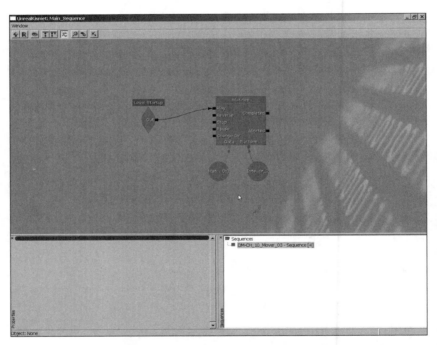

FIGURE 10.25   Take a look at the inputs of the Matinee sequence object.

Also notice that this Platform input also has an object variable connected to it, which corresponds to the InterpActor. This object variable was created and attached automatically because we had the InterpActor selected when we first created the group.

2. Our first step is to make use of the Matinee sequence object's inputs and outputs to cause the animation to play in reverse once it reaches its end. To do this, drag a wire from

the Completed output of the sequence object to the Reverse input on the opposite side of the sequence object (see **FIGURE 10.26**). Do not worry that you are connecting the sequence back to itself; this will not pose a problem.

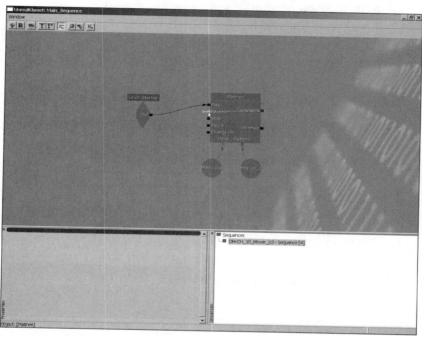

FIGURE 10.26   Notice that the wire crosses back over the Matinee sequence.

3. Test the level. You will now see that the platform crosses the gap, enabling the player to board, and then re-traverses the gap. However, there is currently no way for the player to get back across the gap again. Exit the In Editor Game when finished.

4. The Aborted output can be a bit misleading in name, in that it actually has nothing to do with the sequence being stopped. The Aborted output is activated when reverse playback reaches the beginning of the sequence. Drag a wire from the Aborted output to the Play input of the Matinee sequence object. Once again, you are connecting the sequence object to itself (see **FIGURE 10.27**).

5. Save your level and test again. The platform now moves back and forth across the gap, with two-second pauses on each side. Congratulations on completing your first Matinee sequence!

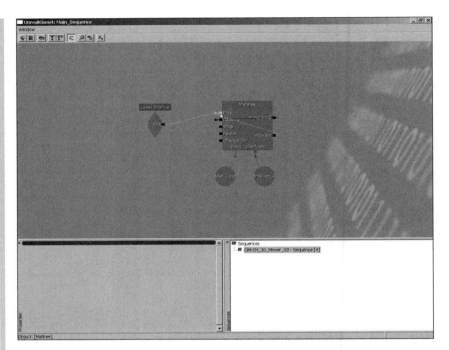

FIGURE 10.27   Connect the Aborted output back to the Play input.

END TUTORIAL 10.4

Accessing Matinee

Matinee is only accessed via Kismet through the creation of a Matinee sequence object. Once you right-click in the Kismet Editor and choose New Matinee, the sequence object appears. Double-clicking on the Matinee object opens the Matinee Editor.

The sequence object contains the Matinee functionality. Connected to each Matinee sequence object is the Matinee Data object, which holds all the animation information, such as keyframes and tracks. Think of the relationship as being similar to a DVD player and an actual DVD. Whereas the Matinee sequence object plays the information and applies to the correct object, the Matinee Data supplies the animation information being used.

The Matinee Sequence Object

The Matinee Kismet sequence object can be thought of as a container that holds a single Matinee animation sequence. This does not, however, mean that a Matinee sequence object can be used to animate only one object. In fact, with just a little bit of clever networking, you can animate any number of objects by using the same Matinee sequence object (see **FIGURE 10.28**).

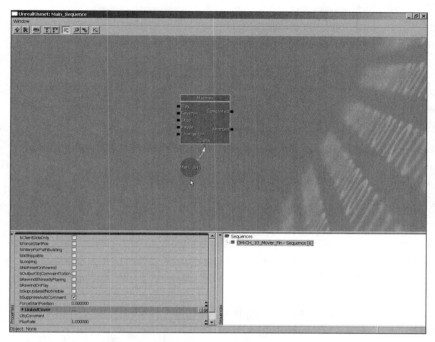

FIGURE 10.28   The Matinee Sequence object. Notice that it automatically comes with a Matinee Data object, which we cover later.

Like all Kismet sequence objects, the Matinee object has a variety of inputs and outputs to control the flow of your sequence, and how your Matinee animation is handled as a part of that sequence. Following is an overview of each of those inputs and outputs, because they are each very important to how your animation flows.

Inputs

The following list contains all of the available inputs on the Matinee Kismet node, which you will use to control basic playback:

- ▶ **Play**—This input causes the Matinee sequence to begin playback of your animation in a forward direction.
- ▶ **Reverse**—This input triggers the Matinee sequence to playback in the reverse direction. For example, if the original sequence animated a value from 0 to 1, playing back in reverse would animate that value from 1 to 0.

> ▸ **Stop**—This input stops the Matinee sequence during playback.

> ▸ **Pause**—This input pauses the Matinee sequence during playback. Triggering this input twice effectively un-pauses.

> ▸ **Change Dir**—This input swaps the current direction that the Matinee sequence is playing. If it was playing forward, it plays in the reverse direction and vice-versa.

Outputs

The following list contains all of the available outputs on the Matinee Kismet node, which are used to trigger other actions:

> ▸ **Completed**—This output is activated if the Matinee sequence reaches the end of the animation while playing forward.

> ▸ **Aborted**—This output is activated if the Matinee sequence is playing in reverse and reaches the beginning. Its name can be a bit of a misnomer—it has nothing to do with playback being stopped or paused.

> ▸ **Event Track Outputs**—These outputs do not initially exist. You can create an event track in your Matinee sequence object, and these tracks can contain named outputs that are fired off at indicated intervals. For instance, you could create an event track and create an event within it named QueueEnemies at the two-second mark. Once added, you would see a new event track output appear on the right side of the sequence object in Kismet, and anything connected to it would be triggered two seconds after the sequence began playback, provided the sequence was playing forward.

Variable Links

The following list contains all of the available variable input links, which are visible on the bottom of the Matinee Kismet node. These are used to send various forms of data into the Matinee system:

> ▸ **Data**—This variable link takes in a single Matinee Data object.

> ▸ **Group Variable Inputs**—These variable inputs, much like the Event Track outputs, do not initially exist. They are created through the generation of groups within the Matinee sequence object. When a new group is created, a new Group Variable input link appears along the bottom of the sequence object. The currently selected actor is automatically placed within an object variable and attached to this new input.

Properties

The Matinee sequence object has several properties that are also used to influence the nature of its playback. These properties are described as follows:

▶ **ClientSideOnly**—This property tells the engine that the sequence does not affect any part of gameplay, and therefore does not need to be replicated, or performed on networked machines. The property also prevents the sequence from playing if none of its associated actors are visible, and causes the sequence to be ignored by dedicated servers.

Basically, when playing in a multiplayer game, this property prevents other computers from seeing the Matinee sequence. If this is set to False for an operation such as opening a door, as soon as the server receives the information that the door has been opened, it then propagates that information to all client machines so that all players see the door open.

▶ **ForceStartPos**—This property tells the sequence to always start playback from the time—or timeline position—indicated by the ForceStartPosition property, which is explained later.

▶ **InterpForPathBuilding**—This property tells the sequence to jump to the time indicated in the Path-Building position in the timeline.

The Path-Building position is a time specified in the Matinee Editor from the Editor's Edit menu. Its purpose is to prevent moving objects from blocking AI paths. Consider this example: You have a path going down a corridor that has a doorway going down it. The door takes 1 second to open in its Matinee sequence. If you set its Path-Building position to 1 second, when you click the Build Paths button in the editor, the door's Matinee sequence jumps to that position in the timeline during the build, thereby opening the doorway so that the path can be built all the way down the corridor. This is important so that the doorway does not block the creation of the path.

▶ **IsSkippable**—This property allows the CANCELMATINEE console command to be used to skip the sequence. If the sequence is skipped in this manner, all events that took place throughout the sequence are triggered.

▶ **Looping**—This property causes the sequence to loop back to the beginning as soon as it is done playing. If this setting is set to True, the sequence never triggers the Completed or Aborted outputs.

▶ **NoResetOnRewind**—This property causes any actors who are affected by movement tracks that are using RelativeToInitial interpolation to use the initial position set at the current location when the sequence is rewound. This means that an actor begins the next loop of the animation from the same location as where the animation ended—or in more practical terms, appears to keep traveling along, never resetting to its original position.

▶ **RewindIfAlreadyPlaying**—This property causes the animation to automatically rewind back to the beginning if a user activates the Play input again during playback.

▶ **RewindOnPlay**—This property causes the animation to always start from the beginning when the Play input is activated, even if the animation was paused.

▶ **SkipUpdateIfNotVisible**—This property causes the Matinee sequence to be ignored if bClientSideOnly is True and none of the actors affected by the Matinee sequence are visible.

▶ **ForceStartPosition**—This property holds a designated position along the timeline from which to start the animation when the Play input is activated. This setting is only used if the bForceStartPos is also set to True. The value can also be exposed in Kismet, allowing this value to be adjusted during gameplay due to various events and actions.

▶ **PlayRate**—This property serves as a multiplier for the final speed at which the animation plays back. A value of 1 is equal to normal real-time speed.

Matinee Data Object

The Matinee Data object contains all the animation information that is used by the Matinee sequence object. This animation data is stored in keyframes, which record a property value at a given time. The system then interpolates between these recordings as time progresses, and you have animation. Matinee Data objects contain the groups used in the sequence. These groups in turn contain the individual tracks for each of the properties that will be animated, and each of these tracks contains a variety of keyframes (see **FIGURE 10.29**).

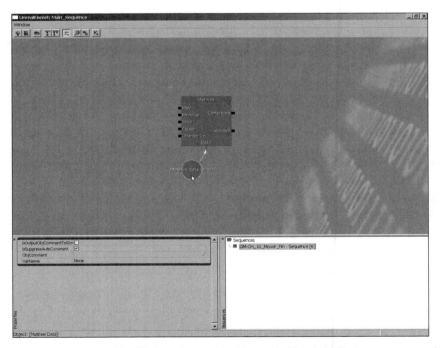

FIGURE 10.29   The Matinee Data object is created by default whenever you make a new Matinee sequence object.

Each Matinee sequence object can be powered by one, and only one, Matinee Data object. However, a single Matinee Data object can be used on multiple Matinee sequence objects. However, when doing this, all movement animation should be using the RelativeToInitial method, or else all actors associated with the animation move to the exact location within the level.

InterpActors

In previous versions of the Unreal Engine, animated game objects were typically handled through movers. *Movers* were special actors that held animation data, or keys, which could be used to animate the object based on the settings of its properties.

As of Unreal Engine 3, the Mover object has been replaced by the InterpActor. These are special mesh actors that use polygon models from static meshes, but differ from static meshes in that they can be dynamic, or move during gameplay. Unlike movers, InterpActors contain no animation data in and of themselves; all of their animation is passed to them through Matinee sequence objects.

> **NOTE**
>
> When placing an InterpActor, you may notice a Mover option. This is not to be confused with movers from previous versions of Unreal Engine. This option simply places an InterpActor with a Mover event in Kismet and a Matinee sequence already created and ready to be animated.

The InterpActor is not always used for motion, however. Because of their dynamic nature, they can also be used in areas where you need a mesh whose material changes in the game—an ability that standard static meshes do not have. They can also be used to cast dynamic shadow buffer shadows through textures that are using an alpha map. This process is described in Chapter 7, "Introduction to Lighting."

Following are some of the notable properties of the InterpActor:

- ▸ **StopOnEncroach**—This property causes the InterpActor to stop moving when it collides with another actor, such as the player. Without this property activated, the InterpActor continues to progress forward, and can be used to crush or kill the player.

- ▸ **CloseSound**—This property contains a sound cue that is played when the InterpActor begins playback of the animation in reverse.

- ▸ **OpenSound**—This property contains a sound cue that is played when the InterpActor begins playback of the animation in the forward direction.

Mover Kismet Event

The Mover Kismet sequence event (Event > Physics > Mover) works in conjunction with an InterpActor to provide a way to create a simple, event-driven animated object that is much more like the original mover in previous versions of the Unreal Engine.

When created, the Mover event consists of an event that is pre-wired to a new empty Matinee sequence object. You'll notice that the first two outputs of the Mover event involve the attaching and detaching of an actor. In simpler terms, this refers to when an actor—such as the player— gets onto the InterpActor or gets back off of it. This means that the mover is perfectly suited to creating objects like simple lifts, moving platforms, trap doors, or anything else that a player could stand on and that needs to move.

In order for the Mover event to function properly, it must be created in one of two ways. The first way is by choosing New Event Using [InterpActorName] -> Mover from the Context menu in Kismet with the InterpActor selected in the viewport. The other way is to create the Mover event by choosing New Event -> Physics -> Mover, right-clicking on the resulting event, and choosing Assign [InterpActorName] to Event(s) with the InterpActor selected in the viewport (see **FIGURE 10.30**).

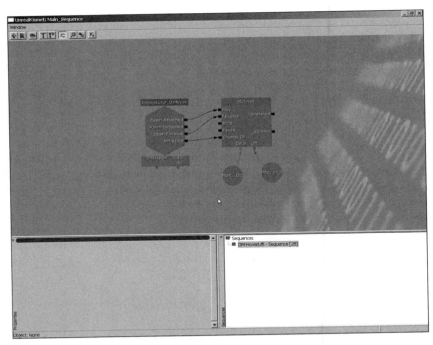

FIGURE 10.30   The result after creating a Mover event for an InterpActor

The Mover event contains the following outputs:

> ▸ **Pawn Attached**—This output is activated whenever a pawn attaches to the InterpActor. Typically, this means that a player is standing on the InterpActor.

10

▶ **Pawn Detached**—This output is activated whenever the attached pawn is detached from the InterpActor. This would mean that the player that was standing on the InterpActor has stepped or jumped off of it.

▶ **Open Finished**—This output is activated after forward playback is complete, and after the time indicated in the StayOpenTime property of the Mover event has elapsed.

▶ **Hit Actor**—This output is activated if the InterpActor collides with another actor. This means you can use this output to tell the InterpActor what to do in such circumstances as the player walking into the path of an oncoming lift.

The Matinee Editor

The heart of the Matinee system, as well as the primary tool for creation and editing of animated sequences, is the Matinee Editor. The Editor provides a visual interface for establishing animation groups and tracks, adding keys, setting values, and working with interpolation curves (see **FIGURE 10.31**).

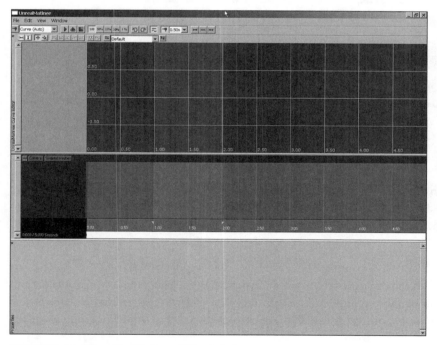

FIGURE 10.31   The Matinee Editor interface

The editor consists of five key areas, covered in the following sections: Toolbar, Curve Editor, Group/Track List, Timeline, and Properties.

Toolbar

This area provides quick icon-based access to a variety of common functions, including playback, looping, stopping, adjusting playback speed, setting keys, and more (see **FIGURE 10.32**).

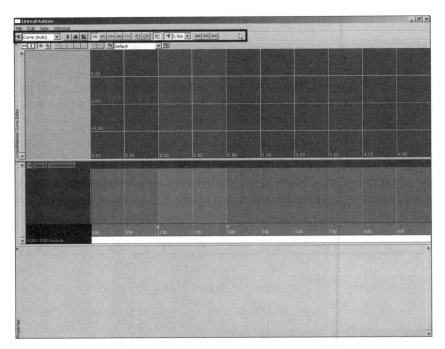

FIGURE 10.32   The Matinee Editor toolbar

Curve Editor

This area, hidden by default, can be made visible by clicking on the Toggle Curve Editor button ⇌. The Curve Editor enables you to manipulate the interpolation curves that run between keys (see **FIGURE 10.33**). For more information on using the Curve Editor, please see Appendix B.

Group/Track List

This area lists off all the different groups used in your Matinee sequence, as well as the various tracks within each of those groups. It is within this area that you can create new groups and tracks. When a director group is present, this section is divided with the director group in the top section and all other groups in the bottom section.

Groups within the Group/Track List can also be divided into tabs to help with organization. In fact, you can see the first three default tabs across the top of the Kismet Editor: All, Cameras, and Static Meshes.

10

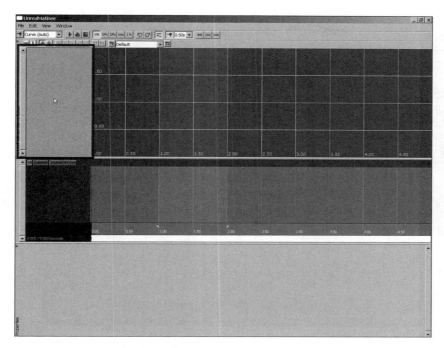

FIGURE 10.33   The Curve Editor

Creating a new tab is easy—simply right-click on a group and choose Create New Group Tab from the Context menu. You are asked to input a name for this tab, and then the new tab appears at the top of the Group/Track List. If you then click on this group, only the groups added to it are visible in the list (see **FIGURE 10.34**).

You can add existing groups to custom tabs by right-clicking on them, choosing Add to Group Tab, and selecting the name of the tab from the Context menu. Also, to remove a group from a custom tab, you can right-click on any of the groups within it and choose Remove from Selected Group Tab.

Timeline

This is the functional timeline for the animation, upon which you can place keys and set the current position of the animation for previewing purposes. The timeline contains the time slider, which is a bold black line that indicates the current time for the animation. This time slider begins at time interval 0.00, meaning that it cannot be easily seen at first. Simply drag the slider from the 0.00 interval or press Play, and it will be visible. The time slider can also be "scrubbed" (dragged back and forth) to test the results of the animation.

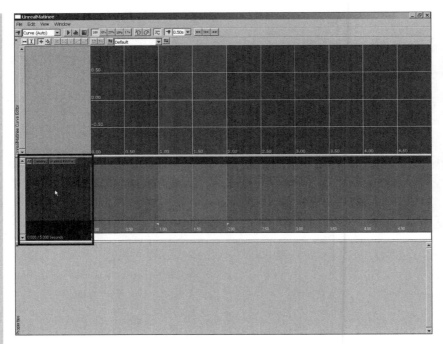

FIGURE 10.34   The Group/Track List

The loop section is a portion of the timeline that is designated by a green shaded area within the timeline itself. This section of the sequence is looped when the Loop Preview Playback button is pressed. The keys located within the green area can also be modified through some functions found in the Edit menu, such as Stretch Selection, Delete Section, and Select Keys in Selection. The size of the green area is changed by moving the green flags located at the bottom of the timeline.

The sequence markers, displayed as small red triangles at the bottom of the timeline, are used to designate the length of the entire sequence. When the sequence is played using the Play input, it plays from the first sequence marker until it reaches the second. The first marker is located at time interval 0.00 and cannot be moved. The second marker should be adjusted in order to set the desired duration for the sequence (see **FIGURE 10.35**).

Properties

Located at the bottom of the interface, this is a typical properties window, as it appears throughout several areas of Unreal Editor. It is used to adjust and edit properties for the various groups and tracks of a sequence.

10

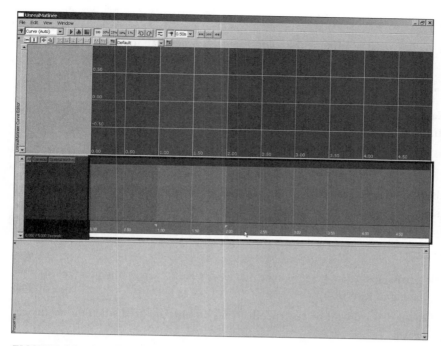

FIGURE 10.35   The timeline

Types of Tracks

There are several different types of track that can be created in the Matinee Editor, each designed for a different purpose. This section covers a list of each of these tracks, as well as a description covering the general uses for each one.

Anim Control

This track is used to play skeletal animations, such as those used with characters. The Anim Control track requires a SkeletalMeshActorMAT with an AnimTree and AnimSet associated with it to be selected when the track itself is created.

Important Property:

► **SlotName**—This property holds the name of the AnimNodeSlot in the AnimTree you want to use. This can only be set when creating the track by choosing from the dropdown list of the available slots.

Color Property

Color Property tracks are used to animate the color of objects other than materials, such as lights and height fog actors.

Important Property:

▶ **PropertyName**—This is the name of the property the track affects. This can only be set when creating the track by choosing from the dropdown list of the available properties.

Event

Event tracks enable you to create outputs on the Matinee sequence object that serve as events to trigger other actions. These events are activated at their indicated time in the timeline. The event track can activate these events during both forward and reverse playback.

Important Properties:

▶ **FireEventsWhenBackwards**—If set to True, the track's events are fired when the sequence is playing in reverse.

▶ **FireEventsWhenForwards**—If set to True, the track's events are fired when the sequence is playing forward.

▶ **FireEventsWhenJumpingForwards**—If set to True, the track's events are fired even if the sequence is skipped using the CANCELMATINEE console command.

FaceFX

The FaceFX track is used to play FaceFX animations. FaceFX is a specialized facial animation system that is integrated into Unreal Editor. However, as this is an introductory text, the use of FaceFX falls outside the scope of the book and are not covered.

Important Property:

▶ **FaceFXAnimSets**—This is an array of AnimSets to be used in addition to the AnimSets of the group this track belongs to.

Float Material Param

This track animates a MaterialInstanceConstant's ScalarParameter value. The track does not affect the MaterialInstanceConstant directly, but instead affects a MaterialInstanceActor, which is in turn connected to the material instance.

Important Property:

▶ **ParamName**—This property holds the name of the ScalarParameter in the material that this track controls.

10

Float Particle Param

This track animates a parameter of a particle system.

Important Property:

▶ **ParamName**—This property holds the name of the parameter in the particle system that this track controls.

Float Property

The Float track animates a float property for certain actors. All dynamic actors can have their DrawScale property animated in this way. Actors with properties supported by this track include HeightFog, Light, Camera, RB_RadialForceActor, and RB_Thruster.

Important Property:

▶ **PropertyName**—This property holds the name of the property the track affects. This can only be set when creating the track by choosing from the dropdown list of the available properties.

Morph Weight

The Morph Weight track animates the weighting of a morph target assigned to a Morph node in the AnimTree belonging to a skeletal mesh actor.

Important Property:

▶ **MorphNodeName**—This property holds the name of the Morph node in the AnimTree of the skeletal mesh actor that this track controls.

Movement

This track animates the location of dynamic actors such as InterpActors, moveable lights, particle emitters, and so on.

Important Properties:

▶ **AngCurveTension**—This property controls the tightness of the curve for the rotation path.

▶ **DisableMovement**—This property disables previewing of this track, which can be used when animating another object relative to the group this track belongs to.

▶ **Hide3DTrack**—This property disables rendering of the path of this track in the viewports.

- ► **ShowArrowAtKeys**—This property displays arrows at each key in the viewports representing the rotation of the object.

- ► **ShowRotationOnCurveEd**—This property displays the rotation curves when the track is viewed in the Curve Editor (this only works if bUseQuatInterpolation is set to False).

- ► **ShowTranslationOnCurveEd**—This property displays the translation curves when the track is viewed in the Curve Editor.

- ► **UseQuatInterpolation**—This property forces the track to use quaternion interpolation between keys, which means it uses the shortest distance to get to the next key's rotation. This interpolation is linear only, so it does not support easing in and out.

- ► **LinCurveTension**—This property controls the tightness of the curve for the translation path.

- ► **LookAtGroupName**—This property is the name of the group to use when using the IMR_LookAtGroup RotMode.

- ► **MoveFrame**—This property determines whether the movement of this track should be relative (IMF_RelativeToInitial) or absolute (IMF_World). This can only be set through the Context menu of the track and is set to IMF_RelativeToInitial by default.

- ► **RotMode**—This property determines whether the rotation of this track uses keyed values (IMR_Keyframed) or always faces the group specified in the LookAtGroupName (IMR_LookAtGroup).

SkelControl Scale

The SkelControl Scale track animates the weighting of a SkelControl node in the AnimTree belonging to a skeletal mesh actor.

Important Property:

- ► **MorphNodeName**—This property holds the name of the SkelControl node in the AnimTree of the skeletal mesh actor that this track controls.

Sound

The Sound track allows SoundCues to be played at specific intervals. When adjusting the curves for a Sound track, the X and Y curves represent volume and pitch, respectively.

Important Properties:

- ► **ContinueSoundOnMatineeEnd**—This property causes the sound of the track to keep playing if it is not finished when the sequence finishes.

- ► **SuppressSubtitles**—This property suppresses any subtitles for the sound being played.

Effects Toggle

The Effects Toggle track activates or deactivates the particle system of an Emitter actor.

Important Property:

▸ **bActivateSystemEachUpdate**—If True, the particles system will have ActivateSystem called every update. If False, the particle system is only activated if it is not already active.

Vector Material Param

The Vector Material Param track allows for animation of a MaterialInstanceConstant's vector parameter. Like the Float Material Param track, this track does not directly affect a MaterialInstanceConstant, but instead affects a MaterialInstanceActor, which must be placed in the level and associated to the material instance.

Important Property:

▸ **ParamName**—This is the name of the VectorParameter in the material that this track controls.

Vector Property

This track animates a vector property of certain actors. All dynamic actors can have their DrawScale3D property animated in this manner. Actors with other properties currently supported are Cameras and PhysicsVolumes.

Important Property:

▸ **PropertyName**—This is the name of the property the track affects. This can only be set when creating the track by choosing from the dropdown list of the available properties.

Director Group-Specific Tracks

The following tracks can only be created within a director group, and all affect the camera in some way. Mastering the use of these tracks can result in much more professional cutscenes in your game.

▸ **Color Scale**—This track animates the ColorScale property of the current camera, allowing for a variety of color-based effects.

▸ **Director**—The director track is used to handle cuts between cameras. In reality, it simply switches between groups. If the group being switched to contains a camera, that camera becomes active. If the group that is switched to is the director's group itself, or another group that is not associated to a camera, the player's camera becomes active.

▶ **Fade**—This track fades the active camera to or from black.

▶ **Slomo**—This track enables you to animate the game speed. This effects everything in the level, including physics, particle systems, Matinee animation sequences, animated materials, and so on.

Matinee Considerations

The following are some general things to keep in mind when using Matinee:

▶ Movement tracks can only be used on dynamic actors who have their Physics property set to PHYS_Interpolating. If some dynamic object does not seem to move when you animate it with Matinee, make sure to double-check the Physics property!

▶ It is usually a good idea to set an initial key for all tracks at time interval 0.00 with the actor in its default position in the level. This helps to avoid any popping when the sequence is played in-game.

▶ When a key is selected in the Matinee Editor, a message is visible in the viewports saying ADJUST KEY #. This message alerts you that you are in Interpolation Mode, and that a key is active. If you edit the property associated with that key through the group, you are adjusting the value of that key at the designated time.

▶ InterpActors have their CollisionType property set to COLLIDE_NoCollision by default. This must be changed to either COLLIDE_BlockAll or COLLIDE_BlockAllButWeapons for the player to be able to collide with the InterpActor.

▶ When Matinee is open, you cannot hold Shift while moving objects to automatically have the camera follow the movement.

Over the next several tutorials, you use Matinee to construct a moderately advanced lift system, including doors and animated materials. In **TUTORIAL 10.5**, we establish the initial Matinee sequence that drives the lift's motion.

TUTORIAL 10.5: Creating a Lift, Part I: The Lift Animation

1. Launch Unreal Editor and open the DM-CH_10_Lift_Start.ut3 map file and the Chapter_10_MatineeDemo package included on the DVD in the files for this chapter (see **FIGURE 10.36**).

2. In the side viewport, you can see that there is an InterpActor already at the bottom of the shaft serving as a lift. Select the lift and open the Kismet Editor. Right-click in the Kismet work area and create a new Matinee sequence object. Set the ObjComment property of this new object to Lift (see **FIGURE 10.37**).

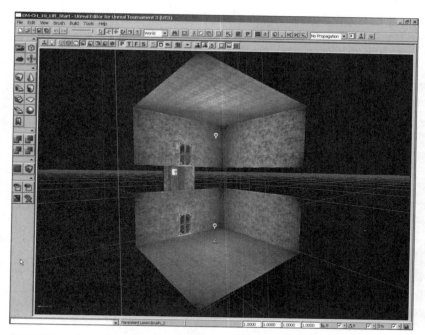

FIGURE 10.36 The DM-CH_10_Lift_Start level provides a simple floor-to-floor lift setup.

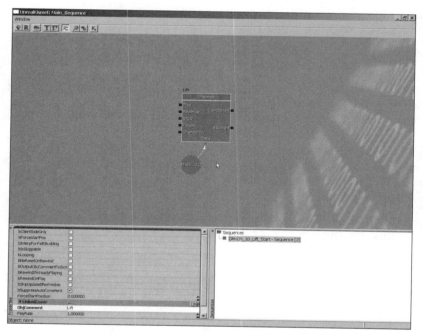

FIGURE 10.37 The new Lift Matinee sequence object

3. Double-click the new Matinee sequence object to open the Matinee Editor. Create a new group by right-clicking in the Group/Track List and choosing Add New Empty Group from the Context menu. Name the new group Lift and click OK (see **FIGURE 10.38**).

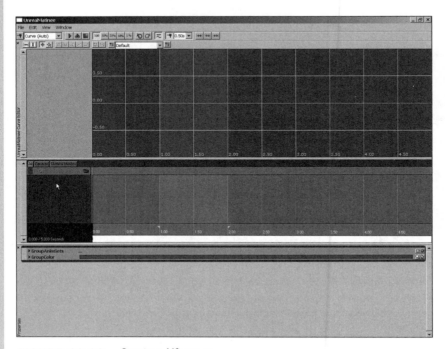

FIGURE 10.38   Create a Lift group.

4. Right-click on the Lift group and choose Add New Movement Track from the Context menu. Locate the end sequence marker. The marker appears at the bottom of the timeline at the 5.00 second mark, and looks like a small red triangle. Drag the end sequence marker to 2.00, which sets the duration of the sequence (see **FIGURE 10.39**).

> **NOTE**
>
> You may need to zoom in (mouse wheel) to get the marker to exactly 2.00.

5. Move the time slider to 2.00—the end of the sequence—and press the Enter key to add a new key (see **FIGURE 10.40**).

10

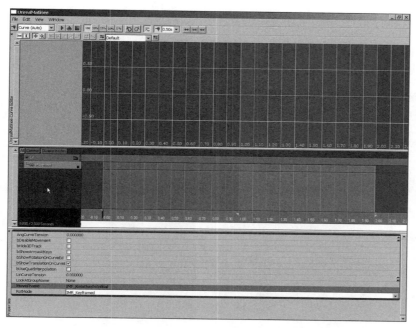

FIGURE 10.39 The movement track is added and the duration has been set.

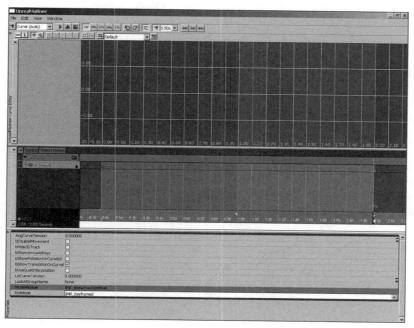

FIGURE 10.40 Place a key at the end of the sequence.

6. While the time slider is still at 2.00, go back to the side viewport. Notice the words *ADJUST KEY 1* in the lower-left corner of the viewport. Move the lift InterpActor up in the Z-axis so that it is flush with the floor of the second story of the level. Notice the yellow path appear in the viewport while you move the InterpActor (see **FIGURE 10.41**).

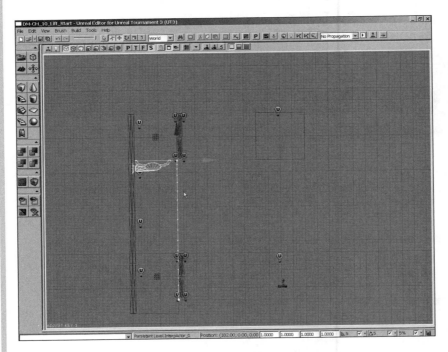

FIGURE 10.41   The yellow line indicates the motion of the InterpActor.

7. Back in the Matinee Editor, locate the Loop Section markers, found at the bottom of the timeline as small green triangles. Set these to 0.00 and 2.00, either manually or by pressing the View Fit Loop Sequence button ⟷, to select the entire sequence, and then click the Loop Preview Playback button ⬆ to view the animation in the viewport.

8. Save your progress.

> **NOTE**
>
> When Matinee is open, you cannot hold Shift while moving objects to move the camera in tandem.

> **NOTE**
>
> Make sure that the Realtime Preview button 🔘 is active in the Perspective viewport, or else you will not be able to see Matinee playback in your viewport!

END TUTORIAL 10.5

10

Please complete **TUTORIAL 10.5** before continuing, or open the DM-CH_10_Lift_01.ut3 map file provided on the DVD with the files for this chapter. The lift mesh has two materials applied to it: One material provides the look of the main lift body, whereas the second is used on the gears that are set into the tracks on the shaft wall. The material on the gears has been built with a scalar parameter that in turn drives a panner, giving the gears the appearance of spinning.

In **TUTORIAL 10.6**, we are going to animate that scalar parameter through Matinee using a Float Material Param track. The Float Material Param track in turn controls a MaterialInstanceActor, which must be placed in our scene and associated with the material instance that is applied to the gears.

TUTORIAL 10.6: Creating a Lift, Part II: The Lift Gears Animation

1. Open the Actor Classes browser and select the MaterialInstanceActor. This actor is associated to a material instance, enabling you to animate it with Matinee. Right-click and place the actor anywhere in the level, although it would make the most sense to place it somewhere near the lift (see **FIGURE 10.42**).

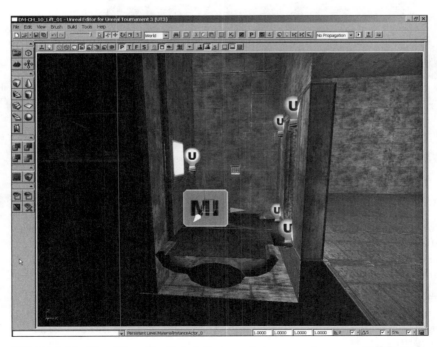

FIGURE 10.42   Place the MaterialInstanceActor somewhere near the lift shaft.

2. Select the MaterialInstanceActor in the viewport and open its Properties Window with the F4 key. Use the Generic browser to set the MatInst property to the matInst _lift_gears material instance.

3. Make sure that the MaterialInstanceActor is selected in the viewport. Open the Kismet Editor and double-click the Matinee sequence object to open the Matinee Editor. Right-click in the Group/Track List and choose Add New Empty Group from the Context menu. Name the new group LiftGears and click OK (see **FIGURE 10.43**).

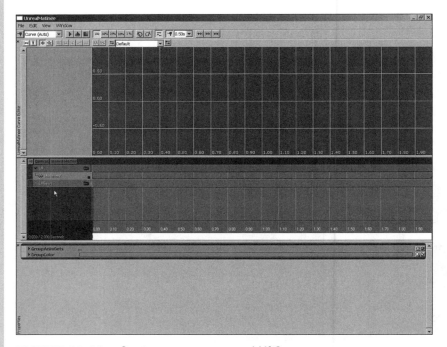

FIGURE 10.43   Create a new group named LiftGears.

4. Right-click on the new LiftGears group and choose New Float Material Param Track from the Context menu. In the properties for the new track, set the ParamName property to LiftGearSpeed. This property is named after a scalar parameter located in the material instance (see **FIGURE 10.44**).

5. With the time slider at 0.00, press Enter to create a new key. The key is located in the Float Material Param track, and is visible as a dark orange triangle. Right-click on it and choose Set Value from the Context menu. Verify that the value is set to 0.0 and press Enter (see **FIGURE 10.45**).

10

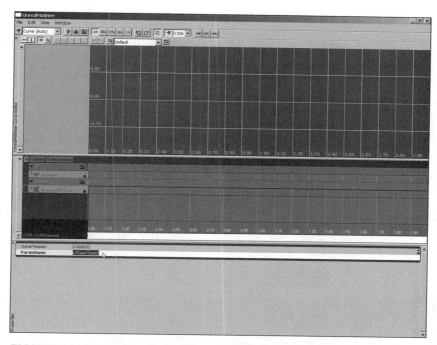

FIGURE 10.44 Add a new Float Material Param track.

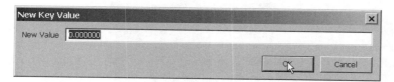

FIGURE 10.45 Make sure the Set Value window shows a value of 0.0.

6. Move the time slider to 2.00 and press Enter to create a second key. Right-click on the new key and choose Set Value from the Context menu. Set the value to 2.0 and press Enter (see **FIGURE 10.46**).

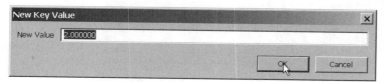

FIGURE 10.46 Set the key at 2.00 seconds to a value of 2.0.

7. Use the Loop Preview Playback button placeholder to preview the animated material in the Perspective viewport.

8. Save your progress.

END TUTORIAL 10.6

Please complete **TUTORIAL 10.6** before continuing, or open the DM-CH_10_Lift_02.ut3 map file provided on the DVD with the files for this chapter. In **TUTORIAL 10.7**, we set up the lift events that trigger our lift to start working once the player gets in and uses the keypads located at the top and bottom.

TUTORIAL 10.7: Creating a Lift, Part III: Basic Lift Events

1. Add a Trigger actor to the map by right-clicking and choosing Add Actor > Trigger. Position this Trigger actor in the lift shaft, and right in front of the lower control pad (see **FIGURE 10.47**).

FIGURE 10.47   Place the trigger right in front of the control panel in the lift shaft.

10

2. Duplicate the trigger and place the duplicate in front of the control pad on the upper level (see **FIGURE 10.48**).

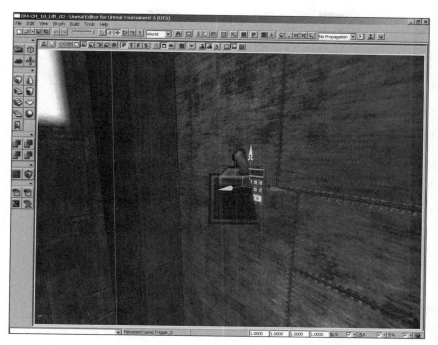

FIGURE 10.48   Move a duplicate in front of the other control pad.

3. Select both Trigger actors, and open the Kismet Editor. Right-click in the main workspace and choose Create New Events using... > Used. This creates two Used events, one for each trigger (see **FIGURE 10.49**).

4. Set the following properties for both Used events:

InteractDistance: 256

MaxTriggerCount: 0

5. You need to verify which Used event corresponds to the trigger at the top and bottom. Connect the output of the Used event for the bottommost trigger to the Play input of the Matinee sequence object. Then, connect the output of the opposite Used event to the Reverse input of the Matinee object (see **FIGURE 10.50**).

6. Save and test your map. You can now enter the lift, face the control panel, and use it to send the lift to the top or bottom.

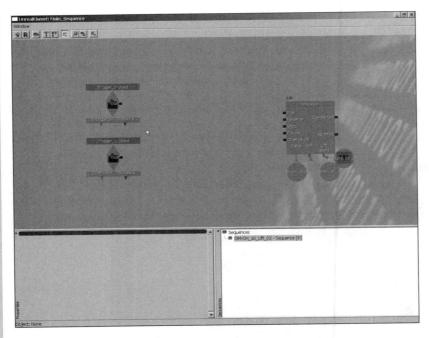

FIGURE 10.49
Create two new
Used events for the
triggers.

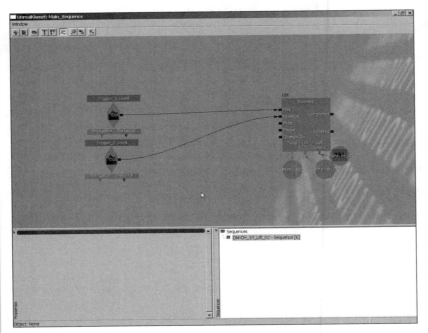

FIGURE 10.50
The Used event for
the bottom trigger
should connect to
Play, whereas the
other should con-
nect to Reverse.

10

END TUTORIAL 10.7

Please complete **TUTORIAL 10.7** before continuing, or open the DM-CH_10_Lift_03.ut3 map file provided on the DVD with the files for this chapter. In **TUTORIAL 10.8**, we set up the first of four door InterpActors that operates at the top and bottom of the lift.

TUTORIAL 10.8: Creating a Lift, Part IV: Animating the First Door

1. Continuing from **TUTORIAL 10.7**, open the Generic browser and select the sm_hall_deco_door_2 static mesh, which can be found within the Matinee_Demo package.

2. In the Perspective viewport, right-click and place this mesh into the map as an InterpActor (Add Actor > InterpActor: StaticMesh Matinee_Demo.sm_hall_deco_door_2), and then position it so that it fits in the right half of the lower doorway, as shown in **FIGURE 10.51**.

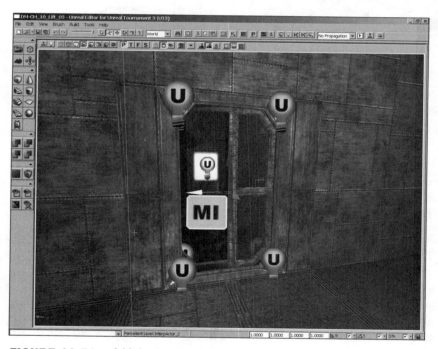

FIGURE 10.51   Add the door mesh as an InterpActor and position it in the right half of the doorway.

3. Press F4 to open the Properties window for the actor. Expand the Collision tab, and set the CollisionType property to COLLIDE_BlockAll. This causes the mesh to be able to collide with everything.

4. Make sure that the InterpActor is still selected, and open the Kismet Editor. In the main Kismet workspace, create a new Matinee sequence object, and set its ObjComment property to Lower Doors. When finished, double-click it to open the Matinee Editor (see **FIGURE 10.52**).

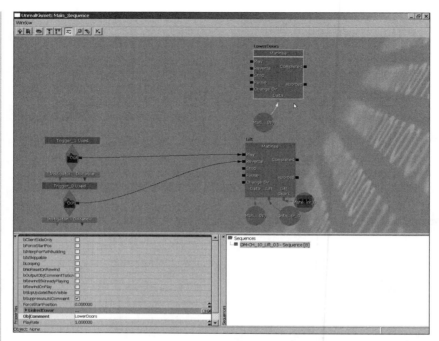

FIGURE 10.52　Make sure to comment the new Matinee sequence object as Lower Doors.

5. Add a new group to the Matinee Editor by right-clicking on the Group/Track List and choosing Add New Empty Group from the Context menu. Name the group LiftDoor and press Enter (see **FIGURE 10.53**).

6. Right-click on the new LiftDoor group and choose Add New Movement Track from the Context menu.

> **NOTE**
>
> Remember to zoom into the timeline with the mouse wheel if you need extra precision.

7. We start by establishing the duration of our animation. Set the end sequence marker (small red triangle) to 1.00. Then use the Loop Section markers to highlight the entire area between 0.00 and 1.00 (see **FIGURE 10.54**).

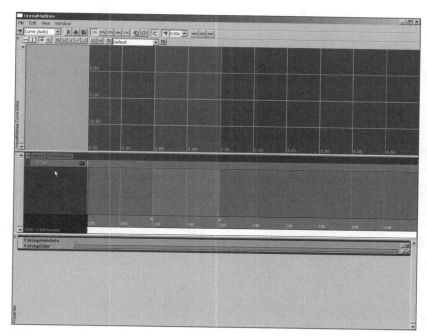

FIGURE 10.53 Add the LiftDoor group.

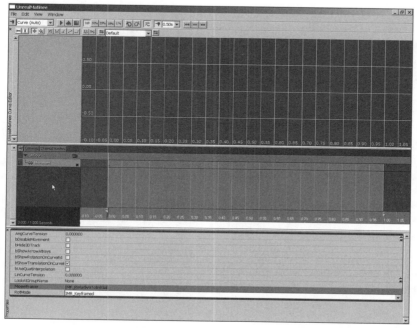

FIGURE 10.54 Set the duration to 1 second and set the Loop Section markers to both ends.

8. Move the time slider to 1.00 and press Enter to create a new key. Select this key to enter Interpolation Mode, noting the ADJUST KEY 1 that should appear in the lower-left corner of the viewports. While in this mode, move the door InterpActor 56 units in the negative Y direction, or into the door frame (see **FIGURE 10.55**).

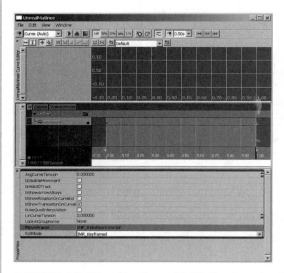

FIGURE 10.55   At a time of 1.00, the door should open.

9. Save your level's progress. Feel free to click the Loop Preview Playback button ⬛ to see your animation so far. Close the Matinee Editor when finished.

END TUTORIAL 10.8

Please complete **TUTORIAL 10.8** before continuing, or open the DM-CH_10_Lift_04.ut3 map file provided on the DVD with the files for this chapter. In **TUTORIAL 10.9**, we finish up the animation for the door and then duplicate it.

TUTORIAL 10.9: Creating a Lift, Part V: Duplicating the Animated Door

1. Make sure that the Matinee Editor is closed. Duplicate the door InterpActor and rotate it 180 degrees around Z. Make sure this new door fits perfectly into the opposite side of the doorway (see **FIGURE 10.56**).

2. With the new InterpActor selected, open the Kismet Editor. Right-click on the LiftDoor input on the bottom of the Matinee sequence object and choose New Object Var Using InterpActor. This creates a new object variable for your duplicated door and wire it into the Matinee sequence object (see **FIGURE 10.57**).

10

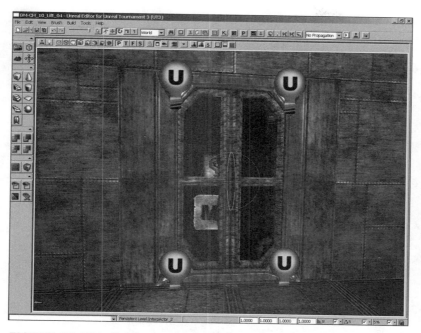

FIGURE 10.56   Duplicate and rotate the door to make the opposite door.

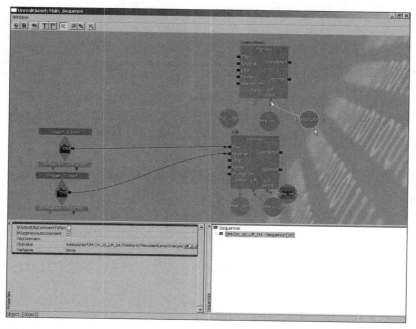

FIGURE 10.57   Adding this new object variable causes the Matinee sequence object to affect the new door.

3. Select both of the InterpActors and duplicate them, moving up the duplicates to fit into the doorway at the top of the lift shaft (see **FIGURE 10.58**).

FIGURE 10.58   Duplicate both doors into the upper doorway.

4. In the Kismet Editor, select the Matinee sequence object and copy it with Ctrl-C, Ctrl-V. On the new duplicate, break all wires to the LiftDoor variable link by holding Alt and left-clicking on it. *Do not* break the link to the existing Matinee Data object (see **FIGURE 10.59**)!

5. Set the ObjComment property for the newly duplicated Matinee sequence object to Upper Doors.

6. Make sure that the newly duplicated InterpActors are selected in the viewport, and then right-click on the LiftDoor input of the Upper Doors Matinee sequence object. Choose New Object Vars Using… (see **FIGURE 10.60**).

7. Save your progress. If you play either one of the Matinee sequences using their respective Matinee sequence objects, you'll see the doors opening and closing appropriately. This is because, by default, the movement tracks are using the RelativeToInitial movement type, which moves them from their initial position.

10

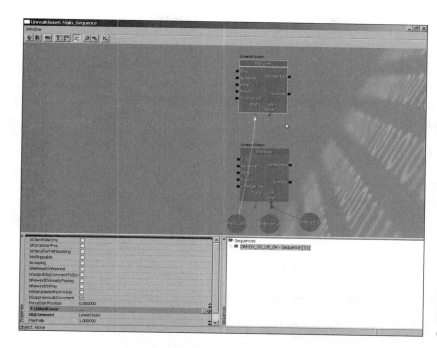

FIGURE 10.59
Duplicate the Matinee sequence object.

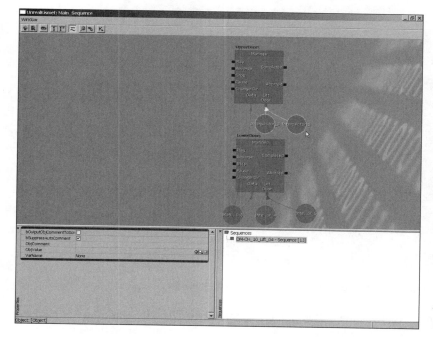

FIGURE 10.60
The two upper doors have now been connected to the Upper Doors Matinee object.

END TUTORIAL 10.9

Please complete **TUTORIAL 10.9** before continuing, or open the DM-CH_10_Lift_05.ut3 map file provided on the DVD with the files for this chapter. Our lift is just about set up. All we need to do now is set up the events that open and close the doors. In **TUTORIAL 10.10**, we establish these events.

TUTORIAL 10.10: Creating a Lift, Part VI: Finalizing Lift and Door Events

1. Continuing from **TUTORIAL 10.9**, right-click the Cube button 🔲 and set the following dimensions:

   X: 192

   Y: 256

   Z: 256

   Click Build and Close when finished, and then center the Red Builder Brush on the bottom doorway in all three axes (see **FIGURE 10.61**).

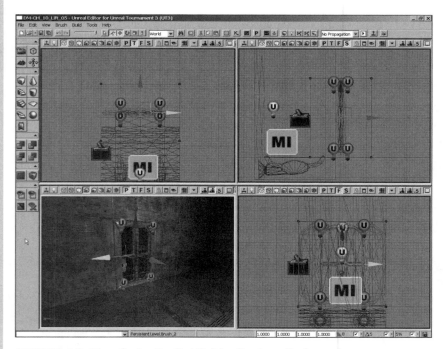

FIGURE 10.61   Center the Red Builder Brush on the lower doorway.

2. Right-click on the Add Volume button 🔲 and choose TriggerVolume. Move the Red Builder Brush out of the way and select the new TriggerVolume. Duplicate it, and move the duplicate upward 768 units in the Z-axis. Make sure to center the duplicate on the upper door in all three axes (see **FIGURE 10.62**).

10

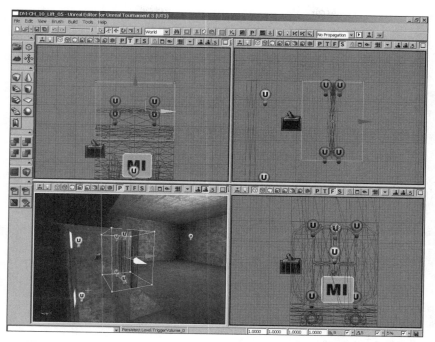

FIGURE 10.62   Add the volume and duplicate it to the upper doorway as well.

3. Select both TriggerVolumes and open the Kismet Editor. Right-click in the workspace and choose New Event Using... > Touch. This creates two new Touch events: one event for each volume (see **FIGURE 10.63**).

4. Set the MaxTriggerCount property for both events to 0.

5. Make the following connections to finish your sequence, which gets the doors working (see **FIGURE 10.64**):

   ▶ TriggerVolume_0 (Upper Volume): Touched → Upper Doors Matinee: Play

   ▶ TriggerVolume_0 (Upper Volume): UnTouched → Upper Doors Matinee: Reverse

   ▶ TriggerVolume_1 (Lower Doors): Touched → Lower Doors Matinee: Play

   ▶ TriggerVolume_1 (Lower Doors): UnTouched → Lower Doors Matinee: Reverse

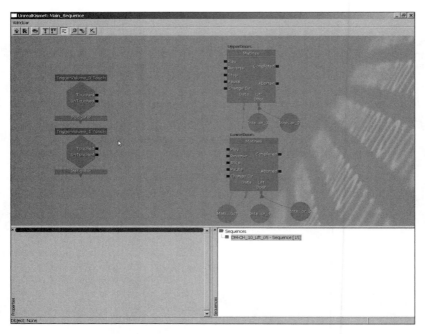

FIGURE 10.63   Create a Touch event for both volumes.

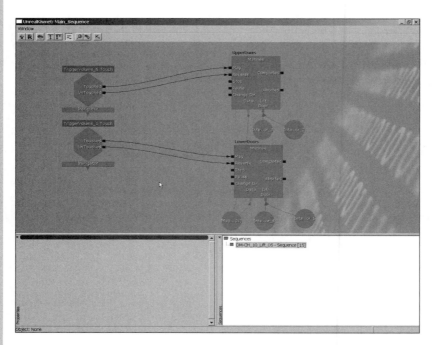

FIGURE 10.64   The sequences should be connected as shown.

6. Follow up by also making these connections, which serve as a failsafe system to prevent the lift from getting stuck on the level opposite our player. Think of them as a proximity-triggered call button (see **FIGURE 10.65**):

   ▶ TriggerVolume_0 (Upper Volume): Touched → Lift Matinee: Play

   ▶ TriggerVolume_1 (Lower Doors): Touched → Lift Matinee: Reverse

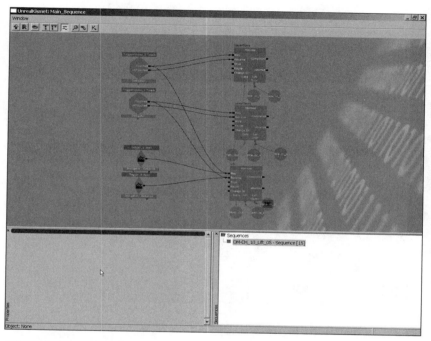

FIGURE 10.65   Making these final connections prevents errors in which the player is on the opposite floor from the lift.

7. Save and test your level. You should now notice that your doors and lift are working properly.

END TUTORIAL 10.10

Over the next several tutorials, we set up a flushing toilet for a restroom, which is comprised of several different effects and sequences. In **TUTORIAL 10.11**, we start the basis for our system by establishing our sound effect. We can then use the timing of the sound to create the rest of our animation.

For your convenience, the necessary Trigger actors, emitters, InterpActors, and MaterialInstance Actors have already been added to the level. These actors, however, have not been connected to anything. In **TUTORIAL 10.11**, we set up their functionality through Matinee.

TUTORIAL 10.11: Restroom Scene, Part I: Flush Sound

1. Open the DM-CH_10_Restroom_Start.ut3 map file and the Chapter_10_MatineeDemo package included on the DVD in the files for this chapter. This level is a simple and slightly oversized purgatorial bathroom, with no way in or out (see **FIGURE 10.66**).

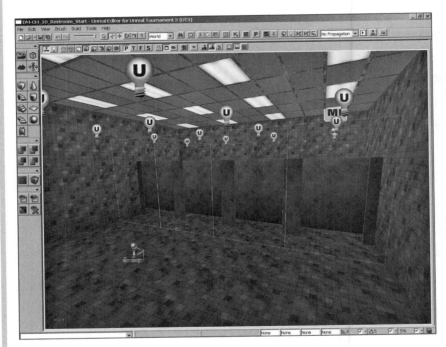

FIGURE 10.66   This is the DM-CH_10_Restroom_Start level.

2. In the Top viewport, select the toilet static mesh in the upper-left corner stall. Open the Kismet Editor and create a new Matinee sequence object (see **FIGURE 10.67**).

3. Check the Matinee sequence object's bRewindOnPlay property. This makes sure that the toilet flushes again each time it's triggered, as long as the sequence is not already playing.

4. Double-click on the Matinee sequence object to open the Matinee Editor. Right-click in the Group/Track List and create a new group. Name the group FlushSound (see **FIGURE 10.68**).

10

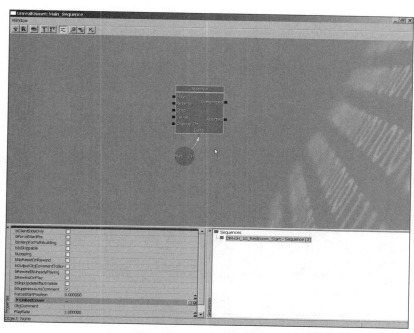

FIGURE 10.67   The new Matinee sequence object has been created.

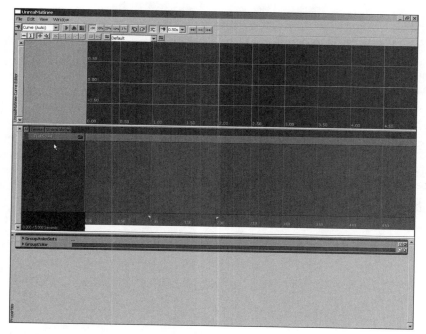

FIGURE 10.68   Add the FlushSound group.

5. Create a new Sound track in the FlushSound group. Because you had the toilet static mesh selected, the mesh is used to spatialize the sound (see **FIGURE 10.69**).

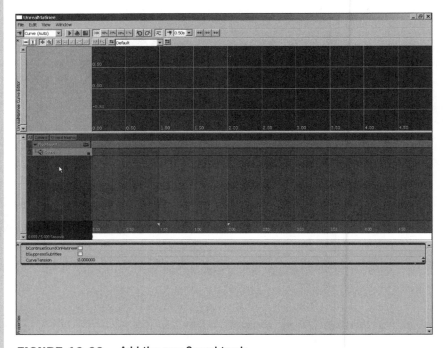

FIGURE 10.69   Add the new Sound track.

6. Open the Generic browser and select the toilet_FlushCue, located in the Chapter_10_MatineeDemo package. If you have not selected a SoundCue, you cannot place keys in a Sound track.

7. With the time slider at 0.00, press Enter to create a new key. This key is associated with the selected SoundCue (see **FIGURE 10.70**).

8. Move the end sequence marker (small red triangle) so that it is even with the end of the sound's playback length. This should be at about 19.065.

9. Close the Matinee Editor and the Kismet Editor. Save your progress so far.

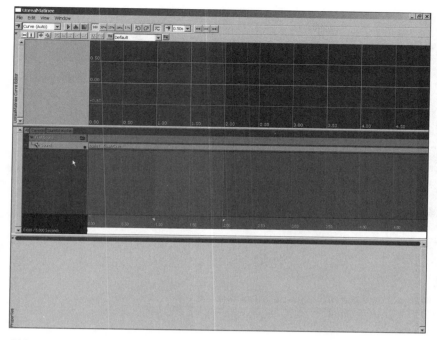

FIGURE 10.70 The SoundCue appears in the timeline.

END TUTORIAL 10.11

Please complete **TUTORIAL 10.11** before continuing, or open the DM-CH_10_Restroom_ 01.ut3 map file provided on the DVD with the files for this chapter. In **TUTORIAL 10.12**, the actual movement of the plane of water within the toilet is set up.

TUTORIAL 10.12: Restroom Scene, Part II: Flush Movement Track

1. Continuing from **TUTORIAL 10.11**, select the water InterpActor that is located inside the toilet in the upper-left corner of the room. This should be the same toilet you selected in **TUTORIAL 10.11**. Open the Kismet Editor and double-click the Matinee sequence object to open the Matinee Editor.

2. Create a new group in the Matinee Editor named Flush. Add a new movement track to this group (see **FIGURE 10.71**).

3. Move the time slider to 5.00 and press Enter to add a key. Set your Drag Grid to 1, and then move the water plane InterpActor down 9 units in Z, and then toward the back wall 2 units in X.

4. Move the time slider to 9.00 and press Enter to add another key. Move the water InterpActor down -11 units in Z and then toward the back wall 6 units in X.

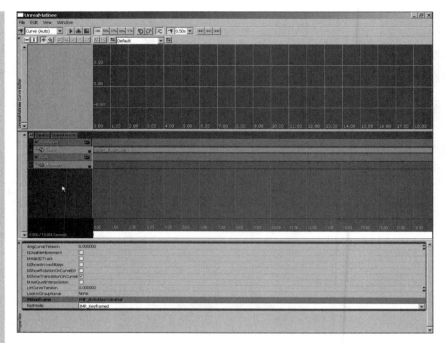

FIGURE 10.71   The Flush group has been added, along with a movement track.

5. Move the time slider to 13.00 and press Enter to add yet another key. Move the InterpActor up 10 units in Z and 6 units away from the back wall in X.

6. Move the time slider to 16.00 and press Enter to place a key. Move the InterpActor up 5 units in Z and away from the back wall 1 unit in X.

7. Move the time slider to the end of the sequence, and press Enter to place our final key. Move the InterpActor up 5 units in Z and away from the back wall 1 unit in X (see **FIGURE 10.72**).

8. We now duplicate all but our last keys, which creates pauses in the animation at various levels as the toilet flushes. Marquee-select by holding Ctrl-Alt and dragging to select all but the very last key. In the Matinee Editor's Edit menu, choose Duplicate Selected Keys. Holding Ctrl, move the newly duplicated keys so that they are 1.5 seconds to the right of the original keys.

9. Move the Loop Selection indicators to envelop the entire sequence, and press Loop Preview Playback to see how the playback is working. Close the Matinee Editor and save your progress when finished.

10

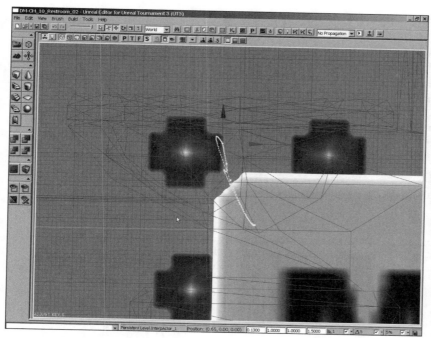

FIGURE 10.72 The viewport now shows the path of the water going down and back up.

END TUTORIAL 10.12

Please complete **TUTORIAL 10.12** before continuing, or open the DM-CH_10_Restroom_02.ut3 map file provided on the DVD with the files for this chapter. In **TUTORIAL 10.13**, we animate the scale of the toilet's water surface object so that it does not stick out of the sides of the toilet.

TUTORIAL 10.13: Restroom Scene, Part III: Flush DrawScale Track

1. Open the Kismet Editor and double-click the Matinee sequence object to open the Matinee Editor. Select the Flush group, and add a new Float Property Track using the DrawScale property (see **FIGURE 10.73**).

2. Make sure the time slider is at 0.00 and press Enter to set an initial key.

3. Move the time slider to 5.00 and press Enter. Right-click on the new key, choose Set Value from the Context menu, and enter 0.10.

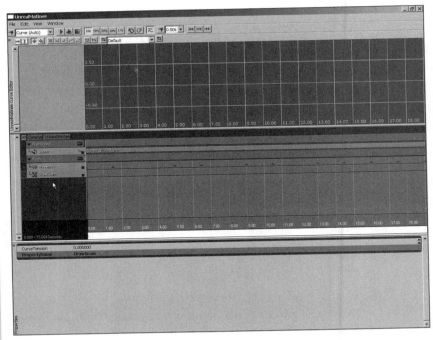

FIGURE 10.73   Add a new DrawScale track.

4. Using the method from Step 3, create keys at the following times with the designated values:

   ▶ Time = 9.00; Value = 0.06

   ▶ Time = 13.00; Value = 0.09

   ▶ Time = 16.00; Value = 0.12

   ▶ Time = End; Value = 0.13

5. Once again, we duplicate all the keys to create pauses. Marquee-select all but the last key, and from the Edit menu, choose Duplicate Selected Keys. Hold Ctrl and move the duplicated keys 1.5 seconds later (to the right) than the original keys (see **FIGURE 10.74**).

6. Use the Loop Preview Playback feature to preview your animation and make any adjustments ready. Save your progress when finished.

10

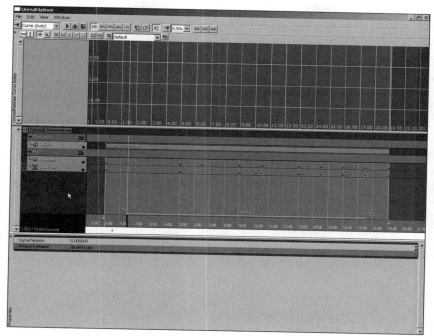

FIGURE 10.74   The timeline should look like this when finished.

END TUTORIAL 10.13

Please complete **TUTORIAL 10.13** before continuing, or open the DM-CH_10_Restroom_03.ut3 map file provided on the DVD with the files for this chapter. In **TUTORIAL 10.14**, we animate a parameter that is driving a Linear Interpolation material node, which blends between the standard water surface and the swirling one.

TUTORIAL 10.14: Restroom Scene, Part IV: Flush Material Linear Interpolation

1. Select the MaterialInstanceActor located within the toilet in the upper-left corner, as seen from the top viewport. This should be the same toilet you were working on in **TUTORIAL 10.13**. Once the actor is selected, open the Kismet Editor and double-click the Matinee sequence object to open the Matinee Editor (see **FIGURE 10.75**).

> **NOTE**
>
> So that you can focus strictly on the Matinee sequence, the MaterialInstanceActor has already been associated with the matInst_toilet_water_1 material instance constant.

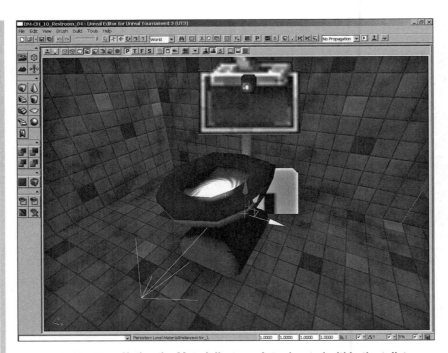

FIGURE 10.75   Notice the MaterialInstanceActor located within the toilet.

2. Create a new group named FlushMaterial. Add a Float Material Param track to this new group, and set the ParamName property of the new track to TextureInterp (see **FIGURE 10.76**).

3. With the time slider at 0.00, press Enter to set your initial key. This key contains whatever value the material instance constant had at the time of key creation.

4. Right-click the new key and set its value to 1.0 (see **FIGURE 10.77**).

5. Using the skills gained so far in this chapter, set the following keys in the track, with the associated values:

  ▶ Time = 3.50; Value = 0.75

  ▶ Time = 5.00; Value = 0.5

  ▶ Time = 9.00; Value = 0.75

  ▶ Time = 10.00; Value = 1.0

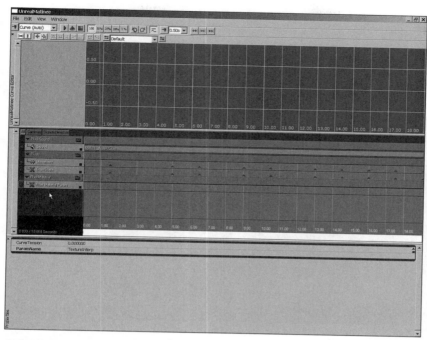

FIGURE 10.76 The new Float Material Param

FIGURE 10.77 The Set Value window

6. Use the Loop Preview Playback feature to preview your animation and make any adjustments ready. Save your progress when finished. Your toilet water blends to the swirl, but there is currently no spin (see **FIGURE 10.78**).

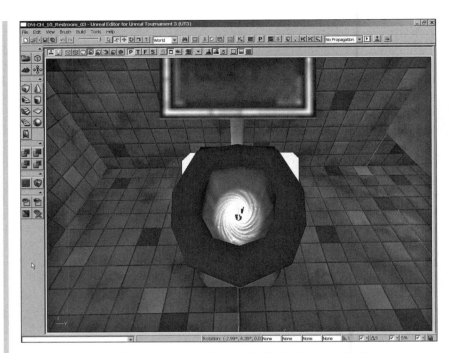

FIGURE 10.78   You can now see the swirl effect when you play the sequence.

END TUTORIAL 10.14

Please complete **TUTORIAL 10.14** before continuing, or open the DM-CH_10_Restroom_ 04.ut3 map file provided on the DVD with the files for this chapter. In **TUTORIAL 10.15**, we set up the system to animate the swirling of the water material. Most of this functionality has already been set up on the material beforehand. In **TUTORIAL 10.15**, we attach the animation sequence that powers its transition.

TUTORIAL 10.15: Restroom Scene, Part V: Flush Material Spin

1. Open the Kismet Editor and double-click the Matinee sequence object to open the Matinee Editor.

2. Right-click the FlushMaterial group and add a new Float Material Param track. Set the ParamName property of this new track to WaterSpinSpeed (see **FIGURE 10.79**).

3. With the time slider set to 0.00, press Enter to place an initial key. The value of this key is automatically set to the current value of the WaterSpinSpeed property of the matInst_toilet_water_1 material instance constant.

10

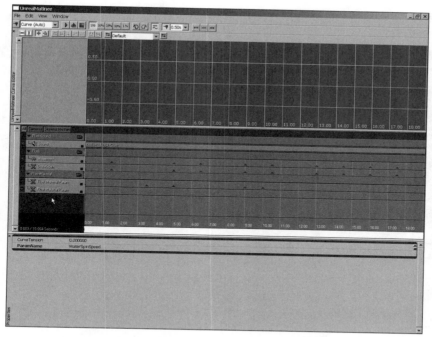

FIGURE 10.79   The new Float Material Param track has been added.

4. Using the skills gained so far in this chapter, create keys at the following times using the associated values:

   ▶ Time = 2.00; Value = 0.0

   ▶ Time = 5.00; Value = 0.5

   ▶ Time = 7.00; Value = 1.5

   ▶ Time = 8.75; Value = 3.0

   ▶ Time = 9.00; Value = 0.0

5. Holding Ctrl, select the first, second, and third keys. Right-click on any one of them and choose InterpMode > Linear from the Context menu (see **FIGURE 10.80**).

6. Save your progress when finished. You should now see the swirl spin when the sequence is played.

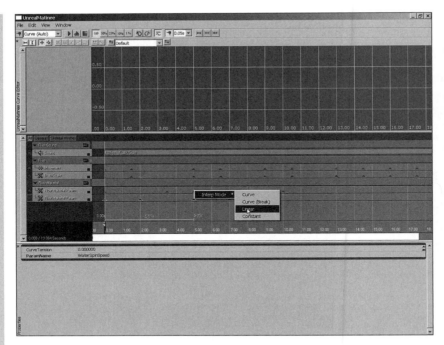

FIGURE 10.80   The InterpMode Context menu

END TUTORIAL 10.15

Please complete **TUTORIAL 10.15** before continuing, or open the DM-CH_10_Restroom_ 05.ut3 map file provided on the DVD with the files for this chapter. In **TUTORIAL 10.16**, we reuse the animation that we have set up for the first toilet to drive the other toilets in the restroom.

TUTORIAL 10.16: Restroom Scene, Part VI: Duplicating Sequences, Assigning Objects, and Setting Up Trigger Events

1. Open the Kismet Editor. Select the Matinee sequence object, and set its ObjComment property to Toilet 1 (see **FIGURE 10.81**).

2. Select the Matinee sequence object, as well as the variables currently connected to the FlushSound, Flush, and FlushMaterial group inputs. Duplicate all of these with Ctrl-C, Ctrl-V. Change the ObjComment to Toilet 2.

   Repeat this process two more times, creating sequences for Toilet 3 and Toilet 4 (see **FIGURE 10.82**).

> **NOTE**
>
> Your newly duplicated Matinee sequence objects should still be connected to the original Matinee Data object.

10

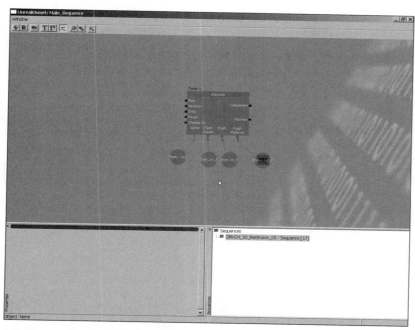

FIGURE 10.81 The Matinee object is now commented.

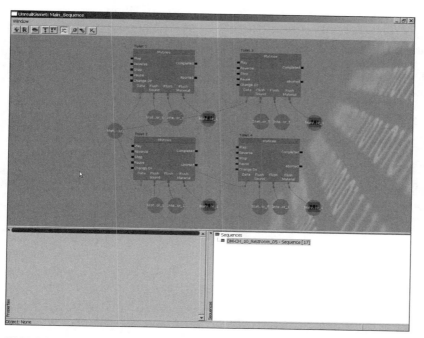

FIGURE 10.82 You should now have four total Toilet Matinee sequence objects.

3. In the top viewport, select the static mesh for the second toilet from the left. In the Kismet Editor, locate the Toilet 2 Matinee sequence object, and right-click the object variable assigned to its FlushSound group. Choose Assign StaticMesh_6 To Object Variable(s). This places the new mesh into the object variable.

   Repeat this process for the other two Matinee sequence objects, associating the appropriate toilet with each sequence.

4. Select the water plane InterpActor inside the second toilet. In the Kismet Editor, locate the Toilet 2 Matinee sequence object and right-click on the object variable connected to its Flush group. Choose Assign InterpActor_2 To Object Variable(s).

> **NOTE**
>
> The reason this setup is working on each individual toilet, rather than changing the material on all the toilets at once, is because each of the toilet bowl water objects has its own copy of the material instance constant for the water material.

   Repeat this process for the other two Matinee sequence objects, associating the appropriate InterpActor with each sequence.

5. Select the MaterialInstanceActor that is with the second toilet. In the Kismet Editor, locate the Toilet 2 Matinee sequence object and right-click on the object variable connected to its FlushMaterial group. Choose Assign MaterialInstanceActor_2 To Object Variable(s).

   As before, repeat this process with the other two Matinee sequence objects, associating the appropriate MaterialInstanceActor with each sequence.

6. Select all four of the Trigger actors that are next to each toilet. In the Kismet Editor, right-click and choose New Events Using Trigger_0... > Used. Set the MaxTriggerCount property for all these events to 0 (see **FIGURE 10.83**).

7. Make the following connections to finalize the toilet systems (see **FIGURE 10.84**):

   ▶ Trigger_0: Out → Toilet 1 Matinee: Play

   ▶ Trigger_1: Out → Toilet 2 Matinee: Play

   ▶ Trigger_2: Out → Toilet 3 Matinee: Play

   ▶ Trigger_3: Out → Toilet 4 Matinee: Play

8. Take a moment and play each sequence individually to make sure everything is working properly. Save your progress.

10

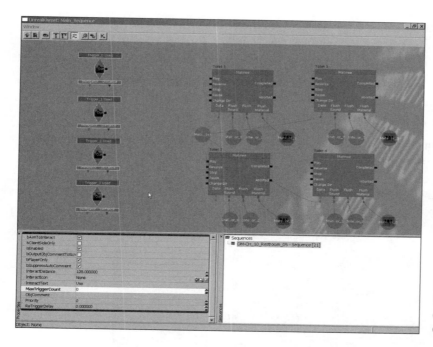

FIGURE 10.83
Four new Used events have been created.

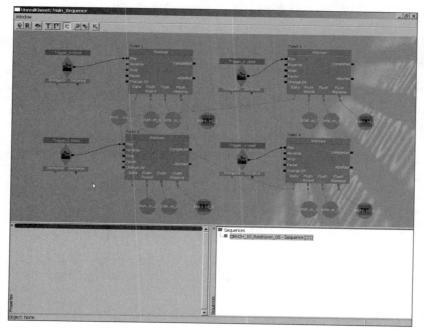

FIGURE 10.84
Connect each of the Used events.

END TUTORIAL 10.16

Please complete **TUTORIAL 10.16** before continuing, or open the DM-CH_10_Restroom_ 06.ut3 map file provided on the DVD with the files for this chapter. In **TUTORIAL 10.17**, we use the emitter that is already placed over the first toilet to give the effect that the toilet breaks the first time it's flushed.

TUTORIAL 10.17: Restroom Scene, Part VII: Flush Spray

1. Open the Kismet Editor, and select the Matinee Data object connected to the Matinee sequence objects. Duplicate the Data object with Ctrl-C, Ctrl-V (see **FIGURE 10.85**).

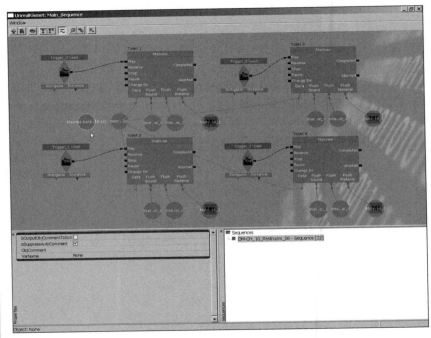

FIGURE 10.85   Make a duplicate of the Data object.

2. Disconnect the original Matinee Data object from the Toilet 1 Matinee sequence object, and connect the new duplicate to it. We are doing this so that we can adjust the animation for the first toilet without affecting the others.

   As soon as you disconnect the original Matinee Data object, all your groups—and therefore all your other connections—vanish. Reconnect the connections after you attach the newly duplicated Data object (see **FIGURE 10.86**).

3. In the Perspective viewport, select the Emitter located within the first toilet (see **FIGURE 10.87**).

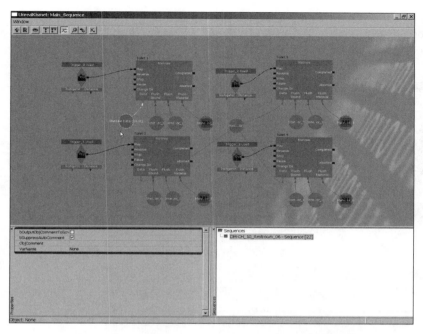

FIGURE 10.86 The first Toilet sequence now has its own Data object.

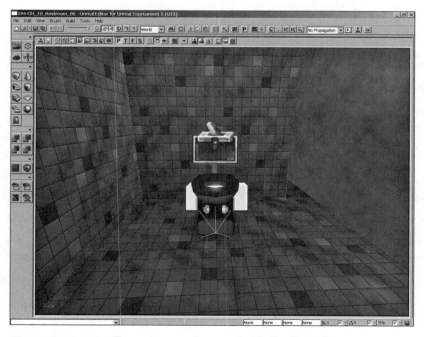

FIGURE 10.87 The emitter can be seen inside the first toilet.

4. In the Kismet Editor, double-click on the Toilet 1 Matinee sequence object to open the Matinee Editor. Create a new group named FlushSpray. Add a new Float Particle Param track to this new group (see **FIGURE 10.88**).

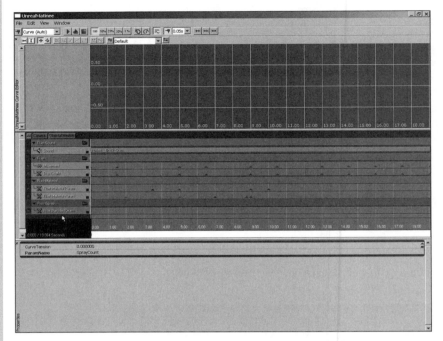

FIGURE 10.88　The FlushSpray and Float Particle Param track have been added.

5. Set the ParamName property of the new Float Particle Param track to SprayCount.

6. Using the skills gained so far, create the following keys in the Float Particle Param track, and set the designated values:

- ▸ Time = 8.75; Value = 0.0
- ▸ Time = 10.00; Value = 50.0

7. Drag the end marker of the sequence to 10, so that the rest of the animation is ignored.

8. Finally, uncheck the bRewindOnPlay property on the Toilet 1 Matinee sequence object. Alternatively, you could set the MaxTriggerCount property for Trigger_0 to 1.

9. Save your progress, and play through the sequence to test the result (see **FIGURE 10.89**).

10

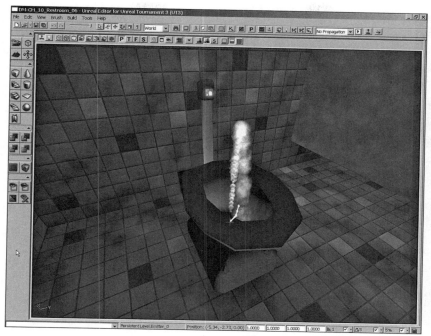

FIGURE 10.89   The toilet now breaks and shoots particles.

END TUTORIAL 10.17

Please complete **TUTORIAL 10.17** before continuing, or open the DM-CH_10_Restroom_ 07.ut3 map file provided on the DVD with the files for this chapter. In **TUTORIAL 10.18**, we set up the stall doors so that they open when we approach them.

TUTORIAL 10.18: Restroom Scene, Part VIII: Stall Door Animations

1. Continuing from **TUTORIAL 10.17**, select the InterpActor for the stall door on the left-most stall, as seen from the top viewport. With the InterpActor selected, go into the Kismet Editor and add a new Matinee sequence object. Set the ObjComment for this new object to Stall Door 1 (see **FIGURE 10.90**).

2. Double-click this new object to open the Matinee Editor. Create a new group named StallDoor, and add a movement track to it. In the track's properties, set the bUseQuatInterpolation property to True.

   This property makes sure that the doors take the shortest possible rotation to their destination, which helps prevent odd rotation when animated (see **FIGURE 10.91**).

3. Use the end sequence marker to set the duration of the sequence to 1.00 seconds.

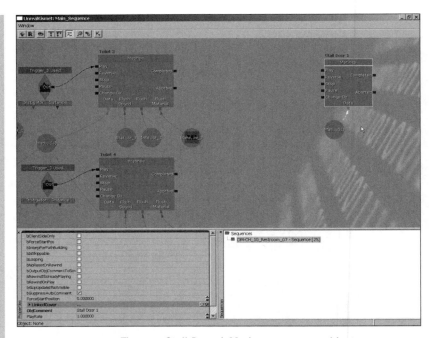

FIGURE 10.90   The new Stall Door 1 Matinee sequence object

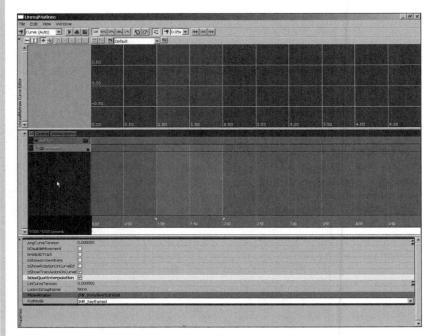

FIGURE 10.91   The StallDoor group and a new movement track have been added.

4. Set the time slider to 1.00 and press Enter to set a new key. In the top viewport, rotate the stall door InterpActor - 95.63 degrees around the Z-axis. This should cause the door to open inward (see **FIGURE 10.92**).

> **NOTE**
>
> It helps if your Rotation Grid setting is set to 5, which is the default.

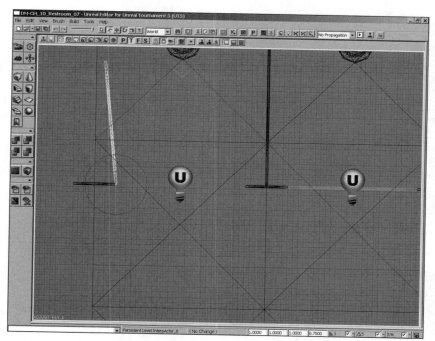

FIGURE 10.92   Key 1 should rotate the door inward -95.63 degrees.

5. Select the Stall Door 1 Matinee object, as well as the object variable connected to it. Duplicate it with Ctrl-C, Ctrl-V, and set the ObjComment property for the duplicate to Stall Door 2.

Repeat this process two more times to create Matinee sequences for Stall Door 3 and Stall Door 4 (see **FIGURE 10.93**).

6. Select the stall door InterpActor for the second stall, and then right-click the object variable connected to the Stall Door 2 Matinee sequence object. Choose Assign InterpActor_7 To Object Variable(s).

Repeat this process to assign the appropriate stall doors to the remaining sequences.

7. Select the four TriggerVolumes in the viewport. In the Kismet Editor, right-click and choose New Events Using TriggerVolume_1... > Touched. While all four events are selected, set the MaxTriggerCount property for all the new events to 0 (see **FIGURE 10.94**).

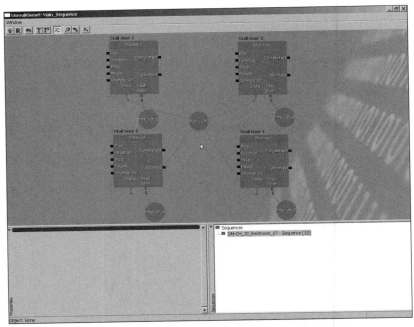

FIGURE 10.93   You should now have four copies of the Stall Door sequence, each named accordingly.

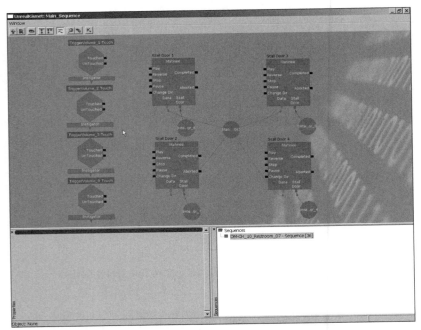

FIGURE 10.94   You should now have four new Touched events.

8. Make the following connections to finalize the door sequences (see **FIGURE 10.95**):

> ▶ TriggerVolume_1: Touched → Stall Door 1 Matinee: Play

> ▶ TriggerVolume_1: UnTouched → Stall Door 1 Matinee: Reverse

> ▶ TriggerVolume_2: Touched → Stall Door 2 Matinee: Play

> ▶ TriggerVolume_2: UnTouched → Stall Door 2 Matinee: Reverse

> ▶ TriggerVolume_3: Touched → Stall Door 3 Matinee: Play

> ▶ TriggerVolume_3: UnTouched → Stall Door 3 Matinee: Reverse

> ▶ TriggerVolume_0: Touched → Stall Door 4 Matinee: Play

> ▶ TriggerVolume_0: UnTouched → Stall Door 4 Matinee: Reverse

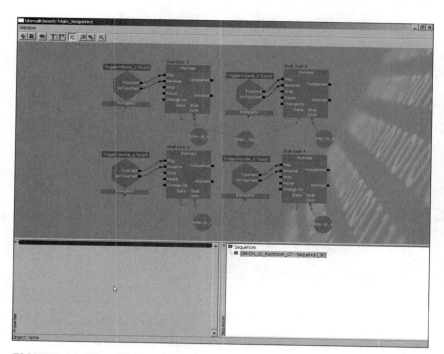

FIGURE 10.95 All the sequences have now been connected.

9. Save your progress and test the map in the In Editor Game. Your doors should now open and close as you move close to and away from them.

END TUTORIAL 10.18

Please complete **TUTORIAL 10.18** before continuing, or open the DM-CH_10_Restroom_08.ut3 map file provided on the DVD with the files for this chapter. In **TUTORIAL 10.19**, we create a new Matinee sequence that flickers a light.

TUTORIAL 10.19: Restroom Scene, Part IX: Flickering Light Brightness

1. Select the light against the back wall in the stall on the far right. This is a PointLightMoveable actor, which is dynamic and can therefore be animated (see **FIGURE 10.96**).

FIGURE 10.96   The light in the far-right stall is dynamic.

2. With the PointLightMoveable selected, open the Kismet Editor and create a new Matinee sequence object. Set the bLooping property for this new sequence to True, which causes the animation to play back over and over continuously. Also, set the ObjComment property for this sequence to Light Flicker (see **FIGURE 10.97**).

3. Double-click the new Matinee object, and in the Matinee Editor, create a new group named LightFlicker. Add a new Float Property track to this group, and choose Brightness from the dropdown of available properties (see **FIGURE 10.98**).

10

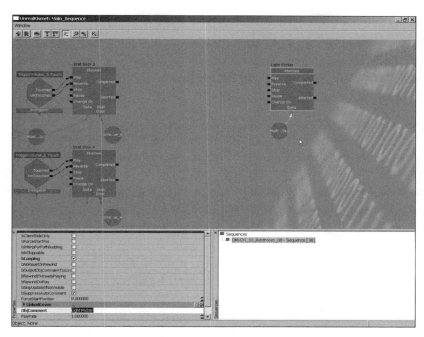

FIGURE 10.97 The new Light Flicker Matinee sequence object

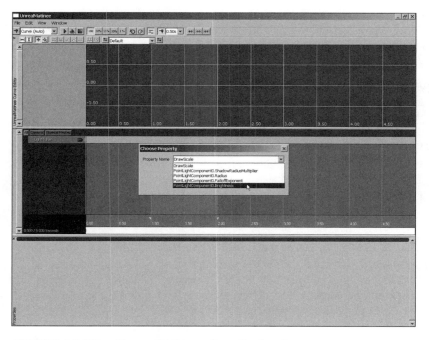

FIGURE 10.98 Choose Brightness from the dropdown.

4. Set the end sequence marker to 4.00 to set duration.

5. With the time slider at 0.00, press Enter to set your initial key, using the light's current Brightness value. Then, move the time slider to 4.00 and press Enter again, which means the sequence begins and ends with the same value.

6. Set the following keys using the designated values:

> ▶ Time = 0.20; Value = 0.20
>
> ▶ Time = 0.40; Value = 0.05
>
> ▶ Time = 0.70; Value = 0.05
>
> ▶ Time = 0.80; Value = 0.15
>
> ▶ Time = 1.70; Value = 0.17
>
> ▶ Time = 1.90; Value = 0.02
>
> ▶ Time = 2.70; Value = 0.02
>
> ▶ Time = 2.80; Value = 0.22
>
> ▶ Time = 3.00; Value = 0.22
>
> ▶ Time = 3.10; Value = 0.06
>
> ▶ Time = 3.90; Value = 0.06

7. If you previewed the animation now, the effect would be very slow. To speed it up, close the Matinee Editor, and select the Matinee sequence object. In the Kismet Properties window, set the PlayRate property to 10. This gives the flicker a much more natural appearance.

8. Save your progress.

END TUTORIAL 10.19

Please complete **TUTORIAL 10.19** before continuing, or open the DM-CH_10_Restroom_ 09.ut3 map file provided on the DVD with the files for this chapter. In **TUTORIAL 10.20**, we animate the material that corresponds to the flickering light. For your convenience, the material instance constant that handles this operation has already been set up and applied.

TUTORIAL 10.20: Restroom Scene, Part X: Flickering Light Material

1. Continuing from **TUTORIAL 10.19**, select the MaterialInstanceActor that is located in the upper-right corner of the room, as seen from the top viewport. This actor is already associated with the material for the light in that corner, enabling us to animate the brightness of the material's emissive property (see **FIGURE 10.99**).

10

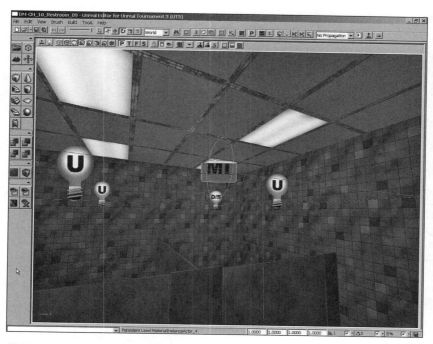

FIGURE 10.99 The MaterialInstanceActor in the upper corner of the room is associated with the material for the light in that area.

2. Double-click on the Light Flicker Matinee sequence. In the Matinee Editor, create a new group named MaterialFlicker, and add a new Float Material Property track to it. Set the track's ParamName property to Flicker (see **FIGURE 10.100**).

3. With the time slider at 0.00, press Enter to set your initial key. Move the time slider to 4.00 and press Enter again to set the final key.

4. Create keys at the following times with the corresponding values:

   ▸ Time = 0.20; Value = 0.90

   ▸ Time = 0.40; Value = 0.25

   ▸ Time = 0.70; Value = 0.25

   ▸ Time = 0.80; Value = 0.85

   ▸ Time = 1.70; Value = 0.90

   ▸ Time = 1.90; Value = 0.10

   ▸ Time = 2.70; Value = 0.10

   ▸ Time = 2.80; Value = 1.10

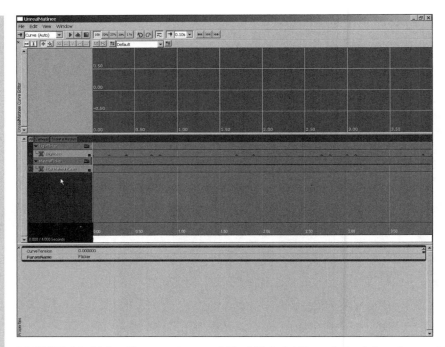

FIGURE 10.100   The new group and Float Material Property track have been added.

> ▸ Time = 3.00; Value = 1.10

> ▸ Time = 3.10; Value = 0.30

> ▸ Time = 3.90; Value = 0.30

5. In the Kismet Editor, create a Level Startup event and connect its Out output to the Play input of the Light Flicker Matinee sequence. Preview the animation and make any tweaks desired.

6. Save your progress and test your level when finished.

END TUTORIAL 10.20

Summary

Over the course of this chapter, you have seen several ways in which Matinee can be used to animate in-game events. In the past, animation was mainly limited to moving objects. With the introduction of Matinee, the possibilities are far greater. Whether you are controlling particles or materials, or modifying lights, or playing animations, it is clear that Matinee is a very powerful tool for any level designer. And, when you factor in the fact that it is completely integrated inside of Kismet, it is often hard to come up with ideas that cannot be achieved. The sheer power of Matinee can be seen when viewing the cinematic sequences found within Gears of War or Unreal Tournament 3. These were all created with the help of Matinee and serve to show off what it can do in the hands of knowledgeable designers.

Chapter 11

Level Optimization

OK, you've worked hard to build all these digital assets. You've put 'em all together. You now have a level—congratulations. You're done, right? No way. Just throwing everything together is a good way to deliver a level that won't perform well during gameplay. Not everyone has 64 gigs of memory, a super-mega-32-core processor and a state-of-the-art video card—and even if they did, it's all too easy to create a game that'll transform their hardware into cold molasses! You need to understand how your game level will perform on real-world systems. If you're building a PC game, you need to set realistic hardware requirements (ideally, without disqualifying 99% of your potential customers!) Above all, you need to optimize your game so it plays well on equipment mere mortals actually own. That's what this chapter is about: simple (and relatively simple) tweaks you can use to deliver faster, more responsive levels—without compromising the stuff that makes your game so great.

General Optimization

In previous versions of the Unreal Engine, level optimization had mainly to do with dividing your level into zones within which objects could be hidden en masse based on whether the player could see the boundaries of the zone. As of Unreal Engine 3.0, however,

11

this type of optimization is obsolete, because all objects can automatically occlude one another. This means that if one object is completely occluded by (or hidden behind) another, it will not be calculated by the rendering engine.

Understanding Overhead

Understanding optimization has to do with understanding overhead, or the amount of effort your computer must go through to run your game. There are two types of overhead that you need to be concerned with: game overhead and rendering overhead. Game overhead comes from the game code itself, controlling what is *happening* during the game. Rendering overhead is the result of the computer trying to actually show your game on the screen.

In this chapter, we focus primarily on rendering overhead. In Unreal Engine 3.0, most of the overhead involved in rendering a level has to do with the interactions between lights and surfaces.

In-Game Performance Diagnostics

Viewing statistics in the editor can give you a general idea of how things will behave in game and how well the scene will perform. However, the only way to know for sure whether your game is playable is to test it during gameplay! Unreal includes a wide variety of in-game console commands to help you tell which direction to look for the culprit of a performance hit. These include lists of statistics that you can render to the screen during gameplay that tell you which calculations are taking up the most time, as well as commands that control what is and is not rendering during gameplay. For instance, if you're only getting 10 frames per second, or 1 frame every 100 milliseconds, you can scan through these lists of statistics and see where all the time is being taken up, or perhaps hide all of your dynamic shadows and see if that helps.

The STAT commands provide various lists of data onto the screen during gameplay. These lists update in real time and can be used to narrow down exactly where to look for performance issues. Following is a list of the most common of these:

>   **STAT FPS**—Shows the current rate of frames rendering per second.

>   **STAT SCENERENDERING**—Shows rendering-specific statistics, such as draw times for lighting, emissive, and translucency, as well as occlusion statistics (see **FIGURE 11.1**).

>   **STAT MEMORY**—Shows statistics dealing with memory usage.

>   **STAT ENGINE**—Shows rendering-specific statistics such as terrain, foliage, HUD, and skeletal mesh draw times.

>   **STAT STREAMING**—Shows statistics dealing with streaming of levels.

>   **STAT AUDIO**—Shows statistics dealing with the playing of sounds.

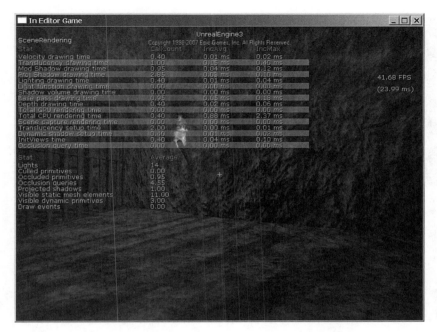

FIGURE 11.1   Both the STAT FPS and STAT SCENERENDERING commands have been activated.

The SHOW commands enable you to hide or display a variety of game elements and effects. There are many things that can be shown with these commands, although these are a few of the most commonly used in terms of performance. Their definitions are fairly self-explanatory, as follows:

> **SHOW BSP**—Shows the BSP in a level (see **FIGURE 11.2**).
>
> **SHOW DYNAMICSHADOWS**—Useful for hiding dynamic shadows.
>
> **SHOW UNLITTRANSLUCENCY**—Helpful for testing whether unlit transparency is affecting your gameplay.
>
> **SHOW POSTPROCESS**—For diagnosing complex post-processing effects as a source of performance drops.
>
> **SHOW PARTICLES**—Helpful for levels that make heavy use of particles.

FIGURE 11.2   Here you can see the result of the SHOW BSP command. Notice that the floor, made of a BSP brush, has disappeared.

SHOW FOLIAGE—Helpful for terrain levels.

SHOW RIGIDBODY—Useful for making sure that rigid bodies aren't slowing things down too much.

The VIEWMODE commands enable you to change the way the game displays during play, showing a variety of information regarding rendering. Listed next are some of the most common:

VIEWMODE WIREFRAME—This mode draws the level entirely in wireframe (see **FIGURE 11.3**).

VIEWMODE UNLIT—This mode draws the scene with textures, but with no light or shadow (see **FIGURE 11.4**).

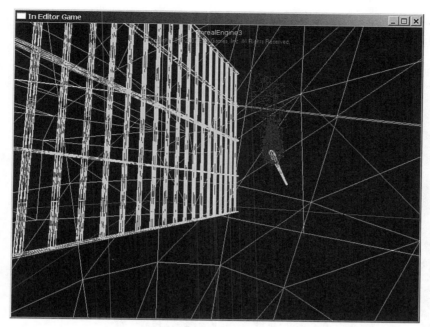

FIGURE 11.3 The result of VIEWMODE WIREFRAME

FIGURE 11.4 The result of VIEWMODE UNLIT

VIEWMODE LIT—This is the default mode for the viewport, showing the scene with texturing, lights, and shadows (see **FIGURE 11.5**).

FIGURE 11.5   The result of VIEWMODE LIT

VIEWMODE LIGHTINGONLY—This mode hides all texture information, showing only how lights and shadows are playing across the surface of the level (see **FIGURE 11.6**).

VIEWMODE LIGHTCOMPLEXITY—This mode draws surfaces using solid colors, which represent the number of non-light-mapped lights affecting a surface (see **FIGURE 11.7**).

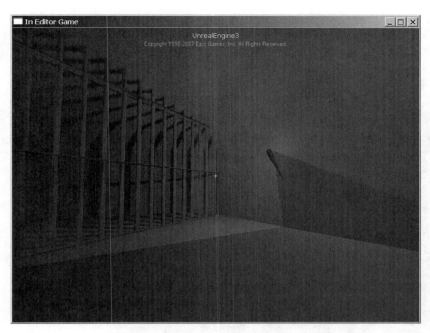

FIGURE 11.6   The result of VIEWMODE LIGHTINGONLY. Notice the effect of the Light Function.

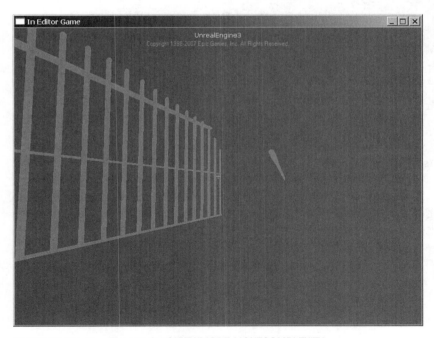

FIGURE 11.7   The result of VIEWMODE LIGHTCOMPLEXITY

11

VIEWMODE TEXTUREDENSITY—This mode draws all surfaces in a solid color, reflecting the complexity of textures on each surface. High-resolution textures show as red, medium in green, and low in blue. This is useful for making sure that you are not squandering high-resolution textures in areas where they aren't necessary (see **FIGURE 11.8**).

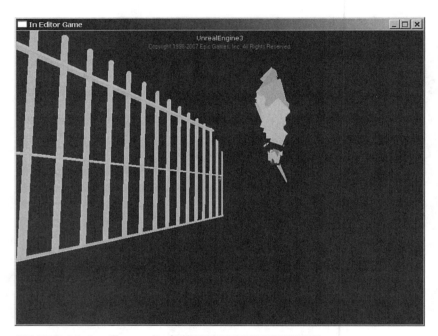

FIGURE 11.8   The result of VIEWMODE TEXTUREDENSITY

VIEWMODE SHADERCOMPLEXITY—This mode draws all surfaces in a solid color, reflecting the complexity of materials in terms of shader instructions on each surface. High instruction counts display in red, whereas low instruction counts display in green. This is useful for determining whether material complexity is causing a performance problem (see **FIGURE 11.9**).

In **TUTORIAL 11.1**, we show how you can activate the Light Complexity render mode, which enables you to visualize how computer memory is affected by your lighting setup. We also demonstrate the Stats system, which gives feedback on how computer resources are used to deliver the game to the player.

FIGURE 11.9   The result of VIEWMODE SHADERCOMPLEXITY

TUTORIAL 11.1: Optimization, Part I: Viewing Light Complexity and Stats

1. Launch Unreal Editor and open the DM-CH_11_LevelOp_Start.ut3 map included on the DVD in the files for this chapter. This map is very similar to the map completed in Chapter 7, "Introduction to Lighting," but with a few minor changes to make optimizations more apparent.

2. Right-click in the Perspective viewport and choose Play From Here, or click the Play In Editor button ▓ to jump in and test the map (see **FIGURE 11.10**).

3. Once the map is loaded, press Tab to open the console across the bottom of the screen. Many commands can be entered into this console during gameplay (see **FIGURE 11.11**).

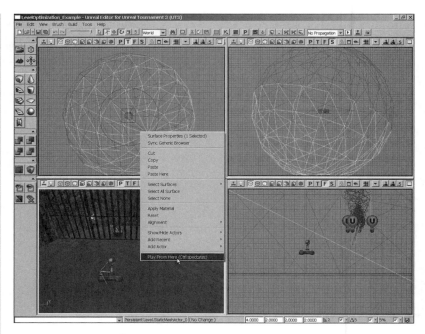

FIGURE 11.10   Choosing Play From Here launches the In Editor Game.

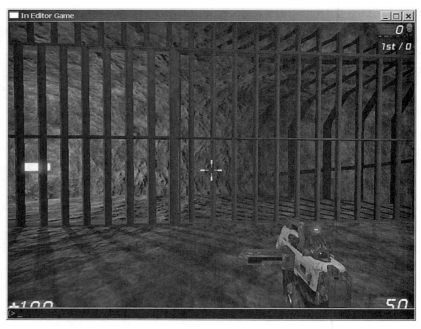

FIGURE 11.11   The console can appears at the bottom of the screen.

4. Enter the command VIEWMODE LIGHTCOMPLEXITY and press Enter. This draws the level in a series of solid colors, reflecting the number of non-light-mapped lights affecting each surface. In the case of this map, most of the surfaces are a shade of yellow, with at least one surface being red (see **FIGURE 11.12**).

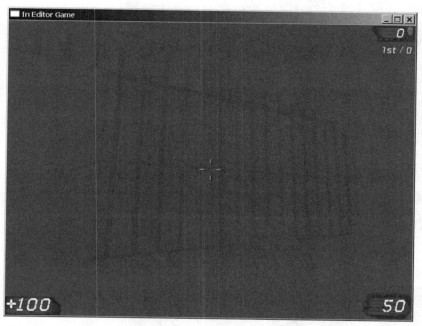

FIGURE 11.12   The LightComplexity viewmode can give you an idea of performance issues concerning lighting.

5. Reopen the console and enter VIEWMODE LIT. This resets the view to its default status. As an alternative, you can press the F3 key.

6. Enter the STAT FPS command into the console. This brings up the current frames per second, which is a good way to gauge performance levels. Make a mental note of the values you see here, so that you can compare them to values taken once you've completed all the optimization tutorials in this chapter (see **FIGURE 11.13**).

7. Enter the STAT SCENERENDERING command into the console. This brings up a list of constantly updating values, which can be useful for determining the precise cause of a performance drop (see **FIGURE 11.14**).

8. Exit the In Editor Game and save your map. You will use this map throughout the chapter.

FIGURE 11.13   The current Frames Per Second is now shown.

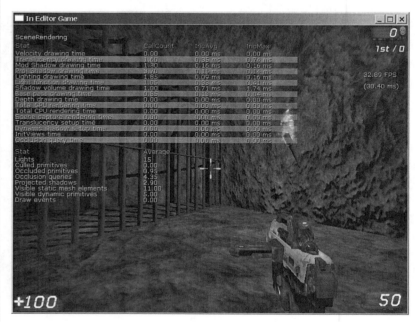

FIGURE 11.14   STAT SCENERENDERING shows many of the rendering-specific level details.

END TUTORIAL 11.1

Occlusion

Occlusion is simply defined as when one object completely obstructs the view of another. This is an important factor in Unreal, because when an object is completely occluded it does not render. The fewer objects there are to render, the better your performance will tend to be (see **FIGURE 11.15**).

Unreal calculates occlusion using the bounding box of each object. If any portion of the bounding box is visible to the viewpoint (the player's screen), that object is rendered. Only if the bounding box is completely hidden will the object be culled, or omitted from the render.

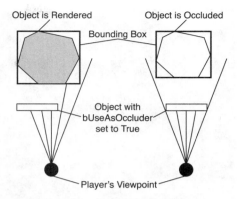

FIGURE 11.15 This diagram demonstrates the concept of occlusion.

If an object is so small that it is unlikely to occlude anything, you can remove it from the occlusion calculations by setting its bUseAsOccluder property to False. This property is found in a variety of locations within each type of object's property window. Following is a list of where the bUseAsOccluder property can be found on a variety of objects:

- ▸ **BSP Brushes**—Collision > CollisionComponent.
- ▸ **Static Meshes, Skeletal Meshes, and InterpActors**—Collision > CollisionComponent > Rendering.

It is also noteworthy that whenever the viewpoint falls *within* an object's bounding box, that object will never be culled. This becomes a factor when creating static mesh buildings, because it means that once inside the building, the geometry of the building will never be culled (see **FIGURE 11.16**).

If occlusion is not working for you—as in perhaps there is an object that you do not need to render, although its bounding box is not completely occluded—you can use the FREEZERENDERING console command. This command shuts down the occlusion calculations in your level, meaning that any objects that are occluded at the time the command was input are not rendered (see **FIGURE 11.17**).

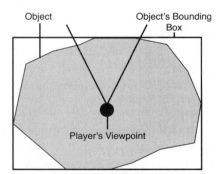

FIGURE 11.16 When the viewpoint is within an object's bounding box, that object will never be culled from the render.

You then use the VIEWMODE WIREFRAME console command (or the F1 key during gameplay) to see the level's wireframe. Parts that are occluded at the time the FREEZERENDERING command was given are colored gray, whereas parts that are visible appear in teal.

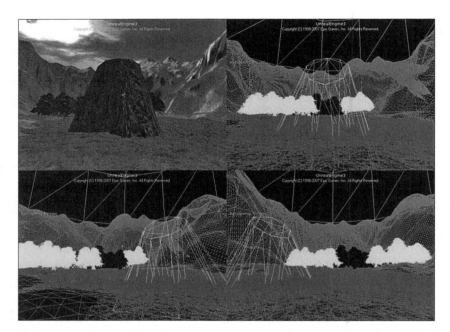

FIGURE 11.17   The FREEZERENDERING command stops the occlusion calculation.

CullDistance and CullDistanceVolumes

The CullDistance property can be found in the Rendering section of the components of most actors. This can be an invaluable tool when working with large outdoor environments because it enables you, as the level designer, to specify the distance from the camera at which any actor is no longer rendered, even if it would not be culled otherwise because of occlusion or any other factor. A value of 0 for this property means the CullDistance will be ignored for the actor.

CullDistanceVolumes provide a method for level designers to specify the CullDistance properties for all the actors within a given area without having to manually set the property for each individual actor. If actors within the CullDistanceVolume already have their CullDistance property set, the lower of the two values between its CullDistance property and the value it would be given by the CullDistanceVolume will be used. The CullDistances array of the CullDistanceVolume allows various sizes (this is the radius of the bounding sphere of the actor) and distances to be set. In order to show how these values work, let's look at an example:

- [0]
    - **Size:** 0.0
    - **CullDistance:** 0.0

   ▶ [1]

        ▶ **Size:** 1000.0

        ▶ **CullDistance:** 2000.0

   ▶ [2]

        ▶ **Size:** 10000.0

        ▶ **CullDistance:** 20000.0

Any actors within this CullDistanceVolume between the sizes of 0.0 and 1000.0 will be culled when more than 2000.0 units from the camera. Actors between the sizes of 1000.0 and 10000.0 will be culled when more than 20000.0 units from the camera.

Levels of Detail

Making use of the Levels of Detail (LOD) system for static meshes provided by Unreal Engine 3 can help to improve performance. This system allows for switching between several meshes of varying complexity at various distances from the camera. This means an extremely detailed mesh can be used when the player is close to the object, but less detailed and more efficient meshes can be used as the player gets farther and farther away from the object. In conjunction with the standard occlusion scheme used by Unreal Engine 3 and the CullDistance property or CullDistance Volumes, static meshes can become extremely efficient.

Optimizing Lights and Shadows

Dynamic shadows are a major concern for lighting optimization, especially shadow buffer shadows. These shadows use a shader, which blurs the edges of the shadow. This shader, however, comes at the cost of heavy performance drain, especially when the shadow takes up a considerable percentage of screen space. Possible solutions to this problem include making sure that light sources for such shadows are kept far enough away from dynamic objects that their shadows cannot become overly large.

Light Maps

Keep in mind that light maps are pre-rendered, and are essentially "free," adding only to the amount of memory the level uses. Because of this, light maps should be used whenever possible for shadowing. In cases where a particular object should not be able to receive a dynamic shadow, you can activate the bForceDirectLightMap property. This property forces that surface to only use light maps for shadowing, instead of shadow buffer shadows. However, this setting can be bypassed by modulated shadows, which can be used on top of light maps.

Light Environments

Light Environments are another important way to optimize the lighting for your level, especially where dynamic shadows are concerned. Rather than having to deal with multiple shadows from different sources, a Light Environment calculates only a single modulated shadow based on proximity to all relevant lights (see **FIGURE 11.18**). Naturally, this results in a massive performance gain over using dynamic shadows, especially for characters and movers. For more information on Light Environments and setting them up, see Chapter 7.

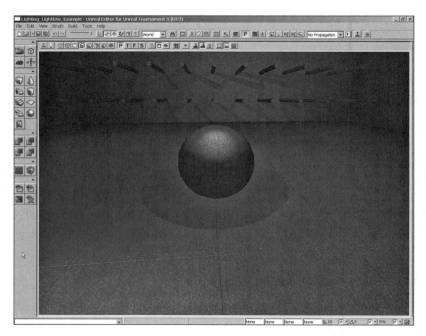

FIGURE 11.18   Light Environments can give you the illusion of using multiple dynamic lights with only a fraction of the overhead.

Light Functions

At the time of this writing, applying Light Functions to a light prohibits the use of that light within any light maps. This means that Light Function lights are always being calculated, and should therefore be kept to an absolute minimum if not avoided altogether.

Casting Light onto Unlit Materials

Another lighting concern comes from objects whose materials are set to the MLM_Unlit lighting model. Naturally, if an object's material appears unlit, that object doesn't need to receive lighting. You can help out your performance a bit (not to mention keep Unreal Editor from giving you warnings at build time) by setting the bAcceptsLights property to False on all objects whose materials are using MLM_Unlit.

The Primitive Stats Browser

The Primitive Stats browser provides a great deal of information regarding the meshes in your scene (static and skeletal meshes, terrain, and BSP) and how much calculation is required for each one (see **FIGURE 11.19**). The statistics available are listed and defined as follows.

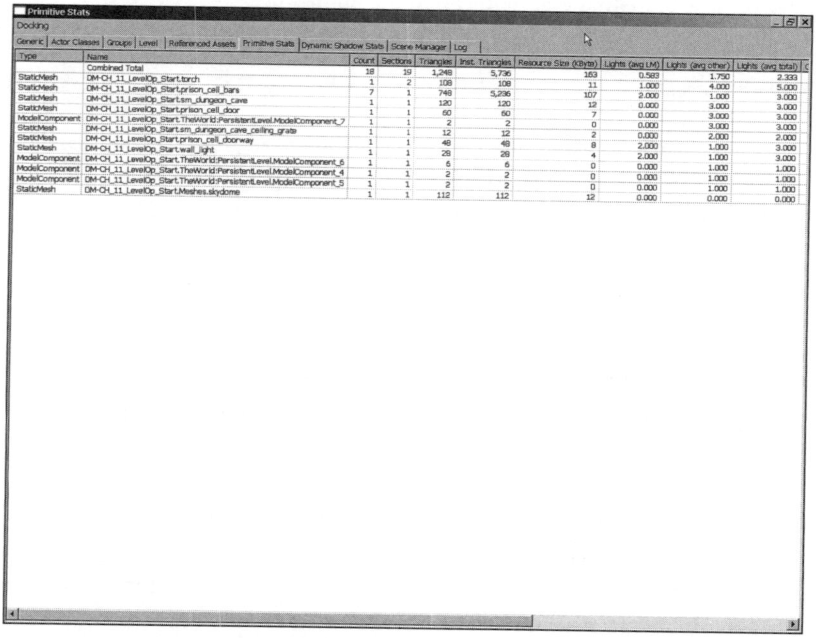

FIGURE 11.19   The Primitive Stats browser can help you determine the amount of overhead caused by various meshes in your level.

- ▸ **Type**—This lists the type of object being analyzed.
- ▸ **Count**—The number of copies, or instances, of that object that are in the level.
- ▸ **Sections**—This is the number of pieces, or separate parts, that make up an object.
- ▸ **Triangles**—The total number of triangles in each instance of the object.
- ▸ **Inst. Triangles**—The total number of triangles in all instances of the object combined.
- ▸ **Resource Size**—This reflects the amount of memory that a particular object is using, listed in Kilobytes. This information is pertinent only for static meshes and skeletal meshes.

11

- ▶ **Lights (avg LM)**—The average number of light-mapped lights affecting each instance of an object.

- ▶ **Lights (avg other)**—The average number of non-light-mapped lights affecting each instance of an object.

- ▶ **Lights (Avg total)**—The average number of light-mapped and non-light-mapped lights affecting each instance of an object.

- ▶ **Obj/ Light cost**—This number reflects the number of times a static mesh is re-rendered during each frame. It is calculated in the following manner:

  - ▶ Total number of non-light-mapped lights affecting an object

  X

  - ▶ Total number of pieces in the static mesh

  X

  - ▶ Total number of instances of the static mesh within the level

- ▶ **Note**—Light-mapped lights are not taken into account in terms of memory usage, because they are calculated before gameplay.

- ▶ **Lightmap**—This is the total amount of memory used for an object's light map.

- ▶ **Shadowmap**—The total amount of memory used for an object's shadowmap.

- ▶ **LM Res**—This is the average resolution of the light map for each instance of an object.

- ▶ **Radius (min/max/avg)**—Min/max/average radius of the bounding box for each instance of the mesh.

By analyzing the information provided in the Primitive Stats browser, you can locate a variety of different overhead problems. For instance, by checking stats such as Count, Triangles, and Resource Size for very similar static meshes, you may be able to determine that one mesh could be replaced with a simpler mesh for a gain in performance. Checking the Light statistics can be very important as well, as it provides you with a way to find areas where too many non-light-mapped lights are affecting meshes, which can lead to a significant drop in performance.

Dynamic Shadows and the Dynamic Shadow Stats Browser

Dynamic shadows are another likely source of performance overhead. This problem can be diagnosed by launching your level, and then using the SHOW DYNAMICSHADOWS command to turn off dynamic shadow casting. It may also help to use the STAT FPS command to show frame rates. If performance increases significantly when dynamic shadows are off, you know you've got a problem.

Once you've diagnosed dynamic shadows as having an overly negative effect on performance, you need to figure out which objects are creating the bulk of those shadows. This can be done using the Dynamic Shadow Stats browser, which is located in the Browsers window. However, when you first open this browser, you see that it is completely blank.

In order to fill in the Dynamic Shadow Stats browser, you must first run the game in the editor, and during gameplay press F10, or enter DUMPDYNAMICSHADOWSTATS into the console. When you exit the In Editor Game and return to the browser, you find that it is full of information, enabling you to quickly see which lights are creating the most dynamic shadows, and from what objects those shadows are being cast (see **FIGURE 11.20**).

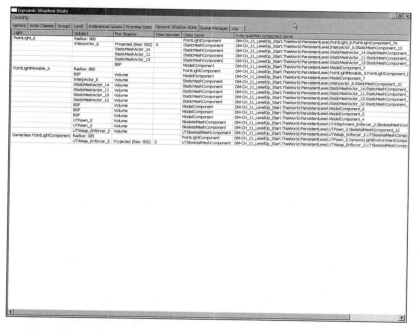

FIGURE 11.20   The Dynamic Shadow Stats browser enables you to see the sources of all dynamic shadows in your level.

For **TUTORIAL 11.2**, please continue from **TUTORIAL 11.1**, or open the DM-CH_11_LevelOp_01.uts map file provided on the DVD with the files for this chapter.

TUTORIAL 11.2: Optimization, Part II: Forcing Light Maps on Geometry

1. Open the Generic browser and click on the Primitive Stats tab (see **FIGURE 11.21**). We are most concerned with the Lights(avg other) and Obj/Light cost columns. Ideally, we would like the Lights(avg other) to be filled with 0's, as this would mean that all our surfaces are using light maps and should incur little to no performance penalty. Of course,

this cannot always be the case in every level. In this case, we have several objects that could be using light maps but are not causing a performance drop.

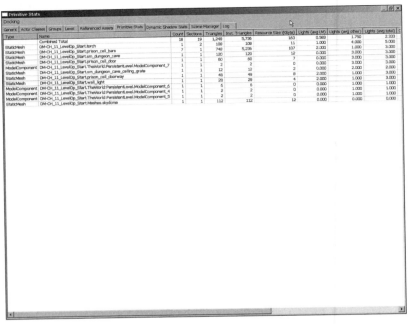

FIGURE 11.21   The Primitive Stats tab shows you a great deal of information regarding your level's efficiency.

2. In the Perspective viewport, select the cave static mesh, right-click on it, and choose Select all StaticMeshActor. This selects all static meshes in the scene.

3. Press F4 to open the Properties Window. Under the StaticMeshActor tab, open StaticMeshComponent and find the Lighting category. Notice that some of the checkboxes are filled with a checker pattern, meaning that some of the selected static meshes have multiple values for those properties (see **FIGURE 11.22**).

   Activate the bForceDirectLightMap property, so that all static meshes will use light maps. This property is on by default, but was deactivated so that some of the static meshes could receive dynamic shadows.

4. Select the floor surface and press F5 to open the Surface Properties window. Select the Force Lightmaps option to cause this surface to use light maps.

5. Now that all visible static meshes and BSP are using light maps, rebuild your lighting with the Build Lighting button ![icon] or Build All button ![icon]. Open the Primitive Stats browser once again and notice that there are far fewer lights displayed in the Lights (avg other) column, meaning that we are using fewer non-light-mapped lights.

The torch mesh is still being affected by four lights. However, because those lights are all using Light Functions, they cannot (at the time of this writing) be used in the light map. In order to force light maps upon them, we need to kill off the Light Functions.

6. Select all the lights surrounding the torch, and press F4 to open the Properties Window. Under Light > LightComponent, click on the right side of the Function property to display the Clear All Text button ▢. Click this button to clear all Light Functions from these lights (see **FIGURE 11.23**).

7. Still in the Properties Window for the four lights, check the UseLightMap option and set the LightColor property to a shade of orange. We used RGB values of 255,132, 40.

8. Build all of your lighting and save your map. In the Primitive Stats browser, all static meshes and BSP are now affected by one non-mapped light.

The reason we still have a single non-mapped light is because some of our lights are dynamic, or in motion. The only way we could do away with the overhead of this light is to eliminate its animation, making it a static light. This is an instance in which one must consider the trade-off of performance over visual effect. If the wavering light is necessary to your final effect, then you'd simply have to find a way to deal with its resultant overhead.

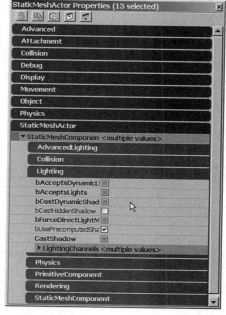

FIGURE 11.22   A checkered filling in an option means that the selected objects have differing values of that property.

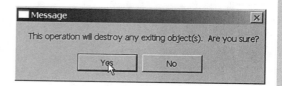

FIGURE 11.23   Removing the Light Function makes the level more efficient, though at the cost of some visual effect.

END TUTORIAL 11.2

Material Optimization

There are several considerations for working with materials in your level that can help a great deal with performance. Like all optimizations, some of the issues listed here can sometimes not be avoided in your level. The key is moderation, and using such things only when you need them.

11

Multiple Materials per Object

Although it can be useful from a design standpoint to have multiple materials on an object, it can result in a performance hit if overused. In some instances, however, this technique is unavoidable. One example would be in the case of characters, who typically use one material for the head and a separate material for the body, even though the head and body are joined as one piece (see **FIGURE 11.24**). The key is to not get carried away, and to use as few materials as possible to achieve the desired result.

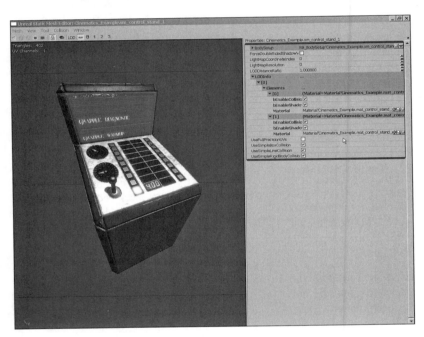

FIGURE 11.24   This object is using multiple materials.

Material Instructions

As discussed in Chapter 6, "Introduction to Materials," some materials require more instructions, or calculations, than others. The most complex materials you can create will only be two to three times more complex than an average material, but having too many such materials on too many objects in one area can potentially be a drain.

> **NOTE**
>
> It is important to note that although materials are rarely the bottleneck in performance, too many complex materials can incur a performance hit.

Unlit Translucency

Unlit translucency occurs when you are using a material with a blend mode of BLEND_translucent and a lighting model of MLM_Unlit. The problem is that this can cause severe *overdraw*, which is when a pixel is drawn over the top of a previously drawn pixel (see **FIGURE 11.25**). This can cause a serious performance hit.

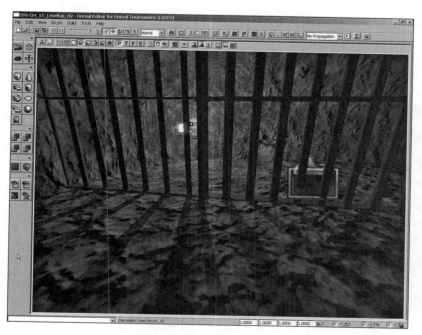

FIGURE 11.25   This diagram illustrates the concept of overdraw.

Because of this potential, you should limit your use of unlit translucent materials. However, you can determine if unlit transparency is causing a significant problem by showing the frames per second during gameplay (STAT FPS console command) and then using the SHOW UNLIT-TRANSLUCENCY console command. If your frame rate increases when unlit translucency is turned off, you know you've got a problem on your hands.

Please continue from **TUTORIAL 11.2**, or open the DM-CH_11_LevelOp_02.ut3 map file provided on the DVD with the files for this chapter. In **TUTORIAL 11.3**, we look at optimizing the dynamic shadow cast by the prison cell door. In order to do this, we utilize a LightEnvironment.

11

TUTORIAL 11.3: Optimization, Part III: Using Dynamic Shadows on Light-Mapped Geometry

1. Select the prison cell door and press F4 to open its Properties Window. Expand DynamicSMActor > Light Environment > LightEnvironmentComponent and activate the bEnabled property. This forces this object to receive light from a Light Environment.

2. Using the Light Environment on the door may cause other shadows to look too dark by comparison. To fix this, we adjust the other shadows. Select the light next to the fixture inside the cell. Open the Properties Window and set the LightShadowMode property to LightShadow_Modulate. This causes the shadows to have similar contrast, because Light Environments automatically use modulated shadows (see **FIGURE 11.26**).

FIGURE 11.26   The modulated shadows have a similar contrast to the other shadows in the level.

3. Build your lighting and save your map. Feel free to test the level. Notice that the shadows are now equal in contrast.

4. While in the In Editor Game, try applying the VIEWMODE LIGHTCOMPLEXITY and STAT FPS console commands and notice the difference in performance that you now have based on your optimizations (see **FIGURE 11.27**).

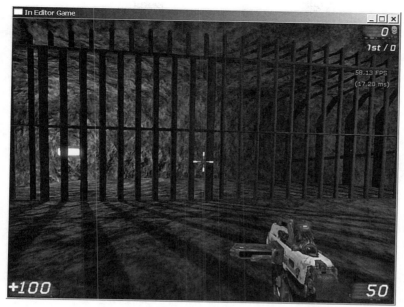

FIGURE 11.27   Throughout the chapter, this level has become much more efficient.

END TUTORIAL 11.3

Summary

In this chapter, we looked at many of the tools Unreal Engine 3 provides for analyzing your levels. There are many ways to go about looking for the cause when performance problems arise in a map. However, when most beginning designers run up against a trouble area in a map, it is usually because of not following good practices when creating the map instead of a matter of needing to employ some sort of optimization technique. This is the reason we have tried throughout the entire book to provide you with the knowledge of how things should best be done in order to prevent these problems from ever arising in the first place. By following these guidelines and using the diagnostic tools contained within the engine, you should easily be able to avoid most problems and easily find the cause of any others, making your maps playable and enjoyable for yourself and others within the Unreal community.

Chapter 12

Level Streaming

In the previous chapter, you learned several great ways to optimize your levels. In this chapter, we focus on a powerful new approach introduced with Unreal Engine 3.0: *level streaming*. With level streaming, you can load and unload level from memory during gameplay, on the fly. The concept itself is simple: A level doesn't technically "exist" in the game until you approach it, and it ceases to exist as you leave it behind. You save crucial memory, even as you build games with enormous playable areas.

Some new games use level streaming to brilliant effect: In fact, it's the key means of game progression in Gears of War. Other games, such as fast-paced multiplayer games like Unreal Tournament 3, don't lend themselves as well to the technology. But, if it fits your game, it can open amazing new vistas in game design.

We'll tell you straight up: This chapter's more advanced than most of what we've shown you before. You need to be comfortable with Kismet (see Chapter 9, "Introduction to Unreal Kismet"), Matinee

12

(see Chapter 10, "Unreal Matinee"), and with using Geometry Mode on brushes (see Chapter 4, "A Universe of Brushes: World Geometry In-Depth").

One more thing before we get started: In level streaming, precise level naming is absolutely essential. That's why we aren't providing individual files for use with each of this chapter's tutorials. You need to complete this chapter's tutorials in order from start to finish. (We do, of course, provide completed versions of this chapter's levels in the Chapter_12_Complete folder.)

Level Streaming Benefits

In previous versions of the Unreal Engine, most optimizations were handled through *zoning*, a process by which your level would be divided up into occluding zones, and visibility of the various zones would be handled based on whether or not the player could see the zone. This had its benefits, but suffered from the fact that only visibility was being affected; larger levels would still require vast amounts of memory. Level streaming solves this problem by allowing levels to be completely removed from memory when not visible; thus, it is a far more efficient means to optimize your levels for playability.

The benefits of level streaming extend in different directions—not only just the benefit to computer resources. The first is collaboration; because all the levels beings streamed together are each contained in their own file, multiple level designers can work on one consistent streaming world by each designing their own level. Another important factor is the ability for each level to have unique Kismet sequences, meaning that each level has its own individual control over virtually every major aspect of gameplay (see **FIGURE 12.1**).

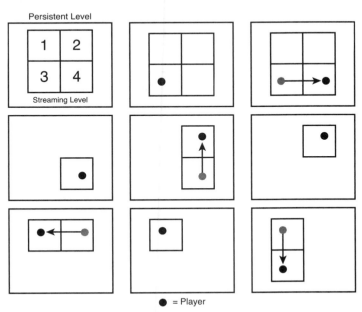

FIGURE 12.1   This diagram illustrates the basic idea behind level streaming.

Testing Level Streaming

An important thing to keep in mind about level streaming is that you can't really test it out in the In Editor Game. This is because all levels of the scenario are already loaded into memory, and the streaming process only adjusts the visibility of the levels themselves. In order to accurately test your streaming setup, you need to test the game away from the editor, preferably on the actual gameplay platform.

For Unreal Tournament 3, this simply requires that you publish the map and then open it from within the Instant Action menu.

Streaming Methods

There are two basic methods for level streaming: Distance and Kismet. One of these methods must be selected whenever a level is imported in for streaming purposes. The difference is simple and self-explanatory; Distance uses the player's distance from a given point to stream the levels together, whereas Kismet enables you to stream the levels together using scripted sequence events and actions. You can mix and match the methods however you like, based on which is the most appropriate for your level.

When using the Kismet method, the level designer also has the options of using LevelStreaming Volumes, which provide an extremely intuitive way to handle the streaming process. There is also a special technique that can be used as a way to stream multiple level-streaming scenarios together; we discuss this later in this chapter.

Persistent Levels Versus Streaming Levels

There are two types of levels involved in a level-streaming scenario: persistent levels and streaming levels. A persistent level is, as the name suggests, always present during gameplay. It is the basis from which all the other levels are loaded and unloaded. The persistent level is a requirement of any level-streaming scenario, as it is the initially loaded level that begins the streaming process. In many cases, this level is simply a PlayerStart actor that is floating in empty space. The actual playable levels are then streamed into this persistent level.

Because every level in a level-streaming scenario can contain its own Kismet sequences, the persistent level must contain any sequences that are used by all levels. This includes any Kismet that is actually handling the streaming process, as well as any variables that must be used in the Kismet sequences for multiple levels, such as Music Track Banks.

The levels that are actually streamed through the persistent level are called streaming levels. Although there technically is no limit on how many streaming levels you can place in your streaming scenario, you should realize that there could be a performance hit with loading extremely high numbers of streaming levels to each persistent level. As a reference, Epic's Gears of War typically streamed around 20 streaming levels to each persistent level.

Size is also a factor when streaming levels. Streamed levels should be created so that when streamed together, they are contiguous, not overlapping. This means that you are limited in the size of your level-streaming scenarios by the size of the grid. However, this is rarely a serious design concern, due to the massive size of the usable grid. For example, if we assume the average height of a player (96 Unreal units) is about 6 feet, the grid (at $376,832^2$ units) provides you with almost 20 square miles of space to lay out your level! Plus, that's only if you're thinking two dimensionally. There's no reason you couldn't stack different levels on top of one another in the Z-axis, giving you nearly 90 cubic miles of space to play with!

> **NOTE**
>
> Some care should still be used if you plan on creating extremely massive worlds. Certain precision problems can arise on levels that approach the edges of the grid!

Finally, you should be aware that although in typical circumstances a streaming level is just a regular level that is being streamed into a persistent level, it is possible to stream in other persistent levels, forming a type of hierarchy. This process is not as seamless as standard level streaming, as there is a marked load time from one persistent level to the next. However, it does still make use of loading content on the fly. For those who have played the game Gears of War, this is how different chapters of the game were streamed together and why the game would typically go to a cutscene in between chapters. The loading was taking place, but was not completely seamless; showing an animation kept the player entertained while loading happened.

The Level Browser and Scene Manager

The central tool of level streaming is the Level browser, which is tucked inside the Browsers window under its own tab (see **FIGURE 12.2**). From the Level browser, you can add streaming levels to your persistent level. All the loaded levels, both persistent and streaming, are listed within this browser. You can also view and edit the properties of any of the levels, associate LevelStreamingVolumes with their appropriate level, and set the current level.

You may have noticed that Unreal Editor does not have a typical "Save" option under its File menu. Instead, it has Save Current Level. The reason for this is that while working with multiple streaming levels at once, you need to be able to designate which level you are currently adjusting, so that you can save your changes into the proper level. This designation is known as making the level "current." Only the current level actually receives any new actors that are placed into the

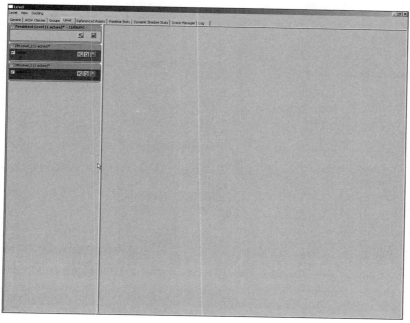

FIGURE 12.2   The Level browser

level. It is important that when working with multiple levels, you always adjust your current level to reflect the level you are working on so that you do not save changes into the wrong level. The current level is denoted in the level list of the Level browser by a label that reads –CURRENT-.

The levels listed in the Level browser can be color coded to help with organization. Each level can be individually saved, and the Kismet sequences for each level can be accessed through the browser as well.

The Scene Manager is a spreadsheet-style browser that enables you to see all the actors in a level, as well as a way to get access to the WorldInfo properties of the level itself (see **FIGURE 12.3**). However, when you first go to the Scene Manager, it appears to be empty. In order to see a level within the manager, you must select the level from the level list in the Level browser, right-click on it, and choose Show Selected in Scene Manager from the Context menu.

While in the Scene Manager, you can select, focus on, and delete actors from the level. You can also easily filter the list to focus on any type of actor that you like.

12

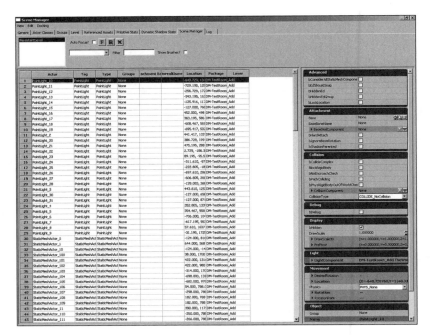

FIGURE 12.3   The Scene Manager

Map Changing

One of the unique abilities of the level-streaming system is the ability to actually change from one persistent level to another through the use of map changing. In a sense, this is like streaming between multiple level-streaming scenarios. As mentioned earlier, this is slightly different than standard level streaming and requires the use of two specialized Kismet sequence objects: Prepare Map Change and Commit Map Change, as follows:

FIGURE 12.4   Prepare Map Kismet sequence object

▶ **Prepare Map Change**—This object starts the loading process for the new persistent level (see **FIGURE 12.4**).

▶ **Commit Map Change**—This object performs the actual transition to a new persistent level (see **FIGURE 12.5**).

FIGURE 12.5   Commit Map Change Kismet sequence object

This technique is different than standard level streaming in that while the loading is taking place in the background, there is a noticeable transition (or "pop") as you jump from one persistent level to another. The designer typically covers up this problem through some distractive mechanism, such as fading to another screen or to a Matinee sequence as the new map loads into memory. This is the technique that was employed in Gears of War.

The basic setup to establish map changing is to create multiple level-streaming scenarios, each with their own persistent and streaming levels. A new "empty" map is created that handles the transition between the different persistent levels. In this case, "empty" means that the level typically only has a PlayerStart actor and some form of Kismet sequence that handles the loading of the first level, as well as the circumstances by which other persistent levels are loaded. Once a persistent level is loaded, each of its corresponding streaming levels are handled automatically, until the next persistent level is loaded.

It is important to note that Changing Maps do not work in the In Editor Game. In order to actually test this process, you must run their master persistent level in the standalone game. This process is outlined in the "Level Streaming via LevelStreamingVolumes" section later in the chapter.

> **NOTE**
>
> Before you begin working on the tutorials in this chapter, make sure you have access to the following levels, all included on the DVD in the files for this chapter:
>
> DM-Ch_12_Level_01
>
> DM-Ch_12_Level_02
>
> DM-Ch_12_Level_03
>
> DM-Ch_12_CityStream_1
>
> DM-Ch_12_CityStream_2
>
> DM-Ch_12_CityStream_3
>
> DM-Ch_12_CityStream_4

In the tutorials in this chapter, we set up a simple system for transitioning from one level to another as you might in a real game. We use the map changing concept outlined in the previous section. To begin, we create the map that will act as the container for the multiple persistent levels that we will stream in. This is going to be a very simple map consisting of a PlayerStart, a single cube brush, and some Kismet to load in the first level. The cube brush is added because the PlayerStart needs some geometry to sit on to build correctly. We need to make sure this geometry is not visible in any of the levels we will stream in, though.

The style of streaming we create can best be described through the diagram in **FIGURE 12.6**.

To sum up, this diagram illustrates that we start from Level_Entry, which immediately streams us to the first of our three persistent levels: Level_01. From there, we can stream

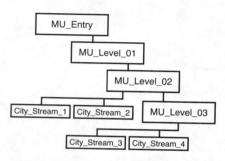

FIGURE 12.6   This diagram illustrates the example of streaming used throughout the tutorials in this chapter (the names are truncated for simplicity).

to our second persistent level, Level_02. Level_02 actually has two streamed levels within it: CityStream_1 and CityStream_2. Once we're done playing in those for a while, we can move on to Level_03, which has its own sublevels streamed in: CityStream_3 and CityStream_4. There's a whole lot of streaming going on, and if you're confused, it would be a good idea to open up the completed versions of the levels, which are included in the Chapter_12_Complete folder in the files for this chapter!

TUTORIAL 12.1: Level Transitioning, Part I: Creating the Entry Level

1. Launch Unreal Editor and start a new additive map. Set the Perspective viewport mode to Unlit.

2. Right-click the Cube button 🔲 and set the following settings in the Cube Builder window:

   X: 256

   Y: 256

   Z: 32

   Click Build and Close when finished; then move the Red Builder Brush down 1,024 units to keep it from being visible when we stream in other levels, and add the Red Builder Brush to the level with the CSG: Add button 🔲 (see **FIGURE 12.7**).

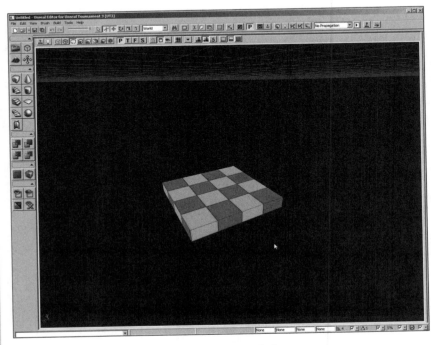

FIGURE 12.7   The new level is just a basic platform.

3. Right-click on the newly created brush and choose Add Actor->PlayerStart to add a player start on the brush (see **FIGURE 12.8**).

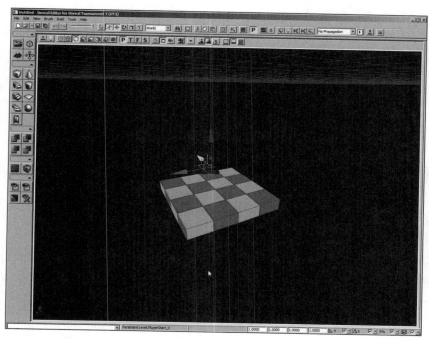

FIGURE 12.8   The PlayerStart actor has been added.

4. Now, Open Kismet so we can set up the sequence to load in the new level. Add a Level Startup event by right-clicking and choosing New Event > Level Startup from the Context menu (see **FIGURE 12.9**).

5. Next, add a Prepare Map Change (New Action->Level-> Prepare Map Change) action and connect the Out of the Level Startup to the PrepareLoad input of the Prepare Map Change (see **FIGURE 12.10**).

Set the following properties for the Prepare Map Change event:

bIsHighPriority: True

MainLevelName: DM-Ch_12_Level_01

FIGURE 12.9   Create a new Level Startup event.

6. Add a Commit Map Change (New Action->Level->Commit Map Change) event and connect the Finished output of the Prepare Map Change to the Commit input of the Commit Map Change (see **FIGURE 12.11**).

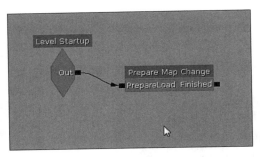

FIGURE 12.10   Add a Prepare Map Change object.

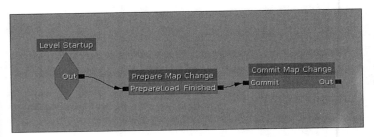

FIGURE 12.11   The Commit Map Change has been added.

7. Add a Toggle Cinematic Mode (New Action->Toggle->Toggle Cinematic Mode) action and connect the Out output of the Level Startup to the Enable input of the Toggle Cinematic Mode. This nullifies the player's ability to control the game while the map change is taking place. It also hides the HUD.

8. Create a Player variable (New Variable > Object > Player) and connect in to the Target variable input of the Toggle Cinematic Mode (see **FIGURE 12.12**).

9. We don't really want the player to ever see this level, so we're going to shift perspective away to a camera that is faded completely to black. This is kind of like cutting to a camera that has its lens cap on. We should note, however, that this technique would generally not be used in conventional game development circumstances. Typically, you would cut to some in-game cinematic or loading screen while such a map change is taking place. However, for sake of simplicity in the proof-of-concept example, we're just going to switch to a blackened camera.

   To do this, we need a new Matinee sequence object and a Camera actor. We'll start by placing the necessary camera. Please follow these steps:

   a. Open the Actor Classes browser and select the Camera actor.

   b. Right-click on the small platform upon which the PlayerStart is resting. Choose Add CameraActor Here from the Context menu.

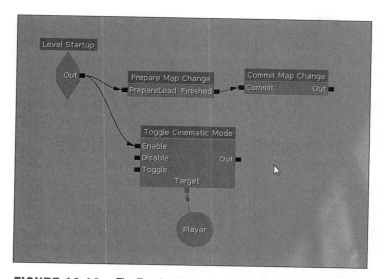

FIGURE 12.12   The Toggle Cinematic Mode and Player variable are now connected.

     c. Using the Translation Widget, move up the camera away from the platform so that it cannot see the platform (see **FIGURE 12.13**).

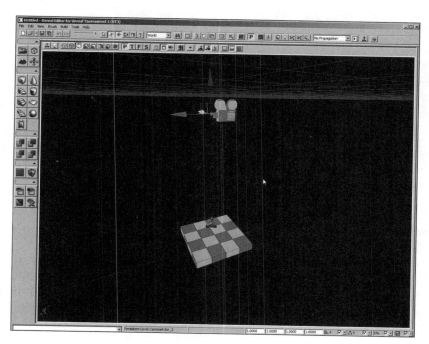

FIGURE 12.13   A new Camera actor sits above the platform.

10. The camera is now in place; we just need to switch to it when the level begins and make sure the player sees through the camera. Do the following:

> **NOTE**
>
> Because the Camera actor was selected, it should automatically be attached into this new group. If this is not the case, you need to create a new variable for the Camera actor and attach it to the group manually.

  a. With the Camera actor selected, go into Kismet. Right-click above the Prepare Map Change object and choose New Matinee. Double-click this new Matinee to open the Matinee Editor (see **FIGURE 12.14**).

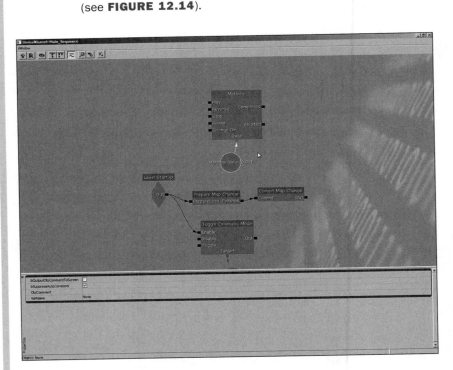

FIGURE 12.14   Place a new Matinee like so.

  b. In the Group/Track List, right-click and choose New Empty Group. Enter Camera into the dialog that appears and click OK (see **FIGURE 12.15**).

  c. Right-click again the Group/Track List and choose New Director Group (see **FIGURE 12.16**).

> **NOTE**
>
> You will notice the ability to create a Camera group within the Context menu of the Group/Track List. This is not so much a "special" group just for cameras as much as it is a group that automatically comes in with a Movement track and a Float Property track set to the camera's FOVAngle property for zooming. Because we'll be using neither of these tracks in this example, it's better practice to just place the camera in an empty group.

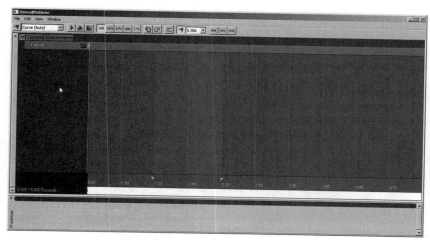

FIGURE 12.15   Add a new group named Camera.

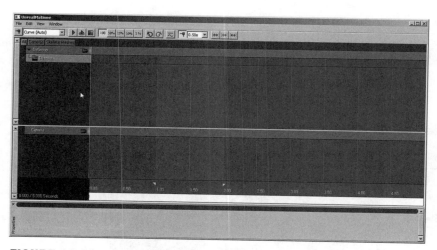

FIGURE 12.16   A new Director group has appeared.

    d. Select the director track that just appeared. Make sure the time slider is on 0.00 and press Enter to place a new keyframe. In the dialog that appears, select the Camera group created earlier, and click OK. This adjusts the player's perspective to this new camera (see **FIGURE 12.17**).

Don't exit Matinee just yet.

11. The last thing in this part of the setup is to make sure the camera is always faded to black.

    a. In Matinee, right-click on the DirGroup and choose Add New Fade Track (see **FIGURE 12.18**).

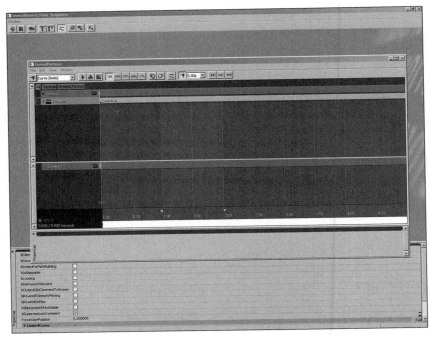

FIGURE 12.17   The Director group is now switching the camera.

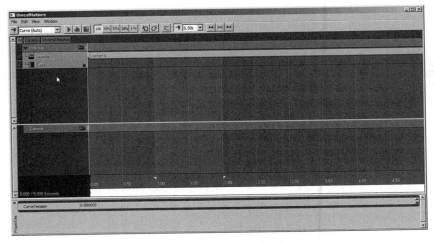

FIGURE 12.18   A new fade track has been added.

b. Select this new fade track, and with the time slider at 0.00, press Enter to set a new keyframe.

c. Right-click on the new keyframe and choose Set Value. In the dialog that appears, set the value to 1.00, which is full fade.

d. Exit Matinee.

e. In Kismet, connect the Out of the Level Startup to the Play of the Matinee sequence (see **FIGURE 12.19**).

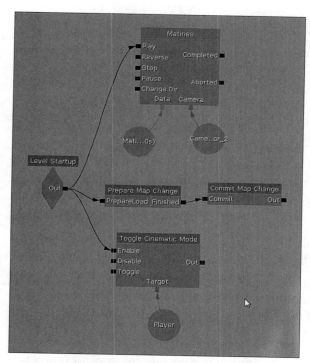

FIGURE 12.19   The Matinee now connects to the Level Startup.

12. Finally, open the Generic browser and switch to the Level tab. Select the persistent level, right-click, and choose Self Contained Lighting (see **FIGURE 12.20**). This setting forces the lighting of a particular level to only affect that level. Without this setting, the lighting will be un-built when a new level is loaded, in which the "LIGHTING NEEDS TO BE REBUILT" message is displayed.

13. Save the map as DM-Ch_12_Level_Entry.

12

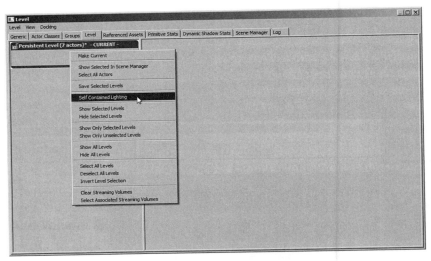

FIGURE 12.20   Make sure to choose Self Contained Lighting.

END TUTORIAL 12.1

When the level is loaded, it pops into view with the player in the same location as it was in the previous level. We need to set up a way to lessen or eliminate the popping from the player's point of view and position the player in the correct location for the new level (see **TUTORIAL 12.2**).

TUTORIAL 12.2: Level Transitioning, Part II: Setting Up DM-Ch_12_Level_01 Beginning Sequences

1. Open the DM-Ch_12_Level_01 map included on the DVD in the files for this chapter. This map is one of the three levels that is streamed into the Entry level created in **TUTORIAL 12.1** (see **FIGURE 12.21**).

> **NOTE**
>
> **TUTORIAL 12.2** makes use of Matinee. For more information on using Matinee, please see Chapter 10.

2. First, we deal with the player's positioning. The player starts out on a block that is floating out in empty space. We change this later using a simple Teleport sequence. Place a Note actor in the center of the concrete slab about 50 units above it and rotate it so its direction arrow (a very thin blue arrow) is pointing in the negative Y direction. This is the destination for the Teleport (see **FIGURE 12.22**).

FIGURE 12.21   The DM-Ch_12_Level_01 map

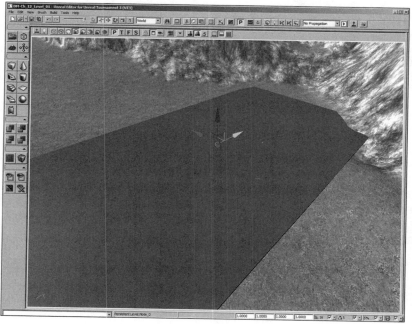

FIGURE 12.22   Place the Note actor as shown.

3. Open Kismet and add a Level Loaded And Visible event (New Event > Level > Level Loaded And Visible), as shown in **FIGURE 12.23**.

> **NOTE**
>
> You'll need to select the Note actor from the Actor Classes browser. Also note that the actor's direction arrow might be difficult to see through its icon!

4. Next, add a Teleport action (New Action > Actor > Teleport) and connect the Out output of the Level Loaded And Visible to the In input of the Teleport action.

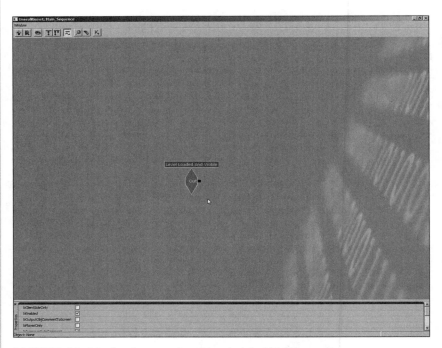

FIGURE 12.23   Create a new Level Loaded And Visible event.

5. With the Note actor selected, right-click on the Destination variable link of the Teleport action and choose New Object Var Using Note_0. Create a player variable (New Variable > Object > Player) and connect it to the Target variable link of the Teleport (see **FIGURE 12.24**).

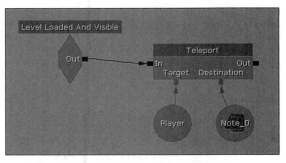

FIGURE 12.24   The new Teleport with Player and Note connected.

6. As you may recall, the camera is black as we leave the Entry level. We need to fade the camera back up, but we'll need to make use of an external camera to make that happen. Please complete the following:

    a. In the Perspective viewport, locate and select CameraActor_1, which is floating above the large concrete pad (or use the Search for Actors window if you prefer).

    b. Back in Kismet, create a new Matinee sequence and connect its Play input to the Out of the Level Loaded And Visible (see **FIGURE 12.25**).

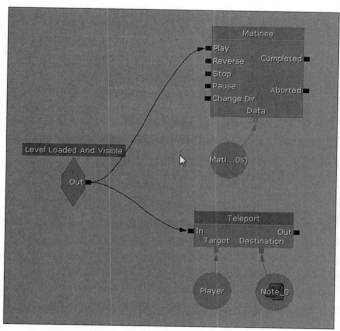

FIGURE 12.25   Connect your new Matinee object like so.

    c. Double-click the new Matinee to open it in the Matinee editor.

    d. Right-click in the Group/Track List and choose New Empty Group. In the dialog that appears, enter the name Camera.

    e. Close the Matinee Editor and verify that the Camera group is attached to an object variable containing CameraActor_1. If it is not, select the camera again, create the variable, and connect it to the Camera group.

7. Now that we have the CameraActor tied into Matinee, we simply need to make sure that we're looking through it when the level begins, and that we fade up from black as the level gets going. Follow these steps carefully:

    a. Double-click the Matinee node to open the Matinee Editor.

    b. Right-click in the track list and create a new Director group.

c. Select the director track. With the time slider at 0.0, press Enter to create a new keyframe. In the dialog that appears, choose the Camera group. This causes the view to look through CameraActor_1 throughout the sequence.

d. Select and right-click the new Director group and create a new fade track.

e. Set keys at time intervals 0.00 and 2.00.

f. Select and right-click on the key at 0.00 and set its value to 1.0.

g. Select and right-click on the key at 2.00 and verify that its value is set to 0.0.

h. Make sure the range of the sequence (denoted by red markers) is set to 0.00–2.00.

i. Exit Matinee when finished (see **FIGURE 12.26**).

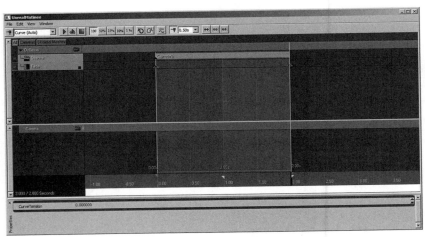

FIGURE 12.26   The Matinee Editor should look something like this when finished.

8. We now need to give control back to the player, as well as set the camera back to the player's perspective.

a. Create a Toggle Cinematic Mode action (New Action > Toggle > Toggle Cinematic Mode) and connect the Completed output of the Matinee sequence to the Disable input of the Toggle Cinematic Mode. This turns on the input that we turned off in the Entry level.

b. Duplicate the Player variable and connect it to the Target variable input of the Toggle Cinematic Mode action.

c. Create a Set Camera Target object (New Action > Camera > Set Camera Target), and connect its In input to the Out of the Toggle Cinematic Mode.

d. Drag wires from the Target *and* Cam Target inputs of the Set Camera Target object to the Player variable (see **FIGURE 12.27**).

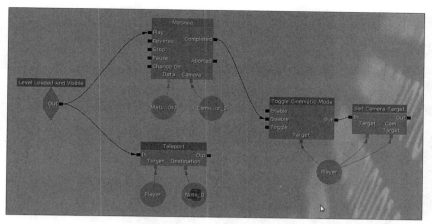

FIGURE 12.27 The new Toggle Cinematic Mode and Set Camera Target should connect like so.

9. Save your changes to the map.

END TUTORIAL 12.2

When loading a new persistent level, there will most likely be some hitching and freezing of the viewport and controls. We need a way to keep the player from noticing this. Just as we had the viewport fade in from black when starting the level, in **TUTORIAL 12.3** we fade the viewport out to black when exiting a level. This provides a consistent experience for the player.

TUTORIAL 12.3: Level Transitioning, Part III: Setting Up DM-Ch_12_Level_01 Ending Sequences

1. Continue with the DM-Ch_12_Level_01 map that was saved at the end of **TUTORIAL 12.2**.

2. Add a Trigger actor (right-click and choose Add Actor > Trigger) on the concrete slab half-way between the Note actor and the edge of the concrete slab on the right (looking in the top viewport). In the trigger's Properties Window under the Display category, set the bHidden property to False (Unchecked). This is where the player triggers the transition to the next level (see **FIGURE 12.28**).

3. With the trigger selected, open Kismet and add a new Touch event for the trigger (New Event Using Trigger_0 > Touch).

4. Duplicate the Toggle Cinematic Mode object, as well as the Player variable connected to it. Connect the Touched output of the new Trigger Touch event to the Enable input of his new Toggle Cinematic Mode (see **FIGURE 12.29**). Be sure to disconnect the lingering wire that connects the duplicate to the Set Camera Target object.

12

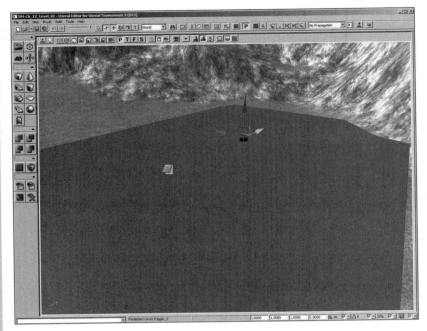

FIGURE 12.28   Place the trigger as shown.

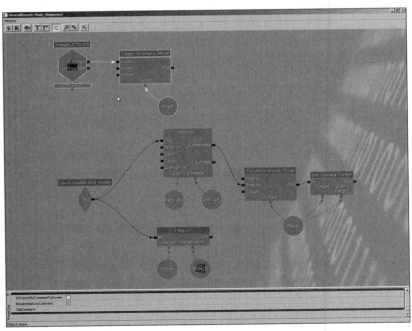

FIGURE 12.29   Duplicate the Toggle Cinematic Mode and connect it to the new Touch event.

5. Create a new Matinee and connect its Play input to the Touched output of the Touch event (see **FIGURE 12.30**). Double-click it to open it in the Matinee Editor. This is used to transition back over to the camera and fade out the viewport, as well as fire off a few events to prepare and commit the next map change.

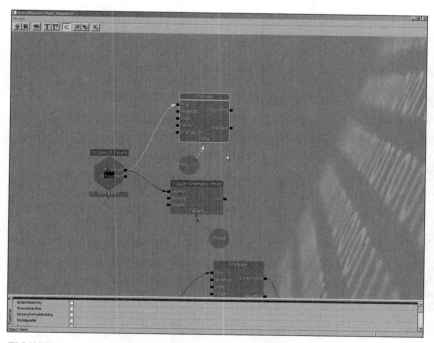

FIGURE 12.30   The new Matinee should connect to the Touch.

    a. Right-click in the Group/Track list and create a new Director group.

    b. As you did in Step 6 of **TUTORIAL 12.2**, create a new empty group named Camera associated with CameraActor_1.

    c. Add a keyframe to the director track at 0.0, and set the group to Camera.

    d. Add a new fade track and set keys at the following times with the corresponding values:

        Time: 0.00   **Value:** 0.00

        Time: 1.50   **Value:** 1.00

Now the camera switches back over to CameraActor_1 and fade to black.

    e. Create a new empty group and name it Events.

f. Create a new event track in the Events group and set keys at the following times with the corresponding values:

> 1.50 -> Prepare
>
> 3.00 -> Commit

g. Make sure the range of the sequence (denoted by red markers) is set to 0.00–3.00 (see **FIGURE 12.31**).

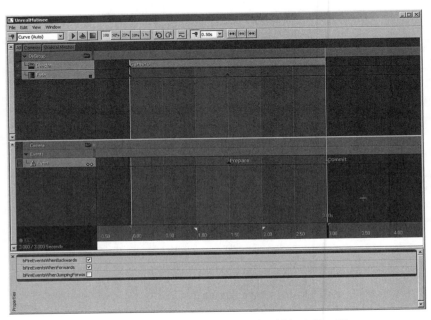

FIGURE 12.31   The new Matinee sequence should look like this.

6. Close Matinee. The Matinee sequence should now have two extra outputs corresponding to the keys set in the event track you created (see **FIGURE 12.32**).

7. Create a Prepare Map Change object (New Action > Level > Prepare Map Change) and connect the Prepare output of the Matinee sequence to the PrepareLoad input of the Prepare Map Change (see **FIGURE 12.33**). Set the following properties of the Prepare Map Change:

> **bIsHighPriority:** True
>
> **MainLevelName:** DM-Ch_12_Level_02

Click Add New Item for InitiallyLoadedSecondaryLevelNames; then set the following:

> **[0]:** DM-Ch_12_CityStream_1

This process loads the new DM-Ch_12_Level_02 persistent level, and also loads in the DM-Ch_12_CityStream_1 streamed level that streams from within Level_02.

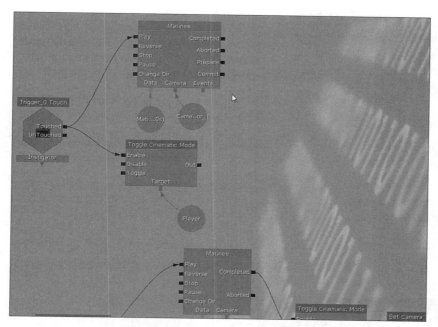

FIGURE 12.32   The Matinee object has new output connections.

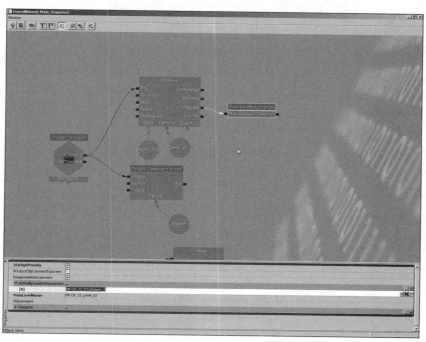

FIGURE 12.33   Connect a new Prepare Map Change object.

8. Create a Commit Map Change (New Action > Level > Commit Map Change) action and connect the Commit output of the Matinee sequence to the Commit input of the Commit Map Change.

9. Finally make the following connections:

> Matinee: Prepare -> Matinee: Pause (this connects back into the same Matinee object).
>
> Prepare Map Change: Finished -> Matinee: Play (again, this wraps back into the same Matinee object).

These connections simply pause the Matinee sequence until the loading process has completed, after which the Matinee resumes. It's like a catch-all in case loading takes longer than the Matinee sequence is expected to run (see **FIGURE 12.34**).

> **NOTE**
>
> As you can see in this example, we use the Matinee sequence to fade the camera to black, hiding from the player any sudden "pop" as the levels transition. However, if loading larger levels, the player might have to stare at a black screen for a considerable time. To avoid this, you can trigger the Prepare Map Sequence much earlier in the sequence, thus shortening the player's wait time. However, this requires that the sequence is then edited to check for the completion of the Prepare Map Sequence and the Matinee sequence before activating the Commit Map Change.

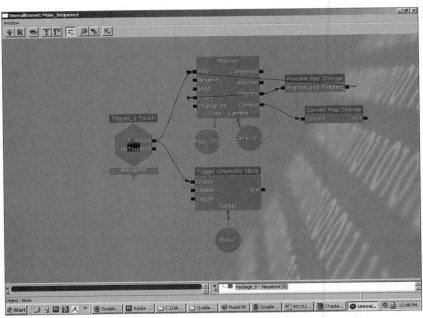

FIGURE 12.34   The new Commit Map Change has been added and the final connections are in place.

10. Save your changes to DM-Ch_12_Level_01.

END TUTORIAL 12.3

Level Streaming via Kismet

Streaming your level through the use of Kismet sequences provides a high degree of flexibility, as you have complete control over when a level is loaded and unloaded, and when it is made visible and invisible. This means that it is far simpler to handle streaming based on gameplay events, scripted sequences, and so on. At the same time, this flexibility comes at the cost of a certain level of complexity in terms of setup. In a nutshell, it can get a bit tricky setting up level streaming using Kismet, and you may find yourself using simpler methods except when you need levels loaded by way of a very specific event or circumstance. Following are some of the more commonly used specialized Kismet sequence objects used in level streaming via Kismet:

▶ **Change Level Visibility**—This sequence object enables you to toggle the visibility of a specific level (see **FIGURE 12.35**).

▶ **Stream Level**—This sequence object enables you to toggle whether or not a level has been loaded, as well as whether it is visible upon loading. The level name passed into this object must be the name of a level that has been placed in the Level browser of the current persistent level (see **FIGURE 12.36**).

▶ **Stream Multiple Levels**—This sequence object is very similar to the Stream Level object, except that it is capable of loading or unloading more than one level at once (see **FIGURE 12.37**).

▶ **Wait for Levels to be Visible**—This object causes the game to pause until the specified levels are visible. This can prevent the player from reaching areas that have not yet fully loaded (see **FIGURE 12.38**).

FIGURE 12.35   Change Level Visibility object

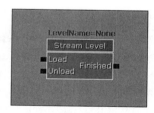

FIGURE 12.36   Stream Level object

FIGURE 12.37   Stream Multiple Levels object

FIGURE 12.38   Wait for Levels to be Visible object

Level Streaming via LevelStreamingVolumes

When importing a level for streaming by using the Kismet method, you have the option of controlling the streaming by using LevelStreamingVolumes. LevelStreamingVolumes use their Touch and Untouch events to perform streaming actions according to a few settings in their properties. The functionality is very simplistic in and of itself; if a player is within a LevelStreamingVolume that is associated to a particular level, that level is loaded and visible to the player. As soon as the player leaves that LevelStreamingVolume, the level is made invisible and unloaded from memory. Logically, this means that LevelStreamingVolumes tend to overlap one another, rather than being contiguous, so that there is no noticeable change in level visibility from one location to the next. While a player is within the overlapping region of two LevelStreamingVolumes, the level associated to both volumes is visible (see **FIGURE 12.39**).

There are several properties that control how a LevelStreamingVolume handles its streaming process. These properties are listed as follows:

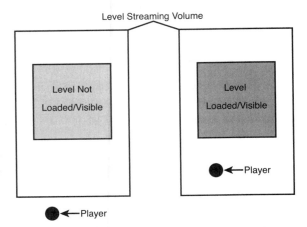

FIGURE 12.39   This diagram demonstrates the concept of using LevelStreamingVolumes.

- ▶ **bDisabled**—This property determines whether or not the volume actually performs any streaming functions. The benefit of the property is that it can be toggled by using a Toggle sequence object within Kismet. When bDisabled is set true, all levels associated to that particular volume reverts to using the Kismet streaming method. It should be noted that toggling this property is not advised unless absolutely necessary.

- ▶ **bEditorPreVisOnly**—This property determines whether the volume should perform its streaming function in the game or only function within Unreal Editor for pre-visualization purposes. When active, and when the Level Streaming Volume Previs button is active, the levels change their visibility based on the position of the Perspective viewport camera.

- ▶ **StreamingLevels**—This property is actually a list of levels with which the volume has been associated. All levels in this list are streamed based on the functions of this volume. Levels are added and removed from this list using the Level browser.

▶ **Usage**—This property controls what function the volume performs on the levels listed within the StreamingLevels property. The following are descriptions of this property's settings:

SVB_Loading—This setting loads the associated level into memory, but does not make it visible. To handle visibility, you would need a separate volume also associated to the same level, and set to SVB_VisibilityBlockingOnLoad. Alternatively, you could use a Kismet sequence to make the level visible.

A typical setup when using this setting is to have a large volume set to SVB_Loading, with a smaller volume inside that toggles visibility. However, you should note that once the visibility is toggled on, it is not toggled off again until you exit the SVB_Loading volume.

SVB_LoadingAndVisibility—This setting loads the associated level into memory and makes it visible while the player is within the volume. As soon as the player leaves the volume, the level is unloaded.

SVB_VisibilityBlockingOnLoad—This setting actually does several things at once. First, it checks to see if the level is already loaded into memory. If it isn't, it starts loading it. It then pauses the game until the load is complete, makes the level visible, and then continues the game.

Because of the ability to pause the game during the load, this setting is perfect as your standard method for toggling visibility, and should be used when the associated level has already been loaded into memory by some other means. The pause acts as a check and balance system to make sure that the player either sees a fully loaded and visible level, or he will experience a pause while the level loads. Either way, they will not see a blank area where an unloaded level should be, which would destroy the game's immersion.

Another use for this setting is for loading an initial map when the level begins, as you are practically guaranteed some sort of loading hitch, which will be least noticeable at the beginning of a particular level.

SVB_BlockingOnLoad—This pauses the game until the associated map is loaded into memory. It should be noted that this setting will not actually trigger the load itself, but instead just verifies the load and pauses the game until the load is complete. You need to begin the load using some other means, such as a Kismet sequence or a separate volume. This setting can serve as a safeguard against slow loading times, and is especially useful in areas where you absolutely must have a level loaded before something else happens, such as entering a new area or beginning a Matinee sequence.

12

SVB_LoadingNotVisible—This setting loads a map into memory, but will not make it visible. It is very similar to SVB_Loading, and will typically be used in a similar setup; a large

> **NOTE**
>
> The "Blocking" settings are there to pause the game during the load. This pause results in a massive increase in loading speed.

volume set to SVB_LoadingNotVisible and smaller volumes within are used to toggle visibility. However, it is different in that when you leave the visibility toggling volumes, but are still within the LoadingNotVisible volume, the associated level will be invisible, but will still be loaded in memory until you also exit the LoadingNotVisible volume.

Keep in mind that LevelStreamingVolumes must be placed within the persistent level and then associated with the various streaming levels by way of the Level browser.

Finally, as you may already have gleaned from this section, streaming levels through using volumes is advised whenever possible, as it is the easiest method to set up. In **TUTORIAL 12.6**, we demonstrate how you can create a streaming scenario using LevelStreamingVolumes.

In **TUTORIAL 12.4**, we establish the basic Kismet network that causes our level streaming to take place.

TUTORIAL 12.4: Level Transitioning, Part IV: Setting Up DM-Ch_12_Level_02 Beginning Sequence

1. Open the DM-Ch_12_Level_01 level saved at the end of **TUTORIAL 12.3**.

2. Open the Kismet Editor, select all sequence objects, and press Ctrl + C to copy the sequences (see **FIGURE 12.40**).

3. Now, open the DM-Ch_12_Level_02 map included with the files for this chapter, open the Kismet Editor, and press Ctrl + V to paste the sequences into the new map. This saves some considerable time over recreating all the sequences in the new level (see **FIGURE 12.41**).

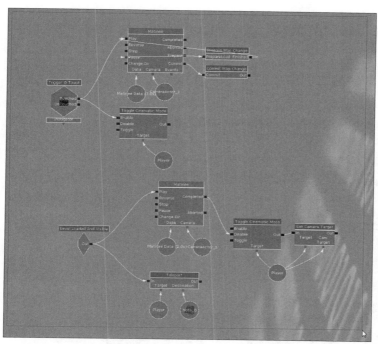

FIGURE 12.40   Select all the sequence objects as shown.

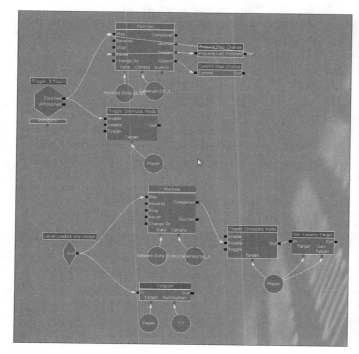

FIGURE 12.41   Paste the duplicates into the new level's Kismet Editor.

12

4. As we did before, we use a Teleport sequence to get the player started. Place a Note actor in the center of the temple's concrete slab about 50 or so units above it and rotate it so its direction arrow is pointing in the negative Y direction (see **FIGURE 12.42**). This is the location for the player to start the level. Go into Kismet, select the object variable connected to the Destination variable link of the Teleport action, right-click on it, and assign the Note actor to it.

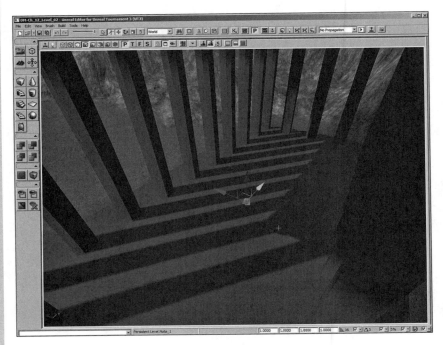

FIGURE 12.42   Place the Note actor like so.

5. Create a new Trigger actor inside the temple and set its bHidden property to False (Unchecked). With the new trigger selected, open Kismet and replace the Touch event with a new Touch event created using the new trigger, making sure to connect it to the same connections used by the original (connect the Touched output to both the Play of the Matinee and the Enable of the Toggle Cinematic Mode).

6. Open the Generic browser and switch to the Level tab. Select Import Level from the Level menu and choose the DM-Ch_12_CityStream_1 level. Then, choose Kismet as the streaming method from the next window and press OK. The map should appear in the Level browser, as well as in the viewports now (see **FIGURE 12.43**).

7. If we tested the level in Unreal Tournament 3 as it is now, the CityStream_1 level would not show up or even be loaded into memory. We need to tell it to load and become visible at some point. In our case, we need the level loaded and visible when the level begins since it is directly in the player's view.

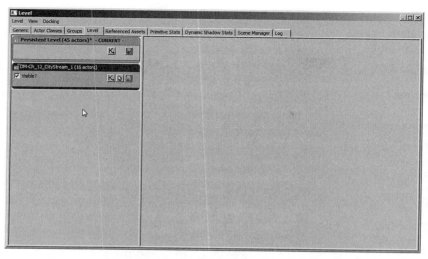

FIGURE 12.43   The new level is now visible in the Level browser.

8. Open Kismet if it is not already and create a Level Startup event (New Event > Level Startup), as shown in **FIGURE 12.44**.

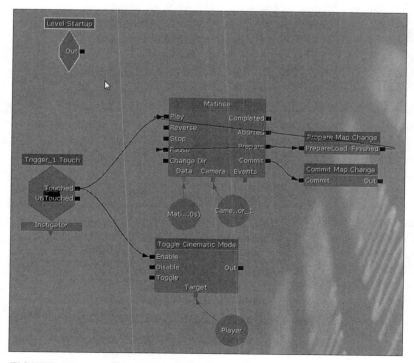

FIGURE 12.44   The new Level Startup event

12

9. Now, create a Stream Level action (New Action > Level > Stream Level). Connect the Out output of the Level Startup to the Load of the Stream Level (see **FIGURE 12.45**). Set the following properties on the Stream Level:

> **bMakeVisibleAfterLoad:** False
>
> **LevelName:** DM-Ch_12_CityStream_1

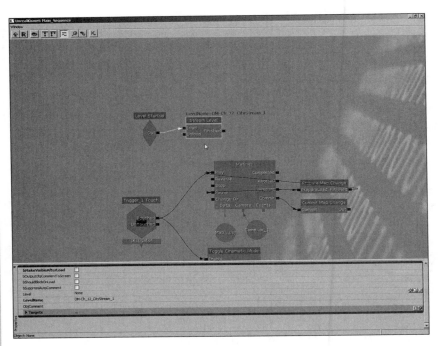

FIGURE 12.45   Connect a new Stream Level.

10. Next, add a Change Level Visibility action (New Action > Level > Change Level Visibility) and connect the Out output of the Level Loaded And Visible event created earlier to the Make Visible input of the Change Level Visibility action (rearrange objects as necessary), as shown in **FIGURE 12.46**. Set the following properties of the Change Level Visibility:

> **LevelName:** DM-CH_12_CityStream_1

NOTE

We are using Stream Level to load the level into memory and Change Level Visibility to make the level visible simply to show their functionality. It should be noted that Stream Level has the ability to do this all by itself, which we show in **TUTORIAL 12.5**.

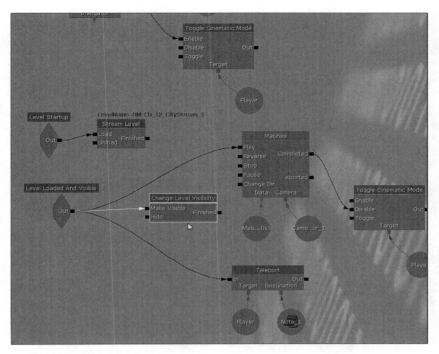

FIGURE 12.46   The new Change Level Visibility has been connected.

11. Save your changes to DM-Ch_12_Level_02.

END TUTORIAL 12.4

In **TUTORIAL 12.5**, we take the network we've established thus far and place it within our other streamed levels.

TUTORIAL 12.5: Level Transitioning, Part V: Setting Up DM-Ch_12_Level_03 Beginning Sequence

1. Open DM-Ch_12_Level_02 that was saved at the end of **TUTORIAL 12.4**, open Kismet, select everything, and press Ctrl + C to copy the sequences (see **FIGURE 12.47**).

2. Now, open DM-Ch_12_Level_03, open Kismet, and press Ctrl + V to paste the sequences into the new map. As before, this saves us a lot of time.

3. As you did in the previous level, place a Note actor in the center of the concrete slab within the temple about 50 units or so above it and rotate it so its direction arrow is pointing in the negative Y direction. This is the location for the player to start the level. Go into Kismet, select the object variable connected to the Destination variable link of the Teleport action, right-click on it, and choose to assign the Note actor to it (see **FIGURE 12.48**).

12

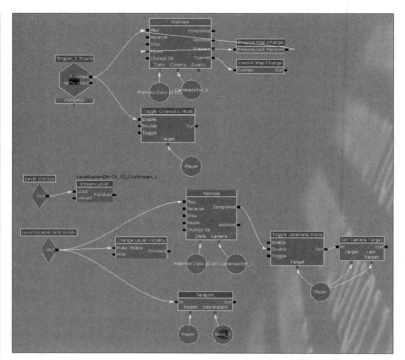

FIGURE 12.47   Select all the sequence objects as shown.

4. Open the Generic browser and switch to the Level tab. Select Import Level from the Level menu and choose the DM-Ch_12_CityStream_3 level. Then, choose Kismet as the streaming method from the next window and press OK. The map should appear in the Level browser as well as in the viewports now (see **FIGURE 12.49**).

5. Open Kismet and set the following properties on the Stream Level object:

> **bMakeVisibleAfterLoad:** True (Checked)
>
> **LevelName:** DM-Ch_12_CityStream_3

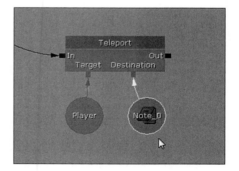

FIGURE 12.48   Make sure the Teleport action points to the new Note actor.

6. Next, delete the Change Level Visibility action because it is not needed. This time we use the bMakeVisibleAfterLoad property within the Stream Level object to handle this functionality.

7. Save your changes to DM-Ch_12_Level_03.

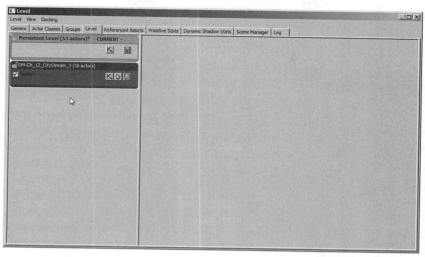

FIGURE 12.49   City_Stream_3 is now visible in the Level browser.

END TUTORIAL 12.5

Level Streaming via Distance

Distance-based level streaming is, as its name suggests, a way for you to stream levels together based upon a player's distance from the level (see **FIGURE 12.50**). Essentially, the designer establishes a spherical radius, and when a player enters that radius, the associated level loads and becomes visible. To handle the creation of this radius, the persistent level's WorldInfo contains the StreamingLevels property, which is an array containing all the levels that are being streamed in (see **FIGURE 12.51**). Each entry in this array has an Origin and a MaxDistance property, which control how the radius is calculated. Origin enables you to designate a point in 3D space that serves as the center of the radius for that

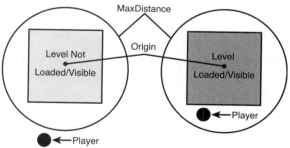

FIGURE 12.50   This diagram illustrates the concept of level streaming via distance.

> **NOTE**
>
> The Origin and MaxDistance properties are only visible if you have imported a level using the distance streaming method.

12

particular level. The MaxDistance property then controls the distance from each origin at which loading begins.

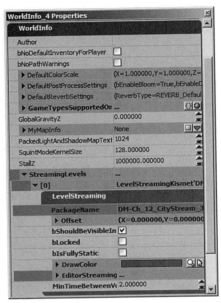

FIGURE 12.51   The WorldInfo properties contain the various radii used for distance-based streaming.

Because the Origin and MaxDistance must be established manually, and because there is (at the time of this writing) no visual indication of the radii when using this type of streaming, you will likely discover that this method of streaming is extremely inflexible and inefficient in terms of setup. In general, it is a good idea to consider using volumes or Kismet to stream your levels whenever possible.

In **TUTORIAL 12.6**, we begin the stream conclusion sequence for our first set of levels.

TUTORIAL 12.6: Level Transitioning, Part VI: Setting Up DM-Ch_12_Level_02 Ending Sequence

1. Open DM-Ch_12_Level_02. In the Generic browser, switch to the Level tab. Select Import Level from the Level menu and choose the DM-Ch_12_CityStream_2 level. Then, choose Kismet as the streaming method from the next window and press OK. The map should appear in the Level browser as well as in the viewports now (see **FIGURE 12.52**).

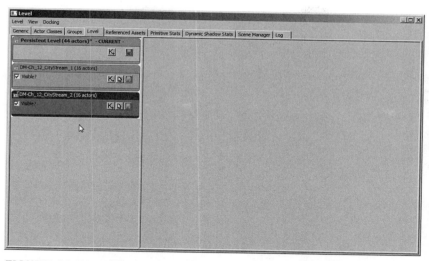

FIGURE 12.52   City_Stream_2 is now available in the Level browser.

Instead of using Kismet sequences to load or make a level visible, we set up some LevelStreamingVolumes to handle this. Volumes work great in this situation because we only want the level to be loaded and visible when the player is about to enter the area where that level is located, and the volumes do this automatically.

2. Right-click the Cube button and enter the following settings:

> **X:** 5120
>
> **Y:** 6144
>
> **Z:** 2080

Click Build and Close when finished (see **FIGURE 12.53**).

Position the Red Builder Brush in the top and side viewports so that the negative X, Y, and Z faces are even with the negative X, Y, and Z edges of the geometry of City_Stream_2. In case you're not sure, CityStream_2 is the left-most level when seen from the top viewport.

Once the brush is in place, right-click the Add Volume button and choose LevelStreamingVolume. Then, move the new volume to the left in the top viewport 464 units in the negative Y direction (see **FIGURE 12.54**).

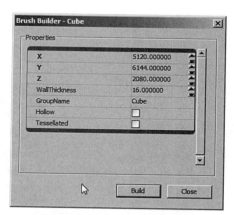

FIGURE 12.53   Cube properties window

12

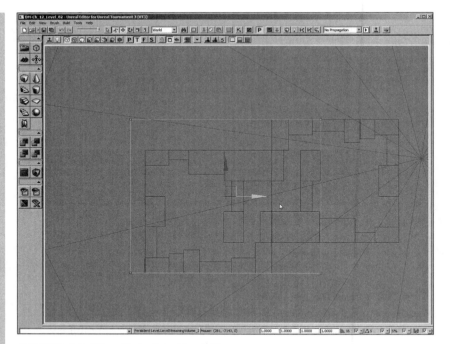

FIGURE 12.54   Place the volume like so.

3. Select the new volume and open its properties. Set the following property:

> **Usage:** SVB_VisibilityBlockingOnLoad

4. Duplicate the volume. Go into Geometry Mode and drag the face on the positive Y side (the right side, as seen from the top viewport) 1,600 units in the positive Y direction (see **FIGURE 12.55**).

> Exit Geometry Mode and set the following property on the duplicated volume:

> **Usage:** SVB_Loading

What's going on here is that the larger volume starts to load CityStream_2 into memory. The second smaller volume queues visibility for the level, but is also prepared to pause the game (block) if loading is not yet finished. Generally speaking, you'd want to make sure your player was never allowed to move forward so quickly that they'd outrun the load, but just in case someone finds a loophole (for a speed run video, maybe), everything halts so that the level can load up.

5. Select both the LevelStreamingVolumes, go into the Level browser, double-click the DM-Ch_12_CityStream_2 level to make it the current level, right-click on it, and choose Set Streaming Volumes (see **FIGURE 12.56**).

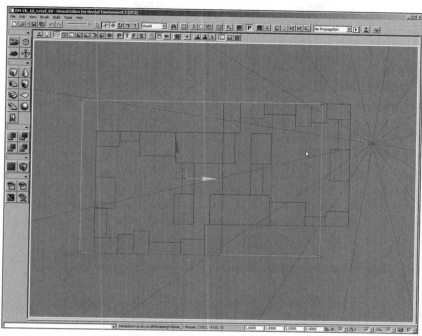

FIGURE 12.55   The volume has been duplicated and edited.

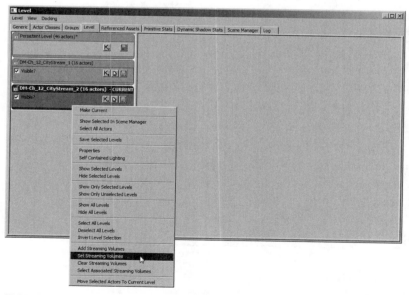

FIGURE 12.56   Level browser Context menu

12

6. Toggle the Visible? Checkbox off and back on. If all went well, both volumes should now not be visible in the viewport. This is because associated level-streaming volumes are not visible unless selected through the Context menu of the Level browser.

7. Press the Kismet button ⊞ of the persistent level in the Level browser to open Kismet and set the following properties of the Prepare Map Change action:

> **InitiallyLoadedSecondaryLevelNames:**
>
> ▸ **[0]:** DM-Ch_12_CityStream_3
>
> **MainLevelName:** DM-Ch_12_Level_03

8. Create a Stream Multiple Levels action (New Action > Level > Stream Multiple Levels) and connect the Prepare output of the Matinee sequence to the Unload input of the Stream Multiple Levels action (see **FIGURE 12.57**). Add and set the following values in the Levels property (you'll need to hit the Add Item button twice):

> **Levels:**
>
> ▸ **[0]:** DM-Ch_12_CityStream_1
>
> ▸ **[1]:** DM-Ch_12_CityStream_2

This pulls the first two CityStream levels (CityStream_1 and CityStream_2) out of memory, since we don't need them anymore.

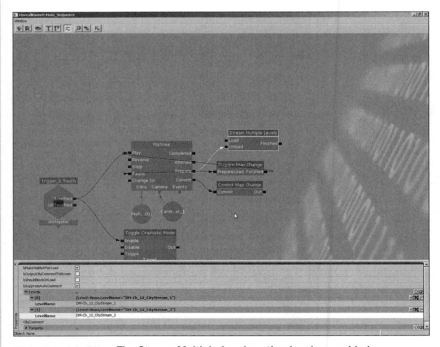

FIGURE 12.57   The Stream Multiple Levels action has been added.

9. Add a Force Garbage Collection action (New Action > Misc > Force Garbage Collection) and connect the Finished output of the Stream Multiple Levels action to the In input of the Force Garbage Collection action (see **FIGURE 12.58**). This completely cleans out any residual memory usage from the unloaded levels.

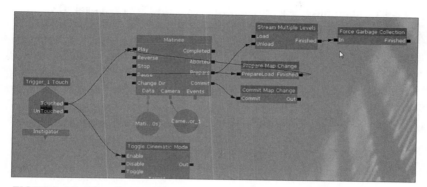

FIGURE 12.58   Connect the new Force Garbage Collection as shown.

10. Save the changes to your level (see **FIGURE 12.59**).

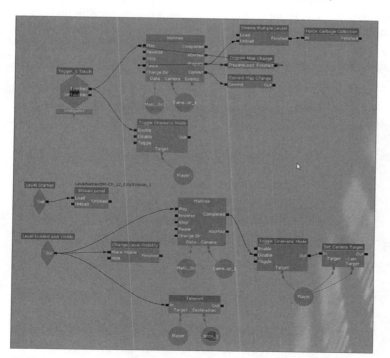

FIGURE 12.59   The entire network will now look similar to this.

END TUTORIAL 12.6

You may notice that **TUTORIAL 12.7** is very similar to **TUTORIAL 12.6**, but in this tutorial we establish the same network using new level names.

TUTORIAL 12.7: Level Transitioning, Part VII: Setting Up DM-Ch_12_Level_03 Ending Sequence

1. Open DM-Ch_12_Level_03. In the Generic browser, switch to the Level tab. Select Import Level from the Level menu and choose the City_Stream_4 level. Then, choose Kismet as the streaming method from the next window and press OK. The map should now appear in the Level browser as well as in the viewports.

2. Right-click the Cube Builder button and create a cube brush with the following dimensions:

    X: 5120

    Y: 6144

    Z: 2080

3. Position the builder brush so the negative X, Y, and Z faces are even with the negative X, Y, and Z edges of the geometry of City_Stream_4, right-click the Add Volume button ![icon], and choose LevelStreamingVolume. Then, move it to the left in the top viewport 464 units in the negative Y direction (see **FIGURE 12.60**).

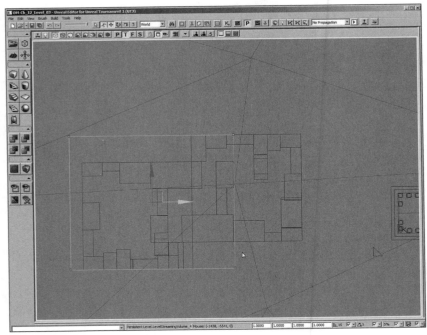

FIGURE 12.60   Position the volume like so.

4. Select the new volume and open its properties. Set the following property:

> **Usage:** SVB_VisibilityBlockingOnLoad

5 Duplicate the volume. Go into Geometry Mode and drag the face on the positive Y side (that's the right side seen from the top viewport) 1,600 units in the positive Y direction (also to the right). Set the following property on the duplicated volume (see **FIGURE 12.61**):

> **Usage:** SVB_Loading

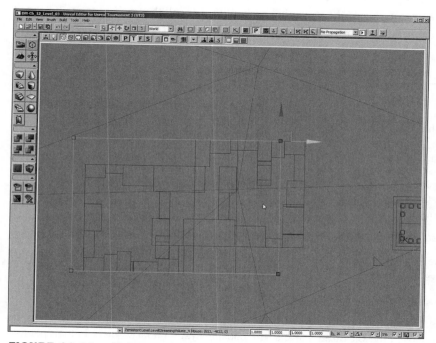

FIGURE 12.61   Make sure the duplicated volume has been edited.

6. Select both the LevelStreamingVolumes, go into the Level browser, double-click the City_Stream_4 level to make it the current level, right-click on it, and choose Set Streaming Volumes.

7. Toggle the Visible? Checkbox off and back on.

8. At this point, you could stop and have a level setup that streamed progressively from Entry to Level_03 and then ended, but as a challenge, see if you can take what you've learned in this chapter and have the player return to Level_01. Here's a hint: All the required Kismet objects are already there and waiting; you just need to change a few properties and add some sort of triggering mechanism!

> If you *don't* want to go any further, it would be a good idea to go into the Kismet setup for the persistent level and delete out the Stream Multiple levels, or anything that would be used to enable the player to exit this level.

9. Save your progress.

END TUTORIAL 12.7

Please continue from the previous tutorials. At this point, we need to test our progress and test out the whole thing in-game. However, playing the game through the In Editor Game does not give an accurate representation of the streaming process, because all the levels are already loaded into memory. We launch the maps within Unreal Tournament 3 in **TUTORIAL 12.8**.

TUTORIAL 12.8: Testing the Map Change Process

1. Open the DM-Ch_12_Level_Entry file saved earlier in this chapter, or open the file of the same name included in the Chapter12_Complete folder, included with the files for this chapter.

> **NOTE**
>
> These steps are designed for use with Microsoft Windows XP.

2. As a safety precaution, it's a good idea to build lighting and geometry for each level before publishing. Click the Build All button. Granted, the Entry level contains no lighting, but if you had moved any geometry, you'd need to build that as well.

3. Also as a safety precaution, save your level before publishing.

4. Click on the Publish button in the main toolbar. In the dialog that pops up that asks if you want to save packages, click No, as we have made no changes to our packages.

   When the commandlet is finished, close it.

5. Repeat this process for Ch_12_Level_01, Ch_12_Level_02, and Ch_12_Level_03. There is no need to publish the CityStream levels; the cooking system notices them in their persistent levels and takes care of them automatically.

   It should become a habitual process: Build, Save, Publish, Repeat.

6. Launch Unreal Tournament 3, go to Instant Action, Deathmatch, and choose DM-Ch_12_Level_Entry from the level selection screen. In the options box, set the number of bots to 0, and click Start Game.

7. If everything went well, you should jump right into Level_01 (you'll never really see the Entry level), and then pass into Level_02 when you hit the Trigger. While in Level_02, you can walk over to the two streamed maps. When finished, hit the Trigger again and go into Level_03, where you have two other streamed maps.

END TUTORIAL 12.8

Troubleshooting

If you made it all the way through the tutorials in this chapter but are experiencing some sort of problem, here are some things you can try out to fix it.

My cameras don't seem to be fading in/out.

Go double-check your Matinee sequences. Verify that your fade track keys are set up with the appropriate values (0.0 for no fade and 1.0 for full fade), and make sure your camera cut is set up in the director track. At the time of this writing, you cannot fade the player's perspective with a fade track.

My map change levels aren't loading.

Make sure you're using the right names for your maps. Check any Prepare Map Change objects and all of their properties, as well as any Stream Level objects. Really, any Kismet object that deals with streaming should be double-checked. Missing a single letter can cause problems.

It could also be that you didn't replace the Trigger Touch event with a new one for the new trigger. That's an easy one to miss. While you're at it, make sure you have no Object variables with question marks in them. They should all be assigned to something—generally the Note actor we're using for teleportation.

Also make sure you're committing any map changes you've prepared (that is, go look at your Matinee sequences).

I can't control/see my player/HUD.

You have probably turned on Cinematic Mode, but there's no sequence or connection in place to turn it back off. Look for a misplaced wire, or a missing Toggle Cinematic Mode. Remember that you want to enable Cinematic Mode when you're leaving a level, but disable it after you arrive in the new level.

My streamed sublevels aren't appearing.

Make sure the levels were loaded into the Level browser, and that the LevelStreamingVolumes are in place and associated with the second level (CityStream_2 or CityStream_4, depending on which persistent level you're in). If it's the first level that isn't loading, make sure that the name is correct in your Stream Level and/or Change Level Visibility.

Level Streaming Considerations

Following are some important guidelines to keep in mind when creating streamed levels of your own:

▶ Although it is theoretically possible to use both additive and subtractive levels in your level-streaming scenarios, you find that because of a variety of potential lighting issues, it is best to only use additive levels.

▶ When streaming between different persistent levels, as described in the "Map Changing" section, you should be aware that the player is added to the new persistent level based on his current location. This means that you should take appropriate measures to make sure that the player does not enter this new map inside a piece of geometry. A safe work-around to this problem is to teleport the player to a new location when the new persistent level loads, or to create a new map that is identical to the previous map, and make it a part of the new persistent level's streamed levels.

▶ Avoid allowing the player to actually see the streaming process. This appears as if large portions of his environment simply pop into existence, thereby killing any sense of immersion the player may have been experiencing.

▶ When streaming through Kismet, using separate actions for loading and visibility can allow the streaming level plenty of time to load before needing to be displayed. This can help avoid hitches or wait times in the game.

▶ Streaming times cannot be fully tested from within the In Editor Game, as all the levels are already resident in memory. When playing the In Editor Game, only the visibility of the levels is actually being affected. In order to fully test streaming, you need to test the level within the Unreal Tournament 3, preferably on the intended platform.

▶ Streaming multiple persistent levels together using the Commit Map Kismet action has no effect on the In Editor Game. In order to see the results, the game must actually be running in a standalone fashion, such as within Unreal Tournament 3.

Summary

Level streaming is a powerful way for you to piece together extremely large gaming experiences. It is, however, very technical in terms of its setup, and care must be taken to make sure that everything is working properly. In the end, the best idea is to plan out everything well in advance. Know what it is you want your players to experience, and tailor the layout to suit. Keep track of what should be streamed together using the Level browser and which parts should be handled with a map change. In no time, you'll find yourself thinking in larger terms of what your levels can be, and of all kinds of ways that you can take your level designs even further!

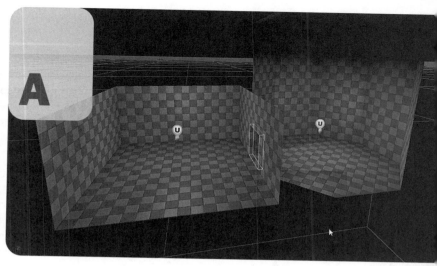

Appendix A

The Unreal Editor User's Guide

This appendix is your working Unreal Editor 3.0 reference. You'll find a complete overview of the program, plus detailed descriptions of its key components.

The Main Menubar

This area is common to many computer applications, and in the Unreal Editor, it is very similar to what you've come to expect. There are seven menus across the menubar (see **FIGURE A.1**), with the following functions:

File   Typical to most modern programs, and functions in the same way. Here, you have access to opening files and saving them, as well as importing and exporting files. The bottom of the menu contains an area for opening recently used files.

A

Edit	Allows for access to Undo and Redo, as well as selecting the current Transform method and visibility of the Transform Widget. It also holds the Search for Actors command, used to locate any actor in your level. The menu includes the Cut, Copy, Paste, Duplicate, and Delete commands. At the bottom, the menu gives access to a wide variety of selection methods, such as Select All, Select None, Invert Selection, and Select by Property.
View	Offers a tentative list of all the windows available in the Unreal Editor, along with some options for the viewports in the program itself. Here you can access all the browser windows, as well as all the properties and options windows for the objects in your level, including the overall properties for the level itself. The menu also has an area where you can adjust their configurations or placement on the interface. You can also toggle the editor into fullscreen mode from this menu.
Brush	This menu contains a wide variety of options for your brushes. Within the brush menu, you can import and export different brushes that you create, and add a wide variety of brushes into your level. Among these are additive and subtractive brushes, as well as volumes. The menu also enables you to intersect and de-intersect brushes.
Build	Enables you to rebuild specific aspects of your levels, in order to update them if changes have been made. Among those objects that you are able to rebuild are geometry, lights, and AI paths. The menu also enables you to play-test your level within the game itself.
Tools	Contains tools for creating a new terrain, checking the map for any errors that are present, and adding pickup lights.
Help	Contains access to toggling on and off the Tip of the Day feature, as well as a link to the Unreal Developer's Network site (www.udn.epicgames.com).

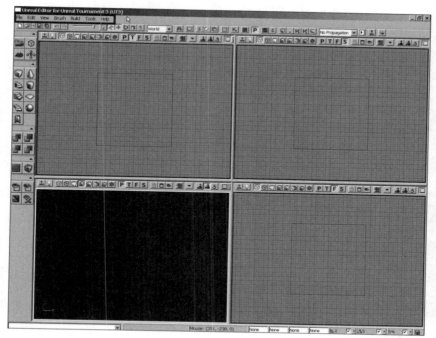

FIGURE A.1   The main menubar

The Toolbar

Underneath the main menubar, you will find the Toolbar (see **FIGURE A.2**). This contains several buttons for quick access to many of the commands found in the menus. The buttons are divided into groups, and the following sections describe each of these groups.

File Options

The first four buttons across the Toolbar contain the File Options. These give the user access to creating a new file, opening an existing file, opening recently opened files, and saving the current file. These work exactly like the corresponding commands found in the File menu.

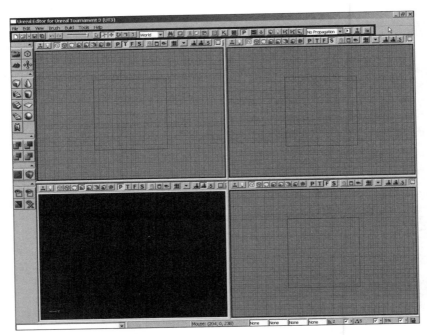

FIGURE A.2   The Toolbar

Undo and Redo

The next two buttons on the Toolbar enable you to Undo and Redo actions in your level. You have many levels of Undos in Unreal Editor, and numerous Redos as well. These commands can also be found in the Edit menu.

Far Clipping Plane Distance

This slider allows the far clipping plane in the editor's viewports to be adjusted in order to increase performance when working on large, heavily-populated maps.

Transform Tools

This series of buttons allows cycling between the various types of transformations that can be performed on actors within the viewports. There is also a button for locking transformations so actors may be selected without accidentally moving them. The dropdown list allows the coordinate system in which the transformations are performed to be chosen.

Search for Actor

This tool is designed to help you find specific actors within your scene in a fast and easy manner. For more information on this tool and how to use it, go to the "Search for Actors" section later in this appendix.

Toggle Fullscreen

This button toggles the editor into fullscreen mode, which hides the title bar and maximizes the editor.

Cut, Copy, and Paste

This series of buttons cut, copy, or paste the selected actors.

Generic Browser

This button opens the Generic browser. For more information on this tool and how to use it, see the "Browsers" section later in this appendix.

Kismet

This button opens the Kismet visual scripting system. For more information on this tool and how to use it, go to Chapter 9, "Introduction to Unreal Kismet."

Toggle Brush Polys

This button toggles the visibility of the polygons of brushes when in Geometry Mode.

Toggle Prefab Lock

This button toggles the ability to select the individual elements of a prefab in the viewport. When selected, only the prefab itself is selectable.

Use Curves Button

As its tooltip suggests, this button causes any distributions to use their actual curves, rather than any baked lookup tables that might have been created for them.

Enable/Disable Socket Snapping

When enabled, the sockets of all skeletal meshes become visible in the viewport, allowing objects to be snapped to those sockets.

A "socket" is an offset position and orientation from a bone in a skeletal mesh, to which you can attach items such as weapons and other objects. For example, if you try to attach a weapon directly to a character's hand, you might notice the handle protruding through the character's wrist. Through the use of sockets, you can specify a location and orientation that more closely corresponds to the character's palm. Then, if you attach the object to the socket instead of directly to the bone, the object appears to be in the character's hand, as if they were holding it.

Building

This area allows for the updating of many aspects of the level when they are changed, including the following commands:

Build Geometry	Allows the Unreal Engine to construct the actual geometry of your level using the data created from your BSP brushes.
Build Lights	Recalculates the lighting and shadows cast in your level. This must be done whenever new geometry is added, and whenever any light properties are changed. When clicked, the Lighting Build Options dialog appears, providing the option to selectively build specific aspects of the lighting in the level, which can significantly speed up iteration.
Build Paths	Enables you to construct the paths that AI-controlled creatures and bots use to navigate the level. Paths are constructed from a variety of different actors, including path nodes, playerstarts, and pickups.
Build Cover Nodes	Builds the cover nodes for the currently visible levels.
Build All	Rebuilds all Geometry, Lights, and AI Navigation paths in the level. This can take considerable time, depending on system speed and the size of your level.

Play Level Area

This area provides functionality for playing the current map inside the Unreal Editor, as well as controlling a map playing in stand-alone mode from within the editor. The dropdown selection box chooses whether to propagate changes from the editor to the stand-alone game, while the button to its right sends the position of the camera in the Perspective viewport to the stand-alone game. The joystick button on the right launches your map inside the editor, so that it can be play-tested. This will become one of your favorite buttons on the interface. The button on the far right publishes the current map so it can be selected from the menu and played in the game.

The Toolbox

The Toolbox contains a huge selection of necessary tools for constructing levels inside the Unreal Editor (see **FIGURE A.3**). Many of these you will use numerous times throughout the level design process. In this section, we cover each of the buttons on the Toolbox, and their various uses and parameters. The Toolbox is broken up into five sections, and each section is expandable and collapsible. Also note that along the right side of the Toolbox is a very thin, green scrollbar for moving through the list of tools, provided your window is not big enough to see them all.

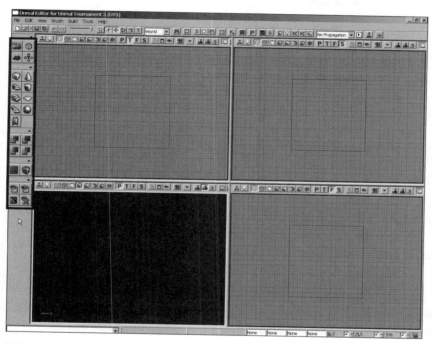

FIGURE A.3   The Toolbox

The following sections walk you through the numerous tools and utilities available in each section of the Toolbox.

Camera and Utilities Area

This area of the Toolbox contains several tools for controlling your camera and other utilities that are used for a variety of functions within Unreal Editor. Following are each of these tools and their settings:

Camera and Movement	Manipulates the camera. At first, this might seem a bit curious, as you can always manipulate the camera with the proper mouse controls. However, aside from enabling you to move the camera as all modes do, this is a general editing mode that enables you to place, move, select, edit, and delete actors and brushes.
Geometry Mode	Manipulates the various components of a brush. For more information on using Geometry Mode, see Chapter 4, "A Universe of Brushes: World Geometry In-Depth."
Texture Alignment Mode	Allows for panning, rotating, and scaling of textures across the surface of a brush. To use the tool, activate it in the Toolbox, and select a texture by left-clicking on the surface to which it has been applied. For more information about using this tool, please see **TUTORIAL 6.8**, "Using Texture Alignment Mode," in Chapter 6, "Introduction to Materials."
Terrain Editing	Brings up the Terrain Editor window, which enables you to create various types of natural-looking terrains by creating 2D monochromatic height maps. This window and all its functionality are covered in Chapter 8, "Terrain."

Brush Primitives Area

This area contains some primitive shapes that can be applied to the Builder Brush in order to add or subtract matter and thereby shape your level. In this section, we cover all these primitives in detail. Right-clicking on any of the buttons in this area brings up a dialog from which you can adjust the parameters for that specific primitive shape.

Cube

This button changes the Builder Brush into a cube for you to use to create BSP in your level. Cubes are usually one of the most frequently-used shapes in your level-building arsenal:

X	Controls the breadth of the resulting Builder Brush. Breadth is defined by the direction of the X-axis.
Y	Controls the width of the brush that is created. The width is defined in the direction of the Y-axis.
Z	Controls the height of the cube from which the Builder Brush is comprised. This height is defined in the direction of the Z-axis.
WallThickness	Controls the thickness of each of the sides of the brush. The value of WallThickness is only relevant if the Hollow parameter is set to True.
GroupName	Enables you to place your brush into a group.
Hollow	Works in tandem with the WallThickness setting. When activated, or set to True, your cube is constructed like an empty box, rather than a solid object.

Tessellated	Divides each of the faces of the object into triangles rather than quadrangles. Tessellating your brush is a key step if you plan to do geometry editing, as such an action can cause your object's faces to possibly become nonplanar, resulting in the Hall of Mirrors effect. If each face is three-sided, and not four, it becomes impossible to generate a nonplanar face.

Curved Staircase

The Curved Staircase is a set of stairs that run all the way up from the floor. As such, it should not be used to create staircases that spiral upward and wrap over themselves numerous times. For such staircases, use the Spiral Staircase brush (see the following section). Also, keep in mind that this particular brush creates a large number of BSP tessellations, which can quickly slow down your level. As such, this brush is rarely used in modern Unreal games, and a static mesh is used whenever such an object is needed:

InnerRadius	Controls the inside radius of the Curved Staircase. It must have a value of at least one. You would want this to be large if you wanted your staircase to travel around an object or area.
StepHeight	Controls the height of each step. This value, multiplied by the number of steps, is the total height of the staircase.
StepWidth	Determines the width of each step. Adding this value to the InnerRadius gives you the total radius of the staircase. For instance, if you had an InnerRadius value of 128, and a StepWidth value of 256, the total radius, or radius from the center of the staircase, would be 384 units.
AngleOfCurve	Enables you to have control over the curve angle of the staircase. Because the stairs are solid and extend up from the ground level, a Curve Angle greater than 270 degrees would cause the stairs to wrap over themselves.
NumSteps	Controls the total number of stairs on the staircase. Multiplying this value by the height of each step gives you the total height of the staircase.
AddToFirstStep	Offsets the entire staircase by the number of units entered. For example, if you need your staircase to begin 256 units in the air, you can enter that value here, and it is added to the height of the first step and to every step thereafter.
GroupName	Enables you to place your brush into a group.
CounterClockwise	When set to True, your staircase winds in a counter-clockwise direction. If this value is set to False, your stairs wind clockwise instead.

Spiral Staircase

This primitive is similar to the Curved Staircase described previously, but does not extend from the floor. Rather, each section of the staircase is only as thick as each individual stair, meaning that you can create a staircase that wraps over itself numerous times, rotating greater than 360 degrees. As with the Curved Staircase, you usually want to use a static mesh whenever you need such a shape:

InnerRadius	Controls the inside radius of the Spiral Staircase. It must have a value of at least one.
StepWidth	Determines the width of each step. Adding this value to the InnerRadius gives you the total radius of the staircase.
StepHeight	Controls the height of each step. This value, multiplied by the number of steps, is the total height of the staircase.
StepThickness	Defines how thick each step will be. This does not have any effect on the height of the staircase—only on the way the staircase appears. For instance, if the StepHeight value is 16, and the StepThickness value is set to 8, each of the steps would be 8 units thick, and there would be an eight-unit gap between each step.
NumStepsPer360	Controls the number of steps in a single 360-degree revolution. For example, if this value is set to 60, it would take exactly 60 steps to complete one full 360-degree revolution.
NumSteps	The actual number of stairs in the staircase. It is used in combination with the NumStepsPer360 value to control how far the staircase will revolve as it goes up. For example, if our NumStepsPer360 was still set to 60, and NumSteps was only 26, we would get half of one revolution, or a 180-degree spiral staircase. However, we have to add one extra stair into this value to get the desired rotation. So we would actually need 61 stairs to get one full 360-degree revolution.
	As a side note, to solve for the total number of steps, you need to get a certain rotation with the following math equation:
	$((NumStepsPer360 *) / 360) + 1 = NumSteps$
	So, if 60 steps were in each full 360-degree rotation, and we needed 270 degrees of rotation, the equation would solve like this:
	$((60 * 270) / 360) + 1 = 46$
	This means that we would need exactly 46 stairs in our staircase to achieve precisely 270 degrees of rotation.
GroupName	Enables you to place your brush into a group.

SlopedCeiling	If this value is set to true, the underside of the staircase will be a smooth ramp. If, however, it is set to false, the underside of the stairs will be stepped instead. Essentially, this aligns the two vertices at the bottom rear of each stair to the two vertices at the bottom front of the next stair.
SlopedFloor	Very much like SlopedCeiling, but this value actually controls whether the bottom surface of the stairs is sloped. In effect, this creates a spiral ramp, rather than a staircase.
CounterClockwise	When set to True, your staircase winds in a counter-clockwise direction. If this value is set to False, your stairs wind clockwise instead.

Linear Staircase

This changes the Builder Brush into a Staircase that moves in a straight line, rather than curving at all. As such, it is quite simpler to use. Still, it is far more efficient for your level to use a static mesh instead of this brush:

StepLength	The length from the front of the step to the rear. This number multiplied by the total number of steps results in the total length of the linear staircase.
StepWidth	Determines the width of each step.
StepHeight	Controls the height of each step. This value, multiplied by the number of steps, is the total height of the staircase.
NumSteps	The actual number of stairs in the staircase.
AddToFirstStep	Offsets the entire staircase by the number of units entered. For example, if you need your staircase to begin 256 units in the air, you can enter that value here, and it will be added to the height of the first step and to every step thereafter.
GroupName	Enables you to place your brush into a group.

Sheet

This command changes the Builder Brush into a single plane, or four-sided polygon. By default, this brush will be created as a square, but its vertices can be edited later. This brush can never block a player:

X	Controls the breadth of the resulting Builder Brush. Breadth is defined by the direction of the X-axis.
Y	Controls the width of the brush that is created. The width is defined in the direction of the Y-axis.
XSegments	Controls the number of divisions in the surface along its width. For instance, setting this to 3 would divide the plane into four equal segments along its width.

YSegments	This parameter is exactly like XSegments, except that it adds divisions along the height of the plane instead of the width.
Axis	Controls the orientation of the brush at the time of its creation.
GroupName	Enables you to place your brush into a group.

Cylinder

This generates a cylindrical Builder Brush, good for pillars, pipes, soda cans, raised daises, and just about anything else that is…well…cylindrical. In most modern Unreal games, however, it is used mostly for cylindrically shaped rooms, while such objects as those described previously are created with static meshes.

Z	Controls the length of the cylinder in the Z-Axis.
OuterRadius	The overall radius of the cylinder, calculated from its center.
InnerRadius	Similar to WallThickness on the Cube primitive, except that this does not cap off the ends. The effect is a pipe-like object. This setting is only relevant if Hollow is set to True.
Sides	Controls the number of polygons that are created around the cylinder. It must have a value of at least 3.
GroupName	Enables you to place your brush into a group.
AlignToSide	If this setting is True, the cylinder will be oriented so that the bottom-most face is parallel to the XY plane, which means that the bottom of the brush would essentially be a flat face. If the value is False, however, the bottom of the brush will be a corner.
Hollow	When activated, or set to True, your cylinder will be constructed like an empty can, rather than a solid object.

Cone

You can think of this primitive as a cylinder in which all the faces at one end have been collapsed down to a single point:

Z	Controls the length of the cone in the Z-Axis.
CapZ	This setting is only valid if Hollow is set to True. This controls how high the inside cap of the brush is. For example, if you were creating a cone-shaped room from a hollow cone, this setting would control the thickness of the floor.
OuterRadius	The total radius of the cone, as calculated from the center.
InnerRadius	Equal to the distance in units from the center of the cone to the inside edge of the cone. Naturally, this is only valid if Hollow is set to True.

Sides	Controls the number of polygons that are created around the cone. It must have a value of at least 3.
GroupName	Enables you to place your brush into a group.
AlignToSide	If this setting is True, the cone is oriented so that the bottom-most face is parallel to the XY plane, which means that the bottom of the brush would essentially be a flat face. If the value is False, however, the bottom of the brush will be a corner.
Hollow	When activated, or set to True, your cylinder will be constructed like an empty can, rather than a solid object.

Volumetric Shape

This primitive is a great tool for creating various texture effects, such as fire, smoke, plasma, trees, and chains, especially where perfect three-dimensional detail is not necessary, or the excess geometric detail would become sub-optimal. It actually consists of a number of sheet brushes rotated about their pivot point in the Z-axis:

Z	Controls the length of the volumetric shape in the Z-Axis.
Radius	Controls the distance each sheet extends from the center of the brush.
NumSheets	The number of actual sheet brushes used to generate the volumetric shape.
GroupName	Enables you to place your brush into a group.

Tetrahedron (Sphere)

This is the closest object to a sphere that you can achieve with a BSP brush. It is a spherical brush comprised completely of triangles. However, the results tend to be very inefficient in terms of performance. It is better to use a static mesh if you require a rounded shape. Generally, this primitive should be avoided!

Radius	Controls the distance each polygon of the tetrahedron extends from the center of the brush.
SphereExtrapolation	Controls how smooth the sphere will be by adjusting the size of the triangles that it is composed of. The higher the number, the more triangles are in the sphere, and the smaller those triangles will be. You could think of this as the resolution of the tetrahedron.
	Note: This setting raises the density of the tetrahedron's geometry exponentially, so you will find that a value of 7 gives you a ridiculously dense sphere.
GroupName	Enables you to place your brush into a group.

CSG Operations Area

The tools in this area are designed to enable you to construct your level through the volumetric modeling method of Constructive Solid Geometry, or CSG. In essence, this is where you go to add, subtract, intersect, or de-intersect your brushes from the world of mass that exists within your level. Also in this area, you will find commands for adding a variety of special-purpose brushes and static meshes. For more information on CSG, see Chapter 4.

Add

This command creates an additive brush, basically inserting mass into the negative space of the world. The new brush will be generated in the exact same location and shape as the Builder Brush. Also, the texture that you have selected in the Texture browser will be applied to the new brush. The resulting additive brush has a tell-tale blue wireframe, so that you are able to identify it as additive in the 2D viewports.

Subtract

This command is essentially the inverse of Add. Rather than inserting volume into your level, this command takes volume away from any additive space it encounters. The new brush will be in the same position and shape as the Builder Brush, but will have a yellow wireframe in the 2D viewports to distinguish it as a subtractive brush. Also, the selected texture within the Texture browser will be applied to the inside of the object.

Intersect

The Intersect command only affects the Builder Brush. It checks the BSP geometry within your level to see where the brush is intersecting, or passing into another brush. The command then performs a Boolean operation on the Builder Brush, based on whether the brush that is intersecting with the Builder Brush is additive or subtractive.

If the Builder Brush is intersecting with an additive brush at the time of the command, only the area of the Builder Brush that is actually passing into the additive brush remains. The rest of the Builder Brush, or the area of the brush that existed outside the additive brush, will be deleted.

If, instead, the brush that is intersecting with the Builder Brush is subtractive, the result is exactly the opposite. The area of the Builder Brush that falls within the intersecting subtractive brush will be deleted, and only the area that was outside the subtractive brush remains. For tutorials involving this function, see Chapter 4.

> **NOTE**
>
> Your Builder Brush can be intersecting both an additive and subtractive brush simultaneously when you perform this command. This can yield some very interesting results. Experiment, and see what you can come up with.

De-Intersect

This command is, in effect, the exact opposite of Intersect. It essentially performs the same checks on the geometry surrounding the Builder Brush, but performs an opposite Boolean operation than Intersect. This means that when the Builder Brush is passing into a subtractive brush, only the area of the Builder Brush that falls within the subtractive brush will be kept, and the area that falls outside the subtractive brush will be deleted.

Conversely, if the Builder Brush is intersecting an additive brush, the area of the builder brush that falls outside the additive shape will be kept, and the area of actual intersection will be deleted.

Additional Brushes Area

The tools in this area allow for the adding of special brushes and volumes to the level using the current builder brush as a template.

Add Special Brush ■

This command brings up the Add Special window (see **FIGURE A.4**). From here, you can create a variety of brushes for specific effect and optimization purposes. Because these types of brushes are not used very often, they have all been grouped within this single command, rather than each having a separate command of their own.

A variety of special brushes can be created from this window by either selecting one or more check-boxes and a radio button for solidity, or selecting a Prefab from the dropdown list:

FIGURE A.4   Add Special dialog

Checkboxes

Portal	Enables you to create a portal. Portals were previously used for zoning levels into separate areas to optimize the speed of rendering, or to designate certain areas of the map. In Unreal Engine 3, portals are no longer needed, making this option obsolete.
Invisible	Disables visibility for your selected Special Brush. Several of the prefabs use this feature. The wireframe for brushes created with this setting alone is pink.
Two Sided	Causes your Special Brush to be double-sided, which means it has a front and back side. This causes the effect of your Special Brush to be visible regardless of which side you are positioned. For example, if you create a sheet brush without checking Two Sided, you will only be able to see one side of the brush: the positive side of the polygons. By checking Two Sided, both sides are visible.

Solidity

Solidity for brushes does not immediately mean exactly what you might assume, in that it does not only specify whether an actor can interact or pass through an object. It also deals with the way your BSP is divided in your level. Because the standard brushes created in your level are solid by default, a solid brush created from the Add Special window works exactly like a normal added brush. For more information on brush solidity, see Chapter 4.

Prefabs

Prefabs are predesigned combinations of various settings from the Add Special window that are commonly used together.

Add Volume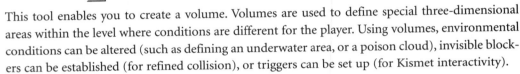

This tool enables you to create a volume. Volumes are used to define special three-dimensional areas within the level where conditions are different for the player. Using volumes, environmental conditions can be altered (such as defining an underwater area, or a poison cloud), invisible blockers can be established (for refined collision), or triggers can be set up (for Kismet interactivity).

Selections Area

This area has the following commands that you can use to control what you see in the viewport.

Show Selected Actors Only	This operation enables you to hide all actors that are not currently selected. The BSP brushes within the level are hidden in the 2D views, but remain visible in the 3D view. This form of isolated viewing is good for fine-tuning specific areas without having to deal with the clutter of surrounding actors.
Hide Selected Actors	This hides only those actors which are selected in a level. This is convenient if you have finished tweaking the properties of a set of actors and need to move on to another area without cluttering your view. This is particularly useful in the 2D viewports where the individual wireframes overlap and can be difficult to differentiate. As before, the BSP brushes within the level are still visible in the 3D view.
Show All Actors	This command unhides all actors in your level. If you have been hiding actors, and seem to have misplaced one or two, be sure you click this button before you replace them.
Invert Selection	This is another of those special commands where the name really seems to say it all. This deselects any currently selected actors, and instead selects all actors that were not included in the original selection.

The Viewports

One of the most important aspects of the Unreal Editor interface is the viewport. Viewports are windows into the Unreal world. They are used to see the level during construction and verify placement of objects (see **FIGURE A.5**). This section discusses the Unreal Editor viewports, along with their various capabilities.

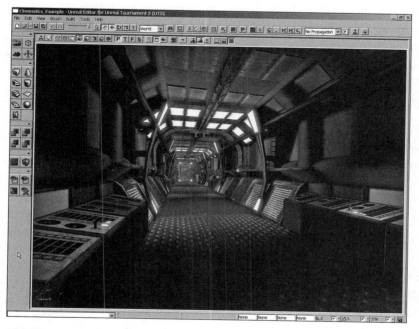

FIGURE A.5   The viewports

The viewports in the Unreal Editor basically come in two different flavors. The first one that strikes our attention is the Perspective viewport. By default this is the viewport in the lower left, and is the only view that actually offers us a perspective view of our level, meaning that it displays depth. It also displays the textures and lighting that have been applied to the actors within the level. The Perspective viewport, however, does have a weakness: It is very difficult (if not impossible) to gauge the precise location of specific objects, such as brushes and static meshes, within this viewport.

It is for this reason that the 2D, or orthogonal, viewports exist. They do not display depth of any kind, nor do they display any of the textures applied to your level. So, although your level appears very much as if it were in blueprint form, you have very precise control over exactly where each object is located within your level. These viewports display from three different angles: Top, Front, and Side.

You will notice that in the lower-left corner of the perspective viewport you see a small icon representing the direction of the world coordinate axes. These display the direction that each axis is pointing at all times, which becomes very important as you are constantly moving and rotating the camera.

Navigation

You can move the camera in the viewports by holding down various mouse buttons or combinations of mouse buttons and moving the mouse. These are different for the perspective and orthogonal viewports.

Perspective

This list includes all of the navigational motions and inputs for the camera in the Perspective viewport:

▶ Holding the left mouse button and moving the mouse forward or backward moves the camera forward or backward. Clicking the left mouse button, and moving the mouse left or right turns the camera in that direction. The effect is much like driving the camera around like a car.

▶ Holding the right mouse button and moving the mouse rotates the camera. Moving the mouse left or right rotates the camera in that direction, whereas moving the mouse forward or backward rotates the camera up and down, respectively.

▶ Holding both the left and right mouse buttons and moving the mouse pans the camera. As you move the mouse left or right, the camera strafes in that direction. Moving the mouse forward or backward pans the camera up and down, respectively.

▶ The mouse scroll wheel zooms in and out of the viewport in the direction the camera is currently pointing.

Orthogonal

This list includes all of the navigational motions and inputs for the camera in the Orthogonal viewports:

▶ Clicking either the left mouse button or right mouse button and moving the mouse pans the camera according to the direction the mouse is moved.

▶ Clicking both the left mouse button and right mouse buttons and moving the mouse or using the mouse scroll wheel zooms the camera in and out.

Maya Camera Tools Emulation

By holding down the U or L keys, you can emulate Maya's camera movement when using the perspective viewport. Holding the U key forces rotation to occur around the center of the viewport, while holding L forces rotation to occur around the current selection's pivot. With U or L held down:

- ▶ Clicking the left mouse button and moving the mouse rotates the camera.
- ▶ Clicking the right mouse button and moving the mouse or using the mouse scroll wheel zooms the camera in and out.
- ▶ Clicking the middle mouse button and moving the mouse pans the camera according to the direction the mouse is moved.

Viewport Controls

There are many places within the editor that you can control the viewports. One of the first of these is within the View menu. In this menu, you will see the Viewport Configuration submenu. From this submenu, you can set up the layout for the viewports that suits you best (see **FIGURE A.6**).

FIGURE A.6   Viewport controls

Just below the Viewport Configuration submenu, you will find the Resize Top and Bottom Viewports Together toggle. When enabled, resizing the viewports horizontally causes both the top and bottom viewports to be resized. When disabled, the individual viewports may be resized independent of one another.

Viewport Toolbar

Each of the viewports has a bar across the top with a selection of buttons. These invoke different view modes and options for each viewport (see **FIGURE A.7**). The following is a list, ordered from left to right across the toolbar, of each of these available controls and what their uses are.

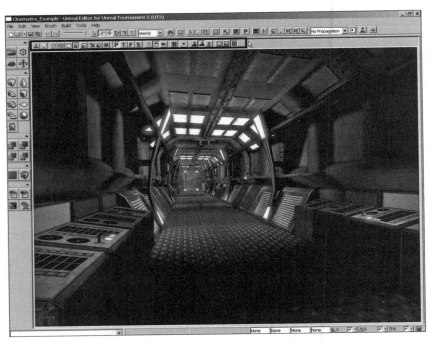

FIGURE A.7   Viewport Toolbar

Realtime Preview

This button enables you to preview ambient audio, particle effects, and any animated materials in real time, as they appear in game. This only has a dramatic effect in the 3D view.

Unlit Movement

This button changes the view mode to Unlit when actively navigating in the viewport. When the camera is not in motion, the view automatically returns to Lit mode. This can significantly increase the speed at which the camera can move, especially when dealing with large levels or levels with lighting not built.

Brush Wireframe

This view mode causes all actors and CSG brushes to be displayed in wireframe. The hotkey for this is Alt + 1.

Wireframe

This view mode causes all meshes to be displayed in wireframe. The hotkey for this is Alt + 2.

Unlit

This display mode shows only the materials on your objects and not the lighting. This is a good way to ascertain texture placement without having to worry about how lights are affecting your scene. You must be careful, however, because many textures look dramatically different when lighting is applied to them. The hotkey for this is Alt + 3.

Lit

This display mode shows all objects as they would be rendered in-game, including lighting and shadows. This is a good way to ascertain exactly how your map looks when others play it without having to actually load up the map in the game. This mode can be slow to navigate when lighting is not built or the level is heavily populated. The hotkey for this is Alt + 4.

Lighting Only

This display mode strips away all textures on your level and shows only how light is playing upon each surface. All surfaces, BSP or otherwise, are rendered in white, and are only affected by the color and type of light that is striking them. This is especially useful for controlling the exact effect of shadows in your level. The hotkey for this is Alt + 5.

Light Complexity

In this view mode, non-lightmapped meshes are displayed with a solid color determined by the number of lights affecting the mesh. It is useful to help gauge whether your light setup is getting too complex for dynamic or non-lightmapped objects in your level. The hotkey for this is Alt + 6.

The various colors visible and the number of dynamic lights designated by each color are covered in the following table.

Number of Lights Versus Color

0	Black – RGB = (0,0,0)
1	Lime – RGB = (0,255,0)
2	Green – RGB = (63,191,0)
3	Olive – RGB = (127,127,0)
4	Dark Red – RGB = (191,63,0)
5	Bright Red – RGB = (255,0,0)

> **NOTE**
>
> On lightmapped meshes, such as BSP surfaces in your level, you will notice that the colors do not match this table. This is normal. Light complexity should only be used to test how the number of lights affect non-lightmapped objects.

Texture Density

When using the Texture Density mode, you see the size of the texture applied to a surface in relation to the area of the surface the texture covers. This is useful when determining which materials may be using textures that are too large for the detail needed for the size of the surface. Different colors are mapped to the surfaces to correspond to different ranges of instruction counts. Blue means small textures compared to the surface area, whereas red means larger textures compared to the surface area. The hotkey for this is Alt + 7.

Shader Complexity

When using the Shader Complexity mode, you see how many shader instructions are being executed over a given part of the screen. This is useful when determining which materials may be too complex. Different colors are mapped to the surfaces to correspond to different ranges of instruction counts. Green means lower counts, whereas red means higher counts.

Perspective P

This display mode shows your level in a three-dimensional wireframe. The brushes in your scene are color-coded as they are in the 2D views.

Display Modes T F S

The last three display mode buttons control the type of 2D view you would like to use. The T, F, and S icons represent Top, Front, and Side, respectively. These enable you to switch quickly between these three modes.

Lock Viewport 🔒

This causes the viewport to ignore the Align Cameras command. Usually, the viewports would all snap to view the selected actor when the Align Cameras command is used. With this button toggled on, the viewport stays positioned and oriented as it is.

Maximize Viewport ▢

This button causes the viewport to be maximized to take up the entire viewport area. This is handy when needing to see small details, which are hard to pick out when the viewports are smaller.

Lock to Selected Actor 👁

The next button in the Viewport Control Bar is not a display mode; rather, it is a very handy tool to relocate objects in your level. This tool snaps the camera to the location of the selected object, and then attaches that object to the camera. In effect, it's a lot like dragging your actor around with a tow truck. To use the Lock to Selected Actor function, click on it to enable it, and then left-click on an actor within your level. Your camera jumps to the current location and orientation of the actor that you selected. Then, move your camera around using your standard viewport controls. When your camera is in the desired location for your actor, disable Lock to Selected Actor, and move your camera. You will see that the actor is now in the exact location and orientation that the camera was in when Lock to Selected Actor was disabled.

Occlusion Parent ⊞

When this button is clicked on a viewport, that viewport becomes the basis for occlusion in all other viewports. This means that only those objects that do not get occluded in that viewport based on its camera position and orientation are rendered in all other viewports. This is great way to preview occlusion within Unreal Editor. When this button is not toggled on for any of the viewports, no occlusion is performed inside Unreal Editor.

Toggle Show Flags ▾

Clicking this button displays a list of all the elements that can have their visibility toggled on or off within a viewport. This makes it easier to focus on just those parts of the level that are needed at any given time.

Level Streaming Volume Previs 👤

Clicking this button causes the viewport to respect any LevelStreamingVolumes present in the map. When the camera is within the limits of a LevelStreamingVolume, the level associated with that volume becomes visible. When the camera leaves the volume, the level will be hidden.

Post Process Volume Previs

Clicking this button causes the effects of any PostProcessVolumes present in the map to be displayed in the viewport when the camera is within the boundaries of the volume.

Toggle "Squint Mode"

Clicking this button turns on squint mode. This mode places a blur across the entire viewport, allowing the level designer to determine if the areas or features of the map that are supposed to draw the player's attention are having the desired effect.

Camera Movement Speed

These buttons allow the speed at which the camera moves in the viewports to be adjusted. This is extremely useful when dealing with very large maps.

Viewport Context Menu

Following are the actions that can be found within the viewport context menu, which can be activated by clicking the Right Mouse Button:

Cut, Copy, and Paste	Provide access to the cut, copy, and paste commands.
Actor Properties	Opens the currently selected actors' properties in the Actor Properties window so that they can be modified.
Level Tools	Contains options dealing with streaming levels. It includes the ability to ad the selected actor(s) to the currently active level, as well as selecting all levels, selecting specific levels, and deselecting all levels.
Find In Kismet	Opens the Kismet editor and focuses on the selected actor. This option is only available if the currently selected actor is referenced somewhere in the Kismet sequences of the current level.
Transform Tools	Contains options for setting the pivot of an actor and mirroring. The pivot tools are used to set the point about which transformations to the selected actor are applied, moved, or snapped. The transform tools provide the ability to mirror the selected actor about any given axis.
Order	Enables you to set the order of the selected CSG brush to first or last. This can be very useful if you need to add a brush to a map late in the development cycle that, because of the nature of CSG, needs to come before other brushes in the operations.

Polygons	Following are the options located within the Polygons submenu of the viewport context menu:
	To Brush—This builds the Red Builder Brush to be identical to the selected CSG brush.
	From Brush—This builds the current CSG brush to be identical to the Red Builder Brush.
CSG	Sets whether the currently selected CSG brush is additive or subtractive.
Solidity	Sets the solidity of the currently selected CSG brush to Solid, Semi-Solid, or Non-Solid.
Add Volume	Adds a volume in the location and shape of the Red Builder Brush.
Select	Selects brushes by solidity, CSG operation, or all.
Align	Provides the ability to perform the following operations on the selected actors:
	Snap to Floor/Align to Floor—These two options move the selected actors down in the Z-axis until they reach a surface and then snap the actors to the grid in the Z-axis. Align to Floor not only moves actors down, but also rotates them to match the alignment of the floor beneath them. If you have multiple actors selected, each actor moves and aligns independently.
	Move Actors to Grid—This option snaps the selected actors to the grid. If you have multiple actors selected, they all move in unison to snap at the active pivot point (as opposed to each actor snapping individually to a different location on the grid).
Toggle Lock Locations	Toggles whether the selected actor can be moved in the editor. When toggled on, some actors may appear to be colored distinctly in the viewport, notifying the user that they cannot be moved but are still able to be selected so that properties can be modified.
Align Cameras	Forces all viewports that are not currently locked to snap to focus on the selected actors.
Selection By Class	Selects actors of certain classes. This is a quick way to access all the actors of a certain type in order to move, delete, or group them, as well as modify their properties.
Snap To Grid	Independently snaps all the vertices of the currently selected BSP brush to the current grid.
Convert To Static Mesh	Converts the selected BSP brush to a static mesh.
Save Brush As Collision	Creates collision for the selected mesh from the Red Builder Brush.
Convert	Converts between static meshes, movers, and physics objects.

Create Archetype	Creates an archetype out of the selected actors.
Create Prefab	Creates a prefab out of the selected actors.
Show/Hide Actors	Shows or hides the selected actors, as well as inverting the selection.
Add Selection	Adds an actor from a list of recently placed actors, from a preset list, or from the currently selected actor in the Actor Browser.
Play From Here	Opens the map in the Play In Editor window, placing the player at the exact position selected in the editor.

A

The Console Bar

The final part of the Unreal Editor user interface is the console bar (see **FIGURE A.8**). This strip across the bottom of the UI contains several tools for controlling the Unreal Editor's behavior, and methods to speed up level construction workflow.

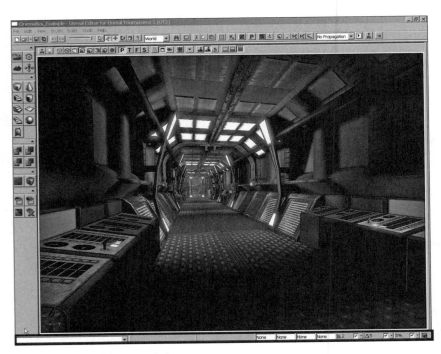

FIGURE A.8   The console bar

Command Line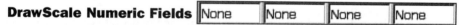

This text field enables you to input console commands directly into the Unreal Editor. There are numerous commands available, and they accomplish a wide variety of tasks, such as recording information in the log file or reporting stats directly in the viewport. The prompt also works as a dropdown menu so that you can access commands that have been previously entered without having to retype them.

Selection Status | Persistent Level.Emitter_3 |

This shows the currently selected actor's name, the number and class of the selected actors (if multiple actors from the same class are selected), or how many actors are selected if multiple actors are selected from different classes.

Transform Status | Mouse: (-1138, -479, 0) |

In an orthographic viewport, this shows the current mouse position within the world. In a perspective viewport, this bar shows the status of the current transformation in progress.

DrawScale Numeric Fields | None | None | None | None |

These fields provide you with a simple method of object scaling. The first field scales the object in all three axes at once, whereas the next three fields scale the object in the X, Y, and Z axes, respectively. The DrawScale system works such that 1.00 is equal to 100 percent, 0.5 would be equal to 50 percent, and so on.

Drag Grid | 2 ☑ ▾ |

This setting snaps entire brushes to points on the grid as they are moved around the level. This is a very important option to have activated when constructing your level. Miniscule (or even imperceptible) distances that occur when aligning objects have the same effect as tremendous distances. For example, if you are trying to connect two subtractive brushes to form a corridor, and there is a space between them that is even a fraction of a unit wide, the distance still renders as a wall, and will be completely impassible. Conversely, if your two subtractive brushes were intersecting each other, you run the risk of creating unwanted holes in your level.

Rotation Grid | 5 ☑ ▾ |

This is another vital setting when creating your level. When enabled, this setting snaps all rotations to the number of degrees specified. This is an invaluable tool when rotating objects in your level, as freely rotating to exact values is likely to be almost impossible. Even though your rotations might appear correct to the naked eye, there could be minor differences that could cause errors.

Scale Grid 5% ☑ ▾

When enabled, this setting snaps all scaling operations to increments of the specified percentage. This enables you to achieve much more precise scales when using the transform tool.

AutoSave

When enabled, the editor automatically saves the current map to a backup file that can be retrieved if an error occurs or some unwanted result happens during the build process. The amount of time between backups can be set here.

Browsers

The assets and information needed to construct an Unreal level can all be accessed within the various tabs of the Generic Browser window. The following section describes each of these tabs, along with their respective functionality.

Generic Browser

The Generic browser is the main portal to all the content contained in packages available within the game (see **FIGURE A.9**). Through the Generic browser, users can edit existing content, or import new content into packages. This is by far the most commonly used browser and is where you will spend a good deal of your time while using the Unreal Editor.

Menu

The menubar contains the following menus and options when the Generic Browser tab is active:

File

New	Opens the new object creation dialog. From this dialog, new objects of various types, such as Materials, SoundCues, or AnimSets can be created.
Open	Opens a file browser from which a package can be loaded into the editor.
Save	Saves the currently selected package.
Save As	Saves the currently selected package with the option of choosing a new name for the package.
Import	Opens a file browser for choosing files to import into packages.
Export	Exports the currently selected asset using the appropriate exporter.
Recent	A list of recently opened packages. This makes opening commonly used packages much faster.

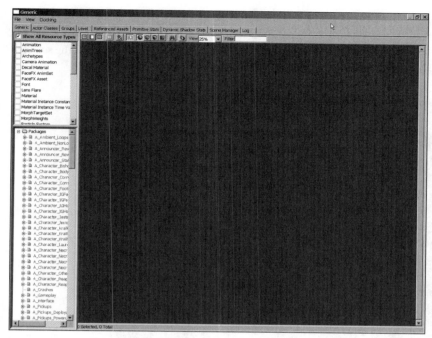

FIGURE A.9   The Generic browser

View

Refresh	Refreshes the Preview window of the Generic browser.
Show Resource Memory Usage	Toggles the display of memory that each item within each package is using. This information can help when optimizing content because sounds or textures might need to use different compression settings to save on memory.

Docking

Docked	Fixes the current browser in the main window as a tab.
Floating	Puts the current browser in its own floating window.
Clone Browser	Creates a new tab in the main window that contains a duplicate of the current browser.
Remove Browser	Removes the current browser from the main window.

Resource Types List

This list contains all types of content that can be viewed in the Generic Bowser (see **FIGURE A.10**). Types whose checkbox is not selected in this list will be filtered out, leaving only the selected types visible. This makes finding specific assets much easier because you can focus your search by type. Double-clicking any type's name de-selects all other types, making only that type visible. The Show All Resource Types checkbox at the top makes all content loaded in the selected packages visible in the browser.

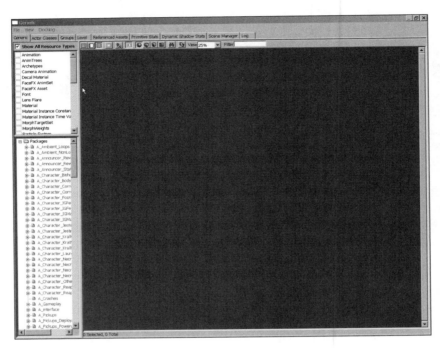

FIGURE A.10   Resource Types list

Packages List

This lists all packages from which any content is currently loaded within the editor (see **FIGURE A.11**). If any packages have groups within them, then the package can be expanded to show the list of groups. It is also possible to group packages within new subfolders for organizational purposes. Packages that contain groups have a + next to their name. Clicking the + expands the list to show the groups within the package.

Right-clicking on a package or group in this list displays the context menu, which provides functionality to save, fully load, or unload the package. Also available from the menu is the ability to import new content, bulk export all content within the package, or export localization data. Packages can be checked for errors from this menu, as well as be placed within a sub-folder within the Packages list. Sound Groups and Texture Groups can also be batch processed from here.

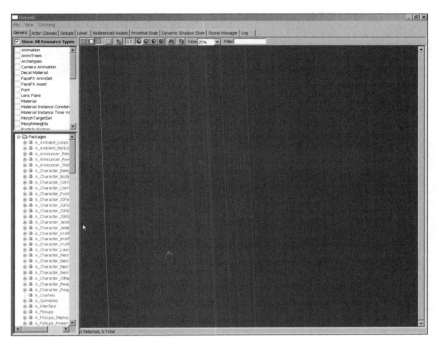

FIGURE A.11   Packages list

Save   Saves the selected package. If the package is not fully loaded, you are prompted with a dialog, enabling you to load the entire package or cancel the save operation.

Fully Load   Loads the entire contents of the current package. When a map is first loaded, only the content used by that map is loaded into memory. This often leads to packages being partially loaded. If you desire to view the remaining assets within those packages, they must be loaded with this command.

Unload   Unloads the package from memory. This is very useful when dealing with a computer with limited memory as packages that are no longer needed can be removed from the browser without having to restart the Unreal Editor itself.

Import   Opens a file browser to select files for import, such as textures, meshes, or sounds. This functionality is available directly from the File menu of the Generic browser as well.

Bulk Export   Exports the entire contents of the package using the associated exporters for each type of content. Most types do not have a specific exporter and use the .T3D file type.

Full Loc Export Exports localization binaries such as .WAV files and also exports content just as the Bulk Export command.

A

Check For Errors	Checks the package for any errors present.
Set Folder	Allows a subfolder within the Packages list to be set for this package. Once set, the package is located under that folder in the list. This information is saved with the package.
Batch Process	**Sound Groups**—Sets all the sounds within the package or group to the selected sound group.
	Cluster Sounds—Groups sounds with similar names* into a SoundCue and connects them to a random node within that SoundCue.
	Cluster Sounds with Attenuation—Groups sounds with similar names* into a SoundCue and connects them to a random node, as well as adding an attenuation node within that SoundCue.
	*Similar names refer to sounds with the same name except for a numeric suffix—that is, ambient_machine01, ambient_machine02, ambient_machine03, and so on.
	Texture Groups—Sets all the textures within the package or group to the selected texture group.

Preview Window

The preview window is the main area of the Generic browser where all the assets are displayed (see **FIGURE A.12**). Through the context menu of the preview window itself, new objects can be created by choosing the appropriate type. The context menu, accessed by right-clicking on items in the preview window, allows for duplicating, renaming, viewing properties, and other functionality specific to each asset type. An asset can be selected here and then placed in the level from the context menu of the viewport. Along the bottom of the preview window, the number of items selected and the total number of items loaded within the current package are displayed.

FIGURE A.12   The three layouts of the preview window

The manner in which content is displayed and the appearance of that content is controlled through the buttons and settings available within the toolbar of the preview window.

Layout Buttons	Determine whether the items in the preview window are displayed as a list, a list with preview, or thumbnails. The thumbnail view is the default, and is most likely the view in which most of your time editing will be spent.
Group By Class	Toggles whether the items in the preview window are sorted by type or by alphabetical order.
In Use Only	Toggles whether all loaded items are displayed or only those which are being used within the current map.
PSys Real-Time Thumbs	Toggles whether the thumbnails for ParticleSystems update in real-time or not.
Display Primitives	Set the shape of the primitive used to display materials within the browser.
Search By Name	Opens the Search By Name dialog, which allows for advanced searches to be performed. This makes finding assets in the browser much easier, especially if you only know part of the name of an asset.
Re-import resources in all selected packages	Causes all the assets within the selected packages in the Packages list to be re-imported from the locations they were imported from previously. This command can take a while if the packages happen to have a large number of assets in them.
Thumbnail Format	Allows the size of the thumbnails in the preview window to be set. Sizes can be set in two ways. One way is to set them as percentages of the actual size of the asset (with textures) or the standard thumbnail size (512x512) for other assets. The other way is to set a specific size for all assets, such as 256x256.
Filter	Filters out assets based on the text entered in the field.

Actor Classes Browser

The Actor Class browser lists all the actor classes available within the engine (see **FIGURE A.13**). This browser is primarily used to insert actors into your level. To do

> **NOTE**
>
> The actual command that appears in the pop-up menu varies greatly based on which type of actor you selected in the Actor Classes Browser.

this, merely select the type of actor you want from the list of classes; then right-click in your viewport where you want the actor to be placed. In the pop-up menu that appears, select the option for placing the selected actor.

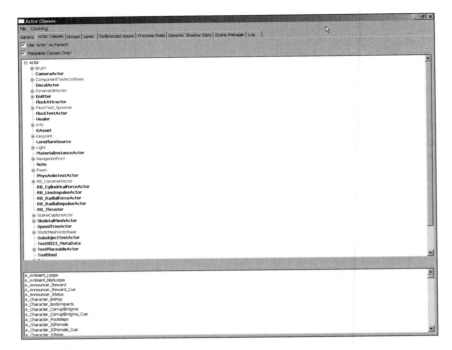

FIGURE A.13   Actor Classes browser

Toolbar

The browser also has interface buttons across the top. Following is a list of each of these buttons, and their functionality.

Use "Actor" as Parent Checkbox	Displays the head of the hierarchy tree as actor, instead of object.
Placeable Classes Only Checkbox	Only displays classes that contain actors who can be placed in the scene.

Menu

The menubar contains the following menus and options when the Actor Classes tab is active.

File

Open Package	Opens a file browser for choosing a package to open.
Export All Scripts	Exports all actor and class scripts to a series of folders and .uc files, so that you can edit them and rebuild them later.

Docking

Docked	Fixes the browser in the main browser window as a tab.
Floating	Puts the browser in its own floating window.
Clone Browser	Creates in the main browser window with a duplicate of this browser.
Remove Browser	Removes this browser from the main browser window.

You can also double-click any actor or class within the browser to access its source code. This is very handy if you need to quickly edit part of the programming code for a specific actor or class. This is a great way to see "behind-the-scenes" of certain actors and classes in order to see what makes them tick. It's also a good way to see how undocumented properties of an actor or class work.

Groups Browser

This browser enables you to create and manage groups of actors in your scene (see **FIGURE A.14**). This can greatly increase the efficiency of your level as you work, because these groups can be hidden from within this browser. After you make a group, you can add objects into it, take them back out again, and edit the properties of objects within the group.

FIGURE A.14   Groups browser

Menu

The menubar contains the following menus and options when the Groups tab is active.

File

New	Creates a new group that you can add actors into, remove them from, edit, and so forth. A dialog appears that enables you to name the group. You can have one or several objects selected when you click this, and all will be added to the group.
Rename	Allows a new name for the selected group to be specified.
Delete	Deletes the selected group from the list. It does not delete the actors.
Add Selected Actors to Group(s)	Enables you to add selected objects into the selected group.
Delete Selected Actors from Group(s)	Removes any selected objects from the highlighted group or groups.
Refresh Group List	Refreshes the groups as you make changes in them. However, in more recent versions of the editor, this button is superfluous because the groups update automatically as you perform actions upon them.
Select Actors	Selects all actors in the selected group.
Deselect Actors	Deselects all actors in the selected group.
Make All Groups Visible	Causes all groups to become visible.

View

Refresh	Refreshes the group list.

Docking

Docked	Fixes the browser in the main browser window as a tab.
Floating	Puts the browser in its own floating window.
Clone Browser	Creates a new tab in the main browser window with a duplicate of this browser.
Remove Browser	Removes this browser from the main browser window.

Within the group list inside the browser, you should see check boxes next to each group. Checking these activates visibility for the corresponding group. In this way, you can quickly hide and show grouped actors in your scene in order to speed up the viewport, or just to stay organized. The major exception to this, however, is BSP brushes. These do not turn invisible in the 3D view, but are hidden in the 2D view.

Selecting all actors within a group can be quite beneficial to speed of workflow. For example, let's say you have a series of lights in your scene that all require the same effect. You can group them all together, select all actors within the group, and make your changes to all the lights simultaneously, rather than having to go light by light.

Actors can be members of more than one group at a time. In fact, a single actor can exist within any number of groups. The main rule that must be kept in mind, however, is that if an actor is a member of numerous groups, then all of those groups must be hidden in order to hide the actor. Let's say, for example, that you have an actor who has been added to GroupOne, GroupTwo, and GroupThree. If you hide GroupOne, the actor remains visible until GroupTwo and GroupThree are hidden as well.

Level Browser

This browser is used for creating, importing, removing, and organizing levels when dealing with level streaming (see **FIGURE A.15**). The use of this browser is explained in greater detail in Chapter 12, "Level Streaming."

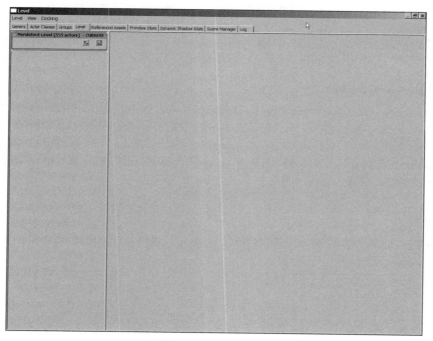

FIGURE A.15   Level browser

A

Menu

The menubar contains the following menus and options when the Level tab is active:

Level

New Level	Creates a new streaming level in which actors can be placed.
Import Level	Imports an existing level into the persistent level for purposes of streaming.
Make Current	Sets the selected level as the currently active level.
Remove Level From World	Removes the selected level from the persistent level's list of streaming levels.

View

Refresh	Refreshes the level list.

Docking

Docked	Fixes the browser in the main browser window as a tab.
Floating	Puts the browser in its own floating window.
Clone Browser	Creates a new tab in the main browser window with a duplicate of this browser.
Remove Browser	Removes this browser from the main browser window.

Referenced Assets Browser

The Referenced Assets browser is very similar to the Generic browser in appearance. It displays a hierarchy, as well as thumbnails, of the assets referenced by the selected actor in the viewport (see **FIGURE A.16**). The Referenced Assets browser is divided into two sections. The section to the left displays the aforementioned hierarchy. This is very handy in determining what assets in which packages are being used by actors within a map.

Menu

The menubar contains the following menus and options when the Referenced Assets tab is active.

View

Refresh	See "Generic Browser."

Docking

Docked	Fixes this browser in the main browser window as a tab.
Floating	Puts this browser in its own floating window.
Clone Browser	Creates a new tab in the main browser window with a duplicate of this browser.
Remove Browser	Removes this browser from the main browser window.

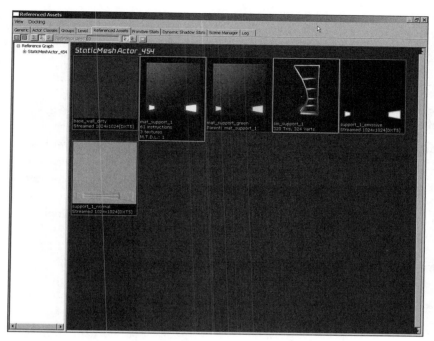

FIGURE A.16   Referenced Assets browser

Toolbar

The browser also has interface buttons across the top. Following is a list of each of these buttons, and their functionality:

List	Displays the referenced actors in a textual list.
Thumbnails	Displays the referenced actors as a series of graphic thumbnails.
Directly Referenced Only	Only displays those assets referenced by the selected actor that are one level away on the hierarchy.
All Referenced	Shows all assets the selected actor is referencing.
Custom Depth	This option and its corresponding numeric entry field control how far down the hierarchy you would like to visualize the referenced assets. For instance, a setting of 2 shows the immediately referenced assets, as well as assets referenced by them.
Include Assets Referenced by Defaults	Shows objects that are referenced by the default properties of the actor's class. For example, a PointLight actor's Component class default settings may reference a material object for the light's icon in the editor.

Include Assets Referenced by Scripts	Shows objects referenced by the UnrealScript code associated with the actor.
Group by Class	Keeps all references of the same type grouped together in the list or thumbnail area.

Primitive Stats Browser

The Primitive Stats browser provides a spreadsheet view of all the geometric objects within the current map and statistics dealing with rendering, lighting, and shadows (see **FIGURE A.17**). This is used a great deal when optimizing levels or when performance problems are encountered. The view can be sorted by column, or stat as it were, in order to provide quick access to the data that is important at any one time. Because this browser is mainly geared toward level optimization, more information on its use can be found in Chapter 11, "Level Optimization."

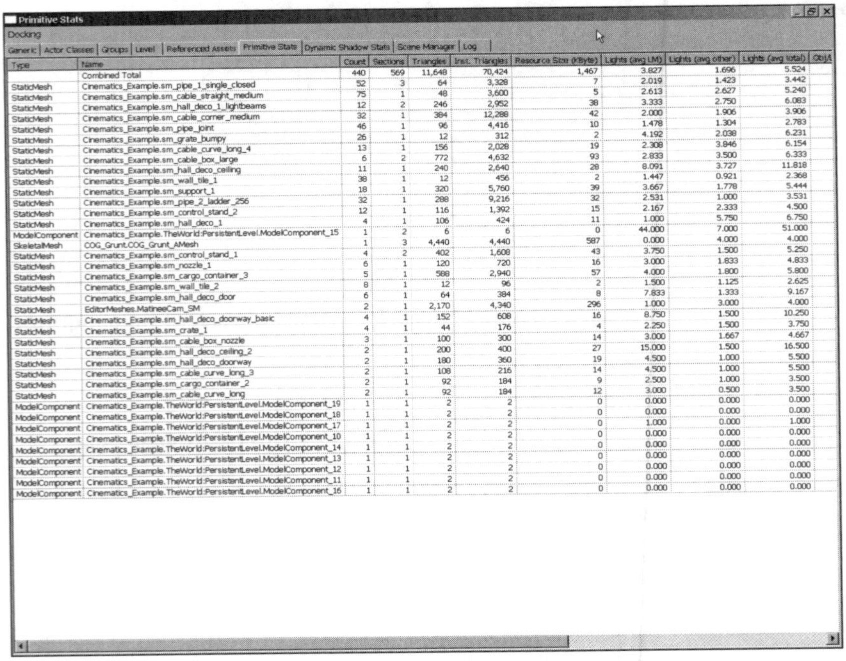

Type	Name	Count	Sections	Triangles	Inst. Triangles	Resource Size (KByte)	Lights (avg LM)	Lights (avg other)	Lights (avg total)	Obj/t
	Combined Total	440	569	11,648	70,424	1,467	3.827	1.696	5.524	
StaticMesh	Cinematics_Example.sm_pipe_1_single_closed	52	3	64	3,328	7	2.019	1.423	3.442	
StaticMesh	Cinematics_Example.sm_cable_straight_medium	75	1	48	3,600	5	2.613	2.627	5.240	
StaticMesh	Cinematics_Example.sm_hall_deco_1_lightbeams	12	2	246	2,952	38	3.333	2.750	6.083	
StaticMesh	Cinematics_Example.sm_cable_corner_medium	32	1	384	12,288	42	2.000	1.906	3.906	
StaticMesh	Cinematics_Example.sm_pipe_joint	46	1	96	4,416	10	1.478	1.304	2.783	
StaticMesh	Cinematics_Example.sm_grate_bumpy	26	1	12	312	2	4.192	2.038	6.231	
StaticMesh	Cinematics_Example.sm_cable_curve_long_4	13	1	156	2,028	19	2.308	3.846	6.154	
StaticMesh	Cinematics_Example.sm_cable_box_large	6	2	772	4,632	93	2.833	3.500	6.333	
StaticMesh	Cinematics_Example.sm_hall_deco_ceiling	11	1	240	2,640	28	8.091	3.727	11.818	
StaticMesh	Cinematics_Example.sm_wall_tile_1	38	1	12	456	2	1.447	0.921	2.368	
StaticMesh	Cinematics_Example.sm_support_1	18	1	320	5,760	39	3.667	1.778	5.444	
StaticMesh	Cinematics_Example.sm_pipe_2_ladder_256	32	1	288	9,216	32	2.531	1.000	3.531	
StaticMesh	Cinematics_Example.sm_control_stand_2	12	1	116	1,392	15	2.167	2.333	4.500	
StaticMesh	Cinematics_Example.sm_hall_deco_1	4	1	106	424	11	1.000	5.750	6.750	
ModelComponent	Cinematics_Example.TheWorld:PersistentLevel.ModelComponent_15	1	2	6	6	0	44.000	7.000	51.000	
SkeletalMesh	COG_Grunt.COG_Grunt_AMesh	1	3	4,440	4,440	587	0.000	4.000	4.000	
StaticMesh	Cinematics_Example.sm_control_stand_1	4	2	402	1,608	43	3.750	1.500	5.250	
StaticMesh	Cinematics_Example.sm_nozzle_1	6	1	120	720	16	3.000	1.833	4.833	
StaticMesh	Cinematics_Example.sm_cargo_container_3	5	1	588	2,940	57	4.000	1.800	5.800	
StaticMesh	Cinematics_Example.sm_wall_tile_2	8	1	12	96	2	1.500	1.125	2.625	
StaticMesh	Cinematics_Example.sm_hall_deco_door	6	1	64	384	8	7.833	1.333	9.167	
StaticMesh	EditorMeshes.MatineeCam_SM	2	1	2,170	4,340	296	1.000	3.000	4.000	
StaticMesh	Cinematics_Example.sm_hall_deco_doorway_basic	4	1	152	608	16	8.750	1.500	10.250	
StaticMesh	Cinematics_Example.sm_crate_1	4	1	44	176	4	2.250	1.500	3.750	
StaticMesh	Cinematics_Example.sm_cable_box_nozzle	3	1	100	300	14	3.000	1.667	4.667	
StaticMesh	Cinematics_Example.sm_hall_deco_ceiling_2	2	1	200	400	27	15.000	1.500	16.500	
StaticMesh	Cinematics_Example.sm_hall_deco_doorway	2	1	180	360	19	4.500	1.000	5.500	
StaticMesh	Cinematics_Example.sm_cable_curve_long_3	2	1	108	216	14	4.500	1.000	5.500	
StaticMesh	Cinematics_Example.sm_cargo_container_2	2	1	92	184	9	2.500	1.000	3.500	
StaticMesh	Cinematics_Example.sm_cable_curve_long	2	1	92	184	12	3.000	0.500	3.500	
ModelComponent	Cinematics_Example.TheWorld:PersistentLevel.ModelComponent_19	1	1	2	2	0	0.000	0.000	0.000	
ModelComponent	Cinematics_Example.TheWorld:PersistentLevel.ModelComponent_18	1	1	2	2	0	0.000	0.000	0.000	
ModelComponent	Cinematics_Example.TheWorld:PersistentLevel.ModelComponent_17	1	1	2	2	0	1.000	0.000	1.000	
ModelComponent	Cinematics_Example.TheWorld:PersistentLevel.ModelComponent_10	1	1	2	2	0	0.000	0.000	0.000	
ModelComponent	Cinematics_Example.TheWorld:PersistentLevel.ModelComponent_14	1	1	2	2	0	0.000	0.000	0.000	
ModelComponent	Cinematics_Example.TheWorld:PersistentLevel.ModelComponent_13	1	1	2	2	0	0.000	0.000	0.000	
ModelComponent	Cinematics_Example.TheWorld:PersistentLevel.ModelComponent_12	1	1	2	2	0	0.000	0.000	0.000	
ModelComponent	Cinematics_Example.TheWorld:PersistentLevel.ModelComponent_11	1	1	2	2	0	0.000	0.000	0.000	
ModelComponent	Cinematics_Example.TheWorld:PersistentLevel.ModelComponent_16	1	1	2	2	0	0.000	0.000	0.000	

FIGURE A.17 Primitive Stats browser

Menu

The menubar contains the following menus and options when the Primitive Stats tab is active:

Docking

Docked	Fixes this browser in the main browser window as a tab.
Floating	Puts this browser in its own floating window.
Clone Browser	Creates a new tab in the main browser window with a duplicate of this browser.
Remove Browser	Removes this browser from the main browser window.

Dynamic Shadow Stats Browser

The Dynamic Shadow Stats browser, much like the Primitive Stats browser, provides access to statistics that are mainly used in optimizing and solving performance problems (see **FIGURE A.18**). Once the stats are dumped to the browser from the game, it is easy to analyze them to see where shadows may be causing performance bottlenecks and where changes need to be made. As with the Primitive Stats browser, more information can be found about this browser in Chapter 11.

FIGURE A.18 Dynamic Shadow Stats browser

Menu

The menubar contains the following menus and options when the Dynamic Shadow Stats tab is active:

Docking

Docked	Fixes this browser in the main browser window as a tab.
Floating	Puts this browser in its own floating window.
Clone Browser	Creates a new tab in the main browser window with a duplicate of this browser.
Remove Browser	Removes this browser from the main browser window.

Scene Manager

The Scene Manager is a quick way to select, delete, focus the camera on, or view the properties of the actors within a level or any streaming levels (see **FIGURE A.19**). You can think of the Scene Manager as being like an advanced search window. The list of actors can be filtered out based on several criteria, including the level containing the actors, the type of actor, and whether a certain string of text is present within the actor's name. When an actor is selected in the list, its properties become loaded into the properties panel on the right, where they can be modified just as in the Actor Properties window.

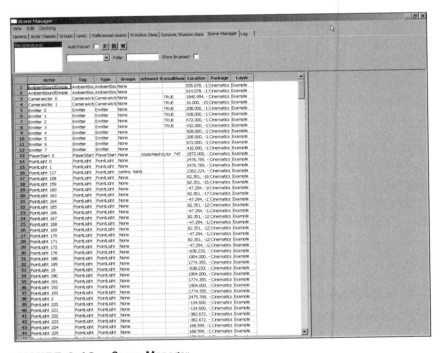

FIGURE A.19   Scene Manager

The Scene Manager is divided up into the following areas.

Filter Criteria

Across the top of the Scene Manager is a set of controls for determining which actors appear in the Actor List, as well as what actions to take once an actor is selected:

Level List	Populates the list with all the levels currently loaded in the editor, including the persistent level and any streaming levels. Selecting one of the levels in this list displays the actors contained in that level in the Actor List.
Auto Focus?	Automatically focuses the camera on the actor when it is selected in the Actor List. This is a great way to find actors within a large map.
Focus On Selected Actor	Focuses the camera on the selected actor when pressed. This is basically the same as the Auto Focus checkbox, but gives the user control over when to focus on an actor and when not to.
Refresh	Refreshes the Actor List in case any updates were made that were not reflected in the Scene Manager.
Delete	Deletes the selected actor from the map. Using this button is the same as selecting an actor in the viewport and pressing the Delete key.
Actor Type List	Filters the Actor List so that only actors of the type selected in this list are shown. When the empty option is selected, all actors are visible in the Actor List.
Filter Text Field	Allows the Actor List to be filtered based on a string. If the string entered in the field is present on the name of the actor, it is shown in the list. The string can be located anywhere within the name of the actor.
Show Brushes?	Shows brushes in the Actor List along with the other actors.

Actor List

The Actor List lists all the actors within the selected level, along with various properties arranged in a spreadsheet layout. Selecting an actor in this list causes the actor's complete properties to be displayed in the Properties Panel. One of the benefits of using the Scene Manager is that multiple actors can be selected in the Actor List with great ease. This makes selecting large groups of actors virtually as easy as selecting one actor within the viewport.

Properties Panel

The Properties Panel is essentially identical to the Actor Properties window. It displays the properties of the selected actors in the Actor List. The properties available change depending on which actor you have selected. They are divided into a series of categories, some of which are standard and can be found on any actor, such as the Display or Movement categories. Other categories are actor sensitive, such as the Light category, which can only be found on actors such as PointLights, Spotlights, or DirectionalLights.

Menu

The menubar contains the following menus and options when the Scene Manager tab is active:

View	
Refresh	Refreshes the Scene Manager.

Edit	
Delete	Deletes the actors selected in the Actor List.

Docking	
Docked	Fixes the browser in the main browser window as a tab.
Floating	Puts this browser in its own floating window.
Clone Browser	Creates a new tab in the main browser window with a duplicate of this browser.
Remove Browser	Removes this browser from the main browser window.

Log

The Log is where errors and messages from the engine are output for the designer to see (see **FIGURE A.20**). It provides a way for designers and programmers to tell exactly what is happening and why problems may occur. Using code, messages can be output to the Log, making debugging much easier. At the bottom of the Log is a command-line text field that functions identically to the command line in the console bar of the main editor window. Console commands can be entered here to perform certain commands.

Menu

The menubar contains the following menus and options when the Log tab is active.

Docking	
Docked	Fixes the browser in the main browser window as a tab.
Floating	Puts this browser in its own floating window.
Clone Browser	Creates a new tab in the main browser window with a duplicate of this browser.
Remove Browser	Removes this browser from the main browser window.

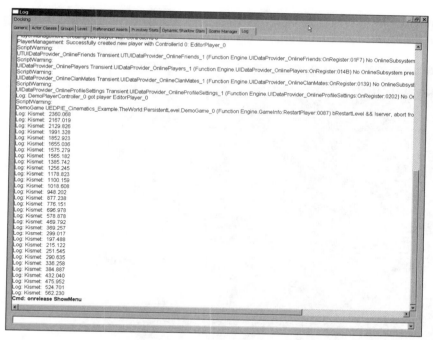

FIGURE A.20 Log

Editors

There are many smaller editors integrated into the Unreal Editor that are specific to the type of content being edited, such as static meshes, particle systems, physics assets, skeletal meshes, animation trees, and so on. Although browsers still exist for the purposes of creating and organizing content, these stand-alone editors have replaced much of the browser functionality available in previous versions of the Unreal Editor and are extremely powerful and sophisticated. Each of these editors is usually accessed by double-clicking on an asset of that particular type from within the Generic browser. Some editors, however, are only accessible from the context menu accessed by right-clicking on the asset in the Generic browser. These editors have been detailed in the chapters associated with the various asset types. As such, they will simply be listed here with a brief description of their function.

Static Mesh Editor

The Static Mesh Editor allows static mesh assets to be viewed, and their properties to be edited (see **FIGURE A.21**). Collision meshes can be added in this editor, as can new UV channels for use with lightmaps. This editor is accessed by double-clicking on, or through the context menu of, a static mesh asset in the Generic browser. See Chapter 5, "Static Meshes," for more detailed information about the Static Mesh Editor.

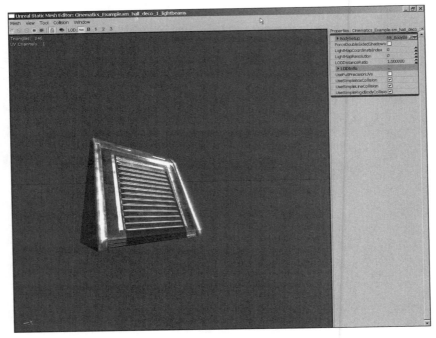

FIGURE A.21   Static Mesh Editor

Material Editor

The Material Editor provides a visual node-based environment for creating materials that can be applied to surfaces within the game (see **FIGURE A.22**). This editor is accessed by double-clicking on, or through the context menu of, a material asset in the Generic browser. See Chapter 6 for more detailed information about the Material Editor.

Kismet Visual Scripting Editor

Unreal Kismet is the visual scripting system within Unreal Engine 3 (see **FIGURE A.23**). It provides complex scripting abilities without the need for writing code. These visual scripts are created within the Kismet Visual Scripting Editor, which is a node-based editor very similar to the Material Editor in appearance. Its editor is accessed through the Open Kismet button on the main editor's toolbar. See Chapter 9 for more information about the Kismet Visual Scripting Editor.

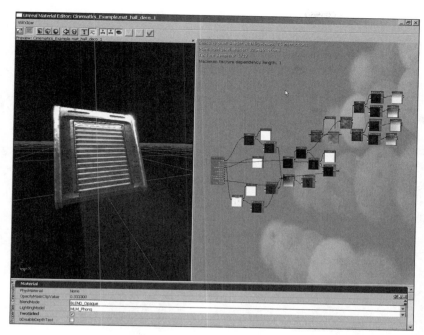

FIGURE A.22
Material Editor

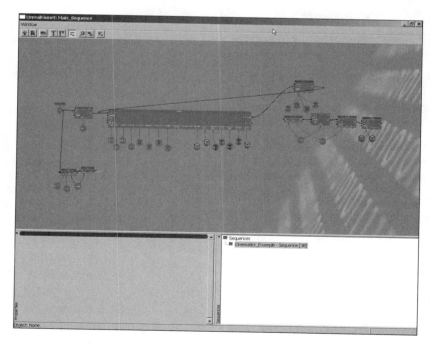

FIGURE A.23
Kismet Visual
Scripting Editor

Matinee Editor

The Matinee Editor is a non-linear animation editor (see **FIGURE A.24**). It allows properties and events to be animated over time during play. One of the main functions of the Matinee Editor is to create cinematic sequences, but it is also used to create movers. The Matinee Editor is accessed by double-clicking a Matinee sequence object within the Kismet Editor. See Chapter 10, "Unreal Matinee," for more information about the Matinee Editor.

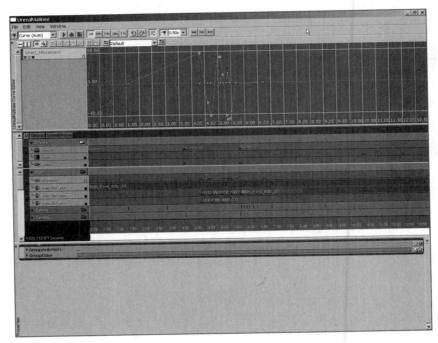

FIGURE A.24   Matinee Editor

PhAT (Physics Asset Tool) Physics Editor

The PhAT Physics Editor is used to set up physics assets for skeletal meshes (see **FIGURE A.25**). These can be used for simulating physical interactions as well as collision. This editor is accessed by double-clicking on, or through the context menu of, a physics asset within the Generic browser.

Cascade Particle System Editor

The Cascade Particle System Editor is used to create special effects through the use of particle emitters (see **FIGURE A.26**). This editor provides the ability to create emitters within a particle system, as well as add behavior and modify the appearance of the particles within those emitters. Cascade is accessed by double-clicking on, or through the context menu of, a Particle System asset in the Generic browser.

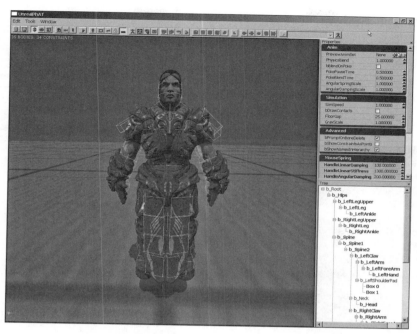

FIGURE A.25   PhAT Physics Editor

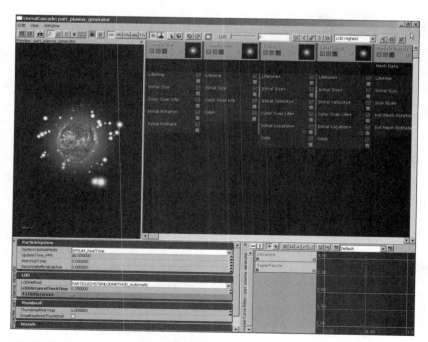

FIGURE A.26   Cascade Particle System Editor

User Interface Scene Editor

The User Interface Scene Editor, or UI Editor for short, is used to set up menus and other on-screen graphical user interfaces for use in the game (see **FIGURE A.27**). It provides the ability to visually lay out the elements of the user interface and uses its own special Kismet visual scripting system to set up their behavior. The UI Editor is accessed by double-clicking on, or through the context menu of, UIScene assets in the Generic browser.

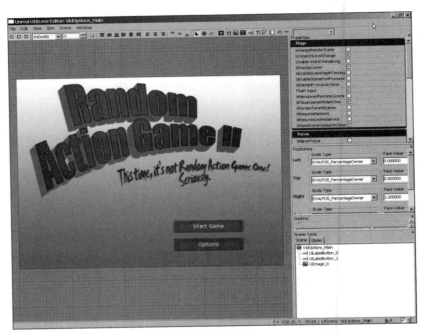

FIGURE A.27   User Interface Scene Editor

SoundCue Editor

The SoundCue Editor provides a visual, node-based environment for adding effects, such as attenuation or modulation, to sounds for use in-game (see **FIGURE A.28**). This editor is similar in appearance to the other node-based editors within the Unreal Editor and is accessed from the context menu of SoundCue assets in the Generic browser.

Post Process Manager

The Post Process Manager is a visual, node-based environment for creating Post Process effect chains (see **FIGURE A.29**). Various effects such as depth of field and motion blur can be chained together to form overall post-process effects. This editor is accessed by double-clicking on, or through the context menu of, Post Process Effect assets in the Generic browser.

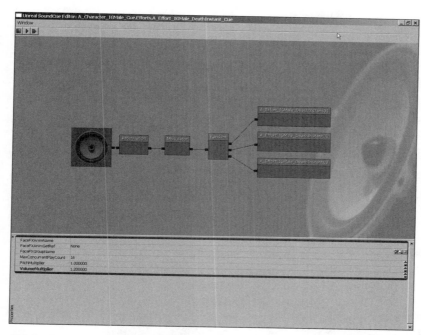

FIGURE A.28 SoundCue Editor

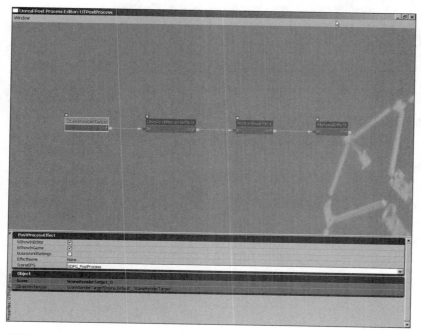

FIGURE A.29 Post Process Manager

AnimSet Editor

The AnimSet Editor allows skeletal meshes to be viewed and for their properties to be modified (see **FIGURE A.30**). In this editor, animations and morph targets can be previewed as well. This is the general purpose editor for all aspects dealing with skeletal meshes, with the small exception of physics and animation trees. This editor is accessed by double-clicking on, or through the context menu of, SkeletalMesh, AnimSet, or MorphTargetSet assets in the Generic browser.

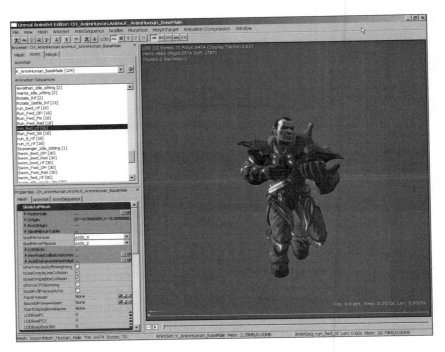

FIGURE A.30   AnimSet Editor

AnimTree Editor

The AnimTree Editor is a visual, node-based editor for setting up animation trees for skeletal meshes (see **FIGURE A.31**). In this editor, nodes can be connected to create complex behaviors with regards to animating skeletal meshes, as well as previewing those behaviors and animations directly inside the editor. It is accessed by double-clicking on, or through the context menu of, AnimTree assets in the Generic browser.

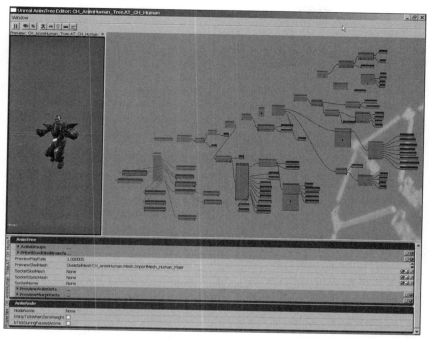

FIGURE A.31   AnimTree Editor

Search for Actors

The Search for Actor command enables you to find and select a specific actor in your level (see **FIGURE A.32**). The command initiates a dialog containing a list of all the actors that currently exist in your level, and you can filter that list by entering text into any of the three text fields on the right side of the window. The list of actors will be filtered as you type. For example, let's say you want to find an actor named BrightLight5. If you just type the first two letters into the name text field, the list automatically shortens to include actors who have names starting with "br." In this case, you would probably get a list containing most of your brushes (as their default name tends to be "brush" and a number), and your BrightLight5 object would also be listed. If, however, you continued to type out the name completely, only actors with that name would be listed—in this case, the desired object.

The tool also includes the Inside Of dropdown, which allows you to choose where you want the search to take place. Within the dropdown, you will find options to search within the Name, Level, Group, Path Name, and Tag of the actors in your level. Beneath the dropdown are the Starting With and Contains options, which enable you to choose between searching either from the beginning of the name or anywhere inside of it, respectively.

This tool can also be accessed from the Edit menu.

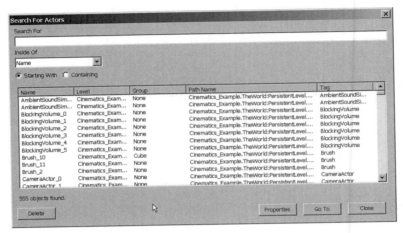

FIGURE A.32   Search for Actors

Property Windows

The property windows give you access to the many properties inherent to any actor or surface in your level. As you construct your Unreal worlds, you will find yourself using these quite often.

Actor Properties

This brings up the Actor Properties window, which gives you access to a tremendous number of parameters for a specific actor (see **FIGURE A.33**). The properties available change depending on which actor you have selected. They are divided into a series of categories, some of which are standard and can be found on any actor, such as the Display or Movement categories. Other categories are actor sensitive, such as the Light category, which can only be found on actors such as PointLights, Spotlights, or DirectionalLights.

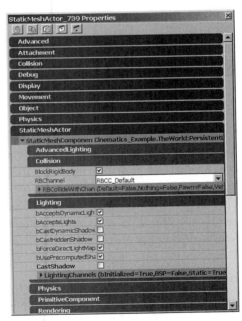

FIGURE A.33   Actor Properties window

Surface Properties

The Surface Properties window is used to control how materials are placed on surfaces (see **FIGURE A.34**). From here, you can pan your materials in the U and V directions, as well as rotate them. The following sections show the options found under each of the four tabs found in the window: Flags, Pan/Rot/Scale, Alignment, and Scale.

Pan/Rot/Scale

This area provides you with a series of tools for panning (moving), rotating, and scaling materials on a BSP surface to help you align them properly.

The Pan group contains buttons for panning, which enable you to move the material in increments of 1, 4, 16, and 64 Unreal units in either the U or V direction. Clicking one of the buttons moves the material that number of units in the given direction. Shift-clicking the button moves the material in the opposite direction.

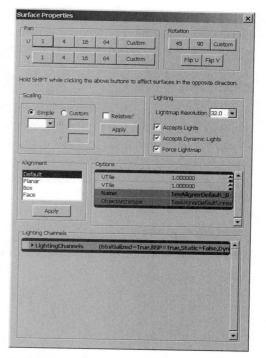

FIGURE A.34   Surface Properties window

The Rotation group rotates the material either 45 or 90 degrees, as well as enables you to flip the material in either U or V.

The Scaling group allows for two different methods for scaling. The first is a simple method that is applied uniformly to the entire surface in both axes, and you can choose a number from the dropdown box. The second allows you to specify your own values for scaling in each axis separately. The relative checkbox enables you to toggle between either absolute scaling or relative scaling based on the material's previous scale. For example, if Relative is checked and you enter a value of 1 into the U and V fields, the material will not scale, regardless of how it has been previously scaled.

Lighting

The Light Map section enables you to control how detailed the shadows will be on individual BSP surfaces. Remember that a lower setting tightens your shadows, giving them more detail, whereas lower values soften your shadows. Over-sharpening your light maps on larger levels can lead to memory problems, as the materials for the light maps get larger.

Also in the Lighting section are checkboxes for setting whether the surface accepts lighting at all or whether it accepts lighting from dynamic lights. The Force Lightmap checkbox determines whether the use of lightmaps will be forced, regardless of the light's settings.

Alignment

This section enables you to control how the materials are projected onto surfaces. The Default system simply enables you to control how materials tile (repeat) in the U and V directions. The Planar method projects the material onto all selected faces from the same direction, which can lead to stretching on some surfaces. The Box method projects the material from six sides, such as a cube. Finally, the Face method produces a separate projection of the material on to each face of the surface.

Lighting Channels

This section allows the lighting channels used by surfaces to be set. For more information on lighting channels, please see Chapter 7, "Introduction to Lighting."

Appendix B

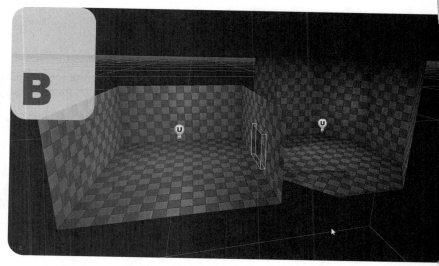

The Curve Editor

As you create your gaming assets, you'll sometimes want to change some property or parameter over time, perhaps to animate an asset. These changes are internally graphed onto a curve, in which Time runs along the bottom of the graph and the value of the property runs up the side (see **FIGURE B.1**).

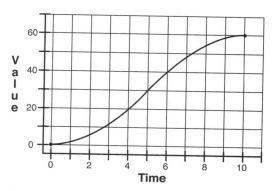

FIGURE B.1   Curve representation

In UnrealEd, you can view and manipulate curves within the Curve Editor. The Curve Editor will appear in two locations: the Cascade Particle Editor and the Matinee System. In each case, its interface and functionality is exactly the same.

In this appendix, we'll walk you through using the Curve Editor. But, before we do, let's take a moment to review a few basic concepts of keyframe-based animation and to learn how curves can be controlled to adjust the animations you create.

Animation Curves

An animation curve is really nothing more than a graphical representation of the change of a property value over time. The final shape of this curve is controlled by two things: keyframes and interpolation curves that connect all the keyframes together.

A *keyframe*—often called a *key* for short in Unreal—is simply the recording of a property's value at a given time. Graphically speaking, you can think of these as the dots in a connect-the-dots game. You could, for example, say that a certain property would have a value of 5 at Time=0, and a value of 10 at Time=3. If you were to plot these two points on your graph, it would look something like **FIGURE B.2**.

Now you know that the property will be one value at a certain time and another value later on. But what happens in between? Fortunately, you don't need to manually designate each and every point along the curve (which is nice; there are an infinite number of points between any two keyframes).

Instead, the computer will do the work for you, creating what are known as *interpolation curves*. If you go back to our connect-the-dots game example, you can think of these as the lines that connect the dots. The great thing is that these lines do not necessarily have to be completely straight as they pass from one key to the next. They can swoop up to the next point, they can meet only at right angles, or they can have a wide variety of other shapes within certain limitations.

Consider, for instance, a curve that started off very flat, but gently became steeper as it approached the next point on the graph (see **FIGURE B.3**). What would be the behavior of such a curve?

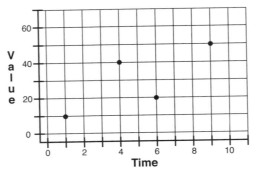

FIGURE B.2   Graphed keyframes

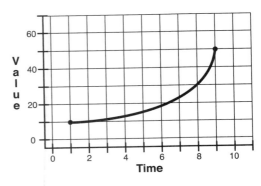

FIGURE B.3   Fast-In curve

This type of curve would define behavior that began with a very slow transition and accelerated, getting faster and faster, right up to the point of the next key. This would be very different from a curve that was simply a straight line connecting the two keys, which would define behavior at a constant rate of change, neither accelerating nor decelerating (see **FIGURE B.4**).

By changing the shape of these curves, you can create a very diverse range of behaviors for your property, all while using the fewest

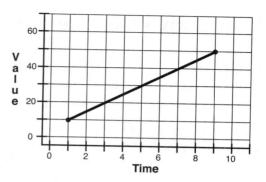

FIGURE B.4   Linear curve

number of keys possible. However, as mentioned previously, there are some limitations. The most important of these is that an animation curve must always evaluate in such a way that if a vertical line were drawn through it at any given point, it would intersect the curve only once. This might sound confusing if you're new to the concept of animation curves, but think about it for a moment. A vertical line on the graph could be used to designate a particular time at a given point, as shown in **FIGURE B.5**.

If the curve were ever allowed to fold back over itself, creating a situation where the vertical line could intersect the curve twice, you would, in effect, have two separate values for the same property at the same time (see **FIGURE B.6**).

This behavior is impossible, and therefore certain shapes for the curve are eliminated.

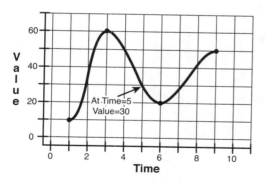

FIGURE B.5   Notice the vertical line designates Time=5.

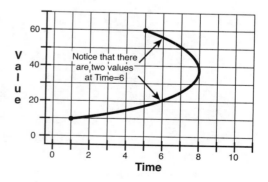

FIGURE B.6   This curve would create two separate property values at the same time.

Controlling Interpolation Curves

So, now that you know generally how an animation curve works, you need to know how you can control its shape in order to get the results you're seeking. This is done in one of two ways: either through the adjustment of *Bezier tangent handles*, which are used to control the angle at which an interpolation curve enters and exits a key; or by changing the type of tangents that the key uses.

We'll start with tangent handles. It helps to first understand what a tangent is. In high school algebra class, you probably learned (or probably will) that a tangent defines the angle of a curve at a given point. That's exactly what we have here. Our point, in this case, is our key. By manipulating these tangents, we can control the angle of the curve at the location of the key.

In UnrealEd's Curve Editor, tangent handles appear as small white lines with a small square handle at the end. By dragging on the small handle, you change the angle at which the tangent intercepts the key, and thereby change the shape of the curve. Also, you'll notice that each key actually contains two handles, one on each side of the key. The handle on the left controls the direction of the curve as it enters the key. The handle on the right controls the direction of the curve as it exits the key (see **FIGURE B.7**).

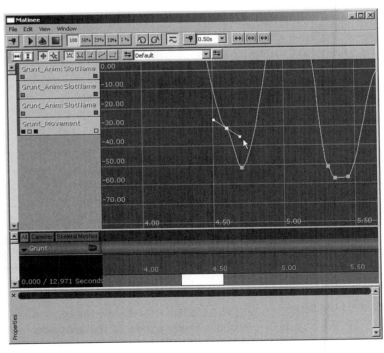

FIGURE B.7   A tangent handle

The second method of controlling a curve involves changing the type of keys used to make the curve. In Unreal, there are five types of keys available to you, as follows:

- Auto
- User
- Break
- Linear
- Constant

Auto

Auto tangents are the default tangent type, and are defined by the computer, rather than being editable by the user. Generally speaking, this type of key creates a very smooth result in which the curve gracefully sweeps from one point to the next (see **FIGURE B.8**). However, this can lead to the problem of overshoot, which we discuss later in this section.

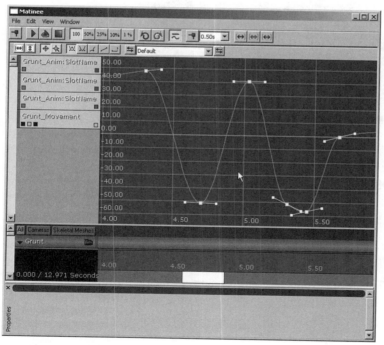

FIGURE B.8   This curve exhibits Auto tangents.

User

User tangents can be adjusted by the designer. This means you can drag on the handle and change the direction at which the curve enters and exits the key. However, as you move the handle, you'll notice that the two handles—the one entering the key and the one exiting it—always remain aligned to one another, appearing as a straight line (see **FIGURE B.9**).

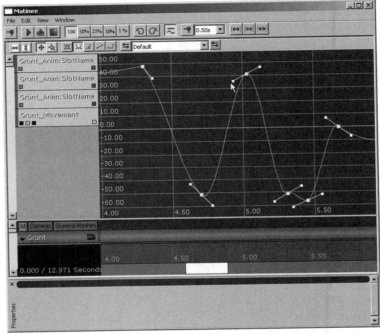

FIGURE B.9   These tangents have been manipulated, meaning they are now User tangents.

Break

Break tangents, like User tangents, can also be adjusted by the designer. However, they differ in that the tangent that enters the key and the one that exits the key will not automatically remain aligned to one another. This means you can point the tangent handles in different directions, which results in a very sharp change in property values over time (see **FIGURE B.10**).

Linear

Linear tangents are by far the most simple, as they merely cause the interpolation curve to create a straight line from one point to the next (see **FIGURE B.11**). The tangents are not editable by the user.

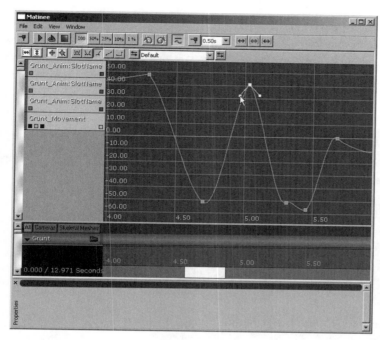

FIGURE B.10   This curve exhibits Break tangents.

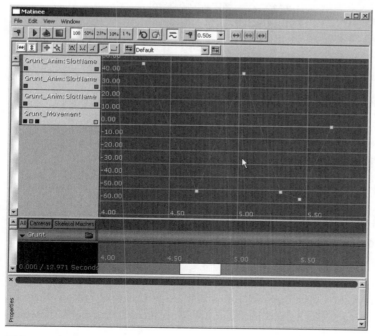

FIGURE B.11   Linear tangents simply cause the curve to create straight lines.

Constant

Constant tangents are unique in that they create a stepped curve that will hold the value of the key until the next key comes along in the graph (see **FIGURE B.12**). This is perfect for animating such things as blinking lights, or any other time when you need an instant transition from one value to another.

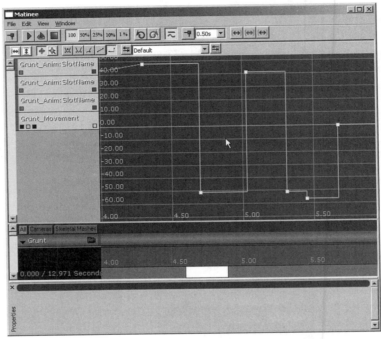

FIGURE B.12   Constant tangents hold the value until the next key comes along.

Curve Editor Interface

The Curve Editor, as mentioned earlier, appears in two key locations in UnrealEd (Matinee and Cascade). It will look and function the same way in both cases. The following is a basic overview of the editor's interface and how it can be navigated. The Curve Editor's interface is divided into three key sections: a toolbar, a curve key list, and the main curve graph.

Curve Editor Toolbar

As with most editors in Unreal, the Curve Editor's toolbar contains a variety of buttons that perform functions that you're going to use most often when working. From left to right, these buttons are listed next.

Fit Visible Tracks Horizontally ⊡

Clicking this button zooms the graph view along the horizontal axis (Time), forcing all the visible curves to fit within the horizontal extents.

Fit Visible Tracks Vertically ⊡

This button zooms the graph view along the vertical axis (Property value), forcing all the visible curves to fit within the vertical extents.

Pan/Edit Mode ⊞

This button toggles on Pan/Edit Mode, which is a navigational mode that still enables you to edit keys and tangents. Navigation of the graph view will be discussed later.

Zoom Mode ⊞

This button toggles on Zoom Mode, which enables you to zoom into and out of the graph view.

Auto Curve ⊞

This converts any selected keys to use Auto tangents, which were described previously.

User Curve ⊞

This converts any selected keys to use User tangents, which were described previously.

Break Curve ⊞

This converts any selected keys to use Break tangents, which were described previously.

Linear Curve ⊞

This converts any selected keys to use Linear tangents, which were described previously.

Constant Curve ⊞

This converts any selected keys to use Constant tangents, which were described previously.

Tabs

Tabs are an aspect of the toolbar that enable you to create your own customized groups of curves, in order to quickly jump to a specific curve or collection of curves.

Create Tab ⊞

Clicking this button creates a new tab and displays a dialog where you can input the name of the new tab.

Tab Dropdown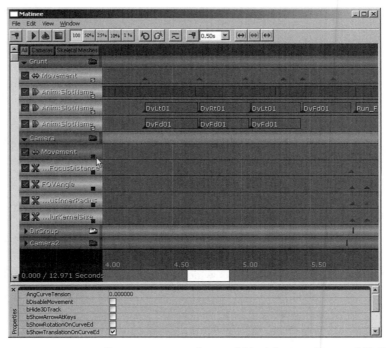

This dropdown shows a list of all the tabs you've created, enabling you to quickly choose one for editing the curves within.

Delete Tab

This button deletes the current tab from the Tab Dropdown. You cannot delete the default tab. Also, keep in mind that this will not destroy the animation curves within the tab.

Curve Editor Curve Key List

The curve key list provides a scrollable list of all the animated properties within the curve editor, and gives you access to the visibility of the curves for those properties. This list is populated by sending curves into the editor. In Matinee, this is done by clicking the small black square that is visible in the lower-right corner of each animated track (see **FIGURE B.13**). In Cascade, there is a similar black box with a curve icon inside visible on each animatable module.

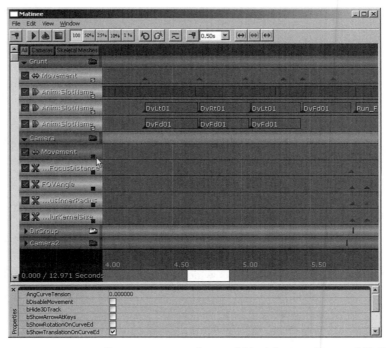

FIGURE B.13   Here you can see the small black box used to send Matinee information to the curve editor.

Visibility Flags

Each entry in the list contains the name of the property being animated, along with a series of small square buttons that control the visibility of each curve in the graph view. The nature of these buttons will change depending on what type of property is being edited, but they all essentially perform the same task: show or hide individual curves.

In the lower-right corner of each entry is a small black box that turns yellow when clicked. This box is the master visibility for the curves of that property. When active, the curve(s) for that property will be visible. When black—or deactivated—the curves cannot be seen.

In the lower-left corner are one to three buttons: red, green, and blue. These control the visibility of individual curves for the property. This is important, especially in the case of vector properties, which have an X, Y, and Z property, because it enables you to control the visibility of individual axes, such as seeing only the X curve. Properties that have only one value show only a red box (X), whereas properties that have an X, Y, and Z value show all three (see **FIGURE B.14**).

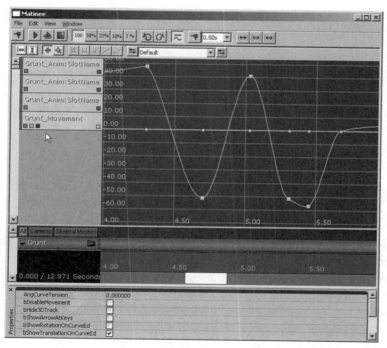

FIGURE B.14   Notice the visibility flags at the bottom of the entry.

Curve Editor Graph View

The graph view is where you'll actually get to see and interact with your animation curves. It consists of a simple graphical representation of value and time, with property values running along the vertical axis and time values spanning across the horizontal. It can be zoomed in each axis individually, allowing for easy navigation of various curves.

You can also create keys in this window, as well as relocate keys along the graph. Moving keys vertically change the value of that key, and moving keys horizontally change the time that the key occurs.

Graph View Navigation

The manner in which you navigate the graph view depends on the mode the graph view is in. The two modes available are Pan/Edit Mode and Zoom Mode.

Pan/Edit Mode Navigation

Pan/Edit Mode serves as the graph view's default navigation mode, providing most of your general navigation abilities. It enables you to move around the graph and adjust keys.

Pan—Drag with the left mouse button to pan the view around and see your curves.

Zoom—You can zoom into or out of the graph view by rolling the mouse wheel. Note that this zoom is uniform in the horizontal and vertical axes.

Select Key—You can select a key by left-clicking on it. Doing so will make its Time and Value visible, and will also display that key's tangent handles.

You can toggle a selection by holding Ctrl and clicking multiple keys.

You can marquee select by holding Ctrl and Alt and dragging a selection.

Moving Keys—You can move a key by first selecting it, and then dragging it while holding the Ctrl key. Dragging left and right will change the key's timing. Dragging up and down will control its value.

Adjusting User Tangents—You can adjust the angle of a User or Break tangents by first selecting a key, and then dragging on the small white tangent handle.

It should be noted to those readers who are accustomed to working with animation curves in certain 2D and 3D animation packages that you cannot adjust multiple tangents simultaneously, nor can you change the weighting of a given tangent.

Right-Click Context Menu—While in Pan/Edit Mode, the user can right-click on a key at any time and change its Time or Value.

Key Creation—You can create your own keys along the curve by holding Ctrl and left-clicking anywhere along the curve. You can then use the context menu to change the time and value for the key.

Zoom Mode Navigation

Zoom Mode is a more specialized navigational mode, enabling you to zoom in individually in the horizontal or vertical axes, or both.

Zoom Value (Vertically)—You can zoom vertically without affecting the horizontal axis by dragging with the right mouse button.

Zoom Time (Horizontally)—You can zoom horizontally without affecting the vertical axis by dragging with the left mouse button.

> **NOTE**
>
> You can zoom nonuniformly in the horizontal and vertical directions by holding both mouse buttons.

Preset Curves

> **NOTE**
>
> At the time of this writing, preset curves are intended for use within Cascade only. In addition, the ability to save your own preset curves is nonfunctional.

As you use the editing tools to create various curves, you may eventually start to realize that you use certain shaped curves over and over. Rather than recreate these curves each time you need one, you can use the preset curve feature to save out a favored curve shape to be reused again and again (see **FIGURE B.15**). On top of this, you can also choose to use a variety of predefined curves, such as sine or cosine waves.

Curve presets can be accessed by right-clicking on any of the curves in the Curve Key List. You will see a context menu appear, giving you the ability to remove the curve from the editor entirely, to place a preset curve for it, or to save out the existing curve as a preset for later use.

Choosing the Preset Curve option opens the Preset Curve dialog. This dialog enables you to choose what type of curve you'd like to place, and in which of the available slots for the property you'd like to place it. For example, if you are animating a property, such as the color of a particle in Cascade, you could apply a sine wave curve to the red value, but still control the other two colors manually.

Using the Preset Curve dialog is as simple as choosing the axis to which you'd like to apply the preset, clicking on the dropdown corresponding to that axis, and choosing which curve you want to use.

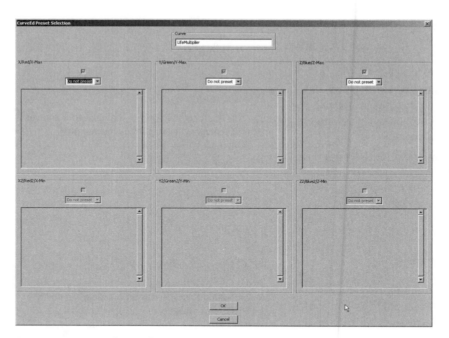

FIGURE B.15   Preset Curve dialog

Available Preset Curve Settings

The following options are available from the Preset Curve dropdowns.

Do Not Preset

This option leaves the curve in its current state, not adding a preset to it.

Cos Wave

This generates a cosine wave over time (see **FIGURE B.16**). When this type of curve is selected, some parameters appear to control the look of the curve. These parameters are as follows:

> **Frequency**—This controls the frequency of the wave as time progresses. At the time of this writing, this is locked to a value between 0 and 1.

> **Scale**—This controls the scale factor of the curve, allowing it to be multiplied by the entered value. As you might know, a sine wave spans between a value of 1 and -1 throughout its life. For example, if you were to set this value to 10, your curve would oscillate between 10 and -10 instead.

Offset—This controls how far you would like to offset the curve once it has been scaled. Say, for example, you wanted a curve that oscillated between 0 and 1; you would need a Scale value of 0.5, which would cause the curve to oscillate between 0.5 and -0.5. You could then set the Offset value to 0.5, which would move the entire curve upwards such that it now oscillated between 0 and 1.

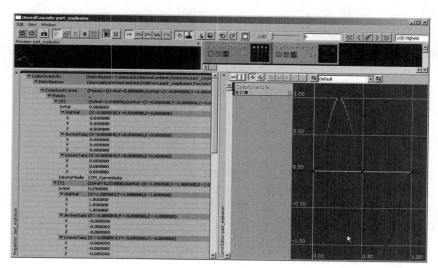

FIGURE B.16   Example of a cosine wave

Sine Wave

This generates a sine wave over time. If this type of curve is selected, the same options described previously for cos waves appear.

Linear Decay

This creates a curve that exhibits linear decay over time (see **FIGURE B.17**). If this type of curve is selected, the following options appear, enabling you to control the setup of the initial curve:

> **NOTE**
>
> Creating a linear decay preset curve will not always result in actual linear decay behavior. This is because the keys that are created are still using Auto tangents. You can solve this problem by selecting each key of the curve and setting their tangent types to Linear.

StartDecay—This is the time at which the decay will start.

StartValue—This is the value at which the curve will begin.

EndDecay—This value sets the time at which the decay will end.

EndValue—This sets the value at which the curve will end.

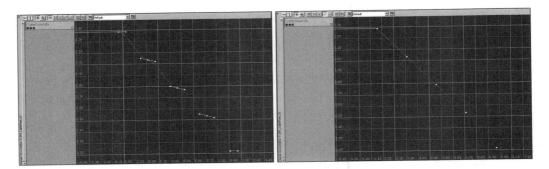

FIGURE B.17   Linear decay curves are not perfectly linear when created. To the right is the same curve with its tangents set to Linear.

User-Set

This option enables the user to load in a pre-curve created earlier. When selecting this type of curve, the UserCurve property appears, enabling you to load in the desirable curve. Please note that these curves appear as objects in the Generic Browser, and that you use the standard Use Current Selection in Browser button to load them in.

Index

Numbers

A

I

Q-R

How can we make this index more useful? Email us at indexes@samspublishing.com

How can we make this index more useful? Email us at indexes@samspublishing.com

SAMS

REGISTER

THIS PRODUCT

informit.com/register

Register the Addison-Wesley, Exam Cram, Prentice Hall, Que, and Sams products you own to unlock great benefits.

To begin the registration process, simply go to **informit.com/register** to sign in or create an account. You will then be prompted to enter the 10- or 13-digit ISBN that appears on the back cover of your product.

Registering your products can unlock the following benefits:

- Access to supplemental content, including bonus chapters, source code, or project files.
- A coupon to be used on your next purchase.

Registration benefits vary by product. Benefits will be listed on your Account page under Registered Products.

About InformIT — **THE TRUSTED TECHNOLOGY LEARNING SOURCE**

INFORMIT IS HOME TO THE LEADING TECHNOLOGY PUBLISHING IMPRINTS Addison-Wesley Professional, Cisco Press, Exam Cram, IBM Press, Prentice Hall Professional, Que, and Sams. Here you will gain access to quality and trusted content and resources from the authors, creators, innovators, and leaders of technology. Whether you're looking for a book on a new technology, a helpful article, timely newsletters, or access to the Safari Books Online digital library, InformIT has a solution for you.

informIT.com

THE TRUSTED TECHNOLOGY LEARNING SOURCE

Addison-Wesley | Cisco Press | Exam Cram
IBM Press | Que | Prentice Hall | Sams

SAFARI BOOKS ONLINE

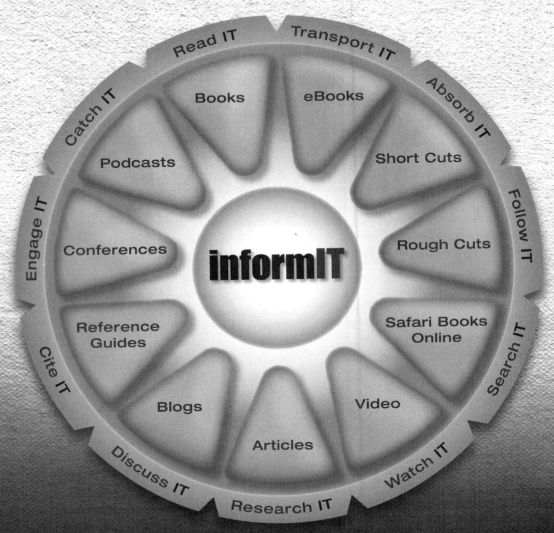

FREE Online Edition

Your purchase of **Mastering Unreal Technology, Volume I** includes access to a free online edition for 45 days through the Safari Books Online subscription service. Nearly every Sams book is available online through Safari Books Online, along with more than 5,000 other technical books and videos from publishers such as Addison-Wesley Professional, Cisco Press, Exam Cram, IBM Press, O'Reilly, Prentice Hall, and Que.

SAFARI BOOKS ONLINE allows you to search for a specific answer, cut and paste code, download chapters, and stay current with emerging technologies.

Activate your FREE Online Edition at
www.informit.com/safarifree

> **STEP 1:** Enter the coupon code: VNNVXFA.

> **STEP 2:** New Safari users, complete the brief registration form.
> Safari subscribers, just log in.

If you have difficulty registering on Safari or accessing the online edition, please e-mail customer-service@safaribooksonline.com

 Addison Wesley   Adobe Press   ALPHA   Cisco Press   FT Press FINANCIAL TIMES   IBM Press   lynda.com   Microsoft Press   New Riders

 O'REILLY   Peachpit Press   PRENTICE   QUE   Darkbooks   SAS Publishing   Sun microsystems   Wharton School Publishing   WILEY